NEUROPSYCHOLOGICAL STUDIES OF APRAXIA
AND RELATED DISORDERS

ADVANCES
IN
PSYCHOLOGY
23

Editors

G. E. STELMACH

P. A. VROON

NORTH-HOLLAND
AMSTERDAM · NEW YORK · OXFORD

NEUROPSYCHOLOGICAL STUDIES OF APRAXIA AND RELATED DISORDERS

Edited by

Eric A. ROY

Department of Psychology
Mount Sinai Hospital and University of Toronto
Toronto, Ontario
and
Department of Kinesiology
University of Waterloo
Waterloo, Ontario

1985

NORTH-HOLLAND
AMSTERDAM · NEW YORK · OXFORD

ISBN: 0 444 87669 3

Publishers:
ELSEVIER SCIENCE PUBLISHERS B.V.
P.O. Box 1991
1000 BZ Amsterdam
The Netherlands

Sole distributors for the U.S.A. and Canada:
ELSEVIER SCIENCE PUBLISHING COMPANY, INC.
52 Vanderbilt Avenue
New York, N.Y. 10017
U.S.A.

Library of Congress Cataloging in Publication Data

Main entry under title:

Neuropsychological studies of apraxia and related
    disorders.

    (Advances in psychology ; 23)
    Includes bibliographies and indexes.
    1. Apraxia. 2. Neuropsychology. I. Roy, Eric A.
(Eric Alexander), 1947-   . II. Series: Advances in
psychology (Amsterdam, Netherlands) ; 23.
[DNLM: 1. Apraxia--physiopathology. 2. Nervous System
Diseases--physiopathology. W1 AD798L v.23 /
WL 340 N4935]
RC394.A75N48 1985   616.85'52   84-24705
ISBN 0-444-87669-3 (U.S.)

PRINTED IN THE NETHERLANDS

Preface/Introduction

Apraxia is a term used to denote a disorder in the performance of limb, oral verbal and oral non-verbal gestures either to command or on imitation with often preserved ability to perform these same gestures outside the clinical setting in the appropriate situation or environment. Over the past century and particularly in the past four decades a great deal of research has focused on understanding the nature of this complex disorder. Problems concerning neural substrates (e.g. association with left versus right hemisphere damage), associated disorders (e.g. agraphia and aphasia), methods of assessment (e.g. command versus imitation) and underlying mechanisms have all been addressed. Considering this current state of knowledge the time seems right for a comprehensive review of this work. Such a review will serve to consolidate what is currently known of apraxia; however, in order to foster a deeper understanding of the nature of this disorder it would seem necessary to go beyond studies of apraxia into areas which have a bearing on praxis and action sequencing, particularly those dealing with motor control.

The first section of the volume, then, is devoted to a review of the current state of knowledge in apraxia. Faglioni and Basso provide a historical perspective to apraxia. Much of the early work by the pioneers in the field is meticulously reviewed. Ennio De Renzi evaluates the various methods for assessing apraxia as they pertain to interpreting the disorder. He considers aspects such as the nature of the movement (e.g., single vs. sequenced) and the mode of input of the command. De Renzi concludes that the crucial factor in apraxia is not the quality of the movement (e.g., symbolic or meaningless, proximal or distal, transitive or intransitive, single or sequenced) but relates to the patient's inability to select from among his repetoire of motor programs when his performance is not assisted by the environmental context.

Leslie Rothi and Kenneth Heilman review much of their work examining the basis of ideomotor apraxia. They apply paradigms used in examining memory in the verbal domain to the study of memory in apraxia. New insights into the nature of this disorder are revealed in this chapter.

Henri Hecaen and Pierre Rondot view apraxia as a disorder to a system of signs. A brief historical review is followed by a consideration of neurophysiological and neuropsychological factors important in uderstanding apraxia. A system for classifying signs is then developed and discussed as it pertains to apraxia.

In his chapter Klaus Poeck continues the discussion pertaining to understanding apraxia by reviewing his extensive work. Both qualitative and quantitative studies are described. Ideational and ideomotor apraxia are considered as to their underlying nature and their relation to aphasia.

Eric Roy and Paula Square examine the commonalities between verbal, oral and limb apraxia using a framework developed by Roy in which praxis is thought to involve the operation of conceptual and production systems. Comparisons include types of errors observed, stimulus and response variables which influence the errors observed and the environmental conditions under which the observed errors occur. The approach in this chapter argues that control of praxis involves both top-down and bottom-up influences which operate in parallel. A full understanding of the neurobehavioural basis for apraxia will arise only when the delicate balance between these influences is focused on in studying these disruptions.

The relationship between apraxia and aphasia is carefully reviewed in the next chapter by Andrew Kertesz. Investigations establish a significant relationship between the two disorders, but dissociations occur in substantial numbers. Aphasia and apraxia coexist either because of anatomical proximity of the mechanisms of language and praxis or because of a sharing of their fundamental mechanisms. Kertesz discusses extensive research, much of it his own, in evaluating the basis of this association. He finds that impairment in comprehension correlates best with apraxia, although comprehension is not the cause of apraxia. The disruption to an underlying general factor of cognitive processing common to both language comprehension and praxis may explain this association.

Anna Basso and her colleagues provide a comprehensive review of advantages and limitations of the various neuroradiological methods currently used to examine brain-behaviour relationships. The focus of the chapter, however, is on the neurobehavioural correlates of apraxia as revealed through CT studies. Large lesions are associated with apraxia more frequently than small ones, while deep lesions alone do not frequently result in apraxia. The importance of the parietal and, to a lesser extent, the frontal regions is confirmed.

The role of cross species studies in understanding apraxia in humans is convincingly presented by Bryan Kolb and Ian Whishaw. The organization of descending motor pathways is considered as it relates to the nature of apraxia. Kolb and Whishaw argue that much additional research is necessary before it will be possible to delineate the anatomical origin of apractic syndromes in either human or nonhuman subjects. The problems of what behaviours to measure and how to quantify the severity of the apractic deficit are also considered as they pertain to studying apraxia in both animals and man. They argue that in order to fully comprehend the nature of apraxia much more consideration must go into what movements are to be examined and how the performance of these movements will be measured. These points are also made by De Renzi in the preceding chapter and by Todor and Smiley and MacKenzie and Marteniuk in subsequent chapters. In a final section Kolb and Whishaw discuss what needs to be considered in making cross species comparisons. One fundamental issue is whether the cerebral hemispheres are equivalent in the non human species to that in humans. Another concern is what behaviour in the animal selected would be appropriate and possibly comparable to that studied in humans.

Sharon Cermak examines the nature of disruptions to praxis in children. The neurobehavioural bases of this disorder are considered in depth. Of particular interest is whether the disorder is a unitary one, a question which has relevance for the study of adult onset apraxia. The relationship between this disorder in children and that in adults is evaluated. Finally, Cermak presents some interesting ideas on how to remediate this disorder.

These chapters in the first section in the book are meant to provide a rather broad perspective on apraxia: the historical roots of apraxia, various views of the nature of apraxia, methods used in assessing the disorder, the relationship of various forms of apraxia with one another and with disorders of speech and language, and the implications of studies of apraxia in animals and children for understanding this disorder in the human adult. While this first section provides a rather complete view of apraxia, a consideration of aspects of motor control provided in the next section complements this one and provides information necessary to gain further insight with the study of this disorder.

The first chapter by Gary Goldberg reviews the evolutionary development of the premotor area, a region of the cortex which has been thought to play an important role in the control of limb praxis. His hypothesis is that the brain has evolved to enable the organization of action across two poles: one pole involving projective action (extrapolating from the current state to a future desired state), and the other pole involving responsive action (adaptation to current specific external inputs). Goldberg proposes that the medial premotor region (supplementary motor area) provides the neural basis for the first pole, while the lateral premotor area subserves the second pole. The implications of these poles of action for the study of apraxia as well as for learning motor skills are discussed.

Donald MacKay in the next chapter presents a theory of the representation, organization and timing of action. A consideration of these issues is important to an understanding of disruptions to the sequential organization of action in apraxia. Adapting concepts he used in describing organizational principles in speech production MacKay has presented a theory relevant to the production of limb actions. Under the theory several types of nodes are thought to be organized into independently controllable systems which provide a basis for producing actions. MacKay discusses the implications of this theory for understanding the nature of errors made by both normals and apractics.

The basis of manual asymmetries is discussed in the next chapter by John Todor and Anne Smiley. A consideration of these asymmetries is important as comparisons of right and left hand performance are often made in apractic patients. As well, it is not uncommon to compare performance of the left hand of apractic patients who frequently have left hemisphere damage to the right hand of right-hemisphere-damaged non-apractic patients as the other hand in each group of patients being contralateral to the damaged hemisphere is often hemiparetic. Todor and Smiley present work which examines asymmetries in several tasks, notably those involving visually aimed movements, and movements requiring fine motor control. Studies using the dual task paradigm are also considered. The implication of this work for understanding manual and hemispheric asymmetries in motor control as well as for the study of apraxia are discussed.

The final chapter by Christine MacKenzie and Ronald Marteniuk focusses on bimanual coordination. Many limb praxis tasks require the coordination of the two limbs, thus, it is important to have some perspective on variables which influence bimanual coordination. In their chapter bimanual coordination and the coordination of movements of a single limb are viewed as special cases of multimovement coordination. They identify a number of dimensions on which bimanual tasks might be classified. Research suggests an intrinsic relationship between the two limbs providing internal constraints on bimanual movements that give rise to preferred, stable modes of control. The implications of this view for understanding motor impairments in apraxia are discussed.

Together the chapters in this volume provide an overview of research into apraxia, examine the relationship of this disorder to other related deficits and review areas in motor control which bear upon an understanding of apraxia. While the volume reviews a bulk of the research on apraxia and related disorders, the work of several scholars, particularly that of Doreen Kimura, Norman Geschwind, Kathleen Haaland, and Edith Kaplan, is not adequately represented here. Unfortunately, these people were unable to contribute chapters due to conflicting commitments. I would urge the serious student to read their fine work referenced throughout the volume.

* * * * *

There are many people to acknowledge in the preparation of this volume. Lori Whippler, Joan Pache and Sherrie Bieman Copland all provided invaluable assistance in preparing the manuscript. Bruce Uttley and Carol Vogt of the Computer Science Centre of the University of Waterloo provided much needed advice as to the preparation of the manuscript on the General Markup Language computer system. I would like to thank Dr. George Stelmach, one of the series editors, for encouraging me to prepare this volume and Dr. K. Michielsen, Editor, for his patience during the process of preparing the volume. Finally, I must express my deepest appreciation to my wife and family for their support throughout this project.

* * * * *

I would like to dedicate this volume to the memory of the late Professor Henri Hecaen who made an immense contribution to the study of apraxia and, indeed, to neuropsychology in general. He kindly accepted my invitation to contribute a chapter to the volume and encouraged me in preparing it, but, unfortunately, was unable to see the finished product.

Eric A. Roy
Toronto and Waterloo
Ontario

CONTENTS

Preface/Introduction   v

Contents   ix

List of Contributors   xiii

PART 1: PERSPECTIVES ON APRAXIA

1. Historical Perspectives on Neuroanatomical Correlates of Limb Apraxia

P. Faglioni and A. Basso.   3

    Liepmann's theory and classification of apraxia   3
    The role of the dominant hemisphere   5
    The role of the subordinate hemisphere   9
    The intrahemispheric localisation of practic functions   11
    Evidence against localization   20
    The role of the corpus callosum   22
    Evidence provided by neurophysiological studies in the normal sub-
    ject   27
    Concluding remarks   30
    References   34

2. Methods of Limb Apraxia Examination and Their Bearing on the Interpretation of the Disorder

Ennio De Renzi   45

    Distinctions based on the nature of the movement   46
    Distinction based on the physiological properties of the movement   53
    Testing apraxia in one modality   56
    Conclusions   59
    References   62

3. Ideomotor Apraxia: Gestural Discrimination, Comprehension and
Memory

Leslie J. Gonzalez Rothi and Kenneth M. Heilman   65

    Two forms of Ideomotor Apraxia   66
    Gestural Comprehension   66
    Gestural Learning and Secondary Memory   68
    Primary Memory   70
    References   74

4. Apraxia as a Disorder of a System of Signs

H. Hecaen and P. Rondot   75

    Anatomo-clinical correlations   77
    Apraxia and motor control deficits   83
    Neuropsychological considerations   85
    References   92

Contents

5. Clues to the Nature of Disruptions to Limb Praxis

Klaus Poeck   99

    Qualitative studies of ideomotor apraxia   100
    Qualitative studies of ideational apraxia   104
    Perspectives for further research   105
    References   107

6. Common Considerations in the Study of Limb, Verbal and Oral Apraxia

Eric A. Roy and Paula A. Square   111

    Control mechanisms in limb praxis: the conceptual-production system   112
    Limb apractic errors   117
    Clues to mechanisms underlying limb apraxia   118
    Mechanisms controlling motor speech production   123
    Clues to mechanisms underlying verbal apraxia   135
    Oral apractic errors   142
    Clues to mechanisms underlying oral apraxia   145
    Commonalities in limb and verbal apraxia   147
    References   150

7. Apraxia and Aphasia. Anatomical and Clinical Relationship

Andrew Kertesz   163

    Oral apraxia, verbal apraxia, and aphasia   165
    Apraxia in aphasia   166
    Praxis and language parameters   167
    Dissociations of apraxia and aphasia   168
    Localization of lesions in apraxia   171
    References   177

8. Methods in Neuroanatomical Research and an Experimental Study of Limb Apraxia

A. Basso, P. Faglioni and C. Luzzatti   179

    Pathological findings   179
    Electrical stimulation   180
    Neuroradiological investigation   180
    Experiment   185
    References   196

9. Can the Study of Praxis in Animals Aid in the Study of Apraxia of Humans?

Bryan Kolb and Ian Q. Whishaw   203

    The problem of anatomy   205
    The problem of measuring behaviour   214
    The problem of quantifying severity   215
    Selecting nonhuman species for study   216
    Summary   219
    References   221

10. Developmental Dyspraxia

Sharon Cermak   225

    Definition   225
    Differences between apraxia in children and adults   226
    Characteristics of the dyspractic child   228
    Theoretical basis/etiology of developmental dyspraxia   232
    Evaluation of dyspraxia   234
    Treatment of developmental dyspraxia   238
    Is developmental dyspraxia a unitary disorder?   241
    References   243

PART 2: CONCEPTS AND ISSUES BEARING ON APRAXIA

11. Response and Projection: A Reinterpretation of the Premotor Concept

Gary Goldberg   251

    The evolutionary theory   251
    The premotor concept   255
    Hypothesis   259
    Summary   262
    References   263

12. A Theory of the Representation, Organization and Timing of Action with Implications for Sequencing Disorders

Donald G. MacKay   267

    Why Morse code?   268
    The theory   269
    Generalization of the theory   279
    Systems controlling action   288
    Attention and errors   299
    Movement disorders   300
    The physiological plausibility of node structure theory   303
    References   306

13. Performance Differences Between the Hands: Implications for Studying Disruption to Limb Praxis

John I. Todor and Ann L. Smiley   309

  Hand differences in manual proficiency   310
  Why are the hands different?   317
  Is the left hand ever superior to the right?   330
  The influence of differential hand use   332
  Summary and implications   333
  References   336

14. Bimanual Coordination

Christie L. MacKenzie and Ronald G. Marteniuk   345

  How shall we classify bimanual coordination tasks?   346
  Acquisition of bimanual coordination   352
  Summary and implications   354
  References   356

Author Index   359

Subject Index   399

List of Contributors

Anna Basso, Ph.D.
    Centro Di Neuropsicologia
    Universita Di Milano
    Via Francesco Sforza, 35
    20122, Milano, Italia

Sharon Cermak, Ph.D.
    Department of Occupational Therapy
    Sargent College of Allied Health Professions
    Boston University
    University Road
    Boston, Massachussetts 02215

Ennio De Renzi, M.D.
    Clinica Neurologica
    Della Universita Di Modena
    Via de Pozzo, 71
    41100 Modena, Italia

Pietro Faglioni, M.D.
    Clinica Neurologica
    Della Universita Di Modena
    Via de Pozzo, 71
    41100 Modena, Italia

Gary Goldberg, M.D. F.R.C.P.
    Department of Rehabilitation Medicine
    Temple University
    Philadelphia, Pennsylvania

Leslie J. Gonzalez Rothi, Ph.D.
    Speech Pathologist - 126
    Gainesville Veterans Administration
    Medical Center
    Gainesville, Florida 32602

Henri Hecaen, M.D.
    Unite de Recherches Neuropsychologiques
    et Neurolinguistiques (U.111)
    I.N.S.E.R.M.
    Laboratoire de Pathologiedu Langage
    Ecole Pratique des Haute Etudies
    E.R.A. No. 274 Au C.N.R.S.
    2ter, Rue D'Alesia
    75014 Paris, France

Kenneth M. Heilman, M.D.
    Department of Neurology
    Box J-236
    J. Hillis Miller Health Center
    University of Florida
    College of Medicine
    Gainesville, Florida 32610

Andrew Kertesz, M.D., F.R.C.P.(C)
          Department of Neurological Sciences
          University of Western Ontario and
          St. Joseph Hospital
          London, Ontario

Bryan Kolb, Ph.D.
          Department of Psychology
          University of Lethbridge
          Lethbridge, Alberta

Donald MacKay, Ph.D.
          Department of Psychology
          University of California at Los Angeles
          Los Angeles, California

Christine L. MacKenzie, Ph.D.
          Department of Kinesiology
          University of Waterloo
          Waterloo, Ontario, N2L 3G1

Ronald G. Marteniuk, Ph.D.
          Department of Kinesiology
          University of Waterloo
          Waterloo, Ontario, N2L 3G1

Klaus Poeck, M.D.
          Vorstand Der Abteilung Neurologie
          Medizinische Fakultat Der
          Technischen Hochschule Aachen
          5100 Aachen, Den
          Goethestrasse, 27-29
          West Germany

Pierre Rondot, M.D.
          Directeur
          Unite de Recherches Neuropsychologiques
          et Neurolinguistiques (U.111)
          I.N.S.E.R.M.
          Laboratoire de Pathologie du Langage
          Ecole Pratique des Haute Etudies
          E.R.A. No. 274 Au C.N.R.S.
          2ter, Rue D'Alesia
          75014 Paris, France

Eric A. Roy, Ph.D., C.Psych.
          Department of Psychology
          Mount Sinai Hospital and
          University of Toronto
          Toronto, Ontario

          and

          Department of Kinesiology
          University of Waterloo
          Waterloo, Ontario

Ann Smiley   Department of Kinesiology
University of Michigan
Ann Arbor, Michigan

Paula A. Square, Ph.D.
Graduate Department of Speech Pathology
University of Toronto
Toronto, Ontario

John Todor, Ph.D.
Department of Kinesiology
University of Michigan
Ann Arbor, Michigan

Ian Q. Whishaw, Ph.D.
Department of Psychology
University of Lethbridge
Lethbridge, Alberta, T1K 3M4

PART 1:

Perspectives on Apraxia

Neuropsychological Studies of Apraxia
and Related Disorders, E. A. Roy (ed.)
© Elsevier Science Publishers B. V. (North-Holland), 1985

HISTORICAL PERSPECTIVES ON NEUROANATOMICAL CORRELATES

OF LIMB APRAXIA

P. Faglioni and A. Basso

Universita di Milano e Universita di Modena

Liepmann's interpretation of apraxia is reviewed and assessed in the light of more recent investigations. There is ample support for the three main points of his theory. 1) The left hemisphere programs the gesture and 2) controls motor activity of the right hemisphere through mid-callosal pathways. 3) Motor planning is the province of the cortex and subjacent white matter. Other aspects of Liepmann's theory appear in need of modification. While he denied the existence of centres specialized in motor planning, there are now many strands of evidence suggesting the role of the parietal cortex in evoking and organizing the motor pattern.

Since Liepmann's (1900) original description of the Regierungsrat's symptomatology, the term "apraxia" has come to be universally accepted to designate a deficit affecting the purposeful organization of voluntary actions, mostly but not necessarily represented by gestures. In the years between 1900 and 1908, Liepmann, drawing often on the work of Pick (1905), Kleist (1906, 1907) and Maas (1907), proposed a theory of gestural functions (1905b, 1907, 1908) which remains the only framework permitting an interpretation of apraxia in anatomical terms. It is our purpose to evaluate the adequacy of Liepmann's interpretation of apraxia in the light of the evidence collected in the 80 years that have elapsed from its original formulation. We shall start with an outline of the theory and will then analyse its main elements.

Liepmann's theory and classification of apraxia

In Liepmann's view, correct execution of a gesture requires the existence of a "motor programme" (Bewegungsentwurf) whereby the spatial arrangement and temporal sequence of the single movements composing the action is evoked and controlled, at least in the early stages of learning. Motor programmes are mainly based on a visual representation of the sequence of which the subject is for the most part aware. The whole cortex would cooperate in building up the programme, with the left hemisphere playing, however, a dominant role.

Inadequate formulation of the motor programme results in ideational apraxia. Gestural activity is most affected when the subject himself must programme the action, and less so when the examiner provides a model, the deficit involves all muscular regions, and its severity is proportional to the complexity of the gesture with errors mainly concerning the direction and correct sequence of movements. Since the dominant hemisphere plays a leading role in conceiving the motor programme, ideational apraxia is associated at least in its most severe and clinically manifest forms with left hemisphere damage alone.

In order to be carried out, a motor programme must be transformed into appropriate "innervations", whose "memory" (kinesthatische und innervatorische Engramme) is located in the "sensomotorium", a region involving, according to Liepmann, the pre- and post-central gyri and the pes of the superior, middle and inferior frontal convolutions. Kinesthetic-innervatory engrams are aroused by the motor programme and thus require the pathways connecting retro-Rolandic areas with the sensomotorium to be undamaged. Their interruption precludes transmission of the motor programme, causing a different form of apraxia, ideomotor apraxia. The patient knows what he has to do, but becomes incapable of calling on the innervations needed to execute the action, whether on verbal command or on imitation. Generally, the deficit is confined to the muscles controlled by the cortical area which does not receive the motor programme and is not related to the complexity of gesture. Clumsiness, distortion, falterings and exaggeration characterize the patient's movements, which become incomplete or overcharged. The patient is aware of his failure and tries to correct them.

Since in right-handers gesture learning is under left hemisphere control, ideomotor apraxia will occur in them following left hemisphere lesions. However, once the action has become automatized as a fixed motor stereotype, the intervention of the left hemisphere is no longer necessary. The relevant innervations are called up unconsciously and carried out under kinesthetic control by the sensomotorium contralateral to the innervated limb. This explains why everyday actions -- like hand-shaking, knocking at the door, buttoning up a shirt, tying shoelaces, knotting a tie, or any habitual gesture of our daily routine -- can be performed correctly by ideational and ideomotor apractics.

Loss of kinesthetic-innervatory engrams consequent to sensomotorium damage causes melokinetic apraxia, which affects all types of gesture, without relation to their complexity and routine character and independently of whether the patient must create or imitate them. The disorder is confined to the muscles controlled by the injured cortex. Gestures will become uncouth, clumsy, "inexpert", and will be preceded by fruitless attempts which only bring the wrong muscles into play. The characteristics of melokinetic apraxia are not dependent on the hemispheric side of lesion.

Left hemisphere control on left limb gestures carried out by the right sensomotorium implies exchange of information through the corpus callosum. By this way sensory information received by the subordinate hemisphere is transmitted to the dominant hemisphere, which utilizes it along with its own data to build up the motor programme. This in turn gains access to the right sensomotorium via the commissures. Apraxia following a lesion of the corpus callosum will be ideomotor in character and will be confined to the limbs controlled by the subordinate hemisphere which is devoid of gestural autonomy. In callosal patients bilateral apraxia will only occur when the information needed for the elaboration of a motor project remains confined to the subordinate hemisphere, for example, when the subject also has a right visual field defect or when the information is projected tachistoscopically into the left visual field.

Having briefly outlined Liepmann's theory, we will now dwell upon some of its main tenets, trying to assess to what extent they have been confirmed or modified by subsequent studies. Our considerations will be limited to ideomotor and ideational apraxia. Autonomy of melokinetic apraxia has in fact been seriously challenged after it had been observed that deficits of dexterity similar to those described by Kleist (1907) and Liepmann (1920) are found in the more mild forms of paresis from lesions of the cortico-spinal pathways and are therefore interpretable as deficits of elementary motility.

The role of the dominant hemisphere

Left-hemisphere dominance for practic functions

It is not from the 1900 study that Liepmann's theory on hemisphere dominance emerged, but rather from later clinical and clinico-pathological investigations. In 1905 Liepmann (1905b) performed what must be probably considered the first systematic neuropsychological research reported in the literature. He tested 41 patients presenting right hemiplegia and 42 patients presenting left hemiplegia for apraxia and found the deficit present in 20 patients of the former group and in none of the latter. From this finding Liepmann inferred that the left hemisphere must have a prominent role in controlling movements that are "innervated" not only by the left hemisphere, but also by the right one.

Definite evidence for left hemisphere dominance was reached by Liepmann investigating the case Ochs which he published with Maas (1907), and on whom he had the chance of performing an autopsy. The patient had a right hemiplegia due to an infarct in the left pes of the pons, and presented remarkably severe apraxia of the upper left limb. For instance, instead of a cigar he would raise the match to his lips, could not clench his fist, nor write a single letter of the alphabet. Severe mistakes were also made when he was requested to perform gestures on command and on imitation. The apractic behaviour of the left limb could not be attributed to the right hemisphere, which was intact, and had to be accounted for by left hemisphere and callosum lesions. They involved the white matter of upper frontal gyrus, the paracentral lobule, the medial portion of the corona radiata, and above all, the left half of the corpus callosum in front of the splenium. Liepmann's hypothesis of left hemisphere dominance was to receive almost unanimous support from subsequent research. Especially relevant to the issue are the studies carried out to assess the occurrence of apraxia in unselected samples of left and right brain-damaged patients. They are summarized in Table 1. With the exception of the first of these studies, the diagnosis of apraxia was always grounded on a quantitative score and made with reference to the poorest, or the poorest but one score achieved by a sizeable group of normal controls. Table 2 reviews studies where the mean scores of left and right brain-damaged patients on movement imitation tests have been compared.

As can be seen, the greater impairment following left brain injury is confirmed by every investigation. The only exception is represented by Arseni, Voinesco and Goldenberg (1958) who studied 32 patients with parietal tumour and found that apraxia was equally frequent following damage to either hemisphere. The value of this research is, however, questionable, as no details are given about the criteria used to establish hemisphere dominance (left- or right-handedness? presence of aphasia?), and to diagnose apraxia.

Possible exceptions to left-hemisphere dominance for practic functions

There are very few cases of right-handed patients in whom a clinically evident apraxia was reported associated with a right hemisphere lesion. Hecaen and Gimeno Alava (1960) gleaned from the literature 16 patients with apraxia and damage to the right brain, but 11 had bilateral lesions and two were left-handed. We are, therefore, left with three patients, who probably correspond to case 9, 10, and 11 of Morlaas (1928). Of these, case 10 was found on autopsy to have a right frontal softening and an undamaged left hemisphere. He had a "light" apraxia (ideomotor type) confined to the left arm, which is not in conflict with Liepmann's theory, for a left hand defect can ensue from the interruption of callosal radiations produced by right frontal lesion. Cases 9 and 11 are more challenging, since they had right posterior

TABLE 1

Incidence of apractics among left (LBD) and right (RBD) brain-damaged patients.

Authors	Apraxia Assessment	LBD			RBD			C^1
		N (Total)	N (Apractics)		N (Total)	N (Apractics)		
De Ajuriaguerra et. al. (1960)	clinical evaluation	206 55*	3 39 8	I IM I+IM	154 (?)	0		none
Pieczuro and Vignolo (1967)	20 gest. imitation	70	32	IM				40
De Renzi et. al. (1968)	10 gest. imitation	160	11 11 34	I IM I+M	45	1 (?)	IM	40
De Renzi et. al. (1980)	24 gest. imitation	100	50	IM	80	16	IM	100
De Renzi et. al. (1982)	24 gest. imitation	150	48	IM	110**	13**	IM	70
	10 obj. use	150	31-59	I	110**	4-7**	I	70

I = Ideative Apraxia (object use)
IM = Ideomotor Apraxia (gestures imitation, symbolic or not, single or multiple)
* = Bilateral lesion
** = Unpublished data
1 = Control Subjects

TABLE 2

Left (LBD) vs right (RBD) brain-damaged patients performance in apraxia tests.

Authors	Test	LBD(N)		RBD (N)	C*
Kimura and Archibald (1974)	Pantomime after verbal order and, if needs be, imitation of 6 objects use	16	<	14	none
	Pantomime after verbal order and, if needs be, imitation of 3 gestures	16	<	14	none
	Imitation of 6 intransitive sequences	16	<	14	none
Kimura (1977)	Sequences of gestures with objects (press a button, pull a handle, press a bar)	29	<	16	none
Roy (1981)	Pantomime after verbal order and, if needs be, imitation of 5 intransitive and 5 transitive gestures	8 (a)　12 (na)	<　=	12　12	none
	5 sequences of gestures with objects (turn, pull, point, slide 4 knobs)	20	<	12	none
Kolb and Milner (1981)	Imitation of 6 sequences of 3 gestures	7 (p)		6 (p)	18
Kimura (1982)	Imitation of 3 sequences	72 (?)	=	46 (?)	?
	Imitation of 5 single gestures	72 (?)	=	46 (?)	?

The sign < means significantly inferior
The sign = means absence of a significant difference
a = aphasic; na = non-aphasic; p = parietal   C = Control Subjects

Sylvian softenings and practic disorders, ideomotor and ideational, respectively. Unfortunately no detail concerning their handedness was given. Another patient at variance with the rule of left hemisphere dominance was described by both von Monakow (1914, case 11) and Brun (1921, case 7). This was a right-handed patient with a right parieto-occipito-temporal lesion and bilateral apraxia. He also had two left-hemisphere softenings, one occipital, and the other temporo-basal, but contrary to von Monakow's claim (1914) these locations can hardly be held responsible for the genesis of apraxia.

The analogy between practic and language dominance is evident and inspired a few authors to advance the hypothesis that praxis and speech utilize the same anatomical structures and are but two different expressions of the same basic mechanism (Kimura, 1976, 1979, 1982; Liepmann, 1913, 1920; Mateer & Kimura, 1977; Mingazzini, 1913; Ojemann, 1982; Ojemann & Mateer, 1979). Many strands of evidence can be adduced which contradict this view, but the most decisive one is represented by case reports showing that one hemisphere is dominant for praxis and the other for speech.

This pattern of alternated dominance has been so far reported in right-handers only by Heilman, Gonyea and Geschwind (1974), who had a patient showing severe ideomotor and ideational apraxia, but no aphasia following middle cerebral artery softening consequent to the occlusion of the left internal carotid. Also relevant to the issue is the patient of Selnes, Rubens, Risse and Levy (1982) in whom a softening involving the frontal and parietal opercula, the angular gyrus and the superior parietal lobule of the left hemisphere produced persistent bilateral apraxia and transient aphasia which quickly recovered leaving only agraphia and inability to spell. It would appear that the right hemisphere was much better equipped to take over language rather than practic functions.

Apraxia in left-handers

More substantial is the number of dissociations between speech and practic disorders reported in left-handers. In the great majority of these subjects apraxia ensues from right brain lesion, which may or may not be associated with aphasia, depending on whether the language dominance has also shifted to the right.

Left-handed patients presenting aphasia and apraxia following right hemisphere damage were reported by Rothmann (1911), Rose (1911), Malaise and Liepmann (quoted by Liepmann, 1911, p. 1310), Guillain, Alajouanine and Garcin (1925), Morlaas (1928: cases 34 and 36), Kleist (1934), Nielsen (1946), Poeck and Kerschensteiner (1971), Signoret and North (1979: case 2), Delis, Knight and Simpson (1983). The left-handed patient repoted by Taterka (1924a,b) is worth noticing as he presented a reversed picture with respect to that described by Liepmann and Maas (1907) in the patient Ochs: following a softening of the right internal capsule and middle corpus callosum (1 cm!), she was found to have left hemiplegia and apraxia in the right limbs.

An approximately equal number of case reports showed apraxia but not aphasia following right brain damage, thus pointing to right hemisphere dominance for movements and left hemisphere dominance for language. Such patients have been reported by Rothmann (1907a,b), Hartmann (1907: case 1), Hildebrandt (1908), Morlaas (1928: case 9, 10 and 11), Heilman, Coyle, Gonyea and Geschwind (1973), Faglioni (1977), Valenstein and Heilman (1979), Margolin (1980) and Poeck and Lehmkuhl (1980). No theory assuming that apraxia is contingent upon the disruption of the same mechanism underlying speech can account for these patients and the idea of a common basis for apraxia and aphasia must, therefore, be abandoned.

There is another aspect of apraxia in left-handers which deserves careful consideration, namely, whether the disorder is always associated with right hemisphere damage. An implicit assumption shared by almost all students is that hand preference and eupraxis are both related to the same cerebral mechanism, conceivable as the ability to program and learn the movement (Geschwind, 1975; Jason, 1983a,b; Liepmann, 1920). This view implies that the side of the brain ruling the most dexterous hand must also be the dominant one in motor planning, viz. apraxia is always associated with a left brain lesion in right-handers and with a right brain lesion in left-handers. Although the great majority of case reports are in agreement with this rule, there are a few remarkable exceptions which seriously challenge the notion of an absolute relationship between handedness and eupraxis. Apraxia in left-handed subjects presenting left sided lesions was reviewed by Signoret and North (1979), who found three apractics in Critchley's (1953) series of 12 brain-damaged patients, three in Ettlinger, Jackson and Zangwill's (1956) series of eight brain-damaged patients, five in Hecaen and Sauguet's (1971) series of 47 brain-damaged patients. It must be admitted that the clinical documentation of these cases is not completely satisfactory and that the issue deserves further investigation, but the notion of an unfailing relationship between handedness and motor control is undoubtedly challenged.

If practic dominance is not determined by manual preference, what other factors are at work? On the analogy of left hemisphere dominance for language, it may be speculated that the basis for asymmetry of function is anatomical, with some cortical (parietal?) areas more developed on the left than on the right in right-handers. Such an asymmetry is known to vary largely for the language specialized areas and it has been argued (Haaland & Miranda, 1982; Naeser & Pieniadz, 1982) that the ability of the right hemisphere to take over language function in patients with left-hemisphere damage is related to the degree of the anatomical asymmetry of their brain. The same line of reasoning may be applied to the pattern of hemispheric representation for praxis, with most of right-handers showing a greater development of the relevant areas of the contralateral cerebral side, some an equal development, and a few an inverted asymmetry.

The role of the subordinate hemisphere

In spite of the leading role attributed to the left hemisphere, Liepmann's theory does not envisage the right hemisphere function as completely passive in the course of movement planning and learning, but rather as cooperating, albeit in a subordinate position: "Let us remember once and for all that the right hemisphere also takes part in eupraxis, especially in relation to the left half of the body" (Liepmann, 1920, p. 531).

The strands of evidence supporting this position are of different weight and relevance, but, taken altogether, suggest that at least in a number of right-handed subjects, the right hemisphere function is not merely executive.

1.   In the first place, clinical evidence suggests the most severe and long-lasting manifestations of apraxia tend to be associated with damage involving both hemispheres (for example, bilateral softening or anoxia, Brun, 1922; Lange, 1936; Liepmann, 1907, 1914). Admittedly, this statement is grounded on clinical impression and not on the findings of a systematic investigation. Rubens, Geschwind, Mahowald and Mastri's (1977) patient can be cited as an example. He still showed left limb apraxia due to callosal damage 14 years after a trauma and had, in addition to callosal damage, atrophy of the supramarginal gyrus and the superior and middle temporal gyri of the right hemisphere.

2.   According to Liepmann (1907, 1911, 1920) and other authorities (Brun, 1922;
        Kleist, 1934; Lange, 1936; von Monakow, 1914), apraxia due to left parietal
        lesion would affect left limbs less severely than the right ones, as though
        they were still to enjoy a certain amount of control by the contralateral
        hemisphere. The evidence supporting this claim is, however, weak, in that
        the only studies which systematically contrasted the motor ability of the two
        limbs following left brain damage failed to find an asymmetry in impairment
        (Kimura, 1977; Kimura & Archibald, 1974; Kolb & Milner, 1981).

3.   When practic abilities are assessed with a quantitative procedure and apraxia
        is diagnosed on an objective basis with reference to the scores of a control
        group, its presence can be brought out in a small, but not negligible percent-
        age of right brain-damaged patients. Moreover, its incidence appears to be
        related to the thoroughness of the testing method. On a ten gesture imita-
        tion test, De Renzi, Pieczuro and Vignolo (1968) found apraxia in 2% of 45
        right brain-damaged patients, while Pieczuro and Vignolo (1967) found it in
        9% of 35 right brain-damaged patients, using a 20 gesture test. The percent-
        age rose to 20% in a sample of 80 right brain-damaged patients when a 24
        gesture test was given designed to survey an extensive range of movements
        (meaningful or meaningless, single or multiple, involving the fingers or the
        whole limb) (De Renzi, Motti and Nichelli, 1980). This finding has recently
        been confirmed (De Renzi, Faglioni & Sorgato, Note 1) in a sample of 110
        right brain-damaged patients, of whom 12% performed in the apractic range.
        In the same investigation, 6% of the same patients also failed when required
        to mime object use on verbal command or on the visual presentation of the
        object, and 4% even when the object was handled.

        Kolb and Milner's (1981) findings suggest that asymmetry in motor control
        varies according to the lobe involved. On a motor sequence imitation test
        seven patients with left parietal damage scored lower than six patients with
        right parietal damage, while no difference in impairment was found when the
        comparison was carried out between patients with left (No. 14) and right (No.
        10) frontal premotor ablation.

4.   Finally, there are patients whose apractic picture points to a complete
        autonomy of the right hemisphere in planning motor activity. Liepmann's
        (1900, 1905a, 1906) Regierungsrat is the most famous example. He was una-
        ble to perform any kind of gesture with his right limbs on verbal command,
        imitation or handling objects, except for the most habitual actions carried
        out under tactual guide (e.g., he could button his shirt if his hand was placed
        upon the button or buttonhole). Gestural activity of the left limbs was, on
        the contrary, unimpaired at least in the course of the testing sessions carried
        out in 1900; later exams showed that he had become partially apractic even
        with the left hand. Since necroscopy disclosed that all the corpus callosum
        except the splenium had been destroyed by the lesion, the right sensomotori-
        um must have become inaccessible to information coming from the left hem-
        isphere and had to function on its own capabilities. Even more amazing was
        the ability of the right hemisphere to carry out movements on verbal com-
        mand, as these are normally decoded by the Wernicke area of the left hemi-
        sphere. In view of the current knowledge on commissural transmission of
        information, it seems unlikely that the left hemisphere could communicate
        with the right sensomotorium via the splenium, the anterior commissure, or
        the hippocampal commissure, as hypothesized by Liepmann (1906). It is more
        likely that the right hemisphere could autonomously control the motor activi-
        ty of the left limbs and also interpret verbal messages.

Another case which points to the equipotentiality of the two hemispheres for practic functions is Geschwind and Kaplan's (1962) patient. He was suffering from a left frontal paramedial glioblastoma and an infarct of the corpus callosum consequent to the surgical tying off of some branches of the anterior cerebral artery. Apraxia affected the left hand but was only apparent in tasks involving oral or written language. As soon as the patient saw the examiner make a gesture, or was allowed to first execute it with his right hand, he was immediately able to repeat correctly the movement with his left hand. Also he successfully demonstrated with the left hand the use of an object he handled. The softening of the corpus callosum explains the inability of the left hand to carry out movements on verbal command, since the decoded message was prevented from reaching the right motor area. By the same token, it must, however, be assumed that the normal performance of the left hand in response to visual or tactile stimuli attests to the autonomous capacity of the right hemisphere to plan gestures.

The intrahemispheric localization of practic functions

An exhaustive interpretation of apraxia must address the question of whether, within the dominant hemisphere, there are areas specialized in planning gestures, or if the hemisphere is engaged in its entirety. While most authors share the former position, other investigators have seen any attempt to identify practic centres with considerable skepticism. The theoretical position of the two schools will be reviewed in this and the next section.

Disconnection and centres theories

Two distinct meanings can be applied to the term "practic zones". Liepmann (1914) thought of them in terms of loci of convergence or passage for the pathways connecting sensory associative areas to motor areas in the cortex that enable them to work together. If they were cut off apraxia would follow because the motor areas would be deprived of the necessary information. The disconnection theory was first proposed by Liepmann when in 1900 he interpreted the right-hand apraxia observed in the Regierungsrat as being due to the "isolation" of the left sensomotorium resulting from the destruction of the corpus callosum and the left parietal white matter. The former lesion was thought to have severed the connections between the left and right hemisphere, and the latter the pathways carrying information from the associative sensory areas of the left hemisphere to the sensomotorium. Cases where apraxia becomes evident when information is conveyed through one sensory modality alone, e.g. on verbal command but not on imitation or on handling objects (this point will be discussed in detail further on) sustain the disconnection theory.

A quite different view of "practic zones" is that implied by the term "practic centres", which are conceived of as cortical areas where gesture-creating information is processed and the movement is "programmed". Damage here would disrupt the motor program assembly and gestural activity would become defective whichever sensory modality were involved. Liepmann firmly denied that he had ever hypothesized the existence of practic centres (Liepmann, 1906, pp. 238-239; 1907, pp. 726-727, 768; 1913, p. 487; 1914, p. 496, 497-498, 503, 506; 1920, p. 529): "I really cannot imagine that there is such a thing as a practic centre, or -- as some people have mistakenly thought me to assume -- that it is to be found in the supramarginal gyrus" (Liepmann, 1914, p. 497). Nevertheless, Liepmann acknowledged that apraxia acquires different qualitative features depending on the locus of lesion. He so summarized his views in his last paper on the subject: "The further back (parieto-occipital) the lesion, the more apraxia has an ideational quality, the further forward (central) the lesion, the more apraxia has a melokinetic quality, while ideo-motor apraxia is brought about by intermediate parietal damage (supramarginal)", (Liepmann, 1920, p. 532). It must be recognized that Liepmann's theory is somewhat ambiguous here, for it is hard to reconcile a pure disconnection hypothesis with the changing quality of apraxia in relation to the locus of lesion. Other authors were, in fact, ready to take up this point and suggested that there were areas of the cortex specialized in gestural programming, localising them either in the frontal lobe (Goldstein, 1911; Hartmann, 1907; Wilson, 1908), or in the parietal lobe (Heilman, 1979a,b; Kleist, 1934), or in both (Kimura, 1982; Luria, 1980).

Recent research on monkeys (reviewed in Faglioni, 1979) and rCBF studies sup-port this hypothesis, corroborating the view that the two "poles of the system" (frontal and parietal) have a specific role in practic functions. Since the turn of the century a great body of data and hypotheses about the existence, localization and specific roles of the "practic areas", either considered as loci of convergence of sensory-motor pathways or as practic centres, has been collected. They will be reviewed and discussed.

The same importance for practic functions is not to be attached to all regions of the cortex and white matter. It would seem that the primary sensory regions (som-esthetic,[1] acoustic, visual) play no role in the performing of gesture. The same applies to the temporal pole and the third temporal convolution, as well as to the cortex of the base of the brain, the cingular gyrus and the hippocampus. The frontal lobe lying in front of the associative motor area is not thought to affect praxis either, except by Luria (1980) who maintains, however, that it is only involved in the programming of complex motor sequences. Finally, lesions of the internal capsule have never been said to cause apraxia. The bulk of data currently available support the opinion that apraxia is critically associated with damage to a region extending from the parietal lobe to the premotor area, with a special emphasis on the supra-marginal gyrus and, to a lesser extent, on the premotor cortex. Some authors have also included in the practic area the first two temporal convolutions, the supple-mentary motor area and some the basal and thalamic nuclei.

The parietal lobe

Since his first study, Liepmann (1900) pointed out the importance of parietal lesions, especially those involving the white matter of the supramarginal gyrus where the occipito-frontal and temporo-frontal pathways carrying to the sensomo-torium the visual and audio-verbal information necessary for programming and call-ing forth gestures run together.

Many authors were to confirm the relevance of parietal damage to apraxia: Strohmayer (1903), von Bechterew (1909), Bychowski (1909), Kroll (1910), Kleist (1911) who reported lesions in the supramarginal gyrus in all 12 of his apractic patients; von Stauffenberg (1911, 1918), Foix (1916, cases 4 and 5), Bremer (1921), Bailey (1924, case 1), Tzavaras (1978, case 2), Signoret and North (1979, 2 cases). Particularly convincing are Morlaas' (1928) cases 4 and 5, who showed a severe ideo-motor and ideational apraxia produced by a lesion confined to the white parietal matter, and case 19 in whom a softening of the superior and inferior parietal convo-lutions spreading into the corpus callosum had caused bilateral ideomotor apraxia, mainly affecting the left limbs. Also von Monakow's (1914) cases 9, 10, 11, 13, 14 and Brun's (1921, 1922) series -- to be discussed at length in the following section -- present substantial evidence in favour of the crucial role played by the parietal lobe.

---

[1] See Liepmann's concept of "sensomotorium"

Proofs of the crucial role of the parietal lobe are also provided by studies that have systematically investigated series of unselected patients and attempted to relate performance to locus of lesion. Arseni, Voinesco and Goldenberg (1958) observed ideomotor apraxia in 11 out of 12 cases with parietal tumor in the "dominant" hemisphere (but also in 11 out of 20 patients with a parietal tumor in the "minor" hemisphere), and ideational apraxia in three cases with a parietal tumor in the dominant hemisphere.

De Ajuriaguerra, Hecaen and Angelergues (1960) reported 13 surgical lesions damaging the parietal lobe among 28 ideomotor apractics, and two from among five ideational apractics. Of particular relevance to the issue of localization are the findings of Kolb and Milner (1981) based on very precisely defined cortical excisions. The seven patients who had undergone left parietal ablation were by far the most impaired group on imitating limb motor sequences, not only with respect to normal subjects (18), but also to the other brain damaged groups (six right parietal patients, 14 left and 10 right frontal patients, 31 left and 29 right temporal patients, three left and two right central patients, and three left occipital patients). Kolb and Milner's (1981) findings were recently replicated by Kimura (1982) and De Renzi, Faglioni, Lodesani and Vecchi (1983). Left brain damaged patients whose lesion was supposed to be parietal only on the grounds of unspecified "clinical and instrumental" data in the former study and ascertained by means of CT in the latter, failed in imitating sequences as well as single manual movements. A still controversial point is whether sequences are in fact more sensitive than single movements to left brain damage in general and to the intra-hemispheric locus of lesion in particular (see De Renzi, this volume). Kimura's (1982) left frontal patients unlike the parietal ones showed normal performance on a single movement test and scored poorly only on a sequence test. Their specific impairment was related to the greater demand that series of movements impose on the system devised to "select the correct postures via a preprogrammed plan". Manual movement test findings suggested to Kimura the existence of a practic system involving the fronto-parietal region with its epicentre in the parietal area. Parietal lesions would thus cause severe arm apraxia, affecting multiple and single movements, and frontal lesions light apraxia showing up only in sequences of movements. However, De Renzi et al. (1980) did not find any difference between the percentage of apractics identified in a sample of 60 brain damaged aphasics with single or multiple manual movements. The same result was obtained in De Renzi et al.'s study (1983); frontal patients failed with respect to normal subjects, but performed better on a sequence and on a single movement test than the parietal patients.

If parietal damage brings about apraxia by severing the pathways transmitting visual and audioverbal information (Liepmann, 1900, 1905b, 1914, 1920) and perhaps also kinesthetic-tactile information (Geschwind, 1965) to the sensomotorium or to a possible supramarginal centrum, then a lesion so located as to interrupt just one channel of information may be expected to produce apraxia confined to a single sensory modality. Single cases attesting to the existence of this dissociation have been occasionally reported by the literature (Heilman, 1973; Liepmann, 1905b; Morlaas, 1928, case 24). Strohmayer (1903) described a patient unable to use even the most common objects but able to make gestures on command. Autopsy revealed a left supramarginal cyst. Damasio and Benton's (1979) patient could make meaningful gestures and demonstrate the use of an object on verbal command, but failed on imitating even the simplest non-symbolic gestures. CT scan showed a lesion in the occipito-parietal area, a location ideal for blocking the flow of visual information, while leaving unaffected the verbal information channel. Klein's (1924) patient failed as soon as he handled an object, that is when he needed to use kinesthetic tactile information: he had a softening located in the interparietal sulcus suited, as Geschwind (1965) maintains, to cut off the connections between primary somesthetic and premotor cortex. Brown's (1972) case 8 presented an analogous picture, though with a less clear dissociation, and his brain scan and EEG showed involvement of the parietal region. Assal and Regli's (1980) patient was able to use and mime the use of objects when they were named, not when she merely saw or handled them. CT scan showed two softenings, one involving the left occipital region and the corpus callosum, which cut the left hemisphere off from any chance of using visual information, and the other involving the left parietal lobe (but sparing the supramarginal gyrus), which blocked tactile information. Thus only audio-verbal information, coming from the temporal lobe, could reach the left premotor area.

De Renzi, Faglioni and Sorgato (1982) sought to come to grips with this problem by systematically investigating the ability of 150 left brain-damaged patients to pretend to use the same 10 objects when they were named, or shown visually but not handled, or handled out of sight. Various types of dissociation emerged. Six patients showed a performance in the verbal modality that was distinctly poorer than in the other two modalities, and six patients showed the same pattern in the visual modality. Many more were markedly impaired on one test in comparison to another: eight on the verbal as against the tactile test, seven on the visual against the tactile, one on the visual against the verbal, one on the tactile against the verbal, and one on the tactile against the visual.

The frontal lobe

After the parietal lobe and next in order of importance comes the premotor area. In Liepmann's (1905b) view the sensomotorium was one of the areas crucial to the genesis of apraxia. More recently, the premotor area alone has been implicated in programming movements since it is the only portion of the sensomotorium to receive direct communications from the associative sensory areas (Geschwind, 1965; Haaxma and Kuypers, 1975; Pandya and Seltzer, 1982, for bibliography). The unanimous acceptance of the crucial role played by the premotor (and perhaps also central) area in practic functioning by so many authors (Angelergues, De Ajuriaguerra, Geschwind, Hecaen, Lange, Liepmann, Morlaas, Sittig and, above all, Hartmann, Goldstein and Wilson) is, however, a bit surprising when one considers how hard it is to find in the literature well documented cases of apraxia with lesions confined to this area.

Table 3 lists in chronological order all the cases that we have been able to glean from the literature in support of this notion. They are 16, but nine can hardly be considered probative of frontal lobe apraxia. Patients No. 2, 3, 4, 8, 13, 14 had apraxia of callosal type, patient No. 5 also had a parietal lesion, in patients No. 12 and 14 the motor disorder is better described as forced grasping, and in patient No. 6 it basically consisted in constructional disability. Convincing anatomo-clinical documentation that apraxia ensued from a left frontal lesion is thus to be found in no more than seven cases (No. 1, 7, 9, 10, 11, 15, 16) and in some of them (1, 11, 15, 16) the lesion was not proven to be restricted to the premotor area.

Liepmann (1905b) sought an indirect proof of the importance of the frontal region, in the frequency with which apraxia is associated with "motor" aphasia (out of 20 right hemiplegics with apraxia, 14 had motor aphasia) which is thought to attest to a frontal lesion. However, it has recently been emphasized (Mohr, Pessin, Finkelstein, Funkenstein, Duncan and Davis, 1978) that a longlasting Broca aphasia suggests the presence of a retrorolandic lesion, in addition to the involvement of frontal convolution. Pieczuro and Vignolo (1967) tried to replicate Liepmann's findings but they found that apraxia was absent in all of the five patients whose only symptom was Brocas aphasia, while it was present in seven of the eight patients whose symptoms (Wernicke aphasia and hemianopia) pointed to a posterior locus of

TABLE 3

FRONTAL LOBE CASES

Apraxia: Side and Features		Etiology and Site of Lesion	Comments
Bilateral: on imitation and object use	1	Left frontal cyst, surgically verified.	"Motor aphasia" without hemiparesis suggests a frontal lesion sparing the central gyri. Surgical verification.
Right limbs; on command, imitation and object use	2	Premotor callosal tumour, encroaching upon left frontal lobe, left basal ganglia, and right mesial frontal lobe.	The lesion was premotor, but increased intracranial pressure was present at the time of examination. Callosal apraxia in left-handed subject?
Left limbs; on command, imitation and object use	3	Tumour of the corpus callosum (from the splenium to the frontal plane of the anterior commissure) infiltrating the cingulate gyrus on the left more than on the right.	Apraxia is explained by the <u>callosal</u> lesion.
Left limbs; on command and object use	4	Post-hemorrhage cyst in the pes of right middle frontal convolution.	Apraxia is explained by lesion of the <u>callosal</u> radiations.
Bilateral; melokinetic	5	Left softenings involving the pes of central gyri, and of the inferior and middle frontal gyri, the superior anterior parietal lobule, the inferior parietal lobule, the superior and middle temporal gyri. Right hemisphere softening involving the posterior limb of the internal capsule. Bilateral softening of the basal ganglia.	Apraxia is explained by the left <u>supramarginal</u> lesion.

P. Faglioni and A. Basso

TABLE 3, continued

Apraxia: Side and Features	Etiology and Site of Lesion	Comments
6 Left limbs melokinetic? object use?	Left softening of the central gyri (hand, arm and leg area). Scar in the lingula.	Right hand was plegic. Attention, memory, and judgment were faulty. Apraxia mainly of constructive type, with agraphia.
7 Bilateral; "for complex actions"	Left softening in the pes of the superior, middle, and inferior frontal gyri, sparing the pars triangularis but partially involving the anterior pars of the precentral gyrus (face and hand area).	Apraxia is described in a single sentence as "incapacity to use limbs for more complex actions" (page 198)
8 Left limbs; "mild" apraxia on command	Right softening in the middle and inferior frontal gyri, inferior two thirds of the precentral gyrus, inferior half of the postcentral gyrus, external and internal capsule.	Apraxia is explained by lesion of callosal radiations.
9 Bilateral (?); transitive and intransitive gestures	Left softening in the inferior third of the post-central gyrus, inferior half of the precentral gyrus and pes of the meddle and inferior frontal gyri. Softenings in the left occipital lobe and in the right angular gyrus.	Bilateral hemianopia with macular sparing.
10 Bilateral (?); mild apraxia only for complex intransitive gestures	Left softenings in the precentral gyrus, and in the pes of the middle and inferior frontal gyri.	Right hemiparesis.
11 Bilateral; on imitation and object use	No autopsy.	Broca aphasia and normal motor and sensory functions suggest a pre-motor focal damage, but there is no evidence of supramarginal integrity.

TABLE 3, continued

Apraxia: Side and Features	Etiology and Site of Lesion	Comments
12 Bilateral; on object use	Callosal glioblastoma extending to the left frontal lobe and partially to the right parietal lobe.	Apraxia or forced grasping?
13 Left limbs; on command, imitation and object use	Left softening of the superior two thirds of the central gyri, the pes of the superior and middle frontal gyri, and a strip of Area 5; "severe degeneration of the corpus callosum".	Right hemiplegia, apraxia is explained by the callosal lesion.
14 Bilateral; on command and object use (?)	Callosal glioblastoma extending to the left frontal lobe and partially to the right.	Left hand apraxia is explained by the callosal lesion. Right hand apraxia was actually a forced grasping.
15 Left limbs; on command and imitation	Left frontal hemorrhage.	Right paresis. Surgical verification.
16 Left limbs; on command and imitation	Left frontal hemorrhage.	Right paresis. Surgical verification.

1 Liepmann, 1905b - Case 5

2-4 Hartmann, 1907 - Cases 1, 2, 3

5 Kleist, 1907, 1922 - Case 5

6 Liepmann, 1912 - Case 3

7 Brun, 1921 - Case 10

8-11 Morlaas, 1928 - Cases 10, 15, 16, 35

12 Bailey, 1929

13 Liepmann, 1929

14 Schaltenbrand, 1963

15-16 Tzavaras, 1978 - Cases 1, 2 (p. 369-370)

lesion. Liepmann (1905b, 1920) himself was aware that frontal apraxia is of mild severity as shown not only by his frequent remarks on this subject, but also by his use of the term "dyspraxia" rather than apraxia for these patients.

Some support for the participation of the frontal lobe in movement organization has recently been provided by a few quantitative investigations. Kolb and Milner (1981) found that patients who had undergone frontal premotor excisions -- 14 on the left side, 10 on the right -- had difficulty in imitating motor sequences and a comparable impairment was reported by Kimura (1982) in 12 patients with left precentral lesions and by De Renzi et al. (1983) in 13 patients with left frontal damage. However, in Kimura's (1982) patients the deficit was confined to imitation of motor sequences and was not apparent on imitation of single movements, as was the case for parietal patients, and even on sequences both Kolb and Milner (1981) and De Renzi et al. (1983) found the parietal group remarkably more impaired than the frontal group. To sum up, it seems that frontal damage can cause apraxia though much less frequently and probably less severely than parietal lesion. This suggests that importance and role are quite different in the two lobes and renders two of Liepmann's basic assumptions highly questionable. The first assumption that no longer holds true is that sensory information necessary to gestural activity, after passing through the parietal white matter, converges in the left sensomotorium, whence it goes to the right sensomotorium. Were this, however, the general rule, the left sensomotorium -- or at least, the left premotor area -- and not, as the data suggests, the supramarginal gyrus, would be the seat par exellence of apraxia-generating lesions. Moreover, the tenet that the role of the parietal lobe basically consists only in forwarding sensory information, needs to be reconsidered. If the area most crucial in the genesis of apraxia is the left supramarginal gyrus, it must then be considered as representing the ultimate point of convergence for all sensory messages; from here practic information is sent to both premotor-motor areas through pathways which in many subjects are separate. It is also conceivable that in this area there is a "practic centre" where practic commands are worked up, as Kleist's (1934) studies and animal experiments (Faglioni, 1979) suggest.

The angular gyrus, the temporal lobe and the occipital lobe

Some authors have emphasized the importance of the posterior parietal lobe (angular gyrus, parieto-occipital area), and of the caudal portion of the superior and middle temporal convolutions with the underlying white matter. In general, damage to these areas, together with supramarginal damage, is invoked to account for the particular severity of apraxia or its ideational quality (Liepmann, 1920). However, to the best of our knowledge, necropsy evidence showing that the lesion was confined to the above areas has not so far been convincingly provided. The angular gyrus was destroyed both in Ciarla's (1913) patient and Brun's (1921) cases 1, 2, 3 and 13, but the damage also extended into the supramarginal gyrus.

Morlaas (1928) emphasized the role of the first temporal convolution, on ascribing to its damage the occurrence of ideational apraxia, or, as he calls it, apraxia of use. He had six cases (1, 6, 8, 11, 12, 13) to back up his theory, but a perusal of his records hardly provides justification for his contention. Case 6 merely showed "hesitation" in using objects and had a lesion extending to the supramarginal gyrus. The other five cases had extensive parietal lesions in addition to damage to the first temporal convolution.

In the series investigated by De Ajuriaguerra, Hecaen and Angelergues (1960) damage to the posterior temporal lobe was frequently found: 16 cases out of 28 had ideomotor apraxia, and four out of five ideational apraxia. Of the latter only three had a tumor in the temporal lobe -- in the other two the neoplasm was located in the parieto-occipital and parieto-temporal regions -- but no details, not even clinical ones, were supplied to prove that the parietal areas were undamaged. Judging by their figure 5, it would seem that the tumor was restricted to the temporal region in one case alone. Both Kolb and Milner (1981) and Kimura (1982) found the imitation of motor sequences unimpaired in subjects with a left temporal or occipital lesion. Yet it is to be stressed that in the former study the posterior temporal lobe was spared (excisions ranged from 4.9 to 6.4 cm from the temporal pole), and in the latter research no information is given on how the lesions were localized. The only available data supporting involvement of the temporal lobe is provided by Basso, Luzzatti and Spinnler (1980) who, based on CT scan evidence, found four out of 16 subjects with damage located below the Sylvian fissure to have ideomotor apraxia on a 10 gestures imitation test.

The supplementary motor area

Although rCBF studies have emphasized the role of the supplementary motor area in motor control, evidence for apraxia following softening of the mesial hemisphere surface is inconsistent. When present, apractic defects are likely due to the concomitant involvement of the corpus callosum, which has the same blood supply (anterior cerebral artery) as the supplementary motor area. This conclusion is justified by the finding that in these patients apraxia only affects the limbs ipsilateral to the dominant hemisphere. This pattern of deficits was reported following a vascular lesion by Hyland (1933), Rubens (1975), Masdeu, Schoene and Funkenstein (1978) and Alexander and Schmitt (1980). In many more cases apraxia was definitely excluded or simply not reported (Goldberg, Mayer & Toglia, 1981; Masdeu, 1980) and this holds true also for patients with small tumors (Arseni & Botez, 1961; Carrieri, 1963; Guidetti, 1957), or who have undergone supplementary motor area excision for relief of epilepsy (Green, Angevine, White, Edes & Smith, 1980). In the latter condition the only problem with motor control was a bilateral difficulty in rhythmic alternating movements (Laplane, Talairach, Meininger, Bancaud & Orgogozo, 1977) or a lack of motor initiative (Damasio & van Hosen, 1980).

The basal ganglia and the thalamus

The classic theory has never implicated the basal ganglia in apraxia genesis and only Kimura (1979) has recently speculated on this possibility, without, however, adducing any piece of evidence. In fact, no convincing case report has ever been published in support of this association. Von Monakow (1914) had two cases (No. 5 and 12) with severe bilateral apraxia and damage to the left basal ganglia. However, one (No. 5) also suffered from hydrocephalus and brain swelling and the other (No. 12) had, in addition to the deep metastasis, metasteses in the left frontal and parietal lobe. The same holds for Kleist's (1922) patients 2 and 7: the softenings were not confined to basal ganglia, but were also present in the parietal or frontal lobe.

Nevertheless, the question deserves further investigation, because the only systematic study (Basso, Luzzatti & Spinnler, 1980), which has attempted to relate the performance on a standardized apraxia examination to CT scan localization, found four apractics in a group of 26 patients with lesions in the region of the thalamus and nucleus lenticularis. Clues that these areas may be relevant to understanding apraxia also come from rCBF studies.

Evidence against Localization

Belief that apraxia is related to a localized lesion in certain regions of the brain has been disputed by some authorities, particularly von Monakow (1914) and his pupil Brun (1921, 1922). According to them, two factors are fundamental to the genesis of severe and long-lasting apraxia: widespread cerebral damage and focal damage of the peri-Sylvian area, not necessarily confined to the left hemisphere. A peri-Sylvian lesion alone would only transiently bring about apraxia, limited to the immediate post-stroke period when the phenomenon of diaschisis causes general breakdown of brain functions. Since support for this hypothesis was derived from so-called "negative cases", viz. patients who, though having lesions in the areas claimed to be crucial for apraxia did not show it, it is worthwhile to scrutinize the evidence adduced.

Three negative cases were reported by von Monakow (1914). Two of them undoubtedly had a lesion located in a crucial area: patient Kuhn (case 13) had a post-hemorrhagic cyst of the left supramarginal-angular region, and patient Mercki (case 14), damage to the posterior part of the left callosum and to the left supramarginal-angular region, consequent to perinatal trauma. What is highly questionable, however, is that these patients were in fact adequately investigated. The mere absence of remarks concerning apraxia in their clinical notes tells us nothing since apraxia only rarely appears in spontaneous behaviour and has instead to be sought with ad hoc tests. It is highly unlikely that any such test were actually carried out in these two patients since Kuhn, as Liepmann (1914) pointed out, died in 1892 and Mercki in 1893, both before apraxia was described (Liepmann, 1900). Moreover, Mercki resided in a psychiatric hospital where apraxia tests were unlikely to have been part of the clinical routine. Von Monakow's (1914) third patient, Koch (case 15), had a left frontal post-hemorrhagic cyst, sparing the premotor area of the first two frontal convolutions and thus he is simply not relevant to the issue of the relation of parietal and premotor areas to apraxia.

Lack of adequate investigation makes two of Brun's (1921) negative cases equally dubious. Patient Ch. (case 4) had a bullet wound in the left supramarginal gyrus and was held to be eupractic simply because "the clinical report in the hospital where the patient was submitted soon after receiving the wound made no mention of an apractic disorder, and not even the Swiss military doctors in the prison camp picked it up". Patient Werner Fr. (case 5) was a nine year old child, epileptic since the age of seven whose behaviour in the hospital showed no signs of apraxia even though he had a central-precentral encephalitis and a foreign body located in the parieto-temporal region of the left hemisphere. A third negative case cited by Brun (1921, case 17) is patient Elmer, who had a glioma spreading from the genu of the corpus callosum into the right and left prefrontal lobes, which, however, did not encroach, as it is apparent from Brun's (1921) description, upon the lateral and medial premotor areas and their connections. Patient H.H., the fourth case Brun (1921, case 9) offers as negative evidence, had a right parieto-temporo-occipital post-traumatic cyst, and could only be considered negative if one were to attribute dominance to the right hemisphere. The same applies to Kudlek's (1908) and Wendenburg's (1909) patients -- both right brain-damaged subjects -- whom von Monakow cites as negative (quoted by Liepmann, 1914; von Monakow, 1914; and Lange, 1936).

Schaffer's case (1910) had bilateral parietal softening, and, although von Monakow (1914) lists him as negative, Liepmann (1914, page 507) claims that: "the author had verbally admitted that the patient had not been tested for apraxia, and that symptoms taken to be ataxic could in part have been apractic".

Lastly, there is Ciarla, who is reported by Mingazzini (1913) to have failed to find apraxia, in spite of appropriate examination, in a patient with a left supramarginal hemorrhage. The puzzling aspect of this case is that clinical and pathological findings do not tally, the former seeming to indicate a lesion in the right hemisphere: the patient had left faciobrachial paresis and suffered from epileptic fits, mostly confined to the left limbs. It is not stated whether he was right- or left-handed.

These are all the "negative cases" we have been able to find. The evidence they provide against Liepmann's theory is far from being impressive, quite apart from the complete absence of any information concerning handedness. In some patients the lesion was in the right hemisphere (Brun, 1921, case 9; Kudlek, 1908; perhaps Mingazzini, 1913; Wendenburg, 1909), in others it did not involve the regions deemed crucial by Liepmann (Brun, 1921, case 17; von Monakow, 1914, case 15), and in others apraxia was simply not tested for (Brun, 1921, cases 4 and 5; Schaffer, 1910, von Monakow, 1914, cases 13 and 14). It may be added that a few patients, e.g., von Monakow's (1914) case 14 and Brun's (1921) case 5, sustained brain damage at an early age, when practic dominance was likely to have not yet developed.

From a review of the literature one gets the feeling that as sometimes happens in scientific quarrels, the divergence between supporters and disclaimers of the localization theory is more a question of words than facts. On the one hand Liepmann (1914) and those who share his view make no bones about admitting that multiple and widespread lesions contribute to the severity and persistence of apraxia. On the other hand, von Monakow himself comes to admit that "apraxia has a predilection for the following sites: firstly, the convolutions between the left postcentral sulcus and the left angular gyrus -- which, according to my experience are almost always involved -- and, secondly, the callosal radiations around the central region. The latter structure is involved in cases with unilateral apraxia, the former mainly in cases with bilateral apraxia" (von Monakow, 1914, p. 543).

Figure 1 is taken from von Monakow's (1914, p. 553) book. He superimposed on a lateral diagram of the left hemisphere the "main locus of lesion found in almost two dozen apractic patients". The figure leaves one no doubt of the paramount importance of the supramarginal gyrus. Exactly the same conclusion can be reached from Brun's data. No less than 15 out of his 16 "positive" cases had lesion of the parietal lobe, and the other one had multiple lesions (Brun, 1922, his table on p. 49).

It is fair to recognize that the question of negative evidence is more complex than the above analysis would suggest, because it is well known that negative cases are less frequently investigated and published than cases confirming an interpretation which has gained wide admission. What we need is a systematic investigation on unselected samples attempting to relate clinical symptoms to locus of lesion. The only study which has met this requirement was grounded on CT scan evidence and has, therefore, the limitation inherent to this localizing technique. Basso et al., (1980) tested 123 left brain-damaged patients with a 10 gesture imitation test carried out with the left hand. Apraxia was found associated with supra-Sylvian, sub-Sylvian, and retro-Sylvian damage and negative cases occurred with each of these locations of lesion. Thus the evidence provided by this study does not really back up the view that specific lesions dictate type of apraxia.

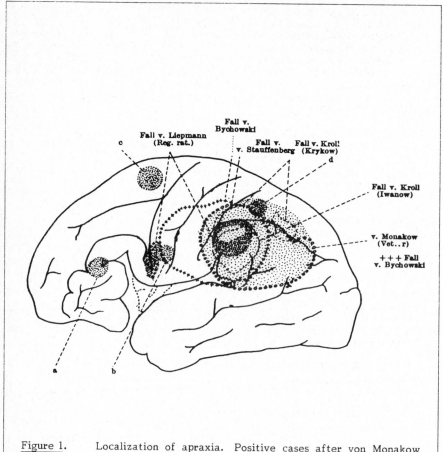

Figure 1.   Localization of apraxia. Positive cases after von Monakow
                (1914). a,b,c,d are little metastases.

The role of the corpus callosum

If one hemisphere plays a decisive role in planning movements and controls the
activity of the other hemisphere, there must be a double exchange of information
between the two sides of the brain. Implicit in the doctrine of dominance is the
notion that motor instructions are transferred from the dominant to the subordinate
hemisphere, while sensory information received by the latter is in turn passed to the
former. Of the commissures linking the two hemispheres, only damage to the corpus
callosum gives rise to apraxia, as Liepmann (1905b) first pointed out, based on the
finding that left limb apraxia ensues damage to this structure. Definite evidence
pointing to this association was provided by Liepmann and Maas's (1907) patients
Ochs and by van Vleuten (1907) and Hartmann (1907, case 2). The latter two
patients had tumors infiltrating the corpus callosum from the genu to the anterior
splenium causing damage to the left cingular gyrus, and, in van Vleuten's patient,
also to the white matter of the left frontal pole. Apraxia was evident on verbal

command, imitation, and use of objects. Case reports with lesions in the mid corpus callosum and apraxia confined to the left limbs rapidly multiplied in the following years. Goldstein (1908, 1909) described a patient with a softening involving the corpus callosum and the right hemisphere in a position that was symmetrical to that of Ochs. Other cases were reported by Forster (1908, 1909, 1913a,b), Claude and Loyez (1913), Bonhoffer (1914), Ciarla (1915: a particularly convincing case, because a cystic lesion was confined to the mid corpus callosum), Mingazzini and Ciarla (1920), Pineas (1924), Foix and Hillemand (1925, case 3), Baldy (1927), Morlaas (1928, cases 17 and 18) and Hoff (1931).

Sweet's (1941) case is exceptionally well documented. He presented severe apraxia of the left hand both on imitation and verbal command, while he could use the right hand normally. An aneurysm of the left anterior cerebral artery had destroyed the corpus callosum lying in front of the splenium, leaving both hemispheres undamaged, even microscopically. More recently, apraxia following a callosal lesion has been reported by Geschwind and Kaplan (1962), Brion and Jedynak (1972) and Watson and Heilman (1983). Rubens et al. (1977) described the only patient known to have a traumatic aetiology with necrosis spreading from the posterior genu to the middle splenium. Left limb apraxia was apparent on verbal command, on imitation, and in miming the use of objects, not, however, in handling objects.

Apraxia limited to the left limbs also results from lesions located, rather than in the corpus callosum itself, in the callosal radiations of the left hemisphere, as shown by Hecaen and Gimeno-Alava's (1960) case 4, or of the right hemisphere, as shown by Westphal's (1907) case, Hartmann's (1907) case 3 and Morlaas' (1928) case 10. Taterka (1924a,b) and Sittig (1931) described two left-handed patients with callosal lesions and apraxia confined to the right limbs.

In all the cases so far reviewed the lesion involved the middle third of the corpus callosum. Available evidence suggests that the critical region for securing transmission of practic information is represented by the anterior half or two thirds of the truncus. No left limb apraxia was observed in the patients reported by Trescher and Ford (1937), Sugishita, Toyokura, Yoshioka and Yamada (1980), and Gersch and Damasio (1981) all of whom had surgical section of the splenium and the immediately anterior part of the corpus callosum in the course of tumor removal. On the other hand, all of Jeeves, Simpson and Geffen's (1979) patients, who for the same reason underwent sections of the anterior and middle parts of the corpus callosum, had great difficulty with a bimanual motor co-ordination test consisting of threading beads. More classical tests for apraxia were unfortunately not used. It would thus seem that eupraxia of the left limbs depends on the integrity of the cortico-cortical connections running in the central body of the corpus callosum.

This assumption is in agreement with Liepmann's (1905b, 1920) theory, which posits that information on movement planning is transmitted through the parietal lobe (supramarginal gyrus) of the dominant hemisphere to the sensomotorium of the same hemisphere, or more precisely, as Geschwind (1965) pointed out, to the association pre-motor area. This in turn controls both the ipsilateral motor area and, through connections crossing the middle corpus callosum, the association pre-motor area and thence the motor area of the right side. The assumption is, however, in agreement with Kleist's (1934) theory of a left parietal praxis centre too; thence connections to the right premotor-motor area can be assumed to run along three alternative pathways. The first one corresponds to Liepmann's route, and seems to fit for some but not for all cases, since apraxia is less frequently associated with frontal than with parietal damage. The second hypothetical route would first cross over to the right parietal and then go forward to the right premotor-motor area.

However, evidence of apraxia ensuing from right parietal damage in right-handers is still lacking, and that means that this route is not normally used. The third possible pathway runs directly from the left parietal lobe (centre) to the subordinate associative motor area through parieto-frontal interhemispheric heterotopic connections.

This last hypothesis, which was first proposed by Kleist (1934, pp. 482-483) predicts that a parietal lesion of the dominant hemisphere will produce bilateral apraxia, and a left frontal premotor lesion apraxia essentially confined to the contralateral limbs. While it is easy to corroborate the first of these assumptions, it is more difficult to show the presence of right limb apraxia following disease of the left premotor area, because the lesion very frequently impinges upon the adjacent motor area, causing paralysis of the contralateral limbs and rendering them inaccessible to testing. It might be argued that the greater weight of the connections going to the right hemisphere through the left frontal lobe is shown by the cases of "sympathetic dyspraxia" (Liepmann, 1905b) -- paralysis of the right side with apraxia on the left -- but for no patient with this pattern of deficits was there compelling evidence that the parietal lobe was undamaged. A stronger case against Kleist's view is posed by the anatomy of the callosal connections determined by monkey studies. These connections appear to be fundamentally homotopic, the exceptions being represented by the inferior parietal lobe areas, thought to correspond to the human supramarginal and angular gyrus which are linked with heterotopic contralateral areas like the caudal insula, the caudal gyrus cynguli, the parahippocampal gyrus and the superior temporal sulcus (Pandya, 1975; Pandya & Vignolo, 1969) and by the premotor area, which has few heterotopic connections with the primary and supplementary motor areas (Pandya & Vignolo, 1971) and with the prefrontal areas (Pandya, 1975). It remains to be seen whether new neuroanatomical techniques, particularly the autoradiograhic ones, will show the presence of heterotopic parieto-frontal (or occpital-frontal, temporo-frontal) connections.

Objections arising from patients with agenesis and surgical section of the corpus callosum

It is fair to recognize that not all the data derived from clinical observations are in agreement with those provided by vascular and tumor cases in pointing out the bearing of the corpus callosum on apraxia.

The first enigma is to be found in the cases of callosal agenesis. This syndrome has remained for decades a fortuitous necroscopy finding, devoid of clinical correlates, except for some aspecific disorders (epilepsy, mental retardation), usually traceable to the effect of other concomitant cerebral malformations (Slager, Kelly & Wagner, 1957). In recent years, more refined examination techniques have enabled us to detect subtle defects in the sphere of motor activity like, for example, a reduced speed and precision of movement, a less skilled bimanual co-ordination (Ferriss & Dorsen, 1975; Gott & Saul, 1978; Sauerwein, Lassonde, Cardu & Geoffroy, 1981), and an inability to transfer manual learning from one hand to the other (Gott & Saul, 1978; Heene, 1966). No symptom of apraxia has, however, been noted, even when specifically sought (Ettlinger, Blakemore, Milner & Wilson, 1972, 1974; Sheremata, Deonna & Romanul, 1973).

Even callosotomy -- a surgical procedure carried out for treatment of drug resistant epilepsy -- results in a remarkable dearth of apractic symptoms. Presplenium section of the corpus callosum, whether carried out alone (as often in Akelaitis' 1944 cases; Akelaitis, Risteen, Herren, van Wagenen, 1942) or along with section of the anterior commissure (Gordon, Bogen & Sperry, 1971; Preilowsky, 1971), does not produce any evident signs of apraxia, except for a difficulty in learning tasks requiring delicate bimanual co-ordination. No more productive of symptoms is the complete section of the corpus callosum (van Wagenen & Herren, 1940). Only following the severing of all the interhemispheric commissures -- the corpus callosum, splenium, anterior commissure, hippocampal commissure, and in most cases the intermediate mass as well, as carried out by Bogen and Vogel (1962) and Bogen, Fisher and Vogel (1965) -- have apractic deficits been reported and then limited to definite testing conditions.

Basing their observations on a series of nine right-handed subjects, Gazzaniga, Bogen and Sperry (1967) describe the syndrome as follows. In imitating gestures tachistoscopically projected to a lateral visual field, patients made errors only when they were required to use the limb ipsilateral to the hemisphere receiving the information and not when the limb was contralateral to the hemisphere, i.e., was directly steered by it. The errors were severe in finger movements, but not in movements of the more proximal limb segments. The patient's most severe errors occurred in the right hand when contradictory commands were simultaneously projected to either hemisphere. In such a case, the right hand was no longer controlled by the ipsilateral hemisphere and followed the directions of the left hemisphere. When written commands were sent to the left hemisphere it was able to control the performance not only of the contralateral, but also of the ipsilateral limb at the cost, however, of a few apractic errors in the distal musculature. When a written command was addressed to the right hemisphere (for example, a word was projected to the left visual field), limb performance immediately became apractic.

Apart from left hemisphere dominance for language, these observations suggest that in commissurotomised patients each hemisphere had independent control over both distal and proximal muscles of the contralateral limbs, but only over the proximal muscles of the ipsilateral limbs.

Zaidel and Sperry (1977) took up the question again more thoroughly using standardized and quantified procedures and testing eight commissurotomised subjects (two with a spared splenium), five to nine years post surgery. They found apraxia of the left limb on verbal commands in patients who had undergone a complete section of the corpus callosum, while the patients had no difficulty in making a gesture with their left hand when imitating the examiner or when they were allowed to make the gesture with their right hand first. Tasks involving delicate bimanual co-ordination, however, were not perfectly mastered.

Gazzaniga, Le Doux and Wilson's (1977) patient showed good control of the contralateral limb by both hemispheres after a complete section of the corpus callosum. He could imitate finger and hand positions correctly using the limb ipsilateral to the visual field in which they were tachistoscopically projected and only made mistakes when field and limb were crossed, namely, when the hemisphere governing the limb did not receive the model it was requested to imitate.

Volpe, Sidtis, Holtzman, Wilson and Gazzaniga (1982) have been able to demonstrate that the interhemispheric transmission of the visual model takes place via the posterior corpus callosum. Imitation with one hand of models presented in the contralateral field was impaired after section of the rearmost three cms of the corpus callosum and did not further deteriorate after section of the rest of the corpus callosum.

In conclusion, in no patient has commissurotomy brought about gestural disruption comparable to that described in the clinical literature as a consequence of mid-callosal vascular and tumor lesions, namely, a severe impairment of the left hand both on verbal command (when the stimulus can be decoded by the left hemisphere alone) and on imitation (when the stimulus can be processed by either hemispheres).

The main difference with respect to the lesions caused by tumor or an infarct is that the picture is far less severe and much more transient, pointing to a functional autonomy of the two hemispheres, which is never found in clinical cases. Sperry, Gazzaniga and Bogen (1969) were inclined to attribute the severity of the "clinical" syndrome to the presence of extra-callosal lesions, which should be bilateral according to Ettlinger (1969). It must be admitted that callosal infarcts are also likely to encroach upon the cerebral convolutions (cyngulate gyrus and supplementary motor area) which share the same anterior cerebral artery blood supply as the corpus callosum. Furthermore, both infarct and tumor can cause diaschisis (von Monakow, 1914). This factor is also at work in patients who have undergone a surgical section and, indeed, during the first week after the operation, the surgical syndrome is to some extent comparable in terms of severity with the clinical one (Gazzaniga et al., 1967). It remains to be said that the clinical syndrome, with very few exceptions has always shown an asymmetry of practic abilities, with one hemisphere overruling the other.

A possible explanation for this discrepancy must be sought in the way asymmetry of practic functions develops. This is an unexplored area about which very little is known. The wealth of data on the maturation of manual dexterity are of only marginal relevance, since patients submitted to callosotomy show a dissociation between their preserved right-handedness and the absence of left hemisphere dominance for praxis.

Genetic factors favouring an anatomical and functional asymmetry of the hemispheres are likely to play a crucial role in promoting left brain control over the motor activity of both sides. The degree of left hemisphere dominance, however, probably differs from subject to subject, as suggested by the fact that also the neurological literature has repoted patients whose hemispheres were equipotential with respect to practic abilities (one such patient was the Regierungsrat himself, who suffered from apraxia of the right limbs alone). Moreover, in the critical periods of early development, neuronal organization and cortical connections display a considerable capacity for rearrangement after surgical resection of their target structures, and this takes place in both cortico-subcortical and cortico-cortical intra- and inter-hemispheric pathways (Goldman-Rakic, 1981). Thus, it is conceivable that early brain damage to the left hemisphere may foster the acquisition of a practic autonomy by the right side of the brain in a way which is analogous to what happens in similar cases for the shift of language abilities to the right. In this perspective, the absence of left limb apraxia in patients with callosal agenesis is not surprising. As for patients who underwent callosotomy, it must be stressed that the operation was not carried out in normal subjects, but in patients who had been suffering from epilepsy since infancy, suggesting the presence of early cerebral damage. It would, therefore, be unrealistic to take them as representative of normal brain organization (Geschwind, 1965; Kennard, 1942; Scharlock, Tucker & Strominger, 1963).

One has to admit that this is a simplified explanation of the conflicting evidence provided by different sources of pathology. Whether it holds true must remain for future invesigations to verify.

Evidence provided by neurophysiological studies in the normal subject

Data relevant to understanding the mechanisms underlying gesture programming are provided by three techniques investigating brain function in the living subject. The chief source of information is represented by the study of the rCBF variation occurring during execution or programming of gestures. The behavioural changes in motor activity consequent to electrical stimulation of the brain are also informative, while recording of cerebral electric potential evoked by movement has as yet given information of only marginal importance.

A general limitation in these sources of data is that the movements they analyse are elementary and repetitive and thus require neither purposeful choice nor sequencing, which are the critical features making a motor action susceptible to apractic disruption.

Cerebral blood flow increases in the motor area contralateral to the hand or foot being moved and this occurs with simple as well as with complex movements. Examples of simple movements and the percentage of rCBF increase associated with them are: clenching and unclenching one's fist, 54% (Olesen, 1971); holding a spring compressed between forefinger and thumb, 17%, compressing and releasing the spring repeatedly, 30% (Roland, Larsen, Lassen & Skinhoj, 1980); pressing one's foot down onto an object, 24% (Orgogozo & Larsen, 1979). Examples of complex movements are opposing the thumb to each finger in succession 2-10% (Halsey, Blauenstein, Wilson & Wills, 1979), or according to a pre-determined pattern, 25-31% (Orgogozo & Larsen, 1979; Roland, Larsen, Lassen & Skinhoj, 1980; Roland, Meyer, Shibasaki, Yamamoto & Thompson, 1982); tracing a spiral in the air, 28%; exploring a maze stepwise on verbal command with index finger, 34-44% (Roland, Skinhoj, Lassen & Larsen, 1980); performing a complex series of foot movements, 30% (Orgogozo & Larsen, 1979). Increase of rCBF is strictly confined to the motor area opposite to the hand being used (Halsey et al., 1979; Olesen, 1971; Roland, Larsen, Lassen & Skinhoj, 1980; Roland, Skinhoj, Lassen & Larsen, 1980; Roland et al., 1982) and the same applies during isometric muscle contractions of hand or foot, e.g., holding a spring compressed (Orgogozo & Larsen, 1979; Roland, Larsen, Lassen & Skinhoj, 1980) or during repeated execution of the same movement, e.g., compressing a spring (Roland, Larsen, Lassen & Skinhoj, 1980).

When the motor sequence is so arranged as to oblige the patient to think out each new step (touching his thumb twice to the forefinger, once to the next, three times to the next, twice to the last, and then repeating backwards), the rCBF increases significantly not just in the sensory-motor area of the opposite hemisphere, but also in the supplementary motor area of both hemispheres: 15% contralateral (Orgogozo & Larsen, 1979), 29% contralateral and 27% ipsilateral (Roland, Larsen, Lassen & Skinhoj, 1980), 22% contralateral and 18% ipsilateral (Roland et al., 1982). Complex foot sequences also show involvement of the supplementary motor area (moving one's toes downwards once, upwards twice, three times to the right, four to the left, 21% contralateral, Orgogozo and Larsen, 1979).

Further areas of the cortex are involved when the movement is carried out in extra-personal space, and not directed to personal space, as in the above examples (Roland, Skinhoj, Lassen & Larsen, 1980). A hand tracing a spiral in the air causes contralateral (ipsilateral recordings are not reported) increase of rCBF in the parietal (16-30%) and premotor (14%) areas, in addition to increase in the contralateral sensory-motor and supplementary motor areas. Bilateral involvement of parietal (16-20% contralateral, 14-20% ipsilateral) and premotor (19-22% contralateral, 14-19% ipsilateral) areas is particularly remarkable in a more complex task requiring subtle spatial analysis. The subject is facing a frame with 7x8 cells and has to move his forefinger from one cell to another following verbal instruction (so many steps in this direction, so many in that, etc). As in the finger-touching sequences mentioned above, the subject has to select a new movement at each step, but here it is directed in extra-personal space (Roland, Skinhoj, Lassen & Larsen, 1980). If the gesture is rehearsed mentally rather than actually carried out, the sensory-motor area remains silent, while rCBF increase in the extramotor areas is of the same magnitude as during actual movements. Thus squeezing a ball on command acti- vates -- besides the central region -- the frontal and parietal regions, which remain the only ones active if the subject limits himself to rehearse the movement mentally (Ingvar and Philipson, 1977). Similarly, when the patient imagines a complex finger sequence without carrying it out, the supplementary area alone is involved (17-21% contralateral, Roland, Larsen, Lassen & Skinhoj, 1980).

In many of the above studies increased rCBF was also recorded in the language areas. This finding was attributed to concomitant verbal activity, either in decoding the verbal command (Ingvar & Philipson, 1977; maze test, Roland, Skinhoj, Lassen & Larsen, 1980) or in covert verbalization (complex finger sequences, Roland, Larsen, Lassen & Skinhoj, 1980).

Roland et al. (1982) have shown that a complex finger sequence, like touching thumb to fingers following a pre-established sequence, bilaterally activates the basal ganglia as well: the pallidum (20% contralateral, 10% ipsilateral), putamen (13% contralateral, 12% ipsilateral), and head of the nucleus caudatus (8% contralateral, 7% ipsilateral). Slight increase in rCBF was also recorded from the thalamic- subthalamic region (6% contralateral, 8% ipsilateral).

This series of data lends itself to some interesting remarks, especially when they are compared with findings from electrostimulation experiments.

The contralateral sensory-motor area is involved at the stage of movement exe- cution but not of movement programming as shown by its increased rCBF when the movement takes place, and its inactivity when it is only "imagined".

The supplementary motor area comes into play when both "actual" and "imag- ined" complex motor sequences take place, but remains inactive during isometric muscular contractions and simple or repetitive movements. Their function, accord- ing to Roland, Larsen, Lassen and Skinhoj (1980), would consist in the assembly of a central motor program, specifying the organization of the motor act (which muscles must be moved, in which order and how many times). They would also be involved in memorizing the programme and calling it up at the moment of action. This hypothesis conflicts, however, with the absence of apractic disorders reported by the clinical literature following a lesion of the supplementary motor area. An alternative and more likely interpretation of its role is that it supplies the necessary "initiative" for gestural activity, whether "actual" or "imagined". Thus in simple and repetitive tasks it would come into play at the outset of the test, and in complex tasks, where every movement must be selected from a possible set, it would be at work throughout the performance. This interpretation is in line with the finding that the most common motor defect associated with supplementary motor area lesion is loss of initiative up to the blockage of action.

There is no research aimed at specifically examining the effects of supplemen- tary motor area stimulation on practic function. It is, however, known that it results not only in complex limb and mouth movements, but also in hesitation, slowing-down and blockage of motor behaviour (Penfield & Welch, 1951), a picture which calls to mind what occurs following damage to this area.

According to Roland, Skinhoj, Lassen and Larsen (1980) the premotor frontal and posterior parietal areas are only activated by tasks carried out in extra-personal space and remain inactive when the movement is performed in personal space. This interpretation rests on the finding that rCBF is increased in these areas during the spiral and maze tests, but not during other apparently equally complex motor tasks directed towards body parts. It must be kept in mind, however, that, to enable the detection of rCBF variations, a motor task has to last several minutes, during which the subject keeps on repeating the same movement or the same sequence in a stereotyped way. This performance has little to do with practic activity, which basically refers to the selection and organization of a new motor pattern. The actual practic stage of the performance occurs before the rCBF measure, when the subject is learning the task. In the course of recording, the movement has become routine and does not involve any purposeful decision as to the movement to be selected. This limitation applies to most of the motor paradigms used in this research, not only simple repetitive movements, but also finger motor sequences, as used by Orgogozo and Larsen (1979), Roland, Larsen, Lassen and Skinhoj (1980), and Roland et al., (1982). The only two tests, which would seem to escape this defect are the spiral and the maze test used by Roland, Larsen, Lassen and Skinhoj (1980), because both require the subject to make new motor choices throughout the performance. It can, therefore, be argued that the parietal and premotor areas are active in these tests because they are the only ones which are demanding at the practic level.

The involvement of the premotor and inferior parietal areas in the course of practic activity is confirmed, as far as the oral movement is concerned, by the stimulation experiments carried out by Ojemann and Mateer (1979) and Ojemann (1982). A thrice repeated movement was disrupted by the stimulation of the premotor area, and a sequence of three different movements by the stimulation of both the premotor and the parietal area, as predictable from Mateer and Kimura's (1977) and Kimura's (1982) findings. Impairment also followed the stimulation of the superior tempoal convolution, but this may be due to the close relationship between oral and verbal movements.

As mentioned above, rCBF increases in the basal ganglia during the execution of complex sequences. Does it mean that they participate in motor programming or is their role restricted to execution? The finding that the increase is bilateral would support the former hypothesis, yet the variation is always slight compared to that occurring at the cortical level, the only exception being the globus pallidus. Here, however, a sizeable variation is recorded from the hemisphere contralateral to the hand being used, analogous to what happens in the sensory-motor area which has a purely executive role.

The lower thalamus and the subthalamic area reveal light activity during complex finger sequences. In fact stimulation of the nucleus ventralis lateralis of the thalamus also affects the reproduction of repetitive or sequential oral movements (Ojemann, 1982). It has, however, been proposed (Ojemann, 1982) that these structures, rather than in gesture programming, are involved in the "focusing of attention that is a necessary part of the motor system". This is confirmed by the fact that stimulatin of this area impairs motor learning.

rCBF findings are in many points in agreement with Liepmann's theory in that they show -- just as Liepmann (1920) maintained -- that the premotor and parietal regions participate in movement planning. There are, however, two important discrepancies between the neurophysiological findings and Liepmann's theory. First, the parietal lobe is more than a mere transit point, where the pathway connecting the occipital and temporal lobe with the frontal lobe runs, but instead plays an active part by means of its own cortex in practic functions. The cortex of the superior parietal lobule as well as that of the supramarginal gyrus and the inferior parietal lobule show an increased rCBF. Although it is not possible from rCBF findings to discriminate between their respective contribution, it may be argued (De Renzi, 1982) that the superior parietal area is involved in spatial analysis while the inferior parietal area provides a spatial "guide" to gestural activity. Second, the areas of the cortex that become active during gesture programming always operate bilaterally, without significant difference between the hemisphere contralateral or ipsilateral to the working hand or between the dominant or subordinate hemisphere. This statement does not deny the existence of a functional asymmetry of the hemispheres, and it is compatible with the doctrine that one of them -- albeit to a degree which varies from case to case -- monitors the activity of both. Such at least would seem to be the outcome of Ojemann and Mateer's (1979) and Ojemann (1982) studies although their experiments only dealt with oral movement. Stimulation of the cortex of the dominant hemisphere has been found to have an extremely disruptive effect on execution of movement sequences, while stimulation of the subordinate hemisphere had none.

rCBF and cortical stimulation findings do not, unfortunately, give any information about the temporal order with which different areas are activated (namely, whether the parietal and premotor areas come into play before the central area). At first sight, the simultaneous recording of electric potentials (evoked potentials, mu phenomenon) from different areas of the cortex may appear to be a procedure more suited to the answering of this question, but again the movements tested in these types of experiment are not relevant to apraxia, since the same elementary action (e.g., bending a finger) must be repeated a great many times (about 100), in order to distinguish the specific potential from the noise (Pocock, 1980; Shibasaki, Barrett, Halliday & Halliday, 1980).

Concluding Remarks

The many clinical and experimental investigations bearing on the question of movement organization, which have been prompted by Liepmann's studies on apraxia, have generally confirmed the anatomical model he proposed, although it seems that some of its aspects need to be modified. The following points epitomize the conceptual framework into which clinical evidence can be integrated.

1.   Gesture programming depends on the cerebral neocortex. A few cases of apraxia caused by lesion of subcortical structures, like the thalamus or the basal ganglia, have been brought out by CT scan studies, but their number is still so small as to leave the role of these structures uncertain.

2.   Although rCBF studies suggest that both hemispheres are engaged in practic functions, the participation of the left side of the brain in programming movements is dominant, as shown by the finding that in right-handers apraxia usually ensues only from left brain damage. Impairment in imitating actions following right hemisphere damage occurs in a minority of cases and can be brought out only by delicate tests. Praxic dominance does not always coincide with language dominance or with manual preference or dexterity. Although it is impossible to identify the factors favouring the hemispheric specialization for praxis, one may hypothesize an anatomical asymmetry on the analogy of what occurs for the speech areas.

3.   The theory that the whole cortex is equally involved in practic activity, and that only large lesions are likely to bring about severe and lasting apraxia has never been substantiated by convincing pathological evidence, and even the

strongest upholders (Brun, 1921, 1922; von Monakow, 1914) of such a thesis have come to admit that there are areas whose damage is crucially associated with apraxia. These areas have been identified with the supramarginal gyrus and the premotor area, but it seems likely that a hierarchy exists between their contribution to movement organization, since the association of damage to the inferior parietal lobe with apraxia has been confirmed by both necroscopy and CT scan findings, whereas the evidence supporting the relation of frontal damage to limb apraxia is scarcer and less compelling.

4.   The left hemisphere exerts its leadership over the subordinate one through the corpus callosum, as pointed out by the many case reports showing left limb apraxia following a softening or a tumor in the callosal truncus. The role of the corpus callosum has been disputed, based on the absence of apractic disorders in epileptics who had undergone callosotomy, but it is dubious to what extent the brain of patients who have sustained cerebral injury at an early age can be considered representative of the cerebral organization of functions in normals.

5.   Two different, though not necessarily self-excluding interpretations of the genesis of apraxia have been advanced. They are known as "disconnection" and "centres" theories. According to the disconnection theory, apraxia occurs when the lesion interrupts the transmission to the motor areas of the sensory information eliciting the required act. This theory does not imply that there is any specific centre which specializes in planning movements, and the existence of areas whose damage is crucially associated with apraxia is accounted for by assuming that lesions located here interrupt the pathways linking associative sensory and motor areas. This is the reason why the white matter underlying the left supramarginal gyrus, where occipito-frontal, temporo-frontal and parieto-frontal fibre bundles travel close to each other, has been given special emphasis in the genesis of bilateral apraxia (Geschwind, 1975; Liepmann, 1905b, 1920). By the same token, damage to the left premotor region, where the pathways described above converge, will also necessarily result in apraxia, mostly confined to the left limbs, because its detection in the right limbs is prevented by paresis. Liepmann endowed the sensomotorium with the function of being the repository of kinesthetic engrams, but did not assign any ascendancy to the left hemisphere with respect to this property, except in the stage of motor learning.

It is not easy to explain the left brain dominance in practic abilities in terms of mere disconnection, except in the case of the inability to carry out movements on verbal command. It has therefore been assumed by some authors that there is in the left hemisphere a centre, sometimes identified with the premotor area (Goldstein, 1911; Hartmann, 1907) though mostly with the supramarginal gyrus (Heilman, 1979a,b; Kleist, 1934), which specializes in organizing the correct sequence of movements needed to reproduce the motor act. Fibres from sensory cortices would converge in this area, conveying information which gives rise to the appropriate motor plans. The supramarginal gyrus being connected with the left premotor area would therefore be in a position to guide its activity when the movement is executed.

Both the disconnection and the centre theories assume that the left prefrontal area receives all types of motor commands, those for the right limbs, which are transmitted to the ipsilateral motor area, as also those for the left limbs which are transmitted to the contralateral premotor area through the corpus callosum and thence to the right motor area. This schema hardly, however, provides sufficient explanation of why left limb apraxia is less frequent and severe (De Renzi et al.,

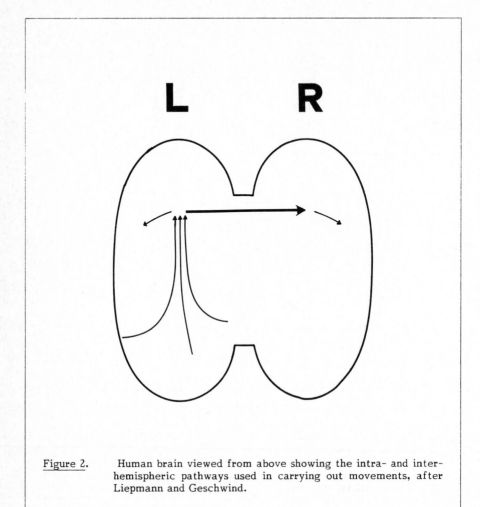

Figure 2.   Human brain viewed from above showing the intra- and interhemispheric pathways used in carrying out movements, after
Liepmann and Geschwind.

1983) following frontal than parietal damage. Kleist (1934) first drew attention to
the dearth of convincing cases with frontal apraxia in comparison to the abundance
of those with parietal apraxia and proposed a direct connection between the left
parietal lobe and the right frontal lobe, designating subordinate functions to the
longer route through the left frontal lobe. Following this view, the left parietal lobe
is credited with a pivotal role in movement control, an assumption which is more in
agreement with the centre rather than the pure disconnection hypothesis. We are
inclined to support this hypothesis.

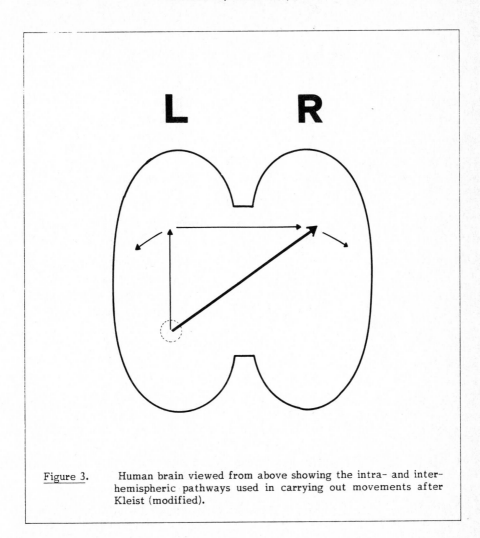

Figure 3.   Human brain viewed from above showing the intra- and inter-hemispheric pathways used in carrying out movements after Kleist (modified).

Acknowledgements

We are grateful to C. Mason for the first English translation and to C. Barbieri for the typing and retyping of the manuscript. Dr P. Nichelli helped us in the preparation of the figure material. Professor E. De Renzi not only gave essential advise about the draft of the paper but also helped to clarify our ideas to improve the text.

REFERENCE NOTES

1.   De Renzi, E., Faglioni, P. & Sorgato, P.   Unpublished data, 1982.

REFERENCES

Akelaitis, A.J.   A study of gnosis, praxis and language following section of the corpus callosum and anterior commissure.   Journal of Neurosurgery, 1944, 1, 94-102.

Akelaitis, A.J., Risteen, W.A., Herren, R.Y. & van Wagenen, W.P.   Studies on the corpus callosum.   3.   A contribution to the study of dyspraxia and apraxia following partial and complete section of the corpus callosum.   Archives of Neurology and Psychiatry, 1942, 47, 971-1008.

Alexander, M.P. & Schmitt, M.A.   The aphasia syndrome of stroke in the left anterior cerebral artery territory.   Archives of Neurology, 1980, 37, 97-100.

Arseni, C. & Botez, M.I.   Speech disturbances caused by tumors of the supplementary motor area.   Acta Psychiatrica et Neurologica Scandinavica, 1961, 36, 279-299.

Arseni, C., Voinesco, I. & Goldenberg, M.   Considerations clinico-statistiques sur le syndrome parietal dans les tumeurs cerebrales.   Revue Neurologique, 1958, 99, 623-638.

Assal, G. & Regli, F.   Syndrome de disconnexion visuo-verbale et visuo-gestuelle. Aphasie optique et apraxie optique.   Revue Neurologique, 1980, 136, 365-376.

Bailey, P.   A contribution to the study of aphasia and apraxia.   Archives of Neurology and Psychiatry, 1924, 11, 501-529.

Bailey, P.   Tumor of the septum lucidum and corpus callosum causing apraxia. Archives of Neurology and Psychiatry, 1929, 22, 614-616.

Baldy, R.   Les syndromes de l'artere cerebrale anterieure.   Paris: Jouve et Cie, 1927.

Basso, A., Luzzatti, C. & Spinnler, H.   Is ideomotor apraxia the outcome of damage to well-defined regions of the left hemisphere?   Neuropsychological study of CAT correlation.   Journal of Neurology, Neurosurgery, and Psychiatry, 1980, 43, 118-126.

Bechterew, W. von   Uber die Lokalisation der motorischen Apraxie.   Monatsschrift fur Psychiatrie und Neurologie, 1909, 25, 42-51.

Bogen, J.E., Fisher, E.D. & Vogel, P.J.   Cerebral commissurotomy: A second case report.   Journal of American Medical Association, 1965, 194, 1328-1329.

Bogen, J.E. & Vogel, P.J.   Cerebral commissurotomy in man.   Preliminary case report.   Bulletin of the Los Angeles Neurological Society, 1962, 27, 169-172.

Bonhoffer, K.   Klinischer und anatomischer Befund zur Lehre von der Apraxie und der "motorischen Sprachbahn".   Monatsschrift fur Psychiatrie und Neurologie, 1914, 35, 113-128.

Bremer, F. Global aphasia and bilateral apraxia due to an endothelioma compressing the gyrus supramarginalis. Archives of Neurology and Psychiatry, 1921, 5, 663-669.

Brion, S. & Jedynak, C.P. Troubles du transfert interhemispherique (callosal disconnection). A propos de trois observations de tumeurs du corps calleux. Le signe de la main etrangere. Revue Neurologique, 1972, 126, 257-266.

Brown, J.W. Aphasia, apraxia, and agnosia, clinical and theoretical aspects. Springfield (Illinois): Charles C. Thomas, 1972.

Brun, R. Klinische und anatomische Studien uber Apraxie. Schweizer Archiv fur Neurologie und Psychiatrie, 1921, 9, 29-64, 194-226.

Brun, R. Klinische und anatomische Studien uber Apraxie. Schweizer Archiv fur Neurologie und Psychiatrie, 1922, 10, 48-79, 185-210.

Bychowski, Z. Beitrage zur Nosographie der Apraxie. Monatsschrift fur Psychiatrie und Neurologie, 1909, 25, 1-32.

Carrieri, G. Sindrome da sofferenza dell'area supplementare motoria sinistra nel corso di un meningioma parasagittale. Rivista di Patologia Nervosa e Mentale, 1963, 84, 29-48.

Ciarla, E. Emorragia nel giro sovramarginale e nel giro angolare di sinistra. Rivista di Patologia Nervosa e Mentale, 1913, 18, 473-493.

Ciarla, E. Contributo clinico e anatomopatologico allo studio della aprassia motoria per lesione del corpo calloso. Policlinico, 1915, 1-17.

Claude, M., & Loyez, M. Etude anatomique d'un cas d'apraxie avec hemiplegie droite et cecite verbale. L'Encephale, 1913, 8, 289-307.

Critchley, M. The parietal lobe. London: Edward Arnold, 1953.

Damasio, A.R. & Benton, A.L. Impairment of hand movements under visual guidance. Neurology, 1979, 29, 170-174.

Damasio, A.R. & van Hoesen, G.W. Structure and function of the supplementary motor area. Neurology, 1980, 30, 359.

De Ajuriaguerra, J., Hecaen, H. & Angelergues, R. Les apraxies. Varietes cliniques et lateralization lesionelle. Revue Neurologique, 1960, 102, 566-594.

Delis, D.C., Knight, R.T. & Simpson, G. Reversed hemispheric organization in a left-hander. Neuropsychologia, 1983, 21, 13-24.

De Renzi, E. Disorders of space explanation and cognition. New York: John Wiley, 1982.

De Renzi, E., Faglioni, P., Lodesani, M. & Vecchi, A. Performance of left brain-damaged patients on imitation of single movements and sequences. Frontal and parietal-injured patients compared. Cortex, 1983, 19, 333-343.

De Renzi, E., Faglioni, P. & Sorgato, P. Modality-specific and supramodal mechanisms of apraxia. Brain, 1982, 105, 301-312.

De Renzi, E., Motti, F. & Nichelli, P. Imitating gestures. A quantitative approach to ideomotor apraxia. Archives of Neurology, 1980, 37, 6-10.

De Renzi, E., Pieczuro, A. & Vignolo, L.A. Ideational apraxia: A quantitative study. Neuropsychologia, 1968, 6, 41-52.

Ettlinger, G. Apraxia considered as a disorder of movements that are language-dependent: Evidence from cases of brain bi-section. Cortex, 1969, 5, 285-289.

Ettlinger, G., Blakemore, C.B., Milner, A.D. & Wilson, J. Agenesis of the corpus callosum: A behavioural investigation. Brain, 1972, 95, 327-346.

Ettlinger, G., Blakemore, C.B., Milner, A.D. & Wilson, J. Agenesis of the corpus callosum: A further behavioural investigation. Brain, 1974, 97, 225-234.

Ettlinger, G., Jackson, C.V. & Zangwill, O.L. Cerebral dominance in sinistrals. Brain, 1956, 79, 569-588.

Faglioni, P. Aprassia. Ricerche di Psicologia, 1977, 1, 67-135.

Faglioni, P. Specializzazione anatomo-funzionale della corteccia e organizzazione del gesto. Contributo della sperimentazione animale allo studio dell'aprassia. Cortex, 1979, 15 (Suppl. To No. 3), 1-32.

Ferriss, G.S. & Dorsen, M.M. Agenesis of the corpus callosum. 1. Neuropsychological studies. Cortex, 1975, 11, 95-122.

Foix, C. Contribution a l'etude de l'apraxie ideo-motrice de son anatomie pathologique et de ses rapports avec les syndromes qui, ordinairement, l'accompagnent. Revue Neurologique, 1916, 23, 283-298.

Foix, C. & Hillemand, P. Les syndromes de l'artere cerebrale anterieure. L'Encephale, 1925, 20, 209-232.

Forster, E. Ein diagnostizierter Fall von Balkentumor. Neurologisches Zentralblatt, 1908, 27, 540-542.

Forster, E. Balkentumor. Neurologisches Zentralblatt, 1909, 28, 1290-1291.

Forster, E. Demonstration des Gehirns eines Patienten, der apraktische Symptome im Leben dargeboten hatte. Monatsschrift fur Psychiatrie und Neurologie, 1913, 33, 196-197. (a)

Forster, E. Apraxie bei Balkendurchtrennung. Monatsschrift fur Psychiatrie und Neurologie, 1913, 331, 493-500. (b)

Gazzaniga, M.S., Bogen, J.E. & Sperry, R.W. Dispraxia following division of the cerebral commissures. Archives of Neurology, 1967, 16, 606-612.

Gazzaniga, M.S., Le Doux, J.E. & Wilson, D.H. Language, praxis and the right hemisphere: Clues to mechanisms of consciousness. Neurology, 1977, 27, 1144-1147.

Gersch, F. & Damasio, A.R. Praxis and writing of the left hand may be served by different callosal pathways. Archives of Neurology, 1981, 38, 634-636.

Geschwind, N. Disconnexion syndromes in animals and man, 2. Brain, 1965, 88, 585-644.

Geschwind, N. The apraxias: Neural mechanisms of disorders of learned movement. American Scientist, 1975, 63, 188-195.

Geschwind, N. & Kaplan, E. A human cerebral deconnection syndrome. Neurology, 1962, 12, 675-685.

Goldberg, G., Mayer, N.H. & Toglia, J.U. Medial frontal cortex infarction and the alien hand sign. Archives of Neurology, 1981, 38, 683-686.

Goldman-Rakic, P.S. Development and plasticity of primate frontal association cortex. In F.O. Schmitt, F.G. Worden, G. Adelman, & S.G. Dennis (Eds.), The organization of the cerebral cortex. Cambridge (Massachusetts): M.I.T. Press, 1981, 69-97.

Goldstein, K. Linksseitige motorische Apraxie. Journal fur Psychologie und Neurologie, 1908, 11, 169-270.

Goldstein, K. Der makroskopische Hirnbefund in einem Falle von linksseitiger motorischer Apraxie. Neurologisches Zentralblatt, 1909, 28, 898-906.

Goldstein, K. Uber Apraxie. Beihefte zur medizinischen Klinik, 1911, 7, 271.

Gordon, H.W., Bogen, J.E. & Sperry, R.W. Absence of deconnexion syndrome in two patients with partial section of the neocommissures. Brain, 1971, 94, 327-336.

Gott, P.S. & Saul, R.E. Agenesis of the corpus callosum: Limits of functional compensation. Neurology, 1978, 28, 1272-1279.

Green, J.R., Angevine, J.B. Jr., White, J.C., Edes, A.D. & Smith, R.D. The significance of the supplementary motor area in partial seizures and in cerebral localization. Neurosurgery, 1980, 6, 66-75.

Guidetti, B. Desordres de la parole associes a des lesions de la surface interhemispherique frontale posterieure. Revue Neurologique, 1957, 97, 121-131.

Guillain, G., Alajouanine, T. & Garcin, R. Un cas d'apraxie ideomotrice bilaterale coincidant avec une aphasie et une hemiparesie gauche chez une gauchere. Troubles bilateraux de la sensibilite profonde. Revue Neurologique, 1925, 32, 116-124.

Haaland, K.Y. & Miranda, F. Psychometric and CT scan measurements in a case of crossed aphasia in a dextral. Brain and Language, 1982, 17, 240-260.

Haaxma, R. & Kuypers, H.G.J.M. Intrahemispheric cortical connexions and visual guidance of hand and finger movements in the Rhesus monkey. Brain, 1975, 98, 239-260.

Halsey, J.H., Blauenstein, U.W., Wilson, E.M. & Wills, E.H. Regional cerebral blood flow comparison of right and left hand movement. Neurology, 1979, 29, 21-28.

Hartmann, F. Beitrage zur Apraxielehre. Monatsschrift fur Psychiatrie und Neurologie, 1907, 21, 97-118, 248-270.

Hecaen, H. & De Ajuriaguerra, J. Les gauchers. Prevalence manuelle et dominance cerebrale. Paris: Presses Universitaires de France, 1963.

Hecaen, H. & Gimeno Alava, A., L'apraxie ideomotrice unilaterale gauche. Revue Neurologique, 1960, 102, 648-653.

Hecaen, H. & Sauguet, J. Cerebral dominance in left-handed subjects. Cortex, 1971, 7, 19-48.

Heene, R. Klinische Untersuchungen bei Defekten des Corpus Callosum. Deutsche Zeitschrift fur Nervenheilkunde, 1966, 188, 62-69.

Heilman, K.M. Ideational apraxia: A redefinition. Brain, 1973, 96, 861-864.

Heilman, K.M. Apraxia. In K.M. Heilman & E. Valenstein (Eds.), Clinical Neuropsychology. New York: Oxford University Press, 1979, 159-185. (a)

Heilman, K.M. The neuropsychological basis of skilled movement in man. In M.S. Gazzaniga (Ed.), Handbook of behavioural neurobiology, Vol. 2, Neuropsychology. New York, 1979, 447-461. (b)

Heilman, K.M., Coyle, J.M., Gonyea, E.F. & Geschwind, N. Apraxia and agraphia in a left-hander. Brain, 1973, 96, 21-28.

Heilman, K.M., Gonyea, E.F. & Geschwind, N. Apraxia and agraphia in a right-hander. Cortex, 1974, 10, 284-288.

Hildebrandt. Dyspraxie bei linksseitiger Hemiplegie. Neurologisches Zentralblatt, 1908, 27, 576.

Hoff, H. Balkentumor mit linksseitiger Astereognosis und Apraxie. Deutsche Zeitschrift fur Nervenkrankheiten, 1931, 123, 89-100.

Hyland, H.H. Thrombosis of intracranial arteries. Report of three cases involving, respectively, the anterior cerebral, basilar and internal carotid arteries. Archives of Neurology and Psychiatry, 1933, 30, 342-356.

Ingvar, D.H. & Philipson, L. Distribution of cerebral blood flow in the dominant hemisphere during motor ideation and motor performance. Annals of Neurology, 1977, 2, 230-237.

Jason, G. Hemispheric asymmetries in motor function: I. Left hemisphere specialization for memory but not performance. Neuropsychologia, 1983, 21, 35-46. (a)

Jason, G. Hemispheric asymmetries in motor function: II. Ordering does not contribute to left hemisphere specialization. Neuropsychologia, 1983, 21, 47-58. (b)

Jeeves, M.A., Simpson, D.A. & Geffen, G. Functional consequences of the transcallosal removal of intraventricular tumors. Journal of Neurology, Neurosurgery, and Psychiatry, 1979, 42, 134-142.

Kennard, M.A. Cortical reorganization of motor function. Studies on series of monkeys of various ages from infancy to maturity. Archives of Neurology and Psychiatry, 1942, 48, 227-240.

Kimura, D. The neural basis of language qua gesture. In H. Whitaker, & N.A. Whitaker (Eds.), Studies in Neurolinguistics. New York: Academic Press, 1976, 145-156.

Kimura, D. Acquisition of a motor skill after left-hemisphere damage. Brain, 1977, 100, 527-542.

Kimura, D. Neuromotor mechanisms in the evolution of human communication. In H.D. Steklis & M.J. Raleigh (Eds.), Neurobiology of social communication in primates: an evolutionary perspective. New York: Academic Press, 1979, 197-219.

Kimura, D. Left-hemisphere control of oral and brachial movements and their relation to communication. Philosophical Transactions of the Royal Society of London, 1982, B298, 135-149.

Kimura, D. & Archibald, Y. Motor functions of the left hemisphere. Brain, 1974, 97, 337-350.

Klein, R. Zur Frage der zentralen Mechanismen der Apraxie. Medizinische Klinik, 1924, 12, 395-396.

Kleist, K. Ueber Apraxie. Monatsschrift fur Psychiatrie und Neurologie, 1906, 19, 269-290.

Kleist, K. Kortikale (innervatorische) Apraxie. Jahrbuch fur Psychiatrie und Neurologie, 1907, 28, 46-112.

Kleist, K. Der Gang und der gegenwartige Stand der Apraxie-forschung. Ergebnisse der Neurologie und Psychiatrie, 1911, 1, 343-452.

Kleist, K. Die psychomotorischen Storungen und ihr verhaltnis zu den Motilitatsstorungen bei Erkrankungen der Stammganglien. Monatsschrift fur Psychiatrie und Neurologie, 1922, 52, 253-302.

Kleist, K. Gehirnpathologie vornehmlich auf Grund der Kriegserfahrungen. Leipzig: Barth, 1934.

Kolb, B. & Milner, B. Performance of complex arm and facial movements after focal brain lesions. Neuropsychologia, 1981, 19, 491-503.

Kroll, M. Beitrage zum Studium der Apraxie. Zeitschrift fur die Gesamte Neurologie, 1910, 2, 315-345.

Kudlek, F. Zur Physiologie des Gyrus Supramarginalis. Deutsche Medizinische Wochenschrift, 1908, 17, 722-725.

Lange, J. Apraxien. In O. Bumke, & O. Foerster (Eds.), Handbuch der Neurologie, Vol. 6. Berlin: Springer, 1936, 885-960.

Laplane, D., Talairach, J., Meininger, V., Bancaud, J. & Orgogozo, J.M. Clinical consequences of corticectomies involving the supplementary motor area in man. Journal of the Neurological Sciences, 1977, 34, 301-314.

Liepmann, H. Das Krankheitsbild der Apraxie (motorischen Asymbolie). Monatsschrift fur Psychiatrie und Neurologie, 1900, 8, 15-44, 102-132, 182-197.

Liepmann, H. Der weitere Krankheitsverlauf bei dem einseitig Apraktischen und der Gehirnbefund auf Grund von Serienschnitten. 1. Monatsschrift fur Psychiatrie und Neurologie, 1905, 17, 289-311. (a)

Liepmann, H. Die linke Hemisphare und das Handeln. Muenchner Medizinische Wochenschrift, 1905, 49, 2322-2326, 2375-2378. (b)

Liepmann, H. Der weitere Krankheitsverlauf bei dem einseitig Apraktischen und der Gehirnbefund auf Grund von Serienschnitten. 2. Monatsschrift fur Psychiatrie und Neurologie, 1906, 19, 217-243.

Liepmann, H. Ueber die Funktion des Balkens beim Handeln und die Beziehungen von Aphasie und Apraxie zur Intelligenz. Medizinische Klinik, 1907, 3, 725-729, 765-769.

Liepmann, H. Drei Aufsatze aus dem Apraxiegebiet. Berlin: Karger, 1908.

Liepmann, H. Ueber die wissenschaftlichen Grundlagen der sogenannten "Linkskultur". Deutsche Medizinische Wochenschrift, 1911, 37, 1249-1252, 1308-1312.

Liepmann, H. Anatomische Befunde bei Aphasischen und Apraktischen. Neurologisches Zentralblatt, 1912, 31, 1524-1529.

Liepmann, H. Motorische Aphasie und Apraxie. Monatsschrift fur Psychiatrie und Neurologie, 1913, 34, 485-494.

Liepmann, H. Bemerkungen zu von Monakows Kapitel Die Lokalisation der Apraxie in seinem Buch: Die Lokalisation im Grosshirn (1914). Monatsschrift fur Psychiatrie und Neurologie, 1914, 35, 490-516.

Liepmann, H. Ergenbnisse der Gesamten Medizin, 1920, 1, 516-543.

Liepmann, H. Klinische und psychologische Untersuchungen und anatomischer Befund bei einem Fall von Dyspraxie und Agraphie. Journal fur Psychiatrie und Neurologie, 1929, 71, 169-214.

Liepmann, H. & Maas, O. Ein Fall von linksseitiger Agraphie und Apraxie bei rechtsseitiger Lahmung. Monatsschrift fur Psychologie und Neurologie, 1907, 10, 214-227.

Luria, A.R. Higher cortical functions in man. New York: Basic Books, Inc., 1980. (2nd edition)

Maas, O. Ein Fall von linksseitiger Apraxie und Agraphie. Neurologisches Zentralblatt, 1907, 26, 789-792.

Margolin, D.I. Right hemisphere dominance for praxis and left hemisphere dominance for speech in a left hander. Neuropsychologia, 1980, 18, 715-719.

Masdeu, J. Aphasia after infarction of the left supplementary motor area. Neurology, 1980, 30, 359.

Masdeu, J.C., Schoene, W.C. & Funkenstein, H. Aphasia following infarction of the left supplementary motor area. Neurology, 1978, 28, 1220-1223.

Mateer, C. & Kimura, D. Impairment of nonverbal oral movements in aphasia. Brain and Language, 1977, 4, 262-276.

Mingazzini, G. Aprassia - Patogenesi e sintomatologia. In G. Mingazzini (Ed.), Anatomia clinica dei centri nervosi. Torino: UTET, 1913 (2nd edition), chapter 37.

Mingazzini, G. & Ciarla, E. Klinischer und pathologisch-anatomischer Beitrag zum Studium der Apraxie. Jahrbuch fur Psychiatrie und Neurologie, 1920, 40, 24-98.

Mohr, J.P., Pessin, M.S., Finkelstein, S., Funkenstein, H.H., Duncan, G.W. & Davis, R. Broca aphasia: Pathologic and clinical neurology. Neurology, 1978, 28, 311-324.

Monakow, C. von Die Lokalisation im Grosshirn und der Abbau der Function durch Kortikale Herde. Wiesbaden: Bergmann, 1914, 489-574.

Morlaas, J. Contribution a l'etude de l'apraxie. Paris: Amedee Legrand, 1928.

Naeser, M.A. & Pienadz, J.M. Reversed cerebral asymmetries. Archives of Neurology, 1982, 39, 601.

Nielsen, J.M. Agnosia, apraxia, aphasia. Their value in cerebral localization. New York: Hafner Publishing Company, 1946 (2nd edition).

Ojemann, G.A. Interrelationships in the localization of language, memory, and motor mechanisms in human cortex and thalamus. In R.A. Thompson, & J.R. Green (Eds.), New Perspectives in Cerebral Localization. New York: Raven Press, 1982, 157-175.

Ojemann, G. & Mateer, C. Human language cortex: Localization of memory, syntax, and sequential motor-phoneme identification systems. Science, 1979, 205, 1401-1403.

Olesen, J. Contralateral focal increase of cerebral blood flow in man during arm work. Brain, 1971, 94, 635-646.

Orgogozo, J.M. & Larsen, B. Activation of the supplementary motor area during voluntary movements in man suggests it works as a supra motor area. Science, 1979, 206, 847-850.

Pandya, D.N. Interhemispheric connections in primate. In F. Michel, & B. Schott (Eds.), Les syndromes de disconnexion calleuse chez l'homme. Lyon: Hopital Neurologique, 1975, 17-40.

Pandya, D.N. & Seltzer, B. Association areas of the cerebral cortex. Trends in Neurosciences, 1982, 5, 386-391.

Pandya, D.N. & Vignolo, L.A. Interhemispheric projections of the parietal lobe in the rhesus monkey. Brain Research, 1969, 15, 49-65.

Pandya, D.N. & Vignolo, L.A. Intra- and inter-hemispheric projections of the precentral, premotor and arcuate areas in the rhesus monkey. Brain Research, 1971, 26, 217-233.

Penfield, W. & Welch, K. The supplementary motor area of the cerebral cortex. Archives of Neurology and Psychiatry, 1951, 66, 289-317.

Pick, A. Studien uber motorische Apraxie und ihre nahestehende Erscheinungen, ihre Bedeutung in der Symptomatologie psychopathologischer Synptomenkomplexe. Leipzig: Deuticke, 1905.

Pieczuro, A. & Vignolo, L.A. Studio sperimentale sulla aprassia ideomotoria. Sistema Nervoso, 1967, 19, 131-143.

Pineas, H. Ein Fall von linksseitiger motorischer Apraxie nach Balkenerweichung. Monatsschrift fur Psychiatrie und Neurologie, 1924, 56, 43-46.

Pocock, P.V. The spatial and temporal distribution of alpha activity and their modification during motor preparation. In G. Pfurtscheller, P. Buser, F.H. Lopes da Silva, & H. Petsche (Eds.), Rhythmic EEG activities and cortical functioning. Amsterdam: North Holland, 1980, 135-177.

Poeck, K. & Kerschensteiner, M. Ideomotor apraxia following right-sided cerebral lesion in a left-handed subject. Neuropsychologia, 1971, 9, 359-361.

Poeck, K. & Lehmkuhl, G. Ideatory apraxia in a left-handed patient with right-sided brain lesion. Cortex, 1980, 16, 273-284.

Preilowski, B.F.B. An investigation of perceptual-motor learning and bilateral transfer in partial commissurotomy patients. Biology Annual Report, 1971, 117.

Roland, P.E., Larsen, B., Lassen, N.A. & Skinhoj, E. Supplementary motor area and other cortical areas in organization of voluntary movements in man. Journal of Neurophysiology, 1980, 43, 118-136.

Roland, P.E., Meyer, E., Shibasaki, T., Yamamoto, Y.L. & Thompson, C.J. Regional cerebral blood flow changes in cortex and basal ganglia during voluntary movements in normal human volunteers. Journal of Neurophysiology, 1982, 48, 467-480.

Roland, P.E., Skinhoj, E., Lassen, N.A. & Larsen, B. Different cortical areas in man in organization of voluntary movements in extrapersonal space. Journal of Neurophysiology, 1980, 43, 137-150.

Rose, F. Un cas d'apraxie ideomotrice gauche chez un gaucher. L'Encephale, 1911, 6, 536-542.

Rothmann, M. Diskussion zu: "Klinisch-Anatomischer Beitrag zur Lehre von der Bedeutung der linken Hemisphare und des Balkens fur das Haudeln" von Liepmann, H. und Maas, O., Berliner Klinische Wochenschrift, 1907, 757-758. (a)

Rothmann, M. Zur Symptomatologie der Hemiplegie. Berliner Klinische Wochenschrift, 1907, 1002. (b)

Rothmann, M. Apraxie der rechten Hand bei linksseitiger Hemiplegie beim Linkshander. Deutsche Zeitschrift fur Nervenheilkunde, 1911, 41, 271-272.

Roy, E.A. Action sequences and lateralized cerebral damage: Evidence for asymmetries in control. In J. Long & A. Baddeley (Eds.), Attention and Performance. Hillsdale, N.J.: Erlbaum, 1984, Vol. 3, 487-499.

Rubens, A.B. Aphasia with infarction in the territory of the anterior cerebral artery. Cortex, 1975, 11, 239-250.

Rubens, A.B., Geschwind, N., Mahowald, M.W. & Mastri, A. Post traumatic cerebral hemispheric disconnection syndrome. Archives of Neurology, 1977, 34, 750-755.

Sauerwein, H.C., Lassonde, M.C., Cardu, B. & Geoffroy, G. Interhemispheric integration of sensory and motor functions in agenesis of the corpus callosum. Neuropsychologia, 1981, 19, 445-454.

Schaffer, K. Uber doppelseitiger Erweichung des Gyrus supramarginalis. Monatsschrift fur Psychiatrie und Neurologie, 1910, 27, 53.

Schaltenbrand, G. Uber einen Fall von Personlichkeitsspaltung infolge Balkentumor. Archiv fur Psychiatrie und Zeitschrift fur die Gesamte Neurologie, 1963, 204, 521-530.

Scharlock, D.P., Tucker, T.J. & Strominger, N.L. Auditory discrimination by the cat after neonatal ablation of temporal cortex. Science, 1963, 141, 1197-1198.

Selnes, O.A., Rubens, A.B., Risse, G.L. & Levy, R.S. Transient aphasia with persistent apraxia. Uncommon sequela of massive left-hemisphere stroke. Archives of Neurology, 1982, 39, 122-126.

Sheremata, W.A., Deonna, R.W. & Romanul, F.C. Agenesis of the corpus callosum and interhemispheric transfer of information. Neurology, 1973, 23, 390.

Shibasaki, H., Barrett, G., Halliday, A.M. & Halliday, E. Scalp topography of movement related cortical potentials. In H.H. Kornhuber, & L. Deecke (Eds.), Motivation, Motor and Sensory Processes of the Brain, Progress in Brain Research, 1980, 54, 273-242.

Signoret, J.L. & North, P. Les apraxies gestuelles. Paris: Masson, 1979.

Sittig, O. Uber Apraxie. Berlin: Karger, 1931.

Slager, U.T., Kelly, A.B. & Wagner, J.A. Congenital absence of the corpus callosum: Report of a case and review of the literature. New England Journal of Medicine, 1957, 256, 1171-1176.

Sperry, R.W., Gazzaniga, M.S. & Bogen, J.E. Interhemispheric relationships: The neocortical commissures; syndromes of hemisphere disconnection. In P.J. Vinken, & G.W. Bruyn (Eds.), Handbook of clinical neurology, Vol. 4, Disorders of speech, perception and symbolic behaviour. Amsterdam: North Holland, 1969, 273-290.

Stauffenberg, W.F. von Beitrage zur Lokalisation der Apraxie. Zeitschrift fur dei Gesamte Neurologie und Psychiatrie. 1911, 5, 434-444.

Stauffenberg, W.F. von Klinische und anatomische Beitrage zur Kenntniss der aphasischen, agnostichen und apraktischen Symptome. Zeitschrift fur die Gesamte Neurologie und Psychiatrie. 1918, 39, 71-212.

Strohmayer, W.   Uber subkortikale Alexie mit Agraphie und Apraxie.   Deutsche Zeitschrift fur Nervenheilkunde, 1903, 24, 372-380.

Sugishita, M., Toyokura, Y., Yoshioka, M. & Yamada, R.   Unilateral agraphia after section of the posterior half of the truncus of the corpus callosum.   Brain and Language, 1980, 9, 215-225.

Sweet, W.H.   Seeping intracranial aneurysm simulating neoplasm.   Archives of Neurology and Psychiatry, 1941, 45, 86-104.

Taterka, H.   Partielle Apraxie des rechten Armes nach linksseitiger Hemiplegie bei einer Linkshanderin.   Zeitschrift fur die Gesamte Neurologie und Psychiatrie, 1924, 90, 573-579. (a)

Taterka, H.   Partielle Apraxie des rechten Armes bei einer Linkshanderin nach halbseitiger Hemiplegie.   Berliner Gesellschaft fur Psychiatrie, 1924, 35, 446-448. (b)

Trescher, J.H. & Ford, F.R.   Colloid cyst of the third ventricle.   Report of a case; operative removal with section of posterior half of corpus callosum.   Archives of Neurology and Psychiatry, 1937, 37, 959-973.

Tzavaras, A.   Les apraxies unilaterales.   In H. Hecaen & M. Jeannerod (Eds.), Du control moteur a l'organisation du geste.   Paris: Masson, 1978, 359-379.

Valenstein, E. & Heilman, K.M.   Apractic agraphia with neglect-induced paragraphia.   Archives of Neurology, 1979, 36, 506-508.

Vleuten, C.F. van   Linksseitige motorische Apraxie: Ein Beitrag zur Physiologie des Balkens.   Allgemeine Zeitschrift fur Psychiatrie, 1907, 64, 203-239.

Volpe, B.T., Sidtis, J.J., Holtzman, J.D., Wilson, D.H. & Gazzaniga, M.S.   Cortical mechanisms involved in praxis: Observations following partial and complete section of the corpus callosum in man.   Neurology, 1982, 32, 645-650.

Wagenen, W.P. van & Herren, R.Y.   Surgical division of commissural pathways in the corpus callosum.   Archives of Neurology and Psychiatry, 1940, 44, 740-759.

Watson, R.T. & Heilman, K.M.   Callosal apraxie.   Brain, 1983, 106, 391-403.

Westphal, A.   Uber einen Fall von motorischen Apraxie.   Allgemeine Zeitschrift fur Psychiatrie. 1907, 64, 452-458.

Wilson, S.A.K.   A contribution to the study of apraxia.   Brain, 1908, 31, 164-216.

Zaidel, D. & Sperry, R.W.   Some long-term motor effects of cerebral commissurotomy in man.   Neuropsychologia, 1977, 15, 193-204.

Neuropsychological Studies of Apraxia and Related Disorders, E.A. Roy (ed.)
© *Elsevier Science Publishers B.V. (North-Holland), 1985*

METHODS OF LIMB APRAXIA EXAMINATION AND THEIR BEARING

ON THE INTERPRETATION OF THE DISORDER

Ennio De Renzi

Universita di Modena

There are many variables of the movement and of the
way it is examined that have been claimed to be crucial
in apraxia, but few of them withstand scrutiny and
deserve special consideration in test construction. The
main requirements an adequate apraxia examination
must fulfill are that it can be given also to patients with
comprehension deficit (because many apractics are
aphasics), that it allows the distinction between ideomotor and ideational apraxia and that it is suitable to
ascertain whether the deficit is contingent on the
modality through which the order eliciting the movement
is conveyed. The basic tests that a battery should
include are: 1. A movement imitation test, made up of
different types of action (meaningful and meaningless,
postures and sequences, etc.). It can be administered to
severe aphasics and is suited to assess ideomotor apraxia.
2. Use-of-object pantomimes on verbal command and
object presentation. Since no model is present, the
patient must evoke the movement shape and thus the
ideational component of the deficit may be disclosed. A
dissociation between the performance on verbal and visual administration hints at a modality specific apraxia.
If test 2 is failed, it is useful to require 3. A third type
of test involving the actual use of objects with items of
graded difficulty, from single object manipulation to the
coordinated use of more than one object.

There is a discrepancy between the interest apraxia deserves as a symptom
clearly pointing to left hemisphere dominance in a non-linguistic realm and the relatively scanty number of studies that have been devoted to its investigation, especially if compared with the mass of research centering on aphasia. Also, clinicians
tend to pay little attention to this disorder in the course of neurological examination
and thus, underestimate its frequency following left brain damage. Probably, very
few of them would guess apraxia occurs in 50% of unselected acute left brain-
damaged patients, as has been shown in a systematic investigation carried out with a
standardized procedure (De Renzi, Motti & Nichelli, 1980). The reason for this neglect is probably to be found in the fact that apraxia rarely appears in everyday situations and in spontaneous motor behaviour, predominantly emerging when gestures
are produced out of context as a purposeful response to an artificial request. While
aphasia is immediately perceived by the patient or others around him, even when it
is of mild severity, apraxia is to a large extent an examination-bound symptom and
is, therefore, not liable to attract the doctor's attention, unless expressly looked for.
Another circumstance that conspires to obscure its detection is that apraxia is normally associated with aphasia; 80% of unselected aphasics are apractic as against

only 5% of non-aphasic left brain-damaged patients (De Renzi et al., 1980). However, this link is due to the anatomical contiguity of the structures subserving the two symptoms and not to a causal relation. Since the most common way to test apraxia is to request gestures by verbal commands, severe aphasics tend not to be examined, on the assumption that they would not be able to understand the order.

The above considerations stress the importance of a proper examination, and the need to carefully assess the variables of the movement and of the testing procedure which could play a role in the patient's inability to carry out purposeful motor actions, despite the absence of paralysis or sensory deficits. The purpose of this chapter is to analyze the potentials and pitfalls inherent in the different procedures that have been proposed to examine apraxia and to evaluate what implications can be drawn from their use for understanding the nature of the deficit.

Before probing specific issues, a general comment is in order concerning the hand to be tested. Brain-damaged patients frequently present with muscular weakness of the contralateral limbs, namely, right-sided paresis or plegia in the case of left hemisphere injury, which may render the evaluation of apraxia difficult or even impossible when the movements are to be carried out with the preferred hand. However, this is not a real drawback, since it has been shown (De Renzi, Faglioni & Sorgato, 1982) that in normal right-handers the two hands are equally proficient in performing a series of apraxia tests and that no difference exists between the scores achieved with either hand by non-hemiplegic left brain-damaged patients on a movement imitation task (Kimura & Archibald, 1974). Thus, when unselected brain-damaged patients are investigated, the limb ipsilateral to the lesion will be used.

Distinctions Based on the Nature of the Movement

The definition of apraxia as a disorder of purposeful movements which is not explicable in terms of elementary motor or sensory deficit is very broad and leaves open the question of whether there are features of the movement which make it selectively sensitive to disruption following a left brain lesion. Movements may be analyzed from different viewpoints, but the classification more frequently adopted with reference to apraxia is that based on the aim the motor action purports to fulfill, namely whether it is meant to manipulate objects, to communicate ideas, to express feelings, or is devoid of any pragmatic and symbolic value. The schema shown in Table 1 will serve as a guide in our analysis.

Meaningful movements, which are the only ones deserving the name of gestures, may be grouped in two broad categories, those directed to manipulate objects, which are also called transitive movements, and those meant to express ideas or feelings, which are called intransitive movements. The psychological foundation of this differentiation is obvious, but our concern here is whether it is also justified on clinical grounds, and, if so, what advantage the diagnosis of apraxia may be expected to accrue from it.

Transitive Gestures and the Question of Ideational Apraxia

Two sets of reasons have been advanced in support of the view that object use should be given special consideration. Some authors have stressed the point that demonstrating how familiar objects are used is a very simple task, both because it refers to a frequently experienced behaviour and because it is favoured by the assistance that tactile cues and the reference points for manipulation present in objects give to movement execution. The facilitation effect of the latter condition was first pointed out by Liepmann (1900) in connection with the preserved ability of the

Table 1

Classification Schema of Movements used in Limb Apraxia Testing

```
Transitive gestures
        Action with single objects
        Action with multiple objects
        Simple pantomimes
        Complex, narrative pantomimes

Intransitive gestures
        Symbolic gestures
        Natural, expressive gestures

Meaningless movements
        Single movements
        Sequences
```

Regierungsrat to button up and unbutton his jacket, a task that is usually performed entirely under tactile guidance without visual aid.[1]

In this perspective the aim of examining object-use would mainly be to test the lower limits of performance of severely impaired patients with an elementary task, which differs from those involving intransitive gestures in terms of difficulty, not of nature. Its inclusion in an apraxia battery would thus be optional and, as a matter of fact, it is often substituted by the more exacting and supposedly more discriminative task of pantomining the use of objects in their absence, a performance not aided by contextual cues and one which calls for an effort of imagination.

Traditionally, however, use-of-object tests have been viewed as playing a more specific role in apraxia examination, in that they would provide the only way to bring out that particular form of apraxia called ideational apraxia (IA). Its independence with respect to ideomotor apraxia (IMA) is controversial. Liepmann (1908) accepted its autonomy viewing it as consequent to the disruption of the plan of action, while Sittig (1931) and Kleist (1934) were inclined to consider it as an extreme form of IMA, showing up also when the performance is facilitated by the use of objects, a position shared, albeit with some reservation, by Zangwill (1960) in his review of the subject. Understandably, authors, like Geschwind (1965, 1975) and Goodglass and Kaplan (1963), who propose object use as an easy test of apraxia, are apparently not interested in the issue related to IA, or at least they never mention it in their studies. At any rate, the majority of students accept IA as an autonomous

---

[1] A case with a selective difficulty in manipulating objects with the left hand without the aid of vision has been recently reported by Yamadori (1982). The patient showed inability in buttoning, putting on gloves, slipping his hand into the pocket of his trousers and was clumsy in handling objects. The deficit was attributed to the loss of an active sense of moving fingers (inspite of preserved sense of passive movement), which was also held responsible for astereognosis. Movements on visual imitation were much less impaired. Yamadori called palpatory apraxia this picture, but the legitimacy of designating as apractic a disorder of this type confined to the left hand in a right-hander is questionnable.

symptom, which emerges when the patient is required to manipulate objects and betrays a loss of the ability to evoke and organize the appropriate gestures (see also Poeck, this volume). Two experimental investigations have provided data upholding this position.

The idea that IA is but an extreme form of IMA implies that it can be demonstrated only in patients who irremediably fail on executing intransitive gestures, even when they are imitated and thus do not require the building up of an ideational program. Conversely, patients with no or mild disorders on this task will not show IA. De Renzi, Pieczuro and Vignolo (1966) tested this hypothesis by examining a large sample of left brain-damaged patients with a symbolic gesture imitation task and with a use-of-object task. Only a moderate correlation (0.41) was found between the two scores and there were 11 patients who performed within the normal range (i.e., above the cutting score, determined in a normal control group) on the imitation task and were defective (i.e., scored below the cutting score) on the use-of-object test. For at least three of these patients the discrepancy was striking with almost perfect scores on the former task and extremely poor scores on the latter.

These findings were replicated in a recent study (De Renzi, Faglioni & Sargato, 1982) comparing the performance of left brain-damaged patients (N:150) on an imitation test and a use-of-object test, both presented in the visual modality. The former test required the patient to copy meaningful and meaningless gestures made by the examiner, the latter to pantomime the use of objects that were shown, but neither handed to the patient nor named by the examiner. Since different movements were involved by the two tests, it was first determined whether normal subjects (N:70) found them of dissimilar difficulty by computing the difference between the two scores, which were previously standardized. The majority of subjects scored somewhat lower on the imitation test and only two performed poorer on the use-of-object test, the maximum difference being of one point. As the scores ranged from zero to 20, only a difference greater than five points (which represents the 25 percentile) was accepted as evidence of a disproportionally poor performance on the use-of-object test. There were 13 patients exceeding the five point difference. This proportion is significantly higher than that which would be expected to occur by chance in the normal population and cannot, therefore, by attributed to a random fluctuation in performance. Most of these 13 patients were apractic also on imitation, although less strikingly so than on the use-of-object test, but two performed in the normal range on imitation and failed dramatically on pantomimes. The authors argued that what distinguishes the two performances and explains the selective impairment on pantomimes is that they demand the patient to conjure up in memory the movement pattern, an ability that comes before and must be differentiated from that of implementing the evoked motor plan. IA would correspond to a disruption occurring at the former stage and, while in the majority of cases the lesion will probably hamper both levels, it can predominantly or even exclusively affect evocation.

A clinical description of a patient who performed worse in using objects than on intransitive movements was given by Brown (1972, case 8), while Poeck and Lehmkuhl (1980a) reported a patient presenting with unmistakeable signs of severe IA at a time of disease when the ability to produce symbolic and meaningless arm movements either on verbal command or on imitation had completely recovered. These patients must necessarily be rare, because of the contiguity of the neuronal networks underlying the two symptoms, but they would probably turn out to be less exceptional than it is thought, if systematically looked for. In any event, even a single case is sufficient to challenge the notion that IA is dependent on IMA.

It must be emphasized at this point that two views have been advanced concerning the intimate nature of the deficit underlying IA and that they have important implications for the choice of the testing procedure. Most authors (Pick, 1905; Liepmann, 1920; Lange, 1936, Poeck, 1982) view IA as a disruption in the sequential organization of the gestures required to carry out a complex performance, due to the disintegration or inadequacy of the plan of action. Errors would mainly affect the order in which the single components of the sequence must be produced or consist in the omission, and perseveration of some of them. It logically follows from this conception that the only appropriate way of testing IA is with tasks requiring the manipulation of more than one object, where cooperative gestures must be programmed in order to attain a goal (e.g., hanging a picture to the wall, preparing a cup of coffee, opening a tin, etc., see Poeck and Lehmkuhl, 1980a,b). On the contrary, failure to use a single object would reflect an executive disruption and point to IMA.

A different stance was taken by Marcuse (1904) and especially Morlaas (1928), who maintained that IA may appear in complex sequences as well as in the use of single objects, since the basic deficit underlying the disorder is the inability to evoke the gesture appropriate for the utilization of the object, in spite of its correct identification and the preserved cognition of what in theory its use is. To define the nature of the deficit, Morlaas proposed the name of "agnosie d'utilization" (agnosia of utilization). Evidence in support of this position can be adduced from some cases that have been described as typical examples of IA, whose errors are by no means restricted to the disruption of performances implying the use of multiple objects. Pick's (1905) original case used a razor as a comb, and scissors as a pen, Brown's (1972) case 8 used a toothbrush for brushing his nails, Poeck and Lehmkuhl's (1980a) patient, requested to open a tin, repeatedly beat the tin with the opener, and requested to heat water with a water immersion heater in order to prepare a cup of coffee, dipped the plug of the heater into the water pot and stirred around with it. What these and many similar observations suggest is that the patient literally does not remember how to use the object: he looks at it perplexed, turns it over in his hands and eventually makes an attempt that may be totally wrong. Obviously, the more complex the task, the easier the appearance of errors and it is conceivable that they may take the form of omissions and derange the proper order of acts when the performance requires the combined use of multiple objects, but the basic deficit remains one of evocation, which in moderate to severe cases can be brought out also by the use of single objects.

A word of caution is, however, in order before leaving this subject, warning not to take the failure of using objects as prima facie evidence of IA, since it may as well result from disruption in movement execution, consequent to a severe IMA. In principle, the error quality should be discriminative, the performance of IMA patients still bearing a certain resemblance to the intended movement in spite of its awkwardness, and that of IA patients being more skillful, but conceptually wrong. However, it is fair to recognize with Sittig (1931) that this differentiation may be hard to draw in clinical practice and that a sounder basis for the diagnosis is provided by the finding of a striking discrepancy between the performance on imitation tasks in comparison to conditions where the gesture must be evoked by the patient.

Intransitive Gestures

Intransitive gestures are traditionally considered a convenient measure of IMA, because they relate to a repertoire of motor acts that are well practiced, precisely designable with a verbal label and have a definite conformation, which makes them easy to request and to compare with a standard.

In the schema proposed by Hecaen (1978, see Hecaen & Rondot, this volume) symbolic gestures (e.g., salute, make the sign of cross, etc.) are kept separate from expressive gestures (e.g., threaten somebody, smell something bad, etc.) as they would reflect different psychological purposes subserved by discrete neuronal mechanisms. The legitimacy of this distinction appears to be questionnable because it applies to gestures made in a real situation, not to gestures purposefully produced out of context: to pretend to beg somebody in response to a verbal command can hardly be contrasted with waving goodbye, as the performance is not sustained by the emotional mechanisms implicated when the gesture is spontaneously produced. There would seem to be, therefore, little basis for retaining this dichotomy. Another distinction which also seems of questionnable relevance to apraxia is that concerning the direction of the movement, whether towards or away from the body, which has been advocated by Brown (1972) with respect to intransitive movements and Hecaen (1978) with respect to pantomimes. It is hard to see why saluting should be analyzed separately from waving goodbye or combing oneself from turning a key, simply because the former movements are body-directed and the latter not. There is some evidence, however, that movements centred around the body (egocentric space) may be more affected in apraxia than movements made in extrapersonal space in both adult-onset (Kimura, 1979) and developmental (see Cermak, this volume) apraxia.

The question may be raised as to whether the inability to produce a symbolic, or expressive movement in response to a verbal command necessarily points to IMA. Could it not be due in some cases to a deficit in conjuring up the pattern of the gesture, similar to what occurs in using objects and thus suggestive of an ideational component in the defective performance? The doubt is justified when a patient without comprehension deficits gives no response or makes a totally incorrect movement which does not bear any resemblance to the requested gesture. From a logical viewpoint, there is no reason to restrict the evocative deficit to use of objects, as claimed by Morlaas (1928), and not to conceive of it as encompassing any movement pattern, which has been learned and stored. We will discuss the issue later; for the time being, it is sufficient to point out that no absolute relation links intransitive gesture impairment with IMA and that a performance must always be evaluated keeping in mind that it can be thwarted at different levels.

Meaningless Movements

Until now we have been dwelling on gestures, namely, movements that fulfill a pragmatic or communication need and that for this very reason have been learnt and repeatedly practised by the subject. One might infer that both or either of these features-being meaningful and being overlearned - constitute a prerequisite for making a movement liable to disruption by apraxia and that, consequently, only gestures are fit for testing the disorder. Although the majority of authors who have investigated apraxia have stressed a testing approach based on gestures and pantomimes and have only marginally or not at all mentioned meaningless movements, a few studies carried out in recent years clearly show that such a neglect is by no means justified.

Pieczuro and Vignolo (1967) must be credited for having been the first to provide convincing evidence that meaningless movements are more and not less effective than meaningful movements to bring out a deficit in imitation which is specific to left brain-damaged patients. Since this paper has been somewhat overlooked by the literature, probably because published in an Italian journal, it is worth summarizing in some detail. Seventy left brain-damaged patients, 40 right brain-damaged patients and 40 normal controls were required to imitate 20 movements made by the examiner. Ten of them were symbolic gestures and 10 meaningless movements of comparable motor complexity and each item was scored 2,1,0 according to whether the execution was correct, partially incorrect or totally incorrect.

There was a slight tendency on the part of normal subjects to imitate symbolic better than meaningless gestures, with 17 subjects scoring at the same level on both tests, one outranking on the meaningless test and 22 on the meaningful test. To ascertain whether the same pattern also held in brain-damaged patients, Pieczuro and Vignolo determined how many brain-damaged patients showed a difference between the two scores higher than the maximum difference found in normals, one point when it was the meaningless test which was to be performed better and three points when the meaningful test was superior. One right brain-damaged patient and two left brain-damaged patients had a difference greater than one favouring mean-ingless movements as against one right brain-damaged patient and 18 left brain-damaged patients having a difference greater than three in favour of meaningful movements. It is apparent that right brain-damaged patients performed like nor-mals, while patients with left hemisphere lesions found imitation of meaningless movements significantly more difficult (p < 0.001) than imitation of meaningful movements in comparison with control subjects. From this finding the authors inferred that it is not the symbolic nature of the movement to determine its sensi-tivity to ideomotor apraxia, but rather the extent to which the nervous system is engaged in controlling its execution. Meaningless movements, being unpracticed, require a higher degree of motor control than conventional, overlearned gestures and are, therefore, more easily disrupted.

Subsequent studies have confirmed that the symbolic nature of the movement does not make it more sensitive to apraxia. Kimura and Archibald (1974) found left brain-damaged patients more impaired than right hemisphere patients on imitating meaningless movements as well as on imitating gestures, although in their rather small sample a significant deficit was confined to copying manual sequences (e.g., closed fist, thumbs sideways on table) and did not extend to copying hand gestures (e.g., open hand, extended fingers spaced apart). A direct comparison of the power of symbolic and meaningless movements to bring out a deficit following left brain damage was carried out by De Renzi et al. (1980) who examined 100 control patients, 70 right brain-damaged patients and 100 left brain-damaged patients, on a a 24 item test, made up of an equal number of the two types of movements. A cut-ting score was determined, based on the performance of the worst control subject and brain-damaged patients falling below it were identified as apractic. An equal number of apractics (42) was found among left brain-damaged patients on either test. The bulk of evidence bears out, therefore, the conclusion that meaningless movements are at least as suitable as gestures for IMA examination. The only limi-tation with meaningless gestures is that they do not lend themselves to easy verbal labelling and are, therefore, unsuited to be administered with oral commands, par-ticularly considering that most apraxics are aphasic. However, this does not repre-sent a real drawback for testing IMA.

Sequential Movements

Some investigators have recently called attention to the increased diagnostic power of apraxia examination which accrues from requiring patients to imitate sequences of unrelated movements. As mentioned above, Kimura and Archibald (1974) found that left-brain-damaged patients' impairment was confined to copying multiple movements, while copying hand postures was not poorer than in patients with right-sided lesions. From this dissociation they inferred that the basic deficit underlying apraxia was the inability to control the rapid transition from one motor act to another. The claimed insensitivity of single movements to apraxia is at vari-ance with the results of Pieczuro and Vignolo's (1967) investigation, which was mainly based on the imitation of static positions, and clearly showed the poorer performance of left brain-damaged patients. Also De Renzi et al. (1980) failed to find evidence for a better identification of apractics with multiple rather than single movement imitation and one is led to suspect that Kimura and Archibald's results were contingent upon the particular movements they chose for posture imitation, which were too simple to be sensitive indicators of apraxia. For example, in our experience two of the six items of their test (a closed fist, an open hand) are performed flawlessly by almost every patient and for this very reason we use them for demonstration. Kimura herself (1982) has subsequently recognized that the sequential nature of the performance is not crucial and that apraxia shows up also with postures, at least in moderately to severely impaired patients.

Yet, it has been held that the two kinds of performance deserve separate treatment, because they would manifest a differential sensitivity not only to the severity of apraxia but also to the locus of lesion causing it (Kimura, 1982). In a group of 72 left brain-damaged patients, those with injury primarily restricted to a single lobe were identified and their performance on a hand posture and a multiple hand movement task was compared. Parietal patients were impaired on both tasks, frontal patients on the multiple movement task only. These data are interesting, because they open a path to unravel the contribution of discrete cerebral areas to the organization of motor performances, with the parietal lobe implicated in the control of every type of movement and the frontal lobe only in the execution of a complex sequence. It is worth reminding that Luria (1966; see also Roy, 1978) had already emphasized the role of the frontal lobes in steering motor actions consisting of rapidly alternating movements and that his claim has found support in a recent study of Kolb and Milner (1981), carried out mainly in epileptic patients who had undergone cortical ablations restricted to one lobe. They were patients with a relatively mild impairment and thus provide information that properly complements Luria's findings, which were mainly drawn from patients with tumors of undefined size, possibly accompanied by signs of increased intracranial pressure.

Kolb and Milner's patients were given meaningless movement sequences to imitate and both frontal and parietal patients were found to be defective in comparison to normal controls. Although in general agreement with Kimura's data, Kolb and Milner's findings differ in two respects: 1) parietal patient's impairment was significantly more marked than that of any other cortical group, the frontal one included; 2) damage to either frontal lobe and not only that confined to the left side resulted in a decrement in performance. The patients in this investigation were not apractic when examined with conventional apraxia tests, such as pantomiming the use of objects and making symbolic gestures on verbal command, but they were not systematically tested on single meaningless movement imitation and it remains, therefore, uncertain whether their deficit was confined to sequences or also involved single movements.

We (De Renzi, Faglioni, Lodesan & Vecchi, 1983) have data that allow us to answer this question. Sixty control and 60 left brain-damaged patients were given two imitation tests, one made up of single movements, the other of three unrelated movements carried out in a sequence. To avoid the interference of memory problems, sequences were repeated three times before the patient began to imitate and, in addition, three photographs displaying the units of each sequence were laid down on the table in front of the patient as a reminder. Both tests significantly differentiated left brain-damaged patients from controls, but the test by group interaction was practically zero. The same result obtained when frontal and parietal patients were identified on the basis of CT scan findings and their performance was compared. Posterior patients scored significantly poorer than frontal patients on either test and the interaction fell far short of the significance level. It follows from these findings that requiring serial actions does not enhance the sensitivity of motor performance to left brain damage nor to the intrahemispheric locus of lesion and that the basic deficit underlying apraxia resides in the inability to select the correct motor innervation.

Viewed in conjunction with the data of Kolb and Milner (1981) and Kimura (1982) the above findings concur to challenge an interpretation of apraxia in purely disconnectionistic terms, namely, that it is dependent on the interruption of the pathways connecting the information processing areas with the motor areas and that the relevance of parietal damage to the disorder is simply due to the involvement of the white matter underneath the supramarginal gyrus, where the fibres directed to the frontal lobe are running (Liepmann, 1920). In this perspective left parietal and frontal lesions would be expected to be equally conducive to apraxia, whereas the finding that the deficit is much more marked following the former rather than the latter injury favours a hierarchic conceptualization of function, with the left parietal cortex playing a leading and unreplaceable role in programming manual movements. The left premotor area would act at a subordinate level and its function may be in a number of cases superseded by the homologous right cortex, at least as far as left limb movements are concerned. Much remains to be investigated to define the specialization of cortical areas in motor control and in particular to trace the pathways linking the left parietal lobe with the frontal lobe, but I believe that this aspect of Liepmann's theory needs revision.

Distinction based on the Physiological Properties of the Movement

So far we have analyzed the relation the nature of limb movements bears to apraxia mainly in psychological terms, focusing on the value they have for the subject and the goal they purport to fulfill, i.e., whether movements are intended to manipulate objects, convey ideas, express feelings or make arbitrary actions. None of these distinctions has been found to play a crucial role in bringing out apraxia, except for the circumstance that the gesture must be purposefully executed, out of context. One may wonder, however, whether the issue would not be more fruitfully addressed from a physiological rather than a psychological viewpoint, differentiating movements on the basis of the neural pathways involved in their execution and thus putting the study of apraxia in the same perspective as the study of other movement disorders (see also Kolb & Whishaw, this volume).

Distal versus Proximal Limb Movement

An obvious distinction that immediately comes to mind is that between isolated finger movements, which are under exclusive control of the contralateral pyramidal tract, and more proximal limb movements, which are subserved by other descending motor pathways. Is it the case that apraxia affects skillful distal movements more than movements implying the arm, forearm or whole hand? This distinction is certainly pertinent to understanding one aspect of apraxic phenomena, namely, the pattern of movement disruption found in a limb when the contralateral motor cortex is disconnected from the centres where the information instigating the action is processed. Such a condition typically occurs in patients submitted to the section of the commissures when they are investigated with appropriate procedures and it betokens the extent to which the motor cortex is able to control ipsilateral limb movements. The available evidence confirms that ipsilateral control is ineffective with respect to fractionated finger movements. For example, imitation of hand postures flashed in a visual hemifield and carried out with the contralateral hand (e.g., left field-right hand) has been found to be poor when the response requires single finger movements, but to be adequate when it involves shoulder and arm muscles or even the most simple hand postures, like making a fist or opening the fingers (Gazzaniga, Bogen & Sperry, 1967; Volpe, Sidtis, Holtzman, Wilson & Gazzaniga, 1982). The same result obtains (Zaidel & Sperry, 1977) for motor performances carried out with the left limb in response to verbal commands. Although the right hemisphere proves to be able to decode them, something fails at the moment of transforming the information into motor programs if they refer to isolated finger movements.

Skillful, Repetitive Movements

In the above examples the selective impairment of finger movements following the section of the commissures was viewed as a consequence of the inaccessibility of the motor cortex to the stimuli instigating the action. One may raise the more general question of whether there is any evidence that left hemisphere dominance for motor abilities is more manifest for movements strictly contingent upon the functioning of the contralateral motor cortex and less marked for movements that can also be steered by the ipsilateral motor cortex and the nonpyramidal system. The issue may be addressed relying upon normal and pathological data. In the former case the question is tantamount to asking whether right limb preference differs in normal subjects according to whether the task involves the proximal arm musculature or the distal musculature. The answer appears to be negative. When limb proficiency was tested by requiring the patient to tap a key either with finger movements or with movements mainly involving the wrist, the elbow or the shoulder, the degree of the left-right asymmetry did not change, whether it was assessed in terms of tapping rate (Kimura & Davidson, 1975) or of tapping variability (Todor, Kyprie & Price, 1982).

As to the clinical evidence, the only systematic study (De Renzi, et al., 1980) which addressed the question of whether motor performances involving isolated finger movements were more vulnerable to left brain damage than performances involving whole hand position failed to show any difference. Comparisons between movements at the shoulder and the wrist joint and movements at the metacarpophalangeal joint have not been carried out.

Negative evidence is also provided by measures from performances requiring skillful, repetitive finger movements, since they have for the most failed to discriminate left from right brain-damaged patients, in striking contrast with what is found when the same groups were given movement imitation tests. Thus no hemispheric asymmetry has been reported by Pieczuro and Vignolo (1967) on a test measuring the time needed to unscrew 10 screws with the hand ipsilateral to the lesion. Although apractic and non-apractic left brain-damaged patients were not compared in this study, the correlation of the unscrewing test with a movement imitation test was found to be rather low (0.31) in the group with left-sided lesion. On an analogous screw rotation task comparable results were obtained by Kimura (1979), who also found no difference between left and right brain-damaged patients on a finger tapping test (Kimura, 1977). The latter finding is in agreement with the outcome of a study by Carmon (1971), while a mild decrement in finger tapping speed associated with left hemisphere disease was reported by Wyke (1967). Heilman (1975) contrasted the tapping rate of apractic and non-apractic left brain-damaged patients and found apraxics impaired, but since no comparison was carried out with a right hemisphere-damaged group, it is unclear whether the difference was due to apraxia or to the group difference in the size of lesion.

In conclusion, the bulk of evidence does not appear to support the idea that distinctions based on the differential central control of the proximal and distal limb musculature provide clues critical to the understanding of apraxia mechanisms.

Limb versus Axial Movements

Data from callosal patients show that some aspects of apraxia find a plausible interpretation if one takes into account the alternative pathways that the brain is forced to choose, when the passage of information through the fibre system specialized to accomplish the task is thwarted. Geschwind (1975) suggested that the same mechanism can be invoked to account for other apractic phenomena. One of them would be the preservation of axial body movements, such as those involving neck and trunk muscles, in response to verbal commands in patients who present with severe limb apraxia. When asked to bow, kneel, walk backwards and even dance or take the position of a boxer, the patient would respond correctly without hesitation, in marked contrast with the wavering and deranged performance that characterizes such commands as "wave goodbye" or "show me how you would stamp out a cigarette". This apparent contradiction is explained by assuming that axial movements are carried out by nonpyramidal pathways arising from the temporal lobe and thus directly activated by the commands, while limb movements require the participation of the pyramidal system, and the integrity of the fibre bundles linking Wernicke's area with the pre-Rolandic motor area. Any lesion disconnecting the two areas will, consequently, affect limb movements, but not whole body movements. This interpretation is plausible, but there are some problems with the basic data inspiring it.

Body Parts Used as Objects

The same line of interpretation has been extended by Geschwind to account for a peculiar behaviour shown by apractics, when they are required to pretend to use objects on verbal command. Goodglass and Kaplan (1963) have pointed out that a typical error coming out of this kind of task is to use the hand as the instrument, instead of positioning it as if holding the instrument and then making the appropriate movement. Thus, for example, the patient will use his fist as a hammer, pounding the table with it, will brush his teeth with the index finger as the toothbrush and will rake his hair with his extended fingers as the teeth of a comb.

Given these errors Geschwind proposes that patients are switching from the utilization of the pyramidal system, which has been made inaccessible by the lesion, to that of the nonpyramidal system, at the cost, however, of substituting differentiated finger movements by gross hand positioning. I must confess to have some difficulty in accepting the view that the substituted movements are less taxing than the pyramidal system than the correct movements. Let us take the example of hammering. In either case the patient has to keep his fist closed -- a hand position that makes minimal demand on finger motor control -- and the difference only refers to wrist movements, present when the patient is pretending to handle a hammer, absent when he is pounding the table with his fist. In other instances, the use of a body part as instrument is even more demanding at the level of isolated finger movement than a correct pantomime: it is hard to see why rubbing the teeth with the extended index finger, instead of moving the closed fist sideways in front of the mouth, would be a convenient way to bypass the block of the pyramidal system, when the patient is confronted with the task of brushing his teeth. I am therefore, inclined to agree with the original interpretation advanced by Goodglass and Kaplan (1963, p. 718) "BPO (body part as object) may permit the aphasic to evade the difficult task of reproducing a movement sequence outside of the concrete context which ordinarily elicits it. It offers the "reality" of acting on an object and, one conjectures, permits a more vivid experience of the affective component of the pretended action".

Testing Apraxia in One Modality

We must now address an aspect of the apraxia examination which has not been fully considered but which deserves careful consideration, because it can open new avenues to the understanding of the disorder. The motor performances we test may differ not only in their intrinsic features, but also in the way they are elicited, i.e., the modality through which the order given by the examiner is conveyed. Although a certain degree of verbalization is nearly always needed to explain the general requirements of the task to the patient, a variety of procedures can be followed when the single items are administered: verbal commands, visual or tactile imitation, presentation of an object in a single modality, etc. Since discrete abilities and nervous networks are involved by these approaches, it is important for the examiner to be aware of the potentialities and limitations, inherent in each mode of testing.

Verbal Modality

Verbal commands are probably the procedure preferred by clinicians to elicit movements at the bedside, because they permit a convenient and expeditious evaluation of a wide range of symbolic gestures and pantomimes, easily labelled with a name. In spite of these advantages, and of the information provided on the integrity of the connections linking Wernicke's area with the motor area, the results of this approach need to be evaluated with caution and to be complemented by other testing procedures. Since aphasia and apraxia frequently coexist in the same patient, the burden of proof that the inability to carry out the gesture is not due to a defective decoding of the command lies on the examiner. Although in some patients this can be shown beyond any reasonable doubt, a margin of uncertainty will probably remain in the majority of cases and will result in the exclusion of aphasics with moderate to severe comprehension deficit from the examination. This not only the presence of apraxia will be missed in a number of patients, but a sampling bias will be introduced in studies carried out in consecutive patients. Some authors have proposed the patients who fail on verbal command be required to imitate the same gestures performed by the examiner, and to consider apractic only those who also make errors on imitation. But then one questions the use of the verbal test. Would it not be simpler to just employ imitation tasks?

One particular limitation of assessing apraxia to verbal commands is that this mode of presentation does not lend itself to an easy description of meanginless movements, which results in the tendency not to test these kinds of movements. Also poor performance to verbal command alone cannot provide an answer to the question of whether the impaired performance is due to defective recall of the movement pattern or to its distorted implementation.

Visual Modality

There are two ways orders can be given in the visual modality, either by requiring movement imitation or by presenting objects out of reach for the patient to pantomime their use. Imitation tasks may involve any type of movement and have the great advantage that the requests they make to the patient are self-explanatory and need at the most the aid of some pointing gesture, but only minimal verbal explanation, which permits testing almost every aphasic, with the exception of some severe Wernicke and global aphasics, who are totally incommunicado.

A further asset of imitation tasks is that they can be easily and reliably assessed, as any deviation the copy presents from the model is immediately apparent, whereas, for instance, pantomimes leave a certain margin of freedom in performance to the patient and of uncertainty in evaluation to the examiner. In many respects imitation can be recommended as the first choice procedure for testing apraxia, because it entails only minimal patients' selection, but it must be kept in mind that it tells nothing of the ability to evoke the gesture. Somewhat more demanding at the level of verbal comprehension is the procedure whereby an object is presented with the aim of having the patient pantomime its use. Yet in most aphasics a few examples are generally sufficient to convey the message and to induce the appropriate learning set.

Tactile Modality

The same objects employed for the visual modality can be handed to the patient, out of his sight, with the request to demonstrate their use, either when he is still handling them, or when he has laid them down. It is preferable to have the test carried out with the left hand, unless one can be certain that the right hand has no motor or sensory deficit. In the absence of sensory-motor impairment, a haptic equivalent of the visual imitation test can also be used: a limb is passively placed in a given position, and the patient is required to copy the same position with the other limb.

In principle, one might think of other sensory modalities to elicit use-of-object movements (e.g., by presenting their sound or flavour), but these procedures are cumbersome and applicable to a limited number of objects, so that it is understandable that no one has so far employed them.

Intermodal Dissociation

This variety of approaches to the apraxia examination deserves consideration not only because it permits a comprehensive view of the deficit, which would not be provided by any single procedure, taken in isolation, but also because it affords the opportunity to compare performances carried out through the activation of different pathways and thus to verify some implications of the disconnection hypothesis. This theory, which in spite of its inadequacies is the only interpretation of apraxia that has gained wide acceptance, predicts that a strategically placed lesion will interrupt the pathway transmitting a certain type of information (e.g., the verbal one) and leave other pathways undamaged (e.g., those connecting the visual centres with the motor area), so that the patient will be found apractic, with the order given in one modality, but not when it is given in an other.

The occurrence of a verbal-visual dissociation has been emphasized by Geschwind (1975) and adduced as evidence that apraxia results from the interruption of the fibre bundles linking the centres processing the information with those executing the movement. The symptomatology of patients who fail on verbal command, but perform well on imitation or when handed an object is explained by assuming that the lesion is restricted to the fibres connecting Wernicke's area with the premotor area and does not encroach upon fibres transmitting visual and tactile information. The cogency of this hypothesis is, however, somewhat weakened by the fact that movements to verbal command and to imitation are not strictly comparable performances, in that the former also imply the recall of the action pattern and can, therefore, be considered as more exacting from a motor programming viewpoint. The anatomical interpretation would be strengthened, were it possible to show that gestures requiring an equal effort of evocation are differentially impaired depending on the modality used to elicit them, especially if not only a verbal-visual dissocation, but also a visual-verbal dissocation or some other type of dissociation could be brought out. Assal and Regli (1980) reported a patient who remarkably improved his imitation and demonstration of object use when the name of the gesture or of the object was provided by the examiner, while Klein (1924) had a patient who correctly pantomimed the use of objects presented visually, but failed when he was handed them.

A systematic investigation of the performance of left brain-damaged patients on three tests requiring the use of the same 10 objects has been carried out in our department (De Renzi, et al., 1982). In one condition the patient pantomimed the use of the object in response to a verbal command, in another in response to the presentation of the object, which was neither named nor handed, and in a third condition he was blindfolded, handed the object and had to demonstrate its use. Thus the information eliciting the movement was merely verbal in the first case, visual in the second case and tactile in the third case. The maximum score was 20 for each modality and control patients performed almost perfectly on each of them. The proportion of left brain-damaged patients falling below the worst score of normals was significantly smaller on the tactile as compared with the verbal and visual modality, which in turn did not differ from each other. This advantage is attributable to the wealth of information that an object conveys when it is handled during its use and in fact no modality difference emerged in a subsequent study, where the patient pantomimed the use of the object, after having laid it down.

Our main concern was whether there were patients who performed more poor in one modality than in another. To ascertain this we looked for a difference in score greater than five points, i.e., greater than 25 per cent of the total scale. Out of the 150 left brain-damaged patients examined 14 were found to be markedly impaired on the verbal modality in comparison with the visual modality (mean difference: 9.67 points). It must be pointed out that all of the patients admitted to this investigation had been shown to be able to decode the names of the objects utilized in the test and that there were patients selectively impaired on the verbal modality who showed minimal or mild comprehension deficit. It is, therefore, unlikely that their inability to carry out movements on verbal command is to be attributed to aphasia and a block of the connections linking Wernicke's area with motor centres appears to be a more convincing explanation.

Seven patients were poor in the visual modality compared with the verbal modality and 13 compared with the tactile modality. There were also two patients who failed selectively on the tactile modality, one with respect to the verbal modality, the other with respect to the visual modality.

We think that this intermodal dissociation provides evidence in support of the notion that apraxia may result from lesions disconnecting the areas where stimuli instigating the movement are processed from the centre where the plan of action must be evoked and programmed in order to activate the motor cortex neurons. The existence and location of this centre is still a question on which opinions diverge: Liepmann (1908) spoke rather vaguely of the left sensomotorium, a region corresponding to the pre- and post-Rolandic central gyri; Geschwind (1965, 1975) has never made an explicit reference to its existence and role; Heilman (Heilman, Rothi & Valenstein, 1982) located it in the inferior parietal lobule, which would be the storage of visuokinesthetic motor engrams.

I am inclined to share Heilman's opinion, since there is a large body of evidence pointing to the critical role played by damage to this area in causing apraxia and, it seems to me, that the concept of left hemisphere ascendancy in motor control cannot be explained in terms of fibre dominance and, therefore, implies a dominant centre. What, however, such a centre would exactly store is open to question. Heilman (1979) speaks of visuokinesthetic engrams, which would "program sequences of movements needed to perform skilled acts", but he and his colleagues (Heilman et al., 1982) have shown that parietal apractics fail in identifying a gesture named by the examiner from among alternative gestures projected in succession in a film, a finding which would imply that the idea of the gesture and not simply the organization of its motor components is disrupted in these patients. It may be tentatively surmised that more posterior lesions (angular gyrus, adjacent temporo-occipital cortex?) impair the ability to evoke the general shape of the movement, while the contiguous rostral cortex (supramarginal gyrus?) is engaged in selecting the appropriate pattern of innervation needed to implement the idea of the movement in a sequence of discrete motor acts. These two stages of movement planning correspond to the two levels of breakdown, represented by IA and IMA. The contiguity of the two areas would account for the frequent association in the same patient of ideatory and ideomotor elements, which is for the astute examiner to disentangle.

Conclusions

The above analysis strongly suggests that the crucial factor in determining apraxia is not the quality of the movement, but rather the artificial condition of its evocation and planning. Whether the movement is symbolic or meaningless, transitive or intransitive, confined to the distal or the proximal musculature, plays only a minor role and there is no convincing evidence that motor sequences requiring the rapid transition from one manual posture to another are more suited to bring out the deficit than single postures. Rather the gist of the deficit appears to reside in the patient's inability to deliberately make a choice from among his repertoire of motor innervations, when his performance is not assisted by a facilitating set of circumstances. The same gesture which is failed when it must be produced in response to an arbitrary order is often correctly executed when it is elicited by contextual cues or by the inner needs of the patient; for example, the patient is unable to wave goodbye on verbal command and even on imitation, but spontaneously makes the appropriate gesture when the examiner waves to him, leaving the room.

This voluntary-automatic dissociation, which Jackson (1932) had already emphasized nearly a century ago not only in the realm of aphasia but also as a feature of oral apraxia, suggests that the right hemisphere can take over motor planning under appropriate conditions of stimulation, but that the visuo-motor engrams it stores have a higher threshold of excitability and can be only imperfectly called upon in an intentional way. Liepmann (1920) accounted for the preservation of highly practiced gestures in apractics, conjecturing that once a motor act has become automatic, thanks to its repeated production, the corresponding kinetic engrams are stored in either sensomotorium, so that the right hemisphere is able to monitor its execution with the left limb in the absence of the aid provided by the dominant hemisphere. However, the availability of these engrams is heavily dependent on the condition of their evocation, as the above example shows. The participation of the right hemisphere in movement control, even if in a subordinate position, is borne out by the clinical observation that in most cases bilateral damage is necessary to produce a manual impairment so severe as to be present also in concrete situations (generally, under the form of an extreme clumsiness).

It follows from these considerations that, at least as far as IMA is concerned, it is to a certain extent indifferent what kind of movement the patient is required to perform, while the modality through which the request is transmitted is of much greater import for practical and theoretical reasons. In clinical testing the screening of patients presenting with apraxia is more validly accomplished with imitation tasks, which do not call for verbal comprehension and thus avoid the risk of mistaking aphasia for apraxia or of renouncing to test the patient. A quantitative score is easily obtained if, in the case of failure on the first presentation, each item is repeated two more times and 3,2,1 or 0 points are assigned depending on whether a correct performance is achieved on the first, second, third presentation or never. Of course other methods of evaluating the performance can be adopted (e.g., see Kolb & Milner, 1981).

If the examiner is confident that the patient is able to understand language, testing can go on with verbal commands requiring symbolic gestures and use-of-object pantomimes, which will inform on the ability to evoke motor patterns and on the integrity of the pathways connecting Wernicke's area with motor centres. Both imitation and verbal tasks can be conveniently and rapidly administered at the bed-side, without the need of objects or special procedures, so they may be recommended to the clinicians as the first choice method of examination. If aphasia does not assure a reliable level of comprehension, it is preferable to turn to the visual presentation of objects for assessing use-of-object pantomimes. Probably the coupling of imitation tasks with visually elicited pantomimes represents the most convenient way to evaluate the presence of apraxia in an experimental setting when the study is carried out on an unselected series of patients. A discrepancy between the performance on imitation and on pretended object manipulation should alert one to the presence of an evocative component in the deficit and prompt one to sharpen the error analysis. Do the errors suggest that the patient is forgetful of the general shape of the movement, as he makes unrelated gestures, or remains hesitant and perplexed, sometimes repeating to himself the object name? This behaviour hints at an evocative, or ideational deficit, which may be due to either the disruption of the engram storage, or its unaccesibility, because the lesion interrupts the pathways transmitting the order to it. The latter hypothesis may be entertained if there is a visuo-verbal or a verbo-visual dissociation, namely, the performance is much better for stimuli conveyed through one modality than the other. An impairment crossing through both modalities calls for testing the use of actual objects to establish whether the aid provided by tactile information and the more concrete and vivid situation helps recalling the movement pattern. Items of graded difficulty -- from single object manipulation to the coordinate use of more than one object -- are desirable to strengthen the sensitivity of the examination. Although in severe ideational apraxia the patient also fails in this testing condition, the ideational (or evocative) deficit may span over a continuum of progressive intensity and thus may not be confined to the use of multiple objects but retraceable whenever the model of the gesture must be called upon from memory.

If apraxia is as severe on imitation as on pantomimes, it is likely that the deficit has to be attributed to ideomotor apraxia, namely to the inability to implement the general idea of the movement into a proper sequence of discrete muscle innervations. Something must be added apropos of imitation tasks. In principle, it would appear preferable to have exactly the same gestures carried out in the imitation and pantomime test, so as to make their comparison straightforward, but this would greatly limit the gamut and skillfulness of the to-be-tested movements. Normal subjects, who are not professional mimes, tend to perform pantomimes rather crudely, rarely going beyond sketches of the actual gesture which are not sharply differentiated from each other (think to the pretended use of a key and a screwdriver) and make little demand on motor adroitness. At least for experimental purpose, it is, therefore, better to test imitation with a separate set of items, chosen among meaningless and meaningful movements, which provide the opportunity to examine adept manual and finger actions. Obviously, the comparison with the use-of-object test must be carried out on standardized scores or on rank-transformed scores, so as to allow for the differential difficulty of the two tasks.

Heilman et al. (1982) maintain that a distinction can be made between a form of ideomotor apraxia due to the disruption of visuokinesthetic engrams consequent to a parietal lesion and a form due to the interruption of the pathways linking the inferior lobule with the premotor and motor region, based on the inability of apractics of the former, but not of the latter type to discriminate between correct and incorrect gestures performed by the examiner or a third person. In a small group of patients this hypothesis was tested and supported, in that parietal apractics were the only group impaired on the gesture recognition test. The cogency of this finding is not, however, beyond question. The attribution of the recognition deficit to loss of visuokinesthetic engrams implies that their activation gives rise to a detailed and precise representation of the movement, which will serve as standard of reference for evaluating the perceived gestures.

Patients deprived of this ability would be expected to show ideational and not simply ideomotor errors in their motor performance, since recall is a more and not a less demanding task than recognition. Yet this was not the case for Heilman et al.'s patients who were admitted to the investigation only if the gestures they produced on verbal command exhibited a generally correct, albeit clumsy correspondence with the requested movement. It seems contradictory that they were able to evoke the general configuration of the gesture and, nevertheless, failed to discriminate in the recognition test the target not only from its clumsy variants, but also from correct, but completely different alternatives. I would suggest that the occurrence of this kind of errors betokens an evocative defect not confined to the smooth sequencing of movements, but including the general shape of the gesture and thus pertaining to IA rather than to IMA. It is appropriate to mention in this context that aphasic patients with IA have been reported (Lehmkuhl and Poeck, 1981) to score significantly poorer than aphasics without IA and right brain-damaged patients on a test requiring them to rearrange sets of 5-7 photographs portraying manipulation of objects (e.g., opening a bottle of wine, preparing a cup of coffee, etc.), which were presented in a random order. The deficit was specific for this particular type of items and bore no relationship to the severity of aphasia or of ideomotor apraxia. Thus a cognitive deficit would appear to characterize IA; its investigation is certainly worth pursuing (see Roy, 1981, 1983 and Roy & Square, this volume).

REFERENCES

Assal, G. & Regli, F. Syndrome de disconnexion visuo-verbale et visuo-gestuelle. Aphasie optique et apraxie optique. Revue Neurologique, 1980, 136, 365-376.

Brown, J.W. Aphasia, apraxia and agnosia. Springfield: Thomas, 1972.

Carmon, A. Sequenced motor performance in patients with unilateral cerebral lesions. Neuropsychologia, 1971, 9, 445-449.

De Renzi, E., Faglioni, P., Lodesan, M. & Vecchi, A. Impairment of left brain-damaged patients on imitation of single movements and motor sequences. Frontal- and parietal-injured patients compared. Cortex, 1983, 19.

De Renzi, E., Faglioni, P. & Sorgato, P. Modality-specific and supramodal mechanisms of apraxia. Brain, 1982, 105, 301-312.

De Renzi, E., Motti, F. & Nichelli, P. Imitating gestures. A quantitative approach to ideomotor apraxia. Archives of Neurology, 1980, 37, 6-10.

De Renzi, E., Pieczuro, A. & Vignolo, L.A. Ideational apraxia: A quantitative study. Neuropsychologia, 1966, 6, 41-52.

Gazzaniga, M.S., Bogen, J.E. & Sperry, R.W. Dyspraxia following division of the cerebral commissures. Archives of Neurology, 1967, 16, 606-612.

Geschwind, N. Disconnexion syndromes in animals and man. Brain, 1965, 88, 237-294.

Geschwind, N. The apraxias: neural mechanisms of disorders of learned movement. American Scientist, 1975, 63, 188-195.

Goodglass, H. & Kaplan, E. Disturbances of gesture and pantomime in aphasia. Brain, 1963, 86, 703-720.

Hecaen, H. Les apraxies ideomotrices. Essai de dissociation. In H. Hecaen & M. Jeannerod (Eds.), Du controle moteur a l'organisation du geste. Paris: Masson, 1978.

Heilman, K.M. A tapping test in apraxia. Cortex, 1975, 11, 259-263.

Heilman, K.M. Apraxia. In K.M. Heilman & E. Valenstein (Eds.), Clinical neuropsychology. New York: Oxford Press, 1979.

Heilman, K.M., Rothi, L.J. & Valenstein, E. Two forms of ideomotor apraxia. Neurology, 1982, 32, 342-346.

Jackson, J.H. Remarks on non-protrusion of the tongue in some cases of aphasia. In J. Taylor (Ed.), Selected Writings. London: Hodder and Stoughton, 1932, vol. 2.

Kimura, D. Acquisition of a motor skill after left-hemisphere damage. Brain, 1977, 100, 527-542.

Kimura, D. Neuromotor mechanisms in the evolution of human communication. In H.D. Steklis & M.J. Raleigh (Eds.), Neurobiology of social communication in primates. New York: Academic Press, 1979.

Kimura, D. Left-hemisphere control of oral and brachial movements and their relation to communication. Philosophical Transactions of the Royal Society. London B 298, 1982, 135-149.

Kimura, D. & Archibald, Y. Motor functions of the left hemisphere. Brain, 1974, 97, 337-350.

Kimura, D. & Davidson, W. Right arm superiority for tapping with distal and proximal joints. Journal of Human Movement Studies, 1975, 1, 199-202.

Klein, R. Zur der zentralen Mechanismen der Apraxie. Medizinische Klinik. 1924, 20, 395-396.

Kleist, K. Gehirnpathologie. Leipzig: Barth, 1934.

Kolb, B. & Milner, B. Performance of complex arm and facial movements after focal brain lesions. Neuropsychologia, 1981, 19, 491-503.

Lange, J. Apraxien. In O. Bumke & O. Foerster (Eds.), Handbuch der Neurologie, Berlin. Springer, 1936, Vol. 6, 885-960.

Liepmann, H. Das Krankheitsbild der Apraxie (Motorische Asymbolie auf Grund eines Falles von einseitiger Apraxie) Monatsschrift fur Psychiatrie und Neurologie, 1900, 8, 15-44, 102-132, 182-197.

Liepmann, H. Drei Aufsatze aus dem Apraxiegebiet. Berlin: Karger, 1908.

Liepmann, H. Apraxie. Ergebnisse der gesamten Medizin. 1920, 1, 516-543.

Luria, A.R. Higher cortical functions in man. New York: Basic Books, 1966.

Marcuse, H. Apraktische Symptome bei einen Falle von seniler Demenz. Zentralblatt fur Neurologie, 1904, 15, 737-751.

Morlaas, J. Contribution a l'etude de l'apraxie. Paris: Legrand, 1928.

Pick, A. Studien uber motorische Apraxie und ihre nahestehende Erscheinungen: ihre Bedeutung in der Symptomatologie psychopathischen. Symptomen-Komplexe. Leipzig: Deuticke, 1905.

Pieczuro, A. & Vignolo, L.A. Studio sperimentale sull'aprassia ideomotoria. Sistema Nervoso, 1967, 19, 131-143.

Poeck, K. Klinische Neuropsychologie. Stuttgart: Thieme, 1982.

Poeck, K. & Lehmkuhl, G. Ideatory apraxia in a left-handed patient with right-sided brain lesion. Cortex, 1980, 16, 273-284(a).

Poeck, K. & Lehmkuhl, G. Das Syndrom der ideatorischen Apraxie und seine Localization. Nervenartz, 1980, 51, 217-225(b).

Roy, E.A. Apraxia: A new look at an old syndrome. Human Movement Studies, 1978, 4, 191-210.

Sittig, O. Ue ber Apraxie. Berlin: Karger, 1931.

Todor, J.I., Kyprie, P.M. & Price, H.L. Lateral asymmetries in arm, wrist and finger movements. Cortex, 1982, 18, 515-523.

Volpe, B.T., Sidtis, J.J., Holtzman, J.O., Wilson, D.H. & Gazzaniga, M.S. Cortical mechanisms involved in praxis: observations following partial and complete section of the corpus callosum in man. Neurology, 1982, 32, 645-650.

Wyke, M. Effect of brain lesions on the rapidity of arm movement. Neurology, 1967, 17, 1113-1120.

Yamadori, A. Palpatory apraxia. European Neurology, 1982, 21, 277-283.

Zaidel, D. & Sperry, R.W. Some long-term motor effects of cerebral commissurotomy in man. Neuropsychologia, 1977, 15, 193-204.

Zangwill, O.L. Le proble.me de l'apraxie ideatoire. Revue Neurologique, 1960, 102, 595-603.

*Neuropsychological Studies of Apraxia
and Related Disorders, E.A. Roy (ed.)*
© *Elsevier Science Publishers B.V. (North-Holland), 1985*

IDEOMOTOR APRAXIA: GESTURAL DISCRIMINATION,

COMPREHENSION AND MEMORY

Leslie J. Gonzalez Rothi and Kenneth M. Heilman

University of Florida

We have proposed that the visuokinesthetic engrams
responsible for programming skilled motor movements
are stored in the left parietal lobe. Both gestural discrimination and comprehension studies showed that two
forms of ideomotor apraxia could be identified. Unlike
patients with anterior lesions, those with parietal lesions
could not discriminate or comprehend gestures. Apractic
patients with parietal lesions could process gestural
information in primary memory in much the same manner as normal subjects and nonapractic aphasics. Secondary memory or long-term retention (consolidation),
however, was impaired in these patients. These observations provide support for the hypothesis that visuokinesthetic motor engrams are stored in the left parietal
lobe and that destruction of these engrams may induce
discrimination, comprehension, and memory disorders for
gestures.

Although Liepmann was not the first to describe a case of apraxia, he is credited with the original description of the mechanism underlying this syndrome (see
Kimura, 1980). Addressing Marie and the argument of the day regarding mass action
versus localization, Liepmann laid down the principle of left hemisphere lateralization for the guidance of left and right-sided skilled motor movements. He believed
that acquisition of skilled motor movements required the acquisition of a "movement formula" and of an "innervatory pattern" that would communicate the formula
information to the appropriate primary motor areas. These movement formulas, he
proposed, contained the "time-space-form picture of the movement" and assisted in
adapting these memories to environmental conditions. Liepmann believed that the
left parietal lobe was crucial in supporting the "movement formula", but his localization within the parietal lobe remains unclear (Kimura, 1980).

Heilman, Rothi, and Valenstein (1982) used the biological term for memory
(engram) in reference to Liepmann's movement formula. We proposed that these
visuokinesthetic engrams are supported by the left inferior parietal lobule and that
lesions which destroy the engrams should be behaviourally dissociable from lesions
that spare but disconnect the engrams from primary motor areas.

The primary purpose of this chapter is to review recent studies we designed to
examine the possible dissociation of two forms of ideomotor apraxia dependent on
the involvement of the left parietal lobe. Second, although Liepmann originally
described the motor formula that directs the skilled motor movements as a memory
system, no one has examined gestural memory in patients with ideomotor apraxia
from left parietal lesions. Therefore, we shall review the results of two studies that
examine the gestural memory systems of patients with lesions suspected of destroy-
ing the visuokinesthetic engrams.

Two Forms of Ideomotor Apraxia

In 1905 Liepmann, arguing against apraxia as a form of asymbolia, noted that many apractic patients could not adequately produce skilled motor movements but could "understand" gestures produced for them (Kimura, 1980). We proposed (Heilman et al., 1982) that the area of visuokinesthetic motor engram programs skilled motor movements in much the same way as Wernicke's area programs linguistic acts. Along with the notion that visuokinesthetic engrams mediate skilled motor movement, we believe that these engrams have a crucial role in discriminating those features of gestural movements that are distinctive; therefore, these engrams are crucial to normal gestural, receptive functions. Like the aphasia caused by destruction of Wernicke's area, destruction of the visuokinesthetic motor engrams could cause disruption of input processing as well as performance deficits. In contrast, although apractic, persons whose engrams for skilled motor acts are preserved but disconnected from motor areas should be able to perform a gestural discrimination task of differentiating between well-performed and poorly performed motor acts. Therefore, we proposed (Heilman et al., 1982) that we could dissociate two forms of ideomotor apraxia on the basis of gestural discrimination performance. Further, we proposed that those patients with a gestural discrimination deficit would have lesions consistent with inferior parietal lobe involvement.

Twenty patients were classified into one of four groups depending on the suspected locus of a lesion (anterior versus posterior) and the presence or absence of apraxia. All patients had had a unilateral left infarction with some degree of aphasia except that one left-handed patient had a right hemisphere lesion and no aphasia. Lesion locus was based on speech fluency and, when possible, radiologic confirmation. Classification of apraxia was based on performance on the Florida Apraxia Screening Test (Table 1), which includes 15 gestural commands. Nine or fewer correct answers are considered the criteria for apraxia. The examiner instructed patients to choose from among three acts which one best depicted a particular gestural target. The error foils for 16 trials were semantic movement foils (e.g., clumsily produced aberrations of the target or use of a body part for the object).

Our results showed that patients with ideomotor apraxia and suspected posterior lesions had more difficulty discriminating between correctly and incorrectly performed acts. Three of the four apractic patients with posterior lesions had CT confirmation of inferior parietal involvement. Therefore, our conclusion was twofold: first, visual kinesthetic motor engrams support gestural discrimination function; and second, the inferior parietal lobule contains these visual kinesthetic motor engrams.

Gestural Comprehension

Because the apractic patients with posterior lesions had difficulty identifying the unique gestural features necessary to distinguish one hand movement from another, they could also have had difficulty comprehending the meaning of gestures. Using the semantic foil trials, we found that the performance of apractic patients with posterior lesions was poorer than that of all other patient groups. In addition to the explanation of a gesture comprehension deficit, there were several others as well. First, because the task involved a verbal stimulus, its processing could have been impaired by aphasia. Second, because apractic patients with posterior lesions have difficulty distinguishing between distinctive gestural features, a task in which they must choose from among several alternative gestures may prove exceptionally difficult. Last, in this study the apraxia patients may have suffered retroactive or proactive interference -- that is, the foil gestures may have interfered with recognition of the correct gesture. Therefore, we were interested in whether apractic

```
┌─────────────────────────────────────────────────────────────────────┐
│                                                                       │
│                           Table 1                                     │
│                                                                       │
│                     Florida Apraxia Screen                            │
│                                                                       │
│   NAME:                                                               │
│   DATE:                                                               │
│   EXAMINER:                                                           │
│   -----------------------------------------------------------         │
│   SCORE:  X=wrong     C=clumsy  O=body-part-as-object                 │
│           Checkmark=correct                                           │
│   -----------------------------------------------------------         │
│   SHOW ME HOW YOU:          SPONTANEOUS  IMITATION  OBJECT            │
│   -----------------------------------------------------------         │
│   1.  use a scissor                                                   │
│   2.  use a saw                                                       │
│   3.  wave good-bye                             ----                  │
│   4.  use a hammer                                                    │
│   5.  use a key                                                       │
│   6.  wind a watch                                                    │
│   7.  brush your teeth                                                │
│   8.  flip a coin                                                     │
│   9.  write with a pencil                                             │
│   10. dial a telephone                                                │
│   11. snap your fingers                         ----                  │
│   12. hitchhike                                 ----                  │
│   13. use a screwdriver                                               │
│   14. comb your hair                                                  │
│   15. open a bottle of                                                │
│       ketchup                                                         │
│                                                                       │
└─────────────────────────────────────────────────────────────────────┘
```

patients with posterior lesions could attach meaning to gestures when the stimuli were not presented verbally and the response did not involve distinguishing among several gestural alternatives (Rothi & Heilman, Note 1).

A group of apractic patients with lesions that included posterior areas were compared with aphasic and normal control groups. Each subject was presented a videotape showing an actress performing a gesture. A response page of four pictures lay before the subject, who was told to choose the picture that "went with the gesture". We found that the apractic patients produced significantly more errors in selecting an appropriately matched picture than did the aphasic or the normal subjects. Although our task was nonverbal, both aphasic and apractic groups produced more errors than did the normal subjects. Therefore, this gestural comprehension deficit still may result from a linguistic deficit (aphasia or asymbolia). The ability to provide a link between gesture and picture may be linguistic in nature, and the aphasia may interrupt the formation of that association. However, the aphasics produced fewer errors than did the apractics, and because the severity of aphasia was equivalent in the aphasic and the apractic groups, it is unlikely that a language deficit accounts for the differences in gesture comprehension.

The results of these studies (Heilman et al., 1982; Rothi & Heilman, Note 1) would be consistent with the suggestion that the left parietal lobe contains visuokinesthetic (space-time) motor engrams that form an integral portion of a praxis functional system, independent of language. These engrams not only program motor areas for gesture production but also may be necessary for comprehension and discrimination of gestures.

Gesture Learning and Secondary Memory

When ideomotor apraxia results from destruction of visuokinesthetic motor engrams, apractic patients not only should be unable to discriminate and comprehend gestures but also should no longer have the memory mechanism for retaining new gestures. If, however, the area of visuokinesthetic motor engram is spared but disconnected, these patients should be able to learn and consolidate gestural lists in their memory system and any errors that do occur should be consistent with difficulties of retrieval from memory.

Therefore, we (Rothi & Heilman, Note 2) examined whether apractic patients with parietal lesions had difficulty learning lists of gestures and whether the performance deficits they displayed were caused by an inability to consolidate this information in memory or by an inability to retrieve the information once stored. The Buschke (Buschke, 1973; Buschke & Fuld, 1974) paradigm of selective reminding allowed us to examine these issues. Specifically, Buschke repeatedly presented supra-span lists of linguistic stimuli to normal subjects and plotted acquisition and retention. On each successive repetition subjects were presented only those stimuli that they had never remembered (selective reminding) or had not recalled on a preselected number of trials (restricted reminding). For example, if subjects were presented stimuli A through K and recalled only A, B, C, the examiner then reminded them only of D through K. Buschke assumed that there were two explanations for failure to recall a stimulus when it had been previously successfully recalled. First, the item may never have been stored or may have been lost from memory (forgetting). Second, the item had been stored, but the subject may have been temporarily unable to access it or call it out when needed. Therefore, by looking at the learning, storage, and retrieval of an item over time, one might infer one of these explanations for a previous production failure.

On our initial attempts to use the Buschke paradigm, we found that selective reminding -- when the subject was reminded only of those he had never recalled -- was too severe and that brain-damaged (aphasic and apractic) patients tended to respond less and less as time progressed, eventually losing interest in the task completely. Therefore, we used a modified version in which we arbitrarily decided to remind after two consecutive recall failures.

We used four gestural lists each containing 12 gestures. The examiner performed the 12 gestures on the list consecutively and asked the subjects to recall as many as they could possibly remember. On seven subsequent trials the subjects were reminded only of those gestures they had never reproduced or those they had failed to reproduce on two consecutive occasions. Four lists of 12 gestures with eight trials gives a possible maximum of 384 and a minimum of 48 presentations per subject per list.

Each patient's responses were scored along seven dimensions: (1) never learned -- the number of items on each list never produced once; (2) acquisition rate -- the average number of times the examiner had to present an item to subjects before they produced it for the first time; (3) retrieval errors -- the number of items the subjects failed to recall once but subsequently recalled without reminding; (4) consolidation errors -- produced an item at least once but failed to recall it on two or more consecutive subsequent occasions; (5) reacquisition rate -- the average number of times the examiner had to remind subjects before they reproduced an item previously forgotten; (6) recalled -- number of times a subject recalled items in a list without being reminded; and (7) total productions -- those recalled, produced with reminding, or after initial presentation.

To summarize the findings, we found that apractic patients with posterior lesions had difficulty acquiring lists of gestures as evidenced by the fewer number of gestures acquired, slower rate of acquisition, and fewer total number of responses produced than those by aphasic or normal groups.

As with the discrimination and comprehension studies, one explanation for this gesture acquisition deficit might be that it is induced by a language deficit. We found that the performance of normal subjects was better than that of both the aphasic and the apractic groups, which supports this language deficit hypothesis. However, although equally aphasic in degree, aphasics performed better than did apractics on this task, which suggests that the significant gestural acquisition deficit of the apractics could not be accounted for by a language deficit.

The motor performance system is that which programs the primary motor system consistent with the complex programs supplied by the primary gestural memory system. Although destruction of the motor systems may result in loss of precise movements, disconnection from the visuokinesthetic motor engrams contained in the primary gestural memory system would cause difficulty in voluntarily performing complex motor movements (performance deficit hypothesis). Both destruction of motor systems and disconnection of visuokinesthetic motor engrams may induce a performance deficit. That the apractic patient's performance deficit may have been responsible for poor acquisition is supported by the findings that they were slower to learn the gestural lists and acquired fewer of the items. However, the distinction made by Buschke (Buschke, 1973; Buschke & Fuld, 1974) between retrieval and consolidation errors is that the latter errors represent a loss from memory, whereas the former represent a failure resulting from a performance difficulty. Therefore, the present study did not support the performance deficit hypothesis because the apractic groups had an increased number of consolidation errors in the presence of a normal number of retrieval errors. The possibility remains that the arbitrary choice of two consecutive recall failures as criteria for a consolidation error may have been in error, thus falsely increasing the number of "consolidation" errors in the apractic group. This possibility is refuted, however, by the finding that once apractics failed, they took longer than the other groups to reacquire the gesture, which suggests that in fact it was not a performance problem but that the gestures actually did have to be relearned.

Another alternative is that a patient may fail to accurately reproduce a stimulus because he misperceived it when presented. This misinformation introduced into the system would cause a misinformed motor output system, and in turn, result in a failure. The finding that apractic patients acquired fewer gestures than did other patient groups supports this perceptual deficit hypothesis. However, the inordinate number of consolidation errors by the apractic group shows that often these patients accurately reproduced the item at least once; therefore, they had correctly perceived the gesture.

The many consolidation errors made by the apractic patients indicate that the mechanism underlying their failures was not associated with performance or perceptual difficulties. Instead, these patients displayed a primary gestural memory deficit possibly associated with deficits in two mechanisms -- the input encoding system or the visuokinesthetic motor engrams.

After primary visual and visual association areas perform a sensory and percep tual analysis, the percepts must be transformed into a code that allows the engrams to be stored. A hypothetical input encoding system may transform the sensory information into a coded form. As with other functions (e.g., reading), the input encoding system for praxis may involve multiple encoding strategies, such as verbal or visuospatial. In the present study the groups did not differ from each other in processing meaningful versus nonmeaningful gestures. Specifically, meaningful stimuli were easier to retain than were nonmeaningful stimuli. Probably these stimuli were encoded verbally and meaningful stimili were easier to provide with a verbal code than were nonmeaningful stimuli. During testing, subjects sometimes verbalized during recall. The resulting hypothesis (encoding deficit hypothesis) would be that apractic patients have a specific deficit of visual motor-to-verbal transcoding. Again, this is not a general linguistic deficit (aphasia) but a sensory-specific encoding deficit of visual-to-verbal conversion. Ebbinghaus (1964) suggest-ed that verbal labels enhance encoding into memory. Therefore, apractics would have a retention deficit similar to that found in this study. That is, they rely on an ineffective encoding strategy. This hypothesis, however, is refuted by the finding that the groups did not differ in how they responded to meaningfulness of stimuli.

Finally, the apractic patient group may have had an impairment of the visuoki-nesthetic motor engrams. These space-time engrams control purposeful skilled movements, in that they help program the motor association cortex to make the correct movements, which, in turn, program the motor cortex. Destruction of the visuokinesthetic motor engrams would have resulted in a preponderance of consoli-dation errors, as in the present study. In contrast with an encoding difficulty, this engram deficit would cause an inability to discriminate gestures, such as we found in the study of apractic patients with parietal lobe lesions (Heilman et al., 1982). Considering that all of the patients in the present study had infarctions of the left parietal lobe, the previous findings (Heilman et al., 1982) may provide evidence sup-porting the visuokinesthetic motor program deficit hypothesis. Unfortunately, how-ever, the Buschke (Buschke, 1973; Buschke & Fuld, 1974) paradigm does not allow a clear delineation between the encoding deficit hypothesis and the visuokinesthetic motor program hypothesis. If the visuokinesthetic motor program hypothesis is cor-rect, patients with anterior lesions that induce apraxia by disconnection of the visuokinesthetic motor engrams from the motor systems should not make consolida-tion errors. This remains a topic for further research, however.

Primary Memory

A person may use at least two strategies for consolidating gestures in memory — a linguistic-verbal strategy and a sensory-perceptual strategy (visuospatial-kinesthetic). When an apractic person fails to consolidate gestures, the failure may be due to an inability to form an engram either from the sensory perceptual trace or from the verbal linguistic trace or from both. Unfortunately, the Buschke (Buschke, 1973; Buschke & Fuld, 1974) paradigm could not help distinguish between these two alternatives.

A paradigm that examines this distinction is the Brown-Peterson task (Brown, 1958; Peterson & Peterson, 1959). In this paradigm the subject is presented a set of stimuli to retain, then a response delay of increments up to 18 seconds is imposed while a distractor task is presented. This is followed by the subject's reproduction of the stimuli. Brown (1958) and Peterson and Peterson (1959) found that informa-tion was lost rapidly when the distractor task was employed and no further forget-ting was noted by the end of the 18-second interval. This paradigm was expanded to include measurement immediately after presentation and also measurement with a response delay up to 18 seconds when no distractor task was imposed. By comparing the subject's performance when distracted, one can see the forgetting that takes place at each time interval. If a subject is not distracted, the information may be maintained over time by at least two methods -- (1) by "rehearsal" and (2) by encoding directly into secondary and distraction-stable memory. Although the term rehearsal implies a verbal strategy, we use it here to describe any method -- verbal or otherwise -- used to maintain information in distraction labile or primary memory. Since the distractor task interferes with rehearsal, the information maintained after 18 seconds of distraction is that which has been consolidated into secondary memory. Posner and Konick (1966) showed that the more similar the distractor is to the information being maintained, the more information is lost.

In apractic subjects, if a verbal distractor results in forgetting of gestural information, it would suggest that the subjects were rehearsing using a verbal code and could not consolidate this information. In contrast, if a hand movement distractor causes forgetting, it would suggest that the apractic subjects were using a sensory-perceptual rehearsal strategy and could not consolidate this information.

Twenty-one patients were tested: 15 were aphasic and six were without brain damage. The aphasic group was composed of patients who had had a unilateral cerebral vascular infarction within the left cerebral hemisphere. Depending on their performance on the Florida Apraxia Screening Test, subjects were placed in an apractic-aphasic group or a nonapractic-aphasic group, hereafter referred to as the apractic group and the aphasic group, respectively. Seven subjects, who scored nine or below on this test, were classified as apractic; eight subjects, who scored 10-15, were classified as aphasic (nonapractic). The groups did not differ from each other in the time since onset of disorder or in aphasia quotient on the Western Aphasia Battery (Kertesz, 1979). The normal control group comprised six men who had no history of central nervous sytem damage. All were right-handed. None of the groups (aphasic, apractic, or normal) differed from each other in age or years of education.

All subjects were individually tested while seated before a video monitor and were asked to remember three gestures produced by an actor on the video. There were 32 trials of three gestures. The examiner indicated to the subjects immediately or after an 18-second delay that they were to respond, and their responses were recorded on a score sheet. During the 18-second-delay condition subjects were either to sit quietly, to perform a finger movement distractor, or to perform a number-counting distractor as indicated by the examiner.

The content of the distractor tasks (finger movement and number counting) varied for each subject and was determined by a method described by Flowers (1975). For the number-counting distractor task, six levels of difficulty were possible. The subjects were asked to count backwards by ones from various two-digit numbers represented on 3 by 5-inch cards. If successful, they were asked to count backward by twos and then by threes. If they were unsuccessful, they were asked to count forward by ones, twos, or threes. This procedure continued until the subjects could not say three two-digit numbers in 18 seconds. The finger-movement distractor task had two levels of difficulty: the more difficult task was to touch (with the thumb) the index finger, ring finger, middle finger, and little finger, respectively, as fast as possible. The less difficult task was simply to touch each finger with the thumb moving from the index finger to the little finger in consecutive order as fast as possible. Again, if subjects failed to perform the more complex task three times in 18 seconds, they performed the less complex task. All subjects could at least perform the less complex task three times in 18 seconds.

When the subjects responded, they were to report the three gestures they were to remember in one of two ways -- recall or recognition. In the recall response mode the subjects were to reproduce the gestures using their own hand. In the recognition response mode the subjects were presented a sequence of nine gestures by video and asked to indicate which of the nine (by a yes or no response) was one of the three they were to remember on that trial.

The subjects were observed under each of eight combinations of response mode (two levels) by distraction condition (four levels). The response mode levels included recall and recognition. The distraction condition levels included immediate response, 18-second delay with silence, finger-movement distractor, and counting distractor. The grouping factor included apraxia, aphasia, and normal. The resulting observations were analyzed through a repeated measures analysis of variance model. Significant effects were further analyzed by Duncan's multiple range tests.

A group effect (p < .0001) was observed, with the normal subject group performing generally better (p < .05) than the aphasic and apractic groups, who did not differ from each other.

Analysis of group by response mode yielded a significant effect (p = .0224), which indicated that the groups differed in how they responded to a response mode paradigm of recall versus recognition. Specifically, the performance of the apractics was better (p < .05) during recall than during recognition, whereas the response modes were equally difficult for the aphasic and the normal groups. These procedures were used because we were concerned that a performance deficit would masquerade as a memory deficit. If this had been the case, recognition would have been superior to recall performance. Perhaps the apractics had more difficulty with recognition compared with recall because the recognition procedure induced retroactive interference -- that is, successive stimulus presentations acted as distractors.

There was a distractor condition effect (p < .0001) without regard for group, because performance during silence was better than that with no delay, which was better than that with the counting distractor. The group by distractor condition interaction was not significant.

To examine the difficulty of the distractor tasks by group, we recorded the number of numbers counted and the number of fingers touched for each subject. ANOVA of the number of numbers by group was not significant, but ANOVA of the number of fingers touched was (p < .002). T-tests showed that the apractics did not differ from the aphasics but that the normals differed from the aphasics (p < .01) and the apractics (p < .0006).

In summary, in this study designed to examine whether apractic patients with left parietal lesions encode and maintain gestural information in their primary memory system in a manner similar to that used by nonapractic subjects, we found that all groups spontaneously maintained information when not distracted. This indicated that for maintaining information for short intervals, the apractic patients were using a memory control process much like that which the comparison groups used. We found, however, that the normal and aphasic groups consolidated even more information as undistracted time progressed, whereas apractic patients simply maintained the information that they had acquired immediately after presentation of a stimulus. Therefore, it would appear that the memory process used by all of these groups to control primary memory was somewhat less efficient in the apractic group.

How the groups coded information into primary memory was addressed by examining the differential effects of the distractor tasks. Specifically, all groups were distracted by a number-counting distractor, which suggested that all groups were using verbal rehearsal. The finger-movement distraction did not induce forgetting in any group, which suggested that either the perceptual information was directly consolidated into secondary memory (engram information) or the visuospatial-kinesthetic code was not used for rehearsal in primary memory or both.

REFERENCE NOTES

1. Rothi, L.J. & Heilman, K.M. In preparation, a. Acquisition and retention of gestures by apractic patients.

2. Rothi, L.J. & Heilman, K.M. In preparation, b. Retention of gestural information, memory encoding, and ideomotor apraxia.

REFERENCES

Brown, J. Some tests of the decay theory of immediate memory. Quarterly Journal of Experimental Psychology, 1958, 10, 12-21.

Buschke, H. Selective reminding for analysis of memory and learning. Journal of Verbal Learning and Verbal Behaviour, 1973, 12, 543-550.

Buschke, H. & Fuld, P.A. Evaluating storage, retention, and retrieval in disordered memory and learning. Neurology, 1974, 24, 1019-1025.

Ebbinghaus, H.E. Memory. A Contribution to Experimental Psychology. Dover, New York, 1964.

Flowers, C. Proactive interference in short-term recall by aphasic, brain-damaged nonaphasic and normal subjects. Neuropsychologia, 1975, 13, 59-68.

Heilman, K.M., Rothi, L.J. & Valenstein, E. Two forms of ideomotor apraxia. Neurology, 1982, 32, 342-346.

Kertesz, A. The Western Aphasia Battery. London, Ontario: University of Western Ontario, 1979.

Kimura, D. Translations from Liepmann's Essays on Apraxia. Research Bulletin 506, Department of Psychology. London, Ontario: University of Western Ontario, 1980.

Liepmann, H. Apraxia. Ergebnisse der Gesamten Medizin, 1920, 1, 516-543.

Peterson, L.R. & Peterson, J.M. Short-term retention of individual verbal items. Journal of Experimental Psychology, 1959, 58, 193-198.

Posner, M.I. & Konick, A.W. On the role of interference is short-term retention. Journal of Experimental Psychology, 1966, 72, 221-231.

Neuropsychological Studies of Apraxia and Related Disorders, E. A. Roy (ed.)
© Elsevier Science Publishers B. V. (North-Holland), 1985

APRAXIA AS A DISORDER OF A SYSTEM OF SIGNS

H. Hecaen and P. Rondot

CNRS, Paris

Since Steinthal, who was the first to use the word "apraxia", and Liepmann, who provided the neuropathological base, the concept of apraxia has widely developed and is now applied to a variety of clinical syndromes related to different sites: apraxias by lesions of the retrorolandic regions of the dominant and non-dominant hemisphere, i.e. dressing apraxia and constructional apraxia, apraxias attributed to frontal lesions. The role of the corpus callosum received a new impetus from observations of commissurotomies. In these cases, two types of motor disorders manifested themselves: a left hand apraxia to verbal command and a constructional apraxia of the right hand. The coexistence of apraxia and aphasia was also observed. Could this be due to the proximity of the anatomical regions, or is it a more global disturbance, which affects these two major means of communication? In fact, there is a relation between language disturbances and certain types of apraxia. It seems to be necessary to define precisely the different modalities of gesture to establish their relations with language disturbances and take into account the difficulties in motor apprehension.

In 1870, Fritsch and Hitzig were the first to report on the motor effects caused by the stimulation of the cortical area which was later to be classified as the primary motor strip. In doing so they revealed the origin of pyramidal motricity, a system which, despite its complexity, is by now well understood. Interestingly, it was in that same year that Steinthal proposed the name apraxia to designate a disorder of movement inplicating an organization of motricity the complexity of which has not yet been clearly determined. He distinguished this disorder clearly from paralysis. For Steinthal (1871), apraxia involved a disturbance in "the relationship between movements and the objects with which the movements were concerned". For thirty years, the boundaries of this disorder remained unclear.

Using the name asymbolia, Finkelburg (1870) described disorders related to apraxia. For this author, it was a question of a generalized disturbance in the capacity to express or comprehend symbols in any modality, including verbal and gestural symbols. In subsequent work, Finkelburg expanded the concept, incorporating disorders in the recognition of place, persons and objects. The disorders of the voluntary control of intentional movements were considered to be part of a central communication disorder related to a defective capacity for recognition.

This concept of asymbolia was taken up again by Wernicke (1884-1895) who, in distinctly separating aphasia from asymbolia, assigned the origin of asymbolia to a loss of memory images, including images of the utilization of objects. For Meynert (1890) asymbolia, as it had been re-examined by Wernicke, comprised several notions. He distinguished between sensory asymbolia and motor asymbolia. The latter manifested itself as the patient's inability to utilize objects in the absence of paralysis and in this case it referred to apraxia. If Meynert's conception did not receive the recognition it deserved, it was because the clinical case that he presented to support his analysis contained too many other confounding problems (cortical blindness, ataxia, paralysis) for his position to be clear and generally acceptable.

This conception of motor asymbolia corresponded exactly with Liepmann's conception of apraxia. Liepmann justifiably receives credit for establishing apraxia as a distinctive neuro-pathological category. His first report on apraxia (1900) was the famous case of the Imperial Counsellor M.T. This man exhibited defective gestural behaviour affecting the right arm and leg and the head, face and tongue while his left hand was normal for movements to verbal command and imitative gestures, with or without objects. No visual recognition disorder was present; verbal comprehension was good and general intellectual capacity was to a large extent preserved.

Liepmann's conception is opposed to that of Kussmaul, for whom apraxia was due to the failure to recognize objects. Adopting the distinction established by Meynert, Liepmann compared apraxia to motor asymbolia, which was characterized by a dissociation between the idea of movement and its execution. However, such a definition could have also included the notion of "psychic paralysis" which had been the object of several studies by Nothnagel (1887). In fact, for Liepmann, apraxia was not psychic paralysis; the latter corresponded either to an akinesia, in which case it could disappear in the presence of strong stimulation, or to hysteria.

After having thus established the boundaries of apraxia, Liepmann set out to give a precise anatomical description of his case, concluding that the lesions related to apraxia were located sub-cortically in the fronto-rolandic region and were accompanied by destruction of the corpus callosum and of the left posterior parietal area.

For different circumscribed cortical lesions, there existed corresponding varieties of apraxia, which Liepmann was to specify following studies by Bonhoeffer (1903), Stromayer (1903), and Pick (1905). For Liepmann, apraxia was a unitary phenomenon, a disturbance in the voluntary control of purposive movements, the different varieties resulting from dysfunction of different links of the mechanism of movement construction. Following is his overall analysis.

Molokinetic apraxia (called "innervatory apraxia" by Kleist, 1907) represented the loss of kinetic memories for a single limb; it resulted from a mild lesion in the cerebral motor cortex insufficient to produce paralysis.

Bilateral ideomotor apraxia (primitive motor apraxia) resulted from isolation of the sensorium (left parietal region) from the zones of execution. If the lesion involved the corpus callosum, isolating only the right hemispheric zone of execution, the result could be a unilateral left ideomotor apraxia.

Ideational apraxia (called "ideomotor apraxia" by Pick, 1905) referred to disorders of gestural behaviour at a more abstract or ideational level. In this form the sequential kinetic activity remained functional, but the overall conception of the nature of the movement to be carried out was lost. This resulted from lesions that were more diffuse and which included a posterior parietal locus.

This classification of apraxia was not to be accepted without some reluctance; in 1914 von Monakow reproached Liepmann for having espoused such a non-physiologically oriented point of view and for having placed apraxias - which were just as ideational as they were ideomotor - in a category apart, separate from more elementary forms of afferent system disorders. He considered apraxia to be a disorder of automatic movements resulting from a change in the excitability of cortical areas and provoking interference between certain reflexive arcs. He recognized motor and sensory varieties of apraxia. Brun (1921, 1922) and Sittig (1931) continued in the same direction by analyzing the different types of impairment of automatic movement and by stressing the similarities between apraxia and paralysis, pointing out the existence of intermediate disorders on a continuum between them.

There were other attempts at unifying gnosic and praxic disorders (Poppelreuter, 1914-1917; Foix, 1916; Morlaas, 1928; Lhermitte, 1939, Grunbaum, 1930; Schilder, 1935) under the name apractognosia. This syndrome was subjected to neuropsychological examination by Hecaen, Penfield, Bertrand and Malmo (1956). Goldstein (1948) carried the non-localizationist tendencies further, believing that a general loss of abstract behaviour could be manifested by the inability to execute pantomimed actions.

New varieties of apraxia were described after the three main types isolated by Liepmann. Constructional apraxia was defined by Strauss (1924) and Kleist (1907, 1930, 1934) and was said to be related to a left posterior parietal lesion. Later, the disorders of constructional activity with visuo-spatial defects due to right hemisphere lesions were elaborated by McFie, Piercy and Zangwill (1950), Hecaen, Ajuriaguerra and Massonnet (1951); Hecaen et al. (1956); Piercy, Hecaen and Ajuriaguerra (1960); Piercy and Smith (1962). In 1941, Brain characterized the syndrome of dressing apraxia.

Denny-Brown (1958) attempted to give apraxia a more physiological basis in describing two types of unilateral kinetic apraxia: the first was frontal or magnetic apraxia; the second, parietal or repellent apraxia. This description incorporated the pathology of reflexes within movement disorders since, for Denny-Brown, "what we call willed movement is in fact the learned ability of the organism to utilize movements that are primarily reflex for purposes that involve a more tenuous stimulus situation".

Anatomo-clinical Correlations

Each lesion site confers to apraxias a particular set of characteristics. Thus apraxias related to retro-rolandic lesions of either the major or the minor hemisphere as well as apraxias due to callosal and/or frontal lesions can be distinguished. Of course, it is necessary that the lesions be strictly unilateral if they are to fit into this pattern. Even split-brain cases, observed after commissurotomy, must be interpreted in the light of the hemisphere lesions which motivated surgery in the first place.

Apraxias resulting from retro-rolandic lesions of the major hemisphere

These lesions give rise to bilateral ideomotor and ideational apraxias as well as to a type of constructive apraxia which exhibits certain peculiarities. In a series of 415 cases of retro-rolandic lesions studied by Ajuriaguerra, Hecaen and Angelergues (1960), ideomotor apraxia was associated with temporal and parietal lesions and ideational apraxia was caused by more extensive posterior (parietal and temporo-parietal) lesions. These two varieties of apraxia have not been observed when only the minor hemisphere is damaged. De Renzi, Pieczulo and Vignolo (1968), in a study focussing on ideational apraxia, found disturbed manipulation of objects to be related only to left hemisphere lesions.

We may thus infer that posterior parietal and temporo-parietal lesions (supramarginal and angular gyri) in the dominant hemisphere play an important role in the production of ideomotor and ideational apraxias. Nevertheless, Hecaen (1972) did not find significant correlations between the specific posterior lobe involved and either ideomotor or ideational apraxia.

Recently, based on a hypothesis by Geschwind (1965), Heilman, Rothi and Valenstein (1982) proposed a distinction between two varieties of ideomotor apraxia depending on lesion site. Apraxia would result from a lesion located in "Wernicke's arc" which links Wernicke's area to the associative motor cortex through the arcuate fasciculus. One variety of apraxia would correspond to a lesion in the parietal cortex where the programming of an act is assumed to be elaborated. The other variety would be caused by a disconnection between this parietal area and the associative motor cortex. In the first variety, both imitative and response-to-command movements are badly executed and the patient's ability to recognize whether a movement by the examiner is poorly or correctly executed is impaired. In the second variety, which is related to a more anterior lesion, movement is impaired as in the preceding variety, but here the patient is able to judge whether or not a movement presented to him on film is correctly or poorly executed. The first variety bears directly on the problem of an agnosia at the origin of the apraxia. This problem will be examined in more detail below. Heilman et al. themselves do not overlook it. They recognize that, in cases where the connections between the visual area and the area responsible for storage of motor engrams are interrupted, conditions for agnosia are met.

Also, constructional apraxia is significantly related to damage in this area of the parietal lobe (Hecaen, 1972).

Apraxias resulting from retro-rolandic lesions of the minor hemisphere

Next to unilateral left apraxias due to lesions in the corpus callosum, right hemisphere damage is suggested in other cases of left unilateral apraxia by such accompanying symptoms as hemisomatognosia, spatial agnosia and/or left hemianopia. Unilateral gestural disorders thus resemble a deficit in recognition of the hemicorp: deprived of its bodily reference, the movement loses its meaning. It should be pointed out, however, that in the majority of cases, other clinical signs favour accompanying left hemisphere damage.

Two other types of apraxia, namely dressing apraxia and constructional apraxia, are more strictly correlated with lesions in the minor hemisphere. Dressing apraxia appears with the same set of symptoms as visuo-constructional disorders resulting from right hemisphere lesions located at the parieto-temporo-occipital junction.

Constructional apraxia due to right lesions seems to follow mostly from spatial disorders while constructional apraxia due to left lesions seems to be related to a programming disorder (Warrington, James & Kinsbourne, 1966; Hecaen & Assal, 1970).

Although a mass effect is more marked in this hemisphere than in the language dominant hemisphere (the three retro-rolandic lobes of the right hemisphere having a greater tendency to equipotentiality of function than those of the left hemisphere), a significant correlation with constructional apraxia was found for parietal lobe lesions and a significant correlation with dressing apraxia was found for lesions of the parietal and occipital lobes (Hecaen, 1972). Frontal lobe lesions were significantly excluded as causes of either of these two types of apraxia.

Apraxias resulting from frontal lesions

Several types of apraxia are attributed to frontal lesions: melokinetic apraxia, bucco-linguo-facial apraxia, and certain unilateral apraxias. For Kleist (1930, 1934) melokinetic apraxia was due to a controlateral lesion situated in the anterior region of the motor cortex. Fulton (1937) demonstrated motor defects of a melokinetic type in the chimpanzee with ablations of area 6. Nielsen (1946) proposed areas 4 and 6, but this suggestion is more in keeping with a primarily motor defect than an apractic disorder. Furthermore, most authors, Denny-Brown in particular, refuse to consider symptoms connected with melokinetic apraxia as apractic.

Bucco-linguo-facial apraxia is most often associated with lesions in the dominant hemisphere, especially because of the frequent co-occurence of motor aphasia and right facial paralysis. However, some observations of cases in which the lesion was lateralized to the right have also been reported (Hartmann, 1907; Rose, 1908; Goldstein, 1909).

An anterior lesion site in the damaged hemisphere is suggested by the frequency of bucco-linguo-facial apraxia in the initial stages of Broca's aphasia, although expressive phonemic disorders are not always associated with apraxia of bucco-linguo-facial movements. For Nathan (1947) bucco-linguo-facial apraxia is caused by anterior lesions in the fronto-rolandic operculum. Many other authors have referred to lesions in F1 and F2.

Nevertheless, the frontal region is not the sole site of this kind of apraxia: Alajouanine and Lhermitte (1960) pointed out their presence in cases of Wernicke's aphasia. For Geschwind (1965, 1975) the lesions may occur either in the motor association cortex anterior to the motor region for control of the face, near Broca's area, or in the region of the supramarginal gyrus. In the case of a posterior lesion, bucco-linguo-facial apraxia would result from a disconnection of the posterior language areas from the motor association cortex. In the case of a frontal lesion, apraxia would occur because the connections between the motor association cortex and the left motor face area and the origins of the callosal fibers to the right face area would be destroyed.

Ohigashi, Hamanaka and Ohashi (1981) have demonstrated that bucco-linguo-facial apraxia should be divided according to the anterior/posterior lesion site line. Imitation of complex oral movements was more disturbed in the case of fluent aphasias than in the case of non-fluent aphasias. The reverse was true of non-fluent aphasias; that is, simple oral movements were more disturbed here than in the fluent aphasia group. Furthermore, errors were of different types for the different groups. Based on these results, the authors concluded that bucco-linguo-facial apraxia resulting from anterior lesions was caused by a motor realization disorder, and that bucco-linguo-facial apraxia resulting from posterior lesions was caused by a motor programming disorder.

The role of the supplementary motor area, described by Penfield and Welch in 1951, has not been well defined until recently. For Travis (1955), ablation of this area caused a transient grasp-reflex and spasticity of the proximal muscles. Actually, its function is more complex. Regional cerebral blood flow studies in the monkey (Sokoloff, 1961; Cooper & Crow, 1975) and in humans (Olesen, 1971; Roland, Larsen, Lassen & Skinhoj, 1980) disclosed the importance that this structure seems to have in the programming of movement, probably via modulation of the primary motor cortex (de Vito & Smith, 1959; Pandya & Vignolo, 1971; Muakassa & Strick, 1979). Activation of the supplementary motor area arises when movements involving a sequence are programmed or executed; a simple movement -- lifting a finger, for example -- does not seem to involve it. More recently, by ablation of the supplementary motor area, particularly when this area was contralateral to the non-preferred hand, Brinkman (1981) was able to reveal an important disturbance in the coordination of the two hands. Both hands had the tendency to perform a task assigned to the preferred hand. Furthermore, it happens that the hand does not exhibit any anticipatory postures, and instead executes a movement that is no longer goal oriented: the hand remains flat with fingers outstretched on a hole-ridden plate instead of searching for the reward. In this manner it became possible to distinguish two types of abnormal motor behaviour: one due to imitation and the other very strictly related to apraxia. It is undoubtedly a question of a very particular kind of apraxia given the fact that it only manifests itself when the required movements involve coordination of the two hands. We have already verified similar circumstances in split-brain cases (Tzavaras et al., in preparation).

In the case of ablation of the supplementary motor area, the motor disorder is dependent upon a physiopathological mechanism which is very likely the reverse of that of the split-brain cases. Indeed, the tendency of one hand to imitate the other is attributable to the bilateral action of the single remaining supplementary motor area. This undoubtedly explains why the disorder appears especially when the damaged supplementary motor area is situated contralaterally to the non-preferred hand (Brinkman, 1981). As a matter of fact, we know that each supplementary motor area is connected to the ipsilateral and contralateral primary motor areas via the corpus callosum (de Vito & Smith, 1959; Pandya & Vignolo, 1971).

A lesion in the supplementary motor area, more precisely a lesion in the non-dominant hemisphere, is therefore liable to cause a particular type of apraxia in that it affects essentially coordinated movements involving both hands. This type of apraxia is thus related to the subordination of both primary motor areas to the single supplementary area, which in turn causes a conflict in the coordination of the motor program for both hands.

The importance of associative motor cortex lesions for apraxia in humans has been ill defined. Some studies on animals show that the destruction of this region in the monkey produces disorders of complex movements without primary motor or sensory deficit. Deuel (1977) notes that a bilateral lesion of the periarcuate cortex in monkeys produces delays in the relearning of a motor task which requires a sequence of movements learned preoperatively while isolated movements are performed readily.

As for unilateral apraxias, various anatomo-clinical correlations have been noted by different authors. Left sympathetic apraxia accompanies Broca's aphasia and often accompanies right hemiplegia. Imitative gestures as well as gestures in response to verbal commands are disturbed. The lesion responsible is situated subcortically under the left motor area and Broca's area, and it interrupts connections which pass via the corpus callosum to the right hemisphere.

Within the domain of unilateral apraxia, Denny-Brown (1958) distinguished two varieties of "kinetic apraxia". The first, called magnetic apraxia, results from mesially placed lesions of the frontal lobe and represents a "defective kinetic projection of behaviour" for which the prototypical reaction is instinctive grasping. Here Denny-Brown broadened the framework of a reflex anomaly by including the release of a cutaneous reflex of a particular type (the grasp reflex) in order to consider it as a behavioural anomaly. The whole of the upper and lower limbs suffer the repercussions of the grasping action. However, the extension of a reflex reaction to a whole limb should not in itself be a sufficient criterion for the integration of this motor behaviour into the classification of apraxia. Exaggeration of myotactic reflexes in spasticity or the exaggeration of reflexes in flexing also condition special behaviour on the part of the limbs and yet these do not represent instances of apraxic behaviour. In trying "to relate the various manifestations of apraxia to a physiological disorder of movement as a whole", has Denny-Brown not in fact yielded to the opposite temptation, that of integration a physiologic disorder into the framework of apraxia?

This tendency becomes even more clear when we consider the second type of kinetic apraxia, which is correlated with parietal lesions and which Denny-Brown called repellent apraxia. Here a mechanism - the "avoiding reaction" - is found as well. The general behaviour of the limb is one of persistence in an avoiding reaction which is caused by an anterior connection. We believe that the reservations expressed above regarding magnetic apraxia are applicable to repellent apraxia as well. The stereotypic nature of the motor behaviour in both kinds of kinetic apraxia is unusual when compared to other kinds of apraxia.

Unilateral ablation of the premotor cortex causes deficits in the optic guidance of movement (Moll & Kuypers, 1977). Using the limb contralateral to the lesion, the animal tries to seize a visible object directly through a transparent partition when it can reach this object only by introducing the ipsilateral limb into a hole in the partition that is not far from where the food is placed. As an explanation, the authors put forward a disinhibition of subcortical mechanisms that control the movement of the anterior limb toward a visual object.

Apraxia and callosal disconnection

The role of a corpus callosum lesion in left apraxia was suspected by Liepmann and verified later by Liepmann and Maas in the anatomical study of the Ochs case (1907). It was confirmed as well by observations of softening in the region of the anterior cerebral artery (Bonhoeffer, 1914; Foix & Hillemand, 1925; Nielsen, 1946; Geschwind & Kaplan, 1962). A new impetus in the study of callosal disconnections came from observations of commissurotomies which allowed for a stricter interpretation of signs pertaining properly to a corpus callosal lesion. Right or left cortical lesions accompanied softening of the anterior cerebral arteries. After the disappointing results of the first cases studied (Akelaitis, Risteen, Herren, & Van Wagenen, 1942), a series of tests were developed in order to point out the praxic disorders of split-brain patients (Gazzaniga, Bogen & Sperry, 1967; Sperry, Gazzaniga & Bogen, 1969) and the specific characteristics of the unilateral left apraxia that they produced (see De Renzi, this volume).

Akelaitis et al. had not noticed major changes in motor behaviour after section of cerebral commissures. A few days after surgery, however, they did note the existence of a "diagonistic apraxia" which was later confirmed by Gazzaniga et al. (1967): the two hands carried out antagonistic movements. With one hand, the patient might attempt to pull on his trousers, while with the other hand, he would lower them. With the right hand, he might beckon to or enlist aid from his wife, while with the left hand he would push her away aggressively.

Later, a study of commissurotomy cases performed by Vogel proved to be particularly revealing (Gazzaniga et al., 1967) owing to the systematic observation of performances obtained through stimuli that implicated connections between the motor area and ipsi- or contralateral hemisphere areas. Schematically, two types of motor disorders manifested themselves: a left-hand "apraxia" to verbal commands and a constructional apraxia of the right hand.

The unilateral left apraxia to verbal commands is the major symptom, while gesture returns to normal when the patient is asked to imitate. These patients are unable to raise their left arm, move their left foot or close their left fist when asked to do so; yet all these movements are correctly executed on imitation. For Geschwind and Kaplan (1962) and Sperry et al. (1969) this improvement based on visual input suggested that apraxia is conditioned by the right hemisphere. Given such conditions, it is difficult to call this disorder apraxia since it is based not on a movement execution disorder, but rather on a comprehension disorder.

Motor control of the right hand proves to be normal. Usually left-hand performance improves in a week although in some patients the disorder may persist for several years. Initially, motor control of the proximal part of the left upper limb is re-established while fine movements of the hand remain poor. Thus, in response to visual stimuli to the left hemisphere or to verbal stimuli, the left hand can point to objects and trace their external contours, could write words and can carry out arithmetic operations. The crude and hesitant writing of the left hand becomes impossible if proximal arm movements are impeded. Right hemispheric control of the left hand is normal for all non-verbal tests. Right hemispheric control of the right hand is the most deficient, poor performance being found on all but the simple pointing-to-object and outline-tracing tests.

Exploring independent hemispheric control of motor function, Akelaitis et al. (1942) and Gazzaniga et al. (1967) found impairment in the ability to do two different things concurrently with both hands. However, unlike normal subjects, the commissurotomized patients could perform two visual tasks (e.g. respond to colour discrimination vs respond to brilliance discrimination) with the same reaction time for both hands.

Examining eight subjects having undergone commissurotomy six to eight years previously, Zaidel and Sperry (1977) noted the persistence of a mild left-sided dyspraxia and impaired ability to copy with the right hand. These subjects had no performance deficit, although they were slower in performance on tests of motor coordination and dexterity than normal persons; they were even slower than subjects with unilateral hemispheric lesions. However, with tests demanding interdependent manual coordination or with alternating bimanual movements, the split-brain subjects were clearly impaired.

Sperry et al. (1969) concluded that the possibility of hemispheric control of motor behaviour, both contralateral and ipsilateral, may be preserved if the callosal section is pure - that is, if there are no hemispheric lesions. However, hemispheric control of the ipsilateral limbs is inefficient and incomplete, especially for distal movements and movements requiring delicate control.

Motor disorders caused by either vascular lesions or tumors, by virtue of their associated frontal lesions, add to the disconnection syndrome picture. In a case of corpus callosal sarcoma which had spread to the left hemisphere, Vleuten (1907) observed, in addition to apraxia of the left hand, a tonic perseveration of the right hand. Similarly, a patient of Goldstein (1908) sustaining softening in the area of the right anterior cerebral artery including the whole corpus callosum, exhibited left hand apraxia and a grasping reaction. When the callosal disconnection is caused by a tumor or a vascular disorder, left-handed movements do not always improve under imitation, as they do in the cases of split-brain (Brion & Jedynak, 1975).

While the right hand executes movements on verbal command without difficulty, it will nevertheless have difficulties in copying geometric figures. This disorder varies in duration and intensity in different patients. It points to the superiority of the minor hemisphere for spatial construction tasks.

Thus, in pure cases of callosal disconnection, motor performance is altered in both hands but in a different way for each. The left hand responds poorly to verbal commands while the right hand suffers from constructional apraxia. An important point needs to be emphasized: these two disorders will improve steadily and quite often disappear, once again showing that each of the hemispheres can assume the function of the other. Furthermore, only constructional apraxia of the right hand deserves to be called apraxia; the left hand does not execute verbal commands because these are momentarily no longer transmitted to it, but it is not apraxic.

Apraxia and motor control deficits

Visual adjustment disorders

Does one observe disorders of an apraxic nature attributable to lesions disrupting visuo-motor connections? If so, what is the site of these lesions? Movements under visual control can be disturbed in the absence of paralysis, sensory disorders and visual disorders. This syndrome, called optic ataxia (Balint, 1909) or visuo-motor ataxia (Rondot, De Recondo & Ribadeau Dumas, 1977) can be limited to a visual half-field and to a single hand depending on whether the ipsi- or contralateral visuo-motor connections are interrupted. It is essentially a question of faulty coordination of visual information and motor commands, and is therefore not an apraxia. However, after posterior parietal partial lobotomy affecting occipito-frontal connections in the monkey, Haaxma and Kuypers (1975) noted that in order to seize food, the hand contralateral to the damaged hemisphere no longer formed a thumb-index finger grip. Instead, it explored the surface with all fingers, indicating an anomaly in the terminal adjustment of the upper limb. Is this disorder akin to apraxia? It is more likely that this behaviour became necessary in order to permit more extensive exploration of the surface, given the lack of information required to execute a movement with a certain precision. However, Kuypers (1978) noticed in the same animals that the hand opposite the damaged hemisphere was incapable of adapting to new motor strategies such as seizing food through an opening placed 10 cm above the ground. The ipsilateral hand performed the task without difficulty while the contralateral hand was not able to follow the indirect route required: it persistently attempted to seize the food by hitting the transparent plate in which the opening was provided.

In humans, grasping anomalies similar to those of the monkey after posterior parietal partial lobotomy can also be observed. Before seizing the target, the hand corresponding to the side of the visuo-motor ataxia, does not flex the fingers with thumb in opposition (Garcin, Rondot & De Recondo, 1967). It therefore seems that in humans as in the monkey, we are dealing with an exploration mode intended to compensate for the deficiency in visual information. Tzavaras and Masure (1975) observed the grasping movement with respect to an object inserted in a narrow container which necessitated the exclusive use of the thumb-index finger grasp, following a protocol used by Haaxma and Kuypers (1975). In two cases of right visuo-motor ataxia, the absence of final adjustment of the hand seemed to them to correspond to an apraxia. However, in both cases an associated ideational and an ideomotor apraxia were present. The debate concerning the possible participation of apraxia in cases of visuo-motor ataxia thus remains open. If such participation exists, it is certainly minor.

Apraxia as a disorder of temporal sequencing of movements

In describing a special type of apraxia which he named efferent apraxia and which he attributed to lesions in the premotor cortex, Luria (1947, 1966) already considered that the apraxia in question represented a deficit in the organization of motor processes in time, while both spatial organization and the direction of motor impulses remained intact. The premotor cortex is responsible for "the innervation of the individual links of a complex motor act and for the smooth flow from one motor link to another". When this area is damaged "pathological inertia of the individual motor links" develops and the "kinetic melody" is disturbed.

More generally, one may consider that control over motor output is carried out differently by each hemisphere, and that each hemisphere has its own mode of treating information (Levy, Trevarthen & Sperry, 1972). The control deficit caused by left hemisphere lesions could represent the basis of praxic disorders. Research such as that of Wyke (1971) allows us to recognize the control which the left hemisphere exercises over bilateral voluntary motricity.

Kimura and Archibald (1974) found that lesions of the left hemisphere, in contrast with lesions of the right hemisphere, impaired the performance of complex motor sequences, regardless of whether the sequences were meaningful or not. Patients with left-brain damage were more impaired than patients with right brain damage on a task in which they imitated unfamiliar sequential movements of the hand and arm. The same patients who showed a disorder of imitating sequential movements showed no difficulty in producing isolated finger flexion or in imitating a static hand posture. Correlation analyses showed that isolated finger flexion tasks and copying of sequential movements were not related. Further analyses showed no statistical correlations between the movement disorders induced by left hemispheric lesions and disorders of language or disorders of perception of the meaning of gestures. The authors concluded that the defect was an impairment of motor control. For Kimura the unique functions of the left hemisphere, in speech as well as in voluntary control of movement, might be related to motor sequencing rather than to symbolic or language function. Later Kimura (1977) put less emphasis on the role of the left hemisphere in the sequencing of movements. She noted that patients with left hemispheric lesions are more affected than patients with right hemispheric lesions in the acquisition and subsequent performances of a motor skill which involves several changes in hand posture. According to her, the left hemisphere contains a system specialized for producing the correct limb posture and for controlling the transition from one position to another.

Similarly, Heilman, Schwartz and Geschwind (1975) demonstrated defective motor learning in ideomotor apraxia. Haaland, Porch and Delaney (1980), with a group of apractic patients, also found a deficit in certain tests of motor skills. These included static steadiness, in which the subject had to put a stylus in each of 9 holes within 15 seconds; a test of motor coordination involving a maze with a stylus; a test with a grooved pegboard; the making use of feedback in order to correct mistakes; and the requiring an inhibition response of finger and arm movements. Haaland et al. granted that their apractic patient's lesions seemed to affect the frontal lobe more particularly, and thus their results appear to agree with Luria's (1966).

These results could aid in the comprehension of the apraxias, but it would appear rather difficult to consider that the impairment of motor sequencing could be sufficient to account for such complex disorders as ideomotor apraxias (but see Rothi & Heilman, this volume). Nevertheless, one could consider that a basic defect either underlies all the apraxic varieties or that it is only related to certain of these varieties.

Neuropsychological Considerations

Apraxia and language disorders

For a long time, gestural disorders have been considered an aspect of a more general communication disorder. According to Finkelburg (1870), deficits in the ability to use conventional signs -- language included -- should all be grouped under the general term "asymbolia". Meynert (1890), however, divided asymbolia into motor and sensory varieties.

As early as 1905, Liepmann was insistent on the relation between ideomotor apraxia and aphasia, stressing the occurrence of language disturbances in 17 out of 24 cases of apraxia (see Kertesz, this volume). One may remark, however, that most of these were cases of motor aphasia. On the other hand, in 42 observations of left hemiplegia, there was no sign of impaired gesture in the upper right limb. Thus the role of left hemispheric lesions and the frequent association between impaired performance of movement and language disorders was being asserted as far back as 1905. In this series, however, seven cases in which apraxia was not associated with aphasia were already noted.

Since then, the part played by left hemispheric lesions in producing ideomotor apraxia has been confirmed by the study of extensive series of cases (De Ajuriaguerra, Hecaen & Angelergues, 1960; Goodglass & Kaplan, 1963; De Renzi et al., 1968). Controversy remains, however, and discussion on the nature of the relation between apraxia and aphasia depends on whether we believe that this relationship is merely a matter of anatomic proximity of the underlying structural correlates or whether we believe in a global disturbance of communication compromising both linguistic and paralinguistic behaviour.

Goodglass and Kaplan (1963) studied these questions by testing groups of aphasic and brain-damaged non-aphasic subjects matched in age and IQ. They administered a battery of quantifiable tests of gestural behaviour, including natural expressive gestures, conventional gestures, simple and complex narrative pantomime, and descriptions of objects and of object usage. They found disorders of gestural behaviour to be significantly more severe in the aphasic group; there was no clear relation between the severity of apraxia and that of aphasia. Essentially, the aphasics differed from the non-aphasics in that the performance on the aphasics did not improve with imitation. This suggests a disorder of voluntary control of movements and not a disorder of symbolic formulation. In the absence of aphasia, left hemispheric lesions produced more impaired gestural movements than right hemispheric lesions did. The authors concluded that the gestural deficiency of aphasics was an apraxic disorder due to left hemispheric lesions and that it was not an aspect of a general communication disorder. However, the relations between ideational apraxia, language disorders, and general intellectual dysfunction seem to be strong. De Ajuriaguerra et al. (1960) found a high degree of association among these disorders.

De Renzi et al. (1968) studied the capacity for object manipulation in a large group of subjects with unilateral cerebral lesions and in a group of normal controls. Deficient object use was found in 34% of aphasics and 6% of subjects with left hemispheric lesions without aphasia, but this defect was not found following right hemispheric lesions. Correlational studies revealed a high degree of correlation between ideational apraxia (defined as impaired object use) and impaired verbal comprehension but a relatively low correlation between ideational apraxia and general intelligence level or ideomotor apraxia. The results of this study confirmed the previously observed relationship between left hemispheric lesions, ideational apraxia, and aphasia. On the other hand, no support was found for the belief that ideational apraxia is dependent on impaired general intellectual functioning, attention, or memory. These authors proposed that the defective ability to associate an object with its corresponding action may be related to the defective ability of aphasics to associate designs of common objects with their corresponding colours or with their corresponding sounds. All of these defects represent an impaired ability to associate different aspects of the same concept. For De Renzi et al. (1968), this impairment, a defect in concept formation, may be inherent to aphasia. Nonetheless these authors have not completely rejected the possibility that the liaison between these disorders and aphasia may be anatomic proximity.

There is no clear and definite relationship between constructional apraxia and aphasia. In the De Ajuriaguerra et al. (1960) series, disorders of language were present in only 72% of cases of constructional apraxia due to left hemispheric lesions. Patients with severe sensory aphasia who did not have constructional apraxia were frequently observed too. These observations suggest the possibility of an indirect, rather than direct, association of constructional apraxia and aphasia.

Thus, the relation between language and gesture disorders may only be indirect and only depend, on the other hand, on the type of apraxia. A study of 249 cases of left-sided lesions, 36 of which exhibited apraxia, has shown that an association between language disorders and gestural disorders -- excluding those disorders appearing only on verbal command -- really exists only for certain aspects of ideomotor apraxia (conventional symbolic gestures and expressive gestures, Hecaen, 1978).

Apraxia as a disorder of a system of signs

It is therefore necessary to define these gestural modalities and the nature of the disturbances affecting them before it is possible to understand the different types of relations they have with language disorders. Using various criteria, we have searched for the common denominator of the several classifications that have been suggested, in the hope that commonality among them might serve as a basis for isolating the modalities of gestural behaviour and its impairments. A first approximation is suggested by clinical and behavioural findings as well as by the usual descriptions of gesture. These yield the inventory of different types of gestures. This inventory is given below, and can provide a foundation for subsequent, less empirically oriented discussions.

I. Gestures displayed in the absence of objects.

A.   Codified gestures substitutes for oral language, e.g., the manual language of deaf-mutes, the language of artificial gestures.
B.   Gestures which accompany spoken language.
C.   Conventional symbolic gestures, e.g., the sign of the cross, the military salute, etc.
D.   More or less conventional expressive gestures, e.g., menacing gestures, gestures indicating the presence of a bad odour, etc.
E.   Descriptive gestures:
    1.   gestures related to one's own body:
       (a) gestures that do not involve the utilization of an object, e.g., twirling the ends of one's moustache, smoothing down one's hair, etc.
       (b) gestures involving the use of an object, e.g., smoking, eating, placing a ring on one's finger, etc.
    2.   gestures that simulate the use of objects:
       (a) non-sequential acts, e.g., turning a key in its lock, cutting with scissors, etc.

(b) gestures requiring the cooperation of both hands and consisting of sequences of different acts, e.g., driving a nail with a hammer, sharpening a pencil.

II. Acts of manipulation of real objects

A. Acts which do not directly pertain to one's own body:
    1. simple acts, e.g., the manipulation of a pair of scissors, a watering can, a key, etc.
    2. actions consisting of a sequence of acts, e.g., lighting a candle, putting a letter into an envelope.
B. Actions with respect to one's own body:
    1. simple acts, e.g., putting on one's glasses, or combing one's hair.
    2. actions consisting of a sequence of acts, e.g., dressing oneself.

III. Acts of graphic representation and construction..

Notice that a classification scheme, no matter how "naive", is at least in partial agreement with gestural dissociations encountered in pathology. Lesions causing disorders in speech, in sign language or in finger spelling of the deaf, are not associated with either ideational or ideomotor apraxia (Chiarello, Knight & Mandel, 1981). Furthermore, gestures which accompany language can be preserved in the presence of apraxia. Categories I: C,D,E correspond to ideomotor apraxias. Category IIA corresponds to ideational apraxia and category IIB to dressing apraxia; these two types are mutually exclusive given a unilateral lesion. Finally, when category III gestures are disturbed, we are dealing with constructional apraxia.

This inventory of gestures and acts may serve as a starting point. Let us remember, however, that while certain of the actions listed above may be disturbed in isolation by pathology, the disorganization of others occurs only as part of a picture of multiple deficits. Furthermore, we can now attempt a classification based on a logical distinction between signs and symbols, such as has been proposed by Pierce (1932), whose wider significance has been underlined by Jakobson (1964).

Symbolic Gestures.

(a) strictly codified and systematically organized.
(b) conventional, less rigorously defined symbolism, with a link of artificial contiguity between signifier and signified.

Iconic Gestures.

Mimicry, more or less codified expressive reactions, hence the necessity to speak of iconic symbols. The link between signifier and signified is one of similarity.

Indexical Gestures.

Acts that describe the utilization of objects; the link between signifier and signified being one of real contiguity.

With Jakobson we hasten to emphasize that this tripartite division of signs rests more on the hierarchy of their properties than on the properties themselves. This explains, for example, the need to speak of iconic symbols.

But a description of gestures must also take account of their simultaneous or successive character (see Table 1). Thus, successiveness marks substitute gestural language which belongs to the manipulative acts performed in the presence or absence of the object to be manipulated. By contrast, simultaneity characterizes above all conventional symbolic gestures and the majority of expressive gestures. Thus, we can add a new dimension to the preceding classification.

This temporal dichotomy cuts across the preceding classification. Of course, this temporal aspect is not the only dimension; there is also a spatial aspect that should be considered.

Table 1

Characteristic of Sign	Temporal Aspect

1. Symbolic Gestures
  (a) codified system, language
      substitute
  (b) conventional symbols
	successiveness
	simultaneity (for the most part)

2. Iconic Expressive Gestures	simultaneity

3. Indexical Gestures
  (a) descriptive of the
      utilization of objects	

1. simple 2. sequential	simultaneity successiveness
(b) manipulation of real objects	
1. simple 2. sequential	simultaneity successiveness

Finally, another distinction must be maintained, that of the relationship between the response and the stimulus eliciting it. Is the action executed (1) on verbal command, (2) in imitation of the visually perceived action of the experimenter, (3) as a reproduction of a movement imposed on the passive subject, i.e., kinesthetically perceived, or (4) as a descriptive gesture following visual or auditory presentation of the object? It should not be surprising that pathology does not offer us rigorous distinctions between the different types of gestures and acts.[1] In addition to this,

---

[1] Just recently, De Renzi, Faglioni and Sorgato (1982) reported that, in patients suffering from left hemisphere lesions, performance on tasks involving the handling of objects varied according to the modality of presentation of the objects. They conclude that here apraxia results from the disconnection between the areas where information is processed and the areas where the movement is programmed.

all too often our clinical data are not sufficiently precise: we have only the results of more or less rapid observation and not of proper experimentation with systematic use of control groups.

The analysis by Piaget (1960) on the development of the systems of coordinated movements as functions of either some result (goal) or some intention, leads to the recognition of developmental stages (sensory motor coordination stage, intermediary stage with the appearance of the symbolic function, stage of representations with a twofold aspect -- symbolic and operative) corresponding to the three main groups of gestural disorders, which De Ajuriaguerra et al. attempted to describe in 1960. In our last group, which we would now be more inclined to call programming apraxia, the disorders appear to indicate damage to at least two different gestural abilities. The first subgroup concerns disorders of "gesture language" (being viewed as a system of coding, not formally conventionalized, characteristic of particular socio-cultural levels); it could correspond to Piaget's figurative level and include the ideo-motor apraxias with impairment of symbolic and expressive actions (symbolic icons). The second subgroup is represented by the disorder of the propositional use of objects (Denny-Brown, 1958) or of the programming of sequential actions, and corresponds finally to the operative level. Ideational apraxia (impairment of actual handling of objects) evidences disturbance at the level of concrete operations, whereas ideomotor apraxia, which affects actions pantomiming the use of objects, shows a disorder situated at an intermediary level between the aforementioned and a level of more complex structuring and interiorization, where damage results in constructive apraxia of the programming process.

It might be satisfactory to distinguish a gestural "language", depending essentially on the socio-cultural standards of a given society, from a programming activity; and, at the same time, to consider that both involve only indirect relations with linguistic activity. However, such distinctions cannot be absolute; Zangwill's observations (1967) show that movements simulating the handling of objects may be preserved, whereas actual handling of objects may be impaired. Again, given the sequential nature of certain expressive or symbolic actions and the need for some kind of programming for the execution of these movements, it is possible that they may be disordered by a lesion affecting the area controlling programming, whereas other non-sequential actions remains unaffected.

In 1978, Hecaen reported the results obtained from 249 right-handed patients with left hemispheric lesions. They were submitted to a battery of tests based on this classification. Only 36 patients made errors when the tests consisted of imitation of the observer's gestures. The praxic tests included four categories of gestures: conventional symbolic gestures, expressive gestures and descriptive gestures either on the body or of object use. Ideational praxis was also explored. Analysis of the results seems to point out quite clearly the existence of two types of disorders in classical ideomotor apraxia: apraxia of conventional and expressive gestures on the one hand and apraxia of descriptive gestures either on the body or of object use on the other, no correlation having been noted between these two types. Besides, the disorders of the last group are the only ones to be correlated with ideational apraxias.

One can also admit that the difference between ideomotor apraxias concerning descriptive gestures and ideational apraxia depends only on the degree of complexity of tasks. The presence of the object would facilitate the realization of the adequate gesture that is either impossible or distorted when the patient is asked to simulate the utilization of the object in its absence.

Ideational apraxia and disturbances of descriptive gestures of object use, then, seem to constitute the same group that ought to be separated from ideomotor apraxias only including disorders of expressive gestures or conventional symbols.

One is then tempted to look for the origin of the disorders of real or simulated manipulation of objects in the difficulty of sequencing, or programming of partial acts required for the action. The more pronounced the disorder, the longer the sequence needed for the action.

Nevertheless, one should bear in mind the conclusions reached by De Renzi et al. (1982) regarding the need to distinguish between ideomotor and ideational apraxia. They reported that several of their patients suffering from left lesions performed more poorly on tasks involving the handling of objects when the objects were presented visually than when the patients had to imitate the gestures of an examiner who simulated the object's use. They concluded that the patients were unable to evoke gestures involved in the use of objects, while at the same time, they refused to consider ideational apraxia as a deficit in sequencing a series of acts directed to achieve a goal. Their conception thus resembles that proposed by Morlaas (1928). For the latter, ideational apraxia was nothing more than an agnosia for the use of objects.

As for the disorders of expressive gestures and those of conventional symbols, they might involve a disorganization of a communication code that bears no more than an indirect relation to language disorders; the disturbance affects only the encoding since the comprehension of the meaning of the observer's gestures is preserved (Kimura & Archibald, 1974; Gainotti & Lemmo, 1976; Hecaen & Ruel, to appear). In this case a sensori-motor disorder, insufficient as such to account for apractic disorders, might also constitute the necessary condition.

In a study which has not yet been published (Hecaen & Ruel) we reported the results of two tests: a motor learning test and a test of motor sequencing (Kimura's Copying Hand Movements). No significant differences were found between left and right lesions. However, on the first two tests, the performance of the apractic patients (10 cases) was significantly poorer. We should emphasize that the sequencing disorder seemed to be only a motor defect since in the Corsi's Block tapping task (where the motor task is quite simple and where the execution of the sequence depends mostly on the visual channel) only the subjects with right lesions performed poorly when compared with subjects suffering from left lesions and even with apraxic patients. Nevertheless one should bear in mind the results of Lehmkuhl and Poeck (1981). In a task involving the correct sequencing of photographs representing the different stages of an action (telephoning, for example), they found a deficit only in those subjects exhibiting ideational apraxia. This deficit was independent of the presence and intensity of ideomotor apraxia. These authors observed that Liepmann defined ideomotor apraxia as the inability to perform complex sequential motor actions. For them, it is the conceptual organization of the actions which is disturbed.

Finally, in the group of subjects with left-sided lesions but no apraxia, Hecaen and Ruel found that those subjects with aphasia were significantly inferior to those without aphasia on a test of motor sequencing. Therefore only a delay in motor learning seemed to characterize the apractic group: all the apractic patients manifested a more or less severe aphasia.

While looking for learning disturbances and sequential motor control disorders, we ought to have found evidence of them in all six cases in which ideomotor dyspraxia concerned mainly the descriptive gestures of simulated or real manipulation of objects. But the impairment on the hand movement copying test was severe in only three patients, and mild in the other three. On the other hand, in the only patient whose conventional and expressive gestures were impaired in the absence of ideational apraxia, performance on Kimura's test was good but motor learning was impaired. Thus a motor learning deficit seems to be the only constant across all cases of apraxia, independent of the type of gesture affected.

These results are, of course, too limited to allow us to draw definitive conclusions. If they are confirmed, however, they will provide us with evidence of the proposed dissociation in ideomotor apraxia and of the mechanisms that might account for it.

REFERENCES

Ajuriaguerra J. De, Hecaen H. & Angelergues R. Les Apraxies: Varietes cliniques et lateralisation lesionnelle. Revue Neurologique. 1960, 102, 566-594.

Akelaitis, A.J., Risteen, W.A., Herren, R.Y. & Van Wagenen, W.P. Studies on the corpus callosum. III. A contribution to the study of dyspraxia following partial and complete section of the corpus callosum. Archives of Neurology and Psychiatry. 1942, 47, 971-1007.

Alajouanine, T.H. & Lhermitte, F. Les troubles des activites expressives du langage dans l'aphasie. Leurs relations avec les apraxies. Revue Neurologique. 1960, 102, 604-629.

Balint, R. Seelenlahmung des "Schauens", optische Ataxie, Raumliche Storung der Aufmersamkeit. Monatschrift fur Psychiatrie und Neurologie. 1909, 25, 51-81.

Bonhoeffer, K. Casuistische Beitrage zur Aphasielehre. II. Ein Fall von Apraxie und sogenannter transcorticaler sensorischer Aphasie. Archives fur Psychiatrie. 1903, 37, 800-825.

Bonhoeffer, K. Klinischer und anatomischer Befund zur Lehre von der Apraxie und der "Motorischen Spraihbaher". Monatschrift fur Psychiatrie. 1914, 35, 113-128.

Brain, R. Visual disorientation with special reference to the lesions of the right cerebral hemisphere. Brain, 1941, 64, 244-273.

Brinkman, C. Lesions in supplementary motor area interfere with a monkey's performance of a bimanual coordination task. Neurosciences Letters, 1981, 27, 267-270.

Brion, S. & Jedynak. Les troubles du transfert inter-hemispherique. Congres de Psychiatrie et de Neurologie de Langue Francaise. 73eme session, Paris: Masson, 1975.

Brun, R. Klinische und anatomische Studien uber Apraxie. Archives suisses de Neurologie et de Psychiatrie. 1921, 9, 29-64; 1922, 185-210.

Chiarello, C., Knight & Mandel, M. Aphasia in a prelingually deaf woman. Brain, 1981, 105, 29-51.

Cooper, R. & Crow, H.J. Changes of cerebral oxygenation during motor and mental tasks. In D.H. Ingvar & N.A. Lassen (Eds.), Brain Work, Copenhagen: Munksgaard, 1975, 389-392.

Denny-Brown, D. The nature of apraxia. Journal of Nervous and Mental Disease, 1958, 126, 9-33.

De Renzi, E., Faglioni, P. & Sorgato, P. Modality specific and supramodal mechanisms of apraxia. Brain, 1982, 105, 301-312.

De Renzi, E., Pieczulo, A. & Vignolo, L.A. Ideational apraxia: A quantitative study. Neuropsychologia, 1968, 6, 41-52.

Deuel, R.K. Loss of motor habits after cortical lesions. Neuropsychologia, 1977, 15, 205-216.

De Vito, J.L. & Smith, O. Projections from the mesial frontal cortex (supplementary motor area) to the cerebral hemispheres and brain stem of the macaca mulatta. Journal of Comparative Neurology, 1959, 111, 261-278.

Finkelnburg, R. Vortrag in der Niederheim Gesellschaft der Aerzte. Bonn, Berlin, Klinische Wochenschrift, 1870, 7, 449.

Foix, C. Contribution a l'etude de l'apraxie ideomotrice. Revue Neurologique, 1916, 1, 285-298.

Foix, C. & Hillemand, P. Les symptomes de l'artere cerebrale anterieure. L'Encephale, 1925, 20, 209-232.

Fritsch, G. & Hitzig, E. Uber die elektrische Erregbarkeit des Grosshirns. Arch. Anat. Physiol. wissenschaft Med., 1870, 37, 300-332.

Fulton, J.F. Forced grasping and groping in relation to the syndrome of the premotor area. Archives of Neurology and Psychiatry, 1937, 31, 27-42.

Gainotti, G. & Lemmo, M.A. Comprehension of symbolic gestures in aphasia. Brain and Language, 1976, 3, 451-460.

Garcin, R., Rondot, P. & De Recondo, J. Ataxie optique localisee aux deux hemichamps homonymes gauches (etude clinique avec presentation d'un film). Revue Neurologique, 1967, 116, 707-724.

Gazzaniga, M.S., Bogen, J.E. & Sperry, R.W. Dyspraxia following division of the cerebral commissures. Archives of Neurology, 1967, 12, 606-612.

Geschwind, N. Disconnexion syndromes in animals and man. Brain, 1965, 88, 237-294 and 585-644.

Geschwind, N. The apraxias in phenomenology of will and action. In E.W. Strauss & R.M. Griffiths (Eds.), The second Lexington conference on June and applied phenomenology. Pittsburg: Duquesne University Press, 1967.

Geschwind, N. The apraxias: Neural mechanisms of disorders of learned movement. American Scientist, 1975, 63, 188-195.

Geschwind, N. & Kaplan, E. A human cerebral deconnection syndrome. Neurology, 1962, 12, 675-685.

Goldstein, K. Der makroskopische Hirnbefund in einem Falle von linksseitiger motorischer Apraxie. Neur. Centralblatt, 1909, 28, 898-906.

Goldstein, K. Language and Language Disturbances. New York: Grune & Stratton, 1948.

Goodglass, H. & Kaplan, E. Disturbance of gesture and pantomime in aphasia. Brain, 1963, 86, 703-720.

Grunbaum, A.A. Aphasie und Motorik. Z. ges. Neurol. Psychiat., 1930, 130, 385-412.

Haaland, K.Y., Porch, B.E. & Delaney, H.D. Limb apraxia and motor performances. Brain and Language, 1980, 9, 315-323.

Haaxma, R. & Kuypers, H.J.G.M. Intrahemispheric cortical connexions and visual guidance of hand and finger movements in the rhesus monkey. Brain, 1975, 98, 239-260.

Hartmann, F. Beitrage zur Apraxielehre. Monatschrift fur Psychiatrie und Neurologie. 1907, 21, 97-118; 248-270.

Hecaen, H. Introduction a la Neuropsychologie. Paris: Larousse, 1972.

Hecaen, H. Les apraxies ideomotrices. Essai de dissociation. In H. Hecaen & M. Jeannerod (Eds.), Du controle moteur a l'organisation du geste. Paris: Masson, 1978, 333-358.

Hecaen, H., Ajuriaguerra, J. De & Massonnet, J. Les troubles visuo-constructifs par lesions parieto-occipitales droites. Role des perturbations vestibulaires. L'Encephale, 1951, 1, 122-179.

Hecaen, H. & Assal, G. A comparison of construction deficits following right and left hemispheric lesions. Neuropsychologia, 1970, 8, 289-304.

Hecaen, H., Penfield, W., Bertrand, C. & Malmo, R. The syndrome of apractognosia due to lesions of the minor cerebral hemisphere. Archives of Neurology and Psychiatry, 1956, 75, 400-434.

Heilman, K.M., Goneya, E.F. & Geschwind, N. Apraxia and agraphia in a right hander. Cortex, 1974, 10, 284-288.

Heilman, K.M., Rothi, L. & Valenstein, E. Two forms of ideomotor apraxia. Neurology, 1982, 32, 342-346.

Heilman, K.M., Schwartz, H.D. & Geschwind, N. Defective motor learning in ideomotor apraxia. Neurology, 1975, 25, 1018-1020.

Jakobson, R. On visual and auditory signs. Phonetica, 1964, 11, 216-220.

Kimura, D. Acquisition of a motor skill after left-hemisphere lesion. Brain, 1977, 100, 527-542.

Kimura, D. & Archibald, Y. Motor functions of the left hemisphere. Brain, 1974, 97, 337-350.

Kleist, K. Korticale (innervatorische) apraxie. Jahrbuch fur Psychiatrie und Neurologie. 1907, 28, 46-112.

Kleist, K. Gehirnpathologische und lokalisatorische Ergebnisse 4. Mitteilung uber motorische Aphasien. Journal fur Psychologie und Neurologie. 1930, 40, 338-346.

Kleist, K. Gehirnpathologie. Leipzig: Barth, 1934.

Kuypers, H. Etudes sue les systemes neuroniques gouvernant les mouvements chez le singe Rhesus. In H. Hecaen & M. Jeannerod (Eds.). Du controle moteur a l'organisation du geste. Paris: Masson, 1978, 315-321.

Levy, J., Trevarthen, C. & Sperry, R.W. Reception of bilateral chimeric figures following hemispheric disconnexion. Brain, 1972, 95, 61-78.

Lehmkuhl, G. & Poeck, K. A disturbance in the conceptual organization of actions in patients with ideational apraxia. Cortex, 1981, 17, 153-158.

Lhermitte, J. L'Image de notre corps. Nouvelle Revue Critique, Paris. 1939.

Liepmann, H. Das Krankheitsbild der Apraxie (motorischen Asymbolie). Monatschrift fur Psychiatrie und Neurologie, 1900, 8, 15-44, 102-132; 182-197.

Liepmann, H. Die linke Hemisphare und das Handeln. Muenchner Medizinische Wochenschrift, 1905, 49, 2375-2378.

Liepmann, H. Drei Aufsatze aus dem Apraxiegebiet. Volume 1. Berlin: Karger, 1908.

Liepmann, H. & Maas, O. Fall von linksseitiger Agraphie und Apraxie bei rechtseitiger Lahmung. Journal fur Psychologie und Neurologie. 1907, 10, 214-227.

Luria, A.R. Traumatic Aphasia. Moscow: Academy of Medical Sciences Press, 1947. English Translation, The Hague: Mouton, 1969.

Luria, A.R. The higher cortical function in man. New York: Basic Books, 1966.

McFie, J., Piercy, M.F. & Zangwill, O.L. Visual spatial agnosia associated with lesions of the right cerebral hemisphere. Brain, 1950, 73, 167-190.

Meynert, A. Cited by H. Liepmann, 1900.

Moll, L. & Kuypers, H.G.J.M. Premotor cortical ablations in monkeys: contralateral changes in visually guided reaching behaviour. Science, 1977, 198, 317-319.

Monakow, C. von. Die Lokalisation im Grosshirn und der Abbau der Funktion durch kortikale Herde. Verlag von Bergmann, Wiesbaden, 1914.

Morlaas, J. Contribution a l'etude de l'apraxie. Paris: Amedee Legrand, 1928.

Muakassa, K.F. & Strick, P.L. Frontal lobe inputs to primate motor cortex: evidence for four somatotopically organized "premotor" areas. Brain Research, 1979, 179, 176-182.

Nathan, P.W. Facial apraxia and apraxic dysarthria. Brain, 1947, 70, 449-478.

Nielsen, J.M. Agnosia, apraxia, aphasia: Their value in cerebral localization (2eme edition). New York: Hoeber, 1946.

Nothnagel, 1887, cited by H. Liepmann, 1900.

Ohigashi, Y., Hamanaka, T. & Ohashi, H. Tentative de demembrement de l'apraxie buccofaciale. Studia Phonologica, 1981, 15, 31-41.

Olesen, J. Contralateral focal increase of cerebral blood flow in man during arm work. Brain, 1971, 94, 635-646.

Pandya, D.M. & Vignolo, L.A. Intra and interhemispheric projections of the precentral and arcuate areas in the Rhesus monkey. Brain Research, 1971, 26, 217-233.

Penfield, W. & Welch, K. The supplementary motor area of the cerebral cortex. Archives of Neurology and Psychiatry, 1951, 66, 289-317.

Piaget, J. Les praxies chez l'enfant. Revue Neurologique, 1960, 102, 551-565.

Pick, A. Studien uber motorische Apraxie und ihr nahestehende Erscheinungen. Leipzig: Deuticke, 1905.

Pierce, C.S. Speculative Grammar. In collected papers. Vol. 2, 129. Harvard University Press, 1932 (cited by R. Jakobson, 1964).

Piercy, M. & Smith, V.O. Right hemisphere dominance for certain nonverbal intellectual skills. Brain, 1962, 85, 775-790.

Piercy, M., Hecaen, H. & De Ajuriaguerra, J. Constructional apraxia associated with unilateral cerebral lesion, left and right cases compared. Brain, 1960, 83, 225-242.

Poppelreuter, W. Die psychischen Schadigungen durch kopfschuss im Kriege, 2 volumes. Leipzig: Voss, 1914-1917.

Roland, P.E., Larsen, B., Lassen, N.A. & Skinhoj, E. Different cortical areas in man in organization of voluntary movements in extrapersonal space. Journal of Neurophysiology, 1980, 43, 137-150.

Rondot, P. Le geste et son controle visuel. Ataxie visuo-motrice. In H. Hecaen & M. Jeannerod (Eds.). Du controle moteur a l'organisation du geste. Paris: Masson, 1977, 330-342.

Rondot, P., De Recondo, J. & Ribadeau Dumas, J.L. Visuo-motor ataxia. Brain, 1977, 100, 355-376.

Rose, F. De l'apraxie des muscles cephaliques. Sem. Med., 1908, 18, 193-198.

Schilder, P. The image and appearance of the human body. London: Routledge and Kegan Paul, 1935.

Sittig, O. Uber Apraxie. Eine Klinische Studie. Abh. aus der Neur. Psychiat. Psych. und ihre Grenzen, Berlin: Karger, S. Verlag, 1931, 63, 1-248.

Sokoloff, L. Local cerebral circulation at rest and during altered cerebral activity induced by anaesthesia or visual stimulation. In S.S. Kety & J. Elkes (Eds.) Regional Neurochemistry, New York: Pergamon, 1961, 107-117.

Sperry, R.W., Gazzaniga, M.S. & Bogen, J.E. Interhemispheric relationships: the neocortical commissures; syndromes of hemisphere disconnection. In P.J. Vinken & G.W. Bruyn (Eds.). Handbook of Clinical Neurology. Amsterdam: North Holland Publishing Co., 1969, 273-290.

Steinthal, P. Abriss der Sprachwissenschaft, Berlin, 1871.

Strauss, H. Uber konstruktive apraxie. Mtschr. f. Psychol., 1924, 56, 65-124.

Strohmayer, W. Uber subkortikale Alexie mit Agraphie und Apraxie. Dtsch. Z. Nervenhk, 1903, 24, 372-380.

Travis, A.M. Neurological deficiencies following supplementary motor area lesions in Mocaca Mulatta. Brain, 1955, 78, 174-198.

Vleuten, C.F. van. Linksseitige motorische apraxie. Ein beitrag zur physiologie des Balkens. Allgemeine Zeitschrift fur Psychiatrie, 1907, 64, 203-239.

Warrington, E.K., James, M. & Kinsbourne, M. Drawing disability in relation to laterality of lesion. Brain, 1966, 89, 53-92.

Warrington, E.K., James, M. & Kinsbourne, M. Drawing disability in relation to laterality of lesion. Brain, 1966, 89, 53-92.

Wernicke, C. Zwei Falle von Rindenlasion. Arbeit aus das Psychiatrie. Klinische in Breslau, 1895, 11-35.

Wyke, M. The effects of brain lesions on the learning performance of a bimanual coordination task. Cortex, 1971, 7, 59-72.

Zaidel, D. & Sperry, R.W. Some long-term motor effects of cerebral commissurotomy in man. Neuropsycholgia, 1977, 15, 42-48.

Zangwill, O.L. L'apraxie ideatoire. Expose au Seminaire de Neuropsychologie. E.P.H.E., Paris, 1967.

Neuropsychological Studies of Apraxia
and Related Disorders, E.A. Roy (ed.)
© Elsevier Science Publishers B.V. (North-Holland), 1985

CLUES TO THE NATURE OF DISRUPTIONS TO LIMB PRAXIS

Klaus Poeck

Abteilung Neurologie, RWTH Aachen

This chapter is based on the traditional distinction between ideomotor and ideational apraxia, the two varieties of motor apraxia. A defining feature of apraxia is not that the patient performs an action in a clumsy way but rather that the observer notes parapractic errors, i.e. inappropriate movements or inappropriate elements within a movement. Qualitative studies of ideomotor apraxia have demonstrated that apraxia is not a mere deficit in sequential activity. The inappropriate selection of motor elements within a motor sequence is of equal importance. Perseveration was also seen as a characteristic behaviour. A systematic study revealed that axial movements were not preserved in ideomotor apraxia, and no relation to aphasic syndromes was found. Ideational apraxia was found much less frequently. Qualitative error analysis pointed again to perseveration as the most important error. Ideational apraxia did not depend on aphasia. It appears that it is the consequence of a disturbance in the conceptual organization of movements.

There are two varieties of motor apraxia, which are traditionally termed ideomotor and ideational apraxia. These terms reflect the views on the organization of psychological processes in the brain developed at the end of the last century. In particular, they imply a two-stage model of motor processing, similar to the traditional two-stage model of sensory processing (perception and apperception) developed during the same period. It appears convenient, however, to adapt these terms also in modern research provided they are used as neutral denominators not conferring a priori theoretical implications. The two varieties of motor apraxia are brought about by disruption of "higher order" motor processes. The disruption occurs in two ways: impaired selection of the elements which constitute a movement and impaired sequencing. Both aspects, selection and sequencing, are of equal importance, as will be shown below.

Limiting the discussion of apraxia to the ideomotor and ideational variant excludes several neuropsychological syndromes which are sometimes discussed also under the heading of apraxia, although they certainly belong to a different class of neuropsychological syndromes. Constructional apraxia must be treated apart, because it is basically a spatial and not a motor disturbance. It is the motor or efferent aspect of visual-spatial desorientation, which, again, might not be a unitary symptom but rather the result of visual, proprioceptive, or vestibular dysfunction due to parietal lobe damage. Likewise, "dressing apraxia" can easily be traced back to spatial disorientation and/or left-sided neglect. "Apraxia of gait" (Meyer & Barron, 1960) cannot be included in the discussion of motor apraxia, because these patients just perform a certain motor function, e.g. walking, in a clumsy way without performing "parapractic", i.e. inappropriate movements. There is neither a selection nor a sequencing disturbance in the walking problems of these patients. Furthermore, motor apraxia must be defined in neurophysiological terms: it is observed for movements of certain parts of the body which have a distinct representation in the motor system. This is the case in oral and limb apraxia. Actions, like dressing or walking do not have a cerebral representation.

The classical definition of motor apraxia presupposes that the motor disorder is not explained by paresis, sensory impairment, disturbance in coordination of movement, problems in understanding the task because of language disturbance or by impairment in intellectual and cognitive performance. This definition excludes limb kinetic apraxia as described by Kleist (1934) which is just the impairment in fine distal movements of the fingers (and, of course, also the toes) indicating functional disturbance in primary motor pathways.

Motor apraxia is observed only in man. Animals do not develop apraxia as a consequence of a brain lesion, no matter where this lesion is located (Ettlinger, 1969). Consequently, it is hard to conceive of an animal model which might help to develop concepts for the physiological explanation of the apraxias (but see Kolb and Whishaw, this volume). Unfortunately, up to now there has neither been a serious attempt to relate the clinical syndromes to the body of experience of motor physiology in man. Unlike research in the field of aphasia which has strongly capitalized on modern linguistic as well as neuroanatomical experience, apraxia research is still being conducted along the traditional lines developed by Liepmann (1905a,b) and Pick (1905). Patients are asked to perform the sign of the cross or the military salute, either on verbal command or on imitation, and the scoring system is limited, at least in most of the studies, to noting pass or fail, without analyzing the qualitative aspects of the errors (for exceptions see below). Pertinent tasks used in many aphasia studies are listed in De Renzi, Pieczuro and Vignolo (1966) or, more recently, in Lehmkuhl, Poeck and Willmes (1983), where also bimanual tasks and tasks for leg movements are included. Axial movements have been studied systematically by Poeck, Lehmkuhl and Willmes (1982). Some researchers have recognized the need to get off the traditional path of apraxia study. De Renzi, Faglioni and Sorgato (1982) has studied the most interesting problem of modality specific apraxia, other researchers have tested more basic skills like tapping (Heilman, 1975), performance on the pursuit rotor (Heilman, Schwartz & Geschwind, 1975), speed of arm movements towards a target (Wyke, 1967), manual activity during speaking (Lomas & Kimura, 1976), and motor learning after left hemisphere damage (Kimura, 1977; Roy, 1981). These studies certainly illuminate the motor functions of the left hemisphere. It is an open question, however, to what extent they contribute to our understanding of the motor apraxias. Given that bridging the gap between motor physiology and apraxia research is still a postulate, this chapter necessarily has to rely on more or less traditional studies in spite of the criticism voiced above.

Qualitative studies of ideomotor apraxia

David Efron (1941) was the first to apply sophisticated methods for the description of expressive movements in a study on gestural behaviour. He used the term linguistic to denote the referential aspect of symbolic movements. However, his analysis was focussed only on movements as a whole and did not include the single components of movements. These were systematically studied by Birdwhistle (1970) who applied the methods of structural linguistics to the study of normal movements. He recognized posture and movement as patterned behaviour, and he developed a notation system which permitted him to describe a hierarchy of motor elements similar to the description of speech elements in linguistic hierarchy. For Birdwhistle, kinemes and kinemorphes, as units of movements, corresponded to phonemes and morphemes in the description of language. Birdwhistle developed a notation system lending itself to the precise description of the single elements within a motor sequence. He termed this field of research "kinemics".

Stimulated by this research, Poeck and Kerschensteiner (1975) developed a method permitting the quantitative and qualitative assessment of the single components constituting the apractic movements. They elaborated a code permitting the transcription of the characteristics of the single components of a motor sequence. The possible deviations from the expected motor behaviour in apractic patients were classified in four different categories: substitution, augmentation, deficient performance, and other types of error. We became aware that many, but not all, errors recognized in patients with ideomotor apraxia by the application of this qualitative analysis of motor elements had a great similarity to the linguistic errors observed in aphasia. This parallel, however, was confined to the single elements and did not apply to the way these elements were concatenated in sequences. In other words, there was something like phonology and morphology of movements, but no syntax, a fact that had been mentioned already by Birdwhistle.

The code we developed permitted the transcription of movements, which is illustrated by the following example: The patient performed a motor reaction which contained a perseveratory element, he then talked instead of moving, went on to a fragmentary movement and finished the sequence with a motor augmentation involving the whole body, again perseverating a motor element which had appeared two tasks before. This behaviour was coded as spl/t/f/mabp2. Sequences like these could then be subjected to mathematical analysis. A simplified version of this qualitative description was later on used in an extensive study on types and manifestations of apractic symptoms by Lehmkuhl et al. (1983). For details the reader is referred to Poeck and Kerschensteiner (1975). These studies clearly demonstrated that apraxia cannot be viewed as a mere deficit in sequential activity. It emerged that the inappropriate selection of motor elements within a motor sequence is of equal importance. This finding strongly calls for a more refined analysis of the functional elements in apractic movements beyond the traditional categorization of the whole movement under just two headings, pass or fail.

This requirement also applies to perseveration. It was shown that perseveration was a most characteristic behaviour in apraxia. This, of course, had been reported since Liepmann's (1905a,b) studies on apraxia, and the role of perseveration has also been underlined by Kimura (1977) and Mateer and Kimura (1977). Again, we were able to show that in apraxia perseveration does not only show as the repetition of a whole movement or motor sequence but, much more important, as the appearance of motor elements that had been correctly or incorrectly performed up to 13 tasks before. In other words, the patients do not only repeat the military salute when they are asked to wave good-bye, but they perseverate the rhythmic element of the movement "to show that somebody is nuts" when they are to perform the static movement of the military salute, i.e. they tap at their temple, while the hand is in correct military salute position. The perseveratory tendency is so strong that when asked to perform a movement on imitation the patients are likely to repeat a movement or an element of a movement carried out before against the visual evidence of the correct execution of the movement by the examiner. This is not due to impaired recognition of the demonstrated movement. At least this is suggested by a study by Weniger and Muller (Note 1) who demonstrated good recognition of gestures in brain damaged patients.

Quality of apractic errors and subtypes of aphasia

Ideomotor apraxia is, as a rule, observed in patients with lesions to the hemisphere dominant for language, usually the left hemisphere. Ideomotor apraxia following right-sided cerebral lesion is, in most instances, observed only when the right hemisphere is language dominant (Poeck and Kerschensteiner, 1971). Exceptions to this rule are extremely rare (Heilman, Coyle, Gonyea & Geschwind, 1973). Considering further that most patients with ideomotor apraxia are aphasic, one might wonder whether or not there is a structural relation between the two syndromes. This problem can be studied when the quality of errors in apractic movements is considered. We have studied this problem for oral apraxia (Poeck & Kerschensteiner, 1975) as well as all varieties of limb apraxia (Lehmkuhl et al., 1983). One could have speculated that in patients with Broca's aphasia there is a predominance of fragmentary movements, in contrast to a preponderance of augmentation of movements in Wernicke's aphasia. Since perseveration is an important element of global aphasia, perseveratory errors could have been most prominent in these patients.

Our findings were negative in any respect. For error types in oral apraxia, the profiles for the four subtypes of standard aphasia ran virtually parallel to each other and also to the profile of the whole group of 101 patients. The same was true for limb apraxia. Furthermore, there was no correspondence in degree of severity between aphasia and apraxia.

Are there subtypes of apraxia?

We have studied this problem examining 88 aphasic patients and two groups of controls with a series of 200 tasks for the assessment of ideomotor apraxia (Lehmkuhl et al., 1983). The tasks included meaningful (symbolic) as well as meaningless (non-symbolic) movements. Each task was required on imitation and on verbal command. The examination for limb apraxia was done separately for the left and right arm and for the left and right leg, and we also gave bimanual tasks as well as tasks for oral apraxia. Order of presentation was randomized.

The results were subjected to various statistical procedures. The essential findings in this study were the following: Impaired auditory language comprehension could not be the only reason even for apractic errors in the verbal mode, because even the subgroup with global aphasia solved at least half of these tasks correctly. On the other hand, patients with Broca's and amnesic aphasia did not, on the average, show better performance in the verbal examination than on imitation.

We did not find subtypes of apraxia which were related to the standard syndromes of aphasia. Nonetheless there could exist apractic syndromes independent of the type of aphasia. These could have been characteristized by the differential involvement of parts of the body in relation to the somatotopic organization of the motor and premotor cortex and/or by certain types of error.

Error types did not have a differential distribution, the most frequent error being perseveration. More interesting is the finding that a cluster analysis did not demonstrate apractic syndromes when we considered differential affection of parts of the body. In other words, the traditional distinction between oral and limb apraxia appears quite artificial. On the other hand it can be assumed that patients with limb apraxia for arm movements also are impaired in movements of the leg. So there is no need to examine leg movements provided the patient does not have a lesion in the territory of the anterior cerebral artery. It must be stressed that all our patients had a CVA in the territory of the middle cerebral artery. For bimanual movements there was a very strong intraindividual variability of performance which did not permit a meaningful analysis. Patients with apraxia for leg movements did not have the disturbance of gait described as "apraxia of gait" (see introduction).

Oral apraxia and phonemic paraphasias

De Renzi et al. (1966) have reported that a global analysis shows a high positive correlation between the quantitative occurrence of phonemic paraphasias in aphasic patients and the degree of oral apraxia. This finding raises the question, whether the deficit in the selection and sequential ordering of phonemes which leads to phonemic paraphasias is linguistic or motor in nature. Burns and Canter (1977) have demonstrated that in Wernicke's aphasia the quality of phonemic paraphasias has no relationship to the presence of oral apraxia. When one considers the types of phonemic errors in aphasic patients, i.e. substitution, anticipation, elision and augmentation and compares these to the quality of errors in oral apraxia, it is evident that anticipation is not observed in apractic movements. Furthermore, an analysis of error types in both performances, language and oral movements, did not yield a common pattern.

Sometimes, a CVA in the anterior branches of the middle cerebral artery or in the total territory of the middle cerebral artery leaves the patient unable to utter a sound. During the first days, the patient makes no attempt to communicate verbally. At the same time he is unable to perform non-linguistic oral movements both on verbal command and on imitation. This condition is termed anarthria.

Over the next week, the patient starts carrying out random and obviously parapractic oral movements while at the same time he starts voicing single utterances both spontaneously and in a given situational context. It is tempting to speculate that anarthria is the most severe form of oral apraxia. It must be considered, however, that patients with ideomotor apraxia of the limbs, as a rule, are not unable to move the limbs but rather produce sequences of movements which are partly or completely inadequate. Also, limb apraxia on oral command and on imitation does not prevent the patient from using his limbs spontaneously when the situational context calls for the same movement which he did not carry out during the examination. In my view, it is an open question whether anarthria is an extremely severe form of oral apraxia or a lower order motor deficit which, when it resolves, gives way to the appearance of oral apraxia.

Axial movements in ideomotor apraxia

Axial movements are particularly interesting from the neurophysiological point of view since the axial musculature receives bilateral pyramidal projections. Furthermore, the proximal muscles of the limbs receive projections from the non-pyramidal motor system, as described by Kuypers, Fleming and Farinholt (1962), Lawrence and Kuypers (1968) and Brinkman and Kuypers (1973).

One important subgroup of midline muscles, e.g. the tongue, is severely compromised in apraxia, as evidenced by any study on oral apraxia in the literature, beginning with Jackson's famous paper, "Non-protrusion of the tongue" (1878). It was interesting to examine whether or not axial movements are preserved or impaired in ideomotor apraxia.

A systematic study was carried out by Poeck et al. (1982) in 60 aphasic patients with unilateral, left-sided brain damage of vascular etiology. We found that axial movements were not, as a rule, preserved in patients with ideomotor apraxia. This does not exclude the possibility that certain types of movement are impaired in some patients to a different degree. This, however, only reflects the variability of performance which is common to any neuropsychological syndrome.

Is there a need for therapy?

It is widely held that apraxia has a strong tendency for spontaneous recovery. This is not our experience (see studies cited above). However, ideomotor apraxia shows only under testing conditions. It does not prevent the patient from using his limbs spontaneously, and even with rather severe oral apraxia, the patient is able to swallow. This makes therapy in most instances unnecessary. The only exception is apraxia of speech. However, this condition is not established unequivocally, and lack of personal experience prevents the author from discussing this problem (see Roy and Square, this volume).

Qualitative studies of ideational apraxia

Definition, occurrence and typical behaviour

Ideational apraxia is observed in about 4% of the patients with lesions in the language dominant hemisphere, usually the left. There is only one case on record where the syndrome was a consequence of right-sided brain lesion (Poeck & Lehmkuhl, 1980). This patient was a left-hander and had a right-sided or at least bilateral representation of language functions. It is possible that ideational apraxia is more frequent than reported in papers based on large groups of brain damaged patients (e.g. Hecaen, 1960). This problem will be discussed below under the heading "Perspectives for further research".

Patients with ideational apraxia are seriously impaired when they are to carry out sequences of actions requiring the use of various objects in the correct way and order necessary to achieve an intended goal. In contrast to ideomotor apraxia, these patients are conspicuous in everyday behaviour because they have problems with preparing a meal, even eating breakfast or doing some professional routine they had been used to do for years. The behavioural disturbance of these patients is most frequently misinterpreted as indicating mental confusion all the more since these patients, in addition to ideational apraxia, are regularly aphasic.

When we analyzed videotapes of patients with ideational apraxia (Poeck & Lehmkuhl, 1980; Poeck, 1982, 1983) it was evident that the patients had no problems in the recognition of objects. Also they were not impaired in single, one or two step actions within a longer object-bound motor sequence. Interestingly enough, some of our patients, in spite of aphasia being present, commented correctly on the required tasks. Nonetheless, there were errors like beating on a tin with a tin opener or stirring water in a cup with a water immersion heater. Typical tasks and patterns or behaviour are described in Lehmkuhl and Poeck (1981) and Poeck (1982).

Error analysis

Ideational apraxia is not a very severe degree of ideomotor apraxia. Both syndromes may occur in the same patient, but they vary independently of each other. Definitely, the patients do not manipulate the objects at random. The most frequent type of error is sequential in nature: part of the required action is omitted or is executed using an inadequate object. Hesitation is frequent as is repeated self-correction indicating that the patient is aware of the inadequacy of his motor performance.

Brain localization

While Pick (1905) and even Denny-Brown (1958) considered that ideational apraxia was due to diffuse brain damage, Hugo Liepmann (1905a,b) is to be credited for the recognition that ideational apraxia is brought about by circumscribed lesions in the brain, located in the posterior parietal lobe. CT findings in ideational apraxia have been reported by Poeck and Lehmkuhl (1980). It is still an open question, why some patients with an identical brain lesion do show the syndrome of ideational apraxia and others do not. Obviously the methods of localization offered by CT scan are much too crude to resolve this problem. It is certain, however, that diffuse brain damage is no prerogative for the occurrence of ideational apraxia, as well as, on clinical grounds, the patients are by no means demented or confused.

Relation to aphasia

All patients with ideational apraxia are aphasic. Aphasia, however, cannot explain the syndrome, since the tasks are not given verbally. The patient is confronted with a series of objects which he had handled with no problem at all before the onset of his brain disease. Verbal mediation obviously does not play a crucial role in the execution of these movements. On the contrary, some of our patients gave correct verbal comments on the required task while, at the same time, they were unable to carry out the correct execution (Poeck, 1982).

Perspectives for Further Research

We have suggested (Lehmkuhl & Poeck, 1981; Poeck, 1982) that ideational apraxia is due to a disturbance in the associative elaboration of various inputs with motor programs. Ideational apraxia could be viewed as a disturbance in the conceptual organization of movements, because some patients were also impaired when they had to arrange pictures illustrating actions requiring the use of various objects in the correct order. These observations, however, are still at an impressionistic stage, and the receptive aspect of ideational apraxia awaits further systematic study (see Roy & Square, this volume).

The Relation between Aphasia and Apraxia: Parallels and Discrepancies

At the neurological level, all reliable data indicate a localization of the lesion underlying both aphasia and apraxia syndromes in the hemisphere dominant for language. At the semiotic and structural level language and praxis are structured activities, and their elements must be adequately selected and organized in the appropriate order. Errors in both syndromes are morphological, semantic and sequential in nature.

However, there is no parallel variation in degree of severity. We did not find a relation between subtypes of aphasia and error patterns in apraxia. Both syndromes, aphasia and apraxia, cannot be explained by the assumption of a higher order central communication disorder. On the other hand, it is not justified to consider apraxia and aphasia as two aspects of motor disturbance related to left-sided brain damage. At the present stage of our knowledge it does not make very much sense to postulate a common psychological disturbance underlying both syndromes ("Grundstorung"). There are too many problems to be solved in both fields, aphasia and apraxia, and it appears premature to offer speculations on the relation or mutual dependence of these syndromes (but see Kertesz, this volume).

REFERENCE NOTES

1. Weniger, D. & Muller, R. Recognition and imitation of gestures in brain damaged patients. Paper presented at the International Neuropsychological Symposium in Oxford, England, June 19-23, 1978.

REFERENCES

Birdwhistle, R.L. Kinemics and Context. Philadelphia: University of Pennsylvania Press, 1970.

Brinkman, J. & Kuypers, H.G.J.M. Cerebral control of contralateral and ipsilateral arm, hand and finger movements in the split brain rhesus monkey. Brain, 1973, 96, 653-674.

Burns, M.S. & Canter, G.J. Phonemic behavior of aphasic patients with posterior cerebral lesions. Brain and Language, 1977, 4, 492-507.

Denny-Brown, D. The nature of apraxia. Journal of Nervous and Mental Diseases, 1958, 126, 9-33.

De Renzi, E., Pieczuro, A. & Vignolo, L.A. Oral apraxia and aphasia. Cortex, 1966, 2, 50-73.

De Renzi, E., Faglioni, P. & Sorgato, P. Modality-specific and supramodal mechanisms of apraxia. Brain, 1982, 105, 301-312.

Efron, D. Gesture and Environment. New York: King's Crown, 1941.

Ettlinger, G. Apraxia considered as a disorder of movements that are language-dependent: Evidence from cases of brain bisection. Cortex, 1969, 5, 285-289.

Hecaen, H. Les apraxies. Revue Neurologique, 1960, 102, 541-550.

Hecaen, H. & Angelergues, R. Etude anatomo-clinique de 280 cas de lesions retro-rolandiques unilaterales des hemispheres cerebraux. Encephale, 1961, 6, 533-562.

Heilman, K.M., Coyle, J.M., Gonyea, E.F. & Geschwind, N. Apraxia and agraphia in a left-hander. Brain, 1973, 96, 21-28.

Heilman, K.M. A tapping test in apraxia. Cortex, 1975, 11, 259-263.

Heilman, K.M., Schwartz, H.D. & Geschwind, N. Defective motor learning in ideo-motor apraxia. Neurology, (Minneap.), 1975, 25, 1018-1020.

Jackson, J.H. Remarks on non-protrusion of the tongue in some cases of aphasia. Lancet, 1878, 1, 716-717.

Kimura, D. The neural basis of language qua gesture. In H. Whitaker & H.A. Whitaker (Eds.), Studies in Neurolinguistics, Volume 2. New York: Academic Press, 1976.

Kimura, D. Acquisition of motor skill after left hemisphere damage. Brain, 1977, 100, 527-542.

Kleist, K. Gehirnpathologie. Leipzig: Ambrosius Barth, 1934.

Kuypers, H.G.J.M., Fleming, W.R. & Farinholt, J.W. Subcortico-spinal projections in the rhesus monkey. Journal of Comparative Neurology, 1962, 118, 107-131.

Lawrence, D.G. & Kuypers, H.G.J.M. The functional organization of actions in patients with ideational apraxia. Brain, 1968, 91, 1-14, 15-36.

Lehmkuhl, G. & Poeck, K. A disturbance in the conceptual organization of the motor system in the monkey. Cortex, 1981, 17, 153-158.

Lehmkuhl, G., Poeck, K. & Willmes, K. Ideomotor apraxia and aphasia: An examination of types and manifestations of apraxic symptoms. Neuropsychologia, 1983, 21, 199-212.

Liepmann, H. Uber Storungen des Handelns bei Gehirnkranken. Berlin: Karger, 1905.(a)

Liepmann, H. Die linke Hemisphare und das Handeln. Munchener medizinische Wochenschrift, 1905, 52, 2322-2326, 2375-2378.(b)

Lomas, J. & Kimura, D. Interhemispheric interaction between speaking and sequential manual activity. Neuropsychologia, 1976, 14, 23-33.

Mateer, C. & Kimura, D. Impairment of nonverbal oral movements in aphasia. Brain and Language, 1977, 4, 262-276.

Meyer, J.S. & Barron, D.W. Apraxia of gait: A clinico-physiological study. Brain, 1960, 83, 261-284.

Pick, A. Studien uber motorische Apraxie und ihre nahestehende Erscheinungen ihre Bedeutung in der Symptomatologie psychophologischer Symptomenkomplex. Leipzig: Deuticke, 1905.

Poeck, K. & Kerschensteiner, M. Ideomotor apraxia following right-sided cerebral lesion in a left-handed subject. Neuropsychologia, 1971, 9, 359-361.

Poeck, K. & Kerschensteiner, M. Analysis of the sequential motor events in oral apraxia. In K.J. Zulch, O. Creutzfeldt and G.C. Galbraith (Eds.), Cerebral Localization. Berlin-Heidelberg-New York: Springer, 1975.

Poeck, K. & Lehmkuhl, G. Das Syndrom der ideatorischen Apraxie und seine Lokalisation. Nervenarzt, 1980, 51, 217-225.(a)

Poeck, K. & Lehmkuhl, G. Ideatory apraxia in a left-handed patient with right-sided brain lesion. Cortex, 1980, 16, 273-284.(b)

Poeck, K. The two types of motor apraxia. Archives Italiennes de Biologie, 1982, 120, 361-369.

Poeck, K., Lehmkuhl, G. & Willmes, K. Axial movements in ideomotor apraxia. Journal of Neurology, Neurosurgery and Psychiatry, 1982, 45, 1125-1129.

Poeck, K. Ideational apraxia. Journal of Neurology, 1983, 230, 1-5.

Roy, E.A. Action sequencing and lateralized cerebral damage: Evidence for asymmetries in control. In J. Long & A. Baddeley (Eds.), Attention and Performance IX. New Jersey: Erlbaum, 1981.

Wyke, M. Effect of brain lesions on the rapidity of arm movement. Neurology, (Minneap.), 1967, 17, 1113-1120.

*Neuropsychological Studies of Apraxia
and Related Disorders, E.A. Roy (ed.)*
© *Elsevier Science Publishers B.V. (North-Holland), 1985*

COMMON CONSIDERATIONS IN THE STUDY OF

LIMB, VERBAL AND ORAL APRAXIA

Eric A. Roy and Paula A. Square

University of Toronto and Mount Sinai Hospital

Contemporary empirical research regarding both verbal and limb apraxia is considered within the framework of a neuropsychological perspective which views the apraxias as involving dysfunctions of either a cognitive-linguistic system or a motor-production system. The apractic disorders are compared as they reflect disruptions to these two systems. Comparisons include types of errors observed, stimulus and response variables which influence the errors observed and the environmental conditions under which the observed errors occur.

A persistent issue in the study of apraxia concerns the relationship between disorders to limb praxis and speech/language disorders. The observation that these disorders frequently co-occur has prompted an interest in determining the underlying basis for this association. While considerable research has been devoted to studying the relationship between type of aphasia, nature of language/speech disorder (e.g. comprehension) and limb apraxia (e.g. Kertesz, 1979), the relationship between apraxia of speech, oral apraxia and limb apraxia has received somewhat less attention. Work by De Renzi (De Renzi, Pieczuro & Vignolo, 1966) in the mid 1960's and more recent work by Kimura (e.g. Kimura, 1982) and Kolb and Milner (1981) represent the bulk of the research into this relationship. Given that the motor control processes in the speech and limb systems are similar (De Renzi, Pieczuro & Vignolo, 1966) disruptions to verbal and limb praxis should also follow similar principles. The importance of studying these disorders together in the same patients is clearly a means of testing this prediction. This chapter describes one perspective on the nature of the relationship between these forms of apraxia which arises from a consideration of principles of organization of the action system (Roy, 1982, 1983). The chapter is partitioned into sections. The initial three sections evaluate mechanisms and errors observed in limb, verbal and oral praxis, respectively. A model of the organization of action is applied throughout these sections to provide a basis for understanding disruptions to praxis. In this model, control is thought to rely on the operation of conceptual and production processes: the former encompass a knowledge base for action and the latter provides the mechanisms for movement. In the final section we evaluate commonalities in errors observed in limb and verbal apraxia. This notion of a conceptual-production system as a basis for action is used as means for studying the relationship between disorders to limb and verbal praxis.

Control Mechanisms in Limb Praxis: The Conceptual-Production System

Acting in the world may involve the operation of two systems (Roy, 1983): a conceptual system which provides an abstract representation of action and a production system which incorporates a sensory motor component of knowledge (generalized action programs) as well as encompassing the perceptual-motor processes for organizing and executing actions (c.f., Newell & Simon, 1972). We will first discuss this model (see Table 1) as it applies to limb praxis. The model will then be used as a basis for discussing the nature of disruptions to limb, verbal and oral praxis.

The Conceptual System.

The conceptual system is thought to incorporate three types of knowledge relevant to limb praxis: knowledge of objects and tools in terms of the action and functions they serve, knowledge of actions independent of tools or objects but into which tools or objects may be incorporated, and knowledge relevant to the seriation of single actions into a sequence. Knowledge of objects or tools as they relate to their functions may have internalized linguistic referents. The linguistic referents may be similar to functional associates (e.g., Goodglass & Baker, 1976) which form part of the semantic field for objects descriptive of the actions performed with or on them (e.g., pushing, pulling). This notion of action fields surrounding objects relates to work which considers the role of functional information in knowledge about common objects (Nelson, 1979; Rosch, Morris, Gray, Johnson & Boyes-Braem, 1976). For example, Nelson proposes that functional information involving descriptions of goal activities and use provides a core of information about objects. Out of this functional core during development other information important in categorical knowledge, e.g., perceptual attributes, develops. Elaborating on the role of functional information in categorical knowledge, Rosch et al. (1976) proposed that the motor patterns involved in interacting with objects serve as common attributes of these objects.

In addition to these "internalized" functional referents perceptual referents provide an externalization of knowledge about function performed with objects (Roy, Notes 1 and 2; 1982). The perceptual attributes of tools and objects proffer one source of information here. The performer learns through experience with objects that certain perceptual features enable certain actions. The perceptual attributes afford the actions which are possible, e.g., an object which shares perceptual attributes with a hammer would afford hammering (Gibson, 1977). The other source of information concerns the environmental/situational context in which tools are normally used. Bransford (Bransford & McCarrell, 1974) stresses the importance of these sources of perceptual information in knowledge about objects.

An examination of errors in normality provides support for this type of conceptual representation of action. For example, one type of error, a discrimination failure, occurs when the performer confuses contextual or perceptual aspects of objects (e.g., Norman, 1981; Roy, 1982, 1983). Such errors arise from a number of confusions (Reason, 1979) - perceptual, e.g., objects are observably similar; spatial, e.g., objects are used in close spatial proximity; and functional/procedural, e.g., objects are functionally similar. All of these types of information may, then, contribute to the formation of active memory structures which include descriptions of functions performed on various tools or objects in various situations. Furthermore, there may be networks of these memory structures formed on the basis of common or shared features. Two objects which share some features may be confused and, so, used or acted upon inappropriately.

Table 1

Outline of the Conceptual-Production System

Level	Operational Details	System
I		
Abstract Knowledge of Action	Knowledge of Object Function Knowledge of Action Knowledge of Serial Order Linguistic-Conceptual Sensory-Perceptual	Conceptual (Top-Down)
II		
Knowledge of Action in Sensorimotor Form	Attention at Key Points Action Programs Information in Programs Translation of Programs into Action Activation of Programs	Production (High Level)
III		
Mechanisms for Movement Control	Environment Muscle Collectives	Production (Low Level)

In these memory structures perceptual (e.g., shape, size) and contextual (e.g., spatial location) attributes are mapped on to sets of procedures defining various functions performed on objects. These perceptual/contextual attributes provide descriptions which may be used to activate the actions on to which they are mapped. It would seem that this activation process may require little attention (Roy, 1982, p. 290). As such these perceptual/contextual attributes may provide a rather direct link between perception and action.

This first component in the conceptualization of action has its focus on the object or tool which is to be used for a particular function. The second component focuses on the actions performed in carrying out these functions. These actions may be somewhat independent of the tool or object with which they are usually associated. In a way knowledge of action is "decontextualized". That is, it is not associated with any particular object. Knowing what action is to be performed the performer incorporates into the action (i.e., uses) a tool or object which would enable the goal to be achieved. In selecting an object to perform an action perceptual attributes are important: if the appropriate object is not nearby the performer may use an object or tool which shares attributes with the appropriate one. The person uses his practical knowledge about objects based on perceptual attributes, e.g., a shoe would make a good hammer, rather than his lexical knowledge, e.g., a shoe is in the category of footwear (see Miller, 1978).

The linguistic aspect to this component involves verbal descriptions of the relationships of the agent, e.g., the hand, and the implements or objects moving in a particular spatiotemporal pattern (Miller & Johnson-Laird, 1976, Roy, 1983). The perceptual aspects of this component concerns the body-relevant and environment-relevant consequences of action. In the production system this perceptual information is used in generating the appropriate actions (see below). In the conceptual system, however, it forms a basis for knowing about action which may enable the performer to recognize and learn actions, for example, through visual imagery techniques. Assessment of this knowledge component of action forms a part of the limb praxis examination in our studies of apractic patients (see Roy, 1983).

The third aspect in the conceptualization of action concerns the seriation of these single actions into a sequence and is assessed in some intelligence tests and is of recent interest in the study of apraxia (Poeck & Lehmkuhl, 1980; Roy, 1981b). In the initial stages of acquisition of an action or in the process of performing a novel sequence this knowledge may be important in directing the production system, through the processes of verbal mediation (c.f. Luria, 1966). In this way the production system is driven in a top-down fashion in contrast to bottom-up control in which the environment may play a role in directing the production system (see below and Roy, 1982, 1983).

The Production System.

Having considered the conceptual system for action with regard to limb praxis, we now move on to the production system which is concerned with effecting action on the environment. Through examining the types of errors made both in normality and pathology (Roy, 1982) several important principles are evident about the operations of the production system (see also McKay, this volume). One of the key points here is that errors arise principally during periods when the performer is not attending to the unfolding action. These errors occur when the performer fails to verify "the progress of an action sequence at 'key choice points'" (Reason, 1979). These critical points arise when a number of actions are associated with a given situation or with one another and when sequences share common actions (Roy, 1982). If attention is not directed at these points the sequence may be diverted into an action which 1) is similar to but more well learned or familiar than the appropriate one; 2) has been more recently performed than the next intended action in the sequence; or 3) is more frequently associated with the previous action than the intended one. While these observations suggest that attention is important, unintended actions are performed well, apparently without attention. That an action may be performed under these minimal attention conditions suggests that control has shifted from a level which normally uses conscious, attention-demanding processes to one in which attention is somewhat less demanded.

How might action be controlled in these lower systems? At one level action may be directed by generalized programs thought to be abstract conceptualizations of the movement patterns involved in behavioural acts directed at effecting change in the environment (Roy, 1983). These programs represent actions which might be thought to be of ecological importance, e.g., hammering, stirring. As such they are a representation in the production system of knowledge of action in the conceptual system. These programs are not specific to any particular effector unit (e.g., hand, foot) but are able to direct any of these units in producing an action. As such they confer immense flexibility on the action system: an action, a series of movements which effect some environmental change (e.g., writing the letter "A") removing the lid from a coffee jar, may be performed using any one of a number of effectors.

In considering the information content of these programs it is important to understand that all of the information relevant for action is not "in your head", so to speak. Rather, much information relevant to action is "out there" in the environment. The perceptual attributes of tools and surfaces (affordances) inform the performer as to what actions are possible. The interaction of object surfaces, e.g., the pen on paper when writing, constrains the action in a way that only a relatively small number of movements are possible for any particular effector unit. Finally, certain consequences of action are relevant to the environment and to the body (see below for body-relevant consequences) and, so, provide information about the changes in the environment related to action. Since people are able to imitate actions outside of this environmental context, an ability to represent action in gesture, suggests that there must be some internalized information about action. An examination of these gestural representations (see Roy, 1983) would suggest that these action programs contain information about space, i.e., the orientation of objects and movements and the positioning of the fingers in a grasp, and time.

Since the neuromotor system forms the basis for action, this information about changes in limb position over time and through space must be expressed to some extent in the language of this system, the pattern and duration of muscle activation. There is considerable evidence now that there are constraints on this system such that muscles work together in groups or collectives (e.g., Easton, 1972; Turvey, Shaw & Mace, 1978). The existence of these collectives suggests that information in these programs pertaining to muscle activation is not in the form of commands to individual muscles but rather to muscle groups which when activated are constrained to work together in a coordinative fashion (e.g., Keele, 1980). As such this information may be rather simple as it does not involve the details of individual muscle action.

Considerable work examining the structure of motor programs suggests that action sequences which are relatively unstructured in temporal or rhythmic patterns may be represented as event-to-event associations (Keele & Summers, 1976), while sequences which are structured temporally or rhythmically appear to be represented hierarchically as rules which are employed in generating the movement sequence. The timing of action events in a sequence appears to be an integral part of the program.

While efferent information may form an important part of these programs, information as to the expected consequences (e.g., visual, auditory, kinesthetic) of ensuing actions must also be incorporated. These consequences provide information as to what the action should look, feel and sound like. That people are able to visually identify the movement patterns of others as representative of a particular action (Heilman, 1979; Roy, 1983) suggests that this type of information must be available.

Considering that unintended actions occur a number of action programs are apparently activated at one time. This activation may occur in parallel at a number of levels in the production system. Although it may subside at higher levels, e.g., the person changes his mind, other lower levels remain activitated. Given the necessary set of environmental conditions, an action, in this case the wrong one, is selected and triggered (Roy, 1982, 1983).

What might be the basis for this multiple activation? Actions which share cer tain common features may form associative networks such that activating any one in the network results in all of them being activated and prepared. This idea relates to Gottsdanker's (1980) notion of common preparation. Actions related to the intended one in regards to the context of performance and the object on or with which they are performed occur as errors, i.e., discrimination failures (Reason, 1979). One set of features by which actions programs are related may then be provided by these perceptual/contextual aspects. Another dimension on which action programs may be defined is by response compatibility (Shulman & McConkie, 1973): programs in which similar effector units must be prepared or activated may be related. Finally, errors in which an intended action is "directed" into an unintended one which seems to share a common action component with it (i.e., branching errors, Reason, 1979; Roy, 1982) suggests that like action program sequences may be related and organized into networks on the basis of shared action programs.

How is information in these action programs translated into action? This process of translation may largely take place through the operation of the muscle collectives alluded to above. Following selection of collectives through the process of biasing and setting parameters, control shifts from the program to a level in which these muscle collectives control working out the details of the movements in the action through interaction with the environment. As suggested above the environment sets constraints on movement (e.g., perceptual attributes and environment-relevant consequences) such that working out the details is to a large extent constrained or guided by the environment.

At this level the environment in conjunction with spinal neuromotor processes appears to direct action. The role of the environment in controlling action is exemplified by errors in which information in the environment induces an unintended action (i.e., data-driven errors, Norman, 1981) which arise when attention is diverted from the current action. Perceptual and/or contextual information, then, may directly access or select an action program with which it is associated. At this level, then, control seems provided by a rather direct link between perceptual/contextual information and action. This dynamic interface between the environment and the performer has been referred to as a coalitional style of control (Turvey et al., 1978). A type of bottom-up control of action is thus provided (Roy, 1982).

One important source of information in producing action is spatial. The position of body parts relative to one another as provided through posture and grasp form a static aspect of spatial information. The other source is dynamic and involves the interaction of object surfaces and the planes of orientation of body parts through space. The former seems not to be specific to any effector unit. The objects must assume this type of spatial interaction (e.g., orientation of pen on paper) regardless of which effector unit is used (e.g., pen in hand, mouth or foot). As such this might be termed object space. The latter aspect is specific to the effectors used in action and so is termed effector space (Roy, 1983).

The integration of this sensory information with motor commands plays an important role in the execution of movements involved in actions (e.g., MacNeilage, Sussman & Stolz, 1975). From a neurophysiological perspective sensorimotor integration may have both cortical and subcortical components (e.g., Trevarthan, 1978) with the latter subcortical mechanisms providing the neural basis for the interface between the action system and environmental demands exemplified in bottom-up control of action which appears to demand little attention.

Action programs may control action principally between the critical choice points alluded to above (Reason, 1981). Since these programs appear to operate with minimal attention in an open-loop mode, one might think that feedback is of little importance. Schmidt (1976) and more recently Roy (1982) have argued, however, that open-loop control does not mean that feedback is not processed but rather that these processes apparently demand little attention. The fact that action adapts to meet the demands of the environment gives evidence of another level of control here, one below that of the action program.

The production system is comprised, then, not of a single system but a number of parallel systems which may operate somewhat independently. Further, control may shift from one level to another. More generally, these observations indicate that the performance of actions involves a delicate balance between processes sub-served by higher level systems which demand attention and the more autonomous operations subserved at lower levels. Operations at higher levels keep the action sequence directed toward the intended goal through corrections for selection (goal-directed) errors. Those at lower levels involve action programs which operate with minimal attention demands and in which adaptations to environmental constraints are made through existing neural systems.

Limb Apractic Errors

Errors in performing actions concommitant with lesions to the cerebral cortex, particularly those which occur in limb apraxia, have been described in detail (e.g. Hecaen & Albert, 1978; Heilman, 1979, Roy, 1978, 1981). One major type of error involves a disorder in performing the action itself. Errors in performing the sequence of movements are characterized as omissions, repetitions, disturbances to the order of movements in the sequence, a difficulty in terminating movements when required and a difficulty in coordinating the limbs in time and space. One of the commonest of these errors is the tendency to repeat (perseverate) actions (e.g. Kimura, 1977; Roy, 1981). There also appear to be errors involved in performing the movement elements which form the sequence. These errors have been described by Kimura (1977) and Heilman (1979) as 'clumsiness'. The movements lose the smooth-ness; they become jerky and ataxic-like. Fine finger control may be adversely affected (Heilman, 1975).

The second major type of error is one in which the actions are performed cor-rectly, but they are inappropriate for the situation at hand. The patient may use an object or tool in an inappropriate way, for example, using a pencil as a comb. In this case the action of combing may be performed correctly; it is just the wrong action to be used with this implement (or the wrong implement to be used with the action of combing). In another case the patient may perform an action which for him has been associated with a particular situation, even though it may not be the one requested of him. A third example here is errors which are environmentally induced, i.e. the environmental context precipitates an error. These errors are fre-quent in the pathology, as brain damage often leaves the patient in a much more context-dependent state (Luria, 1973).

The third major type of error involves the omission of an action completely. The patient may forget what action it was he was about to perform. In other cases the patient is cognizant of what he should do with an object, for example, but he cannot demonstrate how to use it. In such cases the patient may attempt to indi-cate how or where the object is to be used. The use of parts of the body (body as object), of facial expressions (gestural enhancement), of verbal explanation or exc-lamations, or of pantomime to indicate the situational setting in which the desired movement is made may be seen (Goodglass & Kaplan, 1963). Finally, the patient may be aware of what it is he is to do and can describe how to do the action, but he cannot initiate the action on command.

Clues to Mechanisms Underlying Limb Apraxia

Limb Apraxia: A Disorder of the Linguistic Conceptual System

One of the earliest views of limb apraxia was that it represented a form of symbolic disorder. More recently Denny-Brown (1958) coined the term apractagnosia (agnosia for object use) to describe a type of conceptual disorder he thought might underlie some forms of apraxia. While the view that apraxia is a symbolic/ conceptual disorder has been refuted by some (e.g., Kimura, 1977; see Roy, 1982 for a review), others (De Renzi, Pieczuro & Vignolo, 1968; Kertesz, 1979; Roy, 1981, 1983) have provided some support. Evidence that a form of conceptual disorder may underlie apraxia comes from a number of sources. In one line of investigation apractics are asked to indicate whether the actions pantomimed by a model are appropriate for the implement or tool presented. The patient's knowledge or concept of what the correct action looks like, it is reasoned, is reflected in his ability to judge the appropriateness of the presented actions. Using this method Heilman (Heilman, 1979; see also Rothi & Heilman, this volume) found that some apractics (call them group A) accepted as appropriate presented actions which were apractic, like the ones they themselves produced, while other apractics (group B) correctly rejected such actions. Based on these findings Heilman proposed two forms of ideomotor apraxia. One form (group A apractics), he suggested, reflected a disruption to the visuospatial engram for movement and, one might argue, represented a form of conceptual disorder. The other form (group B apractics) was thought to involve more a disruption on the translation of the engram into movements.

More recent work by Roy (1983) also using this method found that apractics clearly know what actions were appropriate and grossly inappropriate, e.g., using a comb as a hammer, but frequently accepted actions depicting body part as object errors, e.g., hitting the table with a closed fist to depict hammering, as appropriate. From this Roy (1983) suggested that part of the reason these apractics make body-part-as-object errors may be due to the fact that they conceptualize these types of action as being correct. Considering the model presented above one might envisage a disruption in effector space relating to the posture and group associated with the object whose use is to be pantomimed.

Another approach to the study of the conceptual basis of apraxia involves assessing the patients knowledge of object function. Work by Whitehouse, Caramazza, and Zurif (1978) and Goodglass and Baker (1976) examining object naming in aphasics, found that patients with Wernicke-type aphasia had difficulty using functional information (how to use an object or what the object is used for) in structuring lexical items. That is, this functional information was not represented completely in their word knowledge. This difficulty integrating functional and perceptual information was thought, in part, to underly the impairment in naming objects. Many patients with apraxia are also aphasic and have damage to posterior cerebral areas similar to that observed in patients described by Goodglass. Some of the difficulty these patients have with demonstrating actions, then, may occur because of a similar problem in using functional information. The disorder described by Goodglass and Baker (1976) involved a disruption of semantic fields, while that thought to be associated with apraxia was termed a disruption of action fields (Roy, 1983).

Roy (1983) has examined the integrity of this functional information using two tasks. In one task the patient is asked to point to objects that serve particular functions named by the examiner, e.g., show me the object used for driving nails into wood. In this task the perceptual referents for the objects pertaining to their function are available to provide rather direct information about object use. The other task requires the patient to evaluate the functional properties of objects with less direct reference to this perceptual information. In one case, for example, the patient must indicate which two objects from a choice of four (a screw driver, a dime, a feather and a pencil) might be used to turn a screw into wood. To answer correctly (the screwdriver and the dime) the patient must understand the functional properties of the objects involved and, in the case of the dime, go beyond its normal function. Preliminary findings indicate that apractics have little difficulty with the first task but frequently make errors in the second task. This selective deficit is suggestive of a disruption in knowledge of object function. Much additional work is required, however, before such a conclusion is warranted.

A third means of assessing the integrity of conceptual processes in apraxia has been used in the context of action sequences. In one series of studies the knowledge of action component is examined. In this task the patients are required to perform a series of actions according to a sequence indicated by an array of action picture cards (see Roy, 1981). While a number of errors were examined, the one of particular interest here concerns what actions are substituted for the correct one when an error is made. In designing the task the individual actions were chosen such that three of them shared features of finger positioning and initial movements, while the fourth was quite dissimilar in these features. Using the notions of categorical memory in free recall (Tulving, 1968) if the patients understand the action concepts involved, then, the errors should involve subsituting actions which are similar to (within the same category as) the one which should have occurred at that point in the sequence and, hence, a preponderance of within-category errors.

In examining three groups of patients (right hemisphere, left hemisphere aphasic and non-aphasic) Roy (1981) found that for the patients (left hemisphere) who made the most errors in learning the sequence the non-aphasics displayed predominantly within-category, i.e., related, substitutions (as did the right hemisphere patients), while the substitutions for the aphasics were evenly distributed between the related and unrelated categories.

These findings argue that the left non-aphasic patients had some concept of the actions involved in the sequence, while the aphasic patients did not. For the non-aphasic subjects the difficulty in sequencing actions did not lie in a poor conceptualization of the actions involved. Rather, the problem may have been more related to the serial ordering of these actions. For the aphasic subjects, on the other hand, the problem in action sequencing may have related to a poor conceptualization of the action elements involved.

Another aspect of knowledge relevant to action sequence which has been examined involves the serial order of actions in the sequence. Poeck (Poeck & Lehmkuhl, 1980) has shown that an apractic patient who was unable to carry out a series of actions correctly also had difficulty in arranging a series of action cards into the appropriate sequence. Similarly, in the movement sequencing task described above Roy (1981) found that patients who were not able to perform the sequence of actions also had difficulty in appropriately arranging a series of action-word cards, each of which contained a word describing an action in the sequence, e.g., push, pull. Subsequent analyses revealed a relatively high correlation (.87) between performance on these alternate versions of the task.

While there is a substantial body of findings which at least suggest that some form of conceptual disorder may underlie limb apraxia, there is also much evidence to counter this view. With regard to single gestures, if apraxia were a symbolic/conceptual disorder, we might reasonably expect that symbolic gestures (e.g., salute; object pantomime gestures) would be more disrupted than nonsymbolic ones, e.g., meaningless hand gestures. Such an expectation is not observed. Both types of gesture seem to be equally affected in apraxia (Kimura & Archibald, 1974). Other research suggests that although unable to accurately pantomime the way to use objects, apractics are frequently able to denote an object's function and to correctly indicate which actions are appropriate and inappropriate for particular objects. With regard to sequences of action while Roy (1981) found that a substantial number of left hemisphere patients, principally aphasics, made random substitutions, suggesting a disruption in the knowledge of action component (see above), an equally large number of left-damaged patients, who were as impaired at learning the sequence as the aphasics, made within-category substitutions which suggested that the knowledge of action component was intact.

Considering all of this evidence it may be that there are two subgroups of apractics: one in which a conceptual disorder contributes substantially to the apractic condition and another in which apraxia is largely independent of a conceptual disorder. Further, it may turn out that the former group is largely composed of patients with a concomittant aphasia involving substantial comprehension problems, while the latter group may be mostly nonaphasic patients or patients with a more expressive-type disorder. Kertesz (see chapter in this volume) has frequently noted the association between comprehension and praxis arguing that the two processes may both, in some way, be associated with a more global conceptual disorder.

Limb Apraxia: A Disorder of the Production System

While the conceptual basis for apraxia has generated considerable research interest, apraxia as a disorder to the production system has been of interest much longer. Three perspectives are prevalent here: apraxia as a disruption to the temporal-sequential programming of action, as a spatial disorder; and as a disorder to fine motor control. Each of these will be discussed in turn.

Temporal-Sequential Disorder. Liepmann (1908) was the first to suggest that apraxia was a movement disorder. The left supramarginal gyrus was seen as the critical region for the control of limb (or oral) movements without objects in which external (visual guidance) control is minimal. Damage to this region resulted in ideational apraxia in which the ideational outline, an idea of the body parts as well as the rhythm, speed and sequence of movements to be used, was thought to be disturbed.

Elaborating on this position Kimura (1977, 1979, 1982) has suggested that the supramarginal region of the left hemisphere contains a system which controls the selection and/or execution of limb positions/postures bilaterally. This control is not exerted over the sequential ordering of positions/postures in an action, but rather over the transition from one position to another.

Heilman (1975, 1979) has proposed a scheme which also alludes to the importance of the supramarginal region of the left hemisphere. Due to the destruction of visuokinesthetic engrams used to program the motor association cortex which innervates the motor neurons pools used to execute the motor act, damage to this area is thought to result in apraxia. "The motor association cortex programs movements (more than one muscle) and visuokinesthetic motor engrams in the parietal cortex program sequences of movement..." (Heilman, 1979, p. 172). Heilman's (1979) emphasis on the importance of the posterior regions of the left hemisphere in limb praxis concurs with Kimura's viewpoint; however, the mechanism he alludes to may be different. The sequencing of movements and external visual guidance seem to be features of his scheme.

For Luria apraxia may result from disorders to the input (afferent apraxia) to the system or to the output from the system (efferent apraxia). Damage in the parietal-occipital areas was thought to result in afferent apraxia. The analysis of spatial coordinates within which movement takes place is disrupted with lesions in these regions. Action disintegrates primarily with respect to the spatial organization of action, impairing performance of practic activity. Damage in the anterior regions of the cerebrum also precipitated apraxia (frontal and premotor apraxia), but for different reasons. The prefrontal areas were thought to play an important role in integrating afferent information, in the regulation of action by speech and in directing the behavioural act toward the goal, i.e., planning. The premotor area of the frontal region, on the other hand, was thought important in the organization of action over time. It was thought particularly important in actions requiring the sequencing of different movements over time (cf. Haaland et al., 1980). In this case apraxia was seen more as an output disorder (Luria, 1966, 1973).

Elaborating on Luria's views Roy (1978) suggested that apraxia involved disturbances to one or more functions in a cognitive, information-processing system. Damage to the frontal or parietal-occipital areas disrupts planning, while damage to the premotor and sensorimotor regions disturbs the execution of action, either in terms of the sequence of a number of movements (premotor damage) or poor control over isolated movements in a sequence (sensorimotor damage).

More recent work by Roy (Roy, 1981; Roy & Elfeki, 1979) has examined action sequencing disorders using tasks involving sequential finger or arm actions. In one study Roy and Elfeki (1979) found that left hemisphere patients made significantly more errors in a finger sequencing task, particularly in a condition in which visual monitoring of the fingers was prevented. In a more recent study (Roy, 1981) the task required the patient to learn a sequence of four arm actions. As Kimura (1977) had found fewer left hemisphere patients learned to correctly sequence the actions, and for those who did learn the task, significantly more trials were taken to do so. An examination of various types of errors revealed, as Kimura had found, that the left hemisphere patients made more perseverative errors than the right hemisphere group. Further analyses of these perseverations revealed something of the nature of these errors.

Analyses of the serial position of the point of origin of these perseverations as well as the number of times an action was repeated showed a trend which was somewhat different for the aphasic and non-aphasic left hemisphere patients. For the non-aphasic patients, perseverations originated equally often from each position in the sequence, and these patients tended to repeat an action only once. The aphasic subjects, on the other hand, tended to have higher order perseverations such that the frequency of repeating an action twice or even three times (the maximum number in this task) was much higher than in the non-aphasics. As a result perseverative errors originated at the first two positions more frequently in this group. Disruption to a mechanism concerned with transitions between postures or positions in a sequence, then, seems most exemplified in only one of these left hemisphere groups, the aphasics.

Additional insight into the nature of perseverative errors was enabled by comparing performance in the action sequencing task with a comparable task which required the patient to place a series of action-word cards in the appropriate sequence. The motor or action component was reduced in this task but the conceptual component remained. In this task the left hemisphere patients made a number of sequencing errors comparable to that observed in the action sequencing task. Perseverations were, however, dramatically reduced, suggesting that perseverations were not apparently conceptual in origin. The patient did not repeat actions because of a persistence of the "idea" of the previous action. Rather, perseverations appear to be a motor phenomenon, since they were apparent almost exclusively when action was involved (see Roy, 1983).

Analyses of sequencing errors was also revealing as to the nature of motor control processes. One analysis involved classifying sequencing errors in terms of their complexity. A "simple" error was one in which one action was in the wrong order and the wrong position in the sequence. Errors involving higher position/order combinations were considered "complex". Examination of the pattern of these errors revealed that a significantly larger proportion of complex errors were made by the left hemisphere group. Using this measure of complexity, then, it appears that damage to the left hemisphere is associated with a more severe deficit in the sequential ordering of actions, implicating the role of the left hemisphere in the control of the serial ordering of actions (see Roy, 1983).

Finally, Kelso and Tuller (1981) provide an approach derived from the notion that the motor system is organized heterarchically, i.e., there is no one executor or controller, and involves a coalitional style of control based on a dynamic interface between the performer and the environment (see Turvey, Shaw & Mace, 1978). One of the cornerstones of this view of the motor system is that of tuning, whereby supraspinal influences bias or change brainstem and spinal organization to provide the 'postural context' in which a circumscribed class of movements may occur. In their view apraxia may result from brain insults which disrupt these supraspinal influences on brainstem and spinal organization, preventing the patient from specifying the appropriate postural context for actions he is requested to perform.

Spatial Disorder. One type of error frequently seen when the patient is demonstrating how to use an object involves improper spatial orientation of objects and movements. The object (if it is to be grasped in the examination) may be held in an orientation which is not appropriate for its use, e.g., a pencil is held with the eraser end on the writing surface. In other cases the object may be oriented appropriately, but the movements are in the wrong spatial plane. The crucial importance of spatial orientation to effective action is exemplified in these errors. The spatial errors apparent in the apractic suggest that both of the spatial coordinate systems (object and effector space) alluded to in the previous section are disrupted.

In attempting to understand these errors it will be recalled that apractics usually recognize that a depicted action is spatially incorrect, suggesting that the difficulty in generating actions which are aligned correctly in space is not due to a disorder in the conceptual system, but rather a disorder in the production system. The patient is unable to generate the necessary metric constraints on the neuromuscular system so that the correct movement pattern is produced. Some evidence originally reported by Semmes, Weinstein, Ghent and Teuber (1963) and alluded to more recently by Kimura (1979) relates damage to the left hemisphere, the pathology most frequently seen in apraxia, to a disorder in egocentric or body-centred space which may contribute to this problem. Since many patients are able to perform an action to imitation, it seems that when spatial information (body-relevant consequences of action) is provided by the examiner the patient seems able to generate the necessary constraints.

Disruption to Fine Motor Control. Heilman (1975) has characterized the movements of the apractic patient as being clumsy or lacking in fine control. He employed a rapid single finger tapping as a measure of fine control. He found the average rate of tapping to be significantly lower in his apractic than in his nonapractic patients. Others (Haaland et al., 1980; Kimura, 1979; Pieczuro & Vignolo, 1967) examining this aspect of fine control using tapping and other tasks, e.g., screw rotation, have found no differences between left and right hemisphere patients nor between apractics and non-apractics. Further, Kimura (1979) reported that the deficit in manual dexterity was not bilateral in patients with left hemisphere damage but was apparent in the hand contralateral to the damaged hemisphere and was associated with somatosensory loss.

These more recent findings suggest that a deficit in manual dexterity may not be an indication of a disruption to this praxis control system in the left hemisphere, although this difficulty with fine motor control undoubtedly contributes to the problems experienced by the apractic in manipulating objects and tools. Rather, these fine control deficits would seem to represent a disorder at a relatively low level in the production system concerned with the fine details of movement production.

Mechanisms Controlling Motor Speech Production

Theoretical models of speech production have been traditionally developed from assumptions underlying linguistic theory. As such, motor speech production has been thought to be governed by the linguistic conceptual system. This supposition in turn, has dictated that most theoretical models of language-speech production be organized hierarchically. In other words, until recently, the major question regarding the production of speech has been, "How does language control the speech process?".

A traditional representation of these philosophies is depicted in Figure 1. Implicit within this model are the assumptions that cognition supersedes all other aspects of the process. From the cognitive processes comes an idea which the speaker wishes to express. Lexical items and grammatical rules are selected to express the idea. Next a phonological representation of the segments of the message is developed which, in turn, dictates what the spatial goals of the vocal tract will be. This plan or blue-print for the vocal tract goals which is based upon the distinctive features of the phonological representation is executed neuromotorically. This results in certain speech muscle contractions and movements of the vocal tract. The entire process results in a listener perceiving a message based upon his proficiency to analyse the acoustic signal emitted from the speaker's mouth. If the listener wishes to respond the entire top-down process is assumed to be repeated from conceptualization through production of an acoustic signal. In other words, verbal communication has traditionally been thought to be linguistically programmed and, in particular, motor speech production has been thought to be governed by the phoneme and its features.

Two major criticisms follow from such models. The first criticism is derived from the assumption that motor speech production is dictated almost completely by open-loop top-down control. The second criticism centres on the concept of invariant phonological features which dictate motor speech production irrespective of environmental or contextual constraints. The concept of invariant phonological features has been developed from linguistic description and theory and the reality of such constructs has not been proved. That is, we know neither the status of the reality of phonemes nor that these linguistic units possess neuromuscular correlates (MacNeilage, 1973). Moll, Zimmermann and Smith (1977) succinctly review the literature which demonstrated that neither acoustic, articulatory, nor muscle action potential studies has been able to substantiate the reality of invariant linguistic units, which are purported to drive the speech motor system in traditional top-down control models. That is, variation, not invariance results in the measurement of output and thus the concept of invariant central rules (i.e., phonemes) has been argued.

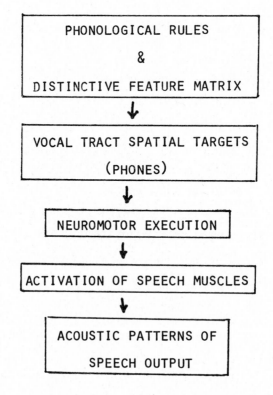

HIERARCHICAL SPEECH PRODUCTION PROCESS

PHONOLOGICAL RULES
&
DISTINCTIVE FEATURE MATRIX

VOCAL TRACT SPATIAL TARGETS
(PHONES)

NEUROMOTOR EXECUTION

ACTIVATION OF SPEECH MUSCLES

ACOUSTIC PATTERNS OF
SPEECH OUTPUT

Figure 1.   Traditional Conceputalization of Hierarchical Control of
Speech Production

An alternative model of motor speech control has been proposed by MacNeilage

(1970). His model assumes that vocal tract postures result not from linguistic (phoneme) commands but instead from commands which delineate spatial targets based upon an internalized quantum knowledge of the vocal tract. MacNeilage stated, "the essence of the speech production process is not an inefficient response to invariant central signals, but an elegantly controlled variability of response to the demand for a relatively constant end" (p. 184). However, he highlighted that these spatial targets are achieved predominantly via open loop control and are "... 'known' independently of any peripheral contingency" (p. 190). Thus, while traditional motor theories of speech production assume phoneme and distinctive feature control (Liberman, Cooper, Harris, MacNeilage & Studdert-Kennedy, 1967; Stevens & Halle, 1967), the model proposed by MacNeilage assumes spatial target commands. Nevertheless, both types of models assume primarily top-down and predominantly open-loop control.

The question as to whether the command system for motor speech production is phonemically based or based upon spatial targets is unresolved. Nevertheless, it cannot be argued that language, to a large degree, does not control motor speech production. Most evidence has come from research concerning spoonerisms (Boomer and Laver, 1968; Nooteboom, 1969; MacKay, 1970; Fromkin, 1971) and word blends (Fromkin, 1971; Hotopf, 1980). By definition, a spoonerism is a transposition of the segments of speech, usually of phoneme size, which may be close in approximation or occur over a considerable stretch of speech. An example offered by Garrett (1982) is, "And this is the larietal pobe" (parietal lobe). A further example is "tasted the whole worm" for "wasted the whole term" Papp, 1975). Word blends, on the other hand, involve the combination of phonological elements from two lexical items which are roughly antonymic. Garrett (1982) offered three such examples: "Dinner is ret" (ready/set) "... more protein than meef" (meat/beef), and "... burnt out cimber" (cinder/ember).

Both spoonerisms and word blends are thought to result from linguistic selection errors. It may very well be that the level of linguistic selection has inherent attentional demands which are ignored when such errors occur. Both phenomena appear to result from the erroneous selection of appropriate phonological features and rules (see Figure 1) or the translation of these phonological features into spatial targets. However, the errors most likely arise from malfunctions of higher levels. Spoonerisms may result from faulty phrase/sentence level selectional processes (Garrett, 1982) while word blend errors may result from faulty lexical selectional processes.

That it is the higher levels of language ordering, i.e., above the theoretical phonological level, which result in these speech errors can be substantiated by several examples offered by MacNeilage and MacNeilage (1973). In fact, the supposition is that morphophonemic rules and phonological rules renormalize sequences which are incorrectly structured at higher levels. At the morphological/phonological level consider the following anomalous and renormalized sequences: "a Kice ream cone" for "an ice cream cone". The form of the indefinite article was changed in the erroneous utterance to be consistent with a noun initiated by a consonant. Further at the phonological level consider "flay the pictor" for "play the victor" in which the transposed "v" was changed to an unvoiced "f" since "fl" occurs in English but "vl" never does. Thus, it may be that lexical and syntactic selection processes demand attention. However, once selection errors have been made at these levels, phonological and morphological rules renormalize the utterance and this may occur independent of attention.

The above examples are just a few of many which lend credence to the importance of language and cognitive processes such as attention for the control of motor speech. However, as Kelso and Tuller (1981) point out, the concept of hierarchical organization presumes two tenets, the linear chaining of events and unidirectionality of information flow which in turn dictates content independence. The notion of the linear chaining of events presumes a unidirectionality of information flow from the control program to the periphery. Evidence that at least some aspects of speech production such as the initiation of speech (MacNeilage, Krones & Hanson, Note 3), the coordination of several speech articulators which act simultaneously (Abbs & Netsell, 1970), and the ability of the articulators to reach certain static articulatory targets or positions when orosensory deprivation (Lindblom, McAllister & Lubker, Note 4) or resistance to movement is mechanically applied (Folkins & Abbs, 1975) have all highlighted the importance of feedback in the motor control of speech. Thus, the concept of linear cha ning dictated by the principles of hierarchical organization cannot be accepted with regard to motor speech production.

The concept that speech movements occur independent of the phonemic context in which they occur also cannot be supported. Measurements of articulatory position (Gay, 1977; Kent & Moll, 1972; MacNeilage & DeClerk, 1969), acoustic signals (Ohman, 1966, Stevens & House, 1963), and electromyographic activity (Fromkin, 1965; Gay, 1977; Harris et al., 1968) have all shown that speech sounds may be differentially produced based upon the phonemic environment, i.e., context, in which they occur. These findings directly refute models of control like the one depicted in Figure 1 which assume invariant phonemic commands and hierarchical, top-down control. Further, these findings indirectly highlight the importance of feedback in the control of motor speech production.

The most obvious examples of bottom-up control include the effects of speech production which derive from environmental influences which occur both naturally or which are experimentally applied. It is a well-known fact that when a speaker must compete with environmental noise, he automatically increases the loudness of his speech. Reduced pitch variation and a slightly higher overall pitch also result. This phenomenon is known as the Lombard effect and is accompanied by physiological readjustments to the respiratory and laryngeal/pharyngeal mechanism as well as to the articulators of the oral cavity during speech production (Ladefoged, 1972). Similar changes can be induced experimentally by applying masking to speakers' ears, thereby eliminating the effect of self-monitoring of speech production by the speaker. Among stutterers, masking has been shown to decrease the frequency of dysfluencies (Chase & Sutton, 1968; Ham & Steer, 1967; Wingate, 1970) probably because of the physiological readjustments to the speech mechanism which occur as the speaker tries to overcome the masking rather than the lack of auditory monitoring per se (Adams & Moore, 1973).

The effects of delayed auditory feedback (DAF) on motor speech production must also be considered when speaking to the topic of the role of auditory feedback on motor speech production. When normal speakers receive delayed feedback (100 to 400 msec) of their own speech, dysfluencies in the form of aberrant syllable durations and phonation/time ratios and longer reading times, as well as increased reading errors occur (Ham & Steer, 1967; Logue, Note 5; Neelley, 1961). Thus, it appears that when the temporal relationships between speech production and auditory self-monitoring are disrupted, the motor speech control mechanism malfunctions especially with regard to the regulation of fluency or prosody of speech output.

Masking and delayed auditory feedback highlight the role of audition in bottom-up control of motor speech production. Both of these environmental disruptions, when abruptly applied, result in gross changes in speech output. However, it is interesting to note that within the adventitiously deaf population and especially among those who have incurred sudden deafness, immediate changes in speech output, other than slight changes in loudness, never occur. Although articulation errors, especially distortions of the more finely controlled speech sounds and slight changes in place of articulation, may develop gradually after loss of hearing, speech motor control, at least as judged perceptually, appears to remain fairly well intact. Thus, although DAF and masking studies have demonstrated that audition plays a role in control of motor speech production, studies of adventitiously deaf adults indicate that audition may be relatively unimportant to the control of speech output once the speech learning process is complete.

The speech production control mechanism has also been shown to respond to environmental demands which disrupt orosensory feedback. Scott and Ringel (1971) experimentally demonstrated the perceptual and acoustical effects of reduced oral sensation on speech output. Application of Xylocaine which eliminated sensation of the oral surface receptors resulted in distortions of those speech sounds which required the finest motor control as well as slight changes in lip and tongue postures. Thus it appears that once speech has been learned, pathophysiological changes which disrupt either audition or oral sensation result only in the deterioration of the most refined gestures needed for distinct speech production and in slight changes in posturing or targeting. However, none of these changes are pronounced enough to jeopardize intelligibility, i.e., understandability.

Several further studies have helped to delineate the nature of orosensory feedback in the control of motor speech production. Gay and Turvey (1979) found that subjects were able to produce appropriate vocal tract configurations and acoustic outputs for isolated vowels after application of oral topical anesthesia. However, Abbs (1973) reported aberrations in speech production of CVC syllables when dynamic measurements of jaw displacement, velocity, and acceleration were taken after selective anesthetization of the mandibular branch of the trigeminal nerve. Although it may be disputed that such anesthetization selectively disrupted the gamma motor system, results of this sensory disruption experiment clearly demonstrated aberrations for the imitation of speech movements as well as demonstrating the contributory role of feedback in the facilitation of movements which demand relatively larger values of acceleration, velocity and displacement. That closed loop control is particularly active during the initiation of speech at least with regard to jaw position has also been established by MacNeilage et al. (Note 3).

The role of feedback in the control of speech production has also been investigated under conditions of disruption of the physiological environment due to application of biomechanical forces. Folkins and Abbs (1975) studied the effects of various resistive loadings to the jaw by physiologically monitoring changes in the labial-mandibular-lingual system during speech production. In general it was found that resistive loads to the jaw resulted in reciprocal compensation by other speech articulators, especially the lips. Further, it was speculated that supraglottal feedback may possibly even affect motor control of the larynx since voice offset time was delayed during some jaw loading conditions. It was proposed that on-line afferent feedback probably contributes to the intercoordination of the organs of speech in that the motor control system makes dynamic and instantaneous adaptations to peripheral changes in the state of the speech mechanism. Thus, motor equivalence as measured by movement reciprocity of the speech articulators is observed.

Lindbloom et al. (Note 4) have also reported on the effects of biomechanical changes to the oral region and the effect on speech. Productions of isolated vowels under the condition of significantly abnormal jaw productions were essentially normal in quality indicating that compensatory adjustments to biomechanical constraints were accomplished by the oral mechanism probably due to afferent feedback. Further, when the same biochemical constraints were applied in conjunction with oral topical anesthesia, several trial-and-error attempts were needed by subjects before appropriate acoustical outputs and vocal tract configurations were achieved. Most probably, the auditory system compensated for orosensory depriva- tion. Thus, it is clear that closed loop feedback is an integral aspect of motor speech control. Further, it appears that the central program interacts with periph- eral feedback and, most probably, gamma loop control to produce a refined speech output. As Abbs (1973) pointed out in his review of the literature on gamma loop control, gamma motoneurons not only operate on a peripheral level correcting length errors between extrafusal and intrafusal muscle fiber systems. Most likely, gamma motoneurons also communicate information via cortical-cerebellar-cortical interconnections for further refinements of cortical activity. Thus, central linguis- tic programs may be reciprocally and concurrently affected at both central and peripheral levels by peripheral feedbacks in a coalitional style of control. In other words, reciprocal boundaries as dictated by both initial posture and the required movement are established and utilized coalitionally to produce accurate speech movements (Kelso & Tuller, 1981).

Perkell (1980) proposed a model of coalitional control in which central phonetic features were constrained by context. The basic aspects of his model are depicted in Figure 2. The central component labelled the feature matrix provides for the speech segments (S)1, i.e., phonemes, their corresponding distinctive features (F) and the durations (D) of suprasegmental aspects of speech. It is assumed within this model that the distinctive features of speech sounds have corresponding sensory goals.[1] These sensory goals are static in nature but are translated into a sensory goal "score" similar to a musical score. Figure 3 elaborates this aspect of the model and highlights the dynamic coalitional controls utilized in motor speech production. In this Figure, the "Look Ahead" box represents the strategies employed in anticipa- tory coarticulation (Henke, 1967). Previous research has demonstrated that the speech mechanism may respond to an upcoming segment (phone), in some cases, up to four phones before the target occurrence (Daniloff & Moll, 1968). By utilizing scanning ahead procedures of upcoming linguistic units, the system sets sensory goal urgencies for upcoming linguistic units, i.e. the system makes adaptations. Thus, it is at this level that the invariant segmental central command (i.e., the phoneme) loses its invariance.

At the level of Intergoal Reorganization, each of the feature specified sensory goals and the sensory urgencies are reorganized thereby producing "overlapping effects of different goals on the same articulator" (Perkell, 1980, p. 360). Each articulator (i.e., tongue, lips, jaw, velum) is commanded to achieve a certain muscle tension via feature-to-sensory-goal transformation. However, due to intergoal reorganization, the "effects sum to produce a single articulatory target or motor goal for each articulator" (Perkell, 1980, p. 360). Of course, it is these spatial goals which correspond to MacNeilage's articulatory targets.

It should be noted that throughout this process peripheral and internal feedback is being used to provide constraints for operations at each level. In particular, how- ever, it should be noted that at the level of intergoal reorganization, participation of the gamma motor system may be especially important. Perkell (1980) explains

---

[1] This hypothesis is developed further by Stevens and Perkell (1977). For example, all speech sounds which are produced by creating a narrow constriction at some point along the vocal tract in which pressure is built up behind the constriction are noted as (+obstruent), the distinctive feature. This distinctive feature has the correlated sensory goal of heightened intraoral pressure which is estimated as 100 to 200 grams over the pharyngeal region of the tongue surface and somewhat greater than this amount on all pharyngeal surfaces. Thus, the sensory goal for (+obstruent) would be heightened intraoral pressure.

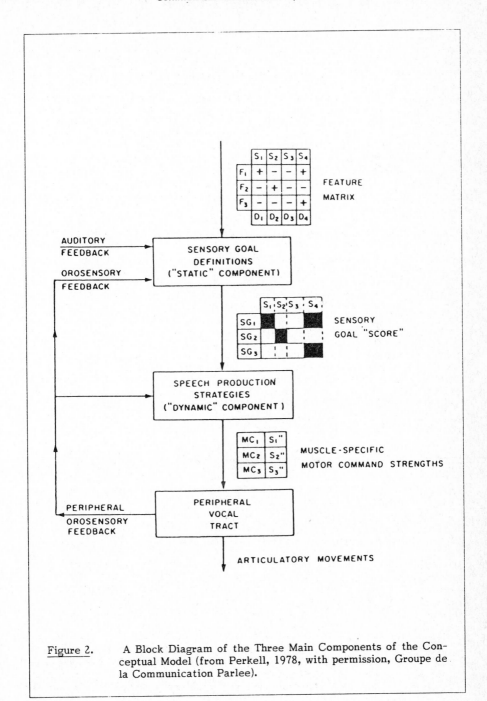

Figure 2.   A Block Diagram of the Three Main Components of the Conceptual Model (from Perkell, 1978, with permission, Groupe de la Communication Parlee).

that the reorganizational process involves knowledge of the relationship of the sen-

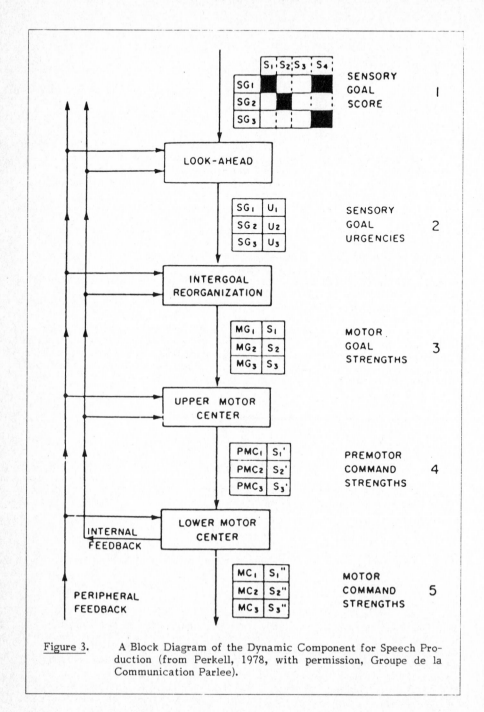

Figure 3.   A Block Diagram of the Dynamic Component for Speech Pro-
              duction (from Perkell, 1978, with permission, Groupe de la
              Communication Parlee).

sory goals (which are static) and the actual positions of the articulators based upon muscle tension feedback. Speculating even further, one structure which may be responsible for the mixing of the sensory goals, sensory urgencies, and knowledge of current states or positions of the articulators is the cerebellum which has been shown to receive gamma motoneuron information (Ruch, Patton, Woodbury & Towe, 1967).

The mixing process at the level of intergoal reorganization results in continuously changing motor goal strengths. The conversion of the dynamically changing motor goals to motor commands is also dependent upon feedback for it is at this level that further adjustments are made based upon the current state of the system. It is because of moment-to-moment adjustments that motor equivalence occurs in speech such that reciprocity between articulators rather than invariant specific targets for each articulator is observed in repeated productions of a specific speech segment (Hughes & Abbs, 1976). Finally, it is the motor goal strengths which feed into the development of premotor commands. Also, it is speculated that, at this level, closed loop feedback is utilized to both elaborate and correct errors in the premotor commands before these are translated into motor commands.

The robustness of the model developed by Perkell (1980) resides in the facts that it considers environmental constraints upon the process of speech production both with regard to articulatory context, i.e., phonemic environment, and the biomechanical and positional constraints as dictated by the production systems, itself. Of course, not considered are environmental effects on higher linguistic processes, i.e., verbal formulation, release of verbal stereotypies, etc. which are also integral aspects of the productive process but which precede actual motor speech control processes. The appeal of the productive model by Perkell (1980) is that it provides for a fit between content (phonemic rules) and context (environments) and allows for viable constraints of each upon the other at various levels resulting in coalitional organization of control of the speech process (Kelso & Tuller, 1981).

Verbal Apractic Errors

Apraxia of speech has been defined by Darley (Note 6) as, "An articulatory disorder resulting from impairment, as a result of brain damage, of the capacity to program the positioning of speech musculature and the sequencing of muscle movements for the volitional production of phonemes... Prosodic alterations may be associated with the articulatory problem, perhaps in compensation for it." This definition highlights the two salient features of erroneous verbal output among apractic patients - articulatory errors and prosodic abnormalities. Both of these error types will be considered individually in the discussion which follows with special consideration given to those studies which have relied on perceptual analysis of errors versus those which have instrumentally studied the errors of apractic subjects.

Articulatory Errors - Perceptual Analysis. In the late 1960's a resurgence of interest in Broca's aphasia occurred among linguists, speech pathologists and speech scientists. In particular, interest in the analysis of articulatory errors, i.e., errors in speech sound production, pervaded. Fry (1959), Shankeweiler and Harris (1966), Johns and Darley (1970), Poncet, Degos, Deloche, and LeCours (1972), Trost and Canter (1974) and LaPointe and Johns (1975) were among the first to report on the articulatory characteristics of apraxia of speech. These early studies attempted to determine the relative frequencies of consonant and vowel errors; the types of errors which most frequently occurred, i.e., substitution, omission, distortion, and/or addition; errors as they occurred with regard to place of consonant articulation and manner of consonant articulation; errors as they occurred with regard to the complexity of phonological context; and consistency and predictability of errors.

These early studies indicated that consonant production was predominately erroneous although vowel errors did occur. Further, substitution errors were observed far more frequently than other error types, i.e., omission, distortion, and/ or addition. With regard to the classes of consonants most likely affected by erroneous production, fricatives (s, z,ʃ,ʒ, f, v) and affricates (tʃ,dʒ) were found to be particularly vulnerable although other classes of speech sounds were found also to be in error especially when they occurred in a complex phonetic context. Further voicing errors usually in the direction of voiceless for voiced occurred although this finding of direction was not consistent across studies (LaPointe & Johns, 1975). Concerning velar coordination, oral/nasal errors rarely occurred (Trost, Note 7).

Place of articulation was found to be significantly more frequently affected than manner of articulation. In particular, tongue tip sounds (apicoalveolar) and lip sounds (bilabial) were most often preserved, while consonants produced at other points along the vocal tract were less well preserved and most frequently, if produced erroneously according to the place dimension, were off by one place. With regard to phonetic environment, apractic speakers were more likely to err on phonemes which occurred in more complex environments such as consonant clusters or polysyllabic words than those which occurred in simple environments. Further, although erroneous substitutions were more likely to be closely related to the target in that they usually differed by only one phonetic feature, some substitutions appeared to be more complex than the intended production.

With regard to the position in which most errors occurred, the initial position was more frequently erroneous than other positions when all initiative attempts at an utterance were analysed. However, when errors of just the final utterance were tabulated, initial articulatory errors were not found to predominate (LaPointe & Johns, 1975; Square, 1981).

Apractic speakers demonstrated highly inconsistent speech output in that phonemes were sometimes produced correctly and sometimes not and this variability was frequently related to phonemic content. While the ability of apractic speakers to predict errors was found to be an individual characteristic, ability to recognize erroneous productions was a group characteristic (Deal & Darley, 1972).

With regard to the sequential aspects of phoneme production, LaPointe and Johns (1975) reported that 7% of all errors committed by their subjects were sequential and that anticipatory errors outnumbered perseverative errors by a ratio of 6:1. In their study, errors of metathesis rarely occurred. However, the stimuli which were used in this study were single words. Sasanuma (Note 8) reported that 71% of the oral reading errors of one apractic subject were sequential errors while 20% were random substitutions and 9% were additions, omissions and repetitions. A higher proportion of sequential errors is also found among normal subjects engaged in oral reading. However, it seems unlikely that the 71% of sequential oral reading errors reported by Sasanuma were due totally to mode of stimulus input.

A more recent perceptual study has added to our knowledge of the vowel articulatory characteristics of apraxia of speech. Keller (1978) reported on the analysis of vowel substitution errors among apractic speakers. Distinctive feature analyses revealed a "...strong tendency for lower vowels to replace higher targets" (p. 265) and for substitutions to be closely related to the target, a finding also reported for consonant substitutions (Blumstein, 1973a,b; Johns & Darley, 1970; Martin & Rigrodsky, 1974; Trost & Canter, 1974).

Controversy surrounding the theoretical interpretation of the articulatory characteristics of apraxia of speech has raged in the literature and will be discussed fully in a subsequent section. However, it is imperative to mention at this point that this controvery exists primarily because subjects studied have been aphasic as well as apractic, i.e., Broca's aphasic, anterior putamel, and conduction aphasic patients. In fact in all the aforementioned studies, subjects used were aphasic-apractic although cases of "pure apraxia" or "pure anarthria" have been repeatedly cited in the literature (Alajouanine, 1952; Alajouanine, Omberdane, & Durand, 1956; Benson & Geschwind, 1971; Brown, 1972; Goodglass & Kaplan, 1972; Lebrun et al., 1973; LeCours & Lhermitte, 1976).

Only two studies of perceptual analyses of the articulatory characteristics of pure apractic patients have been reported (Mlcoch, Note 9; Square, Note 10). In her analysis of both the articulatory and prosodic deviances evidenced in single-word production under four different modes of stimulus presentation among four pure apractic subjected, Square (Note 10) reported results similar to those cited above. However, one important difference in results emerged; the pure apractic subjects were found to make more errors of distortion than substitution. This result emerged due to perceptually distinguishable vowel distortions; voicing delays and/or devoicing delays of consonants; fricative and affricate distortions; and velar-articulatory incoordination, i.e., assimilative nasality or delayed or premature nasalization. Although the results reported by Square (Note 10) were consistent with instrumental data which will be discussed below, she speculated that her results may have differed from those reported by investigators who studied aphasic-apractic subjects for two reasons: 1. vowel and consonant errors were considered collectively in the study by Square, and 2. substitutions may predominate in the speech of mixed patients due to the combined effects of aphasia plus apraxia of speech.

Mlcoch (Note 9) perceptually studied the speech output of three of the pure apractic subjects used by Square (Note 10) as well as three additional subjects. Error frequency, consistency and variability were analysed within the contexts of three types of connected speech, self-formulated, oral reading, and automatic recitation. Results indicated that essentially the same number of articulation errors as well as the same degree of error consistency and variability occurred on all three samples of speech. Unlike previous studies where word length and difficulty of initial phoneme were found to be positively correlated to occurrences of errors, subjects of this study did not demonstrate this effect. It appeared that the use of contextual speech versus isolated word cancelled these effects. Further, subjects, especially severe ones, tended to err in consistant phonetic contexts across conditions. A similar finding was previously reported for oral reading by five minimally aphasic but apractic subjects (Deal, 1974). Nevertheless, the variability of the error was greater in difficult phonetic contexts such as polysyllabic words versus monosyllabic words, a finding also consistent with previous research in which aphasic-apractic subjects were asked to repeat monosyllabic words (Johns & Darley, 1970).

Articulatory Errors - Instrumental Analyses. Recently, speech output and control mechanisms of aphasic-apractic speakers have been subjected to instrumental analyses. Acoustic measurements (spectrographic analyses), as well as physiological measurements (EMG, fiberoptics, x-ray microbeam tracking, and movement transducers) have been undertaken. Early spectrographic studies focussed on voice onset and offset times, collectively referred to as VOT studies (Blumstein, Cooper, Zurif & Carramazza, 1977; Blumstein, Cooper, Goodglass, Statlender & Gottlieb, 1980; Dibrell & Marquardt, Note 11; Freeman, Sands & Harris, 1978; Jaffee & Duffy, Note 12; Sands, Freeman & Harris, 1978). Voice onset times for production of both voiced, e.g., "b", "d", and "g", and voiceless, e.g., "p", "t" and "k", stop consonants among normal adult speakers have been long established and the times for these two categories of sounds do not overlap (Lisker & Abramson, 1964, 1967). Among apractic speakers, however, it has been found that voicing times of these two classes of sounds often fall between the two well-established dichotomous ranges (voiced and unvoiced) as well as within the two ranges. This, of course, is what Square reported as "hearing" and classified as distortions in the speech of her pure apractic subjects. The overlap of timing ranges of these two classes of sounds, as well as an overall compressed range of times and the variability in repeated productions among apractic speakers have lead most of the VOT researchers to conclude that apractic speakers are impaired and extremely variable in their abilities to temporally coordinate laryngeal (air flow phonation) with supralaryngeal (articulation) events.

Other acoustic studies have analysed the durational aspects of both consonants and vowels (Bauman, Wangler & Prescott, Note 13; Di Simoni & Darley, 1975; Gawle & Duffy, Note 14; Kent & Rosenbek, 1982; Lebrun, Buyssens & Henneaux, 1975). Each of these studies have indicated that apractic speakers produce abnormal durations of consonants and/or vowels and these durations have generally found to be abnormally long. Further, these studies have also highlighted the salient feature of intra-subject variability.

The dimensions of variability and inability to temporally coordinate and sequence speech movements have also been reported in physiological studies which have been specifically designed to observe the dynamic movement of the articulators during speech production. Itoh, Sasanuma, and Ushijima (1979) observed the movements of the velum during production of meaningful and nonmeaningful linguistic materials using fiberoptics. Velar movements of the apractic subject studied were less regular than those observed in normal subjects. Repetitions of the same utterance revealed that both velar height and segmental durations varied over the repetitions. Thus, although a trend toward normal production was demonstrated in that the velum tended to elevate on oral consonants and depress on nasal consonants, variability of control was a salient feature of production.

Using an x-ray microbeam system to track the movement patterns of the articulators during speech production, Itoh, Sasanuma, Hirose, Yoshioka and Ushijima (1978) determined that the apractic speaker demonstrated an "apparent disorganization in timing among several articulators". Adjunctively, the speaker demonstrated variability in the timing of oral movements over several productions of the same stimulus item.

Electromyographic (EMG) measurements of the speech musculature have also been found to be grossly abnormal among apractic speakers. In an early study, Shankweiler, Harris, and Taylor (1968) used surface EMG while studying five apractic speakers. Not only were the EMG traces found to be grossly abnormal when compared to normals, but they also highlighted the features of intrasubject variability for sequential timing of muscle innervation as well as the abnormal durational qualities present in apractic speech.

Only one study has been undertaken in which simultaneous measures of articulatory movement (using pressure transducers), muscular innervation (EMG) and speech production were made (Fromm, Abbs, McNeil, & Rosenbek, 1982). Results of the study of speech production of one patient indicated antagonistic muscle contraction, continuous and undifferentiated EMG activity, abnormal muscle activity shutdown, movement dyscoordination, and supraglottic articulatory movement in the absence of appropriate laryngeal function, i.e., phonation. The synthesis of this information led Fromm and her colleagues to conclude that apraxia of speech is primarily a disorder of temporal distortion since there was a substantial degree of dyscoordination between articulators and muscle groups. Further, Fromm, et al. interpreted their results as substantiating the theory of apraxia being a disorder of neuromotor execution within both temporal and spatial parameters.

Articulatory Errors Under Imposing Environmental Conditions. Several investigators have studied the effects of imposed environmental conditions upon the speech production of apractic speakers. Deal and Darley (1972) reported the speech production of apractic speakers with minimal aphasia engaged in oral reading did not change significantly when white noise was applied thus preventing the patients from employing auditory self monitoring. Similarly, delayed auditory feedback was reported not to significantly affect articulation, initiation or duration of word production when apractic patients were asked to read lists of words (Lozano & Dreyer, 1979). However, DAF was found to have a significant effect upon the articulation of Broca's aphasic patients when undertaking a variety of verbal expressive tasks (Chapin, Blumstein, Meissner & Boller, 1981). Although this group of patients was most deleteriously affected by DAF, the pattern of articulatory errors demonstrated by this group did not differ from the pattern which the other groups of aphasic patients, i.e., Wernickes, conduction, transcortical sensory, word deafness, demonstrated while performing the same tasks under DAF. Finally, production of speech during oral reading and while under the effects of auditory rhythmic stimulation had no significant effect upon phonemic accuracy among apractic speakers (Shane & Darley, 1978).

Clues to Mechanisms Underlying Verbal Apraxia

A raging controversy has persisted in the literature for at least the last decade and a half regarding the underlying bases of apraxia of speech. Two schools of thought have emerged. Members of the first adhere to the theory that apraxia of speech is a linguistic disorder and as such is an integral part of aphasia (Martin, 1974). Members of the second school believe that the basis of this disorder resides within the motor system, particularly that aspect of the motor system responsible for motor programming (Darley, Aronson & Brown, 1975). The purpose of this section will be to review the literature concerning apraxia of speech first with regard to that which supports a linguistic-conceptual basis. This will be followed by a review of the literature which support a productive dysfunction as the basis of verbal apraxia.

Verbal Apraxia: A Disorder of the Linguistic-Conceptual System

Linguistic models of speech production assume that deviant speech sound production, if not due to muscle weakness, slowness, or incoordination, i.e., dysarthria, is due then to a deviant linguistic rule system at the level at which phonological features and rules are selected (Figure 1). Support for linguistic models of speech control has been derived from investigations of aphasic individuals. In fact those who propose that the disorder of apraxia of speech has as its underlying basis a rule-governed phonological disorder take the view of Goodglass (1975) when he stated, "...it does not work to draw the lower limit of 'language' at word finding and grammatical formulation, and to exclude from aphasia disorders which are chiefly in phonology" (p. 31). Because aphasia is generally accepted as a disorder of irretrievable language rules, all deficits to aspects of symbolic communication including speech sound production are thought to be based within the linguistic-conceptual system.

Evidence which has been offered to support the linguistic nature of the "speech" deficit which so often occurs with aphasia has been derived primarily from the observation that the articulatory substitution errors which occur appear to be rule-governed. For example, the most common substituted manner of articulation for intended fricatives is stop plosives or the most commonly used places of articulation are lingua-alveolar and bilabial. Numerous investigations can be cited in which it has been assumed that apraxia of speech is a linguistic disorder at the phonological level merely because substitutions appear to follow certain patterns thus allowing linguistic "rules" to be written which may account for these articulatory trends (Bauman et al., Note 13; Blumstein, 1973a,b; Fry, 1959; Klich, Ireland & Weidner, 1979; LeCours & Lhermitte, 1969, 1973; Martin & Rigrodsky, 1974a,b). However, such a position appears dangerous at best. First, linguistic theory is being used to substantiate linguistic theory. That is, linguistic theory assumes that speech production is rule-governed at the phonological level. Thus, the ability to write "rules" to explain deviant output is being used as an argument to substantiate the original theory of phonological rules underlying speech production. It may be, however, that consistencies in the articulatory substitutions of many dysarthric speakers could also be derived such that "linguistic" rules may appear sufficient to explain such disorders. In reality, however, dysarthria is due to neuromuscular dysfunction. Second, only one aspect of apractic output has been considered in such studies, i.e., articulatory substitutions. As reviewed in previous sections, articulatory substitutions account only for a small part of the deviant output observed in apractic speech production. And, third, in none of the previous substitution investigations cited were pure apractic subjects studied. All subjects were identified as aphasic patients who also demonstrated apraxia of speech. It will be recalled from the section on verbal apractic errors, that Square (Note 10) and Square et al. (1982) found that articulatory distortions, not substitutions, predominated in the speech of apractic subjects who did not also demonstrate aphasia. Thus, even if one accepts the justification of theory with theory, or substantiation for deviant phonological rule systems because of an orderliness to sound substitutions, it cannot be overlooked that "substitutive" behaviour has been shown not to predominate in the speech of patients with verbal apraxia and little or no coexisting aphasia.

Another line of reasoning used to substantiate the theory that this speech deficit is linguistic in nature has been to investigate the inter-relationships of the linguistic levels of syntax, semantics, and phonology. Martin (1974) proposed that if, in fact, the phonological impairment in aphasia were purely motor in nature, the effects of syntax, lexicon, and semantics should be minimal on articulation. However, in their investigation of lexical influences, Dunlop and Marquardt (1977) found that the abstractness ratings of words were positively related to the incidences of articulatory errors. Further, Hardison, Marquardt and Peterson (1977) found articulatory efficiency to be influenced by semantic and syntactic factors. While Dunlop and Marquardt (1977) acknowledged the fact that the "aphasic" component of their subjects' disorders could have influenced performances, Hardison et al. (1977) reported that none of their subjects had significant aphasia. They, however, did not explain how this was determined. Nevertheless, performances were felt to reflect the co-dependencies of various levels of language among normal as well as pathological subjects and to support the fact that speech production deficits among left-hemisphere lesioned patients are more linguistically dependent than motorically dependent.

Another line of reasoning used to support the linguistic-conceptual basis of verbal apraxia has been to compare speech errors made using differing stimulus-input modes which differentially tax linguistic formulation. Farmer, O'Connell and Jesudowich (Note 15) found that Broca's aphasic patients made fewer sound substitution and lexical errors on reading tasks as opposed to correlative confrontation naming tasks. However, Square et al. (1982) reported that although fewer articulatory errors were made by pure apractic patients on reading tasks than on correlative naming tasks, more articulatory errors occurred on a correlative repetition task despite the fact that no speech perceptual deficits could be observed in her patients. Since the repetition task was the least linguistically taxing in the study by Square, the explanation offered by Farmer et al. (Note 15) that the greater demands of linguistic lexical selection, i.e., naming, accounted for the decreased efficiency of articulation cannot be substantiated.

The effects of linguistic load was also studied by Mlcoch (Note 9) and reported by Mlcoch, Darley and Noll (1982). Six pure apractic subjects, i.e., without clinical evidence of aphasia, were asked to recite a memorized passage, read a passage and, describe a series of drawings. It was hypothesized that if, in fact, verbal apraxia was a linguistically-based disorder, deviant articulatory characteristics would increase as psycholinguistic demands increased. The major finding of this study failed to support this linguistic hypothesis. That is, the type of contextual speech task had no significant effect on articulation. No significant differences between the number of articulation errors nor the error consistency nor variability occurred over tasks. Mlcoch (Note 9) concluded that "...the type of articulatory behaviour exhibited by the subjects in this investigation tended to support the idea that apraxia of speech is a motor disorder unaffected by linguistic factors" (p. 164).

Further to this discussion regarding the interaction of linguistic levels and the effect that such an interaction has on articulatory output, our attention should return to spoonerisms and word blends, both of which are thought to occur as the result of linguistic selection errors. It will be recalled from our previous discussion that Garrett (1982) explained that spoonerisms may result from faulty phrase/ sentence level selection processes. It is interesting to note that studies of verbal apractic subjects either with or without aphasia have not been undertaken to determine if either spoonerisms or word blends are more easily elicited among this population than normal speakers. Further, it would be of interest to determine if conduction aphasic subjects, a group of subjects for which a linguistic short-term memory deficit has been proposed as the principle dysfunction underlying this disorder (Warrington & Shallice, 1969; Warrington, Logue & Pratt, 1971) differ from pure apractic and normal subjects. Such an investigation, it would seem, would help to resolve the question as to whether linguistic selection and/or attentional processes underlie the deviant articulatory outputs of these populations of patients.

For now, all that can be stated with regard to phoneme selection processes being disordered is that which can be inferred from errors of phoneme sequencing with regard to anticipation, perseveration and metathesis. It will be recalled that LaPointe and Johns (1975) reported that only seven percent of the substitutive errors made by their apractic speakers could be classified as sequential in nature. Further, anticipatory errors outnumbered perseverative errors by a ratio of 6:1. The incidence of metathetic errors was found to be negligible by LaPointe and Johns (1975) as well as by Square (Note 10).

One line of reasoning may consider errors of phoneme sequencing to be representative of phoneme selection errors at the phonological-rule-selection level of language (Figure 1). However, studies of coarticulatory behaviour among normal subjects (Kent & Moll, 1972; MacNeilage & DeClerk, 1969; Ohman, 1966) have demonstrated that speech production will be modified based upon phonetic context up to four phonemes in advance of actual production of a target (Daniloff & Moll, 1968). An ability to predict and modify production based upon environment seems to indicate preserved phonological knowledge. Because most sequential errors in apractic speech are anticipatory, it would appear that predictive linguistic knowledge is preserved. Further, it may be that this preserved linguistic knowledge is overdriving an impaired motor system thus resulting in errors of articulatory anticipation. Further research in this area is needed.

Other evidence of preserved linguistic knowledge at the phonological level comes from those studies which have shown that apractic speakers follow normal trends of reducing the durations of vowels when they precede voiceless consonants (Gawle & Duffy, Note 14) and in stem words as the words increase in length (Collins, Rosenbek & Wertz, 1983; Fager & Deutsch, Note 16). These trends have been interpreted as evidence that linguistic phonological rules are retained. Intrasubject variability in the context of these trends has been interpreted as further evidence that the disorder represents an impairment of the motoric system, especially with regard to temporal aspects of motor control.

The evidence to date is neither robust enough nor complete enough to warrant acceptance of the theory that verbal apraxia is a linguistic-conceptual disorder. In fact, there is more empirical evidence which dictates against this theory than which supports it. Further, the fact that several investigators have identified verbal apractic patients who did not demonstrate clinical evidence of aphasia, i.e., language dysfunction (Brown, 1972; LeCours & Lhermitte, 1976; Mazzocchi & Vignolo, 1979; Mlcoch, Note 9; Mohr et al., 1978; Schiff et al., 1983; Square, Note 10) would indicate that either the phonological rules of language are selectively impaired or that verbal apraxia is not a linguistic-conceptual disorder. Because apractic patients have been found to have retained abilities to perceive subtle phonological differences while not being able to produce them (Blumstein, Cooper, Zurif & Carmazza, 1977; Square, Note 10; Square, Sommers & Darley, 1981), it has been assumed that verbal apraxia is a motoric disorder. That this could be a linguistic-conceptual disorder with a dissociation of analogous linguistic knowledge on the perceptual and productive levels seems implausible.

The facts remain, however, that few pure apractic subjects exist. The majority of patients with left hemisphere damage and a "speech disorder" are aphasic as well. Since aphasia involves inaccessibility to linguistic knowledge, it also seems implausible that the speech disorders which aphasic-apractic patients evidence have a purely productive basis. That is, it would seem likely that the speech disorder would be a combination of a motoric productive disorder plus a linguistic conceptual disorder in patients who demonstrate both aphasia and apraxia of speech.

Some of those who strongly support the theory that apraxia of speech is a motoric disorder imply that all articulatory and prosodic disturbances which accompany aphasia but which are not dysarthric in nature are, in fact, apractic errors with a motor productive basis. Thus, authorities such as Darley (1982), although not adhering to an aphasic classification system, believe that not only the articulatory/ prosodic disturbances associated with Broca's aphasia are of an apractic nature. Those articulatory errors, i.e., phonemic or literal paraphasias, which occur in the context of the fluent output of Wernicke's aphasic patients and those which occur in the context of semi-fluent output and especially worsen during repetition activities and which are thought to be associated with conduction aphasia are also thought to be apractic in nature. In fact, there is empirical data to support this notion. Both oral practic function (DeRenzi et al., 1966; Kimura, 1978; Mateer & Kimura, 1977) and verbal practic-function (Mateer & Kimura, 1977) have been found to be deviant among both fluent and nonfluent patients. This, however, appears extremely plausible in view of the fact that the left parietal region is thought to be responsible for both selection of limb and oral postures (Kimura, 1977, 1979, 1982) and, more importantly, the sequential programming of movement (Heilman, 1979; Kimura, 1981). Since sites of lesion in conduction aphasia almost always involve the parietal lobe and since sites of lesion in Wernicke's aphasia are rarely confined to the superior and posterior borders of the temporal lobe, it seems reasonable to assume that parietal lobe damage would account for at least a partial praxis dysfunction in association with Wernicke's and conduction aphasia.

On the other hand, the articulatory disorders observed among these two groups of patients might also be partially due to linguistic-conceptual dysfunction. This assumption is strengthened by the findings of Blumstein et al. (1977) that both speech perception and production are impaired among patients with posterior lesions and that errors made in production are categorical errors, e.g., "b" versus "p", rather production errors which lie between the two categories of sounds along a continuum.² It is the categorical nature of the errors which seem to support a linguistic-conceptual selection disorder rather than a productive disorder. Thus, among aphasic patients, particularly Wernicke and conduction patients, the articulatory errors observed are probably due to a combination of dysfunction at the linguistic-conceptual and productive levels.

Such is probably the case as well among Broca's aphasic patients. However, the literature supports more strongly a motoric-productive basis than a linguistic-conceptual basis in that intrasubject articulatory productive errors, when measured instrumentally, have been found to be variable and to lie along a continuum rather than being categorical in nature (Blumstein et al., 1977, 1980; Dibrell & Marquardt, Note 11; Freeman et al., 1978; Fromm et al., 1982; Itoh et al., 1979; Jaffee & Duffy, Note 12; Kent & Rosenbek, 1983; Sands et al., 1978). The literature which supports the motor-productive basis of verbal apraxia will be reviewed in the following section.

Verbal Apraxia: A Disorder of the Productive System

Roy (1983) reviewed the literature regarding limb apraxia as a productive disorder with regard to three major areas -- that literature which demonstrated temporal-transitional motor control dysfunction; that which demonstrated dysfunction of spatial orientation; and that which demonstrated disruption of fine motor control. A similar outline will be followed for the discussion of verbal apraxia as a productive disorder.

Temporal/Transitional Motor Control Dysfunction. The literature is replete with evidence which may be interpreted as support for the theory that verbal apraxia is a deficit which is due to dysfunction of the temporal ordering of neural impulses and which results in incoordination of the speech articulators and, thus, deviant speech output (Blumstein et al., 1977, 1980; Freeman et al., 1978; Fromm et al., 1982; Itoh et al., 1975, 1980; Jaffee & Duffy, Note 12; Kent & Rosenbek, 1982; Sands et al., 1978). The majority of these studies have interpreted their instrumental data in such a way as to demonstrate that the linguistic-conceptual selection processes of their subjects remained intact; however, the physiological variability of production of speech indicated that the neuromotor system was either being innervated inconsistently or aberrantly after phonological rules had been selected. Returning to Figure 1, it will be seen that neuromotor execution is believed to occur subsequent to linguistic formulation.

What could account for dysfunction within the realm of neuromotor execution? It has been shown that motor integration involves both cortical and subcortical components (Trevarthan, 1978). Further, historical and contemporary studies of verbal apractic patients have demonstrated that this disorder of speech output may result from lesions to various cortical and subcortical areas including Broca's area (Hecaen & Consoli, 1973; Mazzocchi & Vignolo, 1979; Mohr, et al., 1978); the white

---

² Productions which vary along the continuum between two sound categories such as "p" and "b" are characteristic of Broca's aphasic patients (Blumstein et al., 1977; Freeman et al., 1978) and will be discussed more fully in a subsequent section.

matter immediately deep to Broca's area and including the left basal ganglion, particularly the caudate nucleus, lenticular nucleus, and limb of the internal capsule (Canter, Note 17; Deutsch, Note 18; Luria, 1966; Luria & Huton, 1977; Mazzocchi & Vignolo, 1979; Mohr et al., 1979; Rosenbek et al., 1981; Schiff et al., 1983; Square, Note 10); and/or the parietal lobe (Canter, Note 17; Deutsch, Note 18; Luria, 1966; Luria & Huton, 1977; Square, Note 10). Indeed, it was inferred by Square (1981) and later reported by Square et al. (1982) that differential sites of lesion may have differential effects on speech output among pure apractic patients. Deutsch (Note 18) reported a similar view based upon data collected from aphasic-apractic subjects. The major point to be made here, is one put forth so succinctly by Goodglass and Kaplan (1972) in their discussion of aphemia due to subcortical lesions. They stated that the speech disorder is due to "...an interruption of final outflow of information from Broca's area to the speech effector system without hampering cortical language activity." The intention of this discussion of the neuromotor execution of speech is to take the views of Goodglass and Kaplan (1972) one step further.

As stated previously, Trevarthan (1978) demonstrated that both cortical and subcortical components are involved in motor integration. With regard to speech output, the pathologic literature demonstrates that lesions may occur cortically or subcortically and result in verbal apractic symptomotology and not dysarthria. This should indicate to us that the integrity of communication between neurologic centres is needed in order to maintain a tight temporal patterning of speech movements. As pointed out in our preceeding discussion of mechanisms controlling normal motor speech production, Abbs (1973), among others, has highlighted the importance of cortical-cerebellar-cortical interconnections and the probable participation of gamma motoneuron information in the refinement of cortical motor directives. With specific reference to motor speech output, Rosenbek et al. (1981), described one possible breakdown in this circuitry as resulting in an "ataxico-apractic" symptomotology. In a theoretical discussion, Buckingham (1978) pointed to a need for us to consider verbal apraxia as a disconnection syndrome.

Returning specifically to the temporal aberrations observed in apractic speech, we may cite two major types -- those which seem to represent a breakdown in the tight temporal patterning of two or more articulators (Fromm et al., 1982; Itoh et al., 1979, 1980) and those which appear to be more related to phonetic environment (Kent & Rosenbek, 1982). These latter types of temporal aberrations are represented in several ways: abnormally long steady-state durations of speech sounds and/or transitions between speech sounds and/or inappropriate articulatory hiatuses. In each of these latter cases, however, it appears that the motoric system is incapable of transitionalizing within or between movements. This may in fact be due to disruptions of the neuromotor circuitry. Further, one may speculate that the impaired system requires more time for Intergoal Reorganization as defined by Perkell (1980) in his model of control of motor speech.

One additional aspect of transitionalization must be considered -- that which requires transitions from one action to another in a prescribed order. All experienced clinicians who have worked with verbal apractic patients have observed the great difficulty these patients have on diadochokinetic tests which require repetitions of /pʌtʌkʌ/. Although perseverative (reiterative) errors have not been found to be prevalent in other types of speech tasks, on this particular task, verbal apractic patients appear to demonstrate highly perseverative performances such as "pʌt tʌ...pʌtʌtʌ" or "pʌpʌtʌ...pʌpʌtʌ..." with full awareness of their errors. Mateer and Kimura (1977) in an empirical study reported that on similar diadochokinetic tasks, both fluent and nonfluent aphasic subjects demonstrated significant deficits relative to right- and left-lesioned nonaphasic subjects. These researchers concluded that this impairment was not one of order or sequencing alone but instead represented a deficit in the ability to achieve multiple changes in positioning. In other words, multiple changes in target positioning were difficult due to an inability to transitionalize from one discrete movement to another.

Although the types of errors for such sequenced productions were not fully investigated by Mateer and Kimura (1977) a study of this type appears to be fully warranted. Roy (1981) studied errors made in limb action sequencing conceptualization. Patients demonstrated significantly more errors of perseveration on the former task. The results of this investigation again highlighted the difficulty left-hemisphere lesioned aphasic patients have in the area of transitionalization. More importantly, however, results of Roy's investigation (1981) highlighted the fact that perseverations appear to be a motor phenomenon rather than a linguistic-conceptualization deficit. An investigation of the errors made on diadochokinetic tasks which require multiple target positions among pure apractic as well as aphasic-apractic and aphasic patients would do much to enhance our understanding of the disorder of verbal apraxia especially with regard to our knowledge of neuro-motor transitionalization abilities.

Kelso and Tuller (1981) have very astutely pointed out another aspect of temporal neuromotor execution which may malfunction among apractic patients -- neural pretuning. In connected speech, the preceding phonetic environment provides a boundary condition for subsequent movements. However, in the process of initiating speech, phonetic boundaries are nonexistent. Among normal subjects, however, pretuning of the speech musculature in the form of increased background reflex excitability has been demonstrated (McClean, 1978; Netsell & Abbs, 1975; Since patients with verbal apraxia have unusual difficulty initiating speech as demonstrated by inaudible and audible struggles and phonetic gropes and reapproaches, it may be that either the pyramidal system fails to pretune the brainstem (Kots, 1979) due to neuromotor circuit disconnection or the temporal aspects of this physiological tuning are aberrant. Further research is very much needed in this area in order for us to gleen a better understanding of neuromotor execution among apractic patients.

Spatial Disorientation. Another area which we may look to for providing evidence that verbal apraxia may be a productive disorder is that which indicates that a spatial orientation dysfunction exists. Before reviewing the literature regarding verbal apraxia, let us briefly review those theories of mechanisms controlling normal motor speech production which consider spatial knowledge. The first operates at the conceptual level and consists of spatial target rules rather than phonological rules (MacNeilage, 1970). The second is that which we will be concerned with in this section since its emphasis is on the productive system. That, of course, is the system's use of orosensory feedback in the control of motor speech. Our review of mechanisms controlling normal speech production clearly demonstrated that peripheral feedback is used probably most importantly for intergoal reorganization (Perkell, 1977). Further, this peripheral feedback is probably used in a coalitional style along with internal feedback to constantly reorganize speech production (see Figure 3).

That oral sensory feedback is deviant among verbal apractic subjects has long been recognized (Rosenbek, Wertz, & Darley, 1973; Texiera et al., 1974; Square, Note 19). However, it may be that the significance of this dysfunction has been overlooked.

In his discussion of limb apraxia, Roy (1982) discussed spatial disorientation of the effector surface or effector space as possibly underlying errors in which an action similar to the intended one was produced. A disruption of orosensory feedback, i.e., disruption of spatial information regarding the speech effectors, may also underlie some of the errors of sound substitution in verbal apraxia. For example, many of the substitutive errors observed in apractic speech are produced in the appropriate manner and with appropriate voicing, but in the wrong place of articulation. Thus, an action similar to the intended one is produced but, possibly due to a disruption of effector space, a partially erroneous action results.

Further, it will be recalled that Abbs (1973) reported aberrations in speech initiation and articulatory displacement, velocity and acceleration due solely to orosensory disruption. The fact that similar types of dysfunctions have been noted in the speech of apractic patients (DiSimoni & Darley, 1977; Fromm et al., 1982) should be noted as well as being considered worthy of further investigation.

Disruption of Fine Motor Control. Heilman (1975) reported that among patients with limb apraxia disorders of fine motor control were demonstrated by significantly lower than average rates of finger tapping abilities. Other researchers, however, have reported that patients with and without limb apraxia do not differ significantly on tasks requiring fine motor control (Pieczuro & Vignolo, 1967; Kimura, 1979; Haaland et al., 1980).

A task in speech analogous to finger tapping is diadochokinetic rate for identical targets. Although verbal apractic patients are often found to perform as normal subjects on repetitions of /p / and /t /, rates for repetitions of /k / are often slower than those demonstrated by normal subjects. Kimura (1979) has suggested that slower than normal finger tapping rates among limb apractic subjects were indicative of somatosensory deficits. Following the same line of reasoning, it may be that since the dorsum of the tongue contains fewer sensory receptors than the blade or tip (Sussman, 1972) and since orosensory deficits have been found to often coexist with verbal apraxia (Rosenbek et al., 1973; Square, Note 19), slower rates for repetition of /k / are due to reduced fine motor control.

Roy (1982) stated that "...manual dexterity may not be an indication of a disruption to this praxis control system in the left hemisphere. Nevertheless, this difficulty with fine motor control undoubtedly contributes to the problems experienced by the (limb) apraxic..." (p. 34). It would seem reasonable to postulate the same for the patient with verbal apraxia especially for those patients with a long history of verbal apraxia who appear to have been remediated save for fricative and affricative distortions. It would seem that these distortions reflect a loss of fine motor control, which may or may not in turn be related to an orosensory perceptual deficit. Thus, again, it is seen that the significance of the orosensory deficit among apractic speakers may have been underestimated in the past.

Oral Apractic Errors

Oral apraxia may be defined as the inability to efficiently and immediately produce oral movements on verbal command and/or imitation with preserved ability to produce similar actions semi-automatically. Reports of this disorder have been longstanding in the literature (Jackson, 1878; Wilson, 1908). Anecdotal reports, however, have far outnumbered empirical investigations of the disorder.

Initial research in this area concentrated on quantifying errors which occurred on tests of isolated oral movements among various groups of brain-injured patients (DeRenzi, Pieczuro & Vignolo, 1966). LaPointe (Note 20) and LaPointe and Wertz (1974), however, recognized the need to also quantify errors made by brain-injured adults with regard to performance on sequences of oral movements. Mateer and colleagues (Mateer & Kimura, 1977; Mateer, 1978; Ojemann & Mateer, 1979) continued this work by examining the quality of errors made in the production of sequenc-es as well as ability to learn oral-motor sequences. Poeck and Kerschensteiner (1975) elaborated upon a system of error qualification, while Kimura (1982) pursued developing a theoretical model of neurologic substrata underlying abilities to produce nonspeech oral movements as well as limb movements. Despite these dif-ferent investigative approaches, a common sub-theme of almost all research in this area has been to establish the relationships between oral apraxia, verbal apraxia, aphasia and/or limb apraxia.

Typical testing of oral apraxia include movements such as "sticking out one's tongue", "whistling", "yawning", demonstrating a kiss, and elevating one's tongue either on command or on imitation. In their classic study of oral apraxia as tested by isolated movements, DeRenzi et al. (1966) reported that right-brain damaged as well as a majority of left-brain damaged nonaphasic subjects demonstrated perform-ances similar to normal control subjects on a ten-item test. While left-brain-damaged aphasic patients with no phonemic-articulatory disorders also demonstrated normal or near-normal oral praxis, almost one-half with mild phonemic-articulatory disorders demonstrated impaired oral praxis. Among left-brain damaged aphasic subjects, the majority with severe phonemic-articulatory disorders demonstrated impaired oral praxis, with two-thirds of these demonstrating a severe oral praxis deficit. Further, those two aphasic syndromes demonstrating the most severely impaired oral praxis were Broca's and phonemic jargon. About one-third of the con-duction subjects were impaired while less than 6% of Wernicke's type patients were impaired. While limb apraxia and oral apraxia tended to co-occur, this relationship was not as strong as that between oral apraxia and the presence of phonemic-articulatory disorders.

Poeck and Kerschensteiner (1975) further studied the relationships between "type" of aphasia, incidence of articulatory errors and performances on isolated nonverbal movements both on command and on imitation. Overall results were sim-ilar to those of DeRenzi et al. (1966) in that those patients demonstrating the most erroneous articulatory output also demonstrated the most impaired verbal praxis function regardless of "type" of aphasia demonstrated or presumed associated sites of lesion. This finding led the researchers to speculate that "...particularly precise verbal and non-verbal movements are subserved by similar brain mechanisms" (p. 104).

LaPointe (Note 20) and LaPointe and Wertz (1974) tested brain-injured adults classified as apractic, dysarthric or mixed on both a test of isolated movements and sequenced movements. As a group, the subjects were impaired on both isolated and sequences tasks as compared to normal controls. However, some individual subjects scored within normal limits. Because no relationship between severity of articula-tion and performances on these two types of tasks could be established, it was pro-posed that movements for speech and oral nonspeech movements may be indepen-dent.[3] However, the most significant finding from these studies was that subjects in all three brain-injured groups had difficulty with the sequencing task both with regard to number of errors and number of trials taken to perform the sequence. LaPointe and Wertz (1974) suggested that deficits for sequencing oral movements may be far more prevalent among adults with acquired brain-damage than previously suspected. A startling 75% of their patients had such impairments.

---

[3] The reader must be cautioned that patients with speech disorders due to muscle weakness, slowness and incoordination, i.e. dysarthria, and not just patients with verbal apraxia and phonemic paraphasia, were considered in this correlational analysis.

Mateer and Kimura (1977) further investigated deficits of oral as well as verbal praxis for both isolated and sequenced tasks and specifically contrasted the performances of fluent and nonfluent patients. On the oral praxis tests both nonfluent and fluent patients were significantly impaired in their abilities to sequence movements. Further, the performances of the two groups did not differ significantly on the sequenced tasks. For isolated movements, however, only the nonfluent aphasics were found to be impaired. Mateer and Kimura (1977) thus proposed that there is a dissociation among left-brain injured aphasic adults in their abilities to produce discrete oral movements versus transitionalization from one discrete movement to another in a sequence. It was speculated that the inability to produce sequences of movement was not a sequencing disorder per se but instead an inability to reach targets within a sequence (Mateer, 1978; Mateer & Kimura, 1977). Further, Mateer (1978) reported that while types of errors were difficult to define for nonfluent subjects due to highly amorphous responses, fluent subjects produced more unique errors (e.g., moving the wrong oral structure in the right manner, etc.) than any other brain-damaged group studied, i.e., left-lesioned nonaphasic subjects and right-lesioned subjects. In addition, the left-hemisphere-lesioned patients, aphasic or not, demonstrated more highly perseverative performances. It was thus proposed that the left hemisphere has a highly specialized capacity for production and transitionalization of oral as well as verbal movements.

The issue of error types committed by patients with impaired oral praxis function and especially with regard to performances on oral motor sequencing tasks has not received adequate attention. Although Mateer (1978) attempted to define the quality of errors committed by aphasic subjects on oral motor sequences, she was unable to evaluate the responses of the most impaired subjects, those with nonfluent verbal output.

Poeck and Kerschensteiner (1975) proposed an error classification system but applied it only to performances on isolated oral movement tasks. The system consisted of twelve specific types of errors. The subjects studied included 66 aphasic patients classifed as amnesic, Broca's, Wernicke's or global as well as 20 right-hemisphere lesioned and 20 neurologically normal subjects. Unlike Mateer and Kimura (1977) who reported verbal praxis for isolated movements to be unimpaired among fluent aphasic subjects, Poeck and Kerschensteiner (1975) reported impairment of oral praxis function among all groups of aphasic subjects. However, those subjects with articulatory disorders demonstrated the greatest deficits, albeit a fluent or a nonfluent articulatory disorder. This finding was in accordance with DeRenzi et al. (1966). Further the error profiles did not differ with respect to clinical subtype of aphasia. Among all groups of aphasic subjects, the predominant error type was a semantically unrelated substituted movement. The second most common error was a fragmentation of the intended movement. Talking instead of producing a movement was the third most frequent error among all subgroups of aphasic subjects. Interestingly, amorphous movements ranked second to last in occurrence for all aphasic subjects on isolated movements. The fact that the nonfluent subjects studied by Mateer and Kimura (1977) demonstrated highly amorphous performances for oral motor sequences may indicate that when the motor system is taxed in patients with severe oral practic dysfunction the quality of error also changes and, in fact, motoric organization is drammatically disrupted.

The issue of motoric perseveration has also been inadequately investigated with regard to oral praxis function. Poeck and Kerschensteiner reported that over 43% of the errors which all of their aphasic subjects committed from isolated oral movement on command to the same isolated oral movement on imitation or to subsequent test items consisted of elements of perseveratory responses. That elements of perseveration from isolated event to isolated event was this predominant in the performances of Poeck and Kerschensteiner's (1975) subjects appears to lend credence to Mateer's supposition (1978) based upon left-hemisphered damaged subjects' performances on oral sequences that the left-hemisphere is highly specialized for the transitionalization of movement.

A third issue which has received relatively little attention has been the quality of oral practic function as it relates to the nature of the stimulus, i.e., command vs. imitation. Although most clinicians have observed that stimuli given on verbal command are more frequently erroneous, only Poeck and Kerschensteiner (1975) have studied the quality of responses under these two modes. It was found that errors on verbal command and on imitation were not different in quality and thus lead these researchers to speculate "...that oral apraxia is a disorder of the organization and output of movement, relatively independent of the input channel, auditory or visual, and also of the verbal or nonverbal nature of the stimulus" (p. 106). This finding, of course, disagrees with that of Square et al. (1982) with regard to the influence of stimulus input on the quality of verbal practic function.

Kimura (1982) has recently attempted to identify those neural substrata which underlie oral, both verbal and nonverbal, and limb movements. Based upon a body of empirical data, she has hypothesized that the left parietal lobe is primarily responsible for regulating movement sequences, be they oral or manual. Isolated limb movements are controlled principally by the left parietal lobe while isolated oral movements are controlled principally by the left frontal lobe. Recently, Tognola and Vignolo (1980) presented localizing data to substantiate this last point. They reported that lesions to one of three areas would result in praxis dysfunction for isolated oral movements. These areas are the left frontal and central operculum; the left anterior insula; and a small area of the left first temporal convolution. Kimura (1982) added that because a majority of aphasic patients have frontal and/or parietal lobe damage, deficits of limb, oral and verbal praxis often coexist with aphasia.

Clues to Mechanisms Underlying Oral Apraxia

Because of the limited number of empirical investigations undertaken in the area of oral apraxia, it is a great deal more difficult to find interpretable evidence which may support either a cognitive or productive level of dysfunction. Some preliminary interpretations are offered in the following sections.

Oral Apraxia: A Disorder of the Linguistic-Conceptual System

Several studies have pointed to the fact that among aphasic subjects who demonstrated phonemic-articulatory impairments the incidence of oral apraxia was quite high (De Renzi et al., 1966; Geschwind, 1965; Mateer & Kimura, 1977; Poeck & Kerschensteiner, 1975). Specifically, Poeck and Kerschensteiner (1975) reported that the predominant error type on isolated movements was a semantically unrelated substituted movement and that all aphasic groups (Broca, Wernicke, amnesic, global) demonstrated this error type most frequently.

If one were to view the results of this study in a manner similar to that which linguists view substitutions in verbal apraxia, then these errors might be interpreted as being conceptually based. That is, a wrong movement is selected for execution at the highest level of programming the motoric act. Thus, top-down control is deviant in that knowledge of either motor commands per se or spatial target commands (MacNeilage, 1970) is aberrant. In fact, Mateer (1978) reported that unique movements (substitutions) were demonstrated in oral sequences most frequently by fluent aphasic patients. This "unique substitutive" behaviour may be interpreted in the same manner that linguists interpret literal paraphasias in speech production. The highest order matrices for oral movements (and phonemes) malselects components for the sequence. Nevertheless, the sequence is transitionalized fluently without amorphous movements.

Following a second line of reasoning, it would seem that the question of the conceptual basis of oral apraxia might be partially resolved by describing performances of aphasic patients under two conditions -- imitation of oral gesture versus verbal-command elicitation of the gestures. One could speculate that if the quality of errors on the verbal-command condition were different and more aberrant than on the imitation condition, then faulty conceptualization may at least partially account for the deliterious performances. However, Poeck and Kerschensteiner (1975) reported performances which were qualitatively equivocal under the two input conditions for the four groups of aphasic subjects studied. Further, the aphasic groups could not be distinguished based upon quality of performances. This led Poeck and Kerschensteiner (1975) to conclude ..."oral apraxia is a disorder of organization and output of movement relatively independent of input channel". Thus, analysis of quality of errors under the two input conditions does not resolve the question of the basis of the dysfunction.

But in this same study, analysis of frequency of errors revealed that oral apractic errors may be conceptual in at least one group of aphasic patients -- amnesic or anomic. This group of patients committed substantially more errors on the verbal command than on the imitative condition relative to the other aphasic groups. Poeck and Kerschensteiner (1975) explained that anomic errors on confrontation naming tasks and oral apractic errors upon verbal command may both reflect a deficit in concept realization. While word retrieval as well as oral function are relatively well-preserved in the natural context among these patients, both behaviours are quite deviant in artificial, environmentally-sterile situations. Thus, the lack of environmental context may act to inhibit concept retrieval. These results lend credence to dysfunction at the "cognitive" level of motor control.

A third line of reasoning which might implicate faulty conceptualization as the basis for oral apraxia is again derived from the work of Poeck and Kerschensteiner (1975) and Mateer (1978). In the former study, patients were reported to execute fragmentary movements for isolated movements and, in the latter, to omit portions of sequences. Both behaviours may indicate an attentional deficit and thus may be interpreted as conceptual rather than productive. In the former instance, the environmental context of the movement itself seems not to perpetuate the "motor engram" (Lashley, 1951) for complete execution. In the latter instance, short-term memory for sequences may be impaired. In fact, Mateer (1978) reported the greatest fluency of omissions among the fluent aphasic group. This memory (cognitive) deficit has been previously reported for tasks which also require memory for auditory and visual sequences (Efron, 1963; Brookshire, 1972), particularly among patients with posterior lesions.

Oral Apraxia: A Disorder of the Productive System

The evidence which supports dysfunction of the productive system as the underlying basis for oral apraxia comes primarily from those investigations which have studied performances of aphasic individuals on sequences of oral movements.

Temporal/Transitional Motor Control Dysfunction. Mateer (1979) and Poeck and Kerschensteiner (1975) emphasize the preponderance of perseverative behaviours during production of oral sequences, and on contiguous items when patients were asked to produce isolated movements, respectively. Further, Mateer (1978) reported both immediate and delayed perseverations to occur more frequently among the fluent than the nonfluent aphasic group. Such behaviour was interpreted as a deficit in the ability to transitionalize from one spatial target to another.

Unfortunately, no researchers to date have studied the temporal aspects of production of nonverbal oral sequences, particularly with regard to inter-sequence durational aspects of the components. With the advant of highly specialized video equipment, oral ultrasound imagers and continued use of cineradiography and x-ray microbeam analysis, such valuable studies should augment our understanding of the temporal aspects of oral praxis function as they have in studies of verbal praxis.

Spatial Disorientation. Mateer and Kimura (1977) and Mateer (1978) reported that only nonfluent aphasic subjects demonstrated significant difficulty on isolated oral movements. Further, this same group of subjects usually demonstrated a random continuous amorphous movement when asked to produce an oral sequence. Both studies indicated that this group of patients appeared to be groping for a spatial target which was unobtainable. Further, the ability to achieve spatial targets appeared to be neurophhsiologically independent of the ability to transitionalize since fluent aphasic patients achieved spatial targets quite well but demonstrated severe difficulty transitionalizing.

The question as to whether disability to achieve discrete spatial targets is dependent upon reduced oral sensation and perception is unresolved and warrants further investigation. Mateer and Kimura (1978) reported reduced two-point lingual discrimination thresholds for six aphasic subjects, two nonfluent and four fluent patients, but did not report relationships between this measure and abilities to achieve oral targets and produce oral sequences.

Disruption of Fine Motor Control. No measures of nonverbal oral movements such as "tongue tapping" against the superior alveolar ridge or timed consecutive tongue protrusion have been mentioned in the oral apractic literature. Such measures would be invaluable in order to help determine the integrity of fine motor control among patients with disruptions of oral praxis.

Commonalities in Limb and Verbal Apraxia

Two lines of evidence are suggestive of common mechanisms underlying both limb and verbal apraxia. First, the nature and types of errors observed in these two forms of apraxia seem to bear a striking resemblance (see Table 2). There are errors which are indicative of (1) disruptions to the order of elements in a sequence, (2) disruptions to the spatial positions or planes of movements, and (3) disruptions to motor control processes which normally afford a smooth, unfaltering production of the motor elements in a sequence.

A second line of evidence indicates that these errors observed may have a basis in disruptions to conceptual and/or production processes. Apraxias which seem to have a conceptual basis may be associated with posterior-type aphasias, while those which have more of a production basis seem to involve damage to anterior cerebral and/or subcortical regions. Over the past decade work examining control processes in both limb and verbal praxis have emphasized either a top-down or a bottom-up type of control. Such a dualistic approach has led to two rather dichotomous approaches to the interpretation of apraxia, particularly verbal apraxia, i.e., a linguistic-conceptual-aphasic interpretation or a productive-motoric interpretation. The approach in this chapter argues that control of praxis involves both top-down

Table 2

Similarities in Error Categories in Limb/Verbal Apraxia

	Limb Apraxia	Verbal Apraxia
Single Gesture/ Single Word	Spatial Errors	Substitions of place
	Perseverations	Repetitions
	Verbal Exclamation	Gestural Exclamation
	Groping	Phonetic Grope

	Initiation Errors
	  (Delay)
		Pause, Audible/
		  Inaudible
		  Struggle

	Omission	Omission
	Clumsy	Fricative, Affri- cate/Distortion
	Additional Movements	Additional Sounds
	Self-corrections	Self-corrections
	Substitution	Substitution
	Inappropriate Action	Neologism
	Associated Actions	Distinctive Feature Errors
	Partial Response	Distortion
	Exaggerated Response	Additional Phonetic Features
	Body Part as Object	
Sequence		
	Order	) Metatheses
	Position	)
	Perseveration	Repetition
	Omission	Omission
	Clumsy Elements	Distortion

	Initiation Errors	Pause, Audible/
		  Inaudible
		  Struggle

	Groping on Tran- sition	Vowel Transitions

and bottom-up influences which operate in parallel. A full understanding of the neurobehavioural basis for disruptions to praxis will arise only when the delicate balance between these influences is focused on in studying these disruptions.

While the commonalities in these apraxias are apparent, much of the evidence for these commonalities is based on correlational studies which do not provide insight into whether the mechanisms underlying these disorders are similar. Consequently, much more work is necessary to more clearly understand the basis for the association.

REFERENCE NOTES

1. Roy, E.A. Beyond the reflex: Implications of higher cortical control of behaviour for models of motor behaviour and rehabilitation. Invited address to the Quebec Physiotherapy Association, Quebec City, May, 1978.

2. Roy, E.A. Cerebral substrates of action: Implications for models of motor behaviour and rehabilitation. Paper read at the annual meeting of North American Society for the Psychology of Sport and Physical Activity, Toronto, November, 1978.

3. MacNeilage, P.F., Krones, R. & Hanson, R. Closed-loop control of the initiation of jaw movements for speech. Paper presented at the meeting of the Acoustical Society of America, San Diego, November. 1969.

4. Lindblom, B., McAllister, R. & Lubker, J. Compensatory articulation and the modelling of normal speech production behaviour. Paper presented at the Symposium on Articulatory Modelling, Grenable, France, July 11-12, 1977.

5. Logue, R.D. The effects of temporal alterations in auditory feedback upon the speech output of stutterers and non-stutterers. M.A. thesis, Purdue University, 1962.

6. Darley, F.L. The classification of output disturbances in neurologic communication disorders. Presented in dual session on aphasia to the American Speech and Hearing Association, Chicago, Illinois, 1969.

7. Trost, J. Patterns of articulatory deficits in patients with Broca's aphasia. Unpublished doctoral dissertation, Northwestern University, 1970.

8. Sasanuma, S. Speech characteristics of a patient with apraxia of speech. Annual Bulletin, Research Institute of Logopedics and Phoniatrics, University of Tokyo, 5, 85-89, 1971.

9. Mlcoch, A. Articulatory consistency and variability in apraxia of speech. Unpublished doctoral dissertation, Purdue University, 1981.

10. Square, P.A. Apraxia of speech in adults: Speech perception and production. Unpublished doctoral dissertation: Kent State University, 1981.

11. Dibrell, J.W. & Marquardt, T.P. Apraxia of speech. Voice onset time in initial stop perception and production. Paper presented to the 15th Annual Meeting of Academy of Aphasia, Montreal, 1977.

12. Jaffe. J.W. & Duffy, J.R. Voice-onset time characteristics of patients with apraxia of speech. Paper presented to the American Speech and Hearing Association, San Francisco, 1978.

13. Bauman, J., Wangler, H.H. & Prescott, T. Durational aspects of continuous speech: Comparative measurements based on vowel and consonant production by normal and apraxic speakers. Paper presented at the 50th Annual Convention of the American Speech and Hearing Association, Washington, D.C., 1975.

14. Gawle, C. & Duffy, J.R. Apraxic speakers' vowel duration characteristics in CVC syllables. Paper presented to the American Speech-Language-Hearing Convention, Los Angeles, 1981.

15. Farmer, A., O'Connell, P. & Jesudowich, B. Naming and reading errors and response latency in Broca's aphasia. Paper presented to the Annual Convention of the American Speech and Hearing Association, Houston, 1976.

16. Fager, K. & Deutsch, S.E. Utterance length effects on speech segment durations in apraxics versus normals. Poster session presented at the American Speech Language and Hearing Association, Los Angeles, 1981.

17. Canter, G.J. Classifactory constructs of aphasia. Paper presented to the Annual Convention of the American Speech and Hearing Convention, 1968.

18. Deutsch, S.E. Prediction of site of lesion from speech apraxic error patterns. Paper presented at the Annual Convention of the American Speech-Language-Hearing Association, Atlanta, 1979.

19. Square, P.A. Oral sensory perception in adults demonstrating apraxia of speech. Unpublished masters' thesis, Kent State University, 1976.

20. LaPointe, L.L. An investigation of isolated oral movements, oral motor sequencing abilities, and articulation of brain-injured adults. Unpublished doctoral dissertation, University of Colorado, 1969.

REFERENCES

Abbs, J.H. The influence of the gamma motor system on jaw movements during speech: A theoretical framework and some preliminary observations. Journal of Speech and Hearing Research, 1973, 16 (2), 175-200.

Abbs, J.H. & Netsell, R. An interpretation of jaw acceleration during speech as a muscle forcing function. Journal of Speech and Hearing Research, 1973, 16, 421-425.

Adams, M. & Moore, W. The effects of auditory masking on the anxiety level, frequency of dysfluency, and selected vocal characteristics of stutterers. Journal of Speech and Hearing Research, 1973, 15(3), 572-578.

Alajouanine, T. Centenniere de Pierre Marie. Revue Neurologique, 1952, 36, 753-764.

Alajouanine, T., Ombredane, A. & Durand, M. Le syndrome de desintegration phonetique dans l'aphasie. Paris: Masson, 1956.

Benson, D.F. & Geschwind, N. The aphasias and related disturbances. In A.B. Baker (Ed.), Clinical Neurology, Vol. 1, New York: Harper, 1971.

Blumstein, S. A Phonological Investigation of Aphasic Speech. The Hague: Moulton, 1973a.

Blumstein, S. Some phonological implications of aphasic speech. In H. Goodglass & S. Blumstein (Eds.), Psycholinguistics and Aphasia. Baltimore: John Hopkins, 1973b.

Blumstein, S., Cooper, W., Zurif, E., & Carramazza, A. The perception and production of voice onset time in aphasia. Neuropsychologia, 1977, 15, 371-383.

Blumstein, S., Cooper, W., Goodglass, H., Statlender, S. & Gootlieb, J. Production deficits in aphasia: A voice-onset time analysis. Brain and Language, 1980, 9, 153-170.

Boomer, D.S. & Laver, J.D.M. Slips of the Tongue. British Journal of Disorders of Communication, 1968, 3, 1-12.

Bransford, J.D. & McCarrell, N.S. A sketch of a cognitive approach to comprehension. In W. Weimer & D.S. Palarmo (Eds.) Cognition and The Symbolic Processes. Hillsdale, New Jersey: L. Erlbaum, 1974.

Brookshire, R.H. Visual and auditory sequencing by aphasic subjects. Journal of Communication Disorders, 1972, 5, 259-269.

Brown, J.W. Aphasia, Apraxia and Agnosia. Springfield, Ill.: Charles C. Thomas, 1972.

Brown, J.W. Aphasia, Apraxia and Agnosia: Clinical and Theoretical Aspects. Springfield, Ill.: C.C. Thomas, 1972.

Buckingham, H.W. Explanations in apraxia with consequences for the concept of apraxia of speech. Brain and Language, 1979, 8, 202-226.

Buckingham, H., Whitaker, H. & Whitaker, H. On linguistic perseveration. In H. Whitaker & H. Whitaker (Eds.) Studies in Neurolinguistics. Volume 4. New York: Academic Press, 1979.

Chapin, C., Blumstein, S.E., Meissner, B. & Boller, F. Speech production mechanisms in aphasia: A delayed auditory feedback study. Brain and Language, 1981, 14, 106-113.

Chase, R.A. & Sutton, S. Reply to: Masking of auditory feedback in stutterers' speech. Journal of Speech and Hearing Research, 1968, 11, 222-223.

Collins, M., Rosenbek, J.C. & Wertz, R.T. Spectrographic analysis of vowel and word duration in apraxia of speech. Journal of Speech and Hearing Research, 1983, 26(2), 224-230.

Daniloff, R.G. & Moll, K.L. Coarticulation of lip rounding. Journal of Speech and Hearing Research, 1968, 11, 707-721.

Darley, F.L. Aphasia. Toronto: W.B. Saunders Co., 1982.

Darley, F.L., Aronson, A.E. & Brown, J.R. Motor Speech Disorders, Philadelphia: Saunders, 1975.

Darley, F.L., Aronson, A.E. & Brown, J.R. Motor Speech Disorders. Toronto: Saunders, 1975.

Deal, J. Consistency and adaptation in apraxia of speech. Journal of Communication Disorders, 1974, 7, 135-140.

Deal, J. & Darley, F.L. The influence of linguistic and situational variables on phonemic accuracy in apraxia of speech. Journal of Speech and Hearing Research, 1972, 15, 639-653.

Dejerine, J. Semiologie des Affections du Systeme Nerveux. Paris: Masson, 1926.

Denny-Brown, D. The nature of apraxia. Journal of Nervous and Mental Disease, 1958, 126, 9-32.

De Renzi, E., Pieczuro, A. & Vignolo, L.A. Oral apraxia and aphasia. Cortex, 1966, 2, 50-73.

De Renzi, E., Pieczuro, A. & Vignolo, L.A. Ideational apraxia: A quantitative study. Neuropsychologia, 1968, 6, 41-52.

DeRenzi, E., Motti, F. & Nichelli, P. Imitating gestures: A quantitative approach to ideomotor apraxia. Archives of Neurology, 1980, 37, 6-10.

DiSimoni, F.G. & Darley, F.L. Effect on Phoneme duration control of three utterance length conditions in an apractic patient. Journal of Speech and Hearing Disorders, 1977, 42, 257.

Duncker, K. On problem solving. Psychological Monographs, 1945, 58: 5, Whole No. 270.

Dunlop, J.M. & Marquardt, T.P. Linguistic and articulatory aspects of single word production in apraxia of speech. Cortex, 1977, 13, 17-29.

Easton, T. On the normal use of reflexes. American Scientist, 1972, 60, 591-599.

Efron, R. Temporal perception, aphasia and deja vu. Brain, 1963, 86, 403-424.

Folkins, J.W. & Abbs, J.H. Lip and jaw motor control during speech: Responses to resistive loading of the jaw. Journal of Speech and Hearing Research, 1975, 18, 207-220.

Freeman, F., Sands, E. & Harris, K. Temporal coordination of phonation and articulation time in a case of verbal apraxia: A voice onset time study. Brain and Language, 1978, 6, 106.

Fromkin, V.A. The non-anomalous nature of anomalous utterances. Language, 1971, 47, 27-52.

Fromkin, V.A. Some phonetic specifications of linguistic units: An electromyographic investigation. Working Papers in Phonetics, 3, Los Angeles: University of California, 1965.

Fromm, D., Abbs, J.H., McNeil, M.R. & Rosenbek, J.C. Simultaneous perceptual-physiological method for studying apraxia of speech. In R.K. Brookshire (Ed.), Clinical Aphasiology Conference Proceedings, Minneapolis: BKR Publishers, 1982.

Fry, D.B. Phonemic substitutions in an aphasic patient. Language and Speech, 1959, 2, 52-61.

Garrett, M.F. Production of speech: Observations from normal and pathological use. In Andrew W. Ellis (Ed.), Normality and Pathology in Cognitive Functions, New York: Academic Press, 1982.

Gay, T. Cinefluorographic and electromyographic studies of articulatory organization. In M. Sawashima & F.S. Cooper (Eds.), Dynamic Aspects of Speech Production, Tokyo: University of Tokyo Press, 1977.

Gay, T. & Turvey, M. Effects of efferent and afferent interference on speech production: Implications for a generative theory of speech motor control. Proceedings of the Ninth International Congress of Phonetic Sciences, Copenhagen, Vol. II, 1979.

Geschwind, N. Disconnection syndromes in animals and man. Brain, 1965, 88, 237-294, 585-644.

Geschwind, N. The apraxias: Neural mechanisms of disorders of learned movements. American Scientist, 1975, 63, 188-195.

Gibson, J.J. The theory of affordances. In R. Shaw & J. Bransford (Eds.) Perceiving, Acting and Knowing. Hillsdale, New Jersey: Erlbaum, 1977.

Goodglass, H. Phonological factors in aphasia. In R.H. Brookshire (Ed.), Clinical Aphasiology Conference Proceedings, Minneapolis: BKR Publishers, 1975.

Goodglass, H. & Baker, E. Semantic field, naming and auditory comprehension in aphasia. Brain Language, 1976, 3, 359-374.

Goodglass, H. & Kaplan, E. Disturbances of gesture and pantomime in aphasia. Brain, 1963, 86, 703-720.

Goodglass, H. & Kaplan, E. The Assessment of Aphasia and Related Disorders. Philadelphia: Lea and Febiger, 1972.

Gottsdanker, R. The ubiquitous role of preparation. In G.E. Stelmach & J. Requin (Eds.) Tutorials in Motor Behavior. Amsterdam: North Holland Publishing Company, 1980.

Greenfield, P.M. & Westerman, M.A. Some psychological relations between action and language structure. Journal of Psycholinguistic Research, 1978, 7, 453-475.

Haaland, K.Y, Porch, B.E. & Delaney, H.D. Limb apraxia and motor performance. Brain and Language, 1980, 9, 315-323.

Ham, R. & Steer, M.D. Certain Effects of Alteration in Auditory Feedback. Folia Phoniatrica, 1967, 19, 53-62.

Hardison, D., Marquardt, T. & Peterson, A. Effects of selected linguistic variables of apraxia of speech. Journal of Speech and Hearing Research, 1977, 20, 334-343.

Harris, K.S., Lysaught, G.F. & Schvey, M.M. Some aspects of the production of oral and nasal labial stops. Language and Speech, 1968, 8, 135-147.

Hecaen, H. Apraxia. In S. Filskov & T. Boll (Eds.) Handbook of Clinical Neuropsychology. New York: Wiley, 1981.

Hecaen, H. & Consoli, S. Analyses of language troubles in the course of lesions in Broca's area. Neuropsychologia, 1973, 11, 377-388.

Hecaen, H. & Albert, M. Human Neuropsychology. New York: Wiley, 1978.

Heilman, K.M. A tapping test in apraxia. Cortex, 1975. 11, 259-263.

Heilman, K.M. Apraxia. In K.M. Heilman & E. Valenstein (Eds.) Clinical Neuropsychology. New York: Oxford University Press, 1979.

Heilman, K.M. Apraxia. In K.M. Heilman & E. Valenstein (Eds.), Clinical Neuropsychology. New York: Oxford University Press, 1979.

Henke, W.L. Preliminaries to speech synthesis based on an auditory model. Proceedings 1967 IEEE Boston Speech Conference, 1967.

Hotoph, W.H.N. Semantic similarity as a factor in whole word slips of the tongue. In V.A. Fromkin (Ed.), Errors in Linguistic Performance. New York: Academic Press, 1980.

Hughes, O. & Abbs, J.H. Labial-mandibular coordination in the production of speech: Implications for the operation of motor equivalence. Phonetica, 1976, 44, 199-331.

Itoh, M., Sasanuma, S. & Ushijima, T. Velar movements during speech in a patient with apraxia of speech. Brain and Language, 1979, 7, 227-239.

Itoh, M., Sasanuma, S., Hirose, H., Yoskioka, H. & Ushijima, T. Abnormal articulatory dynamics in a patient with apraxia of speech: X-ray microbeam observation. Brain and Language, 1980, 11, 66-75.

Jackson, J.H. Remarks on non-protrusion of the tongue in some cases of aphasia, 1878. In Selected Writings, Vol. 2. London: Hodder and Stoughton, 1932.

Johns, D.F. & Darley, F.L. Phonemic variability in apraxia of speech. Journal of Speech and Hearing Research, 1970; 13, 556-583.

Keele, S. Behavioural analysis of motor control. In V. Brooks (Ed.) Handbook of Physiology, Motor Control Volume. Washington, D.C.: American Physiology Society, 1980.

Keele, S. & Summers, J. The Structure of Motor Programs. In G.E. Stelmach (Ed.) Motor Control: Issues and Trends. New York: Academic Press, 1976.

Keller, E. Parameters for vowel substitutions in Broca's aphasia. Brain and Language, 1978, 5, 265-285.

Kelso, J.A.S. & Tuller, B. Towards a theory of apractic syndromes. Brain and Language, 1980.

Kent, R.D. & Moll, K.L. Cinefluorographic analyses of selected lingual consonants. Journal of Speech and Hearing Research, 1972, 453-473.

Kent, R.D. & Rosenbek, J. Acoustic patterns in apraxia of speech. Journal of Speech and Hearing Research, 1983, 26(2), 231-249.

Kent, R.D. & Rosenbek, J.C. Prosadic disturbance and neurologic lesion. Brain and Language, 1982, 15, 259-291.

Kertesz, A. Aphasia and Associated Disorders: Taxonomics, Localization and Recovery. New York: Grune and Stratton, 1979.

Kimura, D. Acquisition of a motor skill after left hemisphere damage. Brain, 1977, 100, 527-542.

Kimura, D. Neuromotor mechanisms in the evolution of human communication. In H.D. Steklis & M.J. Raleigh (Eds.) Neurobiology of Social Communication in Primates. New York: Academic Press, 1979.

Kimura, D. Left-hemisphere control of oral and brachial movements and their relation to communication. Philosophical Transactions of the Royal Society of London, 1982, B298, 135-149.

Kimura, D. & Archibald, Y. Motor function of the left hemisphere. Brain, 1974, 97, 337-350.

Klich, R.J., Ireland, J.V. & Weidner, W.E. Articulatory and phonological aspects of consonant substitions in apraxia of speech. Cortex, 1979, 15, 451-470.

Kots, Y.M. The organization of voluntary movement. New York: Plenum Press, 1977.

Ladefoged, P. Three Areas of Experimental Phonetics. London: Oxford University Press, 1972.

LaPointe, L.L. & Johns, D.F. Some phonemic characteristics in apraxia of speech. Journal of Communication Disorders, 1975, 8, 259-269.

LaPointe, L.L. & Wertz, R.T. Oral movement abilities and articulatory characteristics of brain-injured adults. Perceptual and Motor Skills, 1974, 39, 39-46.

Lashley, K.S. The Problem of Serial Order in Behaviour. New York: John Wiley and Sons, 1951.

Lebrun, Y., Buyssens, E. & Henneaux, J. Phonetic aspects of anarthria. Cortex, 1973, 9, 112-135.

LeCours, A.R. & Lhermitte, F. Phonemic paraphasias: Linguistic and tentative hypotheses. Cortex, 1969, 5, 193-229.

LeCours, A.R. & Lhermitte, F. The pure form of the phonetic disintegration syndrome (pure anarthria). Brain and Language, 1976, 3, 88-113.

Liberman, A.M., Cooper, F.S., Harris, K.S., MacNeilage, P.F. & Studdert-Kennedy, M. Some observations on a model for speech perception. In W. Wathen-Dunn (Ed.) Models for the Perception of Speech and Visual Form. Cambridge: MIT Press, 1964.

Liepmann, H. Drei Aufsatze aus dem Apraxiegebiet. Berlin: Karger, 1908.

Lomas, J. & Kimura, D. Intrahemispheric interaction between speaking and sequential manual activity. Neuropsychology, 1976, 14, 23-33.

Lozano, R.A. & Dreyer, D.R. Some effects of delayed auditory feedback on dyspraxia of speech. Journal of Communication Disorders, 1978, 11, 407-415.

Luria, A.R. Higher Cortical Functions in Man. New York: Basic Books, 1966.

Luria, A.R. & Hutton, J.T.A. Modern assessment of the basic forms of aphasia. Brain and Language, 1977, 4, 129-151.

MacKay, D.G. Spoonerisms: The structure of errors in the serial ordering of speech. Neuropsychologia, 1970, 8, 323-350.

MacNeilage, P.F. Preliminaries to the study of single motor unit activity in speech musculature. Journal of Phonetics, 1973, 1, 55-73.

MacNeilage, P.F. Motor control of the serial ordering of speech. Psychological Review, 1970, 77(3), 182-196.

MacNeilage, P.F. & DeClerk, J. On the motor control of coarticulation in CVC monosyllables. Journal of the Acoustical Society of America, 1969, 45, 1217-1233.

MacNeilage, P.F. & MacNeilage, L.A. Central processes controlling speech production during sleep and walking. In F.J. McGuigan & R.A. Scheoner (Eds.) The Psychophysiology of Thinking, New York: Academic Press, 1973.

MacNeilage, P.F., Sussman, H.M. & Stolz, W. Incidence of laterality effects in mandibular and manual performance of dichoptic visual pursuit tracking. Cortex, 1975, 11, 251-258.

Marie, P. Que faut-il penser des aphasies sous-corticales? In Travaux et Memoires, Paris: Masson, 1906.

Marteniuk, R.G. & MacKenzie, C.L. Information processing in movement organization and execution. In R. Nickerson (Ed.) Attention and Performance VIII. New Jersey, Erlbaum, 1980.

Martin, A.D. Some objections to the term "apraxia of speech". Journal of Speech and Hearing Disorders, 1974, 39, 53-64.

Martin, A.D. & Rigrodsky, S. An investigation of the phonological impairment in aphasia. Part I. Cortex, 1974a, 10, 317-328.

Martin, A.D. & Rigrodsky, S. An investigation of the phonological impairment in aphasia. Part II. Cortex, 1974, 10, 329.

Mateer, C. Impairments of nonverbal oral movements after left hemisphere damage: A follow-up analysis of errors. Brain and Language, 1978, 6, 334-341.

Mateer, C. & Kimura, D. Impairment of nonverbal oral movements in aphasia. Brain and Language, 1977, 4, 262-276.

Mazzocchi, F. & Vignolo, L.A. Localization of lesions in aphasia: Clinical-CT scan correlations in stroke patients. Cortex, 1979, 15, 627-654.

McClean, M. Variations in perioral reflex amplitude prior to lip muscle contraction for speech. Journal of Speech and Hearing Research, 1978, 21, 276-284.

Miller, G.A. Practical and lexical knowledge. In E. Rosch & B. Lloyd (Eds.) Cognition and Categorization. Hillsdale, New Jersey: L. Erlbaum, 1978.

Miller, G.A. & Johnson-Laird, P.N. Language and Perception. Cambridge, Mass.: The Belknap Press of Harvard University Press, 1976.

Mlcoch, A.G., Darley, F.L. & Noll, D. Articulatory consistency and variability in apraxia of speech. In R.K. Brookshire (Ed.), Proceedings of the Clinical Aphasiology Conference, 1982.

Mohr, J.P., Pessin, M.S., Finkelstein, S., Funkenstein, H., Duncan, G.W. & Davis, K.R. Broca aphasia: Pathologic and clinical. Neurology, 1978, 28, 311-324.

Moll, K.L., Zimermann, G.N. & Smith, A. The study of speech production as a human neuromotor system. In M. Sawashima & F.S. Cooper (Eds.) Dynamic Aspects of Speech Production, Tokyo: University of Tokyo Press, 1977.

Nebes, R.D. The nature of internal speech in a patient with aphemia. Brain and Language, 1975, 2, 489-497.

Neelley, J.M. A study of the speech behaviour of stutterers and non-stutterers under normal and delayed auditory feedback. Journal of Speech and Hearing Disorders, 1961, Monograph Supplement No. 7, 63-82.

Nelson, K. Explorations in the development of a functional semantic system. In W.A. Collins (Ed.) The Minnesota Symposia on Child Psychology, Volume 12, Children's Language and Communication, Hillsdale, New Jersey: L. Erlbaum, 1979.

Netsell, R. & Abbs, J. Modulation of perioral reflex sensitivity during speech movements. Journal of the Acoustical Society of America, 1975, 58, Suppl. S41.

Newell, A. & Simon, H.A. Human Problem Solving. New Jersey: Prentice-Hall, 1972.

Nooteboom, S.G. The tongue slips into patterns. In A.G. Sciarone, et al. (Eds.) Nomen: Leyden Studies in Linguistics and Phonetics, The Hague: Mouton, 1969.

Norman, D.A. Categorization of action slips. Psychological Review, 1981, 88, 1-15.

Ohman, S. Coarticulation in VCV utterances: Spectrographic measurements. Journal of the Acoustical Society of America, 1966, 39, 151-168.

Ojemann, G. & Mateer, C. Human language cortex: Localization of memory, syntax, and sequential motor-phoneme identification systems. Science, 1979, 305, 1401-1403.

Papp, K.R. Theories of speech perception. In D.W. Massaro (Ed.) Understanding Language, New York: Academic Press, 1975, 151-204.

Perkell, J.S. Articulatory modelling phonetic features and speech production strategies. In R. Carre, R. Descout & M. Wajskop (Eds.), Modelling and Phonetics, Brussels: Groupe de la Communication Parlee, 1978.

Perkell, J.S. Phonetic features and the physiology of speech production. In B. Butterworth (Ed.) Language Production, Volume 1. London: Academic Press, 1980.

Pieczuro, A. & Vignolo, L.A. Studio spermentale sul apraxxia ideomotoria. Sistema Nervoso, 1967, 19, 131-143.

Poeck, K. & Kerschensteiner, M. Analysis of the sequential motor events in oral apraxia. In K.J. Zulch, O. Creutzgeldt & B.C. Gailbraith (Eds.) Cerebral Localization, Berlin: Springer-Verlag, 1975, 98-111.

Poeck, K. & Lehmkuhl, G. Ideatory apraxia in a left-handed patient with a right-sided brain lesion. Cortex, 1980, 16, 273-284.

Poncet, M., Degos, C., Deloche, G. & LeCours, A.R. Phonetic and phonemic transformations in aphasia. International Journal of Mental Health, 1972, 1, 46-54.

Reason, J.T. Actions not as planned. In G. Underwood & R. Stevens (Eds.) Aspects of Consciousness. London: Academic Press, 1979.

Roland, P.E., Larsen, B., Lassen, W. & Skinhoj, E. Supplementary motor area and other cortical areas in the organization of voluntary movement. Journal of Neurophysiology, 1980, 43, 118-136.

Rosch, E.H., Mowis, C.B., Gray, W., Johnson, D.N. & Boyes-Braem, P. Basic objects in natural categories. Cognitive Psychology, 1976, 8, 382-439.

Rosenbek, J.C. & Wertz, R.T. Veteran's Administration workshop on Motor Speech Disorders, Madison, Wisconsin, 1976.

Rosenbek, J.C., Wertz, R.T. & Darley, F.L. Oral sensation and perception in apraxia of speech and aphasia. Journal of Speech and Hearing Research, 1973, 16, 22-36.

Rosenbek, J., McNeil, M., Teetson, M., Odell, K. & Collins, M. A syndrome of dysgraphic and neuromotor speech deficit. In R.N. Brookshire (Ed.), Clinical Aphasiology Proceedings, Minneapolis: BRK Publishers, 1981.

Roy, E.A. Apraxia: A new look at an old syndrome. Journal of Human Movement Studies, 1978, 4, 191-210.

Roy, E.A. Action sequencing and lateralized cerebral damage: Evidence for asymmetries in control. In J. Long & A. Baddeley (Eds.) Attention and Performance IX. New Jersey: L. Erlbaum, 1981.

Roy, E.A. Action and performance. In A. Ellis (Ed.) Normality and Pathology in Cognitive Function. New York: Academic Press, 1982.

Roy, E.A. Neuropsychological perspectives on apraxia and related action disorders. In R.A. Magill (Ed.) Advances in Psychology, Volume 12, Memory and Control of Action. Amsterdam: North-Holland Co., 1983.

Roy, E.A. & Elfeki, G. Hemispheric asymmetries in a finger sequencing task. In G. Roberts & K. Newall (Eds.) Psychology of Motor Behaviour. Illinois: Human Kinetics Publishers, 1979.

Ruch, T.C., Patton, H.D., Woodbury, J.W. & Towe, A.L. Neurophysiology, Philadelphia: W.B. Saunders, 1967.

Sands, E.S., Freeman, F.J. & Harris, K.S. Progressive changes in articulatory patterns in verbal apraxia: A longitudinal case study. Brain and Language, 1978, 6, 97-105.

Schiff, H.B., Alexander, M.P., Naeser, M.A. & Galaburda, A.M. Aphemia: Clinical-anatomic correlation. Archives of Neurology, 1983, 40, 720-727.

Schmidt, R.A. Control processes in motor skills. In J. Keogh & R.S. Hutton (Eds.) Exercise and Sport Sciences Review, Vol. 4. Santa Barbara, California: Journal Publishing Associates, 1976.

Schmidt, R.A. On the theoretical status of time in motor program representations. In G.E. Stelmach & J. Requin (Eds.) Tutorials in Motor Behavior. Amsterdam: North-Holland Publishing, 1980.

Scott, C.M. & Ringel, R.L. Articulation without oral sensory control. Journal of Speech and Hearing Research, 1971, 14(4), 804-818.

Semmes, J., Weinstein, S., Ghent, L. & Teuber, H. Correlates of impaired orientation in personal and extrapersonal space. Brain, 1963, 86, 747-772.

Shankweiler, D. & Harris, K.S. An experimental approach to the problem of articulation in aphasia. Cortex, 1966, 2, 277-292.

Shankweiler, D., Harris, K.S. & Taylor, M.L. Electromyographic studies of articulation in aphasia. Archives of Physical Medicine and Rehabilitation, 1968, 49, 1-8.

Shane, H.C. & Darley, F.L. The effect of auditory rhythmic stimulation on articulatory accuracy in apraxia of speech. Cortex, 1978, 14, 444-450.

Shulman, H.G. & McConkie, A. S-R compatability, response discriminability and response codes in choice reaction time. Journal of Experimental Psychology, 1973, 98, 375-378.

Square, P.A., Darley, F.L. & Sommers, R.K. An analysis of the productive errors made by pure apractic speakers with differing loci of lesions. Clinical Aphasiology Conference Proceedings, Minneapolis: BKR Publishers, 1982.

Square, P.A., Darley, F.L. & Sommers, R.K. Speech perception among patients demonstrating apraxia of speech, aphasia, and both disorders. In R. Brookshire (Ed.) Clinical Aphasiology Conference Proceedings, Minneapolis: BKR Publishers, 1981.

Square, P.A. & Mlcoch, A. The syndrome of subcortical apraxia of speech: An acoustic analysis. In R.N. Brookshire (Ed.), Clinical Aphasiology Conference Proceedings, Minneapolis: BKR Publishers, 1983.

Stelmach, G.E. Motor Control: Issues and Trends. New York: Academic Press, 1976.

Sternberg, S., Monsell, S., Knoll, R. & Wright, C. The latency and duration of rapid movement sequences: Comparisons of speech and typewriting. In G.E. Stelmach (Ed.) Information Processing in Motor Control and Learning. New York: Academic Press, 1978.

Stevens, K.N. & Halle, M. Remarks on analysis by synthesis and distinctive features. In W. Wathen-Dunn (Ed.), Models for the Perception of Speech and Visual Form, Cambridge: MIT Press, 88-102, 1964.

Stevens, K.N. & House, A.S. Perturbation of vowel articulation by consonantal context: An acoustical study. Journal of Speech and Hearing Research, 1963, 6, 111-128.

Stevens, K.N. & Perkell, J.S. Speech physiology and phonetic features. In M. Sawashima & F.S. Cooper (Eds.), Dynamic Aspects of Speech Production, Tokyo: University of Tokyo Press, 1977.

Sussman, H.M. What the tongue tells the brain. Psychological Bulletin, 1972, 77, 262-272.

Teixeira, L.A., Defran, R.H. & Nichols, A.C. Oral stereognostic differences between apraxics, dysarthrics, aphasics, and normals. Journal of Communication Disorders, 1974, 7, 213-225.

Tognola, G. & Vignolo, L.A. Brain lesions associated with oral apraxia in stroke patients: A clinico-neuroradiologic investigation with CT scans. Neuropsychologia, 1980, 18, 257-272.

Trevarthen, C. Manipulative strategies of baboons and origins of cerebral asymmetrics. In M. Kinsbourne (Ed.) Asymmetrical Function of the Brain. New York: Cambridge University Press, 1978.

Trost, J.E. & Canter, G.J. Apraxia of speech in patients with Broca's aphasia: A study of phoneme production accuracy and error pattern. Brain and Language, 1974, 1, 63-79.

Tulving, E. Theoretical issues in free recall. In T.R. Dixon & A.L. Horton (Eds.) Verbal Behaviour and General Behaviour Theory. Englewood Cliffs, N.J.: Prentice Hall, 1968.

Turvey, M.T., Shaw, R.E. & Mace, W. Issues in the theory of action: Degrees of freedom, coordinative structures and coalitions. In J. Requin (Ed.) Attention and Performance VII. New Jersey: Erlbaum, 1978.

Warrington, E.K., Logue, V. & Pratt, R.T.C. The anatomical localization of selective impairment of auditory verbal short-term memory. Neuropsychologia, 1971, 9, 377-387.

Warrington, E.K. & Shallice, T. The selective impairment of auditory verbal short-term memory. Brain, 1969, 92, 885-896.

Whitehouse, P., Caramazza, A. & Zurif, E. Naming in aphasia: Interacting effects of form and function. Brain and Language, 1978, 6, 63-74.

Wilson, S.A.K. A contribution to the study of apraxia. Brain, 1908, 31, 164-216.

Wingate, M.E. Effect of changes in audition on stuttering. Journal of Speech and Hearing Research, 1970, 13(4), 861-873.

Neuropsychological Studies of Apraxia
and Related Disorders, E.A. Roy (ed.)
© Elsevier Science Publishers B.V. (North-Holland), 1985

APRAXIA AND APHASIA. ANATOMICAL AND CLINICAL RELATIONSHIP

Andrew Kertesz

University of Western Ontario

Systematic investigations of aphasia and apraxia reveal a significant correlation between these two disorders, however, dissociations occur in substantial numbers. There are well documented instances of severe aphasia without apraxia. Apraxia without aphasia is also seen. Impairment of comprehension correlates best with apraxia, although comprehension deficit is not the cause of apraxia. Aphasia and apraxia coexist either because of anatomical proximity of the mechanisms of praxis and language or because of the sharing of their fundamental neural mechanisms.

Apraxia will be discussed in this chapter within the framework of Liepmann's clinical definition: impairment of skilled movement which is not attributable to comprehension deficit or paralysis. One could ask, with reason, whether such a phenomenon can be separated from other types of movement disorders such as clumsiness or disturbances of sequencing, or fine motor coordination in speech, drawing, constructing or manipulating objects. Since all of these require skilled movement, the above definition is not entirely sufficient to separate apraxia from related phenomena, which one time or another have been classified with the apraxias. However, apraxia is considered by most clinicians and investigators sufficiently distinct to deserve a separate categorization and attention, as this book testifies.

The most common variety of apraxia encountered in clinical practice is that which is seen in association with aphasia. The nature of this association is an important issue in behavioural neurology and neuropsychology. First of all, it should be stated that dissociations are often observed. There are many aphasics who are not apractic. Similarly, apraxia has been described without significant language impairment. It is important to examine the association as well as the dissociations because they provide insight into the mechanisms of disruption of skilled movements and language.

Few studies have looked at the association of aphasia and apraxia systematically. Liepmann (1905) examined 42 left and 41 right hemiplegic patients in a chronic hospital (excluding severe dementia). He also had five aphasics without hemiplegia with presumed left hemisphere lesions. Only one in that particular series was neither paralyzed nor aphasic, only apractic. He had the patients do a series of intransitive movements such as threaten, wave, throw a kiss, thumb nose, salute and raise a hand to swear, in addition to transitive movements such as knocking, pulling a bell, counting out money, catching flies, playing the organ-grinder and beating time. Some intransitive movements were not iconic, such as snapping fingers and swimming. Manipulating objects, consisting of items of variable complexity were included, such as combing hair, brushing sleeves, sealing a letter or sticking a stamp on an envelope. His left-hemiplegic control group performed these actions promptly, and so did an unspecified number of control patients who were senile and demented, but not paralyzed. Among the right hemiplegics, 20, or about half, showed definite impairment and some of the others were somewhat slow and imprecise, although some of this was attributable to the lack of skill in the left hand. Of the 20 right-hemiplegic patients with apraxia, 14 showed severe speech disturbances, mostly motor aphasia, and of the 21 non-apractic patients only four had aphasia. The example of a man with severe motor, and some sensory aphasia, who had no apraxia, was mentioned. Liepmann also had six non-aphasic right hemiplegics with left sided disturbance of praxis, indicating that apraxia was not dependent on aphasia. Aphasic comprehension deficit was often argued to be the reason why aphasics have apraxia. Liepmann countered this by saying that preserved understanding can be demonstrated in ways other than following commands. Often the beginning of the movement is correct, or the performance is a distortion of the required movement, and finally, with most patients, apraxia persists with imitation even without verbal request.

Liepmann (1905) also established the hierarchy of deficit. In the majority of patients the disability mainly concerned movements from memory, or performance on verbal request. He stated that expressive gestures or intransitive movements were the most involved. However, transitive movements, or pretending to use objects, were also affected. Imitation of movement was not disturbed to the same degree as spontaneous performance on request. Finally, he indicated that object use was failed only by seven of the patients. Liepmann felt that the motor act of speaking is similar to other actions without an object, which utilize mechanisms relying on "memory". Therefore, a motor speech disturbance could be considered apraxia for speech.

Liepmann paid attention to the type of aphasia, noting the high frequency of motor aphasia in cases of apraxia. He also mentioned specifically three sensory aphasics who had no trouble copying movements, and considered these instances representative of ideational apraxia. According to him, the preserved imitation and a greater interchange of movements are the important distinguishing features in ideational apraxia. These "movement-confusions" are analogous to verbal confusions in aphasia (Liepmann, 1913). Amorphic movements are more characteristic of ideokinetic apraxia.

Alajouanine and Lhermitte (1960) did not think there was a direct relationship between apraxia and aphasia. They pointed out that anarthria or motor aphasia can persist without buccofacial apraxia and, on the other hand, buccofacial apraxia is not rare in temporal aphasia where there is no anarthria. Goodglass and Kaplan (1963) examined 20 aphasic patients and 19 non-aphasic brain-damaged controls with an extensive test of gesture and pantomime. Gestures were defined as conventionalized movements and pantomime as a more improvised form of communication, which ordinarily takes the place of speech. Although many interesting items were tested, including complex pantomime recognition, the scoring, which was at three levels of severity, excluded the worst performances because of the possible interference by comprehension deficit. The patients were also ranked on comprehension, object naming, conversational speech, and the performance scale of the Wechsler Intelligence test with the exception of the digit symbol. The pantomime subtests were difficult for both aphasics and controls. Unfortunately the study excluded the most severely affected patients and this undoubtedly contributed to the lowering of the correlation between aphasia and apraxia. They concluded that although the performance of gesture is more impaired in aphasics, the evidence did not fully support the idea of a "central communication disorder". They found that apraxia was not accompanied by aphasia in all cases. Five non-aphasic patients had impaired performance by 24% or more. The only subtest which correlated closely to the severity of aphasia was the complex pantomime which was not corrected for auditory comprehension. None of the aphasic subjects in their sample had any difficulty in handling real objects. Aphasics, however, improved less on imitation than the control group, indicating a disturbance in the execution of movements. They also suggested that the association of language and praxis was related to the contiguity of neural structures involved.

Oral apraxia, verbal apraxia, and aphasia

Oral or buccofacial apraxia has been examined separately because of a postulated relationship to impairment of speech. Nathan (1947) studied facial apraxia in a small sample of head-injured patients whose verbal behaviour he described as apractic dysarthria. Bay (1962) found oral apraxia consistently present in aphasic patients with what he called "cortical dysarthria" and he considered the effort, explosiveness and spasms of oral movements common to both disturbances. Alajouanine and Lhermitte (1960) pointed out that, although oral apraxia is common in Broca's aphasia, it tends to recover better than speech movements because the latter is more complex.

De Renzi, Pieczuro and Vignolo (1966) set out to investigate the relationship between oral apraxia and the phonemic-articulatory disorders in the various clinical syndromes of aphasia, and the relationship between oral apraxia and limb apraxia. He found three non-aphasic patients with oral apraxia but most of the time the severity of oral apraxia correlated with the presence of severe phonemic-articulatory disorders. The correlation between oral apraxia and limb apraxia was higher than the correlation between oral apraxia and phonemic-articulatory disorders of speech. Oral apraxia also occurred independently from limb apraxia in several instances. Eighty percent of Broca's aphasics, 33% of conduction aphasics, and interestingly enough, 83% of jargon aphasics also had oral apraxia. Milder Wernicke's aphasics without jargon had a relatively low incidence of oral apraxia. An interesting finding in this study, which deviates somewhat from the rest of the literature, is the high incidence of phonemic-articulatory disorders as well as oral apraxia in phonemic jargon. They also presented four cases with severe phonemic-articulatory disorders with virtually normal oral praxis. Two of these patients were fairly acute, one with phonemic jargon and the other with the syndrome of "phonetic disintegration", and two others had more chronic Broca's aphasia. They explained the discrepancy by the earlier recovery of non-verbal movements, and for the opposite dissociation they postulated that lesions in the anterior parietal lobe would impair structures subserving oral praxis without involving limb praxis or verbal movements. De Renzi et al. (1966) thought that the coincidence of oral apraxia and Broca's aphasia was not as likely due to concomitant impairment of anatomically associated but functionally independent areas, than to impairment of structures that are common to both praxis and language mechanisms.

Apraxia in Aphasia

We have investigated the relationship of apraxia to language impairment and the distribution of the categories of praxis across aphasic types in an aphasic population and controls (Kertesz & Hooper, 1982). Specifically, 230 consecutively examined aphasic patients were given the Western Aphasia Battery (Kertesz, 1982) and the praxis test consisting of 20 items in four descriptive categories (Table 1). The patients were asked to carry out each movement and if there was no response, or only an amorphous, approximate response, the patient was shown the movement by the examiner and encouraged by words and gestures to imitate. Equal credit was given for the performance on imitation as well as on verbal command to avoid the comprehension difficulty and obviate the need to exclude the more severely affected patients. If a standard performance was achieved by either method, the patient received a score of "3". Impaired but recognizable performance was scored "2", and poor but approximate performance was scored one. For eight items, marked with an asterisk on the table, objects were supplied, and if the patient performed the item with an object only, a credit of "1" was given. No performance, unrecognizable or completely unrelated gesturing, or completely erroneous use of the objects, were scored "0". Maximum score was 60. The population was mostly stroke patients, with a small number with tumour, trauma and degenerative disease included. Most were examined in the first month of their illness, a smaller number at three months and a few in a more chronic stage. Left-handed and ambidexterous patients were excluded. One hundred and twenty-five controls were also examined with the same tests of language and praxis consisting of 21 normal age-matched hospital patients without brain disease and 72 non-aphasic right hemisphere lesions and 32 non-aphasic left hemisphere damaged patients. The patients were grouped into eight diagnostic categories of aphasia based on the scores of the Western Aphasia Battery according to taxonomic criteria published previously (Kertesz, 1979). The sum of their language scores, the aphasia quotient (AQ), was the measure of the severity of aphasia.

The results of the study indicated that global aphasics were the most apractic, with complex and transitive movements being more affected than facial and intransitive upper limb movements. This pattern of difficulty level between the various categories of praxis was similar in other aphasic groups as well. It was interesting to observe that isolation aphasics, although only a small number were observed, seemed to do significantly better on the praxis task than globals. This seemed to be related to their better preserved imitation. However, they still had significantly poorer praxis than Broca's aphasics even though their AQ was higher than Broca's group. Wernicke's aphasics had generally less apraxia even though their comprehension was worse than Broca's aphasics. Transcortical aphasics and conduction aphasics had similar praxis scores even though their fluency, comprehension and repetition scores were significantly different. Anomic aphasics had the best scores, approximating the right hemisphere group. They were different from controls mostly in the complex bimanual movements.

It was also interesting to note that left hemisphere non-aphasic controls had slightly higher total praxis than right hemisphere damaged patients which is somewhat different from what one would expect if the left hemisphere was diffusely dominant for skilled movements.

Generally speaking, intransitive conventional movements were usually the best performed, followed by facial movements and transitive movements; the most difficult of all categories seemed to be complex movements. The differences between the categories were more marked at severe levels of impairment but the hierarchical trend from intransitive to complex movement was similar in all categories.

Table 1

Apraxia Subtests

i)	Facial	1.	put out your tongue
		2.	close your eyes
		3.	whistle
		4.	sniff a flower*
		5.	blow out a match*
ii)	Intransitive	1.	make a fist
	(upper limb)	2.	salute
		3.	wave goodbye
		4.	scratch your head
		5.	snap your fingers
iii)	Transitive	1.	use a comb*
	(instrumental)	2.	use a toothbrush*
		3.	use a spoon to eat*
		4.	use a hammer*
		5.	use a key*
iv)	Complex	1.	pretend to drive a car
		2.	pretend to knock at the door
		3.	pretend to fold a paper*
		4.	pretend to light a cigarette
		5.	pretend to play the piano

* Items for which objects are also used.

Praxis and Language Parameters

Comprehension deficit and the severity of aphasia (AQ) correlated best with apraxia. These two parameters correlated highly with all categories of praxis. There was also a high correlation with drawing, but block design and Raven's matrices showed less correlation than the language parameters. We also found that facial praxis scores correlated best with measures of verbal output such as fluency and repetition. There was a high correlation ($r = 0.73$, $p = < 0.01$) between total praxis and the severity of aphasia (AQ). This conclusion was different from the low level of correlation found by Goodglass and Kaplan (1963), explained mainly by their scoring system which eliminated the worst responses as well as the selection of more mildly affected patients in that study. Hecaen (1978) also found that language parameters and performance on verbal commands correlated significantly, but he emphasized several dissociations and suggested that gesture may be impaired without direct relationship to the degree of language disturbance.

In our study there was no significant difference between "anterior and posterior" aphasics who were matched for severity, such as Broca's and Wernicke's, or transcortical motor and transcortical sensory aphasics. This does not support the concept of different mechanisms for posterior left hemisphere structures versus anterior structures in the performance of complex sequential patterns of movements versus single acts (Kimura & Archibald, 1974). In fact, single intransitive movements appear to be less affected or easier than complex bimanual acts in all types of aphasics. The only category specific feature was that the severity of oral apraxia was more marked than limb apraxia in Broca's and transcortical motor aphasia cases. This reaffirms the conclusions of De Renzi et al. (1966), and corroborates Tognola and Vignolo's study (1980), which showed a preponderance of anterior and central lesions in oral apraxia. Although Geschwind (1965) predicted that conduction aphasia with supramarginal gyrus lesions would have a higher incidence of apraxia, our data failed to show more apraxia in this group. In fact they seemed to have milder apraxia than other aphasic groups, such as transcortical aphasia, who had better overall language scores.

The role of comprehension in apraxia and the relationship of perceptual processes to motor phenomena is quite complex. The idea that an underlying general factor of cognitive processing is needed for language comprehension as well as praxis is suggested by the high correlation between apraxia and comprehension scores, even though the comprehension deficit is excluded as a factor in eliciting the movements by the use of imitation.

Dissociations of Apraxia and Aphasia

We have expanded our investigation of the functional and anatomical relationship between aphasia and apraxia recently (Kertesz, Ferro & Shewan, 1984). For this study we selected 177 left hemisphere stroke patients with lesion localization on CT scans, as well as completed aphasia and apraxia tests. One hundred and fifty-two patients were examined within the first month of illness (acute group), and 143 patients at three or more months post-onset (chronic group). One hundred and eighteen patients had both acute and chronic tests. We were particularly interested in the instances of dissociation where praxis was spared in severe aphasia and where apraxia occurred without aphasia or where recovery appeared to be divergent. We defined the cutoff scores separating apractics from non-apractics, on the basis of 21 age-matched hospital patients without brain damage, as two standard deviations below the mean control scores. None of the normals scored below this point. In the acute group 54.6% of the patients were apractic, contrasting with only 39.9% in the chronic group. Aphasic and apractic patients were further divided into three categories, of severe, moderate or mild impairment, according to their AQ or total apraxia scores. For both scores, mild impairment was defined as the range from the cutoff score to two-thirds of the cutoff score, moderate impairment as the range from two-thirds to one-third of the cutoff score, and severe impairment as the scores below the one-third of the cutoff score. The cutoff score for the aphasics was 93.8 determined by our previous standardization study (Kertesz, 1979). The distribution of patients according to the severity of aphasia and apraxia is tabulated separately for the acute and chronic groups (Tables 2 and 3). This indicates that apraxia was not observed in non-aphasic patients and severe apraxia was present only in severe aphasics. This is partly due to the fact that our population was referred because of symptoms in the left hemisphere, the most prominent being aphasia. In other words "silent" left hemisphere lesions not causing aphasia, which would be located outside of the middle cerebral artery territory, were not as likely to be included in this group. However, these are rarely caused by stroke and do not come to medical attention as often.

Some of the important dissociations between aphasia and apraxia are also indicated in Tables 2 and 3. There were six cases of severe aphasia without apraxia and four cases of moderate apraxia showing only mild aphasia. Some of these dissociations are discussed further below.

Table 2

Acute Patients

APHASIA (AQ)	APRAXIA (total apraxia score)			
	No Apraxia (<51)	Mild (>33-50<)	Moderate (>17-33<)	Severe (<17)
Not Aphasic (>93.8)	9	--	--	--
Mild (>62-93.7)	44	6	3	--
Moderate (>31-61<)	12	17	4	--
Severe (<30)	4	7	15	31

Table 3

Chronic Patients

APHASIA (AQ)	APRAXIA (total apraxia score)			
	No Apraxia (>50)	Apraxia (>33-50<)	Mild (>17-33<)	Severe (<17)
Not Aphasic (>93.8)	17	--	--	--
Mild (>62-93.7)	60	10	1	--
Moderate (>31-61<)	7	11	4	--
Severe (<30)	2	9	13	9

The correlation coefficients between apraxia and aphasia indicated that the severity of aphasia by itself can explain less than 20% of the variance of apraxia. The actual correlation value of r = 0.44, p < 0.001 in the acute and r = 0.41, p < 0.001 in the chronic group was lower than in our previous series mentioned above. This difference could be related to population differences because the severity and number of patients in each type of aphasia would change the degree of correlation. Our previous study showed that this particular relationship varies within the type of aphasia and therefore the actual correlation values would be different from series to series because of the type of aphasics included. The lower correlation in the chronic group appears to be related to the differential recovery of apraxia and aphasia which could be in either direction. In fact, apraxia tends to recover better in some individual cases and this accounts for the several cases of persisting aphasics who have apraxia. We looked at the recovery rates of apraxia in aphasics previously (Kertesz, 1979) and found that global aphasics have somewhat better recovery in praxis than their total language scores. The praxis recovery curve paralleled comprehension more than other language subtests. We had 13 patients with various other types of aphasia, who were followed for one year, and their recovery rates of praxis were, in general, parallel to the recovery rates of language (AQ) and comprehension. However, our more recent studies indicate that divergent recovery is not uncommon. These data need further quantification.

We looked at those cases where severe aphasia was not followed by any gestural disturbances. In one of our cases a small lesion involved the superior temporal gyrus producing a severe stable Wernicke's aphasia. Sparing of occipito-parietal to frontal connections would explain the good performance on imitation. In another patient a small central cortical-subcortical lesion caused a hemiparesis and severe nonfluent aphasia that recovered well. Only minor buccofacial errors were noted on apraxia examination initially. The infarct in this case did not extend into the premotor region to destroy motor patterns and the parieto-frontal connections were also largely spared.

In four other cases, large left hemispheric lesions were present with severe nonfluent aphasia. Two of these patients showed apraxia in the acute stage that recovered quickly while their aphasia remained severe. This accounts for the subsequently observed dissociation. The two remaining patients did not have apraxia to begin with and their recovery of language was also superior to what was expected from their initial severity and aphasia type. In these two patients the occipital skull asymmetry which is usually observed in right-handers was absent and this may relate to bilateral cerebral representation for language and praxis allowing for greater recovery. These cases suggested that in some subjects the visual kinesthetic engrams for gestures may be represented in both hemispheres. Bilateral representation of motor patterns can also account for the rapid recovery of left-handed apraxia in callosum-sectioned patients according to Gazzaniga, Bogen and Sperry (1967).

Dissociations in the other direction also occur. Selnes, Rubens, Risse and Levy (1982) published a case of severe apraxia with recovering aphasia. In this instance, Wernicke's area was spared which was just the reverse situation from one of our cases mentioned above. We also had four cases of moderate apraxia showing only a mild aphasia.

Localization of lesions in apraxia

Most previous studies of the anatomical aspects of apraxia were based on single cases or a series, in which the differentiation was usually restricted to the hemispheres or, at best, to the quadrantic or lobar level. Many authors have doubted that apraxia is associated with a lesion in any particular area. For instance, von Monakow's (1914) study showed that there were apractic as well as non-apractic patients with similar left parietal lesions. Basso's (Basso, Luzzatti & Spinnler, 1980) CT study found no difference in lesion size between patients with or without apraxia, except that non-apractics appeared to have lesions extending deeper than those in apractics (see Basso et al., this volume). Tognola and Vignolo (1980) showed that patients with buccofacial apraxia tend to have frontal and central opercular lesions and involve the anterior insula as well.

We studied the CT correlations of lesions and apraxia in our population of left hemisphere damaged patients. Altogether, 295 correlations of CT lesions were obtained, 152 in the acute stage and 143 in the chronic stage. Patients were scored for apraxia as described above and the CT measurements were made specifically for lesion size and lesion location. The CT lesions were traced on templates by a radiologist who was not aware of the clinical state of the patient (in other words, independently from the aphasia or apraxia test scores). Lesion size was measured by tracing the outline of each lesion with a digitizer program and adding the values for each cut to obtain a volumetric measure. Hemispheric volume was also measured by adding the size of each template in the left hemisphere. Lesions were then grouped according to small, moderate and large categories according to the fraction of hemispheric volume involved. Small lesions were less than one-tenth of the volume and large lesions were more than one-third of the left hemispheric volume. Moderate lesions were those in between.

The results of this study (Kertesz & Ferro, Note 1) indicate that apraxia and lesion size correlates significantly in the acute ($r=0.39$, $p < 0.001$) and in the chronic groups ($r=0.5$, $p < 0.001$). The most striking examples of dissociations were nine acute and three chronic patients whose small lesions were associated with moderate to severe apraxia and at the other end, nine acute and 14 chronic patients had large left hemispheric lesions not associated with apraxia.

The most interesting localization concerned those patients who had moderate to severe ideomotor apraxia with relatively small lesions. Seven patients had subcortical lesions mostly in the frontal lobe and the anterior half of the periventricular white matter. These patients were severely non-fluent aphasics with right hemiplegia and they performed with their left hand only. A typical lesion is seen in Figures 1 and 2. Lesions in this location appear to damage both the white matter connecting the occipital with the frontal lobes and the anterior callosal fibres connecting the premotor areas of both hemispheres. Two other cases with small lesions had more posterior localization. One was in the posterior cerebral artery distribution, which is more often seen with transcortical sensory aphasia. This patient had a Wernicke's aphasia and it was felt that the left parietal lobe was disconnected from visual association areas by the extensive subcortical occipital and callosal lesions. This would prevent gesture-related visual information from reaching the parietal areas where kinesthetic-visual motor patterns are formed. In the second case a moderate size parietal infarct involved most of the supramarginal and angular gyrus; this case is similar to the classical localization described by Liepmann and Maas (1907) and von Monakow (1914). Some of these cases also had a moderate amount of ventricular dilatation although none of them had obvious dementia.

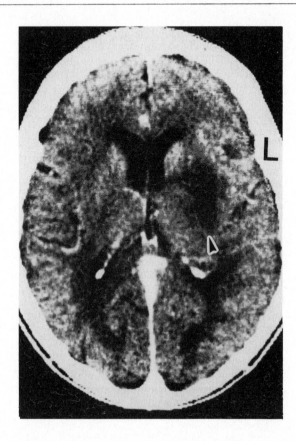

Figure 1.   CT scan of a patient with persistent apraxia and a smaller
             subcortical lesion. The globus pallidus and putamen are
             involved in this cut and the lesion extends to the anterior
             internal capsule. The arrow points to the posterior edge of
             the lesion on the left (L = left).

Patients with large left hemispheric lesions without apraxia were not uncommon. Eighteen percent of the acute and thirty percent of chronic patients (seven of
them being a follow-up of the acute cases) were not apractic. There was a remarkable incidence of uncommon patterns of skull asymmetries among them. LeMay
(1977) suggested that skull asymmetries on the CT scan may be correlated with cerebral dominance. In right handers there is a left occipital prominence balanced by a
less obvious prominence of the right frontal lobe. Such asymmetries may be nonexistent or reversed in left handers. Pieniadz, Naeser, Koff and Levine (Note 2)
suggested that the atypical pattern may be associated with better recovery after
left hemispheric lesions. We measured the occipital and frontal "torques" according
to the methods of LeMay (1977) to investigate these asymmetries. One patient had
a typical left-handed pattern; four patients had larger right occipital torques, and in

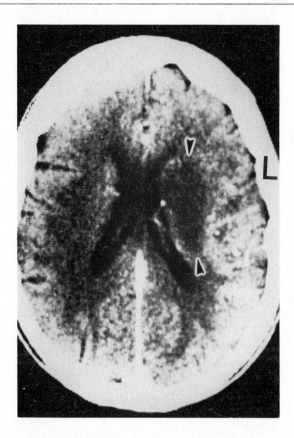

Figure 2.   A higher cut of the same patient as in Figure 1. The lesion is
in the periventricular white matter, which was the common
area for apraxia with small lesions. The anterior and posterior
edges of the lesion are marked with arrows (L = left).

three of them the widths were also larger than in the left hemisphere. In three others the left frontal lobe had a larger torque or width. This indicated that 50% of
these patients had partial or complete reversal of the common right handed pattern
of skull asymmetry, that is, a larger right frontal and left occipital area. There was
also a significant difference in age. The large lesion, recovered group was significantly younger than the persisting apractic group with smaller lesions. Furthermore, a significant difference in the main ventricle/brain ratios, indicated more
cerebral atrophy in the persisting apractic group.

The interpretation of these complex data is important to our understanding of
cerebral mechanisms of praxis or skilled movements. Lesion size explained only
about 25% of the variance of apraxia scores, suggesting that apraxia is not only
related to the amount of left hemisphere damage but that location of the lesions is

important also. The crucial areas concerned with praxis can be inferred from the small lesions that cause a persisting severe ideomotor apraxia as tested by perform-ance on command or imitation of gestures. The most frequent location of these lesions was the anterior half of periventricular white matter and frontal lobe. These relatively small lesions appear to damage the parieto-frontal pathways and callosal connections (Figure 3). This is compatible with Liepmann's (1905) model of apraxia which has been elaborated subsequently by Geschwind (1965) and others. The dis-connection prevents visuokinesthetic information from evoking the frontal motor patterns. We had relatively few cases which had a purely parietal lesion causing apraxia. The role of the parietal lobe in forming visuokinesthetic patterns remains controversial. While many investigators support Liepmann's original idea of the importance of the parietal lobe in praxis, this is not the most common location of lesions producing apraxia.

The association of aphasia and apraxia is partly anatomical and partly function-al. There is a topographic component which is peculiar to vascular lesions. Damage to language and praxis areas are included in the middle cerebral artery territory regardless of their possible functional connections. Therefore, if one takes a series of stroke cases such as Basso and her associates have done, the overlaps of the posi-tive and negative cases may be quite similar because they represent the same arterial distribution. Similarly, the anatomical overlap between the lesions produc-ing aphasia and apraxia may be more coincidental to the arterial distribution of lesions than related to a fundamentally common physiological mechanism.

Cerebral functions may be represented in distinct but interconnected sites. In each cortical area several components of these functions are represented, and each area belongs to several overlapping networks (Mesulam, 1981). Our data suggest that the praxis network may have more bi-hemispheric representation than language. although the difference is not substantial and the left hemisphere is clearly domi-nant for praxis mechanisms as well as for language. The sign language literature indicates that aphasic impairment results in an analogous loss of sign language to that of speech in aphasia. However, a separation of the linguistic components of sign language and non-linguistic gesturing has been observed in brain-damaged sign-ers (Poizner, Bellugi & Iragui, Note 3). Because of the occasional dissociation of praxis from language disturbance the possibility of using sign language for aphasics. as an alternative communication has been considered. "Amerind" sign language was advocated by Skelly, Schinsky, Smith and Fust (1974) as suitable for aphasics because the signs have no grammar and tend to be more representative. Sign sys-tems which are abstract and involve complex syntactic signals are much more diffi-cult for aphasic patients even though they may have less apraxia.

Conclusions

1.   Systematic investigations of aphasia and apraxia established a significant correlation, but dissociations occur in substantial numbers.

2.   There are well documented instances of severe aphasia without apraxia for various apparent reasons: Wernicke's aphasia where imitation or visuoki-nesthetic input is preserved; Broca's aphasia where praxis seems to have recovered more than language; and cases of possible dissociated dominance for language and praxis.

3.   Apraxia without aphasia is also seen, mostly with callosal or subcortical lesions, or in instances of dissociated dominance.

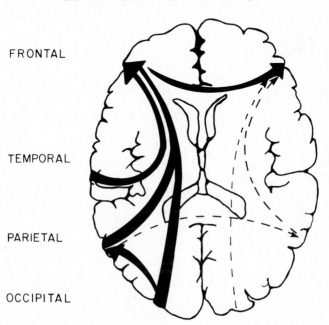

MECHANISMS OF PRAXIS

FRONTAL

TEMPORAL

PARIETAL

OCCIPITAL

Figure 3.   A diagrammatic representation of the neural mechanisms of praxis. Interruption of this network at any point may result in apraxia. Small lesions may affect the system most consistently where convergence of pathways occur. Interrupted lines represent alternate routes that may become active with recovery.

4.   Oral or buccofacial apraxia is more common in Broca's aphasia, although it is certainly seen in other types of aphasia.

5.   Global aphasics may have better recovery of praxis than general language function. Although the recovery of aphasia and apraxia is often parallel regardless of aphasia type, better recovery of praxis in many instances accounts for persisting aphasia without apraxia.

6.   Impairment of comprehension correlates best with apraxia, although comprehension deficit is not the cause of apraxia.

7.   Aphasia and apraxia coexist either because of anatomical proximity of the mechanisms of praxis and language or because of the sharing of their fundamental neural mechanisms. The former is compatible both with the degree of association and dissociation but the latter is not supported by their dissociations.

8.   Relatively small subcortical, periventricular lesions in the left hemisphere may cause severe apraxia more often than lesions in other sites. The classical lesion localization to the left parietal lobe in apraxia is not confirmed.

REFERENCE NOTES

1. Kertesz, A. & Ferro, J.M. Lesion size and location in ideomotor apraxia. Presented at the Academy of Neurology, San Diego, 1983.

2. Pieniadz, J.M., Naeser, M.A., Koff, E. & Levine, H.L. CT scan cerebral hemispheric asymmetry measurements in stroke cases with global aphasia: atypical asymmetries associated with improved recovery. Presented at the 17th Annual Academy of Aphasia Meeting, San Diego, October 16, 1979.

3. Poizner, H., Bellugi, U. & Iragui, V. Apraxia and aphasia for a visual-gestural language, personal communication, 1983.

REFERENCES

Alajouanine, T.H. & Lhermitte, F. Les Troubles des activities expressive du langage dans l'aphasie. Leurs relations avec les apraxies. Revue Neurologique, 1960, 102, 604-629.

Basso, A., Luzzatti, C. & Spinnler, H. Is ideomotor apraxia the outcome of damage to well-defined regions of the left hemisphere? Journal of Neurology, Neurosurgery and Psychiatry, 1980, 43, 118-126.

Bay, E. Aphasia and non-verbal disorders of language. Brain, 1962, 85, 412-426.

De Renzi, E., Pieczuro, A. & Vignolo, L.A. Oral apraxia and aphasia. Cortex, 1966, 2, 50-73.

Gazzaniga, M.S., Bogen, J.E. & Sperry, R.W. Dyspraxia following division of the cerebral commissures. Archives of Neurology, 1967, 16, 606-612.

Geschwind, N. Disconnexion syndromes in animals and man. Brain, 1965, 88, 237-294, 585-644.

Goodglass, H. & Kaplan, E. Disturbance of gesture and pantomime in aphasia. Brain, 1963, 86, 703-720.

Hecaen, H. Les apraxies ideomotrices. Essai de dissociation. In H. Hecaen and M. Jeannerod (Eds.), Du Controle Moteur a l'Organization du Geste. Paris: Masson, 1978.

Kertesz, A. Aphasia and Associated Disorders: Taxonomy, Localization and Recovery. New York: Grune and Stratton, 1979.

Kertesz, A. The Western Aphasia Battery. New York: Grune and Stratton, 1982.

Kertesz, A. & Hooper, P. Praxis and Language. The extent and variety of apraxia in aphasia. Neuropsychologia, 1982, 20, 275-286.

Kertesz, A., Ferro, J.M. & Shewan, C.M. Apraxia and Aphasia. The functional-anatomical basis for their dissociation. Neurology, 1984, 30, 40-47.

Kimura, D. & Archibald, Y. Motor function of the left hemisphere. Brain, 1974, 97, 337-350.

LeMay, M. Asymmetries of the skull and handedness. Journal of Neurological Sciences, 1977, 32, 243-253.

Liepmann, H. Die linke Hemisphere und das Handeln. Mundrener Medzinische Wochenschrift, 1905, 48 and 49.

Liepmann. H. & Maas, O. Ein Fall von linksseitiger Agraphie und Apraxie bei dem Falle Gorstelle. Monatschrift fur Psychiatrie und Neurologie, 1907, 10, 214-227.

Liepmann, H. Motorische Aphasie und Apraxia. Monatschrift fur Psychiatrie und Neurologie, 1913, 34.

Mesulam, M.M. A cortical network for directed attention and unilateral neglect. Annals of Neurology, 1981, 10, 309-325.

Monakow, C. von. Die Lokalisation im Grosshirn und der Abbau der Funktion durch corticale Herde. Wiesbaden: Bergmann, 1914.

Nathan, P.W. Facial apraxia and apractic dysarthria. Brain, 1947, 70, 449.

Selnes, O.A., Rubens, A.B., Risse, G.L. & Levy, R.S. Transient aphasia with persistent apraxia. Uncommon sequela of massive left-hemisphere stroke. Archives of Neurology, 1982, 39, 122-126.

Skelly, M., Schinsky, L., Smith, R. & Fust, R. American Indian sign (Amerind) as a facilitator of verbalization for the oral verbal apractic. Journal of Speech and Hearing Disorders, 1974, 39, 445-446.

Tognola, G. & Vignolo, L. Brain lesions associated with oral apraxia in stroke patients: a clinico-neuroradiological investigation with the CT scan. Neuropsychologia, 1980, 18, 257-271.

*Neuropsychological Studies of Apraxia
and Related Disorders, E.A. Roy (ed.)*
© *Elsevier Science Publishers B.V. (North-Holland), 1985*

METHODS IN NEUROANATOMICAL RESEARCH AND AN EXPERIMENTAL

STUDY OF LIMB APRAXIA

A. Basso, P. Faglioni and C. Luzzatti

Universita di Milano e Universita di Modena

The different techniques used in the study of cerebral localization are briefly reviewed. Problems arising in identification and delimitation of the lesion from CT scan pictures are considered in some detail. The results of an experimental study are reported. One hundred and fifty-two vascular left brain-damaged patients were subjected to CT scan investigation and apraxia examination. Patients were divided into three groups according to apraxia score: apractic, border-line and non-apractic patients. The size and the location of lesion were compared in the three groups.

Localization of cerebral functions has for many decades been based on anatomo-clinical correlations. Some single cases which presented specific and considerable neuropsychological deficits were studied post mortem with anatomical methods in order to identify the cerebral site of typical lesions. "Negative" cases, i.e. patients with a lesion in the critical areas without expected neuropsychological symptom, could not be recognized in this way, and the rare ones which were, have only been briefly described. Notwithstanding its limits, it is the anatomo-clinical method which has given us most of our knowledge on the anatomical structures involved in the different neuropsychological functions. In the last 20 years instrumental techniques allowing the anatomical and functional study of subjects 'in vivo' have been elaborated; they allow the correlation between anatomical findings and the presence or absence of a specific deficit in large series of brain-damaged patients chosen without selection for the presence of the symptom being studied. Normal subjects were also examined while performing gestural activities in order to study anatomo-functional-metabolic correlations. We will consider in the first part of this paper the different techniques most often employed in localization of cerebral function -- use of these same techniques in localization of apraxia producing lesions is discussed in Chapter 1; in the second part we will present some experimental data on CT localization.

Pathological Findings

The nature and the site of the lesion can be established by anatomical study of sections of the brain with higher precision than with any of the techniques used today 'in vivo'. However, with pathological study it is difficult to form a clear view of the relationship between the neuropsychological deficits studied while the patient was alive and the lesions found post mortem. The pathological process can in fact be multifocal as with multiple infarcts, traumas, etc. When it is unifocal, in the case, for example, of a tumour or a softening with perifocal edema, it can cause increased intracranial pressure or "mass effect" which is not always identifiable through anatomical or pathological indices.

What is more, a good deal of time passes between the neurological and the neuropathological examination. When the interval between the two examinations is short, the diaschisis could cause the deficit. On the other hand, during a long interval other cerebral areas with nothing to do with the symptom under study could suffer. Finally, the presence of silent lesions precedent to the damage causing the symptom and which are no longer identifiable as such when the anatomopathological picture is stabilized is not to be ruled out.

Electrical stimulation

The electrical stimulation technique employed for cortical identification during excision of intractable epileptic foci under local anesthesia was first used by Penfield and Roberts (1959) in order to localize a cerebral function 'in vivo'. They evoked naming changes from the classic language areas of inferior premotor and parieto-temporal junction cortex and also from the supplementary motor area of the language dominant hemisphere. Subsequently a great deal of data has been obtained in the same way in mapping the cortex or in mapping deep seated structures during thalamotomies for dyskinesias. For a detailed review of these techniques and related problems see Ojemann (1978, 1980, 1982, 1983; Ojemann & Mateer, 1979a,b).

Neuroradiological investigation

Radio isotope brain scan

Benson (1967) subjected 100 aphasic patients to radio isotope brain scan to study the correlation between fluency and site of lesion (anterior versus posterior). Kertesz, Ghent and Poole (1973) and Yarnell, Monroe and Sobel (1976) used the same technique. With the exception of Karis and Horenstein (1976) a fair correspondence between type of aphasia and site of lesion as might be expected on the grounds of classical doctrine was found. Kertesz, Lesk and McCabe (1977) used diagrams representing the lateral surface of the brain. By retracing the lesion on the lateral diagrams and superimposing them, they obtained composites of lesions.

The radio isotope scan technique has, however, two main limitations (Boller, Patten & Howes, 1973): on the one hand the time factor must be taken into account: in case of vascular lesion, for example, the scan is negative if performed in the first few days or after four to six weeks. On the other hand, small lesions (less than 10 cm3) are generally missed.

Vascular supply analysis

Yarnell et al. (1976) and Rosenfield and Goree (1975) used angiography to study the relationship between fluency in aphasia and locus of lesion (anterior versus posterior). More interesting data however comes from the study of regional cerebral blood flow (rCBF). The principle originally formulated by Roy and Sherrington (1890) is based on the hypothesis of a correlation between functional activity in the brain, O_2 metabolism and cerebral blood flow (Reivich, 1982). Cooper, Crow and Greywalter (1966) and Raichle, Grubb, Gado, Eichling and Ter-Pogossian (1976) found that the increase of the rCBF in the cortical area under examination is related to the use of O_2. The CBF is usually estimated by the initial slope of the clearance of 133 Xenon. The clearance curve is externally registered by a gamma-camera during a variable period (approximately 60 seconds) and mapped onto a lateral diagram using a system of multiple detectors (between 16 and 254).

Study of the rCBF has been carried out in normal subjects (patients without clinical signs of neurological focal damage who underwent a carotid angiography in order to exclude an intracranial pathology) to identify cortical areas active in the programming and execution of specific functional activities (Reivich, 1982).

The study of the rCBF by the clearance of 133 Xenon, however, is not altogether free from limitations. First of all the increase of rCBF in a given area may be due to an increase not only in cortical but also in subcortical metabolic activity, and this is particularly true of the frontal and fronto-parietal regions where the basal ganglia lie at little more than 3 cm from the surface (Hosokawa, Yamashita, Ueno & Caveness, 1977; Maeda, Matsuda, Hisada, Tonami, Mori, Fujii, Hayashi & Yamamoto, 1981). Moreover, the increase in rCBF recorded by the detectors does not correspond to an increase in the rCBF at a given moment (as it is the case when recording electrical activity) but to the mean increase in a certain period (usually 45-60 seconds). This makes it difficult to establish whether the flow increase in a given cerebral area takes place before the beginning of the function under examination or lasts throughout the function, or only finally appears towards the end of it. Lastly, the increase in the rCBF may be due not so much to the function under investigation as to a more or less correlated though different activity. Larsen, Skinhoj and Lassen (1978) studied the rCBF in the right and left hemisphere of control subjects at rest and while engaged in automatic speech (counting aloud); Orgogozo and Larsen (1979), Roland, Larsen, Lassen and Skinhoj (1980) and Roland, Skinhoj, Lassen and Larsen (1980) during simple and complex motor activities of limbs, buccofacial apparatus and eyes.

The relationship between site of lesion and neuropsychological deficits has also been investigated: Soh, Larsen, Skinhoj and Lassen (1978) found in 13 aphasic patients a good correlation between site of lesion according to the classical doctrine and aphasic syndrome, except for Broca's aphasia that seems to be due to a more posterior lesion than is generally thought to be the case, i.e. a lesion in the central area; Kohlmeyer (1979) studied 445 left and right hemisphere damaged patients and found a good correspondence between expected site of lesion and neuropsychological deficit under investigation.

Computed Tomography

CT has substantially modified the problem of anatomopsychological correlations. However it became evident at an early stage that a correct reading could not always be taken straight from a CT picture. Problems arise in identification and delimitation of the lesion in the different pathologies (1, 2) and in correct localization (3).

1) Artifacts and partial volume phenomenon: Lesions in the vicinity of bone structures like the tectus orbitarius or the petrous bone -- for example, lesions in the inferior frontal or temporal convolutions -- can be masked by artifacts due to the sudden passage from high to low density, and by the partial volume phenomenon[1] (Paxton & Ambrose, 1974; Turnier, Hondek & Trefler, 1979).

Artifacts due to the patient's movements during the scanning can also result in false negative or positive identifications. However, movement artifacts are far less important with shorter scan time as with the latest CT scans. Lesions in the inferi-

---

[1] The CT image may be considered as the result of the collapsing of the structures situated in the thickness of the section investigated; a relatively small hypodense lesion like a cerebral infarction, can be masked by the presence in the same section of a structure denser than the normal cerebral tissue (i.e., the bones of the skull).

or face of the brain, on the other hand, can be more easily identified by changing the scan incline.

2) Type and size of lesion, time post-onset and CT images: Small lesions due to softenings can pass undetected and there is widespread agreement in the literature regarding the percentage: between 80 and 100% of lesions under 15 mm diameter and 20% of lesions between 15 and 25 mm diameter give rise to false negative diagnoses (these percentages include recent lesions with possible fogging effect). For non-recent lesions of over 25 mm diameter, no false negative diagnosis has been reported (Alcala, Gado & Torack, 1978; Fullerton & Blanco, 1981; Kinkel & Jacobs, 1976; Ladurner, Sager, Iliff & Lechner, 1979; Mori, Lu, Chiu, Cancilla & Christie, 1977).

Another important parameter is the time interval between onset of CV disease and CT scan. A CT performed less than 24-48 hours post onset can still be negative; there is then a period of low density mainly due to the cytotoxical edema of the lesional focus and to the perifocal (vaso-genical) edema of the healthy tissue; generally the low density zone appears larger during this period than the true softening. Between the 15th and 25th day post onset the CT lesion image often appears less hypodense presumably because of edema resolution, macrophages extravasation, proliferation of capillaries and possible secondary blood extravasation. This phenomenon has been named "fogging effect" by Becker, Desch, Hacker and Pencz (1979), and its occurrence varies according to different authors between 10 and 20% of cases (Alcala et al., 1978; Davis, Taveras, New, Schnur & Roberson, 1975). However, Bech Skriver and Olsen (1981) found a partial fogging effect in 54% of the CT scans studied, and in 30% a fogging effect such as to completely mask the lesion or significantly reduce its size was found.

The low density zone is better demarked after the fourth or fifth week and progressively turns into the well-known low density image of the encephalomalacic cavity. In many cases a shrinkage of the cavity and a dilatation of the ipsilateral ventricle and sulci are present (Davis et al., 1975; Ladurner et al., 1979). After the third month post onset the CT image does not change.

Small lesions due to hemorrhages are easily identifiable and well delimited even in the acute stage due to the highly increased density of the blood clot. Between 15 and 30 days post onset according to the dimension of the hemorrhage, the lesion becomes slowly isodense, but in a rather dishomogeneous way (starting from the periphery). At this stage it is difficult to delimit precisely, or even identify, the lesion. The evolution towards a low density area varies from one case to another; usually an area of encephalomalacia will replace the hemorrhage and the ipsilateral ventricle and sulci adjacent to the lesion will broaden; in a few cases the stabilized lesion will appear much smaller than in the initial stage (with a typical slit-like image) or even completely disappear (Dolinskas, Bilanink, Zimmerman & Kuhl, 1977; Kinkel & Jacobs, 1976). It would thus seem evident that CT images of the cerebral hemorrhage will differ widely in form and dimensions according to when they were taken. The localization of the lesion should accordingly be made as close as possible to the neuropsychological evaluation.

3) Localization of lesions: CT images do not necessarily allow identification of such parameters as are necessary in order to pin-point a lesion. The Sylvian fissure is always adequately visible, but only when a degree -- albeit slight -- of cortical atrophy is in evidence can one hope to distinguish the other fissures of the hemispheric convexity; and these latter vary to some extent in their location. Vignolo (1979), for example, in a survey of 22 adult brains, found a mean angle of 48° between the Sylvian and Rolandic fissures with variations from 36° to 70°, while for

Kido, Le May, Levinson and Benson (1980), 69.5° is the mean angle between the Rolandic and interhemispheric fissures, with variations from 55° to 79°: findings which show that the terms of pre- and post-Rolandic used in interpreting CT pictures are in themselves not a little arbitrary, and hence more precise localization will clearly prove problematic. No strict relationship between the cranial landmarks and the parenchimal structures which lie beneath them has been found (Luzzatti, Scotti & Gattoni, 1979; Tokunaga, Takase & Otani, 1977).

Moreover, the so called axial CT scans are often on an incline, in itself variable enough, in relation to a true axial plane. It is, however, hard to ascertain the exact position of the patient's head, making it difficult to obtain CT sections on a given incline (Du Boulay, Fairbairn & Paden, 1978). There are, however, some parameters unaffected by individual anatomical differences, viz., the system of Cartesian axes along the three orthogonal dimensions, antero-posterior, latero-medial, and craniocaudal. This last entails assessment of level of the first section, degree of possible overlap and section thickness.

Various methods have been elaborated for localizing lesions with CT.

a) Direct localization on axial images or on templates (schematic axial figures taken from the actual CT scan, with the lesion traced in for clearer definition); it is an accurate means of localizing peri-Sylvian and periventricular lesions and lesions of the nucleus caudatus, the nucleus lenticularis, the thalamus and the internal capsule; laterotrigonal lesions are also easily localizable because of the vicinity of the chorioidean plexi which are visible even if not calcified. Boller, Cole, Kim, Mack and Patawaran (1975) localized the lesion in a patient with optic ataxia due to multiple cerebral embolism. Damasio and Damasio (1980) studied localization of lesions in patients with conduction aphasia and Damasio, Damasio, Rizzo, Varney and Gersh (1982) studied language disturbances arising from capsular lesions and lesions of the basal ganglia. Alexander and Schmitt (1980) and Goldberg, Mayer and Toglia (1981) investigated lesions in the anterior artery domain giving rise to aphasia. The site of lesion in patients with ideative and ideomotor apraxia was investigated by Poeck and Lehmkuhl (1980a) and Heilman, Rothi and Valenstein (1982). Maurach and Strian (1981) and Tredici, Pizzini, Bogliun and Tagliabue (1982) studied the motor pathways in the internal capsule; McAuley and Ross Russell (1979), Ostertag and Unsold (1981) and Spector, Glaser, David and Vining (1981) lesions of the posterior optic pathways.

b) Localization on ideal or standardized axial drawings (standard template); it does not, however, take into account variability of scan (incline and starting level) or of anatomical features (size of brain, variability of lobes and fissures, etc.) and the analysis is sometimes only based on a few slices. The advantage of this method is its convenience in very broad series allowing, as it does -- since a slice from any one subject may be compared with the corresponding ones from all the others --, composite drawings to be made up. Standard sections, however, are not generally faithful to reality due to the variability in the scan sections and to differences of head and brain size. Hence it is necessary to make adjustments during the transfer process, which is much to the detriment of precise localization. It is a method that has been used extensively for localization of lesions in aphasic patients (Blunk, de Bleser, Willmes & Zeumer, 1981; Brunner, Kornhuber, Seemuller, Suger & Wallesch, 1982; Hayward, Naeser & Zatz, 1977; Kertesz, 1979; Kertesz, Harlock & Coetes, 1979; Kertesz, Sheppard & MacKenzie, 1982; Naeser, 1982; Naeser, Alexander, Helm-Estabrooks, Levine, Laughlin & Geschwind, 1982; Naeser & Hayward, 1978; Naeser, Hayward, Laughlin & Zatz, 1981). Robinson and Szetela (1980) investigated the mood changes in brain damaged patients and Poeck and Lehmkuhl (1980b) the localization of lesion in ideative apraxic patients.

c)   Transfer of axial figures onto a diagram of the hemispheric convexity; these methods generally aim at localizing the "spatial" seat of the lesion along the three orthogonal dimensions; whence a hypothetical approximation of the corresponding anatomical seat may thus be formed (Naeser, Hayward, Laughlin, Becker, Jernigan, & Zatz, 1981). When scan section incline has not been precisely predetermined, intracranial and cranial anatomical distinguishing features are of the greatest assistance in making the transfer, and in some cases external ad hoc landmarks may be used. These methods permit the representation of deep and superficial lesions with high precision (Cail and Morris, 1979; Luzzatti et al., 1979) and with easily readable images. Lateral diagrams can either reflect the actual size of the brain (i.e., the real antero-posterior diameter of the brain under study) or can be produced as standardized lateral diagrams -- which however take into account the anatomical and CT scan variables --, that can be confronted and superimposed. Lesion site in aphasic patients has been investigated in this way by Basso, Salvolini and Vignolo (1979), Cappa and Vignolo (1979), Mazzocchi and Vignolo (1979), Alexander and LoVerme (1980), Ross (1981) and Rothi, McFarling and Heilman (1982); in ideomotor apraxic patients by Basso, Luzzatti and Spinnler (1980) and Selnes, Rubens, Risse and Levy (1982), and in oral apraxic patients by Tognola and Vignolo (1980). Bisiach, Luzzatti and Perani (1979) and Bisiach, Capitani, Luzzatti and Perani (1981) studied lesion site in unilateral neglect.

Positron Emission Tomography

Some positron emitting radionuclides such as oxygen-15, fluorine-18, carbon-11 or nitrogen-13 can be tagged to physiological active compounds administered noninvasively or little so, and with acceptably low radiation doses. Positron emission tomography (PET) shows the radionuclide distribution through transverse section images using the reconstruction algorithms of transmission CT; it can be used to localize lesional or functional disrupted areas of decreased metabolic activity, or to quantify regional brain metabolism during different neuropsychological activities.

Results and limits are chiefly related to type of radioactive compound used (Ackerman, 1982; Frackowiak, Lenzi, Jones & Heather, 1980). Major technical problems are: low resolution threshold -- mainly due to the high attenuation effect of the skull vault --, thickness of the scan sections (1.5-2.5 cms), and the resulting partial volume effect. Moreover, another technical drawback is the difficulty of getting the patient's head into position inside the tomograph, especially considering the length of scanning time (30-80 minutes) which inevitably requires a correspondingly long evaluation of the function under study.

Some of the most important studies for localization of lesions or of normal brain functions using PET are briefly reported here. Baron, Comar, Bousser, Soussaline, Crouzel, Plummer, Kellershohn and Castaigne (1978), Baron, Comar, Bousser, Plummer, Loc'h, Kellershohn and Castaigne (1979) and Ackerman, Correia, Alpert, Baron, Gouliamos, Grotta, Brownell and Taveras (1981) studied acute stroke lesions and their follow-up. Greenberg, Reivich, Alavi, Hand, Rosenquist, Rintelmann, Stein, Tusa, Dann, Christman, Fowler, MacGregor and Wolf (1981) and Phelps, Mazziotta and Kuhl (1982) evaluated residual cerebral metabolism in normal subjects, presenting different stimuli (simple and complex visual, tactile, verbal, non-verbal and musical acoustic). Roland, Meyer, Shibasaki, Yamamoto and Thompson (1982) repeated with PECT a previous XE 133 rCBF study (Roland, Larsen, Lassen & Skinhoj, 1980) correlating regional metabolism to complex distal voluntary movements unilaterally performed.

For a correct interpretation of PET results on focal brain damage, we consider relevant the work of Kuhl, Phelps, Kowell, Metter, Selin and Winter (1980), who found reduction of both rCBF and metabolism not only in softened areas of CV patients, but also in areas apparently and often clearly undamaged. A cerebral lesion reduces or abolishes the activity not only in the cells directly involved by the lesion, but also in the cells, even distant, that are functionally connected with them. The CT scan shows the lesional focus only, whereas rCBF and PET are able to reveal diminished functional activity, and that could explain the differences found between CT results on the one hand and rCBF or PET results on the other, as is likely the case in Metter, Wasterlain, Kuhl, Hanson and Phelps' work (1981).

Experiment

Our previous attempt with unselected series of brain damaged patients to identify the areas in the dominant hemisphere that are crucial to the genesis of apraxia (Basso et al., 1980) did not give positive results. For that reason we saw fit to reconsider the problem of neuroanatomic correlations of limb apraxia by using a more refined apraxia test and taking into account other variables that could affect its presence, like sex and time post onset. To localize lesions we again used CT because according to us, as just pointed out, it represents the most reliable method of localizing in vivo cerebral lesions that are purely morphologic and not functional too. Lesions were mapped in a slightly different way in order as far as possible to avoid limitations inherent in CT localization techniques.

The purpose of the study was threefold: we specifically wanted to verify whether larger lesions caused apractic symptoms more often than smaller lesions, whether the frontal and parietal areas classically considered crucial for apraxia were effectively so; and whether they had the same relevance or not. Moreover, there are reasons for considering that some neuropsychological functions, like, for example, language (McGlone, 1977) are differently lateralized in the two sexes; we therefore sought to verify whether males and females differed for incidence of apraxia.

Subjects. 152 patients, 46 female and 106 male (mean age = 56.55 $\pm$ 11.78; mean years of schooling = 8.44 $\pm$ 4.40), with clear clinical evidence of a left hemisphere lesion following a CVA, have been examined at the Aphasia Unit of Milan University. A portion of the subjects (n=57) were receiving treatment for a CVA in the wards of the Neurological Department of Milan University. The others (n=59) were seen as outpatients at the Aphasia Unit, and all had been suffering from language disturbances for between one month and 10 years. All patients were given neurological, neuropsychological and CT scan examinations. Patients were excluded from the study 1) if they were left-handed[2] according to the Edinburgh Inventory Test (Oldfield, 1971), 2) if they had sustained more than one CVA, or if they showed CT scan evidence of bilateral lesions, cortical atrophy, or right ventricular enlargement, 3) if they had been given the apraxia examination less than 15 days after their stroke, 4) if they had less than three years schooling, or 5) if the scan pictures were not clear enough to permit an accurate localization.

---

[2] To be considered right-handed patients had to execute no more than one item with the left hand and/or eye or foot.

Procedure: Apraxia examination. All patients were given the movement imitation test described by De Renzi, Motti and Nichelli (1980). The test consists of 24
movements slowly performed by the examiner with the patient reproducing them
with his left arm. Each item was scored 0 to 3 according to the rules set out by De
Renzi et al. (1980), the maximum score being therefore 72. Based on the performance of two different groups of normal controls (De Renzi et al., 1980; De Renzi,
Faglioni & Sorgato, 1982) two cutting scores discriminating a normal from a pathological performance were set at 61 and 52. We used both scores, considering apractic all patients scoring 52 or less, border-line those scoring between 53 and 61, and
non-apractic those scoring 62 or more. On examination 50 (33%) patients were
classified as non-apractic, 33 (22%) as border-line and 69 (45%) as apractic.

Patients were further subdivided into the following four groups, based on time
elapsed between onset of disease and apraxia examination: 1) patients seen between
15 and 90 days post-onset, 2) between 91 and 180 days, 3) between 181 and 365
days, and 4) more than one year post-onset. This was done in view of the possibility
that severity and presence of ideomotor apraxia could diminish or even disappear
with the passing of time, making it difficult to compare a patient examined 15 days
post-onset with another examined many months later. The distribution of patients
in the four groups is shown in Table 1.

Table 1

Number of subjects classified for Apraxia scores and length of illness

Length of Illness (days)	Apraxia Scores		
	0 - 52	53 - 61	62 - 72
15 - 90	31	16	36
91 - 180	13	4	8
181 - 365	9	5	9
> 365	17	3	1

CT scan investigation. Patients underwent a CT scan, when possible at more
than 30 days post-onset. Not all, however, could be examined under these conditions. In some cases patients admitted to the Clinic after a CVA were dismissed
within a month; and, if unable to come back for a further CT between 30-40 days
post onset, their previous CT scan was mapped. In case of an intraparenchimal
hematoma the CT scan was performed approximately at the same time as the apraxia examination (maximum interval: 7 days).

The lesions were mapped onto lateral diagrams following the method proposed
by Luzzatti et al. (1979), slightly modified; in order to obtain standarized diagrams,
length of the anteroposterior and length of the cranio-caudal axis were either mag-
nified or minified according to the case to report them to that of a standard lateral
diagram. The deep and superficial components of the lesions were mapped separately. To better identify the deep structures involved, templates were used for the
deep lesions.

The maps were subdivided according to the size of lesion; small lesions were
also subdivided according to their site which was identified by making reference to

the vascular district involved by the CVA rather than to the lobes. The maps fell into the following groups.

Large lesions (n=59). We defined as large such lesions as involved more than 50% of the maximal antero-posterior diameter of the brain, thus corresponding to the vascular territory of the medial cerebral artery. These lesions consequently are situated in the peri-Sylvian territory, involving the pre- and post-Rolandic areas and the frontal and parietal associative areas to a considerable extent.

Small lesions (n=86). Lesions which involve less than 50% of the maximal antero-posterior diameter. As previously mentioned lesions were further subdivided according to the vascular district affected into the following subgroups:

o "frontal" lesions (n=15): involving the territory of the watershed area between the anterior and middle cerebral artery; pre-frontal artery and pre-Rolandic artery;

o "fronto-central" lesions (n=6): same territory as frontal lesions plus that of the Rolandic artery;

o "parietal" lesions (n=14): ascending parietal artery, posterior parietal artery, angular gyrus artery;

o "temporo-parieto-occipital" lesions (n=12): watershed area between the middle and posterior cerebral artery;

o "temporal" lesions (n=5): superior, middle and inferior temporal artery;

o "occipital" lesions (n=5): posterior cerebral artery (these lesions may therefore involve the inferior surface of the temporal lobe);

o anterior mesial lesions (n=2): frontal polar artery, anterior, middle and posterior internal artery, artery of the lobulus paracentralis, parietal internal artery;

o only deep lesions (n=21): a lesion was defined as deep -- in reference to the convexity of the brain -- if it was seated at more than 2 cms from the surface; the insula is thus considered as being deep;

o multiple lesions (n=6): lesions of vascular domains pertaining to different classification groups.

Negative CT scan (n=7): In seven cases we could not find any CT lesion sign, probably due to the smallness of the CVA; the presence of only moderate focal enlargement of fissures and ventricles, although providing cues of a previous CVA, was ignored because it does not permit localization of damage.

Results

Table 2 shows the distribution of the patients according to length of illness, apraxia scores and size of lesion; patients with small lesions have further been subdivided according to the vascular district involved.

Size of lesion The percentage of small and large lesions differed significantly among the four time groups (X^2 = 34.9512, df = 3, p < .0005). In the group examined at the earliest stage small lesions prevailed over large ones (78% vs 22%). Their

TABLE 2

Size and site of lesion and length of illness in 152 subjects classified for Apraxia scores.

Length of illness (days)	Apraxia scores	Size and site of lesion											
		Large lesions	Small lesions	frontal	fronto central	parietal	carrefour	temporal	occipital	mesial	only deep	multiple	Negative CT scan
15–90	0–52	14	17	3	1	4	7	–	–	–	2	–	–
	53–61	3	12	2	–	1	1	1	1	–	4	2	1
	62–72	1	30	4	1	3	1	4	2	2	12	1	5
91–180	0–52	7	6	–	–	2	2	–	1	–	1	–	–
	53–61	3	1	–	–	–	–	–	1	–	–	–	–
	62–72	2	5	2	–	1	1	–	–	–	1	–	1
181–365	0–52	5	4	–	1	1	–	–	–	–	–	2	–
	53–61	1	4	1	1	1	–	–	–	–	–	1	–
	62–72	4	5	3	–	1	–	–	–	–	1	–	–
>365	0–52	17	–	–	–	–	–	–	–	–	–	–	–
	53–61	2	1	–	1	–	–	–	–	–	–	–	–
	62–72	–	1	–	1	–	–	–	–	–	–	–	–

prevalence decreased in the second and third time groups (52% vs 48% and 57% vs 43%) and they were nearly absent in the latest group (9% vs 91%). The decrease of small lesions from one time group to the other is seemingly due to the fact that patients examined many months (or years) post-onset were seeking aphasia rehabilitation for long-established aphasia probably due to a large lesion.

Table 3

Number (and percentage) of apractic, border-line and non-apractic patients with small and large lesions

	Apractic 0 - 52	Border-line 53 - 61	Non-apractic 62 - 72	Total
Large	43 (73)	9 (15)	7 (12)	59
Small	27 (31)	18 (21)	41 (48)	86

Number of apractic, border-line and non-apractic patients in large and small lesions is reported in Table 3, which yielded a X^2 = 26.6365, df = 2, p < .0005. The general X^2 was partitioned with the method of Brandt and Snedecor (Maxwell, 1961); patients with large lesions were significantly more often apraxic (73%) than those with small lesions (31%) (X^2 = 24.1192, df = 1, p < .0005), whereas no significant difference appeared between border-line and non-apraxic patients (X^2 = 2.5173, df = 1, p = ns).

There were, however, seven cases with large lesions who did not show apraxia: one patient in the first time group, two in the second and four in the third. In the four patients first seen more than six months post-onset recovery could possibly have taken place. The remaining three patients will be briefly described and maps of their lesions are shown in Figure 1.

F.M. was a 45 year old right-handed male with 15 years schooling; he presented with right hemiparesis, hemianesthesia and visual field detect (VFD) 111 days post-onset. His spontaneous speech was nil and his comprehension was severely impaired (Token Test: 14/36); he had no idemotor apraxia: 65/72. Six months later, on second examination, he still presented global aphasia and no apraxia.

L.R. was a 45 year old right-handed female without familial left-handedness and with 13 years of schooling. She was seen 95 days post-onset and showed hemiparesis and hypoesthesia, but no aphasia (she scored 30/36 on the Token Test) or ideomotor apraxia: 69/72.

S.S. was a 42 year old right-handed man with 5 years schooling; when seen 82 days post-onset, he was hemiparetic and hypoesthesic. He presented severe fluent aphasia -- scoring 7/36 on the Token Test -- and no ideomotor apraxia: 64/72.

Only two of these patients really do not confirm the importance of specific regions for the genesis of apraxia: patient L.R. with a large lesion in the praxic and language areas was neither aphasic nor apraxic; she might have had a right hemisphere dominance for both language and praxis.

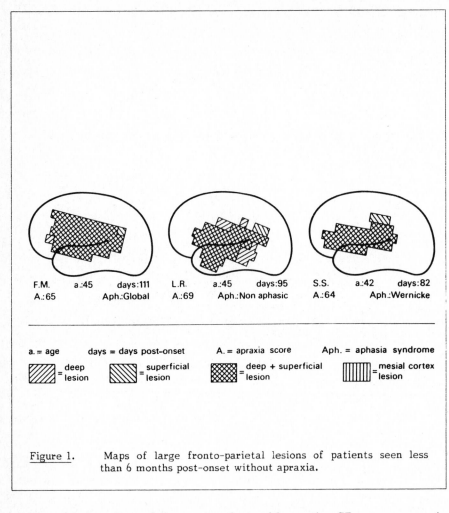

F.M.   a.:45   days:111   L.R.   a.:45   days:95   S.S.   a.:42   days:82
A.:65   Aph.:Global   A.:69   Aph.:Non aphasic   A.:64   Aph.:Wernicke

a. = age   days = days post-onset   A. = apraxia score   Aph. = aphasia syndrome

⫽ = deep lesion   ⧅ = superficial lesion   ⧆ = deep + superficial lesion   ‖‖‖ = mesial cortex lesion

Figure 1.   Maps of large fronto-parietal lesions of patients seen less than 6 months post-onset without apraxia.

Location of lesion. None of the seven patients with negative CT scan was apraxic. The six patients whose CT showed multiple lesions will not be considered for anatomo-clinical correlation.

Twenty-one patients had only deep damage; of these three were apractic. One patient had a thalamic lesion (apraxia score: 42/72), another a lesion of the nucleus lenticularis and the anterior arm of the internal capsule (apraxia score: 48/72), and the third patient had a hematoma encroaching upon the nucleus lenticularis, internal capsule and white matter (apraxia score: 41/72). All three patients presented a fluent form of aphasia which was severe in the thalamic patient and moderate in the other two.

The five patients with lesions confined to the temporal lobe as well as the two with mesial lesions were not apractic. Five patients had occipital lesions. Only one of them was apractic; his map is shown in Figure 2. C.S. was a 50 year old right-

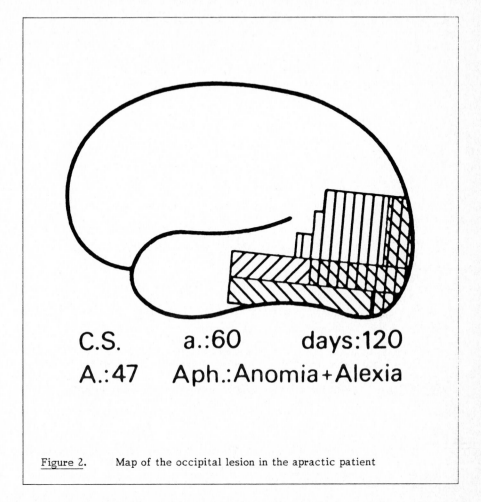

C.S.　　　a.:60　　　days:120

A.:47　　Aph.:Anomia+Alexia

Figure 2.　　Map of the occipital lesion in the apractic patient

handed woman with 4 years schooling. She was first seen at another hospital 2 months post-onset and found to be severely anomic and alexic. When seen by us 120 days post-onset she had a severe right VDF, word finding difficulties in a visual confrontation task, severe alexia without agraphia and she made frequent errors in colour designation. CT scan revealed a left posterior cerebral artery softening encompassing the calcarine area which caused the right VFD. The presence of pure alexia and colour anomia points towards a lesion encroaching upon the splenium (Geschwind & Fusillo, 1966). It can, therefore, be proposed that the visual input for carrying out imitation movement could not reach the praxic area of the left hemisphere, accounting for a specific inability in imitating gestures. Unfortunately, other modalities were not tested.

Lesions were confined to the frontal lobe (frontal and fronto-central lesions) in 21 patients and were predominantly parietal or centered in the temporo-parieto-occipital region (parietal and carrefour lesions) in 26 patients. Number and percentage of apractic, border-line and non-apractic patients in the two groups are reported in Table 4. The majority, i.e. 52% of the frontal patients, were non-apractic, 24% border-line and only 24% were apractic. The reverse was true among the parietal patients, 62% of whom were apractic, 11% border-line and 27% non-apractic (X^2 = 6.6946, df = 2, p < .05). The two lesion groups differed for the contrast between apractic vs border-line plus non-apractic (X^2 = 6.6903, df = 1, p < .01), not for the comparison between border-line vs non-apractic patients (X^2 = 0.0043, df = 1, p = ns).

Table 4

Number (and percentage) of apractic, border-line and non-apractic patients with frontal or parietal lesions

	Apractic 0 – 52	Border-line 53 – 61	Non-apractic 62 – 72	Total
Frontal	5 (24)	5 (24)	11 (52)	21
Parietal	16 (62)	3 (11)	7 (27)	26

Three frontal lesions were particularly small and possibly did not encroach on the premotor area of the hand. Two of these are shown in Figure 3 (EM and EMn); the third lesion was larger involving the premotor area of the face. In the remaining 18 frontal cases the softening encompassed the premotor or motor area of the hand. The supramarginal gyrus was always more or less damaged in all parietal cases except for one non-apractic patient. The maps of the seven non-apractic patients with frontal lesion and of the six non-apractic patients with parietal lesion seen less than six months post-onset, are shown in Figure 3 and 4 respectively.

In line with the hypothesis of a higher incidence of apraxia following a parietal rather than a frontal lesion, the mean performance of the 26 parietal patients was significantly lower than that of the 21 frontal patients (45.96 and 55.33 respectively; t = 1.9554, df = 45, p = .057). However, considering only the 16 parietal and the five frontal apractic patients, the difference in the mean performance vanished (34.64 and 33.00, df = 19, t = 0.2602, p = ns).

Sex. Number of apractic, border-line and non-apractic cases in male and female patients is reported in Table 5, which yielded X^2 = 13.2465, df = 2, p < .005. Females were significantly more often apractic (67%) than males (37%) (X^2 = 12.0894, df = 1, p < .001), whereas no significant difference appeared between border-line and non-apractic males and females. This result cannot be explained by the fact that females are more often apractic because of larger lesions, since large lesions did not prevail in any of the two sex groups (37% among females, 40% among males; X^2 = .0960, df = 1, p = ns).

Discussion

Frequency with which apraxia ensues from a hemispheric lesion has been found to be higher in females than in males. This is a rather unexpected finding when one considers that the hypotheses so far advanced on the different hemispheric specialization in the two sexes point unanimously to a more pronounced lateralization in males (for a review see McGlone, 1980), and one which needs further investigation.

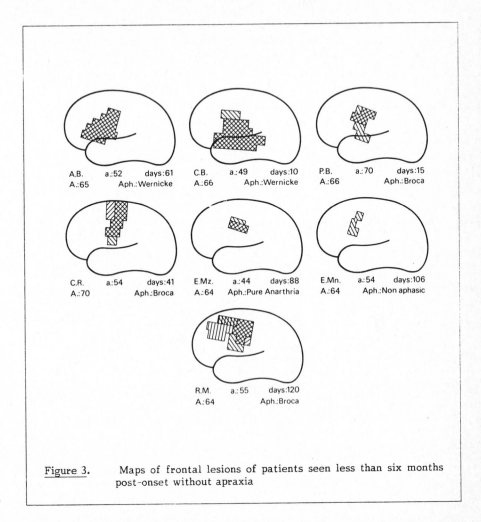

Figure 3.   Maps of frontal lesions of patients seen less than six months
post-onset without apraxia

Large lesions bring about apraxia more frequently than small ones. This can be the consequence of some sort of mass effect or, more plausibly, because large lesions have more chances of encroaching on areas crucial to eupraxia.

If we now turn to consider the identification of the hemispheric areas crucial to the genesis of apraxia, we will find that on the basis of our data no conclusion concerning the participation of the left mesial area alone (only two patients had a mesial involvement and none was apractic) is possible. There were no apractic patients with temporal lesions and only one with occipital lesion: the kind of "apractic" disorder of this patient (Figure 2) has already been discussed.

Apraxia arising from a purely deep lesion has not been frequently reported. The connections classically regarded as bearing on apraxia are rather superficial, and hence a lesion here would probably encroach on the cortical surface. However, in our series three out of 21 deep-lesion patients were apractic (14.3%), which corre-

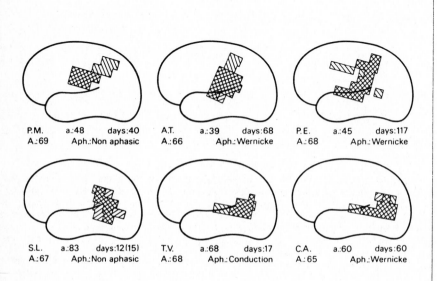

P.M.   a.:48   days:40   A.T.   a.:39   days:68   P.E.   a.:45   days:117
A.:69   Aph.:Non aphasic   A.:66   Aph.:Wernicke   A.:68   Aph.:Wernicke

S.L.   a.:83   days:12(15)   T.V.   a.:68   days:17   C.A.   a.:60   days:60
A.:67   Aph.:Non aphasic   A.:68   Aph.:Conduction   A.:65   Aph.:Wernicke

Figure 4.   Maps of parietal lesions of patients seen less than six months post–onset without apraxia

sponds to the percentage found by Basso et al. (1980) in a different sample (four out of 26 patients or 15.4%). It thus seems possible to hypothesize that certain as yet unspecified deep structures have some importance in the genesis of apraxia.

The importance of the parietal and, to a lesser extent, of the frontal region is confirmed by our data: the majority of patients with parietal lesion (62%) and one fourth (24%) of those with frontal lesion had apraxia. At variance with De Renzi, Faglioni, Lodesani and Vecchi (1983), in our series the deficit arising from frontal lesion, when present, is as severe as apraxia following parietal damage.

Our findings are thus generally in agreement with Liepmann's theory. Some, however, are not compatible. Apart from the presence, already mentioned, of three apractic patients with deep lesion, what is more difficult to reconcile with Liepmann's (1920) schema is the existence of frontal and even parietal patients without apraxia.

Since the long-term evolution of apraxia and natural recovery are unknown quantities, we have chosen to focus on the negative cases seen less than six months post-onset. They were six out of 23 (26%) parietal patients, and seven out of 13 (54%) frontal patients, with apraxia score ranging from 62 to 72. Moreover, there were three out of 20 patients with lesions involving both the frontal and parietal areas who were not apractic.

Table 5

Number (and percentage) of apraxic, border-line and non-apraxic males and females

	Apraxic 0-52	Border-line 53-61	Non-apraxic 62-72	Total
Males	39 (37)	25 (23)	42 (40)	106
Females	31 (67)	3 (7)	12 (26)	46

The frequent absence of apraxia in frontal patients may be explained by Kleist's (1934) hypothesis that the left limbs can be directly controlled by the left parietal area through heterologous left parieto-right frontal callosal connections. However, the negative cases with left parietal damage cannot be explained by the same hypothesis; left ascendency or equipotentiality in motor control may perhaps be invoked even if it is an improbable explanation due to the high number of cases (26%). On the other hand, the existence of negative cases is not an exceptional occurrence in neuropsychological functions and limits inherent to CT method must not be forgotten. Exceptions to the expected localization have been found for functions other than apraxia. Out of 267 cases of left brain damaged right-handed patients Basso, Lecours, Moraschini and Vanier (in press) found 36 patients whose type or presence of aphasia did not correspond to that expected on the grounds of the localization of the lesion, and three of them had lesions inside the speech area without any sign of aphasia.

We cannot offer any satisfactory explanation for the type of exceptions discussed here but it may well be possible that anatomo-clinical correlations for any class of neuropsychological disorder are less absolute than current tenets would have them.

References

Ackerman, R.H. Clinical aspects of positron emission tomography (PET). Radiologic Clinics of North America, 1982, 20, 9-14.

Ackerman, R.H., Correia, J.A., Alpert, N.M., Baron, J.C., Gouliamos, A., Grotta, J.C., Brownell, G.L. & Taveras, J.M. Positron-imaging in ischemic stroke disease using compounds labelled with oxygen 15. Archives of Neurology, 1981, 38, 537-543.

Alcala, H., Gado, M. & Torack, R.M. The effect of size, histologic elements and water content on the visualization of cerebral infarcts. Archives of Neurology, 1978, 35, 1-7.

Alexander, M.P. & Lo Verme, Jr. S.R. Aphasia after left hemispheric intracerebral hemorrhage. Neurology, 1980, 30, 1193-1202.

Alexander, M.P. & Schmitt, M.A. The aphasia syndrome of stroke in the left anterior cerebral artery territory. Archives of Neurology, 1980, 37, 97-100.

Baron, J.C., Comar, D., Bousser, M.G., Plummer, D., Loc'h, C., Kellershohn, C. & Castaigne, P. Patterns of CBF and oxygen extraction fraction (EO^{2}) in hemispheric infarcts: A tomographic study with the $_{15}O$ continuous inhalation technique. Acta Neurologica Scandinavica, 1979, 60, Suppl. 72, 324-325.

Baron, J.C., Comar, D., Bousser, M.G., Soussaline, F., Crouzel, C., Plummer, D., Kellershohn, C. & Castaigne, P. Etude tomographique, chez l'homme, du debit sanguin et de la consommation d'oxygene du cerveau par inhalation continue d'oxygene 15. Revue Neurologique, 1978, 134, 545-556.

Basso, A., Lecours, A.R., Maraschini, S. & Varnier, M. Anatomo-clinical correlations of the aphasias as defined through computerized tomography: On exceptions. Brain and Language, in press.

Basso, A., Luzzatti, C. & Spinnler, H. Is ideomotor apraxia the outcome of damage to well-defined regions of the left hemisphere? Neuropsychological study of CAT correlations. Journal of Neurology, Neurosurgery, and Psychiatry, 1980, 43, 118-126.

Basso, A., Salvolini, U. & Vignolo, L.A. La localizzazione dei sintomi afasici, prime esperienze con l'EMI-scanner. Rivista di Patologia Nervosa e Mentale, 1979, 100, 94-102.

Bech Skriver, E. & Olsen, T.S. Transient disappearance of cerebral infarcts on CTscan, the so-called fogging effect. Neuroradiology, 1981, 22, 61-65.

Becker, H., Desch, H., Hacker, H. & Pencz, A. CT fogging effect with ischemic cerebral infarcts. Neuroradiology, 1979, 18, 185-192.

Benson, D.F. Fluency in aphasia: Correlation with radioactive scan localization. Cortex, 1967, 3, 373-394.

Bisiach, E., Capitani, E., Luzzatti, C. & Perani, D. Brain and conscious representation of outside reality. Neuropsychologia, 1981, 19, 543-551.

Bisiach, E., Luzzatti, C. & Perani, D. Unilateral neglect, representational schema and consciousness. Brain, 1979, 102, 609-618.

Blunk, R., De Bleser, R., Willmes, K. & Zeumer, H. A refined method to relate morphological and functional aspects of aphasia. European Neurology, 1981, 20, 69-79.

Boller, F., Cole, M., Kim, Y., Mack, J.L. & Patawaran, C. Optic ataxia: Clinical-radiological correlations with the EMI scan. Journal of Neurology, Neurosurgery and Psychiatry, 1975, 38, 954-958.

Boller, F., Patten, D.H. & Howes, D. Correlation of brain-scan results with neuropathological findings. Lancet, 1973 (i), 1143-1146.

Brunner, R.J., Kornhuber, H.H., Seemuller, E., Suger, G. & Wallesch, C.W. Basal ganglia participation in language pathology. Brain and Language, 1982, 16, 281-299.

Cail, W.S. & Morris, J.L. Localization of intracranial lesions from CT scans. Surgical Neurology, 1979, 11, 35-37.

Cappa, S. & Vignolo, L.A. Transcortical features of aphasia following thalamic hemorrhage. Cortex, 1979, 15, 121-130.

Cooper, R., Crow, H.J. & Greywalter, W. Regional control of cerebral vascular activity and oxygen supply in man. Brain Research, 1966, 3, 174-191.

Damasio, H. & Damasio, A.R. The anatomical basis of conduction aphasia. Brain, 1980, 103, 337-350.

Damasio, A.R., Damasio, H., Rizzo, M., Varney, N. & Gersh, F. Aphasia with non hemorrhagic lesions in the basal ganglia and internal capsule. Archives of Neurology, 1982, 39, 15-20.

Davis, K.R., Taveras, J.M., New, P.F.J., Schnur, J.A. & Roberson, G.H. Cerebral infarction diagnosis by computerized tomography. Analysis and evaluation of findings. American Journal of Roentgenology, 1975, 124, 643-660.

De Renzi, E., Faglioni, P., Lodesani, M. & Vecchi, A. Performance of left brain-damaged patients on initiation of simple movements and motor sequences. Frontal and parietal-injured patients compared. Cortex, 1983, 19, 333-343.

De Renzi, E., Faglioni, P. & Sorgato, P. Modality-specific and supramodal mechanisms of apraxia. Brain, 1982, 105, 301-312.

De Renzi, E., Motti, F. & Nichelli, P. Imitating gestures: A quantitative approach to ideomotor apraxia. Archives of Neurology, 1980, 37, 6-10.

Dolinskas, C.A., Bilanink, L.T., Zimmerman, R.A. & Kuhl, D.E. Computed tomography of intracerebral hematomas. 1: Transmission CT observations on hematoma resolution. American Journal of Roentgenology, 1977, 129, 681-688.

Du Boulay, G., Fairbairn, D. & Paden, R.S. Precise re-positioning of the head for serial CT examinations. Neuroradiology, 1978, 16, 625-626.

Frackowiak, R.S.J., Lenzi, G.L., Jones, T. & Heather, J.D. Quantitative measurement of regional cerebral blood flow and oxygen metabolism in man, using 15_O and positron emission tomography: Theory, procedure and normal values. Journal of Computer Assisted Tomography, 1980, 4, 727-736.

Fullerton, G.D. & Blanco, E. Fundamentals of computerized tomography (CT) tissue characterization of the brain. Proceedings of SPIE -- The International Society for Optical Engineering, 1981, 273, 256-266.

Geschwind, N. & Fusillo, M. Colour naming defects in association with alexia. Archives of Neurology, 1966, 15, 137-146.

Goldberg, G., Mayer, N.H. & Toglia, J.U. Medial frontal cortex infarction and the alien hand sign. Archives of Neurology, 1981, 38, 683-686.

Greenberg, J.H., Reivich, M., Alavi, A., Hand, P., Rosenquist, A., Rintelmann, W., Stein, A., Tusa, R., Dann, R., Christman, D., Fowler, J., MacGregor, B. & Wolf, A. Metabolic mapping of functional activity in human subjects with the (18_F) fluorodeoxyglucose technique. Science, 1981, 212, 678-680.

Hayward, R.W., Naeser, M.A. & Zatz, L.M. Cranial CT in aphasia. Correlation of anatomical lesions with functional deficits. Radiology, 1977, 123, 653-660.

Heilman, K.M., Rothi, L.J. & Valenstein, E. Two forms of ideomotor apraxia. Neurology, 1982, 32, 342-346.

Hosokawa, S., Yamashita, Y., Ueno, H. & Caveness, W.F. Regional cerebral blood flow pattern in subcortical propagation of focal seizures in newborn monkeys. Annals of Neurology, 1977, 1, 225-234.

Karis, R. & Horenstein, S. Localization of speech parameters by brain scan. Neurology, 1976, 26, 226-230.

Kertesz, A. Aphasia and associated disorders: Taxonomy, Localization and Recovery. New York: Grune and Stratton, 1979.

Kertesz, A., Ghent, C. & Poole, E. Localization of lesions in aphasia. Neurology India, Proceedings, 1973, Suppl. 3, 463-465.

Kertesz, A., Harlock, W. & Coetes, R. Computer tomographic localization, lesion size and prognosis in aphasia and non-verbal impairment. Brain and Language, 1979, 8, 34-50.

Kertesz, A., Lesk, D. & McCabe, P. Isotope localization of infarcts in aphasia. Archives of Neurology, 1977, 34, 590-601.

Kertesz, A., Sheppard, A. & MacKenzie, R. Localization in transcortical sensory aphasia. Archives of Neurology, 1982, 39, 475-478.

Kido, D.K., Le May, M., Levinson, A.W. & Benson, W.E. Computed tomographic localization of the precentral gyrus. Radiology, 1980, 135, 373-377.

Kinkel, W.R. & Jacobs, L. Computerized axial transverse tomography in cerebrovascular disease. Neurology, 1976, 26, 924-930.

Kleist, K. <u>Gehirnpathologie vornehmlich auf Grund der Kriegserfahrungen</u>. Leipzig: Barth, 1934.

Kohlmeyer, K. Disorders of brain functions due to stroke. <u>Correlates in regional cerebral blood flow and computerized tomography</u>. <u>Bayer - Symposium 7: Brain function in old age</u>. Berlin: Springer Verlag, 1979.

Kuhl, D.E., Phelps, M.E., Kowell, A.P., Metter, E.J., Selin, D. & Winter, J. Effects of stroke on local cerebral metabolism and perfusion: Mapping by emission computed tomography of 18FDG and 13NH3 <u>Annals of Neurology</u>, 1980, <u>8</u>, 47-60.

Ladurner, G., Sager, W.D., Iliff, L.D. & Lechner, H. A correlation of clinical findings and CT in ischaemic cerebrovascular disease. <u>European Neurology</u>, 1979, <u>18</u>, 281-288.

Larsen, B., Skinhoj, E. & Lassen, N.A. Variations in regional cortical blood flow in the right and left hemispheres during automatic speech. <u>Brain</u>, 1978, <u>101</u>, 193-209.

Liepmann, H. <u>Ergebnisse der Gesamten Medizin</u>, 1920, <u>1</u>, 516-543.

Luzzatti, C., Scotti, G. & Gattoni, A. Further suggestions for cerebral CT-localization. <u>Cortex</u>, 1979, <u>15</u>, 483-490.

Maeda, T., Matsuda, H., Hisada, K., Tonami, N., Mori, H., Fujii, H., Hayashi, M. & Yamamoto, S. Three dimensional regional cerebral blood perfusion images with single-photon emission computed tomography. <u>Radiology</u>, 1981, <u>140</u>, 817-822.

Maurach, R. & Strian, F. Zur Topologie dur motorischen Leitungsbahnen in der inneren Kapsel. <u>Archiv fur Psychiatrie und Nervenkrankheiten</u>, 1981, <u>229</u>, 331-343.

Maxwell, A.E. <u>Analysing qualitative data</u>. London: Methnen, 1961.

Mazzocchi, F. & Vignolo, L.A. Localization of lesions in aphasia: Clinical CT-scan correlations in stroke patients. <u>Cortex</u>, 1979, <u>15</u>, 627-653.

McAuley, D.L. & Ross Russell, R.W. Correlation of CAT scan and visual field defects in vascular lesions of the posterior visual pathways. <u>Journal of Neurology, Neurosurgery and Psychiatry</u>, 1979, <u>42</u>, 298-311.

McGlone, J. Sex differences in the cerebral organization of verbal functions in patients with unilateral brain lesions. <u>Brain</u>, 1977, <u>100</u>, 775-793.

McGlone, J. Sex differences in human brain asymmetry: critical survey. <u>Behavioural Brain Sciences</u>, 1980, <u>3</u>, 215-263.

Metter, E.J., Wasterlain, C.G., Kuhl, D.E., Hanson, W.R. & Phelps, M.E. 18FDG positron emission computed tomography in a study of aphasia. <u>Annals of Neurology</u>, 1981, <u>10</u>, 173-187.

Mori, H., Lu, C.H., Chiu, L.C., Cancilla, P.A. & Christie, J.H. Reliability of computed tomography: Correlation with neuropathologic findings. <u>American Journal of Roentgenology</u>, 1977, <u>128</u>, 795-798.

Naeser, M.A. Language behaviour in stroke patients. Cortical vs. subcortical lesion sites on CT scans. Trends in Neurosciences, 1982, 5, 53-59.

Naeser, M.A., Alexander, M.P., Helm-Estabrooks, N., Levine, H.L., Laughlin, S.A. & Geschwind, N. Aphasia with predominantly subcortical lesion sites. Archives of Neurology, 1982, 39, 2-14.

Naeser, M.A. & Hayward, R.W. Lesion localization in aphasia with cranial computed tomography and the Boston Diagnostic Aphasia Exam. Neurology, 1978, 28, 545-551.

Naeser, M.A., Hayward, R.W., Laughlin, S.A., Becker, J.M.T., Jernigan, T.L. & Zatz, L.M. Quantitative CT scan studies in aphasia, part 2: Comparison of the right and left hemispheres. Brain and Language, 1981, 12, 165-189.

Naeser, M.A., Hayward, R.W., Laughlin, S.A. & Zatz, L.M. Quantitative CT scan studies in aphasia, part 1: Infarct size and CT numbers. Brain and Language, 1981, 12, 140-164.

Ojemann, G.A. A review of the neurologic basis of human cognition, with special emphasis on language. Allied Health Behavioural Sciences, 1978, 1, 338-374.

Ojemann, G.A. Brain mechanisms for language: Observations during neurosurgery. In J. Lockard & A. Ward Jr. (Eds.), Epilepsy: A window to brain mechanisms. New York: Raven Press, 1980.

Ojemann, G.A. Interrelationships in the localization of language, memory, and motor mechanisms in human cortex and thalamus. In R.A. Thompson, & J.R. Green (Eds.), New Perspectives in cerebral localization. New York: Raven Press, 1982, 157-175.

Ojemann, G.A. Brain organization for language from the perspective of electrical stimulation mapping. The Brain and Behavioral Sciences, 1983, 6, 189-230.

Ojemann, G.A. & Mateer, C. Cortical and subcortical organization of human communication: Evidence from stimulation studies. In H. Steklis, & M. Raleigh (Eds.), Neurobiology of social communication in primates. New York: Academic Press, 1979. (a)

Ojemann, G. & Mateer, C. Human language cortex: Localization of memory, syntax, and sequential motor-phoneme identification systems. Science, 1979, 205, 1401-1403. (b)

Oldfield, R.C. The assessment and analysis of handedness: The Edinburgh inventory. Neuropsychologia, 1971, 9, 97-113.

Orgogozo, J.M. & Larsen, B. Activation of the supplementary motor area during voluntary movements in man suggests it works as a supra motor area. Science, 1979, 206, 847-850.

Ostertag, C.B. & Unsold, R. Korrelation computer-tomographisch dargestellter Infarkte der Sehrinde mit homonymen Gesichtsfeldausfallen. Archiv fur Psychiatrie und Nervenkrankheiten, 1981, 230, 265-274.

Paxton, R. & Ambrose, J. The EMI scanner. A brief review of the first 650 patients. British Journal of Radiology, 1974, 47, 530-565.

Penfield, W. & Roberts, L. Speech and brain mechanisms. Princeton (N.J.): Princeton University Press, 1959.

Phelps, M.E., Mazziotta, J.C. & Kuhl, D.E. Positron computed tomography. Journal of American Medical Association, 1982, 247, 850-851.

Poeck, K. & Lehmkuhl, G. Ideatory apraxia in a left-handed patient with right-sided brain lesion. Cortex, 1980, 16, 273-284. (a)

Poeck, K. & Lehmkuhl, G. Das Syndrom der ideatorischen Apraxie und seine Lokalisation. Nervenarzt, 1980, 51, 217-225. (b)

Raichle, M.E., Grubb, R.L., Gado, M.H., Eichling, J.O. & Ter-Pogossian, M.M. Correlation between regional cerebral blood flow and oxidative metabolism. Archives of Neurology, 1976, 33, 523-526.

Reivich, M. The use of cerebral blood flow and metabolic studies in cerebral localization. In R.A. Thompson, & J.R. Green (Eds.), New Perspectives in cerebral localization. New York: Raven Press, 1982.

Robinson, R.G. & Szetela, B. Mood change following left hemispheric brain injury. Annals of Neurology, 1980, 9, 447-453.

Roland, P.E., Larsen, B., Lassen, N.A. & Skinhoj, E. Supplementary motor area and other cortical areas in organization of voluntary movements in man. Journal of Neurophysiology, 1980, 43, 118-136.

Roland, P.E., Meyer, E., Shibasaki, T., Yamamoto, Y.L. & Thompson, C.J. Regional cerebral blood flow changes in cortex and basal ganglia during voluntary movements in normal human volunteers. Journal of Neuropsychology, 1982, 48, 467-480.

Roland, P.E., Skinhoj, E., Lassen, N.A. & Larsen, B. Different cortical areas in man in organization of voluntary movements in extrapersonal space. Journal of Neurophysiology, 1980, 43, 137-150.

Rosenfield, D.B. & Goree, J.A. Angiographic localization of aphasia. Neurology, 1975, 25, 349.

Ross, E.D. The aprosodias. Archives of Neurology, 1981, 38, 561-569.

Rothi, L.J., McFarling, D. & Heilman, K.M. Conduction aphasia, syntactic alexia and the anatomy of syntactic comprehension. Archives of Neurology, 1982, 39, 272-275.

Roy, C.S. & Sherrington, C.S. On the regulation of the blood supply of the brain. Journal of Physiology, 1890, 11, 85-108.

Selnes, O.A., Rubens, A.B., Risse, G.L. & Levy, R.S. Transient aphasia with persistent apraxia. Uncommon sequela of massive left-hemisphere stroke. Archives of Neurology, 1982, 39, 122-126.

Soh, K., Larsen, B., Skinhoj, E. & Lassen, N.A. Regional cerebral blood flow in aphasia. Archives of Neurology, 1978, 35, 625-632.

Spector, R.H., Glaser, J.S., David, N.J. & Vining, D.Q. Occipital lobe infarctions, Neurology, 1981, 31, 1098-1106.

Tognola, G. & Vignolo, L.A. Brain lesions associated with oral apraxia in stroke patients: A clinico-neuroradiological investigation with the CT-scan. Neuropsychologia, 1980, 18, 257-272.

Tokunaga, A., Takase, M. & Otani, K. The glabella-inion line as a baseline for CT scanning of the brain. Neuroradiology, 1977, 14, 67-71.

Tredici, G., Pizzini, G., Bogliun, G. & Tagliabue, M. The site of motor corticospinal fibres in the internal capsule of man. A computerized tomographic study of restricted lesions. Journal of Anatomy, 1982, 134, 199-208.

Turnier, H., Hondek, P.V. & Trefler, M. Measurements of the partial volume phenomenon. Computerized Tomography, 1979, 3, 213-219.

Vignolo, L.A. Utilita e limiti nella correlazione tra sede delle lesioni e deficit neuropsicologici. In L. Bergamini, C. Loeb, & A. Passerini (Eds.), Utilita e limiti della tomografia computerizzata in neurologia. Italian Journal of Neurological Sciences, 1979, Suppl. 1, 64-73.

Yarnell, P., Monroe, M.A. & Sobel, L. Aphasia outcome in stroke. A clinical and neuroradiological correlation. Stroke, 1976, 7, 516-522.

Neuropsychological Studies of Apraxia and Related Disorders, E.A. Roy (ed.)
© Elsevier Science Publishers B.V. (North-Holland), 1985

CAN THE STUDY OF PRAXIS IN ANIMALS AID

IN THE STUDY OF APRAXIA IN HUMANS?

Bryan Kolb and Ian Q. Whishaw

University of Lethbridge

We argue that the use of animal studies to examine higher functions of the human brain should not be dismissed without a careful consideration of four factors. First, there should be a re-evaluation of the anatomical basis of human apraxia. The anatomical basis of clinical apraxia in humans is unlikely to be neocortical but probably involves combined damage of both cortical and subcortical structures. Second, the behaviours that are studied in apraxic syndromes should be fractionated in such a way that they parallel the anatomical systems that produce different types of movement. Third, the movements should be described and quantified in such a way that the severity and generality of any deficit can be easily assessed. Fourth, mammals display both learned and species-typical behavioural patterns that can be used in the study of praxis. We conclude that further progress in understanding the nature of apractic syndromes will only come through the careful study and quantification of both learned and species-typical movements of humans and other animals and that the study of nonhuman animals can aid significantly in the study of praxis (and apraxia) in humans.

If we phrased the title of this paper in the following way: "Can the study of praxis (movement) in animals aid in the study of praxis in humans?", the answer would be a uniform "Yes"! In fact, there are hundreds of ongoing research projects directed to exactly this problem. If, however, the question is phrased as it is in the title, "Can the study of praxis in animals aid in the study of apraxia in humans?" the answer is usually a loud "No". This is because some scientists, particularly clinical scientists, although willing to accept that there are similarities in the motor system in all animals, also believe that there are classes of movements that humans make that are qualitatively different from those that other animals make, and it is for disruptions of these movements that they reserve the term apraxia. It is to this paradoxical difference in definition that the present paper is addressed. Although we do not insist that rats and monkeys are little men in fur suits, but without socks and shoes, we do subscribe to the view that since they are mammals and have a mammalian nervous system the principles derived from studying brain-behaviour relationships in them will be relevant to the brain-behaviour relationships in humans. We argue that the utility of animal studies in understanding 'higher functions' of the human brain should not be dismissed without careful scrutiny. Three themes are developed in this chapter, each of which derives from methodological errors which are as old as the first neuropsychological experiments conducted by Pierre Flourens in the early part of the last century (e.g., Flourens, 1960). The first is that there must be an adequate definition of the anatomy that is believed to control any particular behaviour under study. The second is that there must be an adequate definition of the behaviour and the development of behaviour to permit quantification. The third is that in comparative studies, some species are more useful than others.

The problems inherent in using nonhuman subjects in the study of apraxia can best be understood by considering the history of the use of animals to make inferences regarding human faculties. The modern history of the use of nonhuman species in neuropsychology can be traced to the early 1820's in the studies of Flourens. Gall and Spurtzheim had hypothesized in their phrenology that psychological functions were localized in the brain in discrete regions of the neocortex. Flourens rejected the concept of localization of function and developed an experimental technique with which to buttress his philosophical arguments: he surgically removed the cerebrum of animals and studied the subsequent changes in their behaviour. From his experiments he concluded that there was no localization of function in the cerebrum and that all intellectual faculties resided there coextensively.

Although it is now generally accepted that Flouren's experiments were devastating to the science of phrenology, it is ironic that they should have been so influential. Most of his experiments were performed with pigeons and chickens, animals with virtually no neocortex, and his behavioural tests were assessments of activities such as eating and wing flapping, behaviours that bore no relation to the cognitive faculties proposed by Gall and Spurtzheim. In spite of these faults, however, Flourens' experiments are important to our discussion of using nonhuman species in the study of apraxia because they illustrate a number of fundamental problems that are encountered in trying to use nonhuman species. (We have written a more general discussion of these and other problems elsewhere (Kolb and Whishaw, 1983) so we shall restrict our current discussion to the specific issue of the study of apraxia.) First, what neuroanatomical systems should we examine in nonhumans? Flourens was clearly on shaky ground in trying to reach conclusions about the question of localization in the mammalian cerebral cortex from his studies using pigeons but the problem is not so obvious in the study of the role of regions such as the posterior parietal cortex of monkeys or rats in the control of praxis. Second, Flourens' experiments lead us to the question of which behaviours in nonhumans can be considered similar enough to those observed in humans to allow generalizations. Wing flapping in the decorticate pigeon is unlikely to be acceptable as a behaviour to be used in the study of apraxia, but what behaviours are acceptable? This is a major issue since in order to determine this we must be very explicit about how apraxia is to be objectively studied in humans. There is little agreement on this question but it must be answered before we are entitled to use nonhuman species. If, for example, it is agreed that apraxia is a failure to follow verbal command or to make symbolic gestures, then we cannot study apraxia in nonhumans. On the other hand, if we agree that movements on some apparatus such as the Kimura manual sequence box (Kimura, 1977) can measure apraxia, then we can study apraxia in nonhumans by constructing some similar apparatus. We must also decide how apraxia is to be distinguished from other movement disorders and how its severity is to be determined. For example, if it is agreed that the opening of a complex puzzle latch might be considered a test of praxis for monkeys, how will we decide what is an apractic response? That is, what grounds do we have for claiming that the behavioural abnormality is an apraxia rather than a form of stupidity, dyskinesia, catalepsy, ataxia, etc.? Third, many of Flourens' experiments used birds as subjects but, given the anatomical difference between birds and mammals, this may not be a defensible choice. The issue to be considered is what is an appropriate choice? We believe that there are certain criteria by which certain species could be selected. For example, we could not use little animals to study disturbances in preparing cups of tea, but we shall illustrate how complex behaviours such as nest building may have many similarities to human tea-making behaviour.

The rationale of this chapter will be to address anatomical and behavioral issues in the study of apraxia in humans so that we have a logical basis to begin to study apraxia in nonhumans. We shall then briefly describe the meagre relevant literature on nonhuman species and suggest directions for future research.

The Problem of Anatomy

Although there have been frequent attempts to relate apractic syndromes to cortical pathology in humans (cf. Geschwind, 1975; Hecaen & Albert, 1978; Heilman, 1979), these discussions have generally ignored the anatomy of the motor systems, concentrating instead upon the syndromes observed in patients with naturally occurring cerebral lesions. This is a valid approach to the question of the neurological basis of apraxia but an alternative approach is to consider the organization of the intact motor systems and then to try to dissect the relative contributions of each component of these systems to the control of movement. We are unaware of any previous attempts to consider human apractic syndromes in this context but we feel that such a conception is essential if one is to make inferences from the study of animals. Furthermore, this new approach may change the perspective one has on the nature of apraxia and suggest a different logic to its study. To illustrate our point we shall briefly review the anatomical organization of the intact motor systems, consider the implications for this organization upon the study of apraxia in humans, and finally consider the implications for the study of nonhuman species.

We do not hope to present a complete detailed description of the anatomical organization of the motor systems but rather we will provide a more general presentation of the features essential to understanding the nature of apraxia. Thus, we shall concentrate upon the descending systems from the forebrain to the spinal cord and the major afferents to these systems. Our discussion derives largely from the work of Kuypers and his coworkers (e.g. Lawrence & Kuypers, 1968) and of DeLong (1974). The reader is directed to Brooks (1981) for a broader description.

The Descending Anatomical Systems to the Spinal Cord

The motor system can be subdivided into a number of general subsystems on the basis of the origin of the pathways in the brain and the final destination of the pathways in the spinal cord. Table 1 summarizes these systems and shows that direct input to the spinal cord originates principally in the cortex (corticospinal systems), red nucleus (dorsolateral systems), and pointine reticular formation, tectum, and vestibular nuclei (ventromedial systems). Most of these systems do not project directly upon motoneurons but rather they project upon interneurons, which in turn project upon the motoneurons.

Corticospinal systems. The majority of the corticospinal projections arise from Brodmann's area 4 (30%) and area 6 (30%), with the remaining 40% arising in the parietal lobe, principally areas 1, 2 and 3. These projections can be subdivided into four subsystems both on the basis of the termination of the projections upon either motoneurons or interneurons of the spinal grey as well as on the basis of function (see Figure 1). Thus, direct projections from areas 4 and 6 that terminate upon the motoneurons in the ventral horn of the spinal grey are involved in the control of relatively independent finger movements. In contrast, projections from these same areas upon interneurons in the intermediate zones of the spinal grey play a role in the control of independent hand, wrist and arm movements. A third projection from areas 4 and 6, which terminates bilaterally on interneurons, plays a role in the control of neck and body movements. Finally, the projection from the somatic cortex (areas 1, 2, 3) project upon sensory neurons in the dorsal horn, possibly indirectly

Table 1

Summary of the Descending Motor Systems

System	Principal Connections
1. Corticospinal	a. direct contralateral projections from cortex (4&6) to motoneurons of ventral horn; allow control of relatively independent finger movements. b. contralateral projections from areas 4 & 6 to interneurons in intermediate zone; control of relatively independent hand and and arm movements. c. contralateral projections from areas 1, 2 & 3 to dorsal horn. d. bilateral projections from area 4 (neck & trunk) & 6 to interneurons in intermediate zone; allow control of body movements and of limbs in locomotion.
2. Dorsolateral	a. originates primarily from red nucleus and projects to contralateral intermediate zone controlling distal musculature, cranial nerve nuclei controlling facial musculature (VII, VIII, XII), and dorsolateral zone controlling limb movements.
3. Ventromedial	a. originates from tectum, medial teticular formation, and vestibular nuclei, projecting to the interneurons of intermediate zones on both sides of the cord; allows control of axial and girdle muscles bilaterally.

influencing a broad range of movements by gating influences on ascending sensory input.

Dorsolateral Systems. The dorsolateral systems originate primarily from the red nucleus and project to the contralateral interneurons of the intermediate zone controlling the distal musculature. In addition, some neurons of the dorsolateral systems terminate en route to the spinal cord upon the cranial nerve nuclei controlling facial musculature (VII, VIII, XII) as well as the sensory trigeminal nucleus and the dorsal column nuclei (cuneate and gracile).

Ventromedial Systems. This group of pathways originates in the brainstem, principally in the medial reticular formation, tectum, and vestibular nuclei, and projects diffusely bilaterally upon interneurons involved in the control of axial and girdle muscles.

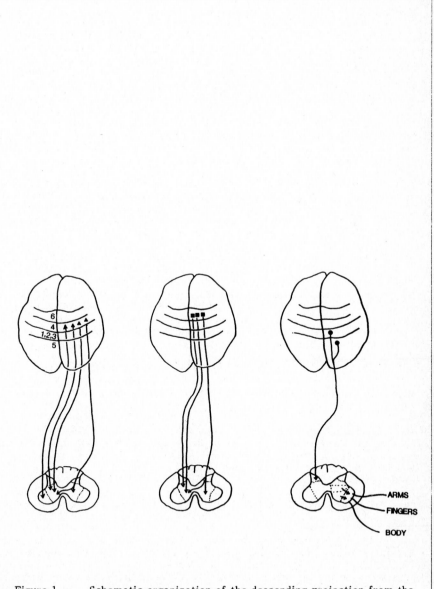

Figure 1.   Schematic organization of the descending projection from the cortex to the spinal cord.

Functional Systems in the Spinal Cord

The descending systems to the spinal cord arise from several points within the cortex and brainstem but they all terminate in the spinal grey and share in the control of movements. Kuypers and his colleagues (e.g. Lawrence & Kuypers, 1968; Brinkman & Kuypers, 1973) have shown that it is possible to conceive of three functional systems directly controlling movement. The first system is responsible for the control of fine movements of the digits and is distinguished by the presence of direct projections from the motor cortex onto the spinal motoneurons in the ventral horn. Damage to this system selectively eliminates independent digital movements. The second system is responsible for the control of independent hand, wrist and arm movements. The projections of this system arise from both the corticospinal and dorsolateral systems and terminate in the more dorsolateral region of the intermediate zone of the spinal grey. If this system is selectively damaged, subjects are capable of independent digit movements but lose control of the limbs. The third system, which controls whole body movements, arises from all three descending anatomical divisions and projects to interneurons in the ventromedial intermediate zone of the spinal grey. Selective damage to this functional system impairs body movements leaving limb and digit movements relatively intact.

Although we have described the routes of direct control of the brain over the spinal motoneurons, many other regions, especially in the forebrain, provide significant input to the descending systems. The three most important inputs in the current discussion are the remaining cerebral cortex, basal ganglia and associated nuclei, and the cerebellum. We shall consider each separately.

Cortical Access to Motor Systems. There are two routes of cortical access to the motor systems. First, all regions of the cortex can influence finger, arm, and body movements through corticocortical connections. These connections arise principally in the parietal, temporal and occipital cortex and project to the prefrontal cortex, which in turn projects to area 6 and eventually area 4. In addition, there are a smaller number of projections from both the somatic cortex and area 5 to area 4. A second source of cortical input comes via callosal fibres originating in the opposite hemisphere. However, in contrast to the input of the ipsilateral corticocortical projections, the callosal projections are restricted to the limb and body regions as the hand and foot areas of the motor and somatic cortex do not receive callosal projections. This difference may be very important in studies of apraxia since one might expect that it would be easier to produce bilateral apraxia in systems that were connected normally.

Basal Ganglia Input. Although the basal ganglia is usually considered to be a 'motor structure' it does not have any direct access to the spinal interneurons or motoneurons. Rather, the basal ganglia form a system with the motor thalamus that takes input from the entire neocortex and substantia nigra and projects back upon the motor cortex as illustrated in Figure 2. This system has some role in the initiation and control of smooth voluntary movements but the nature of this role is uncertain (cf. Kornhuber, 1974). It is likely that the basal ganglia participate in control of both distal and proximal musculature but we are unaware of any data on this point.

Cerebellar Input. Like the basal ganglia, the cerebellum is normally viewed as a 'motor structure', even though there are no direct projections onto spinal neurons. A great deal is known about the anatomy and physiology of the cerebellum (cf. Eccles, Ito & Szentagothai, 1967) but for the current discussion it is sufficient to note that the cerebellum sends projections to virtually all of the motor systems and thus can play a role in virtually all movements. It is unlikely to be implicated directly in

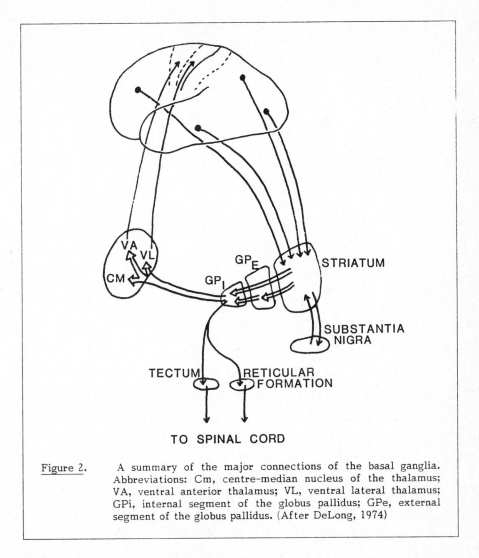

Figure 2.   A summary of the major connections of the basal ganglia. Abbreviations: Cm, centre-median nucleus of the thalamus; VA, ventral anterior thalamus; VL, ventral lateral thalamus; GPi, internal segment of the globus pallidus; GPe, external segment of the globus pallidus. (After DeLong, 1974)

apraxia, however, as the cerebellum apperas primarily to be involved in the timing and patterning of muscle activation during movement (cf. Ghez & Fahn, 1981).

Implications for the Study of Apraxia

Our consideration of the anatomical and functional organization of the intact motor systems has important implications for the study of apraxia; implications that must be considered before we are able to properly consider nonhuman species. We shall consider each in turn.

First, since there are clearly three functional 'motor systems', each with unique anatomical input, studies of apraxia should study separately each type of movement.

Thus, for example, assessment of apraxia syndromes should carefully consider the control of distal (finger, toe and face) movements, hand and limb movements, and whole body movements. Typically, however, these movements are mixed together in the assessment of apraxia as the production of gestures or the copying of movements almost always requires the production of particular finger, limb and body postures. Since the control of these movements is made by separable systems it is likely that subtypes of apraxia can be determined on the basis of the system(s) disrupted. For example, Kolb and Milner (1981) compared the performance of patients with unilateral cortical excisions at the copying of both arm and facial movement sequences and did indeed find evidence of differential input of the frontal and parietal cortex to the control of movement (Figure 3). Whereas left parietal lobe lesions significantly disrupted the copying of arm movement sequences, their lesions had no significant effect upon the copying of facial movement sequences. In contrast, left frontal lobe lesions had relatively little effect upon the copying of arm movement sequences but produced larger impairment in the copying of facial movement sequences. Unfortunately, Kolb and Milner did not try to separate the control of limb, hand and finger movements in their study. Nonetheless, their results show that it is possible to dissociate the relative contribution of different cortical areas to the control of different types of movements. A similar dissociation also has been made by Kimura (1982) in her study of stroke patients. An important additional finding by Kimura, however, was that the complexity of movement was also important. She found that patients with either left anterior or left posterior lesions were inferior to those with equivalent right hemisphere damage on tasks requiring the reproduction of a series of multiple oral or manual sequences. However, on a test requiring the reproduction of single movements the only group significantly impaired was the left anterior group, whereas on single hand postures the only group impaired was the left posterior group.

Second, since the posterior parietal and prefrontal cortex have no direct projections into the spinal cord, theories emphasizing their importance in apraxia must attempt to specify just how it is that these regions might influence movement. Indeed, although it is widely assumed that the posterior parietal and prefrontal cortices are the primary cortical regions for the production of apraxia, patients with circumscribed cortical excisions do not typically demonstrate chronic abnormalities on standard clinical tests of apraxia and, compared to stroke patients, have relatively minor impairments on tests of movement copying (see Figure 4). In order to emphasize this point we have illustrated the extent of surgical excision in several patients from the Montreal Neurological Hospital in Figure 5. It can be seen that even massive removals of the left hemisphere produce rather small movement copying deficits when compared to the performance of patients with naturally occurring lesions, which are summarized in Figure 4. The implication of these observations cannot be underestimated: the direct contribution of the prefrontal and parietal cortex (and the connections between them) to praxis must be less than is generally implied from clinicoanatomical studies. This conclusion is critical for our consideration of animal studies since even large removals of the frontal or posterior parietal cortex in nonhuman species do not produce apractic symptoms similar to those observed in humans with strokes. The failure to observe apraxia-like disorders in nonhuman species may therefore not reflect a species difference as is commonly presumed, but rather may be just the same as is seen in human subjects with cortical excisions. Far more research needs to be done on the motor skills of patients with cortical excisions before the importance of the animal studies can be fairly evaluated and generalizations made.

Third, the importance of the basal ganglia and thalamus in apractic syndromes should be vigorously investigated since these regions provide major access routes for the cortex to influence motor output. Furthermore, the fact that cortical excisions

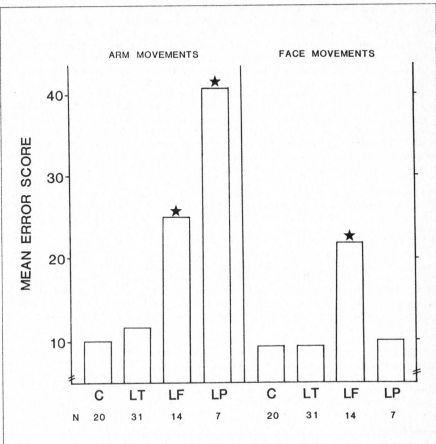

Figure 3.   Copying of arm and face movements. The bars represent the mean errors for each patient group. Data from Kolb & Milner (1981). Abbreviations: C, control; LT, left temporal; LF, left frontal; LP, left parietal.

have far lesser effects upon praxis than do strokes, which presumably affect both the cortex and basal ganglia and/or thalamus, implies that damage to subcortical structures may be essential in order to produce severe clinical apraxia. This conclusion is important because it suggests that studies using nonhuman species should directly compare the effects of cortical, subcortical, and combined cortical-subcortical ablations upon the control of complex movement. Failure to find severe apraxia-like syndromes in laboratory animals with cortical excisions may be reversed if there is also unilateral damage to the basal ganglia or lateral thalamus.

Fourth, since the limbs and face, but not the hands, are connected via the corpus callosum, it should be determined whether or not the extent of bilateral apraxia is similar in tests of hand, finger, face and limb movements. Although the importance of transcallosal connections has been emphasized in accounts of apractic syn-

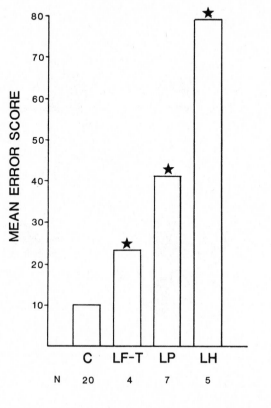

Figure 4.   Copying of arm movements. The bars represent the mean
                 errors for each patient group. Abbreviations: C, control;
                 LF-T, left fronto-temporal; LP, left parietal; LH, left hemi-
                 sphere. The left-hemisphere group is composed of stroke
                 patients whereas the other patient groups have surgical exci-
                 sions.

dromes (cf. Geschwind, 1975; Liepmann, 1908), emphasis usually has been placed
upon the inability of the hand ipsilateral to the speaking hemisphere to perform
movements on verbal command. Few attempts have been made to carefully
describe the abilities of the limbs, fingers and face to perform particular movements (but see Zaidel & Sperry, 1977). In an attempt to consider this problem Milner and Kolb (Note 1) studied the ability of four commissurotomized patients to
copy meaningless sequences of arm or facial movements (cf. Kimura & Archibald,
1974; Kolb & Milner, 1981) with either the left or right hand. The data showed that
the subjects were very badly impaired at copying these movements, even when compared with patients with left parietal lesions. Perhaps most surprisingly, on the arm
movements the patients were equally impaired with either hand, a result that would

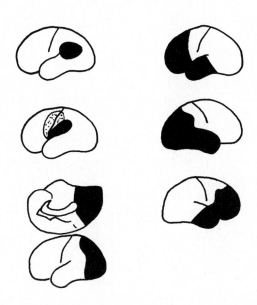

Figure 5.   Examples of cases of surgical excisions studied in tests of movement copying by Kolb & Milner (1981). The left-frontal and left-parietal lobe excisions produced impairments on the copying of face or arm movements, respectively, but not 'clinical apraxia'. The other excisions did not produce any obvious impairments in movement.

not be predicted from previous clinicoanatomical studies (e.g. Geschwind, 1975). Unfortunately, the movement sequences in our study confounded both limb and finger movements although most of the errors of movement appeared to be in the positioning of the arms, rather than the fingers. Since the transcallosal connections of the fingers and arms are different, this impression should be followed up with additional studies.

In sum, when considered in the light of the functional anatomy of the motor systems it is apparent that there are an enormous number of experiments to be done before it will be possible to make educated guesses about the anatomical origin of apractic syndromes in either human or nonhuman subjects. Further, it is clear that although clinicoanatomical studies have been useful in the study of apraxia to date, these studies need to be re-evaluated in the light of what is known about the organization of the intact motor systems.

The Problem of Measuring Behaviour

The problem of developing appropriate measures of praxis for nonhuman species may be understood by considering the definition of apraxia in humans. Strictly defined, apraxia means no action (the Greek praxis meaning action) but the term is hardly ever used in this sense. Rather, apraxia is used clinically to describe all sorts of missing or inappropriate actions that cannot be clearly attributed to paralysis, paresis, or other more primary motor deficits, or to lack of comprehension, 'motivation', etc. Clinically, it has been useful to define subtypes of apractic syndromes (e.g. ideational apraxia, constructional apraxia) on the basis of particular behavioural abnormalities that are observed (cf. Hecaen & Albert, 1978; Heilman, 1979) and various simple clinical tests of apraxia have been devised (e.g. DeRenzi, Pieczuro & Vignolo, 1968). Although these subclassifications of apraxias are very useful clinically as descriptors, they are not very meaningful to the basic neuroscientist, largely because they are defined by clinical examples rather than by a careful description of the qualitative and quantitative aspects of the behaviour. Thus, although it may be clinically informative to describe ideational apraxia as "an inability to carry out a complex gesture (where) although the individual elements of the total act are executed correctly, there is a disruption in the logical and harmonious succession of separate elements" (Hecaen & Albert, 1978), and then to illustrate this with an example patient, this description does not allow us to search for a similar deficit in nonhuman species. Furthermore, it makes clinical diagnosis difficult in the absence of extensive personal experience with apractic patients. We believe, therefore, that a basic obstacle to the study of apraxia in nonhuman species is that the method of studying and defining apraxia in human patients has changed little since Liepmann's now classic investigations at the turn of the century. The time would seem to be right for investigators to capitalize on the knowledge and methodology in experimental psychology (cf. Roy, 1978, 1982) in order to more clearly define the nature of behavioural deficits in apractic syndromes. In contrast to the study of movement disorders by neurological workers, experimental psychologists have concentrated upon the study of the movements of intact subjects (cf. Stelmach, 1976, 1978). Thus, for example, simple movements such as the reaching for and pressing of a button have been analyzed by breaking the movement down into its constituent parts such as: reaction time to initiate the movement; path taken by the limb towards the target; point at which the fingers and hand form the correct posture to contact the target; body posture during the movement, etc. A similar analysis should be applied to the characteristics of movement of patients with all types of movement disorders, including apraxias. By carefully describing the way in which particular movements are (or are not) integrated in complex movements by apractic patients, it should be thus possible to dissociate different subtypes of apraxia, which may or may not conform to the clinically-defined subtypes. A more careful description and quantification of the movement of apractic patients thus has the major advantage that it can provide a classification of apractic disorders that is independent from inferred cognitive processes such as "ideation, realization, conceptualization, etc."; processes that are meaningless when applied to the study of nonhuman species, and that are at best confusing in the study of human subjects.

In addition to carefully describing the details of movements of apractic subjects, it will also be necessary to examine other aspects of the movements. Table 2 summarizes some of the characteristics of movements that must be determined before we have a thorough understanding of the nature of the apractic disorder. For example, it is often suggested that a fundamental difference between ideomotor and ideational apraxia is to be found in the ability of the patients to produce various types of expressive gestures such as wave good-bye, salute, or to pantomime actions such as making a cup of tea. What is not known, however, is what other characteristics of movements might dissociate these patients. How do the patients differ in their ability to make movements to a place versus movements to a thing? How do the patients differ in terms of movements that make contact with the body (or objects) versus movements that do not make contact with the body, etc.? If the answers to these questions were available, it would be far easier to understand the nature of apractic syndromes as well as to design animal experiments to test specific hypotheses.

Table 2

Some examples of characteristics of movements to be considered in the study of apraxia in humans

1. Meaningful versus meaningless movements.
2. Verbal versus nonverbal components.
3. Single joint movements versus multiple joint movements.
4. Facial versus digit versus limb versus body movements.
5. Combinations of movements controlled by different functional systems.
6. Movement to a place versus movement to a thing.
7. Contact versus noncontact movements.
8. Movements requiring speed versus movements requiring accuracy.
9. Learned versus unlearned movements.
10. Copied movements versus internally generated movements.
11. Movements requiring manipulation of objects versus other movements.
12. Repetitive movements versus changing movements.

Note: Each of the above represents a characteristic of movement that should be considered in designing quantitative measures of apraxia.

The Problem of Quantifying Severity

Although it is clinically useful to make qualitative judgements as to whether a behavioural abnormality is an apraxia or not, this type of decision cannot be meaningfully applied to the experimental study of apraxia, especially when nonhuman species are being used. Therefore, we must address the question: when is a disturbance severe enough to be considered an apraxia? This issue is seldom addressed formally in neurological writings but it is critical to the experimental study of apraxia. We may perform scores of elegant experiments using nonhuman subjects but if the observed behavioural impairments can be dismissed because they are not as severe as a human apraxia, then we have reached an impossible impasse if we wish to generalize to humans.

Perhaps the nature of this problem can be best understood by reconsidering our studies of movement copying by patients with cortical excisions (Kolb & Milner, 1981). We were initially struck by the absence of clinical apractic syndromes in our patients with even very large cortical excisions as they had no obvious motor impairments in routine hospital life or even in simple clinical tests of apraxia. This apparent normality of motor control stood in real contrast, however, to their striking difficulty in reproducing sequences of limb or facial movements. Indeed, some patients with large frontal-temporal excisions were completely unable to successfully copy any of the sequences of facial movements. The issue here is whether or not these patients should be considered apractic. If they are to be considered apractic, then what level of performance shall be the 'cutoff'? If they are not to be considered apractic, then does it follow that apraxia is not a condition resulting from cortical ablation? After all, our patients had very large removals and failed to show clinical apraxia.

There is, of course, no satisfactory resolution to this issue. The point to be learned, however, is that we can only proceed with the experimental study of apraxia (and praxis) if we are prepared to quantify the observed behaviour, and then to use the quantification as a measure of severity. As useful as clinical intuition and observation may be, it cannot take the place of quantification in experimental neuropsychology, either in the study of human or nonhuman subjects.

Selecting Nonhuman Species for Study

We now are in a position to consider the use of nonhuman species in the study of brain-behaviour relationships in the control of praxis. We first wish to consider two issues: 1) Which mammalian species are appropriate? and 2) What is the appropriate behavioural analogue in nonhumans of praxis in humans? We shall consider each question separately.

Which Species are Appropriate?

Most nonhuman species can be used validly in the study of human brain-behaviour relationships. It must not be assumed, however, that all species are equally useful for all problems; the choice of species obviously depends upon the nature of the problem under study. We have considered this problem in detail elsewhere (Kolb & Whishaw, 1983) and will not repeat it unnecessarily here. Rather, we shall assume that for the study of praxis it is desirable to choose species with a neocortex (i.e. mammals), and shall ask the question as to which mammals are suitable if we are trying to produce a model of human apraxia?

A fundamental issue to consider is whether or not the cerebral hemispheres, and in particular the 'association cortex' and motor systems, are equivalent in human and nonhuman species.

General structural similarity. Neuroanatomists have long realized that a simple comparison of the brain size of different species is not a valid basis for comparison since brain size is confounded with body size. Thus, horses would be expected to have larger brains than mice simply because it requires more neurons to operate the much larger body of the horse than the mouse.

Motor Systems. The organization of the motor systems of all mammals follows the general organization described earlier. One significant phylogenetic trend, however, is in the number of fibres that project directly onto the spinal motoneurons: There is a general increase in these projections that correlates with the relative amount of cerebral cortex. In fact, there do not appear to be any direct projections in rats, a relatively meagre projection in cats, and a gradually increasing number in primates, proportional to the relative amount of cerebral cortex. The significance of this difference in the study of apraxia is uncertain but it no doubt accounts, at least in part, for the more severe and long-lasting paresis following lesions of area 4 in humans and chimpanzees than is usually seen in rhesus monkeys or in cats or rats. Furthermore, it is obvious that if one wishes to study praxis in distal musculature (face, fingers, toes), it would be wise to choose species with large numbers of direct corticospinal motoneuron connections, and correspondingly superior control of independent distal muscle movements. Thus, rats and cats would not be appropriate choices for studies of digit use or of complex facial movements, but they would be perfectly appropriate for studies of limb or axial praxis.

What is the Appropriate Behaviour to Study?

Each mammalian species has a unique behavioural repertoire that permits the animal to survive in its particular behavioural niche. In view of the diversity of the behaviour of different species it is necessary to identify comparable behaviours across species to allow valid cross species generalizations. Recall that Flourens chose to study eating and wing-flapping in birds in order to draw conclusions about the mental faculties suggested by Gall and Spurtzheim. Few would seriously argue that Flourens chose appropriate behavoiurs. Still, it might be difficult to reach agreement on which behaviours Flourens should have studied had he chosen to study praxis in decorticate monkeys or rats.

There is no simple solution to this problem. Ethologists have successfully utilized the concept of homology in their studies of behavioural evolution and a similar approach is theoretically possible in neuropsychology, but this approach is fraught with difficulties and is unlikely to prove feasible (cf. Kolb & Whishaw, 1983). An alternate approach, that of classifying behaviour in terms of general function (e.g. vision, maternal behaviour, locomotion) has been proposed recently by Warren (Warren & Kolb, 1978) and discussed in detail by Kolb and Whishaw (1983). This technique may provide an alternative to homology that is more attractive to neuropsychologists interested in generalizing about overall brain-behaviour relationships, but it cannot easily be applied to the study of clinically-defined syndrome such as apraxia. Rather, until the definitional problems discussed above have been successfully solved, it would seem that the only reasonable course to take is to attempt to carefully describe (with the help of film or video analysis) the behaviour of animals with different neurological manipulations by using a battery of behavioural tests that include at least three different types of observations: 1) the ability of animals to perform tests of reaching, grasping, walking, etc., in a variety of situations; 2) the ability of animals to learn to execute sequences of discrete movements; and 3) the ability of animals to execute naturally occurring sequences of movements. We shall consider each type of behavioural test separately, using examples from the literature as well as our own work to illustrate.

Simple Movements. In order to be certain that apraxia-like behaviours are not merely the result of more generalized movement disorders (akinesias, paresis, ataxias, etc.), it is necessary to carefully describe the behaviour of animals with damage to each of the three functional motor systems. The elegant work of Kuypers and his colleagues provides an excellent model for this type of approach (e.g. Brinkman & Kuypers, 1973; Haaxma & Kuypers, 1975; Lawrence & Kuypers, 1968; Moll & Kuypers, 1977). These researchers have provided compelling evidence for the existence of separable motor systems in the primate, for the importance of intrahemispheric connections in the visual guidance of relatively independent hand and finger movements, and for the role of the arcuate and supplementary motor cortex in the control of visually-guided reaching. We have conducted similar experiments in rats (Kolb & Whishaw, in press) and Olmstead and Villablanca have performed similar experiments in cats (e.g. Olmstead & Villablanca, 1979). These experiments thus provide the information necessary to interpret the results of tests of more complex motor control.

Learned Sequences of Movements. One way in which to quantify praxis in humans is to have subjects learn a series of movements (e.g. Kimura, 1977; Roy, 1981). An analogue of this type of test in nonhuman subjects may be the acquisition of complex puzzle latches, the acquisition of tool use (in primates), or the performance of a chain of movements to move or displace a series of manipulandae. For example, in her study of the effect of precentral, premotor and parietal lesions on the control of movement, Deuel (1977) examined the postoperative retention of the ability of monkeys to open a complex latch box. Although the animals with premotor lesions recovered apparently normal dexterity and strength, the animals were chronically impaired at opening the latch box, primarily because they made a very large number of sequence errors. That is, the animals were able to manipulate the pieces of the puzzle box but since they did so in the wrong order, the box could not be opened. In contrast, monkeys with posterior parietal lesions were unimpaired and made very few sequence errors. Monkeys with precentral (motor cortex) lesions had chronic loss of strength and dexterity and also were impaired in opening the puzzles, much as might be expected from human subjects with precentral lesions. It would be instructive to test monkeys on several different puzzles in order to determine the ability of the monkeys to distinguish the puzzles. Human frontal lobe patients make a large number of intrusion errors in movement copying tasks by inserting movements from previous sequences into the current sequence (Kolb & Milner, 1981).

Similar experiments have been successfully performed with both rats (e.g. Gentile, Green, Nieburgs, Schmelzer & Stein, 1978; Kolb & Whishaw, 1983) and cats (Webster, Note 2) with the similar finding that frontal, but not posterior parietal, lesions impair the opening of puzzle latches.

Species Typical Behaviours. All animals perform very complex sequences of behaviours that are typical of their species, are relatively unmodified by experience, and are released by particular stimuli. These behaviours are thus considered to be innate and are usually called 'species specific' or 'species typical' behaviours. Virtually all of these behaviours require the animal to chain together a series of discrete movements and require the neocortex for their normal execution (e.g. Kolb & Whishaw, 1981). They thus provide an excellent opportunity for the neuropsychologist to study the effect of neurological manipulations upon the organization of complex movements. An example will serve to illustrate.

Most rodents build nests in the laboratory if nesting material is provided. In our studies of hamsters with various neocortical removals (Shipley & Kolb, 1977; Kolb, Note 3), we were struck by the impairments in nest building observed in hamsters with medial frontal lesions; an inpairment similar in many ways to the difficulties we had observed in rats opening puzzle latches after medial frontal ablations. Table 3 summarizes the nest building behaviour of two hamsters, one with a medial frontal lesion and a second, normal control hamster. When presented with nest material (thin strips of paper towel) the normal animal immediately began to collect it and to transport it to the desired location, before manipulating the amassed paper strips into an intricate web to form a nest. In contrast, although the hamster with a frontal lesion was able to pick up, carry, and manipulate the materials, the order of the behaviours was completely random and even after seven days, no nest was constructed. Similar abnormalities in the organization of behavioural patterns have been observed in a variety of species typical behaviours (e.g. social behaviour, sexual behaviour, maternal behaviour, feeding behaviour, grooming behaviour) in rodents, carnivores and primates (e.g. Kolb & Whishaw, 1981; Nonneman & Kolb, 1974; Myers, 1972) with frontal cortex lesions.

Finally, in the study of learned sequences of movements in normal animals researchers have described a phenomenon that has an apraxia-like appearance. When animals are trained to make a response to obtain a food object, species specific movements usually used for obtaining food, or consummatory movements usually used in ingesting the food, may intrude upon the trained response. For example, a pig trained to press a bar for food may begin to root at the bar (a behaviour that it normally uses in obtaining food), or a rat trained to press a bar for food may begin to bite the bar (the movement it may make to consume the food). Some of these intrusion errors can have fatal consequences. Seals trained to balance a ball to obtain a fish may, if the ball is small, swallow it in anticipation and choke. Many other species specific errors of this type (so called 'instinctive drift') have been described by Breland and Breland (1966). These types of behaviours have some similarity (at least conceptually) to 'body-part as object' behaviours of apractic patients. To our knowledge, there have been no studies of how brain damage effects the frequency of such errors but such studies may be very worthwhile.

Summary

We began this paper by asking whether the study of praxis in animals can aid in the understanding of apraxia in humans. We wish to conclude by reiterating our belief that animal studies can indeed make an important contribution, and that this contribution can best be realized if there are some changes in the approaches used in the study of both humans and animals. First, we have suggested that there should be a re-evaluation of the anatomical basis of human apraxia. We have noted that the anatomical basis of 'clinical apraxia' in humans is unlikely to be neocortical but probably involves combined damage of both cortical and subcortical structures. Second, we have argued that the behaviours that are studied in apractic syndromes should be fractionated in such a way that they parallel, to some degree, the anatomical systems that produce different types of movement. Third, we have argued that the movements should be described and quantified in such a way that the severity and generality of any deficit can be easily assessed. Finally, we have suggested that there are many types of animals that display both learned and species typical behaviours of varying complexity, many of which may be useful in the study of apraxia. If we have been remiss in any regard in this essay it has been in not pointing out that much of human research has been hampered by the belief that the deficits displayed by patients are only gauges to assess the workings of hidden inner activities. This belief is implicit in the assumption that humans are somehow different from other animals, a belief that stems from the Cartesian idea of body as machine controlled by a mind (cf. Vanderwolf, 1983). We subscribe to the hypothesis that the function of the brain is to produce movements. Consequently, we argue that it is the movements themselves that should be studied. Since there are more commonalities than differences between the movements of humans and other animals we believe that comparative studies hold great hope for furthering our understanding of apraxia.

Table 3

Description of nest building behaviour of a normal control hamster and a
hamster with a medial frontal cortex lesion.

Animal   Behaviour

Normal   Material introduced. Pick up in mouth
                (PICK) / Carry to a corner of the cage
                (CARRY) / Manipulate with paws and mouth
                (MANIP.) / DROP / PICK & MANIP. / WALK /
                PICK / CARRY / MANIP. / Adjust all
                collected material with mouth and paws
                (ADJUST) / WALK / CARRY / MANIP. / ADJUST
                / WALK / PICK / CARRY / MANIP. / WALK /
                PICK / CARRY / MANIP. / ADJUST / WALK /
                CARRY / MANIP. / ADJUST / SNIFF / WALK /
                MANIP. / WALK / CARRY / MANIP. / WALK /
                CARRY / MANIP. / ADJUST / All materials
                in corner in less than 10 minutes /
                ADJUSTS with intermittent WALKS for
                3 hours / Nest complete.

Medial   Material introduced. PICK / MANIP. /
Frontal   Push material into cheek pouch (POUCH)
                / SNIFF and WALK / PICK / MANIP. /
                POUCH / WALK around cage with nest
                material in pouch for about 10 min. /
                PICK / MANIP. / DROP / PICK / MANIP.
                / DROP / WALK / SNIFF / DIG in material
                / PICK / MANIP. / DROP / PICK / MANIP. /
                DROP / WALK / PICK / MANIP. / DROP/ PICK
                / MANIP. / DROP / WALK / POUCH / WALK /
                PICK / MANIP. / DROP /WALK / Continues to
                pick-up, manipulate, drop, and walk
                around for three hours / Material never
                collected in one place but rather
                scattered around the cage / No nest
                built.

Note: The control animal worked continually at collecting
        the nest material in one place and manipulating it
        into a nest. The medial frontal animal's behaviour
        was disorganized as it executed the necessary
        components but failed to organize the components
        into a complete normal sequence.

REFERENCE NOTES

1. Milner, B. & Kolb, B. Performance of complex arm and facial movements after cerebral commissurotomy. Unpublished manuscript.

2. Webster, W. Unpublished observations, 1979.

3. Kolb, B. Double dissociation of the role of the prefrontal cortex in practic movements in hamsters. Canadian Psychological Association, Quebec City, 1979.

REFERENCES

Breland, K. & Breland, M. Animal Behaviour. New York: MacMillan, 1966.

Brinkman, J. & Kuypers, H.G.J.M. Cerebral control of contralateral and ipsilateral arm, hand and finger movements in the split-brain rhesus monkey. Brain, 1973 96, 653-674.

Brooks, V.B. Motor Control, Vol. 1 and 2. Baltimore: Williams & Wilkins, 1981.

DeLong, M.R. Motor functions of the basal ganglia: single-unit activity during movement. In F.O. Schmitt & F.G. Worden (Eds.), The Neurosciences Third Study Program. Cambridge, Mass.: MIT Press, 1974.

DeRenzi, E., Pieczuro, A. & Vignolo, L.A. Ideational apraxia: a quantitative study. Neuropsycholgia, 1968, 6, 41-52.

Deuel, R.K. Loss of motor habits after cortical lesions. Neuropsychologia, 1977, 15, 205-215.

Eccles, J.C., Ito, M. & Szentagothai, J. The Cerebellum as a Neuronal Machine. New York: Springer, 1967.

Flourens, P. Investigations of the properties and the functions of the various prts which compose the cerebral mass. In G. von Bonin (Ed.), The Cerebral Cortex. Springfield, Ill.: Charles C. Thomas, 1960.

Gentile, A.M., Green, S., Nieburgs, A., Schmelzer, W. & Stein, D.G. Disruption and recovery of locomotor and manipulative behaviour following cortical lesions in rats. Behavioural Biology, 1978, 22, 417-455.

Geschwind, N. The apraxias: neural mechanisms of disorders of learned movements. American Scientist, 1975, 63, 188-195.

Ghez, C. & Fahn, S. The cerebellum. In E.R. Kandel, & J.H. Schwartz (Eds.), Principles of Neural Science. New York: Elsevier North Holland, 1981.

Haaxma, R. & Kuypers, H.G.J.M. Intrahemispheric cortical connections and visual guidance of hand and finger movements in the rhesus monkey. Brain, 1975, 98, 239-260.

Hecaen, H. & Albert, M.L. Human Neuropsychology. New York: Wiley, 1978.

Heilman, K.M. Apraxia. In K.M. Heilman & E. Valenstein (Eds.), Clinical Neuropsychology. New York: Oxford University Press, 1979.

Kimura, D. Acquisition of a motor skill after left-hemisphere damage. Brain, 1977, 100, 527-542.

Kimura, D. Left-hemisphere control of oral and brachial movements and their relation to communication. Philosophical Transactions of the Royal Society of London, 1982, B298, 135-149.

Kimura, D. & Archibald, Y. Motor functions in the left hemisphere. Brain, 1974, 97, 337-350.

Kolb, B. & Milner, B. Performance of complex arm and facial movements after focal brain lesions. Neuropsychologia, 1981, 19, 491-503.

Kolb, B. & Whishaw, I.Q. Dissociation of the contributions of the prefrontal, motor and parietal cortex to the control of movement in the rat. Canadian Journal of Psychology, 1983.

Kolb, B. & Whishaw, I.Q. Generalizing in neuropsychology: problems and principles underlying cross-species comparisons. In T.E. Robinson (Ed.), Behavioral Contributions to Brain Research. New York: Oxford, 1983.

Kolb, B. & Whishaw, I.Q. Neonatal frontal lesions in the rat: sparing of learned but not species-typical behaviour in the presence of reduced brain weight and cortical thickness. Journal of Comparative and Physiological Psychology, 1981, 95, 863-879.

Kornhuber, H.H. Cerebral cortex, cerebellum, and basal ganglia: an introduction to their motor functions. In F.O. Schmitt & F.G. Worden (Eds.), The Neurosciences Third Study Program. Cambridge, Mass.: MIT Press, 1974.

Lawrence, D.G. & Kuypers, H.G.J.M. The functional organization of the motor system in the monkey. I. The effects of bilateral pyramidal lesions. Brain, 1968, 91, 1-14.

Liepmann, H. Drie Aufsatze aud dem Apraxiegebiet. Berlin: Karger, 1908. (English translation by D. Kimura, Research Bulletin of the University of Western Ontario, 1980, 506.)

Moll, L. & Kuypers, H.G.J.M. Premotor cortical ablations in monkeys: contralateral changes in visually guided reaching behaviour. Science, 1977, 198, 317-319.

Myers, R.E. Role of prefrontal and anterior temporal cortex in social behaviour and affect in monkeys. Acta Neurobiologiae Experimentalis, 1972, 32, 567-580.

Nonneman, A.J. & Kolb, B. Lesions of hippocampus or prefrontal cortex alter species typical behaviour in the cat. Behavioural Biology, 1974, 12, 41-54.

Olmstead, C.E. & Villablanca, J.R. Effects of caudate nuclei or frontal cortex ablations in cats and kittens: paw usage. Experimental Neurology, 1979, 63, 559-572.

Roy, E.A. Apraxia: A new look at an old syndrome. Journal of Human Movement Studies, 1978, 4, 191-210.

Roy, E.A. Action sequences and lateralized cerebral damage. Evidence for asymmetries in control. In J. Long, & A. Baddeley (Eds.), Attention and Performance IX. New Jersey: Erlbaum, 1981.

Roy, E.A. Action and performance. In A. Ellis (Ed.), Normality and pathology in cognitive function. London: Academic Press, 1982.

Shipley, J.E. & Kolb, B. Neural correlates of species-typical behaviour in the Syrian golden hamster. Journal of Comparative and Physiological Psychology, 1977, 91, 1056-1073.

Stelmach, G.E. Information processing in motor control and learning. New York: Academic Press, 1978.

Stelmach, G.E. Motor Control: Issues and trends. New York: Academic Press, 1976.

Vanderwolf, C.H. The influence of psychological concepts on brain-behaviour research. In T.E. Robinson (Ed.), Behavioral Contributions to Brain Research. New York: Oxford University Press, 1983.

Warren, J.M. & Kolb, B. Generalizations in neuropsychology. In S. Finger (Ed.), Recovery from Brain Damage. New York: Plenum Press, 1978.

Zaidel, D. & Sperry, R.W. Some long term effects of cerebral commissurotomy in man. Neuropsychologia, 1974, 15, 193-204.

Zaidel, D. & Sperry, R.W. Memory impairment after commissurotomy in man. Brain, 1977, 97, 263-272.

*Neuropsychological Studies of Apraxia
and Related Disorders, E.A. Roy (ed.)
© Elsevier Science Publishers B.V. (North-Holland), 1985*

DEVELOPMENTAL DYSPRAXIA

Sharon Cermak

Boston University

The majority of the present chapter focuses upon a description of the child with developmental dyspraxia, highlighting characteristics, etiology, theories, evaluation and treatment. The need for early identification and remediation of developmental dyspraxia is emphasized and various treatment approaches are discussed. The concept of developmental dyspraxia is compared to and contrasted with that of adult apraxia. The two definitions are shown to contrast in that dyspraxia involves an impairment in new learning of motor patterns and sequences, whereas apraxia is characterized as a disorder of learned movements. The nature of the disorder also differs in that developmental dyspraxia is seen as a disorder of sensory integration, characterized by problems in planning the movement sequences, while apraxia is seen as largely a problem in execution. Evaluation of apraxia in the adult has emphasized the execution of symbolic gestures and pantomime, primarily to verbal command. In contrast, evaluation of developmental dyspraxia in the child emphasizes the imitation of nonsymbolic gestures. An attempt is made to highlight and clarify the nature of apraxia in adults and children.

Developmental dyspraxia has been used as a categorical label to refer to children demonstrating motor planning disorders. As a descriptor it has come to be favoured over its alternative "childhood apraxia" for several reasons: 1) the physiological mechanisms that have been forwarded to explain the disorder vary considerably from those seen in adult apraxia; 2) the behavioural manifestations are different than those seen in adult apraxia; and 3) evaluation and treatment of the dyspractic child proceed along different dimensions than those used with adults. The purpose of the present chapter will be to highlight some of these differences and, in some instances, to point out similarities in the two types of motoric disorders. In addition, a typology of developmental dyspraxia will be suggested.

Definition

The concept of developmental dyspraxia has been documented since the early 1900's by Collier who used the term "congenital maladroitness" (Ford, 1966). Doctors and therapists in France were, by 1925, calling attention to motor awkwardness in many disabled children, calling it "motor weakness" or "psychomotor syndrome". Orton (1937) considered abnormal clumsiness or "developmental apraxia" to be one of the six most commonly occurring developmental disorders (the other five were in the area of communication). He recognized that disorders of praxis and gnosis might result in a clumsiness of physical performance that was different from that arising from pyramidal, extrapyramidal or cerebellar dysfunction. In the United States, clumsiness was first discussed by Strauss and Lehtinen (1947). But there was no real documentation of developmental dyspraxia until a series of case studies appeared in the 1960's (Walton, Ellis & Court, 1962; Gubbay, Ellis, Walton & Court, 1965.

More recently, Ayres (1972a,b,c) has referred to the clumsiness seen in some learning disabled children as developmental dyspraxia and has defined it as a disorder of sensory integration interfering with the ability to plan and execute skilled or non-habitual motor tasks. She feels that while children can attain reasonably high degrees of skill in specific activities which they have practised, this motor skill remains highly specific to a particular act and does not generalize to other similar activities. Whenever variation is required, the response breaks down and motor behaviour becomes inaccurate and disorganized. Other authors have also emphasized that, in the dyspractic child, there is an excessive expenditure of energy with inaccurate judgement of the required force, tempo and amplitude (Walton et al., 1962).

Gubbay (1975) defined the dyspractic child as a clumsy child whose ability to perform skilled movement is impaired despite normal intelligence and normal findings on conventional neurological exam. For Gubbay, normal intelligence is of primary consideration. He views motor planning itself as an intellectual function and suggests that the child with intellectual retardation will be clumsy on intellectually challenging tasks. Gubbay feels that clumsiness in the retarded child should not be called apraxia, and compares it to calling the retarded child with delayed speech and visuo-spatial functions, aphasic and agnostic. Dawdy (1981) has questioned the mandating of normal intelligence and suggests that the child's motor skills should be compared to his cognitive skills.

Differences Between Apraxia in Children and Adults

The literature on apraxia in adults is, for the most part, widely discrepant from the literature which describes dyspraxia in children. These differences are critical to understand and will be discussed in some detail. For the purposes of this comparison, a description of apraxia, as presented by Geschwind (1975) and colleagues will primarily be used to illustrate apraxia in adults whereas the work of Ayres (1972a,b,c; 1975; 1976a,b; 1980a,b) and Gubbay (1975, 1979) will primarily be utilized for the description of dyspraxia in children. Undoubtedly, the major difference between the two is in the definition of apraxia, Geschwind (1975) defines apraxia as a "disorder of the execution of learned movement which cannot be due to a lack of coordination, a sensory loss, dementia, attentional deficits, etc." In contrast, Ayres (1972a,b,c) defines dyspraxia as an impairment in the performance of new skilled or non-habitual motor tasks. Thus, whereas Geschwind focuses on impairment of already learned motor tasks, Ayres suggests that the dyspractic child can learn motor tasks, and can perform already learned motor tasks but has trouble with new learning or the performance of new motor tasks. One researcher who helps to bridge this apparent discrepancy is Kimura (1977). She has investigated the learning of new motor skills in apractic adults and has found that not only do the subjects have difficulty in performing learned motor tasks, they also have problems in new learning (cf., Roy, 1981, 1983).

Another discrepancy between the adult and childhood literature is the conception of the nature of the disorder. Geschwind (1975) discussed the problem primarily in terms of an executive disorder, whereas Ayres (1972a,b,c; 1975) focuses on the sensory integrative aspects, specifically the planning stage of the movement. The work of Roy (1978) may help to clarify this difference and is discussed in a later section.

Two other major differences between the literature on adults and children concerns the time of the acquisition of the disorder, and the nature of the lesion producing the praxis problems. In children, the problem is congenital or developmental, often related to prenatal, perinatal or neonatal circumstances. Thus, the child has never developed normal motor skills. In contrast, the adult with apraxia did have normal motoric skills but lost them through an acquired problem in later life. Additionally, there is usually an identifiable lesion associated with adult apraxia whereas this is usually not the case with developmental dyspraxia. Studies examining CAT scans of clumsy children did find a higher incidence of abnormality but did not find any consistent pattern of localizable lesion (Bergstrom & Bille, 1978; Knuckey, Apsimon & Gubbay, 1983).

Evaluations of apraxia in adults and children has also been quite discrepant. Apraxia in adults has usually been evaluated by asking the patient to perform gestures to verbal command or to imitation. These gestures are usually symbolic, that is they convey a particular meaning (eg. Show me how you brush your teeth with a toothbrush; show me how you woud cut wood with a saw; show me how you stand like a boxer). In addition to evaluating performance to verbal command and to imitation with the object absent, the patient may be also asked to perform the task using the actual object. Thus, in adults, there are two primary characteristics of the testing. First, symbolic or meaningful gestures are generally assessed. Second, a comparison is made of performance to verbal command versus to imitation, and of performance with and without the actual object.

In assessing praxis in children, the tests have principally assessed nonrepresentational or nonsymbolic gestures. Berges and Lezine (1965) developed a test for children ages three to six in which the child was asked to imitate nonmeaningful arm and hand positions assumed by the examiner. The test developed by Ayres (1980a,b,c) for four to eight year olds, and the test developed by Druker (1978) for 11 to 14 year olds also involve the imitation of nonmeaningful gestures. If indeed, there are differences in performance as a function of the symbolic content of the task, then the use of two types of widely discrepant stimulus material may be of critical importance.

The role of language is another variable which differs between apraxia in adults and children. Many adult apraxia patients are also aphasic, leading many researchers to question whether apraxia is a form of language (symbolic) disorder. However, this linkage is not true to the same extent in chidren. While some researchers have noted co-existing language deficits in some dyspractic children (eg. Ayres & Mailloux, 1981; Eustis, 1947; Garvey, 1980), many researchers have emphasized that dyspractic children are very proficient in language. In fact, for Gubbay (1975), the profile of the dyspractic child is one with relatively good language skills as manifested by a Wechsler Intelligence Scale for Children profile of high Verbal-low Performance. Interestingly, the adult apractic shows the opposite IQ profile, that of low Verbal-high Performance, on the Wechsler Adult Intelligence Scale.

With this in mind, a detailed account of the major characteristics of developmental dyspraxia will be presented.

Characteristics of the Dyspractic Child

While the dyspractic child does not show a single pattern of deficits, there are a number of characteristics that have been repeatedly identified in the literature, and descriptions that have been repeatedly reported by parents of clumsy children.

1. Clumsy

The dyspractic child is frequently described as clumsy and awkward. Although many dyspractic children are not identified until they reach school age, many parents often report a history of clumsiness and associated difficulties. Children are described as falling excessively, continuously knocking into things and dropping things, and having more than the usual number of bruises. Performance on skilled motor tasks is different in quality from the way other children perform the task, and is often characterized by groping and variability. Some children report the need to constantly think about planning their movements -- that movements do not seem to come automatically. One adult described dance lessons while she was a child. She said: "I never could figure out as a kid why I couldn't point my toes. The teacher would say "Point your toes" and it never made any sense to me. I always curled my toes up. Only when somebody sat down with me and actually showed me, did I know that was how you were supposed to point your toes. With the other kids, they just did what the teacher did. Nobody had to stop and tell them."

2. Poor tactile perception abilities

Kephart (1971, 1975) observed that many clumsy learning disabled children seemed to have a poor tactile-kinesthetic sense. Ayres (1965, 1969, 1971, 1972a,b,c, 1977) through clinical observation, and a series of factor analytic studies, has repeatedly identified a relationship between problems in tactile perception and problems in motor planning. Difficulty is experienced in interpreting the spatial and temporal qualities of information received through the sense of touch. Recent research has also identified deficits in kinesthetic judgement in the clumsy child (Hulme, Biggerstaff, Moran & McKinlay, 1982).

3. Inadequate body scheme

Deficits in body scheme have been described in detail by a number of investigators dealing with the dyspractic, learning disabled child. Ayres (1965, 1972a,b,c) has hypothesized a close relationship between problems in processing tactile information, problems in body scheme, and motor planning problems. According to Ayres (1972a), "Motor planning involves the development of a semiconscious motor scheme. This scheme is developed by sensory awareness initiating with the tactile system which is a mature sensory system right at birth. Sensory input from the skin and joints, but especially from the skin, helps develop in the brain, the model or internal schema of the body's design as a motor instrument". As this sensory input is coupled with movement and manipulation, the child learns to plan his actions. Ayres (1972a,b,c) has suggested that "if the information which the body receives from its somatosensory receptors is not precise, the brain has a poor basis on which to build its body scheme". Thus, Ayres views the deficits in body scheme as related to the deficits in processing somatosensory information.

4. Slowness learning activities of daily living

Children who are dyspractic usually have a history of slowness in learning activities of daily living although developmental milestones such as sitting, crawling, and walking are achieved within normal or slow normal limits. Parents of dyspractic children report that the children have unusual difficulty learning dressing skills such as buttoning a coat, managing fastenings, snaps or buckles, or tying shoes. Learning to blow one's nose also presents significant difficulty. Feeding independence including handling a spoon, fork, and knife is often delayed. Particular difficulty is noted in the child's attempt to open various containers such as a milk carton at school. While these tasks are ultimately achieved, they are often achieved at a later age and seem to take extra effort for the child to perform.

The mother of a six year old child described her son's daily living skills by saying ... "He does not take care of his dressing needs, and requires help at the dinner table with pouring and cutting." She described dinnertime as a "nightmare". "John spills things, wiggles in his seat, and usually leaves the table in tears".

One learning disabled adult described her difficulty with personal grooming. She said "It was very difficult for me learning how to put on make up, and to use a hair-blower. It took many hours of trying to learn. For a long time, my finger nails were cut very short because I didn't know how to file them. It still is very hard for me to put on eye make up -- to look in the mirror and try to figure it out". When describing herself as a child, she said "If you looked at me, I probably looked like a lot of the kids you see, ... clothes were not put together properly, shoelaces were untied, my hair was never quite combed properly".

5. Problems in gross motor skills

Although poor gross motor coordination may present as a difficulty with total body balance, ineptness may be even more apparent with complex motor activities. Play skills such as learning to ride a tricycle and bicycle, skipping rope, and catching a ball are often achieved at a later age, and seem to take extra effort. The dyspractic child cannot keep up with his peers in sports. He is often the last to be chosen for the team, or excluded from the activity. Some children prefer to play more sedentary games, to play alone, or to play with younger children.

Physical education class often presents major difficulties. A nine year old described his problems as follows: "When the gym teacher tells us to do something, I understand exactly what he means. I even know how to do it, I think. But my body never seems to do the job" (Levine, Brooks & Shonkoff, 1980). One learning disabled adult described her educational experience as follows: "The hardest course for me was gym. I was unfortunate enough to have the same gym teacher throughout high school. The teacher used to think I was a lazy kid, that I just never wanted to do the exercises. Although I tried, I couldn't do the stunts and tumbling for anything. The other girls would do a somersault and I would still do it like a four year old. I'd just about get over". Another adult described her experiences by saying, "Physical education courses were hell as a child, especially gymnastics where you are forced to leave the ground and swing or walk on balance beams or uneven bars. I cannot begin to explain the terror and disorientation".

6. Problems in constructive manipulatory play and poor fine motor abilities

Fine motor coordination problems are often evident and may be characterized by both poor fine motor control and/or spatial problems. They may be manifested by reluctance to engage in, or incompetence in, small motor tasks such as block building, or constructive manipulatory play such as tinker toys, lego blocks, tracing and colouring, and cutting with scissors. One parent described her preschooler as being "destructive with toys, breaking them while playing". Closer inspection, however, revealed that the "destructiveness" occurred when the child "forced" pieces together because he was unable to adequately manipulate the pieces.

7. Handwriting deficits

One of the most frequently cited educational impairments of the dyspractic child is problems in handwriting. Gubbay (1975) found that 65 percent of his "clumsy child" sample showed problems in handwriting. An even higher percentage was reported by Clements (1966). Impaired handwriting is often characterized both by poor motor control and by spatial disorientation. Handwriting is laboured and spacing problems are evident. Letters are irregular in shape and poorly organized on the page. To compensate for inadequate pencil manipulation, the child may develop a maladaptive grasp which further contributes to making writing prolonged and laborious.

8. Developmental articulatory deficit

Frequently, an articulation deficit accompanies the limb motor planning disorder (Kornse, Manni, Rubenstein & Graziani, 1982; Yoss & Darley, 1974). This is not surprising since articulation requires fine motor planning with the oral and speech musculature. Gubbay (1978) found that approximately one third of five to twelve year old children who were dyspractic also had speech difficulties. One would expect that the younger the child, the greater likelihood of finding an accompanying articulation problem.

9. Accompanying soft neurological signs

Many children with developmental dyspraxia show greater than the usual number of soft neurological signs. Given that motor awkwardness, fine motor incoordination, and awkward gait are considered soft neurological signs, this relationship would, to some extent, be expected. It is interesting that somatosensory involvement including finger agnosia, graphesthesia, and extinction to double tactile stimuli are also considered soft neurological signs, and are consistent with the hypothesis of the relationship between motor planning problems and a somatosensory base.

10. Accompanying learning disability

Many children with dyspraxia also have an accompanying learning disorder. This may be manifested by problems in reading, arithmetic, or spelling, or other academic tasks. In a sample of 39 dyspractic children, Gubbay (1978) found that 50% had difficulty with school work. Gordon and McKinlay (1980) have found that spelling, particularly for irregular words, presented particular difficulty for dyspractic chidren.

11. Test performance patterns

The Wechsler Intelligence Scale for Children is often administered to learning disabled children. In dyspractic children, there is frequently a significant discrepancy between the Verbal and Performance scales, with the Performance score being lower. In fact, for Gubbay (1975), this Verbal IQ-Performance IQ split is the single most important characteristic associated with developmental apraxia. However this pattern has not been consistently found. Henderson and Hall (1982) did not find a lower Performance than Verbal IQ in a sample of clumsy children. Similarly, Conrad, Cermak and Drake (1983) found that learning disabled children with low Verbal-high Performance WISC-R profiles as well as learning disabled children with high Verbal-low Performance WISC-R profiles performed more poorly on tasks of praxis than did their nonlearning disabled peers.

A series of tests which have been used by occupational and physical therapists to identify dyspraxia and other types of learning disorders is the Southern California Sensory Integration Tests (Ayres, 1980b). This consists of 17 tests and related clinical observations which assess performance in the areas of somatosensory perception, vestibular and balance functions, visual perception, and motor functions. In this group of tests, the best single indicator of dyspraxia is a low score on the Imitation of Postures test, a test in which the child is required to imitate the examiner as she assumes a series of nonrepresentational (nonsymbolic) gestures. Difficulty with other tasks that involve motor planning include an eye hand coordination test, a test of copying designs, and a test of bilateral motor coordination. Frequently accompanying the low scores on tests of motor planning, are low scores on tests of somatosensory perception and/or vestibular function. Clinical observations of neuromuscular functions often reveals that the child is often hypotonic and has poor postural mechanisms, especially of the flexor mechanism (Ayres, 1976a,b).

12. Emotional component

Many therapists have noted that the dyspractic child often is whiney, manipulative, and somewhat negative. A number of reasons have been suggested as to why many dyspractic children have these personality characteristics. The first hypothesis considers it to be a reaction to failure. Development of gross motor skills and the child's ability to master his body movements serves to enhance feeling of self esteem and confidence. Children who are clumsy are often ostracized by their peers resulting in feelings of worthlessness. The relationship between motor performance, self image and social interaction is exemplified by this statement of a learning disabled child: "They always pick me last. This morning they were all fighting over which team had to have me. One guy was shouting about it. He said it wasn't fair because his team had me twice last week. Another kid said they would only take me if his team could be spotted four runs. Later, on the bus, they were all making fun of me, calling me a fag and a spaz. There are a few good kids, I mean kids who aren't mean, but they don't want to play with me. I guess it could hurt their reputation" (Levine et al., 1980).

Another explanation of the personality characteristics deals with the suggestion that poor body scheme results in poorly defined concept of self which may cause an identity crisis (Ayres, 1980a,b). The child does not have a good sense of who he is and how he is separate from the external world. Because the child has a tenuous grasp on his sense of self, he may have difficulty being able to pretend, and also being able to separate what he is responsible for versus what others do to him (Ayres, 1980a,b).

The third explanation is similar, and relates to the vestibular system. Some dyspractic children have vestibular processing deficits and are gravitationally insecure. These children have an excessive fear reaction to certain types of vestibular input (Avres, 1980a,b). Since one's relationship to gravity is an important sense of security, when this is deficient, all other relationships are apt to be less than optimal (Ayres, 1980a,b). The child may try to manipulate his environment and other people to avoid fearful situations.

Theoretical Basis/Etiology of Developmental Dyspraxia

Clumsiness in children has been found to occur for a variety of reasons because adequate motor performance is an end product requiring the integrity of many different neurological functions. According to Gubbay (1975), "abnormal clumsiness may arise from virtually any disturbance of the nervous system and not exclusively when there is disruption to the motor system".

In the early literature on the etiology of developmental dyspraxia, Orton (1937) suggested that understanding of acquired language and motor (aphasia and apraxia) losses in adults were the key to the developmental disorder in children. In discussing the relationship between apraxia in the adult and the child, Orton stated: ".. the symptoms observed are a very exact counterpart of those seen in the corresponding syndromes in the adult" (p. 142). He further suggested that since the symptomatology was so similar, that the "determiner for these disabilities in childhood is very closely related physiologically to that which is disturbed by lesions in the critical cortices controlling language (and praxis) in the adult" (p. 142). According to Orton (1937), apraxia was caused by disturbance in the parietal lobe, especially the area anterior to the angular gyrus.

Current research however has emphasized differences between developmental and acquired conditions, and has stated that a failure in original development may well have determinants that are not the same as those operating in an acquired impairment (Finger & Stein, 1982). Goldman and Galkin (1978) have stated that there are major differences between function in brain areas in the developing versus the developed brain. Researchers have emphasized that while the symptomatology may be similar between adults and children, this does not imply a similar locus of lesion. While a lesion in a particular localization in the dominant hemisphere may be a prerequisite for the appearance of an acquired disorder in praxis, the situation is quite different in the child with a congenital problem. In fact, preliminary research on the site of the lesion seen in dyspractic or clumsy children has not indicated a specific locus, although there has been a relatively high incidence in abnormal CAT scans (Bergstromm & Bille, 1978; Knuckey et al., 1983).

In attempting to understand the etiology of dyspraxia, researchers have investigated the birth histories of dyspractic children. Gubbay (1978) found that there was an incidence of about 50% prenatal, perinatal, or neonatal factors. He also found that a higher percentage of clumsy children were first born children. This is consistent with the finding that there is a higher incidence in neonatal problems in first born children. As with other developmental disabilities, there is a higher incidence of males than females. Gubbay (1978) and Abbie, Douglas and Ross (1978) reported an incidence of two males to one female whereas Gordon and McKinlay (1980) found the incidence to be four males to one female.

Since examination of neonatal histories of dyspractic children has frequently revealed problems, it is important to consider the consequences of neonatal problems. The most common problem is hypoxia (Towbin, 1980). Thus it is relevant to consider the consequences of hypoxia. Faro and Windle (1969), in a series of studies, deprived monkeys of oxygen at birth for increasingly longer periods of time. They found that asphyxiation resulted in destruction of brain stem centres and thalamus, especially those nuclei of the thalamus concerned with somatosensory function and hearing. If indeed this pattern of destruction is similar in humans, this might relate to the somatosensory processing dysfunction that is frequently noted in dyspractic children (Ayres, 1972a,b). Additionally, although the visual system was not particularly vulnerable, when the monkeys grew up, they showed problems in visual memory. This would support the ideas that visual perception problems may be an end product and may be affected by dysfunction in a number of areas.

Research with humans and animals has also shown the cerebellum to be disproportionately susceptible to processes affecting brain growth during late pregnancy and early infancy (Dobbing & Smart, 1973). It has been suggested that this may relate to the fact that the growth spurt of cerebellum begins a little later than the rest of the brain and ends earlier (Gordon & McKinlay, 1980). Interestingly, in rats, transient undernutrition or irradiation during the growth spurt has been shown to lead to disproportionate underdevelopment of the cerebellum with observed clumsiness in the mature animal (Dobbing, Hopewell & Lynch, 1971). Similarly, in low birth weight babies who are small for date (eg. poor late intrauterine growth), impaired Performance IQ with normal Verbal IQ scores were found on IQ testing. This, however, was not true for premature babies of the same weight but appropriate for their gestational age. Their PIQ and VIQ were normal, but 25% of the premature babies and 33% of the small for gestational age babies showed learning difficulties even though IQs were greater than 70. In one study of 32 newborn babies who showed symptoms after perinatal asphyxia, long term follow up studies showed that 14 (40%) were clumsy children (Brown, 1976).

In summary there seems to be a relationship between clumsiness and neonatal problems. Further, there are indications that the somatosensory system, auditory system and cerebellum may be especially susceptible to neonatal problems.

Ayres (1972a,b) has suggested, because of the close relationship between tactile tests and a test of motor planning seen in a series of factor analytic studies that the dorsal column medial lemniscal system may be of particular importance in developmental dyspraxia. Traditionally, the dorsal columns have been considered to mediate discriminative touch. Recent research on the role of the dorsal column medial lemnsical system would also support its possible role in the development of motor planning. Wall (1970) and Vierck (1978) looked at the deficits in both man and animals (rats, cats, monkeys) that resulted from dorsal column lesions and identified motor deficits. Studies with primates showed that following dorsal column lesions, monkeys demonstrated problems in complex movement sequences and in refined manual dexterity, clumsiness in handling objects in space, and an impairment with moving and/or manipulating small objects. Similarly, monkeys were noted to have flexion hypotonia of their forelimbs. It is interesting to note that dyspractic children often have similar difficulty with supine flexion (Ayres, 1976a,b).

Other studies with animals have implicated the dorsal column in selective attention, orientation and anticipation (Vierck, 1978). It has been suggested that the dorsal columns may play a role in unravelling competing stimuli, and may be involved in orientation in order to bring in more sensory information. The dorsal columns have also been implicated as being necessary for the anticipatory components of sequential behaviour patterns (Melzack & Southmayd, 1974).

In summary, the dorsal column medial lemniscal system seems to be involved not only in tactile discrimination, but also in complex movement sequences and refined manual dexterity, manipulation in space, selective attention, orientation and anticipation, and programming of complex movement sequences. These functions are clearly relevant to the development of motor planning.

While Ayres (1972, 1975) has emphasized the role of the tactile system in motor planning, Gubbay (1975) has suggested that clumsiness is an all inclusive end product of differing etiologies. He emphasizes that the integrity of many different neurological functions is necessary for the execution of skilled movement including intactness of pyramidal, extrapyramidal and sensory pathways, and basic factors of consciousness, and intelligence. He suggests that praxis involves all levels within the central nervous system incluidng the cortex, basal ganglia, cerebellum, and brain stem, all acting upon the final common pathway through the spinal cord and peripheral nerves.

A number of alternative hypotheses have been proposed to explain why praxis may not develop normally. Hypotheses that have been suggested include: 1) Impairment of innate cerebral mechanisms (Gubbay, 1975); 2) Understimulation of an otherwise intact network due to faulty input pathways (Gubbay, 1975); 3) Failure of integration of different parts of the brain (similar to Geschwind's (1975) disconnection theories) (Gordon, 1979); 4) Delay and or incomplete development of cerebellar functions (Lesny, 1980); 5) Parietal disorder (Lesny, 1980); 6) Failure of interneuron development due to poor nutrition, anoxia or hypoxia, or deprivation (Gordon, 1979); and 7) Sensory integrative dysfunction (Ayres, 1972a, 1980a).

Evaluation of Dyspraxia

There are a number of parameters to consider when evaluating developmental dyspraxia. These parameters have been extensively considered in the literature on apraxia in adults but have been only minimally addressed in discussions of developmental dyspraxia. In the following presentation, a number of parameters will be identified. The rationale for including each parameter and the findings in the adult literature will be briefly presented. The results of investigation of each parameter with children will be presented if it has been studied.

Parameters

The first parameter to be discussed is gross versus fine motor planning. A common means of categorizing psychomotor behaviors, and, therefore, their associated mesures, is by differentiating them as either gross motor (large muscle groups) or fine motor (small muscles or manipulative) (Goodwin & Driscoll, 1980). However, such classification is oversimplified in that even skills normally classified as gross motor (such as balancing), also involve fine adjustments of the muscles (in the feet and ankles). Conversely, electromyographic research has shown that considerable muscle activity takes place in the larger muscle groups during fine motor activities (Goodwin & Driscoll, 1980).

Nevertheless, the distinction between gross and fine motor skills is useful and has been identified by factor analytic studies (Fleishman, 1975). However, even though therapists think in terms of a "gross to fine" continuum, with good performance in gross motor activities needed for the execution of fine manipulative activities, there is evidence that this may not necessarily be true. Most dyspractic children do experience difficulty with both gross and fine motor planning but, a number of therapists working with learning disabled children have observed that some clients have primarily gross motor planning deficits, with relatively better fine motor skills, while others primarily have problems in fine motor planning, with relatively good gross motor skills. It has been suggested that those children with fine motor planning problems exhibit problems in tactile perception, while those clients with problems in gross motor performance evidence dysfunction in vestibular processing (Ayres, 1976a,b). This distinction is supported by the literature in which the dorsal column medial lemniscal system (somatosensory system) is primarily involved in complex movement sequences and in refined manual dexterity (Wall, 1970; Vierck, 1978), whereas the vestibular system is more involved in postural adjustments deQuiros & Schrager, 1979).

A parameter closely related to the gross-fine distinction is the <u>proximal (axial)-distal</u> distinction. Research with adult apractics has found that although some patients are unable to respond to verbal commands using distal limb movements, they can perform commands that involve movements of their midline structures (eg. the eyes, neck and trunk - axial movements). For example, one such patient was unable to correctly show how to hammer, but he could correctly carry out tasks such as "look up", "stand", "kneel", "bend the head" (Geschwind, 1975). Geschwind (1975) suggested that preservation of axial movements in the presence of loss or impairment of distal movements is a function of the organization of the motor systems of the brain. Kuypers (Brinkman & Kuypers, 1972; Lawrence & Kuypers, 1965) suggests, at least anatomically, and perhaps functionally as well, the axial or medial system (head, neck, trunk and proximal limbs) and the distal limb or lateral systems are separable. The lateral system of one side is involved in control of discrete movements of the limbs of the opposite side, especially individual finger movements. In contrast, the medial systems of each hemisphere tend to control the more axial muscles on both sides and also initiate certain coordinated movements of both sides of the body such as turning. While the pyramidal system (lateral system) arises primarily from the precentral gyrus, the nonpyramidal systems (axial) arise from multiple sites in the cortex (Geschwind, 1975). Unfortunately, this parameter has not been investigated in the child with develomental dyspraxia.

One parameter which has been addressed, albeit in a limited way, in both adults and children concerns whether the movement is <u>personal or extrapersonal</u>. Broadly defined, personal movements are those actions performed on the self (eg. "Show me how you comb your hair with a comb") whereas extrapersonal movements are those executed in space (eg. "Show me how you hit a nail with a hammer"). In a study of the development of representational gestures in normal children, ages four, eight, and twelve, Kaplan (Note 1) found that for the eight year olds, implements that could be used on the self, such as a comb, yielded less differentiated (less symbolic) gestural responses than implements used away from the self in extrapersonal space. In contrast, Overton and Jackson (1973) found that self-directed action sequences resulted in a greater proportion of symbolic representation than externally directed action sequences. The major proportion of self-directed action sequences became symbolic between four and six years while this occurred between six and eight years for externally directed representations.

Cermak, Coster and Drake (1980) also examined the personal-extrapersonal parameter in their study of the representation of implement usage in learning disabled boys with a low Verbal-high Performance WISC or WISC-R profile. They found that learning disabled children showed significantly less articulated representation on items executed on the self than did the controls, but were not different from the controls on items executed in extrapersonal space. However, while place of action was a relevant variable for the learning disabled subjects it was not for the control subjects.

Schilder (1950) noted that disturbance in one's own body is usually stronger than in extrapersonal space. The finding of Cermak et al.'s (1980) study was consistent with those observations by Schilder. Moreover, it is consistent with the hypothesis that many learning disabled children are field-dependent and do not have a normal sense of interior body orientation.

The performance of learning disabled subjects in Cermak et al.'s (1980) study was similar to that of Kaplan's (Note 1) normal eight year olds who achieved lower gestural maturity scores for personal than for extrapersonal space. However, this distinction between personal and extrapersonal space did not hold for Kaplan's twelve year old children nor did it hold for the normal readers in Cermak et al.'s study. Cermak et al. suggested that the gestural performance of the learning disabled group more closely approximated their level of reding than it did their chronological age, and suggested that factors involved in the reading process might also be related to the child's ability to gesturally represent the use of implements.

A parameter which has been extensively explored in the adult literature is whether the gesture is performed to <u>verbal command or to imitation</u>. In general, performance of adult apractics has been found to improve on imitation when compared to verbal command (Geschwind, 1975). Although not yet studied in developmentally dyspractic children, the verbal command versus imitation parameter has been studied in normal children. In a developmental study of four, eight and twelve year old normals, Kaplan (Note 1) found a greater differentiation of gestural representation on imitation than on verbal command. However, Overton and Jackson (1973), did not find this distinction with three to eight year olds.

As mentioned imitation versus verbal command has generally not been considered in the evaluation of the dyspractic child. In fact, most tests designed to identify dyspraxia in children involve either imitation of nonmeaningful gestures (Ayres, 1980b; Berges & Lezine, 1965; Druker, 1978) or performance on specific motor tasks (eg. Gubbay, 1975). For the most part, these tasks cannot be performed to verbal command. One study which did examine the parameter of imitation/command in learning disabled children found that both the normals and the learning disabled subjects scored significantly better (more mature level of gestural representation) on imitation than on verbal command (Cermak et al., 1980). While it was suggested that perhaps performance was better on imitation because the subject could use the visual model (the examiner) to compare his performance and, so, self correct, or that perhaps improvement was noted in the imitation condition because verbal mediation was not necessary, the authors noted a limitation in drawing any conclusions. The imitation condition always followed the command condition, thus the subjects had familiarity with the practic tasks. In order to ascertain whether a difference actually existed, it would be necessary to explore the parameter using a counterbalanced presentation.

One other focus of research in apraxia is the possible dissociation of <u>symbolic and nonsymbolic gestures</u>. Symbolic is defined as "possessing communicative value, as being referential, and as having meaning" (Beck, 1982, p. 93). Used broadly, the term includes not only words but also gestures such as saluting, and pantomiming the use of tools. Nonsymbolic refers to "Stimuli or responses, whether oral or manual, which are without communicative significance" (Beck, 1982, p. 93). Because apraxia in adults is commonly seen in conjunction with aphasia, many researchers have suggested that apraxia may be a form of a symbolic deficit. This has led researchers to investigate whether apractics might be more impaired on the representation of symbolic as compared to nonsymbolic gestures (Adams & Victor, 1977; Benson & Geschwind, 1971; Goodglass & Kaplan, 1963; Kimura, 1979; Lehmkuhl, Poeck & Willmes, 1983; Lupert, 1981).

The symbolic-nonsymbolic dichotomy has rarely been studied in children. This is probably in part due to the nature of tests for apraxia used with children. The majority of tests for children involve imitation of nonrepresentational, nonsymbolic gestures (Ayres, 1980b; Berges & Lezine, 1965; Druker, 1978). While Kaplan's original work with representational gestures was done with children, this work was based on normal children, and although it has been extensively applied to the assessment of apraxia in adults (Brown, 1972; Geschwind, 1975) and applied to the assessment of the development of gestural representation in normal children, it has been investigated in dyspractic children only minimally.

One study with learning disabled children demonstrated that learning disabled children with a low Verbal-high Performance WISC-R profile showed impairment in representation of both symbolic and nonsymbolic gestures (Cermak et al., 1980). It was suggested that perhaps in the developing child, the symbolic and nonsymbolic components of praxis were not separable.

A number of parameters have been identified which relate to the type of movement being performed. These include whether the movement is 1) static or dynamic; 2) habitual or non-habitual; and 3) simple or complex. With regard to the static-dynamic dimensions, static movements are those which involve the performance of imitation of a position or posture. They have also been called "postures". In contrast, dynamic movements tend to involve change in position, often involving a movement sequence. Research has suggested that the right hemisphere may be involved in the performance of static postures, perhaps because of their spatial nature (Ingram, 1975; Luria, 1966, but see Kimura, 1982; Kolb & Milner, 1981), while the left hemisphere may be more involved in the performance of dynamic gestures because of its sequential role (Denckla, 1973; Geschwind, 1975; Kimura & Archibald, 1974; Luria, 1966; Wolff, Hurwitz & Moss, 1977) or its role in monitoring position change (Galluscio, 1983; Kimura, 1977). This parameter has been investigated by Conrad et al. (1983) in their work with learning disabled subjects. These authors applied Luria's (1966) model of apraxia to children and examind four types of praxis: kinesthetic, optic-spatial, dynamic and symbolic. Learning disabled subjects were divided according to their WISC-R profiles into high Verbal-low Performance subjects and low Verbal-high Performance subjects. It was hypothesized that because a low Verbal profile would more likely reflect a profile of lesser efficiency of the left hemisphere, subjects would score more poorly on dynamic gestures; similarly low Performance subjects (lesser efficiency of the right hemisphere) would score more poorly on optic spatial (static postures) gestures. Results, however, indicated that there was no difference between learning disabled groups, and that both groups scored more poorly than normal controls on dynamic and optic spatial gestures.

Another distinction that needs to be considered in evaluating praxis is whether the movement is nonhabitual or habitual, viz. whether it is a new skilled (nonhabitual) movement or whether it is a learned (habitual) movement. Ayres (1972a,b,c, 1975) differentiates between the performance of nonhabitual movements (deficits of which she terms dyspraxia) and the performance of habitual motor acts. Roy (1978) has similarly emphasized this distinction. Habitual (ie. programmed, well-learned movement patterns) activities are seen to involve very little in the way of planning (making decisions about the sequential ordering of movements). These movements are well learned patterns which can be carried out with little conscious control.

For nonhabitual or novel activities, planning decisions other than just goal selection are required. These involve decisions about the ordering of the individual movements or units in a movement sequence. Two components cognitive or organizational (frontal) and perceptual (paretal-occipital) are considered to be involved in making decisions about sequential order (Roy, 1978, 1983).

The final distinction to consider is whether the movement is simple or complex. A complex movement is a movement composed of a series of different manoeuvres, with changing properties. This contrasts with a static posture which requires the demonstration of a single stationary posture, and with an automated movement which involves the repetition of a movement, either so simple, or so habitual, that continuous monitoring is not required to sustain it (Beck, 1982). According to this categorization, sequential or dynamic movements can be considered either simple or complex, depending on the monitoring needed to sustain the movement. If this is so, then what is considered a "simple" movement for the average child or adult, may in effect be a complex movement for a dyspractic individual.

Treatment of Developmental Dyspraxia

Educators, therapists, and medical personnel are increasingly cognizant of the need for treatment of the child with visuo-motor and motor coordination deficits (eg. Dare & Gordon, 1970). There is increasingly recognition that help must be given at an early age if secondary emotional and behavioural disorders are to be prevented (Dare & Gordon, 1970; Gubbay, 1978; Kinsbourne & Caplan, 1979). McKinlay (1978) has succinctly stated that "The question is not whether remedial teaching works, but whether particular techniques help particular children".

Professionals who deal with the clumsy child recognize that treatment should take into account and reflect the cause of the clumsiness. For example, Dare and Gordon (1970) have emphasized the need to distinguish perceptual difficulties from motor organization problems. They suggest that if the deficit is due to severe perceptual deficit, then the treatment approach should use verbal mediation and emphasize body awareness and body-in-space exercises. On the other hand, if the deficit is in the building up of patterns and memory of movement, then treatment should include practice, circumventing the problem, and breaking the task into simpler parts. Ayres (1965, 1972a,b,c) also emphasizes the need to identify the cause of clumsiness prior to treatment. For example, if the clumsiness is due to difficulty in sensory processing such as inadequate processing of tactile and vestibular information, then an appropriate form of treatment would be occupational therapy utilizing sensory integration procedures.

Since therapists, educators and neurologists are still trying to determine which "type of child" responds best to "which type of therapy", a number of therapeutic approaches have to be considered. The needs of many dyspractic children can best be met by a comprehensive approach which incorporates aspects of the various approaches. In fact, Gubbay (1979) suggests that an interdisciplinary approach, both towards diagnosis and management is necessary. For purposes of the present discussion, treatment will be discussed under the categories of psychosocial aspects, treatment of the motor disorder itself, and treatment of the underlying problem.

Psychosocial Aspects of Treatment

Understanding the nature of the dyspractic condition, and recognizing that this condition is a real disability and not just excessive carelessness often helps both the parent and the child (Orton, 1937; Gordon, 1979). If the dyspractic child's difficulty is not recognized and dealt with, emotional and behavioural disorders often follow.

The dyspractic child is often told that he is lazy or that he could do better if he tried. In fact, the child may be already trying to a significantly greater extent than his peers (Gordon, 1979). Thus, it is not surprising that he becomes depressed, discouraged, frustrated and angry when he is told he is lazy.

Gordon (1979) suggests that unless the child is severely affected, individual help and understanding may be all that is required. He further stated that dyspractic children will have to try harder than their peers if they are going to succeed, and that this is acceptable to the child if he is suitable praised for his efforts. According to Gubbay (1978), "it is not so much what is being done for the child, but more that something is being done" (p. 157). "Bringing the child into focus by recognition of his problem immediately reduces the pressure to conform" (p. 157).

Orton (1937) has suggested that a considerable measure of feeling of inferiority seems to be unavoidable in apractics or dyspractic children. However, Gordon (1979) suggests that one should attempt to put the child into a position where he can succeed, in addition to giving him as much help as possible to overcome the disability.

According to Gubbay (1979), it is important to reduce the pressures on the dyspractic child to conform to the norms of motor functions such as sporting, drawing, and especially handwriting. Gubbay (1979) feels that "a major ingredient of a successful program is a learning environment that provides a measure of protection for the child until such time as a higher level of central nervous system maturity and integration can be achieved".

Remediation of Motor Deficits

This approach usually involves drill or practice in the deficient skill or skills. Often the skill is analyzed and broken down into simple parts, or is taught in a graded sequence. Programs utilizing this approach include that by Cratty (1975), a physical educator who advocates the use of gross motor activities for motor learning and physical fitness. Arnheim and Sinclair (1979) emphasize the importance of physical fitness and present a developmental motor program for learning disabled clumsy children. The perceptual-motor theorists such as Kephart (1971) also utilize this approach in that they emphasize the underlying foundations for skill (eg. gross motor precedes visual perception), although they do not emphasize the influence of their program on neural organization.

One concern regarding remediation of motor skill deficits is that teaching the child specific skills will result in the development of splinter skills, a term used to describe skills which have been learned by the child but which are inefficient because the child does not have the underlying prerequisite sensory integration, postural functions, or movement patterns. In reality, however, children need certain requisite skills in order to cope in their everyday life. It is therefore important to teach these skills and to provide methods or adapted equipment that allow performance of the skill but prevent the development of maladaptive patterns.

Special educators, educators, and physical and adaptive physical educators most frequently utilize the motor skills approach. The occupational or physical therapist can be of particular assistance in identifying maladaptive patterns and suggesting alternate methods.

Remediation of the Underlying Deficit

The course of treatment, which involves remediation of the underlying deficits, obviously relates to how one views the underlying disorder as well as one's view of the ability to influence the disorder by external means. When dyspraxia is viewed as reflecting an underlying problem in neurological integration, the emphasis of treatment is to influence the neural organization to enable more optimal function. Some clinicians/educators/neurologists believe that you cannot influence brain development. In fact, methods to help a child's brain develop have been called "irrational" (Kinsbourne & Caplan, 1979). However, research on recovery of function (Finger & Stein, 1982), on sensory stimulation and enriched environments (Rosenzweig, Bennett & Diamond, 1972) and on neural plasticity (Finger & Stein, 1982; Goldman & Mendelson, 1977) have certainly given support to the possibility of modifying the central nervous system as well as the modifiability of performance abilities.

According to Gaddes (1980), sensory integration procedures are among the most articulate and well developed programs of this nature for learning disabled children. Sensory integration theory has been primarily developed and articulated by Ayres (1965, 1972a,b,c, 1975, 1977, 1980a,b) and includes concepts drawn from neurophysiology, neuropsychology and development. According to this theoretical framework, certain types of developmental dyspraxia are viewed as reflecting a deviation in neural function, and specifically a dysfunction in the ability to organize and interpret sensory information (Ayres, 1972a,b,c). The basic goal of sensory integration procedures is modification of the neurological dysfunction interfering with learning. It is felt that inadequate processing in the tactile and vestibular systems contributes to poor motor planning and remdiation ought to begin at this level. Ayres has suggested that the optimal functioning of higher level cognition and language are dependent, in part, on the ability of the brain stem/midbrain to organize and integrate sensory processes, particularly from the somatosensory and vestibular senses. The functioning of these systems is considered to influence the functioning of the brain as a whole.

Sensory integration procedures are both conceptually and practically different from those approaches that deal primarily with the direct remediation of the motor problems. Conceptually, the dyspraxia seen in the learning disabled child with sensory integration dysfunction are due to problems in processing sensory input, rather than primarily disorders in the execution of motor skills. The objective of sensory integration procedures in modification of the neurological dysfunction interfering with learning rather than dealing with the specific behavioural skills associated with the dysfunction. Practically, this means that "motor skills are neither taught nor are they the primary objective of sensory integration procedures. Rather, the goal of occupational therapy (using sensory integration procedures) is to improve the individual's somatosensory, auditory and visual perception; to improve the ability to plan skilled movement, to develop speech and language and other cognitive functions; and to improve the capacity to organize behaviour". Treatment focuses on sensory input and its continual interaction with movement. Thus, the child is an active participant in the planning and execution of adaptive goal directed motor response sequences.

A number of factors need to be mentioned about sensory integration procedures. First, sensory integration procedures are considered appropriate only for children with sensory integration problems. Not all learning disabled children benefit from this approach. Ongoing research is attempting to determine which types of children benefit from this approach (Ayres, 1972c, 1976a,b, 1978; Ottenbacher, 1982). Second, sensory integration procedures must be coupled with an educational program to enable optimal integration of sensory and motor functions that subserve language and higher cortical functions (Ayres, 1972a, 1976a,b). Third, vestibular and somatosensory input which are utilized in therapy are powerful types of input. They must be used with caution, and the autonomic as well as the behavioural responses of the child must be carefully monitored. The therapist should be knowledgeable about sensory integration theory and treatment prior to utilizing these procedures.

Is Developmental Dyspraxia a Unitary Disorder?

Many types of apraxia have been described for adults (Brown, 1972; DeAjuriaguerra & Tissot, 1969; Hecaen & Albert, 1978; Luria, 1966) and while the typology is not agreed upon, most would agree that apraxia is not a unitary disorder. Luria (1966) and Roy (1978) have suggested that apraxia must be considered from the standpoint of a disturbance to a complex functional system, that being skilled human motor behaviour.

Despite the fact that various typologies of apraxia have been proposed for the adult, apraxia has almost always been treated as a unitary disorder in children, although there is an increasingly recognition that there are different types of motor planning disorders in children (Cermak et al., 1980; Conrad et al., 1983; Dawdy, 1981).

The recent work on a typology of apraxia by Roy (1978) may aid in the clarification of the nature of apraxia in adults and children. Based on a review of the parameters of apraxia in adults, Roy (1978) suggested classifying the apraxias as a planning or an executive disorder. There are two types of planning disorders, primary and secondary. In primary planning apraxia, the patient has lost the ability to conceptually organize the requisite movement sequences. This conceptual organization problem is not limited to motor acts. This type of apraxia is hypothesized to be due to a lesion in the frontal area. Roy also posits a secondary planning apraxia in which the patient manifests severe spatial disorientation due to a lesion in the parietal-occipital area. Since the frontal planning area depends on sensory information from the parietal-occipital areas in order to plan movements, the patient with a lesion in the parietal-occipital area is considered to exhibit a secondary planning disorder.

The second type of apraxia is executive apraxia. In executive apraxia, the patient is able to conceptualize (eg. plan) the movement sequence necessary for accurate performance but lacks the ability to output the planned action into a coherent movement pattern (see Roy & Square, this volume).

It is interesting to try to apply this conceptualization to the literature on apraxia in children. Most writers identify a clumsiness of performance but do not attempt to differentiate between whether the problem is in the "planning" or execution phase. Ayres (1972a,b,c, 1975) does make this distinction. She hypothesizes that the problem is a planning problem, and not just a disorder in execution. Thus, developmental dyspraxia, as described within a sensory integration theory framework, more closely resembles the planning apraxia described by Roy. Many therapists have clinically observed that children who are developmentally dyspractic also are very disorganized. They never can find their papers; their school desks and dresser drawers are always a mess. Ayres has stated that praxis is more than just motor planning. It involves an overall problem with organization, resulting in poor work habits and poor strategies. Perhaps the problem of the dyspractic child described in this manner is comparable to what Roy describes as primary planning apraxia.

However, not all dyspractic children with planning problems manifest primary planning problems. Perhaps some children have secondary planning apraxia. This concept would be consistent with two lines of evidence in the literature on developmental dyspraxia. First, many children with dyspraxia manifest concomitant visual perceptual problems (Henderson & Hall, 1982). Also, the profile manifested by dyspractic children on the Wechsler Intelligence Scale for Children-Revised (WISC-R) often shows a low Performance-high Verbal profile (Gubbay, 1975, 1979).

The Performance section is highly visual motor in nature and is consistent with the suggestion of visual perceptual problems.

Another factor to be considered is the role of the somatosensory system in praxis. Ayres (1972a,b,c) has hypothesized that somatosensory perception contributes to the development of an adequate body scheme which is essential for the ability to plan motor acts. It is interesting that the literature on body scheme deficits in brain damaged adults implicates the parietal-occipital areas as critical for body scheme (Luria, 1966). It is this same area that Roy (1978) suggests is impaired in secondary planning apraxia.

Finally, therapists have clinically distinguished between the incoordinated child and the dyspractic child. Although quantitative differentiation has not been made, many experienced therapists have observed the quality of movement in clumsy children and have labelled some children as dyspractic, and others as clumsy and incoordinated. This latter group of children appear to know how to approach a task, but seem to be clumsy in the execution. Perhaps these children experience what Roy (1978) refers to as executive apraxia.

Thus, Roy's classification seems to describe adequately the typology of children whose disability falls under the rubric of developmental dyspraxia. Through his terminology, a correspondence between adult apraxia and childhood dyspraxia can be seen. This does not imply that the two disorders are identical, a concern expressed by Russell (1960), Zangwill (1960) and Geschwind (1975). Rather, it suggests that the two share common symptomatology and behavioural manifestations. Certainly there is precedent in the usage of terms such as developmental dyslexia, developmental dysphasia, and developmental acalculia. The acceptance of the commonality of terminology allows further sharing of common findings from adult and childhood research, and an understanding of the commonalities and differences might well, in the future, lead to a more complete understanding of normal central nervous system development of function.

REFERENCE NOTES

1. Kaplan, E. The Development of Gesture. Unpublished Ph.D. Dissertation, Clark University, 1968.

REFERENCES

Abbie, M.H., Douglas, M.H. & Ross, K.E. The clumsy child: Observations in cases referred to the gymnasium of the Adelaide Children's Hospital over a three year period. Medical Journal of Australia, 1978, 1, 65-68.

Adams, R.D. & Victor, M. Principles of Neurology. New York: McGraw Hill, 1977.

Arnheim, D.D. & Sinclair, W.A. The Clumsy Child: A Program of Motor Therapy. St. Louis: C.V. Mosby, 1979.

Ayres, A.J. Patterns of perceptual motor dysfunction in children: A factor-analytic study. Perceptual and Motor Skills, 1965, 20, 335-368.

Ayres, A.J. Deficits in sensory integration in educationally handicapped children. Journal of Learning Disabilities, 1969, 2, 160-168.

Ayres, A.J. Characteristics of types of sensory integrative dysfunction. American Journal of Occupational Therapy, 1971, 25, 329-334.

Ayres, A.J. Sensory Integration and Learning Disorders. Los Angeles: Western Psychological Services, 1972.(a)

Ayres, A.J. Types of sensory integrative dysfunction among disabled learners. American Journal of Occupational Therapy, 1972, 26, 13-18.(b)

Ayres, A.J. Improving academic scores through sensory integration. Journal of Learning Disabilities, 1972, 5, 338-343.(c)

Ayres, A.J. Sensorimotor foundations of academic ability. In W.M. Cruickshank & D.P. Hallahan (Eds.), Perceptual and Learning Disabilities in Children. Volume 2: Research and Theory. New York: Syracuse University Press, 1975, pp. 300-360.

Ayres, A.J. The Effect of Sensory Integrative Therapy on Learning Disabled Children: The Final Report of a Research Project. Pasadena, California: Center for the Study of Sensory Integrative Dysfunction, 1976. (a)

Ayres, A.J. Interpreting the Southern California Sensory Integration Tests. Los Angeles: Western Psychological Services, 1976. (b)

Ayres, A.J. Cluster analyses of measures of sensory integration. American Journal of Occupational Therapy, 1977, 31, 362-367.

Ayres, A.J. Learning disabilities and the vestibular system. Journal of Learning Disabilities, 1978, 2, 30-31.

Ayres, A.J. Sensory Integration and the Child. Los Angeles: Western Psychological Services, 1980. (a)

Ayres, A.J. Southern California Sensory Integration Tests Manual - Revised. Los Angeles: Western Psychological Services, 1980. (b)

Ayres, A.J. & Mailloux, Z. Influence of sensory integration procedures on language development. American Journal of Occupational Therapy, 1981, 35, 383-390.

Beck, C.H.M. Processing of symbolic and nonsymbolic events: A review of comparisons in selected cognitive activities. International Journal of Neuroscience, 1982, 17, 93-107.

Benson, D.F. & Geschwind, N. Aphasia and related cortical disturbances. In Baker, A.B. & Baker, L.H. (Eds.), Clinical Neurology. New York: Harper and Row, 1971.

Berges, J. & Lezine, I. The Imitation of Gestures. London: Heinemann, 1965.

Bergstrom, K. & Bille, B. Computed tomography of the brain in children with minimal brain damage: A preliminary study of 46 children. Neuropadiatrie, 1978, 9, 378-384.

Brinkman, J. & Kuypers, H.G.J.M. Splitbrain monkeys: Cerebral control of ipsilateral and contralateral arm, hand and finger movements. Science, 1972, 176, 536-539.

Brown, J. Aphasia, Apraxia, and Agnosia: Clinical and Theoretical Aspects. Springfield: Thomas, 1972.

Brown, J.K. Infants damaged during birth: Perinatal asphyxia. In D. Hull (Ed.), Recent Advances in Pediatrics - 5. Edinburgh: Churchill Livingstone, 1976.

Cermak, S.A., Coster, W. & Drake, C. Representational and nonrepresentational gestures in boys with learning disabilities. American Journal of Occupational Therapy, 1980, 34, 19-26.

Clements, S.J. Minimal Brain Dysfunction in Children. U.S. Department of Health, Education and Welfare. No. 1415. Washington: Public Health Service Publication, 1966.

Conrad, K., Cermak, S. & Drake, C. Differentiation of praxis among children. American Journal of Occupational Therapy, 1983, 37, 466-473.

Cratty, B.J. Remedial Motor Activity for Children. Philadelphia: Lea and Febiger, 1975.

Dare, M.T. & Gordon, N. Clumsy children: A disorder of perception and motor organization. Developmental Medicine and Child Neurology, 1970, 12, 178-185.

Dawdy, S.C. Pediatric neuropsychology: Caring for the developmentally dyspraxic child. Clinical Neuropsychology, 1981, 3, 30-37.

DeAjuriaguerra, J. & Tissot, R. The Apraxias. In P.J. Vinken & G.W. Bruyn (Eds.), Handbook of Clinical Neurology, Volume 4. New York: American Elsevier Co., 1969.

Denckla, M.B. Development of speed in repetitive and successive finger movements in normal children. Developmental Medicine and Child Neurology, 1973, 15, 635-645.

DeQuiros, J. & Schrager, O. Neuropsychological Fundamentals in Learning Disabilities, San Rafael, California: Academic Therapy, 1979.

Dobbing, J., Hopewell, J.W. & Lynch, A. Vulnerability of developing brain: VII. Permanent deficits of neurons in cerebral and cerebellar cortex following early mild under-nutrition. Experimental Neurology, 1971, 32, 439-447.

Dobbing, J. & Smart, J. Quantitative growth and development of human brain. Archives of the Diseases of Children, 1973, 48, 457-467.

Druker, R. The Finger Position Imitation Test. Unpublished Master's Thesis, University of Southern California, 1978.

Eustis, R. The primary etiology of specific language disabilities. Journal of Pediatrics, 1947, 31, 448-455.

Faro, M.D. & Windle, W.F. Transneuronal degeneration in brain of monkeys asphyxiated at birth. Experimental Neurology, 1969, 24, 38-53.

Finger, S. & Stein, D. Brain Damage and Recovery: Research and Clinical Perspectives. New York: Academic Press, 1982.

Fleishman, E.A. On the relationship between abilities, learning, and human performance. American Psychologist, 1975, 27, 1017-1032.

Ford, F.R. Diseases of the Nervous System in Infancy, Childhood and Adolescence, 5th Edition. Springfield: Thomas, 1966.

Gaddes, W.H. Learning Disabilities and Brain Function. New York: Springer-Verlag, 1980.

Galluscio, E.H. Brain laterality: Differences in cognitive style or motor function? Perceptual and Motor Skills, 1983, 56, 3-9.

Garvey, M. Speech therapy. In N. Gordon & I. McKinlay (Eds.), Helping Clumsy Children. New York: Churchill Livingstone, 1980.

Geschwind, N. The apraxias: Neural mechanisms of disorders of learned movement. American Scientist, 1975, 63, 188-195.

Goldman, P.S. & Galkin, T.W. Prenatal removal of frontal association cortex in the fetal rhesus monkey: Anatomical and functional consequences in postnatal life. Brain Research, 1978, 152, 451-485.

Goldman, P. & Mendelson, M.J. Salutary effects of early experience on deficits caused by lesions of frontal association cortex in developing rhesus monkeys. Experimental Neurology, 1977, 57, 588-602.

Goodglass, H. & Kaplan, E. Disturbance of gesture and pantomime in aphasia. Brain, 1963, 86, 703-720.

Goodwin, W.L. & Driscoll, L.A. Handbook for Measurement and Evaluation in Early Childhood Education. San Francisco: Josey-Bass, 1980.

Gordon, N.S. The acquisition of motor skills. Brain and Development, 1979, 1, 3-6.

Gordon, N. & McKinlay, I. (Eds.), Helping Clumsy Children. New York: Churchill Livingstone, 1980.

Gubbay, S.S. The Clumsy Child. New York: W.B. Saunders, 1975.

Gubbay, S.S. The management of developmental apraxia. Developmental Medicine and Child Neurology, 1978, 20, 643-646.

Gubbay, S.S. The clumsy child. In F.C. Rose (Ed.), Pediatric Neurology. London: Blackwell, 1979.

Gubbay, S.S., Ellis, E., Walton, J.N. & Court, S.D.M. Clumsy children: A study of apraxic and agnosic deficits in 21 children. Brain, 1965, 88, 295-312.

Hecaen, H. & Albert, M.L. Human Neuropsychology. New York: Wiley and Sons, 1978.

Henderson, S.E. & Hall, D. Concommitants of clumsiness in young school children. Developmental Medicine and Child Neurology, 1982, 24, 448-460.

Hulme, C., Biggerstaff, A., Moran, C. & McKinlay, I. Visual, kinesthetic and cross-modal judgements of length by normal and clumsy children. Developmental Medicine and Child Neurology, 1982, 24, 461-471.

Ingram, D. Motor asymmetries in young children. Neuropsychologia, 1975, 13, 95-102.

Kephart, N.C. The Slow Learner in the Classroom. Columbus, Ohio: Charles E. Merrill, 1971.

Kephart, N.C. The perceptual-motor match. In W.M. Cruickshank & D.P. Hallan (Eds.), Perceptual and Learning Disabilities in Children, Volume 1: Psychoeducational Practices. New York: Syracuse University Press, 1975.

Kimura, D. Acquisition of a motor skill after left-hemisphere damage. Brain, 1977, 100, 527-542.

Kimura, D. Neuromotor mechanisms in the evolution of human communication. In H.D. Steklis and M.H. Raleigh (Eds.), Neurobiology of Social Communication in Primates. New York: Academic Press, 1979.

Kimura, D. Left hemisphere control of oral and brachial movements and their relations to communication. Philosophical Transactions of the Royal Society of London, 1982, B298, 135-149.

Kimura, D. & Archibald, Y. Motor functions of the left hemisphere. Brain, 1974, 97, 337-350.

Kinsbourne, M. & Caplan, P.J. Children's Learning and Attentional Problems. Boston: Little Brown, 1979.

Kolb, B. & Milner, B. Performance of complex arm and facial movements after focal brain lesions. Neuropsychologia, 1981, 19, 491-503.

Knuckey, N.W., Apsimon, T.T. & Gubbay, S.S. Computerized axial tomography in clumsy children with developmental apraxia and agnosia. Brain and Development, 1983, 5, 14-19.

Kornse, D.D., Manni, J., Rubenstein, H. & Graziani, L. Developmental apraxia of speech and manual dexterity. Journal of Communication Disorders, 1982, 14, 321-330.

Lawrence, D. & Kuypers, H.J.G.M. Pyramidal and non-pyramidal pathways in monkeys. Science, 1965, 148, 973-975.

Lehmkuhl, G., Poeck, K. and Willmes, K. Ideomotor apraxia and aphasia: An examination of types and manifestations of apraxic symptoms. Neuropsychologia, 1983, 21, 199-212.

Lesny, I.A. Developmental dyspraxia-dysgnosia as a cause of congenital children's clumsiness. Brain and Development, 1980, 2, 69-71.

Levine, M., Brooks, R. & Shonkoff, J.P. A Pediatric Approach to Learning Disorders. New York: John Wiley, 1980.

Lupert, N. Auditory perceptual impairments in children with specific language disorders: A review of the literature. Journal of Speech and Hearing Disorders, 1981, 46, 3-9.

Luria, A.R. Higher Cortical Functions in Man. New York: Basic Books, 1966.

McKinlay, I. Strategies for clumsy children. Developmental Medicine and Child Neurology, 1978, 20, 494-501.

Melzack, R. & Southmayd, J.E. Dorsal column contributions to anticipatory motor behaviour. Experimental Neurology, 1974, 42, 274-281.

Orton, S.T. Reading, Writing, and Speech Problems in Children. New York: Norton, 1937.

Ottenbacher, K. Sensory integration procedures: Affect or effect? American Journal of Occupational Therapy, 1982, 36, 571-578.

Overton, W. & Jackson, J. The representation of imagined objects in action sequences: A developmental study. Child Development, 1973, 44, 309-314.

Rosenzweig, M.R., Bennett, E.L. & Diamond, M.C. Brain changes in response to experience. Scientific American, 1972, 226, 22-30.

Roy, E.A. Apraxia: A new look at an old syndrome. Journal of Human Movement Studies, 1978, 4, 191-210.

Roy, E.A. Action sequencing and lateralized cerebral damage: Evidence for asymmetries in control. In J. Long & A. Baddeley (Eds.), Attention and Performance IX. New York: Erlbaum, 1981.

Roy, E.A. Neuropsychological perspectives on apraxia and related action disorders. In R.A. Magill (Ed.), Advances in Psychology, Volume 12, Memory and Control of Action. Amsterdam: North-Holland Co., 1983.

Russell, W.R. The parietal lobes. In M. Bax, E. Clayton-Jones & R. MacKeith (Eds.), Child Neurology and Cerebral Palsy. Little Club Clinics in Developmental Medicine. London: Spastics Society, 1960.

Schilder, P. The Image and Apperance of the Human Body. New York: International Universities Press, 1950.

Strauss, A.A. & Lehtinen, C.E. Psychopathology and Education of the Brain Injured Child. New York: Grune & Stratton, 1947.

Towbin, A. Neuropathologic factors in minimal brain dysfunction. In H.E. Rie & E.D. Rie (Eds.), Handbook of Minimal Brain Dysfunctions: A Critical View. New York: John Wiley, 1980.

Vierck, C.J. Interpretation of the sensory and motor consequences of dorsal column lesions. In G. Gordon (Ed.), Active Touch: The Mechanism of Recognition of Objects by Manipulation: A Multidisciplinary Approach. Oxford: Pergamon Press, 1978, pp. 139-160.

Wall, P.D. The sensory and motor role of impulses travelling in the dorsal columns toward the cerebral cortex. Brain, 1970, 98, 505-524.

Walton, J.N., Ellis, E. & Court, S.D.M. Clumsy children: A study of developmental apraxia and agnosia. Brain, 1962, 85, 603-613.

Wolff, P., Hurwitz, I. & Moss, M. Serial organization in left and right handed adults. Neuropsychologia, 1977, 15, 539-546.

Yoss, K.A. & Darley, F.L. Developmental apraxia of speech in children with defective articulation. Journal of Speech and Hearing Research, 1974, 17, 399-416.

Zangwill, O.L. Deficiency of spatial perception. In M. Bax, E. Clayton-Jones & R. MacKeith (Eds.) Child Neurology and Cerebral Palsy. Little Club Clinics in Developmental Medicine, No. 2. London: Spastics Society, 1960.

PART 2:

Concepts and Issues Bearing on Apraxia

Neuropsychological Studies of Apraxia
and Related Disorders, E.A. Roy (ed.)
© Elsevier Science Publishers B.V. (North-Holland), 1985

RESPONSE AND PROJECTION:

A REINTERPRETATION OF THE PREMOTOR CONCEPT

Gary Goldberg

Temple University

This paper reviews the principle of evolution of the neocortex which postulates that the neocortex has evolved over phylogeny from separate roots in hippocampal and piriform cortices. In congruence with this principle, the premotor cortex of the frontal lobe of humans and subhuman primates is thought to be organized into two separate but interconnected systems--the mesiodorsal and the ventrolateral. The "core" premotor zone of the mesiodorsal system is the supplementary motor area (SMA) while that of the ventrolateral system is the arcuate premotor area (APA) identified in the primate brain. Evidence is presented to support the proposal that the SMA, as the premotor component of a system capable of generating model-based predictions, is necessary for extended, internally-contingent, projectional action. The APA is hypothesized to be the premotor component of a system concerned with the perception, recognition and association of motivational significance to external inputs. It is postulated to be particularly important in the production of interactive, externally-contingent or responsive action.

The Evolutionary Theory

The cortical mantle of the brain can be viewed as a dynamic, fluid entity which has been shaped over phylogeny by various evolutionary pressures as are all biological entities. In a penetrating examination of the architectonic fields of the human frontal lobe, and in an attempt to link this pattern with functional aspects of the neocortex revealed by neurophysiologic investigation, Friedrich Sanides (1964) independently proposed a theory of the evolution of the architectonic form of the neocortex. This work extended to the human brain and significantly elaborated upon an hypothesis put forward by Dart in 1934 regarding the origins of the neocortex in reptilian brain. Abbie (1940, 1942) had applied the concept to the analysis of the structure of the neocortex of primitive mammalian brain.

The principle recognizes that new architectonic fields arise from phylogenetically older regions, elaborating upon them in a graded fashion. In the human frontal lobe, Sanides (1964) recognized progressive, systematic sequences of architectonic differentiation which he referred to as "protogradations" (Sanides, 1964) or "urtrends" (Sanides, 1970). Such "protogradations" take their origin in the oldest cortical areas and move through progressively more recent fields. Sanides (1964) summarized the principle with the following statement: "The gradations originating from phylogenetically older cortices determine the structure of more recent cortices. Therefore they should be recognized at the same time as evolutional directions of differentiation" (Sanides, 1964, p.280)

Three protogradations could be identified in the human frontal lobe--one rostro-caudal and two coronal directions of development (see Figure 1). The mesiodorsal coronal protogradation takes its origin in the periarchicortical proisocortex of the cingulate "limbic" cortex. This protogradation radiates dorsally, rostrally and ventrally from cingulate cortex on the mesial wall of the frontal lobe. Radiating dorsally, it extends over onto the external surface of the hemisphere. Radiating ventrally, it extends to the ventral surface of the frontal lobe. The supplementary motor area (SMA) can thus be viewed as a component of this trend (see Figure 2 for approximate localization of the SMA and related areas of the human cerebral cortex). Sanides (1964) noted the implications of the theory for the SMA and labelled it the medial "protomotor" area recognizing it as an evolutionarily older area than the primary motor cortex (MI) of the precentral area. As such, the SMA can be viewed as paralimbic cortex derived from the anterior cingulate cortex immediately ventral to it. Tracing the origins of the mesiodorsal protogradation to primitive mammalian (Abbie 1940, 1942) and reptilian (Dart, 1934) brain, it is apparent that it originated from the hippocampus.

The second coronal protogradation is the ventrolateral which takes its phylo-genetic origin in the piriform cortex. In the human frontal lobe, Sanides (1964) identified it as beginning in the peripaleocortical proisocortex of the insular region and radiating dorsally and rostrally over the exterior surface of the hemisphere as well as medially over the ventral surface. Areas of maximal differentiation occur where these two trends meet over the exterior surface and over the ventral surface in the orbital area. On the exterior surface, the two protogradations meet at roughly the inferior frontal sulcus, while in the primate brain, the dividing line, at least in the prefrontal area, is the principal sulcus (Sanides, 1970). The arcuate pre-motor area (see below for further discussion) of the primate and its presently ill-defined equivalent in the human brain, as well as the secondary sensory area SII, would appear to be part of this ventrolateral protogradation. The arcuate premotor area may thus, parallel to the SMA, be considered a lateral "protomotor" zone. Sanides (1970, p.163) states that "considering our ur-trends of differentiation in evolution from archicortex via the cingulate gyrus medially and from paleocortex via the insula laterally, it was conceived that the supplementary motor representation...is an earlier stage of motor control, and the second somatic representation is an earlier stage of sensory control than the respective classic representations."

Sanides (1970, 1972) recognized the correlation between his architectonic theory and the dual nature of prefrontal connectivity noted by Nauta (1964) and thus the possible division of prefrontal cortex into two complementary components--that dorsal and medial to the principal sulcus which tends to project into the cingulum toward mesial cortex and hippocampus, and that ventral and lateral which tends to project via the uncinate fasciculus toward insular and temporal cortex (see also Fuster 1980 for further elaboration).

The third and most recent protogradation identified by Sanides begins with the primary motor cortex (MI) and extends poleward. It is postulated that MI is a rela-tively new innovation which appeared for the purpose of controlling fractionated finely-controlled, isolated movements of a single extremity, a function appearing relatively late in evolution in animals that have adapted to terrestrial life. This function is best developed in humans, whose ability to manipulate objects with finely coordinated hand control represents one of the most powerful evolutionary adapta-tions of terrestrial life. The abilities that evolution has bestowed upon the human hand have given man the adaptive capacities to create and use tools and weapons.

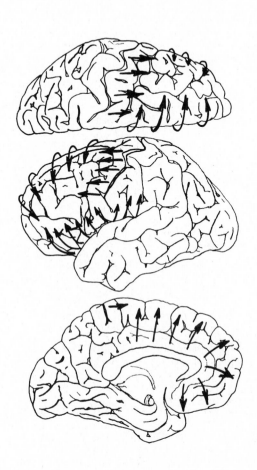

<u>Figure 1.</u>   Human frontal lobe "protogradations" as identified by Sanides
                (1964).

Sanides (1970) speculated that, while the motor centers of the two coronal protogradations, the SMA and the APA "serve a general tetrapod function", the new sensorimotor representations of the classic areas with their distally-emphasized homun-
culi, are related to further adaptation to terrestrial life which required the forel-
imb, particularly, to achieve some independence from "compulsory tetrapody" to
free it to serve specialized adaptive functions. Thus MI, with its high concentration
of large, spinally-projecting pyramidal cells, provides a fast, direct, multiply-
parallel, refined capability for phasic control of extremity musculature which

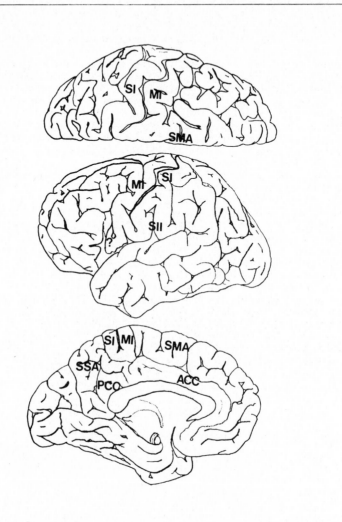

Figure 2.   Localization of functional zones in the human cerebral cor-
                   tex. ACC-anterior cingulate cortex; PCC-posterior cingulate
                   cortex; MI-primary motor cortex; SI-primary sensory cortex;
                   SII-second sensory area; SMA-supplementary motor area; SSA-
                   supplementary sensory area; ? - inferior frontal cortex which
                   may correspond to arcuate premotor area (APA) in primate
                   brain.

enables the elaboration of dextrous limb function. However, a more fundamental
nature of the coordination of skilled movement may be conveyed via the strong projections to MI (and elsewhere) from the medial and lateral protomotor cortices. In

effect, these older areas could be viewed as utilizing MI as a "tool" or elaborated extension while they, themselves, may be viewed as providing the basic infrastructure of movement, particularly in terms of the temporal linkage of component subschema (Arbib, 1981), in which those aspects controlled by MI are embedded.

It is interesting as an aside that the dolphin brain, despite a clearly advanced cortical mantle, has no hypergranular core on the convexity of the hemisphere, but instead, the cortical development appears to have not gone beyond the paralimbic/parainsular (protomotor) stage of architectonic development (Morgane, Galaburda & Jacobs, 1983). Thus, it is likely that the cetacean brain, not subjected to the evolutionary pressures applied to terrestrial mammals, did not develop an architectonic zone analogous to MI but rather, appears to have extended the area of those zones analogous in architectonic structure to the SMA and APA.

How might the functional roles of the dorsomesial and ventrolateral protogradations in the generation of action be distinguished? That is, how can the SMA and APA be differentiated in terms of the general manner in which they participate in the cortical organization of movement? It is postulated that the major clue lies in the recognition that there is a fundamental separation of functions which derives from the fact that these two areas evolved from different sources.

The fundamental dualism of architectonic evolution that follows from the recognition of two simultaneously-developing coronal protogradations--the one (mesiodorsal) arising from hippocampal archicortex and the other (ventrolateral) arising from the piriform paleocortex--leads one to speculate that there may be two fundamental channels through which sensory inputs may be neocortically-processed and associated with limbic structures (Ungerleider & Mishkin, 1982; Bear, 1983) and through which action may likewise be generated (Paillard, 1982; Jeannerod & Biguer, 1982; Bear, 1983). It is the fundamental functional nature of this dualism of systems, particularly as it applies to the organization of action by the brain, which forms the basis for the hypothesis to be developed in this paper.

The Premotor Concept

In 1884, Hughlings Jackson, in his now classic discussions of the hierarchical organization of the central nervous system, and the implications of this organization for the functional effects of lesions at various levels, stated, with respect to the motor functions of the cerebral cortex, that:

"The middle motor centres are the convolutions making up Ferrier's motor region...the highest motor centres are convolutions in front of the so-called motor region". (Jackson, 1884).

"Ferrier's motor region" referred to David Ferrier's study which appeared in 1876, of the electrical stimulatability of the cerebral cortex. Ferrier recognized the ease with which limb movements could be produced with stimulation of the surface of the precentral gyrus and had labelled this the "motor region" for this reason.

Subsequent architectonic analyses of the human cortex by Brodmann (1908), Campbell (1905) and Elliot Smith (1907) identified distinct fields rostral to the magnopyramidal core of the precentral area which, following Jackson's postulation, were felt to play a role in motor function. Campbell, for example, felt that his "intermediate precentral" area was a center of higher motor control. The subsequent introduction of the term "premotor" by Bucy (1933, 1935) and Fulton (1934) to refer to the dorsolateral part of Brodmann's area 6 (the Vogts' area 6a) followed the recognition of a distinctive motor syndrome following lesions of the frontal cortex rostral to the precentral gyrus in primates (see Figure 3) and humans.

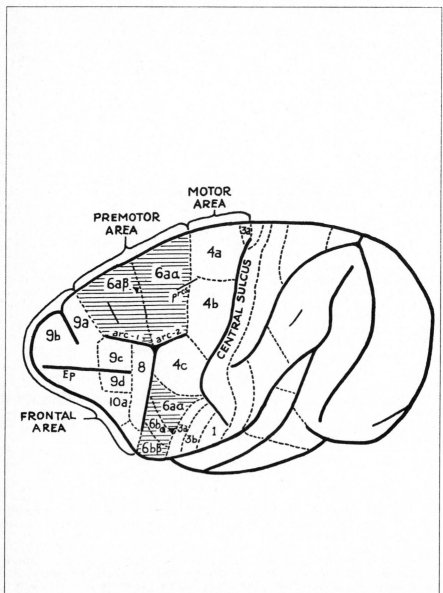

Figure 3. Fulton's localization of the "premotor" area on the architectonic map of the primate brain due to the Vogts (1919) (Reproduced with permission from Fulton (1935))

However, it has been known since Smith (1907) reported his myeloarchitectonic analysis, that Brodmann's area 6 is not structurally uniform. Small cytoarchitectonic differences have also been identified by subsequent investigators who have divided area 6 into subzones (Braak, 1980; von Bonin & Bailey, 1947; Vogt & Vogt, 1919). Additionally, the identification and characterization of distinctive properties of the mesial aspect of area 6--the "supplementary" motor area--by Penfield & Welch (1949, 1951) and Woolsey, Settlage, Meyer, Sencer, Hamuy and Travis (1952) added further complexity to the premotor concept. Along with this, evidence has been brought forward that makes some of the properties of parts of area 6, particularly the rostral, dorsolateral area, difficult to distinguish from those of prefrontal cortex (Goldman & Rosvold, 1970; Sakai, 1978). Even more caudal aspects of dorsolateral area 6 contain a significant proportion of "set"-related units (Weinrich & Wise, 1982). Furthermore, recent studies of unit behavior (e.g. Godshalk & Lemon. 1983; Godshalk, Lemon, Nijs & Kuypers, 1981; Kubota & Hamada, 1978) and the result of lesions in primates (Rizzolatti, Mattelli & Pavesi 1983) suggest that the part of area 6 located low on the lateral convexity adjacent to the spur and lower limb of the arcuate sulcus can also be distinguished functionally from other parts of the "premotor" cortex in that this area appears to be particularly concerned with visually-guided reaching to objects. This is the area which has been labelled as the arcuate premotor area (eg. Schell & Strick 1983) (see Figure 4). Finally, regional cerebral blood flow studies in man have shown that different parts of the premotor area appear to be brought into play depending upon the demands of the task the subject is asked to perform. While there is no significant portion of the premotor area activated with very simple tasks--contralateral sensorimotor cortex seems capable itself in this situation--there is bihemispheric activation of the SMA when the subject is asked to perform an extended, sequential hand task (Orgogozo & Larsen, 1979; Roland, Larsen, Lassen & Skinhoj, 1980). It should be noted that the test task was a practiced, internally-generated skill performed in intrapersonal space--that is, there was no dependence on external context. With dependence on extrapersonal elements in the task, more lateral parts of area 6 were additionally activated bihemispherically (Roland, Skinhoj, Lassen & Larsen, 1980).

Wiesendanger (1981) has proposed that the caudal portion of area 6--6a-(alpha) of the Vogts (1919) or FB of von Bonin and Bailey (1947) (see Figure 3) --is really part of MI containing representation of axial and proximal limb muscles (see also Kwan, MacKay, Murphy & Wong,1978). The precise location of the area 6-area 4 border can be quite difficult to discern since there is no distinct change in density of the pyramidal cells as one moves rostrally from the central sulcus. In fact, one might expect a gradual diminution in the size of the projecting pyramidal cells as well as a decrease in their concentration as one moves from areas responsible for distal muscle control toward areas related to more proximal musculature.

It is relevant to this discussion to recognize that most architectonic maps agree that the rostral part of area 6, constituting what may be the "premotor" area proper, is elaborated mesiodorsally between the upper limb of the arcuate sulcus and the cingulate sulcus, and ventrolaterally between the lower limb of the arcuate sulcus and the Sylvian fissure (see Figure 3).

The present picture of the premotor concept thus appears somewhat confused. It seems clear that a more precise definition of a premotor area is required and that a re-examination of the concept would be appropriate, particularly in view of the suggestion from evidence examined above that area 6 is both structurally and functionally heterogeneous.

With the advent of precise, sensitive techniques for examining neuronal connectivity, it has been possible to distinguish different parts of area 6 in terms of their

Figure 4.   Primate brain with SMA, APA and MI marked
                 1: SMA, 2: APA, 3: MI
                 (Adapted from data of Muakkassa & Strick (1979) and Matsu-
                 mura & Kubota (1979))

projections. While all parts of area 6 project to the cerebellum via the pontine nuclei, area 6 does not project uniformly to MI (Muakkassa & Strick, 1979; Matsumura & Kubota, 1979). In fact, it might be of some use to redefine "premotor area", at least for the primate brain, as referring to those areas rostral to MI which can be shown to project heavily in topographic fashion directly to MI.

Examination of the available horse radish pexiodoxase (HRP) data (Muakkassa & Strick 1979; Matsumura & Kubota, 1979) suggests that there are at least two major areas and as many as four zones satisfying this criterion. The two major foci of neurons projecting monosynaptically to MI from areas just rostral to it are the SMA and the arcuate premotor area (APA) (see Figure 4). Additional somatotopically-organized projections come from the anterior cingulate cortex and the dorsolateral part of area 6 (Muakkassa & Strick 1979). However, these latter areas appear to project less densely particularly when HRP is injected into the more caudal parts of MI (Matsumura & Kubota, 1979, Figure 1C) representing the distally-controlling "core" of the upper extremity map of MI (Kwan, et al, 1978).

The APA can be identified as the premotor area of the ventrolateral protogradation and thus may be identified as the lateral "protomotor" zone, recognizing that it may have appeared earlier in phylogeny than the koniocortical core which is MI. Similarly, the SMA may be identified as the medial "protomotor" area. While the connections of the SMA point to a close relationship to the ventrally-adjacent anterior cingulate cortex and thus its relationship to the limbic flow to cortex via this structure (Papez, 1937; Baleydier & Mauguiere 1980; Damasio, Van Hoesen & Vilensky, 1981), the APA is distinguished from other parts of area 6 by connections to orbital frontal cortex, inferior temporal cortex and the opercular-insular region (Kunzle, 1978). Projections from posterior parietal cortex also appear to differentiate these two areas. Medial parietal cortex and the superior parietal lobule connect with SMA and dorsolateral area 6, while the inferior parietal lobule below the intraparietal sulcus projects to the APA and adjacent ventrolateral area 6 among other zones (Petrides & Pandya, 1983) (see Figure 5). These connections derive, as one might expect, from the evolutionary principle examined in the previous section. Furthermore, the SMA and the APA are anatomically interconnected. Finally, recent data from Strick's laboratory (Schell & Strick, 1983), suggest that the cortical focus of the re-entrant outflow from the basal ganglia via the internal segment of the globus pallidus is the SMA. The transmission of this drive occurs transthalamically to SMA through the VA and VL_0 nuclei. The APA, on the other hand, was found to relate primarily to thalamic nucleus X which receives predominantly cerebellar drive (Kalil, 1981).

Hypothesis

In synthesizing the evidence examined in section 1 and 2, it is possible to hypothesize that there are two separate but interactive intrahemispheric motor programming systems: a medial system with the SMA as its integrating focus and a lateral system with the APA as its focus. These two premotor systems are each parts of larger intrahemispheric limbic-neocortical systems that have developed over phylogeny from their separate sources, namely, the hippocampal archicortex and the piriform paleocortex.

The hippocampally-derived mesiodorsal system, is concerned with the perception and representation of space and time and, through the maintenance of an "internal model" of the external world, is capable of supporting projectional action—that is, action which can be extended forward in time and outward in space using model-based prediction (Bernstein, 1967; Gregory, 1970; Flowers, 1978). This system is dominated by peripheral rather than foveal vision (Ungerleider & Mishkin, 1982). It

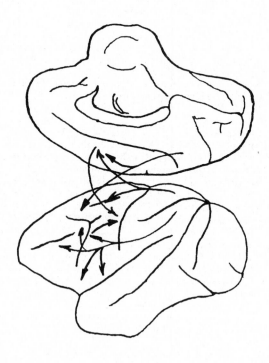

Figure 5.   Parietal projections to premotor areas (Adapted from
                 Petrides & Pandya (1983)).

is more concerned with the problem of the general navigation of the limb through
space and the sequencing of component actions of a skill through time than the
problem of accurately acquiring specific objects in 'peripersonal' (Rizzolatti, Matelli

& Pavesi 1983) or reachable space. Some investigators have differentiated these two components of control in reaching movements into a "space" channel and an "object" channel (Paillard, 1982; Jeannerod & Biguer, 1982). According to Flowers (1978), predictive control allows subjects to "circumvent the handicap of their reaction time, and also to continue appropriate actions in the absence of sensory data—if their predictions are correct". The medial system thus predominates when rapid, well-learned, "skilled" movements are executed relatively independent of the requirement for ongoing feedback monitoring. A feedforward, model- or hypothesis-driven mode of control is thus possible.

An internal model of the task which drives the movement into the future is built up through an opportunity to "learn" the task through practice. How might this process of establishing a model for a new skill occur? The process involves the acquisition of the capacity to recognize a set of selected sensory contexts to trigger or gate component motor subroutines or subschema (Arbib, 1981) that have been assembled in an ordered temporal sequence. The subschema are thus carried out in an anticipatory, feedforward fashion though linkages are tied at critical points to sensory context whose recognition facilitates the transition from one component subschema to the next. The basal ganglia, whose association with the medial system is critical, would provide important assistance to the medial system by rapidly detecting critical task-relevant contexts (Rolls, Thorpe, Maddison, Roper-Hall, Puerto & Perret, 1979) and feeding this information to the SMA.

What if the substrate for prediction—an accurate model—is unavailable? If subjects relied on prediction when a poor model existed, then they would make many errors and would perform poorly. In this case, it would make more sense to operate using corrective, input- or data-driven, closed-loop control. This is the hypothesized mode of action of the lateral motor programming system. The APA, the premotor focus of the lateral system, is tied into a larger intrahemispheric system that involves the orbital frontal cortex, temporal cortex and amygdala which is particularly involved in the perception, identification and assignment of motivational significance to external objects. Thus damage to the APA leads to a deficit of responsive action (Rizzolatti, Matelli & Pavesi, 1983). Responsive action follows from and is dependent upon the availability of specific external inputs. The lateral system is important when prediction is likely to be unhelpful, for example, when one is first learning a new motor skill and is beginning to compose an internal model of the task that will subsequently enable predictive performance. Another situation would be when a task is dependent on sensory input which is inherently inconsistent and unpredictable, such as the tracking of a noise signal. The lateral system would also be relied upon heavily by patients with dysfunction of the medial system, as may well be the case in Parkinsonism, for instance (Cooke, Brown and Brooks, 1978).

Thus the APA would be expected to organize movements responsive to specific external inputs, while the SMA would be more concerned when the movement depends more heavily on internal context. In agreement with this is the finding that units in the APA are readily driven by visual and tactile stimulation (Rizzolatti, Scandolara, Matelli & Gentilucci, 1981a,b) while SMA units are not (Brinkman & Porter, 1979). It would be important to recognize that often these two systems would operate cooperatively in the coordination of action to provide the appropriate balance of control modes. The locus of control would likely shift between the two systems during the course of movement, just as the balance of responsibility of the pilot and the navigator shifts during the course of an airline flight.

Summary

An hypothesis has been put forward which links a theory of how the neocortex was elaborated from limbic sources over phylogeny, to the concept of premotor cortical zones. This hypothesis indicates that the brain has evolved to be able to organize action across a spectrum spanning two poles. At one pole is projective action. In projection, action is determined by modelling the future and thus solving the problem of extrapolating from the current state of affairs to a future desired state (Bernstein 1967). The internal model which makes this possible must be able to reliably anticipate changes in salient task-relevant environmental features, as well as predict the effects that the performance will have on the external conditions and on the state of the organism itself. At the other pole is responsive action which is driven in reaction to specific external inputs. In this mode--analogous to the operation of a computer language interpreter--performance is slower and is dependent on the availability of the required sensory drive. Corresponding to these control modes are the two coronal directions of architectonic development of the cortex, the mesiodorsal and ventrolateral protogradations, and their "premotor" centers--the SMA (medial protomotor area) and the APA (lateral protomotor area), respectively.

The implications of this formulation for the problem of motor skill acquisition should be mentioned. It may be that the process of becoming adept at a particular motor task can be viewed as a gradual transition from the responsive mode to the projective mode of control. Practice at a task would assist in the progressive synthesis of a more and more refined internal model. The manner in which this representation is built up, modified, maintained and utilized in the central nervous system demands further investigation.

With regard to the problem of apraxia, this formulation would imply that lesions of the SMA would tend to produce deficiencies in the performance of spontaneous, extended movements and an inability to learn new motor skills (eg. patient "Ch" in Luria, 1966). Lesions of the more lateral aspects of area 6 would expected to produce abnormalities related to object-dependent movement as has been shown to be the case in primates (Rizzolatti, Matelli & Pavesi, 1983) with peri-arcuate lesions. It remains to be demonstrated whether similar effects can be observed with lesions of homologous areas of the human brain. However, the recognition that damage to frontal lobe structures can lead to a disordered relationship between the presence of action-motivating external objects and the release of object-dependent motor subroutines (Lhermitte 1983) can be viewed as a manifestation of imbalance between the two hypothesized systems.

Acknowledgements

The author would like to thank H.C. Kwan, W.A. MacKay, Y.C. Wong and J.T. Murphy for their encouragement and many stimulating discussions during the development of the ideas presented in this paper. The author was supported by a Centennial Fellowship from the Medical Research Council of Canada.

References

Abbie, A. Cortical lamination in the monotremata. Journal of Comparative Neurology, 1940, 72, 428-467.

Abbie, A. Cortical lamination in a polyprotodont marsupial, Perameles nasuta. Journal of Comparative Neurology, 1942, 76, 509-536.

Arbib, M.A. Perceptual structures and distributed motor control. In V.B. Brooks, (Ed.) Handbook of Physiology. The nervous system. II. Motor control. Bethesda: American Physiological Society, 1981.

Baleydier, C. & Mauguiere, F. The duality of the cingulate gyrus of the monkey: Neuroanatomical study and functional hypothesis. Brain, 1980, 103, 525-554.

Bear, D.M. Hemispheric specialization and the neurology of emotion. Archives of Neurology 1983, 40, 195-202.

Bernstein, N.A. The coordination and regulation of movement. Oxford, Pergamon Press, 1967.

Bonin, G. von & Bailey, P. The Neocortex of Macaca Mulatta. Urbana: University of Illinois Press, 1947.

Braak, H. Architectonics of the Human Telencephalic Cortex. New York, Springer-Verlag, 1980.

Brinkman, C. & Porter, R. Supplementary motor area of the monkey: Activity of neurons during performance of a learned motor task. Journal of Neurophysiology, 1979, 42, 681-709.

Brodmann, K. Beitrage zur histologischen Lokalisation der Grosshirnrinde. VI. Mitteilung: Die Cortexgliederung des Menschen. Journal of Psychology and Neurology. 1908, 10, 231-246.

Bucy, P.C. Electrical excitability and cyto-architecture of the premotor cortex in monkeys. Archives of Neurology and Psychiatry, 1933, 30, 1205-1244.

Bucy, P.C. A comparative cytoarchitectonic study of the motor and premotor areas in the primate. Journal of Comparative Neurology. 1935, 62, 293-331.

Campbell, A.W. Histological studies on the localization of cerebral function. London, Cambridge University Press, 1905.

Cooke, J.D., Brown, J.D. & Brooks, V.B. Increased dependence on visual information for movement control in patients with Parkinson's disease. Canadian Journal of Neurological Sciences, 1978, 5, 413-415.

Damasio, A.R., Van Hoesen, G.W. & Vilensky J. Limbic-motor pathways in the primate. A means for emotion to influence motor behavior. Neurology, 1981, 31, p.60.

Dart, D.A. A dual structure of the neopallium: its history and significance. Journal of Anatomy, 1934, 69, 3-19.

Ferrier, D. The functions of the brain. London, Smith Elder & Co., 1876.

Flowers, K. Lack of prediction in the motor behaviour of parkinsonism. Brain, 1978, 101, 35-52.

Fulton, J.F. Forced grasping in relation to the syndrome of the premotor area. Archives of Neurology and Psychiatry, 1934, 31, 221-235.

Fulton, J.F. A note on the definition of the "motor" and "pre-motor" areas. Brain, 1935, 58, 311-316.

Fuster, J.M. The prefrontal cortex. Anatomy, physiology, and neuropsychology of the frontal lobe. New York, Raven Press, 1980.

Godshalk, M., Lemon, R.N., Nijs, H.G.T. & Kuypers, H.G.J.M. Behaviour of neurons in monkey peri-arcuate and precentral cortex before and during visually guided arm and hand movements. Experimental Brain Research, 1981, 44, 113-116.

Godshalk, M. & Lemon, R.N. Involvement of monkey premotor cortex in preparation of arm movements. Experimental Brain Research supplement 1983, 7, 114-119.

Goldman, P.S. & Rosvold, H.E. Localization of function within the dorsolateral prefrontal cortex of the rhesus monkey. Experimental Neurology, 27, 291-304.

Gregory, R.L. On how little information controls so much behaviour. Ergonomics, 1970, 13, 25-35.

Jackson, J.H. The Croonian lectures: evolution and dissolution of the nervous system. British Medical Journal, 1884, 1, 591-593, 660-663, 703-707.

Jeannerod, M. & Biguer, B. Visuomotor mechanisms in reaching within extrapersonal space. In D.J. Ingle, M.A. Goodale & R.J.W. Mansfield (Ed.) Analysis of visual behavior, 387-409. Cambridge, MIT Press, 1982.

Kalil, K. Projections of the cerebellar and dorsal column nuclei upon the thalamus of the rhesus monkey. Journal of Comparative Neurology, 1981, 195, 25-50.

Kubota, K. & Hamada, I. Visual tracking and neuron activity in the post-arcuate area in monkeys. Journal of Physiology (Paris), 1978, 74, 297-312.

Kunzle, H. An autoradiographic analysis of the efferent connections from premotor and adjacent prefrontal regions (Areas 6 and 9) in macaca fascicularis. Brain and Behavioral Evolution, 1978, 15, 185-234.

Kwan, H.C., MacKay, W.A., Murphy, J.T., & Wong, Y.C. Spatial organization of precentral cortex in awake primates. Journal of Neurophysiology, 1978, 41, 1120-1131.

Lhermitte, F. Utilization behaviour and its relation to lesions of the frontal lobes. Brain, 1983, 106, 237-255.

Luria, A.R. Human Brain and Psychological Processes. New York: Harper & Row, 1966, pp.221-293.

Matsumura, M. & Kubota, K. Cortical projection to hand-arm motor area from post-arcuate area in macaque monkeys: A histological study of retrograde transport of horseradish peroxidase. Neuroscience Letters, 1979, 11, 241-246.

Morgane, P.J., Galaburda, A.M. & Jacobs, M.S. Evolutionary aspects of cortical organization in the dolphin brain. Society for Neuroscience Abstracts, 1983, 9, p.1067.

Muakkassa, K.F., Strick, P.L. Frontal lobe input to primate motor cortex. Society for Neuroscience Abstracts, 1979, 5, p.379.

Nauta, W.J. H. Some efferent connections of the prefrontal cortex in the monkey. In J.M. Warren & K. Akert, (Ed.) The frontal agranular cortex in behavior. New York, McGraw-Hill, 1964.

Orgogozo, J.M. & Larsen, B. Activation of the supplementary motor area during voluntary movement suggests it works as a supramotor area. Science, 1979, 206, 847-580.

Paillard, J. The contribution of peripheral and central vision to visually guided reaching. In D.J. Ingle, M.A. Goodale & R.J.W. Mansfield, (Eds.) Analysis of visual behaviour. Cambidge: MIT Press, 1982.

Papez, J. A proposed mechanism of emotion. American Medical Association Archives of Neurology and Psychiatry. 1937, 38, 725-743.

Penfield, W. & Welch, K. The supplementary motor area in the cerebral cortex of man. Transactions of the American Neurological Association. 1949, 74, 179-184.

Penfield, W. & Welch, K. The supplementary motor area of the cerebral cortex. A clinical and experimental study. American Medical Association Archives of Neurology and Psychiatry, 1951, 66, 289-317.

Petrides, M. & Pandya, D.N. Projections to the frontal cortex from the posterior parietal region in the rhesus monkey. Society for Neurosciences Abstracts, 1983, 9, p.40.

Rizzolatti, G., Scandolara, C., Matelli, M. & Gentilucci, M. Afferent properties of periarcuate neurons in macaque monkeys. I. Somatosensory responses. Behavioural Brain Research, 1981a, 2, 125-146.

Rizzolatti, G., Scandolara, C., Matelli, M. & Gentilucci, M. Afferent properties of periarcuate neurons in macaque monkeys. II. Visual responses. Behavioural Brain Research, 1981b, 2, 147-163.

Rizzolatti, G., Matelli, M. & Pavesi, G. Deficits in attention and movement following the removal of postarcuate (area 6) and prearcuate (area 8) cortex in macaque monkeys. Brain, 1983, 106, 655-673.

Roland, P.E., Larsen, B., Lassen, N.A. & Skinhoj, E. Supplementary motor area and other cortical areas in organization of voluntary movements in man. Journal of Neurophysiology, 1980, 43, 118-136(a).

Roland, P.E., Skinhoj,, E., Lassen, N.A. & Larsen, B. Different cortical areas in man in organization of voluntary movements in extrapersonal space. Journal of Neurophysiology, 1980, 43, 137-150(b).

Rolls, E.T., Thorpe, S.J., Maddison, S., Roper-Hall, A., Puerto, A., & Perret, D. Activity of neurones in neostriatum and related structures in the alert animal.

In I. Divac & R.G.E. Oberg (Ed.) The Neostriatum, Oxford, England: Pergamon, 1979.

Sakai, M. Single unit activity in a border area between the dorsal prefrontal and
premotor regions in the visually conditioned motor task of monkeys. Brain
Research, 1978, 147, 377-383.

Sanides, F. The cyto-myeloarchitecture of the human frontal lobe and its relation
to phylogenetic differentiation of the cerebral cortex. Journal fur Hirnforschung, 1964, 6, 269-282.

Sanides, F. Functional architecture of motor and sensory cortices in primates in the
light of a new concept of neocortex evolution. In C. Noback & W. Montagna
(Eds.), The primate brain, New York: Appleton, 1970.

Sanides, F. Representation in the cerebral cortex and its areal lamination patterns.
In G.H. Bourne (Ed.) The structure and function of nervous tissue, 5, New
York: Academic Press, 1972.

Schell, G.R. & Strick, P.L. Origin of thalamic input to the supplementary and arcuate premotor areas. Society for Neuroscience Abstracts, 1983, 9, p.430.

Smith, G.E. A new topographical survey of the human cerebral cortex being an
account of the distribution of the anatomically distinct cortical areas and their
relattionship to the cerebral sulci. Journal of Anatomy, 1907, 41, 237-254.

Ungerleider, L.G. & Mishkin, M. Two cortical visual systems. In D.J. Ingle, M.A.
Goodale & R.J.W. Mansfield (Eds.), Analysis of visual behaviour Cambridge:
MIT Press, 1982.

Vogt, O. & Vogt, C. Allgemeinere Ergebisse unserer Hirnforschung. J. Psychol.
Neurol. Leipzig, 1919, 25, 277-462.

Weinrich, J. & Wise, S.P. The premotor cortex of the monkey. Journal of Neuroscience, 1982, 2, 1329-1345.

Wiesendanger, M. Organization of secondary motor areas of cerebral cortex. In
V.B. Brooks, (Ed.) Handbook of Physiology. The nervous system. II. Motor
control. Bethesda: American Physiological Society, 1981.

Woolsey, C.N., Settlage, P.H., Meyer, D.R., Sencer, W., Hamuy, T.P. & Travis, A.M.
Patterns of localization in precentral and supplementary motor areas and their
relation to the concept of a premotor area. Research Publications of the
Association for Research in Nervous and Mental Disease, 1952, 30, 238-264.

Neuropsychological Studies of Apraxia
and Related Disorders, E. A. Roy (ed.)
© Elsevier Science Publishers B. V. (North-Holland), 1985

A THEORY OF THE REPRESENTATION,

ORGANIZATION AND TIMING OF ACTION

WITH IMPLICATIONS FOR SEQUENCING DISORDERS

Donald G. MacKay

University of Southern California at Los Angeles

This paper develops a theory for explaining how the components of everyday actions are sequenced and timed (e.g., typing, hammering a nail). Under the theory, a hierarchy of content nodes represents the form of a pre-planned action, while an independently stored set of (sequence) nodes codes the serial order rules for the action and determines sequence in the final output. Another independently stored set of (timing) nodes determines when and how rapidly these action components become activated. The theory also postulates a superordinate organization of content, sequence and timing nodes into systems. Each system has unique characteristics and rules of its own and is independently controllable, enabling thought of particular kinds without the occurence of action. Four systems are discussed in detail: the muscle movement system, the movement concept system the action plan system and the pragmatic system implications of the theory for several related issues are discussed: the physiological bases for action, errors in action of normals and apractics, the nature of attention and intention, and the relations between knowledge, memory, action and speech.

The present chapter examines the question of how everyday behaviors are planned, represented in the brain and executed as sequences of movement. It outlines a theory of the organizational principles underlying skilled behavior and then examines the predictions of this theory for the nature of errors in the behavior of normals and apractics suffering from brain damage. The theory places special emphasis on the sequencing and timing of behavior and was developed originally to explain how words, syllables and phonemes are sequenced and timed in producing speech (see MacKay, 1982). The present study extends the theory by specifying possible neural mechanisms underlying the sequencing and timing of not just speech, but actions involving the arms, hands and fingers as well as the entire body.

The main emphasis of the chapter is the cognitive control of action. The goal of the theory is a detailed specification of the relations between cognition and action. The main problem confronting such a theory is the interaction paradox: In the past, cognition and action have been viewed to involve fundamentally different components and principles of operation, so that the interaction between the two is paradoxical. That is, most theories assume two fundamentally different types of knowledge: cognitive knowledge about actions e.g., lighting a candle and motor knowledge; e.g., the timing, force and direction of particular muscle movements for lighting a particular candle in a particular position. The distinction between these two types of knowledge can be illustrated by the doubly dissociable symptoms of paralysis on the one hand and apraxia on the other (see Roy, 1982). A patient with apraxia can perform the movements for an action such as lighting a candle, but lacks the cognitive control mechanisms that enable the execution of the movements in the appropriate sequence and at the appropriate time. On the other hand, patients with paralysis know what to do and recognize the action when someone else performs it appropriately but cannot move their muscles to perform the action themselves.

Differences between motor and cognitive knowledge are also apparent to introspection. We are generally unaware of how we move our muscles but are usually conscious of what we are doing at a cognitive level. For example, in carrying out an action such as lighting a candle, we can express in words that we are lighting a match and applying it to the wick of the candle. Given these differences between cognitive and motor knowledge, then, how do the seemingly incompatible languages of action interact in the execution of behavior? The theory developed here is designed to resolve this interaction paradox by treating cognitive and motor knowledge within the same framework, with similar underlying components and principles of operation.

Other studies of the neural mechanisms underlying sequencing have concentrated on the locus of the mechanisms for sequencing and timing. For example, Kolb and Whishaw (1980) point to the left cerebral cortex as the usual locus for constructing sequences of voluntary movements. The present study attempts to be precise not so much on the issue of where the processes of sequencing and timing take place, but more on exactly how timed sequences of voluntary movement are represented and executed and the neural principles underlying these execution processes.

We illustrate the theory initially by means of examples from the skill of Morse code and then apply the theory to data on everyday skills such as typing and driving a car.

Why Morse code?

Although there have been many first class studies of Morse code, extending from Bryan and Harter (1899) to Klapp and Wyatt (1979), the experimental literature on piano playing is much more extensive. Moreover, typing is a much more common skill than Morse code, which seems destined to become extinct as a natural skill in the not too distant future. We therefore wish to justify our choice of Morse code rather than typing or piano playing as an initial source of examples for a theory of the control of skilled manual behavior.

Morse code has advantages over both typing and piano playing for anyone with a general interest in the timing and sequencing of behavior. First, Morse code shares formal similarities with both typing and piano playing that neither shares with the other. Like typing, the goal in sending Morse code is to maximize speed and minimize errors, but like piano playing, the motor components (dit, dah and pause) must be precisely timed, an important consideration for anyone interested in the timing of behavior.

Movements for Morse code are readily quantified and involve specifiable muscles, whereas typing movements involve complex distributions of work by the many interacting muscles which control the dynamic links between the arm, elbow, wrist and hands. Only difficult-to-measure, high-speed films can currently capture the movements themselves, let alone the underlying pattern of muscular activation (see Norman and Rumelhart, 1983). Typestroke movements are also variable across individuals and surprisingly large in number: if any pair of the 48 keys of the standard typewriter, taken in either order, allowed only a single movement, there are millions of possible movements. To complicate matters further, each of these movements can both overlap and interact with upcoming movements in the sequence. The result is a cacophonous flow of fingers moving in many directions at once, a phenomenon best described metaphorically as resembling "sea grass weaving in the waves, bending this way and that, all in motion at the same time." (Norman and Rumelhart, 1983, p.47). In contrast, Morse code movements are few in number, discrete in space and time, and virtually invariant across repetitions and between individuals. Such constancy and simplicity is a major advantage for anyone interested in either the muscle movements themselves or, as in our case, the mechanisms responsible for the cognitive control of the skill.

Even so we will see that Morse code is surprisingly complex. It raises issues which concern not just the representation, sequencing and timing of skilled behavior but the nature of memory and cognition in general. Indeed, what follows is not a theory of Morse code. Our treatment of this seemingly simple skill is not meant to be exhaustive. For example, we largely ignore certain aspects of the code (e.g. nonalphabetic punctuation and numerals), and we ignore the mechanisms involved in the actual muscle movements, in the perceptual encoding of the letters to be sent and in the perception of input strings, including the perceptual monitoring that occurs during output. What follows is instead a general theory of the cognitive control mechanisms underlying the timing and sequencing of skilled behavior, using examples from the skill of Morse code for purposes of illustration.

The Theory

A viable theory of action must account for three basis aspects of skilled behavior. First what are the components for organizing actions and how do they combine to allow an infinity of possible sequences. Second, what processes enable these components to become activated in the proper sequence and at the proper time in producing an action. And third, what mechanisms are responsible for the temporal organization of the action, its overall rate and the relative timing of its components. The present chapter deals with each of these aspects in turn, beginning with the components and how they interact.

The basic components for organizing actions in the theory are nodes. Each node consists of one or more neurons but we will forego discussion of the possible neural instantiation of nodes until the end of the chapter. We focus here on the abstract or theoretical properties of nodes. Nodes have three general properties which are relevant to the organization and exectution of behavior: activation, priming and linkage strength.

Activation

Activation of a node is all-or-none in degree and is self sustained, continuing for a specifiable period of time, independently of the state of the source that led originally to activation. Activation is initiated by means of a special activating mechanism and is terminated by inhibition, usually a process of self-inhibition.

Behavior occurs if and only if the lowest level nodes within the muscle movement system become activated. Activation of most nodes is serial in nature and the special activating mechanism determines when and in what order the nodes control-ling an action become activated. During its period of self-sustained activation, a node strongly and simultaneously primes or readies for activation all nodes connect-ed directly to it.

Priming. Priming refers to transmission across a connection which readies a connected node for activation. The level of priming of a node varies in degree from a spontaneous level up to asymptotic level. The level increases via spatial summa-tion (across all simultaneously active connections) and via temporal summation (dur-ing the period that any given connection remains active). Each node has hundreds of connections and continually receives some relatively constant degree of priming from these connected nodes. This contextual or background priming constitutes the spontaneous or resting level of the node and remains relatively constant, varying mainly with the arousal and anxiety of a subject at any point in time.

Priming arrives in two degrees: first-order and second-order. A node receives first-order priming from an activated node and second-order priming from a node which is receiving first-order priming but has not itself become activated. Second-order priming summates to a lower asymptotic level and at a slower rate than first-order priming.

Connections between nodes are both many-to-one and one-to-many. For a many-to-one connection from say Nodes A,B,C,D,... to Node Z, Node Z receives first and second order priming in direct proportion to the activity of A,B,C,D,... However, priming from any number of other nodes over any length of time only summates to some subthreshold, asymptotic level and cannot directly cause activa-tion of a connected node: As already noted, a special activating mechanism is required for activation.

Unlike activation, priming is automatic and parallel in nature, requiring no spe-cial mechanism to determine when and in what order it occurs. Also unlike activa-tion, priming never results in behavior: no movement occurs when the lowest muscle movement nodes become primed. Again unlike activation, priming is neither self-sustaining nor terminated via inhibition. For example, consider a one-to-many con-nection between an arbitrary Node X to its connected Nodes (E,F,G,H,...): when X becomes activated, it starts priming its connected nodes (E,F,G,H,...) but if X ceas-es its activity, priming of E,F,G,H,... stops accumulating and begins to decay to its resting level.

The way that priming summates has important implications for the theory. One is a faster potential rate of output for the later components of a pre-planned output sequence. By way of general example, consider the nodes in Figure 1 (from MacKay, 1981) which illustrate a typical action hierarchy (the set of mental and muscle movement nodes directly controlling an output sequence). The appropriate order for the lowest level output components corresponds to the left to right axis in the figure and the mental nodes controlling the action must be activated in the order shown so that these components can be executed in proper sequence. Activating Node 1 simultaneously primes Node 2 and 5, but since 5 can only be activated after 2, 3 and 4 have been activated, the priming of 5 constitutes "anticipatory priming" which summates during the interval that Nodes 2, 3 and 4 are being activated. Anticipa-tory priming makes it easier to activate the later components in a pre-planned out-put sequence, thereby speeding up the potential rate of output. Anticipatory prim-ing likewise reduces the probability of error for these later components, since as discussed below, increased potential rate and reduced probability of error derive from the same underlying mechanism and are therefore coreferential in the present theory (see MacKay, 1982).

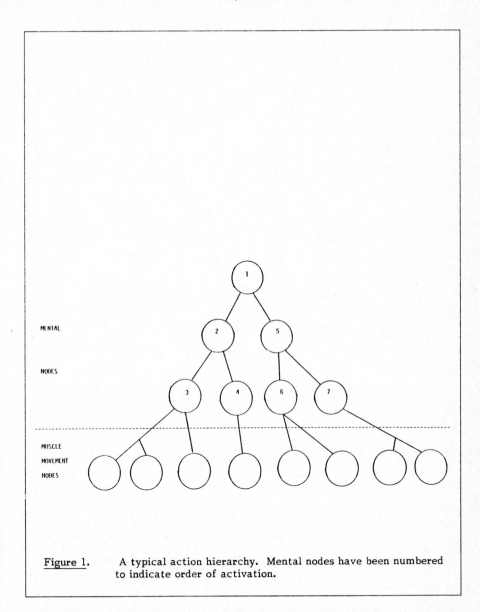

MENTAL

NODES

MUSCLE
MOVLMENT
NODES

Figure 1. A typical action hierarchy. Mental nodes have been numbered to indicate order of activation.

Linkage strength. The priming function in Figure 2 illustrates how the level of priming of a node summates over time from onset of priming up to asymptotic level. As discussed above, the asymptotic level varies with the degree of activity and number of connections simultaneously contributing priming. However, the asymptotic level and the rate of summation per unit time across any one connection (represented by the slope of the priming function) also vary with practice, i.e., the frequency with which the node has been activated via that particular connection in the past. Thus, repeated activation increases linkage strength, reflected in a higher

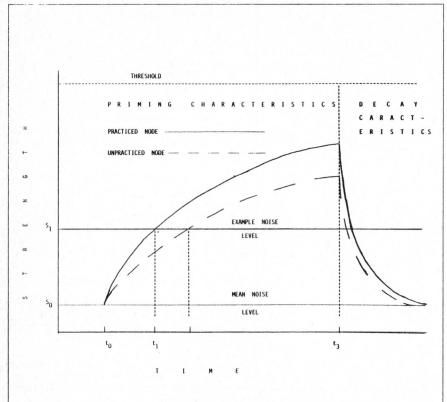

<u>Figure 2.</u>   The priming function (relating degree of priming and time) for
               a practiced and an unpracticed node which are both receiving
               priming from a superordinate node beginning at time t_0 and
               ending at time t_3. Both nodes are part of a hypothetical
               domain of nodes with resting level S_0.

asymptotic level of priming and a faster accrual of priming per unit time across that
one particular connection. Linkage strength is a long-term characteristic of a connection and must be contrasted with the degree of priming, which is a short-term
characteristic of a node, reflecting the extent to which input from any number of
connections has summated on that node at any particular point in time.

The Representation of Actions: Content Nodes

     Content nodes are the theoretical units representing the form or components of
an action and have traditionally been divided into the three categories illustrated in
Figure 3: muscle movement nodes, sensory analysis nodes and mental or association
nodes. Muscle movement nodes represent patterns of muscle movement and are
located in the motor cortex and associated motor pathways.

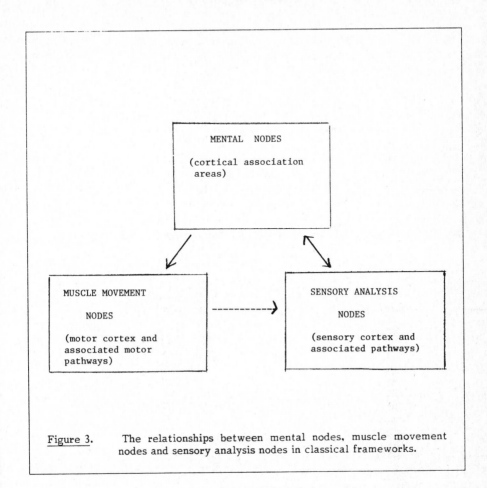

Figure 3.   The relationships between mental nodes, muscle movement nodes and sensory analysis nodes in classical frameworks.

Sensory analysis nodes represent patterns of sensory experience and are located in the sensory cortex and associated sensory pathways. Mental nodes are located within the classical association areas and represent neither muscle movements nor sensory experience but concepts such as 'I lift hammer'. Such concepts are neither sensory nor motoric but play a role in both input and output processes. For example, a node representing the concept 'I lift hammer' constitutes not only the instigator of such an action, but also the highest level perceptual representation of one's own behavior of lifting a hammer. That is, nodes within the visual system (representing e.g., the visual appearance of the arm and hammer) and within other sensory systems (representing e.g., the felt position of the arm) all contribute input to the 'lift hammer' node. However, this node is not responsible for initiating a verbal expression such as 'I am lifting a hammer' or for comprehending such an expression via auditory or other sensory channels. As discussed below, verbal systems are functionally independent of the action systems.

Only the lowest level muscle movement nodes represent specific actions. All other content nodes represent classes of action. For example, the content node representing the concept of lifting a hammer becomes activated whenever a hammer is lifted, whether quickly or slowly, a long distance or a short distance, with the wrist locked or unlocked. These and other ways of lifting a hammer constitute the class of actions the node represents, and the higher the node in the action hierarchy, the larger this class of potential actions.

To illustrate how content nodes are connected to one another, consider the generation of a Morse code dit by a complete beginner. The content node dit (send) represents the entire action and is connected with two other mental nodes, say key down (press) and key up (release) (see Figure 4). These in turn are connected with muscle movement nodes for flexing and extending the muscles of say the right index finger and wrist. These muscle movement nodes are responsible for the actual press and release of the key and are the only truely necessary components for the action. However, without a 'dit' node, the actions of pressing and releasing a telegraph key cannot be represented or understood as a unitary behavioral component with its own characteristic temporal and sequential properties (discussed below).

The Sequencing of Action: Sequence Nodes

Sequence nodes are the special mechanisms for activating content nodes and are distinguished from content nodes by capitalization in the examples to follow. As discussed below, sequence nodes also organize the content nodes into sequential domains and determine the serial order in which the content nodes become activated.

Sequential domains. Each sequence node has a one-to-many connection with a domain of content nodes. By way of illustration, consider again the rank beginner who can send only a single dit or a single dah at any one time, unlike the expert who can send long strings of letters from memory. The content nodes representing the beginner's actions can be represented dit (send) and dah (send) where the class of actions the content node represents is indicated in italics and the domain they belong to in brackets. These content nodes both send and receive a connection from their sequence node SEND (see Figure 4).

Dit (send) is also connected to two content nodes, press key (press) and release key (release). Each of these content nodes have similar connections to and from their sequence nodes, PRESS and RELEASE (see Figure 4). These sequence nodes have much more extensive domains, however. The domain of PRESS, for example, includes nodes representing all the ways of pressing a key; with either hand, with the thumb, with the forefinger or middle and ring fingers in combination. Stated more generally, a sequential domain consists of the set of responses that are possible within a given sequential environment, here PRESS followed by RELEASE or by HOLD and then RELEASE, the only sequential relationships possible among these elements. Phrased in terms of nodes, a sequential domain consists of the set of content nodes serving the same sequential function and activated by the same sequence node.

As noted above, labels such as press key (press) are not intended to carry everyday English meaning or connotation but only to distinguish one node from another within the action system.

Activation and the most-primed-wins principle. When activated, a sequence node can be considered to deliver extremely strong priming to the domain of content nodes connected to it. This priming summates quickly over time with the level of existing priming in these nodes until one of them reaches threshold and becomes activated. This activated node will invariably be the one with the greatest degree of priming prior to receiving input from the sequence node, so that content nodes

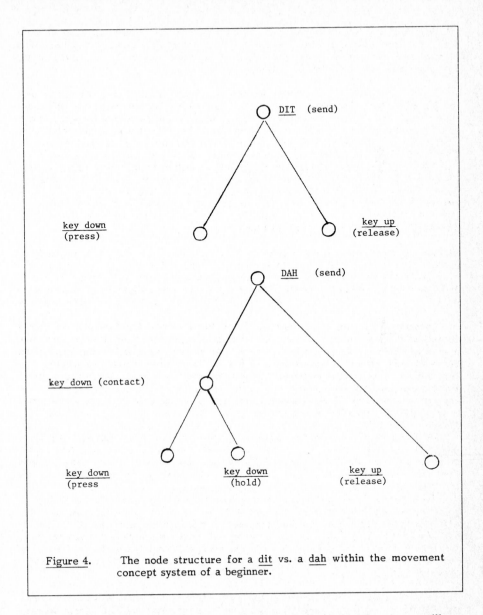

Figure 4.   The node structure for a dit vs. a dah within the movement
concept system of a beginner.

can be said to become activated via a 'most-primed-wins' principle. As we will see,
sequence nodes themselves become activated via this same principle in the case of
automated behavior.

What nodes receive the most priming and become activated under the most-
primed-wins principle? Normally, of course, the node with the most priming in its
domain is the one that has just received priming from its superordinate node in the
action hierarchy. For example, dit (send) in Figure 4a will simultaneously prime

(top-down) key (press) and key (release), so that each of these nodes should have greatest priming in their respective domains. Thus, when PRESS is activated, key (press) will reach threshold before any other node in the (press) domain. Once activated, a content node quickly quenches or inhibits its sequence node so that no other node in its domain can become activated.

Serial order. Classes of actions such as (press) and (release) are governed by serial order constraints: Pressing must precede releasing in the operation of a Morse key or any other device. Connections between sequence nodes represent these serial order constraints and ensure that the content nodes are activated in proper sequence. Specifically, an inhibitory connection between PRESS and RELEASE could ensure the precedence relation between these sequence nodes. Under this proposal, PRESS inhibits RELEASE and dominates in degree of priming when PRESS and RELEASE are simultansously primed. However, once PRESS has been activated it returns quickly to resting level. RELEASE therefore becomes released from inhibition and dominates in degree of priming, thereby determining the sequence (press + release) for movements of this type.

The Timing of Actions: Timing Nodes

Timing and sequencing are closely related processes in the theory. Timing nodes both activate the sequence nodes and determine the rate of behavior. Specifically, timing nodes have a one-to-many connection to the sequence nodes within a system (discussed below) so that when the timing node becomes activated, it strongly primes its connected sequence nodes until it activates the most primed one. The most-primed-wins relationship between timing and sequence nodes can thus be seen to resemble that between sequence and content nodes. The difference is that sequence nodes do not determine what timing nodes become engaged or disengaged. To engage or disengage the timing nodes a high level decision within the pragmatic system (discussed below) is required.

This decision calls for a certain rate of speech or action (e.g. fast or slow). The possible rates are represented by an array of timing nodes each with different endogenous rhythm. When one of the timing nodes becomes engaged, its output is applied to the sequence nodes. The pulses from the timing node therefore determine when the sequence nodes become activated, which in turn determines the temporal organization of the output.

This view of timing leads to some interesting predictions. One is that timing and sequencing are closely related but independent processes. This means that the same sequence of actions can be produced with different timing characteristics or more interestingly, a sequence of actions can be altered while its timing remains intact. This latter phenomenon has been observed in recent studies of transposition errors in skilled typing, e.g. the mistyped as hte by a competent typist. Grudin (1983) found that the pattern of keystroke intervals in a word typed correctly is largely preserved when a transposition error is produced: the wrong letters are typed at the right times, indicating that the order and timing of the letters are independent.

Timing may also be independent of particular motor modalities since simultaneous activities using different effector systems often exhibit the same timing properties. The correspondences that have been observed in the timing of simultaneously generated speech and hand movements are one example. Another is Lashley's (1951) observation that salient rhythms tend to impose their timing characteristics on many different output systems which are active at the same time. Thus a salient musical rhythm can cause a listener to fall in step, speak, gesture with the hands, and even breathe, all in time with the band. The simultaneous temporal coordination of our arms and legs in activities such as swimming is another example. All of these examples may arise from the coupling of different effector systems to the same timing node.

Timing nodes also play an important role in organizing the sequence and content nodes into systems, which are described in detail below. For example, the sequence and content nodes in the examples in Figure 4 are part of the action plan system, and the sequence nodes for this system are connected with a <u>movement concept timing node.</u> By way of contrast, sequence nodes within the muscle movement system are connected with a <u>muscle timing node.</u> These different timing nodes have different average rates of activation. For example, a movement concept timing node has a slower average rate of activation than a muscle timing node, since muscle flexions and extensions are produced faster than the larger behavioral chunks represented by movement concept nodes such as <u>dit</u> (send).

Timing nodes can, of course, only activate a sequence node that has been primed or readied for activation. If no sequence node has been primed, timing pulses can be repeatedly applied without activating any nodes whatsoever. This enables the timing nodes for different systems to begin emitting impulses at the same time. The goal-setting mechanism in the pragmatic systems simply calls for an action sequence at some overall rate and onset time without the need for an additional mechanism to start (and stop) the timing nodes for different systems in cascade, beginning with the timing node for higher level systems such as the movement concept system, and followed in succession by lower level systems, until the muscle timing system has been activated.

A Specific Example

How the timing and sequence nodes interact to determine whether, when, and in what order the content nodes controlling an action become activated is similar for every node within every system. We can therefore illustrate these processes by means of a single example from within the movement concept system: the activation of <u>key</u> (press) and <u>key</u> (release) in producing a novice dit on a Morse key. The reader is referred to MacKay (1982) for a more detailed account and hand simulation of a similar sequence of execution processes in speech production.

The content, sequence and timing nodes in question appear along with the connections between them in Figure 5. Unbroken connections are excitatory and the dotted connection between sequence nodes (in circles) is inhibitory. Some of these connections are built-in and others are formed by a process discussed in detail in MacKay (Note 1). Here we concentrate on the execution processes following the process of connection formation.

The decision to produce a dit simultaneously primes the movement concept <u>dit</u> (send) and starts the movement concept timing node. The first pulse from the timing node activates SEND because of its priming from <u>dit</u> (send). This causes activation of <u>dit</u> (send) which simultaneously transmits first-order priming to <u>key down</u> (press) and <u>key up</u> (release), and second-order priming to their sequence nodes PRESS and RELEASE. the inhibitory link between PRESS and RELEASE temporarily reduces the priming level for RELEASE so that PRESS becomes activated following the first pulse from the timing node. PRESS therefore primes every node in its (press) domain, but one of these, <u>key down</u> (press), having just been primed, has the most priming, reaches threshold soonest, and becomes activated under the most-primed-wins principle (see Figure 5).

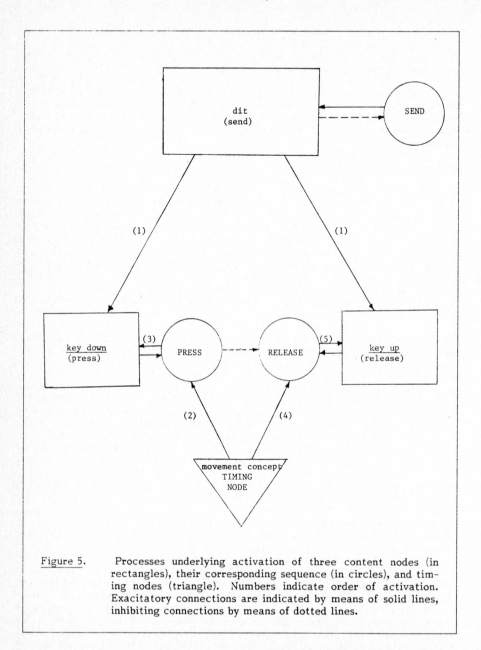

Figure 5.   Processes underlying activation of three content nodes (in
                 rectangles), their corresponding sequence (in circles), and tim-
                 ing nodes (triangle). Numbers indicate order of activation.
                 Exacitatory connections are indicated by means of solid lines,
                 inhibiting connections by means of dotted lines.

Following activation, PRESS returns quickly (via self-inhibition) to its subthreshold resting level. This releases the inhibition on RELEASE which now dominates in
degree of priming and becomes activated with the next pulse from the movement
concept timing node. RELEASE therefore primes the entire domain of (release)
nodes, but having just been primed, key up (release) has more priming than any other
node in the domain, and becomes activated under the most-primed-wins principle.

Generalizations of the Theory

So far we have developed a detailed theory for novice behavior with the following characteristics; a nonpermutable order of activation for the components (e.g. press must precede release), limited generality to the sequential rules such as (press + release), no nonsequential or simultaneous components, and no contextual dependencies in the coding of the components. In the present section we extend the theory to cover expert behavior with permutable behavior sequences, simultaneous components, contextually dependent coding and sequential rules having unlimited generality.

Expert behavior

Expert behavior differs in at least two respects from novice behavior under the theory. First, identical nodes with identical connections can be activated more quickly in expert behavior because of the increased linkage strength between the connections (see MacKay, 1982). Second, many more mental nodes are involved in the organization of expert behavior. For example, compare the novice vs. expert generation of the Morse sequence (dit dit dit dah) for the letter (v). The nodes subordinate to the individual dit and dah nodes (including the ones controlling muscle contractions) are identical for both novice and expert. However, the novice must send the sequence as four separate units, activating one after the other in turn, whereas the expert has additional mental nodes which organize the behavior into a single, automatically executed unit.

These additional mental nodes for generating expert Morse code can be organized in several possible ways. The next two sections describe one of these ways, and the section on individual differences describes another. Here it is only necessary to note that in either of the ways, a single node represents each letter. Figure 6 represents the content and sequence nodes for the expert (Version 1) generating the letter V. The letter node represented I send the letter V (letter) or V (letter) for short is activated to initiate the entire sequence (dit dit dit dah) and is part of a domain consisting of the 26 alphabetic letters, an organization with consequences for the nature of the errors that experts make. As discussed below, actions substituted in error almost invariably belong to the same sequential domain so that experts sometimes substitute one letter for another, an error that is out of the question for the novice. Grudin (1983) noted several other differences in the errors of novice vs. expert typists and these differences can be explained in a similar way within the present theory.

Context-dependent coding. Another difference between the expert and novice is that expert coding is context-dependent. Thus a dit in expert Morse code represents an E if followed by a space, and I if followed by another dit, an S if followed by two other dits or a V if followed by a double dit and a dah.

Sequence is, of course, the essence of this context-dependent code. For example, three dits followed by dah represent V, but three dits preceded by dah represent B. In the description that follows, the components making up a letter have a control structure sensitive to the sequential pattern for the entire letter. We assume that runs are the primary components in this sequential pattern, i.e., single, double, triple or quadruple elements. Thus, V (dit dit dit dah) consists of a triple dit and a dah. Expert Version 1 also codes complex doubles containing intervening elements, represented here in brackets. Thus, dit ( ) dit represents a double dit enclosing a single, double, triple, or quadruple dah as in dit dah dit (R), dit dah dah dit (P), and dit dah dah dah dah dit (apostrophe).

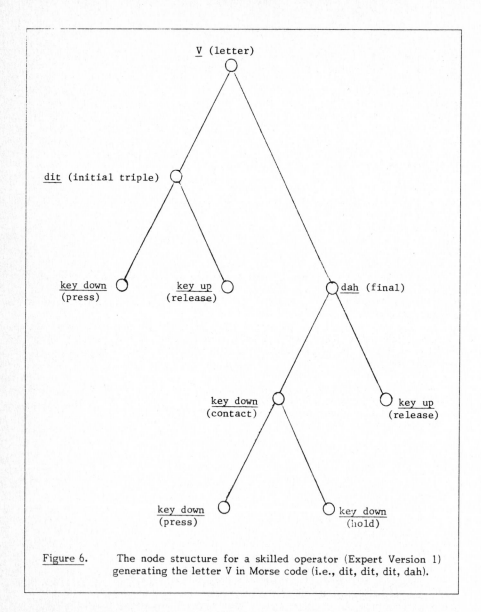

Figure 6.   The node structure for a skilled operator (Expert Version 1)
                   generating the letter V in Morse code (i.e., dit, dit, dit, dah).

Runs of this sort suffice to describe 21 of the 26 letters. The remaining 5 letters, and 4 of the punctuation marks involve alternations i.e., (dit) or (dit dah) dit.
For example, dah dit dah dit (C) is a double (dah dit) and dit dah dit dah dit dah
(period) is a triple (dit dah). These 'alternation' units can be considered secondary
components, derived after the runs have been analyzed or extracted.

In Table 1 we list the complete set of superordinate content nodes (excluding
the letter nodes themselves) that differentiate the expert from the novice under this

analysis. Using these nodes, Morse code can be generated automatically without paying attention to the sequence of operations below the level of the letter. If the letters are input in proper sequence, the preformed connections automatically determine the sequence of the lower level units in the sequence of action.

The present analysis of context-dependent coding can be contrasted with those of Wickelgren (1979) for behavior in general, and Norman and Rumelhart (1983) for skilled typing. Wickelgren (1979) was the first to emphasize that the nodes coding a complex action are sensitive to their sequential environment. In Wickelgren's proposal as many unique units are required for coding a given element of behavior as there are contexts in which the element can occur, where context refers specifically to the elements immediately preceding and immediately following a given element rather than to the sequential pattern of an entire letter as discussed above. Thus, under Wickelgren's proposal, skilled Morse code requires 9 dah nodes and 9 dit nodes. If #, . and _ represent a pause, a dit and a dah in immediately adjacent contextual slots, then the 9 dits can be represented # dit #, # dit ., # dit _, . dit #, . dit ., . dit _, _ dit #, _ dit . and _dit_. Altogether then, there are 18 context-sensitive nodes which become linked by means of unidirectional associations to give the sequence of components for a letter.

The present theory of context-dependent coding involves a much more abstract or conceptual representation of behavior than Wickelgren (1979). The units represent natural groups such as a triple dit that people seem to use in both sending and receiving Morse code. The present theory also predicts errors resembling the ones that actually occur, e.g., the doubling or tripling of the wrong element, whereas the Wickelgren theory has difficulty explaining errors of any sort in Morse code and predicts errors in other behaviors such as speech which simply never occur (see MacKay, Note 1).

The mechanism for sequencing behavior also differs in the two theories. As discussed below, the present theory uses general sequential devices such as DOUBLE and TRIPLE which can apply to any element whereas the Wickelgren theory requires a unique sequential connection for each and every pair of elements.

Hierarchical relations among sequence nodes

Expert generation of Morse code serves to illustrate a further extension of the theory: hierarchical relations among sequence nodes. In the representation of expert Morse code discussed above, a single node, V (letter), represents the sequence dit dit dit dah and is connected to two subordinate nodes; dit (initial, triple) and dah (final). Dit (initial, triple) is connected to two sequence nodes, INITIAL and INITIAL TRIPLE which are hierarchically related in the manner illustrated in Figure 7. Thus INITIAL TRIPLE is a superordinate sequence node which becomes activated at the same time as its subordinate sequence node INITIAL and further primes INITIAL following its first and second activation. However, INITIAL TRIPLE is connected to a counter which enables it to quench rather than further prime INITIAL, following the third activation, so that FINAL can become activated and the sequence completed.

Individual differences

As a general rule, individual differences increase with the degree of skill: the greater the prior practice, the greater the individual differences. This general rule is well documented in the case of skilled typing (see Grudin, 1983 and Gentner, 1983 for example) and almost certainly applies to the generation of Morse code as well. What accounts for this relationship between skill and individual differences? The reason under the theory is that with practice, many different node structures, each

---

Table 1

Content and sequence nodes for generating expert morse code

Expert Version 1

Content Nodes	Example Letters
1. dit (initial)	dit dah dit dit (L)
2. dit (final)	dit dit dah dit (F)
3. dit (initial, double)	dit dit dah (U)
4. dit (final, double)	dit dah dit dit (L)
5. dit (initial, triple)	dit dit dit dah (V)
6. dit (final, triple)	dah dit dit dit (B)
7. dit (quadruple)	dit dit dit dit (H)
8. dit (initial, alternate)	dit dah dit dit (L)
9. dit (final, alternate)	dit dah (A)
10. dah (initial)	dah dit dit dit (B)
11. dah (final)	dah (T)
12. dah (initial, double)	dah dah dit dah (Q)
13. dah (final, double)	dah dah (M)
14. dah (initial, alternate)	dah dit (N)
15. dah (final, alternate)	dah dit dah dit (C)

Other subtle details are required for a complete description of skilled Morse code and these subtleties predict further differences in the errors of experts vs. novices. Here, however, we wish to make a more general point. Although the expert makes use of additional content nodes, the sequence nodes and sequential rules (connections between sequence nodes) for controlling these additional nodes are simple and few in number. Given the content nodes described above, the only sequential rule required to generate all 26 letters is (initial + final + pause).

Expert Version 2

1. INITIAL
2. FINAL

Content Node	Superordinate Sequence Nodes
1. dit (initial)	1. INITIAL DOUBLE
2. dit (final)	2. INITIAL TRIPLE
3. dah (initial)	3. FINAL DOUBLE
4. dah (final)	4. FINAL TRIPLE
	5. FINAL QUADRUPLE

with their own special advantages and disadvantages can be formed to generate the

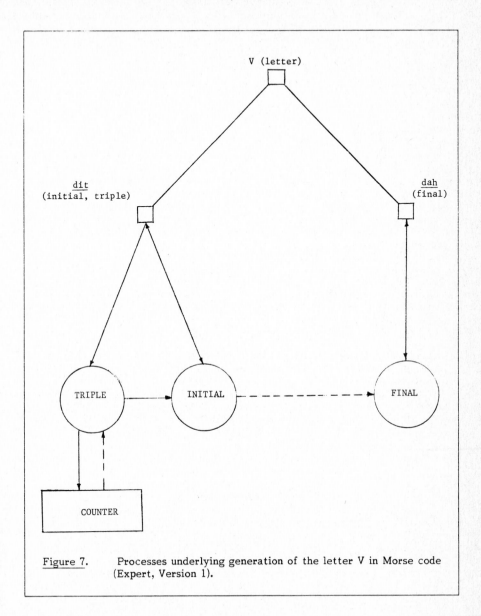

Figure 7.   Processes underlying generation of the letter V in Morse code (Expert, Version 1).

same final output (e.g. sequence of key presses).

To illustrate this point, we describe an alternative and in some ways simpler node structure for generating an expert V. This representation (Expert, Version 2) shifts the burden of sequencing to superordinate sequence nodes and away from the content nodes. Not counting the muscle movement nodes or the letter nodes themselves, only 11 nodes are required to generate all 26 letters: 4 content nodes, 2 sequence nodes, and 5 superordinate sequence nodes (see Table 1.). The connections are in some ways more complex, however. Thus, V (letter) connects with dit (initial) and with INITIAL TRIPLE, as well as dah (final) (see Figure 8.). INITIAL TRIPLE is a superordinate sequence node which is connected with INITIAL and a counter node which enables INITIAL to become activated three times in the same way as for Expert Version 1.

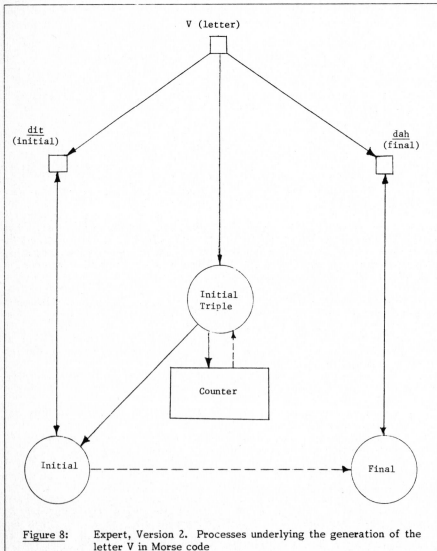

Figure 8:   Expert, Version 2. Processes underlying the generation of the letter V in Morse code

Simultaneous behaviors

As noted in the introduction, the components in Morse code are discrete and sequential at every level: one component ends before the next can begin. However, components for many other behaviors must be executed in parallel. Shifting gears in a standard-shift automobile is an example: the clutch is released at the same time as the accelerator is depressed. Unless these actions are in fact carried out simultaneously, the car may lurch forward and stall.

To illustrate what is involved, consider how the theory might represent the expert shifting of gears from second to third in such an automobile. The highest level node, shift second (third) represents the entire concept of shifting gears from second to third and is connected to a sequence node THIRD. As discussed below, THIRD is part of a general-purpose serial order rule (first + second + third + fourth ...) which can be used to sequence an indefinitely large number of behaviors.

The remaining mental nodes and the connections between them for shifting from second to third are shown in Figure 9. When actually executing the gear shift, the order of events is as follows (see Figure 9.).
Activation of shift second (third) via sequence node THIRD introduces first-order priming to three content nodes, disengage motor (prepare), third gear shift (execute) and engage motor (terminate), and second-order priming to the sequence nodes coding the serial order rule (prepare + execute + terminate). The sequence node PREPARE is therefore activated first, which in turn activates disengage motor (prepare). This primes accelerator (up) and clutch (down) and their corresponding activating mechanisms UP and DOWN. Unlike other sequence nodes (coded verbally with the same names in everyday English), UP and DOWN do not interact with one another to represent a serial order rule: they must be activated at the same time in order to successfully carry out the behavior.

Once accelerator (up) and clutch (down) have been coactivated (simultaneously activated), the most primed sequence node is EXECUTE, which therefore becomes activated and leads in turn to the activation of third gear shift (execute). This in turn primes and leads to the coactivation of gear forward (push) and gear rightward (push), bringing about the smooth flow of movement seen in expert shifting. By way of contrast, beginners usually shift from second to third in three movements (to neutral, to the right, and finally, forward), which accounts in part for their more jerky performance (see Schmidt, 1982).

The remaining primed but as yet unactivated sequence node is TERMINATE, which now becomes activated under the most-primed-wins principle, thereby activating engage motor (terminate). This primes clutch (up) and accelerator (down) which likewise become coactivated in the manner discussed above.

This view of the nodes controlling coordinated behavior not only accounts for the successful execution of everyday actions such as driving a car but allowing reasonable assumptions, makes interesting predictions concerning the nature of the errors that will occur. One frequently occurring error among beginners, predicted under the theory, is omission of the rightward component in the sequence (forward + right + forward) when shifting from second to third. The resulting shift to first rather than third is especially likely under the most-primed-wins principle since the rightward component is relatively unpracticed: forward and backward shifts from neutral are more common (occurring for shifts 1-2, 2-3 and 3-4 as well as reverse) than rightward shifts (occurring only for shift 2-3). Since degree of priming depends on linkage strength, which in turn depends on practice, producing the forward rather than rightward shift is more likely than vice versa under the most-primed-wins principle.

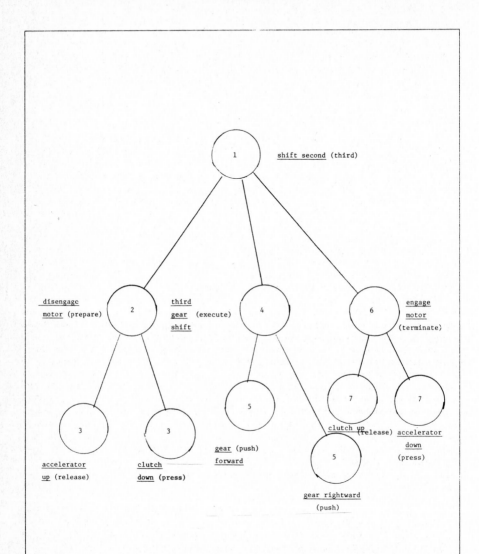

Figure 9.   Content nodes within the movement concept system for
                   shifting gears from second to third in a standard gearshift
                   automobile. The numbers indicate order of activation.

Another error which is especially common when learning to drive is to sequence
rather than coactivate accelerator (up) and clutch (down). The resulting stalls are
explained as follows: Verbal instructions usually refer to clutch and accelerator
positions as up or down, terms which the learner is likely to assume refer not to
cotemporaneous but sequential actions governed by the everyday serial rule (up +
down), seen for example in going up and down stairs or in tapping the foot or finger.
However, releasing the clutch before depressing the accelerator will stall the car,
especially on an incline (see Schmidt, 1982).

A third class of errors predicted under the theory can occur from any gear position and results from the substitution of <u>accelerator</u> (down) and <u>clutch</u> (up) for <u>accelerator</u> (up) and <u>clutch</u> (down) while attempting to disengage the engine. The error is natural enough (the accelerator component has for whatever reason acquired greatest priming in the (down) domain) but has a startling consequence: the car will suddenly accelerate rather than decelerate as expected.

Sequence rules with unlimited generality

The rule discussed above for shifting gears (first + second + third + fourth....) illustrates a general purpose rule that can be used to sequence the activation of any set of mental nodes. All that is required is the formation of a connection between the mental nodes and the appropriate sequence node. For example, a sequence of 10 nonsense syllables could be learned by forming connections between the highest level nodes representing each nonsense syllable and the corresponding sequence nodes (first + second + third ...). However, with sequences greater than 9 or 10 items, humans find such associations difficult to form (many repetitions or practice trials are required for correct performance), perhaps because each sequence node has a large number of prior associations with other content nodes and must simultaneously interact with the 8 or 9 other sequence nodes that are involved.

Permutable sequences and the determining tendency

The final extension of the theory begins with the observation that content nodes provide the basic associations underlying action and cognition, while sequence and timing nodes provide the determining tendency for specifying what domain of association is appropriate and when. Psychologists have long recognized that the basic associations cannot function by themselves: a control process or determining tendency is needed for determining what domain of association is appropriate at any given point in time (see Seltz, 1927). Our ability to either add or multiply any pair of integers (from 1 to 10) nicely illustrates the nature of this more general problem and its solution within the present framework. Consider for example the numbers 6 and 3, their associated product (18), dividend (2), difference (3) and sum (9). How do we retrieve the appropriate association (say the sum) without retrieving and rejecting the other (inappropriate) associations (product, dividend or difference)? In short, what is the determining tendency that facilitates the appropriate association?

Priming from the node representing the operator (+, -, x, /) is the determining tendency under the theory. Consider Figure 10 which illustrates the node structures for representing the propositions 6 + 3 = 9 and 6 X 3 = 18. Note that the integer nodes 6 and 3 are identical in each proposition. This means that the input 6 + 3 will prime the node represented 6 x 3 (components), although not as much as the input 6 x 3. However, this weak priming explains why subjects in a speeded recognition task find it difficult to reject incorrect propositions such as 6 + 3 = 18 and 6 x 3 = 9, where the content nodes have an underlying association but require a different operator.

Finally, note that the same network of nodes can serve to solve equations containing the permuted sequences 9 = 3 + ?, 9 = 6 + ?, 18 = 3 x ?, and 18 = 6 x ?. In these sequences the result and one of the component integers are given so that the remaining integer can be determined by the permutable rule (integer + operator + integer) which enables the integer nodes to become activated in either order.

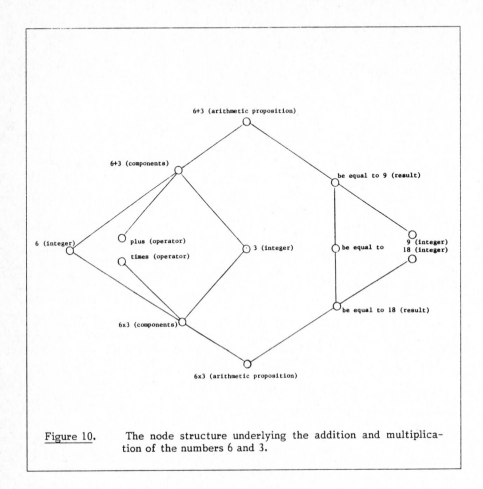

Figure 10.   The node structure underlying the addition and multiplication of the numbers 6 and 3.

Systems Controlling Action

The discussion so far has focused on detailed examples of the control of behavior via content, sequence and timing nodes. However, considering behavior more generally, we find that these nodes are organized into systems, each following the same organizational principles, but each having unique capabilities of its own. As we will see, one of the reasons for this organization into systems is to enable specific types of thought to take place without the occurence of muscle movement or action per se.

Each system is controlled by two sources, one internal to the system itself, the other external. Timing nodes are the internal source of control. Each system has a set of timing nodes which must be engaged if content nodes within the system are to become activated. Each system also has a set of sequence nodes which represent the serial order rules for the components of action the system is responsible for.

Up until now we have been discussing content, sequence and timing nodes within the system known as the movement concept system. Below we discuss this system more systematically, along with its relationship to three other systems that normally play a role in controlling everyday actions; the muscle movement system, the action plan system, and the pragmatic system. Figure 11 illustrates a general schema of the relationship between these systems. Also included for the purpose of comparison are three additional systems needed for the control of speech.

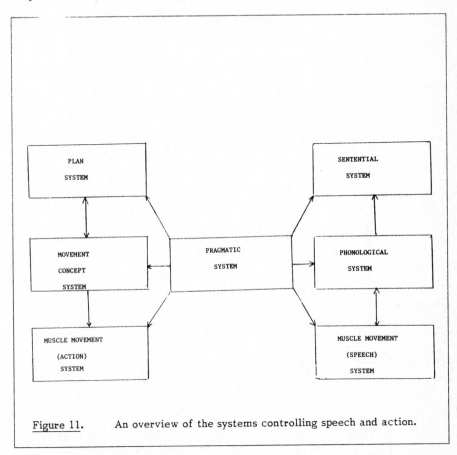

Figure 11.   An overview of the systems controlling speech and action.

Figure 11 must not be taken to represent stages such as those postulated in information processing frameworks. In stage theories, a given type or stage of processing is carried out and then and only then is control passed on to the next stage. Systems, on the other hand, are capable of operating in parallel: it is neither necessary nor usually the case that an action is completely processed within one system before the next system begins processing. Also unlike stages, systems can operate independently: one system can process an action without receiving output (first order priming) from its immediately higher level system and without causing activation within its immediately lower level system.

Muscle movement systems

Muscle movement systems control the organization of muscle movements for the trunk, limbs and fingers as well as internal organs such as the larynx and velum. Full-fledged movement occurs when the lowest level alpha motor-neurons representing specific sets of muscle fibers become activated by their triggering mechanism -- a muscle sequence node. Activated nodes within higher level (mental) systems prime their connected muscle movement nodes but unless a muscle sequence node is activated, only imagined actions occur. These internally generated actions are the basis for mental rehearsal of a movement sequence (see MacKay, 1981).

Nodes within muscle movement systems govern the activation in sequence of particular muscles and sets of muscles. This means that the connections between nodes within these systems are strengthened by practising or repeatedly activating these particular muscle movements. Predictions concerning an individual's relative skill at different muscle movement activities therefore do not depend on nonspecific processes that might be called general motor skill, and existing data support this view. Skill within muscle movement systems is specific not just to a particular limb, but to the strength, speed, and direction of movement of the limb. As Smith (1961, p.219) points out, "Individual differences in limb action abilities (considering reaction latency, strength, and speed as the components of such action) tend to be highly specific to the component, to the limb involved in the action (arm or leg), the direction it is moved (forward or backward), the dynamic or static nature of the action (speed vs. measured strength), and the phase of the action (reaction latency vs. speed of movement). For some of these findings, cross-validation using other published data is available and lends additional support to the hypothesis".

This same general principle applies to different uses of the same muscles. Henry and Whitely (1960) found no significant correlation between static or isometric strength and dynamic or movement strength for a 90-degree horizontal arm swing from the shoulder pivot. They concluded that "neuromuscular control patterns are apparently specific and different when the (same) muscle is moving a limb as compared with causing simple static tension" (p.24).

It should be kept in mind, however, that although we can produce and practice particular muscle movements by themselves, we normally do not do this. Mental nodes (which are not specific to particular muscles) normally control the muscle movements that we practice in everyday life. As a result, practice or repeated activation of these mental nodes can generalize to many different muscle movements and effector systems. Take Morse code as a simple but typical example. Since mental nodes govern this skill, practice in generating Morse code with the right forefinger can be generalized to use of the middle and ring fingers, to the left hand or to the foot. The same basic principle is true of all other complex skills (see MacKay, 1982).

The movement concept system

Nodes within the movement concept system frequently involve body parts for which the sequence of actions is highly automated. We have already discussed two examples in some detail: shifting gears in a car and generation of the letters in Morse code. Movement concept nodes represent not particular muscles but general categories of movement without reference to muscles. For example, a node representing a movement concept such as 'press key' specifies no particular muscle or muscle movement since the key could be pressed with either the left or the right hand, with either one or more than one finger on the key, with either a wrist or finger movement or most likely, both. Sequence nodes within the movement concept system represent serial order rules such as (press + release) for generating a Morse code 'dit', and these sequence nodes are likewise independent of particular muscles or movements.

There are of course many connections between the lowest level movement concept nodes and particular muscle movement nodes, and some of these connections have become very strong as a result of practice, e.g. the connection between say the 'press key' node and the nodes for the muscles controlling the right index finger of the right hand. It is nevertheless possible for a higher level decision (within the pragmatic system discussed below) to override this habit, enabling key press performance with another finger, another hand or the foot. As indicated in Figure 11, this decision may be transmitted directly to the muscle movement system, priming and causing activation of the appropriate limb system.

The action plan system

Content nodes within the action plan system, unlike the movement concept system, are not directly connected to muscle movement nodes and do not represent even broad classes of movements. By way of concrete example, an action plan node can represent an intention such as 'get bread from the bakery', which can be achieved in many different ways such as say walking, bicycling, taking a bus or drive in one's car. Such actions involve many different effector systems and virtually unlimited number of different movements. In contrast, a movement concept such as shifting a gear from second to third involves a relatively limited number of movements and muscle movement systems associated with the right arm. In addition, the action plan system deals with relatively novel rather than automated actions, requires the use of feedback and involves the entire body rather than a body part such as the arm.

To illustrate the action plan system in greater detail, consider the execution of a preplanned shopping trip such as the one illustrated in Figure 12. The plan is to drive to hardware store A, bakery B, clothing store C and furniture store D before returning to home H, where the cognitive representation of A, B, C, D and H has spatial characteristics resembling Figure 12a. Figure 12b represents the nodes and their connections for executing this shopping trip. How these particular nodes become connected differs in important respects from the process of node activation discussed here. Node formation can occur at any time and proceed in any order, unlike node activation which must occur at certain times and in proper serial order.

The execution sequence is as follows (see Figure 12b). The goal node, HBDCAH (goal), representing the entire shopping trip is activated first. This primes both stops (head out) and stops (head back) and the corresponding sequence nodes representing the serial order rule (head out + head back). These sequence nodes (operating under the most-primed-wins principle) active stops (head out) first, which primes its subordinate nodes, store B (near) and store D (far), and the corresponding sequence nodes representing the serial order rule (near + far). The sequence node NEAR now becomes activated under the most-primed-wins principle, which in turn activates store B (near), thereby triggering the action concepts for driving route hb (from point h to point :hpo.b):ehpo.. The most-primed-wins principle now reapplies to activate the sequence node FAR which in turn activates store D (far), thereby triggering the action concepts for driving route bd. The most-primed-wins principle applies to the sequence nodes again to activate stops CAH (head back), which primes home H (final stop) and stores CA (head back) along with their corresponding sequence nodes representing the serial order rule (head back + final stop). The most-primed-wins principle now activates stores CA (head back), which primes store C (near) and store A (far) along with their corresponding sequence nodes represent-

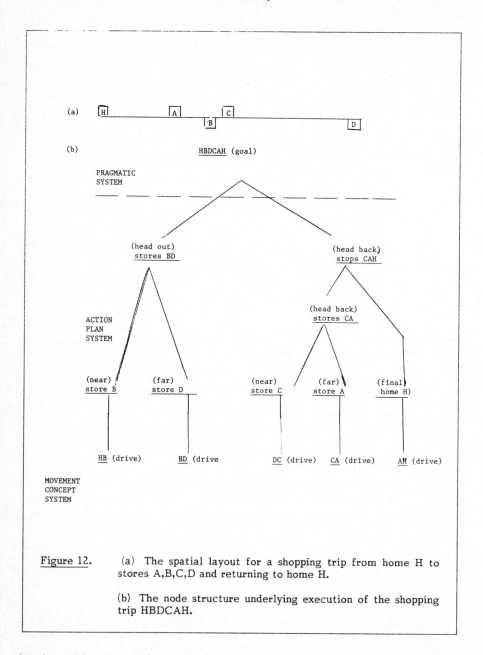

Figure 12.   (a) The spatial layout for a shopping trip from home H to
                 stores A,B,C,D and returning to home H.

                 (b) The node structure underlying execution of the shopping
                 trip HBDCAH.

ing the serial order rule (near + far). The most-primed-wins principle now activates
store C (near), which triggers the action concepts for driving route ca. When the
most-primed-wins principle reapplies again it actives the home H (final) node and
the associated action concepts for driving route ah.

This view of action plans accounts for how broad classes of preplanned behavior are sequenced in everyday life, and with the addition of reasonable assumptions, makes interesting predictions as well. Assume, for example, that the cognitive representation for the location of stores B and D is inaccurate, such that B is represented as the far store and D the near store. Under these circumstances, the most likely error under the theory is to bypass store B during the search for D, since store B will fail to match the memory representation for D.

Vagueness is also easily represented in the model. Suppose, for example, the planner knows that B and D are "head out" stores, but can't remember which comes first. Under these circumstances, the model predicts that the planner will search for store D, B (near), stopping at the first store matching the memory representation of either D or B, and store (far) where = D if near store = B, and = B otherwise.

The pragmatic system

The pragmatic system carries out five major processes or functions discussed below; the integration of perception, speech and action, goal setting, rate setting, evaluative functions, and the determination of output mode.

The integration of perception, speech and action. All forms of behavior and perception become integrated within the pragmatic system. For example, both speech and action originate and receive a common representation within the pragmatic system: A single component or set of components within the pragmatic system can represent an action such as getting up and opening a door and a sentence such as "Could you please open the door?"

The actions of either describing or showing someone the layout of one's home or apartment further illustrate the nature of the rules and representations coded within the pragmatic system. Linde and Labov (1975) had subjects describe their apartment layout and found that most (over 95%) adopted a "tour strategy": they began by describing the room nearest the front door and then described each succeeding room as if it were part of a guided tour, e.g. "A closet is to the left of the front door as you come in and the kitchen is to the right".

This tour strategy provides a means of sequencing large numbers of sentences coded within the sentential system (the analogue of the action plan system shown in Figure 11). Note, however, that the tour strategy is neutral with respect to speech vs. action. The same strategy could be used for guiding the action of showing someone around one's home rather than just describing it.

Like sequence rules, the tour strategy can apply to more than one particular content. One could just as readily use the tour strategy for describing one's place of work or the home of a relative or friend. Extending this observation, MacKay (in preparation) argued that a set of pragmatic sequence rules underlies the tour strategy. Under this proposal, pragmatic sequence nodes code serial order rules such as (left + right) and these rules can be used for sequencing either action (e.g. look first to the left and then to right in giving the guided tour), or speech (e.g. a description such as "The fridge and stove are to the left as you enter the kitchen and the sink is to the right"). Note that such rules are applicable to many other types of behavior, e.g. "step first with the left foot and then with the right" in marching.

The pragmatic system also contains sequence rules for integrating speech and action. Numerous illustrations are found in Schank and Abelson's (1977) descriptions of routine behaviors. For example, consider the stereotypical sequence of events involved in going to a restaurant for dinner. The expected sequence is (1) enter (and get shown to a table), (2) order, (3) eat, and (4) exit (including leaving a tip and paying the bill). Under the theory, pragmatic content nodes represent these expected events along with sequence rules such as (enter + order) and (eat + exit) for determining their order of occurence.

It is of considerable interest that pragmatic sequence rules such as (enter + order) or (left + right) are no more complex than either action plan rules such as (head out + head back) for a return-to-destination trip, or movement concept rules such as (press + release) for a Morse code dit. If the sequence rules for higher and lower level nodes are found to be equally complex in a wide range of behaviors, it might be argued that a fundamentally similar solution to the problem of serial order has been adopted at all levels of the nervous system.

Evaluative processes. The pragmatic system contains evaluative propositions representing attitudes and feelings concerning our social, psychological and physical representations of the world. In addition to many other functions (see Bower, 1981), this evaluative representation can sometimes be used to sequence behavior. For example, sequential rules such as (important + less important) tie into the evaluative representations and enable one to order a series of say, household chores, beginning with the most important and ending with the lease important one.

General goals. The pragmatic system represents the most general purpose of an action sequence, i.e. what the action is intended to accomplish in the outside world. This representation normally includes one's current environmental situation and many other real-world social and psychological constraints on behavior. For example, consider the goal of asking someone to shut the door. The pragmatic system must take politeness constraints into account in determining whether to express this goal as a command, (Shut the door), a question (Could you please shut the door?) or a statement (It's cold in here with the door open). Which of these three means of expression gets chosen under the most-primed-wins principle depends on the degree of priming from other pragmatic nodes coding politeness propositions for the given situation.

The rate of action. The pragmatic system sets the rate or tempo of action by determining how fast the timing nodes for all other systems become activated. How the pragmatic system does this depends on whether or not the action is critically dependent on feedback. Expert Morse code generation is an example of an action which is not critically dependent on feedback. Here the pragmatic system directly determines the rate of output by adjusting the rate seting or activation rate of the (coupled) timing nodes for the movement concept and muscle movement systems.

The situation is rather different for action sequences which are critically dependent on feedback. An example is hammering a nail until flush: since the nail could have changed angle on the previous stroke, the pragmatic system must evaluate the feedback from one stroke before the next stroke can begin.

The shopping trip discussed above is another example of a feedback-timed action sequence. Besides representing the spatial parameters of the trip (illustrated in Figure 12a) and the memory representation for recognizing the stores to be visited, the pragmatic system contains a node representing a concept such as "It is time for shopping." This node primes both HABCDH (goal) and action plan time (shopping trip), the action plan timing node which is engaged for shopping trips. This results in the activation of stores BD (head out) and store B (near), which triggers the behavior of driving route hb. However, subsequent pulses from action plan time (shopping trip) depend on environmental feedback represented in the pragmatic system. This feedback signals that one phase of the shopping trip has been completed so that the next can begin.

Cognition vs. action. The pragmatic system determines the mode of output; thought or imagined action vs. fully articulated action. For fully articulated action, the pragmatic system engages all three timing nodes for the action plan, movement concept and muscle movement systems, but for imagined action, it engages only the higher level timing nodes for the action plan and movement concept systems, so that no muscle movement nodes become activated and no overt behavior takes place. In this way, thought can proceed without the negative consequences that sometimes accompany action.

This is not say that cognition invariably precedes action or that all higher level systems invariably take part in the execution of an action. Two examples serve to illustrate how actions can be executed without the help of higher level nodes. One is Roy's (1982) observation that people sometimes forget the original goal of an action while continuing to carry out its component parts. The other is a hypothetical example dealing with the use of Ameslan (American sign language). For producing Ameslan, a movement concept system for gestures of the arms and hands replaces the phonological system of English for gestures of the respiratory, laryngeal and articulatory organs. However, the higher level sentential nodes representing words and phrases are virtually identical for Ameslan and English. Now consider the case of a person with no knowledge of Ameslan who inadvertently happens to produce the gesture with the arms that means 'tree' in Ameslan. The gesture has been produced as a nonsense action without the help of the higher level nodes that routinely contribute to its production by someone who knows Ameslan.

But although the action is clearly feasible, it is deficient in control, memorability and appropriateness. The person without the movement concepts for Ameslan will not be able to precisely reproduce or even remember the action at a later time. Nor will that person be able to produce the action in appropriate contexts i.e. in a conversation about trees with someone who knows Ameslan. The situation of the apraxic who can produce the components of a action but cannot produce the action as a unit in its appropriate context is in many ways analogous: Due to cortical damage, higher level nodes are no longer contributing to the action, and although the lower level nodes are able to execute the components of the action, there is obvious impairment. The absense of higher level cognitive control can also lead to more subtle deficits: MacKay (1982) experimentally simulated the production of nonsense actions resembling the Ameslan example discussed above and showed that the flexibility and fluency of an action suffers in the absence of higher level nodes.

Errors in Action and Their Relation to Attention and Intention

Errors in everyday behavior provide a challenge for theories of action since theories which cannot account for the erros that occur are incomplete or inadequate as accounts of the mechanisms underlying behavior. To determine whether the present theoretical framework can handle errors in action, we examine three broad categories of error from the everyday behavior of normal individuals. We then explore the relation between intention and errors and develop a way of describing intentions within the present theoretical framework. Finally, we discuss the relation between attention and errors and describe a way of representing attention in the present theory that overcomes some of the problems with earlier theories.

Errors in action

Data driven errors. Irrelevant but simultaneously ongoing perceptual processing sometimes causes errors in action. Meringer and Mayer (1895) and Norman (1981) compiled several naturally occurring speech errors of this type, but the Stroop effect represents a well know experimental demonstration of the same phenomenon (see Norman, 1981). Subjects in Stroop experiments are presented with color names printed in several different colors of ink and the task is to ignore the word and name the color of the ink as quickly as possible. Errors are especially frequent when the color name differs from the name for the ink (e.g. the word green printed in red ink) and the most common error is data driven: the printed name (green) substitutes the required name describing the color of the ink (red).

Data driven errors are readily explained in the present theory as effects of bottom-up priming. The same mental nodes become involved in perception (bottom-up) and behavior (top-down) and the most primed node in a domain becomes activated under the most-primed-wins principle, regardless of whether its source of priming is from above or below. As a consequence, a node receiving bottom-up priming can become activated in error simply because it has acquired more priming than the intended-to-be-activated node in the same domain, i.e., the node receiving priming from a superordinate node in the action hierarchy.

Decay of priming errors. Errors due to decay of priming resemble absent mindedness: The person forgets what they are doing in the process of carrying out an action, and must somehow begin again. Norman (1981) provides a dramatic but otherwise characteristic example where a man went to his bedroom but could not recall what he wanted there until he returned to his work (writing), discovered that his glasses were dirty and returned to the bedroom to fetch the handkerchief he had wanted for cleaning them.

Such absent-mindedness reflects decay of priming in the theory. When activated, an action plan node primes its subordinate nodes which then become activated in proper sequence. However, priming decays over time and with sufficient delay between priming and activation, the subordinate nodes in the action hierarchy can lose so much priming that no action can take place.

Thus, in the above example, an action plan node primed nodes for going to the bedroom, retrieving the handkerchief and cleaning the glasses. However, while actually going to the bedroom, priming of the nodes for retrieving the handkerchief and cleaning the glasses decayed to resting level so that no action could occur. These nodes became reprimed only later during the subsequent attempt to use the dirty glasses for reading.

Capture errors. Capture errors (see Norman, 1981) seem to reflect a combination of decay of priming and bottom-up effects: An action commonly associated with a given environment replaces the intended action (because of decay of priming). The following example from William James (1890) is typical: A man went to his bedroom to change clothes for dinner but forgot what he was doing, put his pyjamas on instead of his dinner clothes, and found himself getting into bed, much to his surprise. Apparently, the bedroom environment had a bottom-up effect on the selection of the higher level plan (going to bed vs. going to dinner) and as Norman (1981) points out, theories of action must make provisions for such bottom-up effects.

Such errors have two possible explanations within the present framework. One involves decay of priming as in the errors discussed above. The bedroom environment primes at least two nodes; one for changing clothes, the other for going to bed. The node for changing clothes is primed from above via the plan to go to dinner, and being the most primed, becomes activated under the most-primed-wins principle. This causes subordinate nodes for removing clothes and for putting on new ones to become primed. Assume, however, that this priming has decayed for reasons similar to those discussed above: The most-primed-wins principle must be applied again to reestablish the superordinate goal. Having accumulated priming from stimuli arising from undressing, from sight of the pyjamas and perhaps other sources as well (e.g. feelings of fatigue), the node for going to bed may have most priming at this point in time and therefore becomes activated, with the ensuing errors, putting on pyjamas and going to bed.

The second explanation resembles the first but requires neither loss of priming nor reapplication of the most-primed-wins principle to superordinate domains. Under this explanation, the error reflects the general principle of subordinate autonomy discussed in MacKay (1982). Specifically, the particular clothes to be worn for a given occasion are unlikely to be specified within a higher level plan: We often delay choosing specific clothes until we have determined what clothes are available in the closet. As a consequence, the pyjamas node may acquire greatest priming (for reasons such as those discussed above) when the activation mechanism is applied to the domain of clothes nodes, so that pyjamas are donned. This primes from below the goal of going to bed, which results in the error of going to bed.

Under this explanation, capture errors closely resemble the "associative errors" in speech recorded by Meringer and Mayer (1895) and Norman (1981). A typical example is the substitution of "Lick Observatory" for the intended "Palomar Observatory," made by a speaker who was highly familiar with Lick Observatory near Stanford. The explanation is as follows: In forming a sentence plan, the noun node for <u>observatory</u> becomes activated. This primes a set of noun phrase nodes from below, including the one for <u>"Lick Observatory"</u> (noun phrase). This node acquires more priming for whatever reason and automatically becomes activated under the most-primed-wins principle, causing the error.

Intention and errors

Errors are closely related to the issue of intention since an intention is by definition violated in producing an error. What are intentions and how are they expressed in action (when they are)?

We are here concerned with intentions during the course of action rather than the knowledge one may have about one's own intentions prior to initiating an action. These 'intentions in action' represent an answer to the question "What are you trying to do" and any theory of action must capture three basic characteristics of such intentions: their indirect relation to action; their multifaceted nature; and their close connection with the units of performance (see MacKay, 1983). We argue below that the present theory captures all three of these characteristics.

Indirect relation between intention and action. Intentions may or may not become expressed in action. Errors represent one example where actions and intentions fail to correspond and context-dependent intentions represent another. For example, one can have a context-dependent intention to light a candle when in need of light but if that need never arises, the intention never becomes expressed in action.

The present theory readily explains this indirect relationship between intention and action. Under the theory, intentions correspond to the priming of sequence and content nodes in preparation for action. These intentions then become expressed in action when the timing nodes for the lowest level muscle movement system become activated. Activating these timing nodes often depends on a specific cue such as darkness in the candle example discussed above. And even when the timing nodes are activated, the intended action does not always occur. Incongruities between intention and action are to be expected in a theory where a node must not only be strongly primed, it must be more primed than any other node in its domain in order to become activated under the most-primed-wins principle.

The multifaceted nature of intentions. One not only intends to execute the components of an action but to execute them in the proper sequence and at an appropriate rate. To illustrate this multifaceted nature of intentions, consider the intention of lighting a candle. Components such as striking a match, applying it to the wick of the candle until it ignites, and blowing out the match are an integral part of the intention. But so is the proper sequence: the sequence "Strike match, blow out match and hold match to candle" clearly violates one's intention to light a candle.

The present theory readily captures this multifacted nature of intentions. The components of an intended action correspond to the top-down priming of content nodes in an action hierarchy and the intended sequence corresponds to the priming of sequence nodes. All that is required for action is the 'go signal' or activation pulse from the appropriate timing node.

The relation between intentions and the units of performance. Intentions are closely related to the units for carrying out a task. Consider for example the units underlying the operation of a lathe (from Welford, 1968, p.193): "At any given instant we should find a detailed muscular action in progress--say, a twisting of the wrist to turn a handwheel on the tool carriage. The action would, however, be only one of a series required to move the tool over the surface of the work. This again would be only one part of the cycle of operations required to machine the article concerned, and the article might be only one of several needed for the job of construction on which the man was engaged". As Welford (1968) points out, the performance units underlying these actions must be hierarchically organized, such that the larger units at each level encompass the smaller, "organizing, coordinating, steering and motivating those that lie below".

Consider now the intentions underlying these actions as reflected in answers to the question "What are you trying to do?" The man is simultaneously intending the action (e.g. gauging), the series of actions (moving the gauge systematically over the wood), the cycle of operations (making a table leg) and the job of construction (making a table). Like the performance units, then, the intentions are hierarchically organized, and vary with the level under consideration.

The present theory readily explains this close relationship between intentions and the units of performance. Since intentions correspond to the priming required to activate the sequence and content nodes, intentions constitute an essential ingredient in the control of action, and the components of intention and action are coreferential in the theory.

Attention and Errors

Current theories sometimes attribute errors to lack of attention, but attention often goes undefined and acquires animistic properties in these theories. In what follows we attempt to develop an alternate view of attention that overcomes some of these flaws.

Under the present theory, attention is the perceptual analogue of intention: it corresponds to the priming of nodes representing an anticipated perception. By way of illustration, consider an example from visual perception (Kaufman, 1974): A subject is instructed to expect a duck when presented with Jastrow's ambiguous rabbit-duck. The subject will see the duck rather than the rabbit because the instructions activate a proposition node representing the concept "A duck will be presented". This proposition node primes the nodes in a visual concept system which represent ducks and their characteristic attributes. These nodes therefore become activated under the most-primed-wins principle and determine perception of the ambiguous figure.

Consider now an example involving attention in action (from Norman, 1981). A man has decided to stop at the fish store on the way home from work but is paying attention to something else at the intersection where he must detour to the fish store. As a result he fails to go to the fish store as intended but goes straight home, his usual pattern of behavior.

Such failures of attention can be explained in the same was as the decay of priming errors discussed above. When we plan an action such as detouring to a fish store on the way home, connections are formed between action plan nodes and nodes within the visual concept system, here the nodes representing the perceptual cues for the turn-off. These visual concept nodes, therefore, become primed during the course of the action, so that when the cues themselves appear, the visual concept nodes become activated under the most-primed-wins principle and strongly prime the plan nodes for making the detour. The outcome is error-free behavior as planned.

What happens when one fails to pay attention and is thinking about some other plan when the cues for making the detour appear? Thinking about some other plan implies that the fish store plan is no longer activated, so that both the plan for making the detour and the visual concept nodes representing the intersection are suffering from decay of priming. As a consequence, bottom-up priming from the visually experienced intersection may fail to reach the action plan node for making the detour in sufficient strength. As a result, the more frequently activated plan of driving straight home may predominate at this critical choice point and become activated under the most-primed-wins principle.

The concepts of critical choice points and competing mental activities are of course not new (see Reason, 1979; Freud, 1914). However, viewing attention as the priming of high level perceptual nodes is new and obviates an appeal to animism seen in earlier theories. For example, Reason (1979) maintained that attention must be devoted at critical choice points in an action sequence to prevent the intrusion of a parallel mental activity as in Freudian and data driven errors. However, attention played the role of a homunculus which must be on the lookout for these choice points when two competing action patterns share common elements or are both associated with same environmental situation. If the homunculus is asleep i.e., insufficient attention is being paid, then the most frequent or most recently activated of the two competing actions will occur, whether correct or not. If the homunculus is awake, it inhibits the stronger habit, allowing the appropriate behavior to occur. As in Freud's theory, civilized behavior requires a homunculus to inhibit stronger or more primitive impulses. In contrast, however, the present theory views appropriate behavior as the result of maintaining the priming of nodes controlling the intended sequence of action.

Movement Disorders

One way of "testing" any theory of skilled action is to determine whether it can account for the errors that occur in the performance of brain-damaged patients. In what follows we test the node structure theory against current clinical data on the movement disorder known as apraxia. As Heilman (1979) points out, complex learned behaviors become disorganized in apraxia but not because of paralysis, weakness, deafferentation, abnormality of tone or posture, abnormal movements such as tremors and chorea, intellectual deterioration, poor comprehension or uncooperativeness. We begin by examing two general phenomena (environmental susceptibility and hemispheric asymmetry) which are characteristic of virtually all apraxias. We then apply the theory to three main forms of apraxia (callosal, ideational and ideomotor) which play a prominent role in the recent literature.

Environmental susceptibility

Environmental susceptibility is a general phonomenon associated with cortical damage: The patient requires the appropriate context or situational props in order to commence and direct an action and becomes easily distracted by irrelevant contextual cues. For example, an apraxic may begin the task of collecting and sorting out the dirty laundry but ends up cleaning the bathroom instead since the environment (a dirty bathroom) primed another course of action (Roy, 1982). Such an error is, of course, less likely to occur when the apraxic maintains a situational prop (the clothesbacket) in hand. Similarly, apractics are often unable to demonstrate the use of a tool except in its appropriate environmental context. If asked to mimic the action of hammering a nail in the absence of both hammer and nail, they have difficulty carrying out the action.

Why does perceptual input play such a dominant role in the behavior of apractics and other patients with cortical damage? Environmental susceptibility introduces serious problems for current theories of motor control (see Roy, 1982), but follows straight forwardly from the present framework. Under the theory, cortical damage impairs the effectiveness of higher level nodes, thereby reducing the degree of top-down priming in an action hierarchy. However, bottom-up priming is by definition unimpaired in apraxia and, therefore, acquires an exaggerated influence on which node receives most priming and becomes activated. No problem arises when these environmental cues are congruent with the required action: The bottom-up priming from the tool or the environmental context will facilitate the appropriate action. However, inappropriate actions become likely in the presence of irrelevant cues, such as the dirty bathroom. These irrelevant cues provide strong bottom-up priming which predominantes over the weaker top-down priming for the intended action, so that inappropriate nodes become activated under the most-primed-wins principle and data driven errors become the norm.

By weakening top-down priming, cortical damage will also increase the likelihood of decay of priming errors: Under the theory, apractics are likely to omit as well as substitute components within a sequence of actions.

Hemispheric asymmetry

A steady stream of findings over the past 20 years indicates that the left hemisphere plays a special role in the sequencing and timing of behavior (whether verbal or nonverbal). For example, left hemisphere lesions in right-handed people selectively impair the sequencing of movements such as pushing a button, pulling a handle and pressing a bar in the Kimura-bar test (Kimura, 1977). However, right hemisphere lesions selectively disrupt spatial abilities: These patients experience difficulty perceiving the spatial relations between objects (as in copying an abstract design or drawing a diagram or map) and positioning objects spatially (as in assembling the pieces of a jigsaw puzzle or building a structure out of blocks).

Current theories are in agreement that deficits arising from right hemisphere lesions reflect an inability to code spatial patterns or relations between objects. The reasons for the left hemisphere effects are more controversial. Almost all cases of apraxia in right-handed people originate from left hemisphere lesions. Since the left hemisphere is usually dominant for language in these patients, it has been suggested that a verbal control system located within the left hemisphere is responsible for directing and sequencing skilled behavior. Thus, left hemisphere lesions cause apraxia by disrupting the control of action via internal speech or other linguistic means.

This view of left hemisphere apraxias has been discredited by both clinical and experimental data. On the one hand, clinical tests of aphasia and apraxia are poorly correlated and surgicaly induced left hemisphere lesions outside the speech area often result in apraxias with no demonstrable aphasic symptoms whatsoever (Kolb and Whishaw, 1980). On the other hand, whole classes of aphasia without apraxia and of apraxia without aphasia are everywhere apparent. For example, animals are capable of generating complexly sequenced actions but are, of course, incapable of speech. Likewise, animals with frontal lesions exhibit apraxic symptoms without even the possibility of a causal language deficit.

The present view of left-hemisphere apraxias is immune to these criticisms. Under the node structure theory, content nodes for speech and action are partly overlapping and partly independent: they become integrated within the pragmatic system but are separate and independent within lower level systems (see Figure 11). Damage to the pragmatic system can, therefore, disrupt both speech and action whereas damage limited to a lower level system can disrupt speech without disrupting action or vice versa. For example, damaging only the phonological system will disrupt speech but not action.

Localized and selective damage to content nodes only cause limited incapacities in specific behaviors and these behaviors are easily relearned. However, apraxia (and aphasia) can arise in another and much more serious way, namely through disconnection or disruption of the sequence and timing nodes for a class of behaviors. Such lesions would not only disrupt the sequencing and timing of many actions but in all likelihood would cause inability to activate many of these behaviors as well. Moreover, because of the role of sequencing and timing nodes in activating, strengthening and forming new connections. relearning these behaviors would be difficult.

Consider now the issue of hemispheric asymmetry. An accumulating body of evidence (Tzeng, Hung & Wang, Note 2) suggests that the sequence and timing nodes are located in the left hemisphere for both speech and action. This being the case, it makes sense that left hemisphere lesions are likely to disrupt the activation, sequencing and timing of speech or action or both, as noted above.

One of the predictions of this view is that left hemisphere lesions should also disrupt the perception of sequence and timing since the same nodes govern both perception and production within higher level systems. Congruent with this prediction lesions within the left but not the right hemisphere interfere with the perception of temporal order (Efron, 1963) and of rhythm (Robinson and Solomon, 1974) for both visual and auditory stimuli. Such findings suggest that sequencing and timing may represent a general function of the left hemisphere, so that the present theory can be viewed as specifying the principles underlying functioning of the left hemisphere. Whether similar principles govern functioning of the right hemisphere remains an open question.

Forms of apraxia

Callosal apraxias. Collosal apraxias result when the corpus callosum becomes severed, thereby disconnecting the left and right cerebral hemispheres. In right-handed patients, the symptoms are as follows: The patient retains virtually normal use of the right hand but has difficulty imitating or performing these same actions on command using the left hand. The ability to use the left hand to demonstrate the characteristic use of a well-known object, e.g. a comb, is also impaired but not as severely (see the above discussion of environmental susceptibility).

These symptoms are readily explained under the node structure theory. In a right-handed person, the control mechanisms for activating, sequencing and timing the higher level aspects of action are localized in the left hemisphere. As a result, callosal lesions disconnect these left hemisphere control mechanisms from content nodes located in the right hemisphere. Since right hemisphere content nodes control the organizaton of action in the left hand, these patients become unable to use their left hand for generating complex actions.

We emphasize again that the above discussion applies only to right-handed persons. For persons who are ambidextrous or left-handed, there is evidence to suggest that the sequencing and timing mechanisms for both speech and action may be represented bilaterally or in the right hemisphere.

Ideational apraxia. Ideational apraxia frequently occurs with lesions to the dominant (usually left) parietal lobe in the region of the angular gyrus and associated subcortical structures (Heilman, 1979). Ideational apractics can imitate actions and demonstrate how to use an object without making errors but have difficulty initiating the same movements on the basis of verbal instructions. The problem is not comprehension of the instructions since these patients can indicate understanding by correctly pointing to a picture of the action.

Performing a series of acts leading to a goal is also difficult for ideational apractics: Even when they can perform the individual acts making up the sequence, they often get the order wrong. For example, when called upon to light a candle, the patient may light the match and then blow it out before applying it to the wick.

Ideational apraxias have several possible bases within the present theory. One is a disconnection syndrome: The lesion has disconnected the systems for action (e.g. the action plan system) from systems for speech (e.g. the sentential system). Since the problem here is not so much with movement per se as with integration of verbal instructions and motor responses, these patients can imitate actions and manipulate objects appropriately, but cannot initiate actions on command (cf., Geschwind, 1975).

The theory suggests a different basis for ideational apractics experiencing difficulties sequencing an action. The sequence nodes are the problem here. If a lesion weakens or distorts the inhibitory interactions between sequence nodes, whole classes of actions will tend to become misordered. Such a lesion may also impair the quenching and self-inhibitory mechanism that enables sequence nodes to return to resting level following activation. This would increase the likelihood of perseveration errors; i.e. repetition of a given behavior or behavior component.

Ideomotor apraxia. Ideomotor apraxia frequently occurs with lesions to the dominant (usually left) parietal lobe and subcortical white matter in the region of the supramarginal gyrus (Heilman, 1979). The plan of action seems intact for these patients but the individual components of a gesture are jerky, clumsy and uncoordinated, whether in performance to command, imitation or use of actual objects. The subgroup with solely cortical damage seems generally incapable of recognizing their own actions as being clumsy. When shown films of smooth vs. clumsy movements, these patients often pick the clumsy act as the correct one (Valenstein and Heilman, cited in Heilman, 1979). When miming an action such as using a hammer, these apractics are also known to use a body part instead of the imagined object (e.g. the fist is used to represent the head of the hammer rather than to hold the handle).

The clumsiness or arhythmia of ideomotor apractics is readily explained under the node structure theory. The rythmicity or smoothness of an action is a function of the timing nodes, which also determine the tempo or rate of action. However, the problem here is not that the overall rate is too fast or too slow but that it is inconsistent: Fast pulses are intermixed with slow ones, so that the sequence of movements appears jerky, clumsy and unpredictable. The fact that some of these apractics cannot distinguish between clumsy and graceful movements is to be expected under the theory, since the higher level nodes for perceiving and producing actions are identical. It is also possible that the higher level systems for analyzing visual concepts have undergone damage in these patients, contributing further to their inability to distinguish clumsy from fluent actions.

The use of a body part as substitute for an imagined object (e.g. a finger for a spoon or a fist for a hammer head) is somewhat more complex under the theory. Here the patients seem to be substituting a similar but inappropriate action (hitting an object with the fist or getting food into the mouth with the finger(s) in these examples). Moreover, the substituted action involving the body part may be generally more frequent, a major contributor to errors of this sort under the theory. The fact that body parts are present in experience whereas an imagined object is not could also contribute to these substitutions (see the above discussion of environmental susceptibility): As expected under the theory, the performance of these patients typically improves dramatically when using an actual rather than imagined object (Heilman, 1979).

The Physiological Plausibility of Node Structure Theory

All theories are intended to go beyond existing data and to stimulate either direct or indirect tests. For theories in human neuropsychology, however, direct tests are often impossible and indirect tests are difficult and time-consuming. Before testing the neural implications of a theory based originally on behavioral data, a preliminary evaluation of its physiological plausibility is desireable: What neural mechanisms are required or suggested by the theory and how plausible are these mechanisms given the current state of our physiological knowledge?

Each node in the theory consists of one or more interconnected neurons and increases in linkage strength for the connections between nodes may reflect the increased efficiency of neural transmission across synapses that results from repeated post-synaptic activation (Eccles, 1972). At least in higher level systems, however, priming cannot be equated with short-term potentiation across a synapse, and activation cannot be equated with the firing of a neuron, since neural potentiation and firing obey very different time characteristics from those required for the priming and activation of higher level nodes. Rather, activation of a node may correspond to rates of firing of a neuron that can be sustained without decrement by means of an excitatory collateral. Priming would then correspond to the range of firing rates which are below the threshold of the excitatory collateral and which cannot therefore sustain activity of the parent neuron. An inhibitory collateral with an even higher threshold may then introduce the self-inhibition that follows activation of the parent neuron.

Given a physiological instantiation such as this, the node structure theory requires a nervous system with five general characteristics, the plausibility of which we examine below. One general characteristic is a large number of components with a multiplicity of connections between them. Since each node consists of one or more neurons, the theory requires billions of neurons with hundreds of connections to and from each one. In line with this requirement, the human nervous system contains over 140 billion neurons (Kolb and Whishaw, 1980) and each of these can synapse with and receive synapses from over 1000 other neurons (Eccles, 1972).

Functionally specific morphological subdivisions within the nervous system are a second requirement of the theory: neurons must be organized into systems and domains or functionally distinct pools. In line with this requirement, the nervous system seems to be organized into many subcomponents with specific although not always completely understood functions. As Brodal (1973, p.687) points out, "It is the rule, rather than the exception that even a small nucleus (or pool of neural cell bodies) can be divided into parts or territories which differ with regard to cytoarchitecture, glial architecture, vasoarchitecture, fiber connections, synaptic arrangements and by its chemistry." Neural compartmentalization characterizes even the lowest level spinal systems controlling muscle movement. Consider the alpha mononeurons for example, the lowest level nodes within muscle movement systems. The cell bodies of alpha-motoneurons are clustered into pools at every level in the spinal cord and like a domain, each pool is functionally distinct, innervating motor units within a single muscle or group of anatomically related muscles (see Schmidt, 1982).

The third general requirement is that the nervous system be organized into motor, sensory and association systems each with a hierarchy of levels of function. Evidence supporting this general organizational structure has been accumulating since the time of Hughlings-Jackson and is well documented in recent literature (see for example Kolb & Whishaw, 1980).

A fourth general requirement is a set of semi-specific activating systems which function like sequence nodes. Recent evidence indicating that the reticular formation contains many individual nuclear groups with semi-specific rather than completely nonspecific activating functions (see Kolb & Whishaw, 1980) renders this requirement physiologically plausible even though the actual function of these nuclear groups remains to be determined.

The fifth general requirement is that voluntary actions be accompanied by a rhythmic activity corresponding to the periodic pulses from the time nodes. This requirement seems physiologically plausible in view of recently observed correlations between the onset of some voluntary activities and rhythmic bursts from mid-brain and forebrain structures in the rat (Bland & Vanderwolf, 1972). The 4 - 7 cps 'theta' pulses from the hippocampus to the forebrain specifically suggested to Kolb & Whishaw (1980, p.241) that the forebrain "is controlling voluntary movements to ensure that they are appropriate in sequence, time and place." Whether pulses from hippocampal timing nodes to sequence nodes in the forebrain are the basis for the theta rhythm is currently unknown but this and other hypotheses concerning the neural substratum for the present theory seem sufficiently plausible to warrant further test.

Acknowledgements

The author thanks Drs. E. Roy, E. Kerr and D. Burke for helpful comments on an earlier version of this paper.

REFERENCE NOTES

1.   MacKay, D.G. The organization of perception and action: Fundamentals of cognitive psychology. Mering, in preparation.

2.   Tzeng, O.J.L., Hung, D.L. & Wang, W. S-Y. (1982). A time-keeping mechanism in the left hemisphere. Paper presented at the Annual Meeting of the Psychonomic Society, Minneapolis, MN.

REFERENCES

Bland, B.H., & Vanderwolf, C.H.   Electrical stimulation of the hippocampal formation: behavioral and bioelectrical effects. Brain Research, 1972, 43, pp.89-106.

Bower, G.   Mood and memory. American Psychologist, 1981, 36(2) pp.129-148.

Brodal, A.   Self-observations and neuro-anatomical considerations after a stroke. Brain, 1973, 96, pp.687-88.

Bryan, W.L., & Harter, N.   Studies in the physiology and psychology of the telegraphic language. Psychological Review, 1899, 4, pp.27-53.

Eccles, J.C.   Possible synaptic mechanisms subserving learning. In A.G. Karyman and J.C. Eccles (Eds.).   Brain and human behavior pp.63-92. New York: Springer-Verlag, 1972.

Efron, R. (1963). Temporal perception, aphasia, and dejavu. Brain, 1963, 86, pp.403-424.

Freud, S. Psychopathology of everyday life (A. A. Brill, trans.). New York: Penguin 1914.

Gentner, D.R.   Keystroke timing in transcription typing. In W.E. Cooper (Ed.) Cognitive aspects of skilled typewriting. p.95-120. New York: Springer-Verlag 1983.

Geschwind, N.   The Apraxias: Neural mechanisms of disorders of learned movement. American Scientist, 1975, 63 188-195.

Grudin, J.T.   Error patterns in novice and skilled transcription typing. In W.E. Cooper (Ed.) Cognitive aspects of skilled typewriting. p.121-144. New York: Springer-Verlag 1983.

Heilman, K.M.   Apraxia. In K.M. Heilman & E. Valenstein (Eds.) Clinical Neuropsychology pp.159-185. New York: Oxford University Press 1979.

Heilman, K.M., Rothi, L.J. & Valenstein, E.   Two forms of ideomotor apraxia. Neurology, 1982, 32, 342-346.

Henry, F.M. & Whitley, J.D.   Relationships between individual differences in strength, speed, and mass in arm movement. Research Quarterly, 1960, 31,(1), pp.24-33.

James, W. The principles of psychology. New York: Holt 1890.

Kaufman, L. Sight and mind. New York: Oxford University Press 1974.

Kimura, D. Acquisition of motor skill after left-hemisphere brain damage. Brain, 1977, 100, 527-542.

Klapp, S.T. & Wyatt, E.P. Motor programming within a sequence of responses. Journal of Motor Behavior, 1979, 8(1) pp.19-26.

Kolb, B. & Whishaw, I.Q. Fundamentals of human neuropsychology. San Francisco: Freeman, 1980.

Lashley, K.S. The problem of serial order in behavior. In A. Jeffress (Ed.) Cerebral mechanisms in behavior. New York: Wiley & Sons, 1951.

Linde, C. & Labov, W. Spatial networks as a site for the study of language and thought. Language, 1975, 51, pp.924-939.

MacKay, D.G. The problem of rehearsal or mental practice. Journal of Motor Behavior, 1981, 13(4), pp.274-285.

MacKay, D.G. The problems of flexibility, fluency and speed-accuracy trade-off in skilled behavior. Psychological Review, 1982, 89(5), pp.483-506.

MacKay, D.G. A theory of the representation and enactment of intentions with applications to the problems of creativity, motor equivalence, speech errors, and automaticity in skilled behavior, pp.217-230. In R. Magill (Ed.). Memory and control in motor behavior. Amsterdam: North Holland, 1983.

Norman, D.A. & Rumelhart, D.E. Studies of typing from the LNR research group, p.45-66. In W.E. Cooper (Ed.) Cognitive aspects of skilled typewriting. New York: Springer-Verlag, 1983.

Norman, D. Categorization of action slips. Psychological Review, 1981, 88(1) pp.1-15.

Reason, J.T. Actions not as planned. In G. Underwood & R. Stevens (Eds.) Aspects of consciousness. London: Academic Press, 1979.

Robinson, G.M. & Solomon, D.J. Rhythm is processed by the speech hemisphere. Journal of Experimental Psychology, 1975, 102, pp.108-511.

Roy, E.A. Action and performance. In Ellis, A. (Ed.) Normality and pathology in cognitive function. London: Academic Press, 1982.

Schank, R.C. & Abelson, R.P. Scripts, plans, goals and understanding: an inquiry into human knowledge structures. Hillsdale, N.J.: Erlbaum, 1977.

Schmidt, R. Motor control and learning. Champaign, Ill.: Human Kinetics, 1982.

Selz, O. The revision of the fundamental conceptions of intellectual processes. In J.M. Mandler & G. Mandler (Eds.) Thinking: From association to gestalt. New York: Wiley, 1927, 1964.

Smith, L.E. Individual differences in strength, reaction latency, mass and length of limbs, and their relation to maximal speed of movement. Research Quarterly, 1969, 32(2) pp.208-20.

Welford, A.T. (1968). Fundamentals of skill. London: Methuen, 1982.

Wickelgren, W. <u>Cognitive</u> <u>Psychology</u>. Englewood Cliffs, N.J.: Prentice Hall, 1979.

Neuropsychological Studies of Apraxia
and Related Disorders, E.A. Roy (ed.)
© Elsevier Science Publishers B.V. (North-Holland), 1985

PERFORMANCE DIFFERENCES BETWEEN THE HANDS:

IMPLICATIONS FOR STUDYING DISRUPTION TO LIMB PRAXIS

John I. Todor and Ann L. Smiley

University of Michigan

The basis of manual asymmetries in motor performance is examined. On selected tasks it is possible to
identify the task demands that maximize observed hand
differences. Identifying the aspect of the movement
most responsible for hand differences provides a frame
of reference from which to contrast experiments that
use similar but not identical tasks. The nature of normal
hand differences should provide some foundation from
which to view disruptions to limb praxis. The merits of
using experimental paradigms that manipulate motor
task parameters as is done in some research into manual
asymmetries should be useful in the study of apraxia.

Although superior dexterity of the right hand for most individuals is overwhelm-
ingly evident, greater motoric capabilities of the right hand are not observed on all
tasks. If one does not consider left handed subjects, there are a variety of motor
tasks on which little or no hand differences are evident (Provins, 1956; Simon, 1964)
and some on which the non-preferred is clearly superior (Benton, Varney & Hamsher,
1978; Maxwell, Note 1; Roy & MacKenzie, 1978). Furthermore, on certain tasks,
slight variations in the conditions of performance may result in varying degrees of
hand differences (Flowers, 1974; Kimura & Davidson, 1975; Todor, Kyprie & Price,
1982; Roy, 1983).

This chapter addresses the issue of hand differences in motoric ability from two
perspectives. The first section focuses on identifying the task variables that underlie the observation of hand differences in performance. Little attempt is made to
review the wide scope of tasks on which hand differences have been investigated.
Rather, subsections are devoted to an indepth analysis of two types of motor tasks
on which hand differences have been systematically studied. In both paradigms,
through manipulation of task variables, the nature of task demands that maximize
the difference between the hands has been identified.

The second section is concerned with why hand differences exist. In one subsection, the relationship between hand differences in performance and cerebral specialization of function is assessed. This evaluation is seriously hampered by the fact
that the revelant studies rely on different assumptions and models of cerebral specialization. An effort is made to articulate and evaluate the assumptions underlying
the various studies, especially as they relate to handedness. In the other subsection,
the extent to which differential use of the hands accounts for hand differences in
manual proficiency is examined. In the summary, implications for the study of disruption of limb praxis are drawn.

Throughout the chapter a view of the typical right-handed subject is presented. As has been documented in a variety of sources, left-handed subjects are more heterogenous as a group (Herron, 1980; Satz, Levy & Reid, 1978; Achenbach & Fennel, 1967). While most of the points raised in this paper would apply to the opposite hands of some left-handers, for others the relative dexterity of the hands is less clear (Doane & Todor, 1978; Levy & Reid, 1978; Parlow & Kinsbourne, 1981; Todor, 1980).

Hand Differences in Manual Proficiency

Rapid Aimed Movements

In 1899 Woodworth observed that in rapid aimed movements the speed and/or accuracy of the non-preferred hand is inferior. However, in simple movements the requirement of speed or accuracy has not always been sufficient to produce significant hand differences (Provins & Glencross, 1968). Rather, in certain tasks, preferred hand superiority only became evident, or more pronounced, when the accuracy demands of rapid movements were increased (Flowers, 1975; Sheridan, 1973). Further, by increasing this dimension of task difficulty the observed hand differences became more stable or reliable (Steingruber, 1975; Todor & Doane, 1977).

These observations have led to the proposition that the preferred hand is superior in using feedback to effect the necessary error corrections to attain the required accuracy (Annett & Sheridan, 1973; Doane & Todor, 1978; Flowers, 1975; Todor & Doane, 1978). Extensive analysis of rapid aimed movements has provided considerable support for the above interpretation of hand differences.

According to Fitts (1954), manipulation of the movement accuracy or movement amplitude influences the information transmission requirements of the task. Fitts found that movement time could be predicted from the following formula which has become known as Fitts' Law:

$$MT = a + b \log2 \, (2A/W)$$

where A is the movement amplitude, W is the width of the target, and a and b are empirically defined constants. Based on this formulation the index of Difficulty (ID) of a movement could be defined by the equation:

$$ID = \log2 \, (2A/W).$$

Keele (1968) and Crossman and Goodeve (1963) proposed a discrete visual feedback explanation for Fitts' Law. Rapid aimed movements toward a target were viewed as consisting of an initial propulsion which contains some error, and subsequently, as many corrective movements as were necessary for the target to be contacted. Since each of these corrections was thought to require a fixed amount of time, either increasing movement amplitude or decreasing target width would necessitate additional error correction and thus increase movement time.

Recent studies have found only one correction in movements towards a target (Carlton, 1981; Langolf, Chaffin & Foulke, 1976), prompting Keele (1981) to modify his multiple correction position. Keele now sees the Howarth, Beggs and Bowden (1971) model as a plausible alternative. Accordingly, when more accuracy is desired, the subject will increase movement time to cover more distance before engaging in error correction. It is assumed that the increased movement time is used to bring the hand closer to the target before the correction, leading to less final error.

In contrast to the multiple error correction model, Annett, Golby and Kay (1958) found two distinct phases to the movement, a rapid movement bringing the hand close to the target followed by a slow terminal phase. Increases in movement time with increases in Fitts' ID seemed to occur in the terminal phase where feedback control is presumed to operate. Recently, Carlton (1979) used considerably higher film speed than Annett et al. (1958). His analysis confirmed and extended their findings. Decreasing the target width failed to modify the initial movement impulse but dramatically increased the deceleration phase of the movement. Further, only one clear corrective movement was observed and it occurred during the latter phase.

Generally, the initial movement propulsion has been viewed as being "ballistic" or preprogrammed and thus unaffected by feedback (Welford, 1971). Perhaps the most convincing evidence of this comes from analysis of electromyographical activity (EMG) during the movement (Hallett, Shahani & Young, 1975; Wadman, Denier, Geuze & Mol, 1979). The EMG activity of rapid aimed movements was found to consist of three temporally separate bursts: first, a burst of activity in the agonists, next a burst of activity in the antagonist, followed by a second burst in the agonist. The agonist-antagonist phasing appeared time locked as it was unmodified by the introduction of movement perturbations. These authors found adjustments to the perturbation to occur only during the second burst of agonist activity. Others have found that increasing the resistance to the movement can result in increased EMG amplitude of the latter phase of the initial agonist firing (Brown & Cooke, 1981; Lee, Lucier & White, 1981). However, the speed of these adaptations suggests they are the result of spinal monosynaptic reflexes that would not be operating in an unconstrained movement involving visual guidance.

Recently Todor and Cisneros (Note 2) replicated and extended the findings of Annett et al. (1958) and Carlton (1979). These experiments systematically contrasted the right and left hands' performance of a rapid aimed movement and the manner by which they accommodated to increased accuracy demands.

In both experiments the subject's task was to move a stylus as rapidly as posible over a fixed distance to a target. The starting plate was positioned laterally to the ear directly above the shoulder joint. The target was fixed along the sagittal plane directly in front of the shoulder. The starting position and target were horizontally aligned at eye level. When the stylus was in the starting position its forward tip and the target could both be in the subject's visual field. The required movement could be accomplished by extending the arm with minimal lateral movement. An accelerometer was mounted near the rear tip of the stylus in an orientation to be maximally sensitive to forward acceleration.

For each trial, the following parameters were derived from the accelerometer trace and target contact:

MT - total movement time
T1 - time to peak positive acceleration
T2 - time from T1 to acceleration reversal
T3 - time from T2 to peak deceleration
T4 - time from T3 to target contact
PA - peak positive acceleration
PD - peak deceleration

In experiment 1 accuracy demands were manipulated by varying the target size. As Fitts' Law predicts, decreasing the target size systematically increased the average movement time. In concert with previous findings the left hand was influenced to a greater extent than the right by decreasing the target size (Flowers, 1975; Sheridan, 1973).

Analysis of within movement components was generally supportive of the two phase pattern, an initial rapid movement followed by a slower terminal phase, described by Annett et al. (1958). However, subjects apparently oscillated between two distinct variants of this pattern across trials which, unless considered, would have confounded contrasts of the within movement patterns used by the hands.

The two movement patterns were distinguished principally by differences in the temporal occurrence of PD, that is, where the greatest deceleration in the overall movement occurred. The most frequent pattern was similar to that described by Annett et al. (1958) and Carlton (1979). Peak deceleration occurred shortly after the limb began decelerating from the initial propulsion. In this pattern ample time would have been available for at least one error correction while the limb was moving at a relatively slow velocity. In contrast, in the other pattern, on the average, peak deceleration occurred within 5 msec of target contact, precluding and subsequent visually guided corrective movements. Since the two patterns did not differ in the initial propulsive phase, if any corrective movements were made earlier than PD in the second pattern, they would have had to occur while the limb was at a high average velocity.

Consistent with the contention that an early PD would permit more effective error correction and thus accuracy, the incidence of early-PD trials increased significantly as the target size decreased. Apparently, this shift in useage of the early-PD movement pattern reflected a general accommodation to the task as there were no significant differences between the hands in the frequency either pattern was used at any target size.

Early-PD was the predominant movement pattern. This was especially evident when the target size was smallest and the observed hand difference was largest. Here it was used on 85% or more of the trials. Therefore, subsequent analysis of quantitative and qualitative differences between the hands used only trials exhibiting an early-PD patterns. Further analysis of only the late-PD trials was not possible since not all subjects exhibited this movement pattern in all conditions.

Increasing the accuracy demands by decreasing the target size resulted in the systematic lengthening of movement time predicted by Fitts' Law. For both hands, 80% of this increase in MT occurred after PD in the T4 phase, i.e., in the period preceding target contact. The left hand took significantly longer in this latter phase regardless of target size. Additionally, a significant hand-by-target size interaction indicated that the left hand was disproportionally affected by decreasing target size. Previous research has indicated that error correction occurs only in this phase, and in this experiment, this is where adjustments to increased accuracy demands predominated. Thus, it is reasonable to conclude that after the initial propulsion towards the target the left hand typically requires a more substantial corrective movement, which takes more time, and/or the time needed to effect error corrections takes longer when executed by the left hand. Unlike previous studies (Annett et al., 1958; Carlton, 1979), less pronounced but systematic adjustments were observed in the early "distance covering" phase. The initial propulsive phase did not vary with target size for the right hand but as the target size decreased the peak deceleration value was less and it occurred later. The net effect of these changes was the maintenance of a higher average velocity for a longer period of time, thus the hand was moved closer to the target before the terminal phase began. It should be noted that while this would presumably make error correction easier to accomplish, dramatic increases in the latency of the final movement phase were still observed.

The accommodation to smaller targets by the left hand differed in several ways which would have resulted in it being even closer to the target before reaching peak deceleration and beginning the final phase of movement where error corrections are presumed. While the left hand's peak acceleration value did not vary across conditions, as the target size decreased it was reached earlier. Additionally, in movements to the smallest target, the left hand's peak deceleration was less pronounced and occurred later than the right hand's. Although it was closer to the target in the plane of the movement, the left hand still required more time than the right in the terminal movement phase.

In spite of exhibiting more pronounced adjustments in accommodation to increased accuracy demands, the left hand had a higher proportion of target misses. This coupled with longer movement times would argue that the observed hand differences could not be attributed to a different speed-accuracy trade-off function being employed by the left hand.

In a second experiment, Todor and Cisneros (Note 2) held the target distance and target size constant and had subjects perform at maximum speed while maintaining either a 20% or 0% error rate. For both hands the movement time increased as the error criterion became more stringent. In both conditions the left hand was slower than the right.

Similar to the manipulation of target size, approximately 80% of the increase in total movement time for either hand occurred in the terminal movement phase. Also, the left hand was markedly slower in this phase, a hand difference which became more pronounced in the 0% error condition.

As with the first experiment, increasing the accuracy demands by reducing the error rate also affected earlier components of the movement. In accommodation to a more stringent error rate, the hands followed a similar pattern. Peak acceleration was not modified but both hands reached this value sooner and the hands accelerated longer. These changes coupled with a decrease in the peak deceleration value would indicate that the hands covered proportionally more distance in the 0% error condition before beginning the terminal phase of the movement. This accommodation was more extreme in the left hand as was the increase in the terminal phase latency.

Previous studies had inferred hand differences in error correction from the observation of a hand-by-target size interaction for overall movement time (Flowers, 1975; Sheridan, 1973). More recently, Annett, Annett, Hudson and Turner (1979) directly observed more corrective movements by the left hand in the terminal phase of a peg shifting task. While consistent with the data reported by Todor and Cisneros (Note 2), there are reasons to question their interpretation. Their data were derived from film recorded at relatively slow speeds with the consequence that the error in detecting events within a movement would have been substantial. Additionally, the hands exhibited markedly different error rates in their study.

In interpreting their data, they refer to the motor output variability model proposed by Schmidt and coworkers (1979). Annett et al (1979) argued that more corrections by the left hand indicated it was inherently more variable in its motor output. Yet, in a peg shifting task this higher error rate could reflect that the hands were predisposed to approach the task in different ways. The task instructions emphasized placing the pegs as rapidly as possible, but did not apparently emphasize direct placement of the peg into the hole. Two grossly different strategies may have been employed. One where a "ballistic" distance covering phase was followed by corrective movements attempting to place the peg directly into the hole. Alternatively, the ballistic or preprogrammed movement phase could, by design, have moved the peg into contact with the board containing the hole, with subsequent corrective movements placing the peg into the hole. Preferential adoption of the latter strategy by the left hand would have resulted in fewer "holes-in-one" and a higher average number of corrective movements as Annett et al. (1979) found. Todor and Doane (1978) found the left hand performed a Fitts type reciprocal tapping task more rapidly when the parameters of movement at a given ID favoured greater distance rather than a narrower target. Hence, in a task like peg shifting, one might expect the left hand to opt for a strategy that optimizes its perforamnce capabilities.

It is argued here that the Schmidt et al. (1979) motor output variability model employed as a post hoc explanation by Annett et al. (1979) does not apply to the slower movements in their experiment or those reported by Todor and Cisneros (Note 2). The model postulates that the output of the muscular system contains noise which leads to variability and this variability determines trial-to-trial variations in terminal accuracy. Accordingly, the variability of a response is directly related to the amount of force which is produced. Increases in movement amplitude or decreases in movement time require a greater force which leads to greater output variability and more errors. Thus, in order to comply with greater accuracy demands, the initial force must be decreased which would lead to longer movement times and less variability.

Unlike the more rapid preprogrammed movements (<200 msec.) investigated by Schmidt et al., the slower movements studied by Todor and Cisneros (Note 2) and Annett et al. (1979) appear to have two distinct phases: a preprogrammed distance-covering phase followed by a phase where homing-in utilizes feedback to make target contact. According to Todor and Cisneros (Note 2), when greater precision is required, the distance-covering phase is modified to bring the hand closer to the target before homing-in occurs. While adjustments occur in both phases, they are most pronounced in the latter. This pattern is in opposition to predictions based on the motor output variability model which would expect a decrease in initial force, and thus velocity, when striving for greater accuracy.

In experiment 1 of the Todor and Cisneros study, the left hand exhibited a higher error rate, a finding which could reflect greater inherent variability in motor output. In experiment 2, movements of maximum speed were obtained while complying with a 20% or 0% error rate. In this experiment, hand differences existed only in the deceleration phase of the movement. Further, a hand-by-error criterion interaction was evident only for the last phase, the interval between peak deceleration and target contact. Since corrective movements have been observed only in this portion of the movement, the primary difference between the hands apparently lies in the speed or efficiency with which they can effect these error corrections. One could argue that the left hand's early propulsive phase may typically produce greater positional error and thus require more time in the terminal phase for correction. However, in experiment 2 the target size and distance were constant and only the error rate was modified. There is no reason to expect the error rate criterion to affect the accuracy of the initial propulsion, yet there was a hand-by-error criterion interaction.

Thus, the rate or efficiency with which corrective movements are effected constituted the major differences between the hands. As a consequence, under certain task conditions the slow error corrective capability of the left hand may force it into a compensatory movement pattern sooner than the right hand. This was observed in experiment 1. If there are hand differences in motor output variability, the data presented by Todor and Cisneros argue that differences in error correction are a major contributor to this variability.

Rapid Finger Tapping

Right hand superiority in the speed of rapid index finger tapping has been frequently observed and is expected in the normal subject (Reitan & Davison, 1974). Accordingly, if there is not approximately a 10% difference between the hands, in favour of the right hand, the empirical data leads one to consider a compromise to the integrity of the motor area contralateral to the hand not conforming to the expection. This prediction is strengthened if performance drops below a critical level empirically associated with brain damage. In this case the integrity of portions of the motor system critical to execution of contralateral control are implicated (Kimura, 1979). However, it is most likely that the underlying cause of normal hand differences are the consequence of planning that precedes this stage of execution.

A number of recent studies have directly addressed the nature of hand differences in rapid finger tapping. The most common meaasure of tapping ability is a global rate variable such as taps per unit time. However, hand differences in the rate of rapid finger tapping are not uniformly evident in all phases of the movement. Todor and Kyprie (1980) report that the shorter average inter-tap interval (ITI) exhibited by the right hand in tapping a Morse code key over a range of 3 mm is attributable to less time being spent in key closure. This movement component most reflects the transition from finger flexion to extension. Peters (1980) has found that the directional reversal phase but not the excursion from up-to-down or down-to-up produce hand differences. Reduction of the finger excursion from 13 mm to about 5 mm increased the average ITI of the left hand but not the right. Apparently the observed hand difference increases under the narrower excursion condition because proportionally more time of each tap is spent in the movement reversal phase.

Peters (1980) has suggested that hand differences are potentially due to lateral differences in force modulation. Accordingly, when the excursion distance is restricted "... in order to maintain performance, much greater subtlety of force modulation is required ..." (p. 67). In a similar vein, Todor and Kyprie (1980) noted that the left hand was both more forceful and variable in the force used to depress the tapping key. At the time they suggested that this erratic application of force may reflect an inability of the left hand to systematically and appropriately terminate the motor out flow necessary to depress the key in each tap.

A recent study by Todor, Smiley and Price (Note 3) directly measured the force exerted during finger tapping and further developed the notion that the hands differ in their force modulation. The index finger was strapped to the tapping key so strain gauges mounted on the key would signal force in both a downward and upward direction. As in their previous study the right hand exhibited a shorter average ITI and dwell (key closure phase) but no hand differences were evident in the slack component of each tap (i.e. the up-down and down-up phase excluding the time in key closure). Tapping by the left hand involved more key depression force and a significantly larger range of force within each tap. Not only did the left hand press the key harder in the down position, but in the up phase the key came close to a zero force level (i.e. the resting or starting position of the key) or moved into negative force implying the key was pulled above the starting position.

Because the right hand minimizes force exertion in both directions one would expect its transit time from either end point to be less than the left hand's. Yet in this experiment the right and left hand slack times, the time between successive periods of depressions, were not different. It should be noted that in addition to reflecting the up and down movement times this measurement contained the time to reverse from extension to flexion. Since the hand differences in the key depression phase were highly significant it was suggested that a lower average peak positive force reflected a more efficient and systematically timed transition from one movement direction to the other. Apparently, the right hand was more adept at establishing the minimum force needed to make key closures and effectively making the directional reversals around this force level. This is not to imply that sensory feedback was used to regulate movement reversals since the transition time in the 70 msec range is below the minimal time estimated for the use of peripheral feedback. Further, while force was the dependent measure in this study it is not necessarily the parameter that a central program utilizes.

Another point that indicates the right hand is more effective in making the directional reversals is the observation of lower variance for ITI and dwell (Peters, 1976, 1980; Peters & Durding, 1978, 1979; Todor & Kyprie, 1980; Todor, Kyprie & Price, 1982). This consistency, especially in the dwell, supports the earlier contention that the right hand more effectively sets a reference interval around which directional transitions are made. Additionally, the left hand exhibited greater variance across taps in the peak force exerted in a downward or upward direction (Todor et al., Note 3), further supporting its failure to execute postural transitions with similar parameters. Todor et al. (Note 3) also found that occassionally the force exerted was insufficient to produce key closure or that there was an insufficient release of force to allow key opening. This resulted in two force peaks within a dwell phase. Both events resulted in increased variance of ITI and dwell. Across subjects the occurrence of these failures to comply with the external task demands did not differ between the hands.

These findings appear to support the contention of Annett et al. (1979) that the motor output of the left hand is inherently more variable. Identifying the task conditions under which this variable output is manifest may help uncover the nature of this variability and possibly identify fundamental processes that differentiate the hands.

Several studies have demonstrated that the left hand is equally capable of regular tapping if external pacing is provided (Brodie, Note 4; Wolff, Hurwitz & Moss, 1977). Brodie trained subjects to tap to a tone of a set frequency. Once subjects successfully matched the specified frequency of tapping the tone was turned off and tapping was to continue at this rate. In general, there were no hand differences in the ability to match the desired frequency, or in the within-tap components. That is, unlike rapid unpaced tapping, the hands did not differ in mean ITI or dwell. The exception occurred at the fastest frequency (200 msec between taps) where, as with rapid unpaced tapping, the left hand had a longer dwell time and a greater dwell variance. At slower tapping frequencies there were no hand differences in the variance of any measures. While the hands differed in the force exerted, it was the left hand and not the right that exerted the least force per tap.

The results of Brodie's study suggest that hand differences in rapid finger tapping are associated with the ability to regulate the tapping sequence. It is conceivable that the training tone assisted the left hand in establishing a parameter around which to set up successive directional reversals. Apparently, increased regularity of the interval between taps also reduces the variability of within-tap components such as the dwell and peak force. This implies that, unaided, the left hand is less adept in establishing an effective framework around which to regulate successive directional reversals.

In summary, by manipulating task parameters, it is possible to identify the nature of the task demands that maximize the performance difference between the hands on two distinct types of tasks. On tasks involving rapid aimed movements, slow enough to permit visual guidance, hand differences increased as accuracy demands became greater. It appears that both hands utilize the same general performance pattern, a ballistic distance covering phase, followed by a slower terminal phase where visually based error correction occurs. It is this latter phase that accounts for the major portion of the hand differences. Thus, it appears that the left hand is slower because it either requires more corrective movements or is slower in executing each error correction. It is not possible to definitively choose between these alternatives at this time, and it is conceivable that both contribute to the observed behaviour. However, data clearly implicate the latter in that manipulation of the error rate while keeping the movement parameters constant results in a markedly greater duration of the terminal phase for the left hand. There is no reason to expect the positional error to vary after the ballistic component when only accuracy rate has been varied. Thus, the left hand must be less efficient in planning and/or executing error corrective movements.

Accommodation to increased precision demands observed in the earlier phase of the movement were qualitatively similar for the two hands. These accommodations occurred in the left hand's performance under less stringent accuracy demands. Further, when accuracy demands caused both hands to accommodate, the adjustments were more pronounced in the left hand. It is likely that the left hand's less efficient error corrective capabilities force compensatory pattern adjustments under less stringent accuracy conditions or require it to make the adjustments more pronounced.

In rapid single finger tapping, hand differences are greatest in the phase of the tap cycle requiring postural transitions. Further, if the range of motion is decreased, increasing the relative contribution of the directional reversal phase to the total tap, the hand differences in overall tapping rate become more pronounced. The left hand appears to be less capable of rapidly carrying out this process because it is more variable in setting a point around which to begin directional reversals.

A second dimension of rapid finger tapping that differentiates the hands appears to be the ability to sequence successive taps. Certainly, this may not be totally independent of the ability to efficiently make directional reversals. Performance after training to an external pacing signal can eliminate hand difference seen in the unpaced condition. However, when the training frequency is rapid, hand differences similar to unpaced conditions are evident. The rate limiting factor seems to be the ability to rapidly make the directional reversal.

Although direct parallels between the two tasks have not been demonstrated, on both tasks hand differences are maximized when components of the task require rapid sequential processing to adjust the movement trajectory.

Why are the Hands Different?

Hand Differences and Cerebral Lateralization

The "split-brain" studies conducted by Sperry and colleagues in the 1960's (Gazzaniga, Bogen & Sperry, 1967; Sperry, 1974) convincingly demonstrated that the two cerebral hemispheres function differently. As a consequence a large number of studies, using both normal and clinical populations, have addressed the nature of this cerebral specialization of function. At present the various models that have been proposed appear to have a limited scope of explanatory power (Allen, 1983). As such, they are usually applicable only to data from a particular experimental paradigm. It is now clear that simple dichotomous models ascribing behaviours to the left and right hemispheres are oversimplications (eg., verbal/visual-spatial ability or sequential/parallel processing modes). It is apparent that predicting lateralized behaviours requires consideration of the processing predisposition or strength of a given hemisphere along with a host of other variables such as: prior or current attention to a particular type of material (Kinsbourne, 1973); relative task complexity (Rizzolatti, Bertoloni & Buchtel, 1979); relative task demands for resources of the two hemispheres (Allen, 1983; Friedman & Polson, 1981; Hellige & Longstreth, 1981); temporal constraints of the task (Peters, 1977).

The following sections will attempt to evaluate the relationship between hand differences in performance and cerebral specialization of function. Three distinct approaches will be taken. In the first section the bases of the assumption that the hands are controlled by the contralateral hemisphere is reviewed. The second section will focus on studies evaluating the effect of performing a motor task concurrently with a task expected to be lateralized to one or the other hemisphere. In the third section tasks on which the left hand is superior are reviewed.

The Structural Bases of Manual Asymmetries

Associations between hand differences in proficiency and hemisphere specializations of function rest heavily on the assumption that the hands are controlled by the contralateral cerebral hemisphere. This position is so well accepted that most studies addressing the above association implicitly or explicitly present contralateral control as "fact" without reference to supportive data. In deference to the work of Kuypers and colleagues (Brinkman & Kuypers, 1973; Kuypers, 1981), it is sometimes acknowledged that exclusive contralateral control may be restricted to movements of the distal portions of limbs. However, as Kuypers (1984) has demonstrated substantial control of the limbs exists in the absence of crossed cortico-spinal pathways. Thus, illumination of the relationship between the functional specialization of the hemispheres and the relative dexterity of the hands requires a less restrictive view.

Kuypers (1981) has described four descending systems of motor control. The brief description prescribed here is intended to highlight key factors which may help illuminate the nature of hand differences and their potential association to cerebral lateralization.

The corticospinal fibres provide the primary basis for the assumption of contralateral control. In descending from the motor cortex the majority of these fibres cross in the medulla to the opposite side of the spinal cord. A small minority apparently descend to segmental levels before crossing to the opposite side of the cord via interneurons. While these fibres end on motor neurons which innervate muscles in the distal portions of the limbs, it is also clear that they innervate proximal muscles as well (Kuypers, 1981). The majority of these fibres innervate motor neurons through interneurons which have collaterals to many motor neurons. A more limited number of cortical motorneuronal fibres exist which directly innervate finger muscles and provide the basis of independent movement of the fingers.

These direct corticomotoneuronal fibres are not present at birth and take 8-12 months to develop in the monkey, paralleling the emergence of differentiated finger movements (Lawrence and Hopkins, 1976). Given the slower maturations rate typically seen in humans the time period for their development may extend well into the first year. The functional capacity of these fibres apparently cannot be subserved by other descending pathways since lesions of the corticospinal tract in the newborn prevents their development.

While little is known about the factors that influence the development of these fibres it is intriguing to consider the implication of a form-function interaction such as that described by Peters (1983). He argues that an early attentional bias promoted by the asymmetrical tonic neck reflex could lead to differential hand use. As a consequence, maturation of neuromuscular systems receiving the most use are facilitated providing a structural foundation for hand differences. In this regard, it is interesting to note that Cress, Taylor, Allen and Holden (1963) found faster maximum nerve conduction velocities of the ulnar and median nerves on the right side of right handed adults. Conversely, left-handed subjects exhibited faster conduction velocities on the left side.

A second crossed descending motor pathway, the rubrospinal tract, originates in the red nucleus. With sectioning of the corticospinal fibres the capacity for differentiated finger movements is lost but the hand as a unit can still be effectively used for grasping. This is apparently carried out via the rubrospinal tract since if it is also sectioned the capacity is severely restricted.

The reticulospinal and vestibulospinal pathways descend ipsilaterally in the spinal cord with fibres projecting bilaterally at segmental levels. These pathways are critically involved in the control of proximal and axial muscles, but characteristically provide poor control of the hands. In experimental animals with other pathways sectioned, attempts at grasping involve the whole limb and appear to be mediated by muscles of the elbow and shoulder. It should be noted that proximal limb muscles do receive corticospinal innervation as well. It is likely that when contralateral control is advantageous, these fibres are involved (Di Stefano, Morelli, Marzi & Berlucchi, 1980; Todor et al., 1982).

Recently, Kuypers (1981, 1984) discovered brainstem pathways that descend ipsilaterally from the subcoeruleo or the raphe nucleus and directly innervate motor neurons of distal muscles. At this time it appears that these pathways do not directly participate in the control of movements. Rather, they apparently modulate the excitability of these motor neurons they innervate. Since they have collaterals which project to multiple levels of the spinal cord they may alter the responsiveness of the motor system. Kuypers (1984) has suggested that these pathways may underlie the increased responsiveness of spinal reflexes when a person engages in the Jendrassik maneouver (i.e. clasping the hands and forcefully pulling).

Given our current level of understanding it is hard to know what involvement these brainstem pathways might have in the manifestation of hand differences. If these pathways contribute to a potentiation of motor neurons that persists after exertion, they may influence the assessment of hand differences. For example, Todor and Lazarus (in press) have found that the order of hand use can amplify or obscure lateral asymmetries in motor overflow. In their study subjects were required to squeeze at various percentages of their maximal force with one hand while the extent of a co-contraction (motor overflow) was measured in the other hand. Motor overflow was measured in both hands with the order of hand use being counterbalanced across the subjects. More motor overflow was observed in both hands if they had previously been active than if it was measured in that hand first. As a consequence, lateral asymmetries in the amount of overflow varied with the order of hand use.

Yakovlev and Rakic (1966) evaluated the course of descending corticospinal fibres in one hundred medullae oblongata of fetal and neonate brains. They found that in 87% decussating bundles of the left pyramid, coming from the left hemisphere, were larger and crossed the midsaggital plane first, i.e. at a higher level than the decussating bundles of the right pyramid. Similarly, Kertesz and Geschwind (1971) found this pattern in 73% of their adult subjects. Although the functional significance of this pattern of crossing is not obvious, it is noteworthy that 13 to 27% of the cases showed an anomalous pattern. Through the use of retrospective questionnaires to relatives, Kertesz and Geschwind established that 17% or more of their anomalous patterns belonged to subjects who had been right handed.

In evaluating the pattern of decussation Yakovlev and Rakic (1966) found that typically the majority of fibres that crossed in the medulla descended laterally in the cord. A smaller number of fibres remained uncrossed and descended medially. These medially descending fibres likely correspond to the corticospinal fibres Kuypers found to cross at segmental levels. Notably, Kuypers found the medially descending fibres to innervate motor neurons of more proximal muscles and the laterally descending fibres to innervate motor neurons of more distal muscles. Remarkably, approximately 33% of the samples did not exhibit the above pattern. Since this is far above the percentage of non-right-handers observed in the normal population, one must entertain the possibility that individual differences exist in the organization of the descending motor system. Thus, one needs to acknowledge that anomalous organization might account for unexpected performance by individual cases.

An additional observation of Yakovlev and Rakic (1966) warrants mention. At a cervical level, they found that the right side of the spinal cord received more pyramidal tract fibres from both cerebral hemispheres. A greater percentage of fibres originating in the left hemisphere crossed over to the right side than crossed from the right hemisphere to the left side of the cord. Further, more fibres from the right hemisphere descended directly into the right side of the cord than on the left side. Since the ipsilaterally descending fibres may cross at segmental levels these findings do not necessarily mean that the right side of the body received more corticospinal innervation. They do, however, indicate a systematic lateral asymmetry of a structural nature.

Cerebral Specialization as a Bases of Manual Dexterity

Assumptions of Dual-Task Paradigms. Dual task paradigms designed to illuminate the relationship between cerebral specialization of function and the manifestation of hand differences in motor performance usually rely on one or more of the following assumptions: (1) If two tasks, requiring functions carried out by the same hemisphere are performed concurrently, interference or facilitation will occur (Kinsbourne & Cook, 1970). An extension of this assumption is the expectation that as the degree of functional overlap within the hemisphere increases, the interference or facilitation will increase (Kinsbourne & Hicks, 1978); (b) A given task may require the co-operative involvement of unique competencies of each hemisphere. Thus, depending on the demands of the concurrent tasks, the two hemispheres may be differentially involved and interference might be unilateral, bilateral, or bilateral but asymmetrical (Allen, 1983; Friedman & Polson, 1981; Hellige & Longstreth, 1981); (c) In most right handers verbalization involves primarily the left cerebral hemisphere (Kimura, 1973).

Several points which are less frequently explicitly addressed but of critical importance warrrant mention. These points are directed at the assumption that the manual activity of each hand is programmed primarily or exclusively by the contralateral cerebral hemisphere. As discussed in the previous section, this assumption requires some qualifications. In addition to considering the functional role of the various descending pathways, it should be noted that preceding a unimanual movement using crossed corticospinal pathways, movement planning may have occurred bilaterally. This movement planning would have involved cortical areas such as the supplemental motor areas, frontal association areas, premotor area and subcortical structures such as the basal ganglia and the cerebellum. Although the motor outflow may be more or less restricted to the motor area of a given hemisphere, it may reflect the converging influence of other intra- and inter-hemispheric structures.

When lateralized cerebral lesions disrupt motor function, the primary deficit is observed in the contralateral limbs (the issue of bilateral decrements occurring due to left hemispheric lesions will be discussed in a separate section). While this reflects the contralaterally descending nature of the corticospinal pathways, it does not explain the robust differences in manual proficiency that the hands exhibit.

In "split-brain" patients, surgical sectioning of the corpus callosum isolates cortical involvement in movement control of distal portions of the limb to the contralateral hemisphere. Kreuter, Kinsbourne and Trevarthen (1972) examined one such patient who was able to simultaneously speak and repetitively tap the left index finger but could not maintain the tapping with the right index finger while speaking. Apparently, concurrent verbalization, a left hemispheric function, disrupted the motor control of the right hand. Conversely, the left hand was not affected, implying that the right hemisphere was capable of unilaterally directing the repetitive finger tapping of the left hand. Examination of "split-brain" drawings (Gazzaniga, 1967) indicates the deficiencies are greatest for competencies frequently attributed to the hemisphere disconnected from the drawing hand. That is, the right hand's drawings of three dimensional objects are strikingly lacking in their spatial configuration. In contrast, the left hand, though effectively representing the spatial aspects of the object, exhibits inferior control over the steadiness of the lines. Conceivably, the latter is attributable to the greater fine motor control normally associated with the right hand. Clearly, a normal individual is able to draw a three dimensional object with his right hand, indicating that planning of movements may draw on the resources of both hemispheres.

In 1971, Kinsbourne and Cook proposed that dual-task performance will decrease proportionally to the extent that the central programs controlling the two tasks compete for the resources of the same hemisphere. In their study, unilateral dowel balancing with the index finger while simultaneously speaking reduced the performance of the right hand but increased the performance of the left hand. Since verbal ability has been lateralized to the left hemisphere, the following inferences have been drawn. First, the right hand decrement occurred because speaking and the motor control of the right hand competed for similar processing capacities of the left hemisphere. Secondly, since the left hand performance was not interferred with, it was apparently controlled by the uninvolved right hemisphere. The enhancement of left hand performance has been difficult to replicate and will not be discussed further.

Investigations designed to replicate and extend these findings generally failed to find a simple unilateral decrement in right hand performance due to concurrent speech. The typical finding, regardless of the nature of the concurrent task, has been to observe a bilateral decrement in motor performance. In some studies the overall magnitude of the decline has been equal in the two hands (Beaton, 1979; Bowers, Heilman, Satz & Altman, 1978; Summers & Sharp, 1979). Others have found a bilateral but asymmetrical decrement. When the concurrent cognitive task involved verbal ability the right hand decrement exceeded that of the left (Bowers et al., 1978; Hicks, Provenzani & Rubstein, 1975; Thornton & Peters, 1982). Conversely, if the concurrent cognitive task required functions assumed to be lateralized to the right hemisphere, the decrement in manual performance was generally bilateral but more pronounced in the left hand (Beaton, 1979; Hellige & Longstreth, 1981).

The fact that bilateral decrements occur seriously challenges the assumption that the hands are programmed and controlled primarily or exclusively by the contralateral hemisphere. The nature of the concurrent tasks employed in these and other studies indicates that to understand the relationship between cerebral specialization and the relative dexterity of the hands, one must consider the following factors: the difficulty of the concurrent tasks; the extent to which the tasks require co-operative use of functions uniquely lateralized to each of the hemispheres; the nature of the tasks or procedures which may dictate which hemisphere gains or assumes control for processing the tasks; and left hemispheric involvement in the control of both hands. There is the potential that a finite processing capacity exists and the demands of the concurrent tasks exceed this limit (Kahneman, 1973). Since this factor does not directly relate to the relationship between hemispheric specialization and handedness it will not be discussed further.

The Difficulty of the Concurrent Tasks. In an earlier section it was argued that hand differences become more pronounced and stable if the demands for precision or accuracy of the movement were increased. Ostensibly, this increase in hand difference occurs because the right hand is superior at executing the necessary error corrections. A number of investigators have argued that these visually guided error-corrections are performed more effectively by the right hand because they involve rapid sequential information processing, a function for which the left cerebral hemisphere is apparently superior (Todor & Doane, 1978). In a similar vein it was argued that hand differences in repetitive single finger tapping were more pronounced if the range of motion was restricted to emphasize the directional reversals or if the dependent measure more directly reflected this component. Additionally, hand differences were evident in the variability with which the force modulation or timing of the directional reversals were made. As with the rapid aimed movements a common processing factor seemed to be the effectiveness with which the sequence of events could be carried out without external assistance.

The position taken above shares with Kimura (Kimura, 1979; Lomas & Kimura, 1976) the proposition that a relationship exists between the movement sequencing ability of the left hemisphere and manifest differences between the hands. However, there are critical points where the positions differ. Kimura suggests that concurrent speaking and sequential movements of the right hand are mutually interfering because both involve regulation of non-visually guided postural transitions. Accordingly, "the term 'sequence of movement' implies that the task does not consist merely in the repetition of the same discrete movement over and over, as in single finger tapping" (Lomas & Kimura, 1976, p. 31).

Support for this position was derived from their finding of only unilateral right hand decrements in multiple key tapping involving the arm or multiple fingers concurrently with speaking. In contrast, when the motor task involved repetitive single finger tapping, concurrent speech caused bilateral decrements.

Subsequent investigations have demonstrated that concurrent speaking and single finger tapping result in bilateral but asymmetrically greater decrements in the right hand (Hellige & Longstreth, 1981; Hiscock & Kinsbourne, 1978, 1980; Summers & Sharp, 1979). Thus, there is reason to question the validity of Kimura and Lomas's definition of movement sequence for which the left hemisphere is uniquely specialized.

As discussed earlier, rapid finger tapping rate is not the dependent measure that maximally differentiates the performance of the hands. As Peters (1980) demonstrated, when a greater range of motion was involved in the tapping task, hand differences in rate were reduced. This introduces the possibility that in dual-task paradigms, task factors could overshadow lateralized differences.

Peters (1980) and Todor (Todor & Kyprie, 1980; Todor, Smiley & Price, Note 3) have argued that single finger tapping involves both delicately timed postural transitions and sequencing of motor acts and that it is these functions that maximally differentiate the hands. Recently, Brodie (Note 4) used measurement techniques designed to assess such aspects of single finger tapping during performance of a variety of concurrent tasks.

The dependent measures Brodie derived from her repetitive single finger tapping task were modelled closely after those obtained by Todor and colleagues (Todor & Kyprie, 1980; Todor, et al., Note 3). This included the mean and within subject variance of the following variables:

Inter-tap Interval	time between successive key closures
Dwell	duration of each key depression
Slack	time between successive key depressions (ITI minus dwell)
Maximum Force	peak force exerted during the key depression phase

Unlike most previous dual-task studies involving repetitive single finger tapping, Brodie's subjects were not instructed to tap as rapidly as possible. Rather, in an effort to equalize the initial performance of the hands, subjects were trained to tap at several different fixed frequencies using a procedure described by Wing (1977, 1980). Consistent with the findings of Wolff et al. (1977), assessment of performance after the training tone was turned off indicated the right hand advantage was eliminated. The exception to this was the observation that the left hand exhibited a greater dwell mean and variance at the fastest tapping frequency. Since this was evident in two separate experiments, it may imply that at the fastest rate the left hand was not capable of effectively using the synchronization tone to facilitate making rapid and consistent directional reversals. There was some indication that the left hand benefitted from the training tone more than the right hand. In control conditions (single task), in three separate experiments, the mean force exerted by the left hand was significantly less than that of the right hand. This is in direct contrast to observations made in rapid single finger tapping (Todor et al., Note 3).

The purpose of the training was to equalize the hands' performance before attempting to observe the effects of concurrent tasks. This technique should have reduced the potential that the dual-task findings could be associated with the hands experiencing different relative degrees of difficulty in performing the task. However, it is conceivable that the training lessens the task demands for functions that produce the interference observed with some concurrent tasks.

Brodie (Note 4) assessed single finger tapping after the training tone was turned off, alone and concurrently with each of the following four tasks:

READ   reading a short paragraph with a post-tapping test for retention.

GEO   examine a complex geometric figure during tapping with a post-tapping matching test.

PRAX   a rapidly executed repeated sequence of the fingers (thumb, middle, little, index, ring).

FLEX   slow single finger flexion at the second joint of one of the fingers on the non-tapping hand.

Of the two cognitive tasks, READ, a verbal task, was expected to selectively disrupt left hemispheric functions and GEO, a spatial task, to interfer with functions of the right hemisphere (Lezak, 1976). Similarly, the motor tasks were expected to cause lateralized interference in different hemispheres. Rizzolatti et al. (1979) found that performance of the PRAX task caused visual half field reaction times to increase bilaterally but to a significantly greater degree when stimuli were projected to the left hemisphere. This occurred regardless of which hand performed the PRAX task. Conversely, the FLEX task has been found to differentially raise lateralized reaction times in the right hemisphere (Anzola, Pulimeno, & Rizzolatti, 1980). Consistent with differential involvement of the right hemisphere in performance of the FLEX task, Kimura and Vanderwolf (1970) found the left hand to be superior to the right on this task.

Brodie (1984) found only a slight bilateral decrement in tapping due to concurrently performing READ or GEO. The fact that previous studies (Hellige & Longstreth, 1981) found a marked bilateral but asymmetrical decrement in unpaced single finger tapping suggests that the training reduced the functional overlap. If this speculation is true, it would imply that the sequential nature of repetitive finger tapping has two relatively distinct components, one regulating individual directional reversals and the other co-ordinating the timing of successive taps.

Concurrently performing the PRAX task while tapping resulted in a significant slowing of the overall tapping rate (ITI) and the directional reversal phase (dwell), in both combinations of tasks and hands. This slowing was not unexpected as both tasks are believed to involve the left hemisphere to some extent. The mean dwell was, however, found to increase to a greater extent in the right hands' tapping. This asymmetry is likely associated with differential left hemisphere demands in the two conditions. Rizzolatti et al. (1979) found the left hand had a more difficult time executing the PRAX task and this resulted in a greater right visual field reaction time than when the right hand performed the PRAX task. Thus, it is conceivable that in the RH-tap/LH-PRAX condition, there is greater concurrent demand for overlapping left hemispheric functions, namely the regulation of directional reversals in the right hand and the PRAX task sequence in the left hand.

A similar pattern of disruptions was observed in the variance of ITI and dwell. Left hemispheric involvement in two motor tasks likely required time sharing which detracted attention from tapping at irregular points in the tapping cycle. As with the increase in mean dwell, a greater increase in right hand dwell variance was likely associated with the greater difficulty experienced by the left hand in performing the PRAX task.

The peak force of tapping increased above control levels when concurrently performing the PRAX task. This supports the position that superior left hemispheric regulation of force contributes to the hand differences seen in unpaced rapid tapping (Peters, 1980; Todor & Kyprie, 1980; Todor et al., Note 3). Failure to find an asymmetrical increase in the peak tapping force of the right hand may indicate that force modulation and regulation of the tap to tap cycle are related. In this experiment the training appeared to differentially aid the force modulation of the left hand.

Concurrent performance of the FLEX task also significantly interfered with the tapping of both hands. When asymmetries were present greater decrements were noted in the left hand's tapping. As with the PRAX task, the dwell component of tapping proved to be most susceptible to interference. The bilateral increase in dwell observed during FLEX was slight in comparison to that observed with PRAX possibly because the FLEX is a less demanding task. The bilateral effect is not unexpected since previous research has indicated FLEX and tapping differentially involve the two hemispheres.

Both task combinations involve both hemispheres. In the RH-FLEX/LH-tap combination, the FLEX task involves the right hemisphere for more abstract planning but translation to motor code would likely involve the left premotor area and be executed through the left side motor area. In the PRAX condition, tapping by the left hand apparently requires some left hemispheric involvement but would also involve translation to motor code and execution by the right hemisphere. Thus both tasks may involve both hemispheres, potentiating some interference. Accordingly, in the LH-FLEX/RH-tap combination, the FLEX task would be planned and executed primarily by the right hemisphere but, as Anzola, Pulimeno & Rizzolatti (1980) found, there is the potential for left hemispheric involvement at least under dual-task conditions. Right hand tapping would be expected to be more lateralized to the left hemisphere for both planning and execution. Dual-task decrements in performance would then, be expected to occur because of some bilateral control of the FLEX task. Thus, the greater potential for interference in the RH-FLEX/LH-tap condition would be expected to have more pronounced effect on tapping.

The fact that mean dwell and dwell variance were found to increase with FLEX task more when the left hand tapped may be associated with bilateral involvement in both tasks in this condition. If the left hand differentially benefitted from the training, i.e. reduced its need for left hemispheric function, the magnitude of the asymmetry may be less with unpaced tapping.

It is apparent that the same variables that maximally discriminate the hands in unpaced single finger tapping are the most susceptible to interference by a concurrent task with overlapping lateralized demands (Brodie, Note 4; Peters, 1980; Todor et al., Note 3). In contrast, the inter-tap interval (or taps/unit time), the more global measure of rate, which also usually differentiates the hands, was equally affected in the two hands. Brodie's paradigm failed to elicit performance decrements in tapping due to concurrent reading. Thus, one cannot completely dismiss Kimura's contention that as single finger tapping involves only sequencing repetitive positions, it is not susceptible to interference. It is, however, very conceivable that global measures of overall tapping rate used by Lomas and Kimura (1976) obscured or confounded measurement of the underlying lateralized function.

Selecting motor tasks that are highly practiced also reduces the potential of observing dual-task effects (Bahrick & Shelley, 1958). Unless considered, this may lead to misleading conclusions regarding the relationship between cerebral specialization and the relative manual proficiency of the hands. This effect was clearly demonstrated by Rizzolatti et al. (1979). In contrast to their novel finger sequence (the PRAX task used by Brodie, Note 4), a repetitive sequence involving the same digits in more natural order (little, ring, middle, index, thumb) failed to produce lateralized decrements. Furthermore, when this automated sequence was performed concurrently with a lateralized simple reaction time, there was only a small increase regardless of visual field. While statistically significant this increase was only a small fraction of the bilateral and asymmetrical increase caused by the novel PRAX task.

Kimura and Lomas (Kimura, 1979; Lomas & Kimura, 1976; Lomas, 1980) have argued that the decrement in manual performance observed during concurrent verbalization occurs because of the competition between the sequencing demands of the manual task and those required in the motor production of speech. Furthermore, Lomas (1980) suggests that lateralized intrahemispheric competition cannot be simply attributed to competition between two activities controlled by the same hemisphere. In his view, lateralized interference has not been demonstrated with right hemispheric tasks and "the failure to produce clearly lateralized right hand interference on visually guided and certain nonvisually performed motor tasks suggests it is possibly unique to competition between control systems for speaking and a control system for non-visually guided limb movements." (Lomas, 1980, p. 147). Recent studies indicate that while motor production of speech does interfere with concurrent manual activities the generalizations regarding intrahemispheric interference are too sweeping.

A number of studies have now convincingly demonstrated lateralized interference on concurrent motor tasks using nonverbal tasks. While it is true that with the one exception (Smith, Chu & Edmonston, 1977), the effects have not been strictly unimanual, they cannot be ignored. Anzola et al. (1980) found the finger flexion task, pioneered by Kimura as a right hemispheric function (Kimura & Vanderwolf, 1970), caused a bilateral but asymmetrical lengthening in simple lateralized reaction time. It was apparent from their study that the right hemisphere was differentially involved in the execution of the flexion task. Similarly, Brodie (Note 4) found this finger flexion task to cause significantly greater disruption of left hand finger tapping, especially the phases reflecting the postural transition. As discussed earlier the bilateral interference is not unexpected if one considers the potential for interhemispheric involvement in tasks.

Hellige and Longstreth (1981) have convincingly shown interhemispheric involvement in the control of one task. Additionally, they systematically demonstrate that cognitive-motor interference occurs independent of the motor production of speech. Further they found concurrent non-verbal right hemispheric tasks produced a greater decrement in left hand performance, a decrease that cannot be totally attributable to the motor component of the task.

In their first experiment rapid single-finger tapping was assessed during concurrent reading either silently or aloud. One half of the sample was instructed to pay close attention to the content of the material read because they would be given a post test. To control for asymmetries in the rate of finger tapping, the reduction in performance was expressed relative to the baseline rate for each hand.

In all conditions the right hand reduction in tapping rate was greater than that observed for the left hand. Consistent with Hicks et al. (1975) they found that overt speech was not necessary to cause a lateralized interference. Reading aloud did, however, result in a more marked decrement in performance indicating that the lateralized interference due to the cognitive and speech-motor aspects of reading are to some extent dissociable. This position gained additional support from the finding of greater interference and hand differences when verbal material was subsequently tested, that is, knowledge of the verbal material was stressed.

In an effort to extend their finding that some interference in manual activity could be caused by cognitive processing they assessed the impact of a concurrent right hemispheric task on rapid finger tapping. They reasoned that prior efforts to demonstrate such an effect may have produced bilateral decrements because the visual-spatial tasks required verbal answers. Since they had demonstrated that overt verbalization disproportionally interfered with the right hand motor activity, bilateral decrement may have occurred. To test this position, they had subjects concurrently perform a known right hemispheric task (Bogen & Gazzaniga, 1965; Galin & Ornstein, 1972; Nebes, 1978), the block design subtest of the WISC-R. To establish the extent to which tapping decrements were a function of a motor-motor interference, in one condition subjects merely manipulated the blocks without reference to their visual characteristics.

In all concurrent conditions tapping rate decreased bilaterally but to a greater extent in the left hand. The asymmetrically greater left hand decrements in tapping rate during the block design condition were essentially twice that of the motor only condition. This clearly indicates that intrahemispheric interference occurred at a cognitive or planning level as well as in simultaneous motor execution. Considering both experiments of Hellige and Longstreth, it is clear that decrements due to concurrent intrahemispheric processing can be demonstrated in either hemisphere.

Bilateral Involvement in Unimanual Tasks

> Because lateralized manual interference effects depend on which cerebral hemisphere is more involved in the concurrent activity, such effects should be a useful converging operation for the study of cerebral hemisphere asymmetry. However, because the interference is determined by a variety of motor and cognitive factors, considerable care must be exercised in design and interpretation of such studies. For example, suppose that the concurrent task required visuospatial processing for which the right cerebral hemisphere is specialized, but also required periodic verbal responses (McFarland & Ashton, 1975, 1978). The present results suggests that the visuospatial processing would tend to be more disruptive of left-hand movements while programming verbal output would be more disruptive of right hand movements. Consequently, it would be difficult to predict or to interpret lateralized motor interference in such a situation. (Hellige & Longstreth, 1981; p. 403)

While the main effect of the Hellige and Longstreth study provides the most direct support for this position, they provide other evidence as well. In their study the manipulation of the blocks with any cognitive demand resulted in a greater tapping decrement for the left hand. They offer two plausible explanations. One, block manipulation involved sufficient spatial processing to differentially involve the right hemisphere. Both activities, placing blocks or rotating blocks, had minimal sequential demands but did require spatial or positional monitoring. Secondly, they suggest that right handers might attend more to right hand movements when performing simultaneous but different manual tasks. As a consequence the left hand performance would suffer.

Beaton (1979) has provided data in line with the Hellige and Longstreth position that both hemispheres may be involved in certain tasks. It should be noted that the interpretation of this study given here differs from Beaton's own.

Beaton had subjects perform a lateralized digit detection task simultaneously with a bimanual sorting task. Each hand engaged in different and separate sorting tasks. One task involved sorting nuts and bolts into separate bins. The second involved sorting two sizes of nuts into bins. The latter nut sorting task was apparently more difficult and determined the rate of bimanual sorting.

When the right hand engaged in the difficult nut-nut sorting, visual input to either hemisphere produced the same magnitude of decrement. When the left hand was performing the difficult sorting, visual digit detection by the right hemisphere, but not the left, impaired manual performance. In line with Hellige and Longstreth's position one might argue that left hand performance suffered when the visual detection occurred in the right hemisphere because of concurrent demands on this hemisphere. Right hand sorting required both hemispheres, the left hemisphere for motor control, the right hemisphere for the tactile-spatial processing. As a consequence of the perceptual-motor nature of the sorting task, lateralized visual detection by either hemisphere would disrupt the rate of sorting.

A similar interpretation of some counterintuitive findings has been posited by Summers and Sharp (1979). Subjects performed three different manual tasks concurrently with a verbal or a visuospatial task. Their bimanual sequencing task involved moving the fingers in a sequence dictated by the ordered onset of eight lights. Movements alternately involved fingers of the right and left hands. They assumed that the lead hand determind which hemisphere was in control (this issue will be discussed in a later section). Subjects performed trials with each hand leading the sequence. The unimanual sequencing was the same as the bimanual except that movements were performed by one hand only. The third motor task was repetitive single finger tapping.

Concurrent verbalization resulted in a generalized decrement, that is, it was independent of lead hand in the bimanual sequencing and affected both hands equally during unimanual sequencing. In contrast, only the right hand was affected by verbalization during single finger tapping. They felt this provided some support for Kimura's (1979) position that the left hemisphere controls "sequences of movement" of both hands but not repetitive tapping. However, similar effects were observed when the concurrent task was of a visuospatial nature, findings that a left hemispheric sequencer alone could not explain. Furthermore, the lateralized decrement caused by the visuospatial task was observed in the right hand conditions not the left as would be expected from right side intrahemispheric competition.

Summers and Sharp (1979) suggested that the spatial task, recalling locations of dots on a grid, was amenable to verbal mediation which would have involved the left hemisphere and accounted for the decrements in the right hand lead and the unimanual right hand movement sequence. Similar left hand decrements were observed because, in spite of possible verbal mediation, the task still involved the right hemisphere.

In an alternative but not necessarily mutually exclusive argument they suggest that movement sequences such as their bimanual and unimanual task are controlled by both hemispheres. Accordingly, the movement sequencing involves two components, ordering the movements into a sequence (left hemisphere) and positioning the fingers in space (right hemisphere). As a consequence concurrent verbalization affected left hemispheric ordering and spatial rehearsal affected the spatial positioning component of the manual sequencing task. Thus, bilateral decrements in performance occurred.

The contention that multiple finger movements to different positions involves both hemispheres might account for the difference between visually and nonvisually guided movement sequences observed by Lomas (1980) and Thornton and Peters (1982). In both studies movement sequencing was performed more rapidly under visual control than without vision. Presumably, the need to rely on an internalized spatial position system increases the overall task difficulty leading to a decrease in performance time.

Hemispheric Priming or Attentional Allocation. A number of theorists have proposed that "... a cerebral hemisphere may be primed, that is aroused or activated prior to presentation of the information to be processed, and that this primed hemisphere then assumes control of the processing" (p. 88, Allen, 1983). Kinsbourne (1970) and Moscovitch (1979) indicate that priming may occur because of a subject's expectancies about the task as well as the prior or ongoing activity of the hemisphere itself. While the effects of priming on cognitive tasks have been given some attention, little consideration has been given to its impact on relative manual proficiency.

There are, however, a number of studies which suggest hemispheric priming or attentional allocation can markedly affect manual proficiency. Several studies have demonstrated superior performance of a bimanual sequencing task when the right hand initiates the sequence (McGlone, Note 5; Hicks et al., 1975; Summers & Sharp, 1979). These results were viewed as being consistent with Oldfield's (1969) position that the preferred hand is superior at leading or initiating a sequence, while the nonpreferred hand is better at following or supporting the movements of the preferred hand.

Peters (1981a) has amplified this position by demonstrating that bimanual performance was markedly affected by varying which hand was required to perform the task demanding the most attention. Additionally, this interaction between hand and task was further affected by which hand initiates or begins the movements (Peters, 1983).

Recently, Todor et al. (Note 3) found that prior activity by one hand may influence subsequent unimanual performance by the other. In rapid single finger tapping rate variables that differentiate the hands were affected by the order of hand use. When performance was assessed in the right hand before the left the expected asymmetries in intertap interval and dwell were highly evident. However, in the left-right order of hand use, the magnitude of the superiority of the right hand decreased or was nonexistent. In this experiment, three consecutive trials were administered to each hand before switching. The effect of order of hand use persisted across all three trials of the second hand used.

Although it is not clear how these priming or attention factors are mediated, it is evident that they could markedly influence the magnitude and possible direction of relative manual dexterity observed. Certainly, a clear understanding of cerebral specialization and its relationship between handedness must account for these effects.

Left Hemisphere Involvement in the Control of Both Hands. A frequently made observation is that unilateral left hemisphere lesions lead to ipsilateral as well as contralateral deficits in limb praxis, whereas right hemisphere lesions are typically followed by only contralateral motor deficits (Haaland, Cleeland & Carr, 1977; Heilman, Schwartz & Geschwind, 1975; Kimura & Archibald, 1974; Liepmann, 1913; Roy, 1981; Vaughan & Costa, 1962; Wyke, 1966, 1967, 1968, 1971). A common element to the tasks showing bilateral decrements due to left hemisphere damage appears to be the need for sequencing of movements.

Kimura (1977, 1979) has argued that the essence of the unique left hemisphere function is not sequencing per se, but rather the ability to internally guide movements to new postures. She states:

> The evidence suggests that the left hemisphere contains a system for
> accurate internal representation of moving body parts, important for

the control of changes in the position of both oral and brachial articulators. Once a position is achieved, however, it can apparently be run
off repetitively without further intervention from this system. The
function controlling accurate positioning of limb and oral articulatory
musculature has been labelled "praxis", from the widely used term for
its disruption "apraxia". The praxis function appears to be dissociable
from another function not selectively mediated by the left hemisphere,
which involves fine finger control and which may depend critically on
somatosensory feedback. (Kimura, 1979; p. 197).

Two issues are of concern here: (1) the extent to which this left hemisphee
function is manifest in the motor performance of normal subjects, especially as it
may impact on the observation of hand differences; and (2) the extent to which the
left hemisphere may be involved in the motor control of both hands in tasks outside
the scope of Kimura's praxis system.

In 1890, Welch observed that if one hand was engaged in a sustained isometric
contraction and the other performed a rhythmic squeezing action, the latter pattern
became evident in the action of the first. Further, when the left hand performed
the rhythmical action it showed up in the isometric action of the right hand to a
greater extent than when the roles were reversed. Although Welch indicated practice reduced the effect, the amount of practice and the extent of reduction was not
specified. It is conceivable that the observed asymmetrical influence occurs
because the left hemisphere is involved in sequencing the repetitive action of the
left hand as well as the sustained contraction of the right hand.

Alternately, this effect may not involve the sequencing attributes of the left
hemisphere, but rather lateral asymmetries in motor overflow. In this phenomenon,
unilateral voluntary contraction may result in an involuntary co-contraction of additional muscle groups, occurring most frequently and most forcefully in the contralateral homologous muscles (Todor & Lazarus, in press). As with Welch's bimanual
act, greatest overflow is usually seen when the left hand is performing the voluntary
activity. The extent to which this effect is associated with an asymmetrical structural coupling between the limbs or is a consequence of differential use, remains to
be established.

Wang (1980) has also found evidence of an interaction between the performance
of the limbs. In his study, when the hands attempted to simultaneously draw different figures, the left hand tended to be more strongly influenced by the right than
the reverse. The direction of influence is opposite to that trend seen in motor overflow studies and may reflect a natural coupling between the phasing of bimanual
acts (Peters, 1977).

Is the Left Hand Ever Superior to the Right?

This section addresses an often ignored aspect of the assumption that hand differences in performance reflect the functional specialization of the contralateral
and controlling hemisphere. This assumption implies that one should be able to
demonstrate that the typically less proficient left hand is superior on tasks that differentially involve right hemispheric functions, or, one should be able to account for
the inability to observe such behaviour.

Early studies explored pressure sensitivity differences between the two sides of
the body. Findings indictated that the left hand, especially the thumb, had a lower
threshold for tactile stimulation than the right hand (Semmes, Weinstein, Ghent &

Teuber, 1960). An alternative to hemispheric specialization was reduced sensitivity of the right hand due to calluses from greater use. Later studies (Ghent, 1961; Weinstein & Sersen, 1961) indicated that left side body parts where differential use was not a variable, such as the inner arm and sole of the foot, were also more sensitive than the right sided counterpart.

Tasks where tactile stimuli are matched to visual stimuli (Benton, Levin & Varney, 1973) and tactile stimuli are matched to tactile stimuli (Harriman & Castell, 1979; Benton, Varney & Hamsher, 1978) add further evidence to a perceptual superiority for the left hand. The stimuli used in these studies included Braille symbols and perception of the orientation of steel rods. In addition, the learning rate of matching two dimensional shapes with letters or numbers was faster using the left hand (Hatta, 1978).

It appears that spatial complexity of the task may be an important variable for the demonstration of laterality differences. Young and Ellis (1979) found the hands were equally capable of tactile dot detection when the dots were presented in an orderly and predictable pattern. However, a left hand advantage was evident in a task where the dots were arranged in a complex, unpredictable spatial pattern. Myers (1976) found no hand differences in counting groups of Braille dots, but this may have been the result of a spatially more simple and predictable arrangement of dots.

Perception of limb location and reproduction of that location has also been studied. Roy and MacKenzie (1978) required subjects to move either arms or thumbs to a stop, return to the beginning position, and then repeat the movement without the stop in place. The task was performed bimanually without visual guidance. If, as Roy and MacKenzie postulate, a bimanual task reduces interhemispheric communication, then performance of the contralaterally controlled thumbs would reflect a right hemispheric superiority. This position was supported as the left thumb showed greater accuracy than the right and was significantly less variable. In contrast, the proximal muscles controlling the arms are innervated by bilaterally descending pathways. As a consequence, both arms would have had access to the right hemisphere which could explain why no arm differences were observed.

The previous studies utilized motor tasks that have a high demand for perceptual acuity. However, tasks with a greater emphasis on a manipulo-spatial dimension also show a left hand superiority (LeDoux, Wilson & Gazzaniga, 1977). Split-brain patients were asked to perform several tasks: replicating block designs, cube drawing, matching of wire figures, and identifying geometric designs from manipulation of fragments of each design. In all cases, the left hand's performance was superior to the right. However, when the same tasks were presented without the manipulative component, i.e., the correct response was made via visual matching, there were no hand differences.

Maxwell (Note 1) has presented data from normal children that are supportive of the manipulo-spatial competencies LeDoux assigns to the right hemisphere. He used a rapid line drawing task which one might expect to show a right hand superiority. However, when the manipulo-spatial capabilities were emphasized, the left hand was superior. The task was a modified version of the Trail Making Test (Reitan & Davison, 1974). Children were directed to draw a continuous line tracing the path of a succession of rabbits facing the direction of the next jump. The rate at which this task could be performed was significantly faster by the left hand.

The Influence of Differential Hand Use

Frequently, research by Provins (1956, 1958; Provins & Glencross, 1968) is cited to support the position that differential practice can account for hand differences. However, a close examination of these studies indicates that this factor alone is insufficient.

In one study, finger tapping ability was compared to toe tapping with the rationale that finger tapping might be influenced by differential practice, but toe tapping would not be (Provins, 1956). Therefore, the finding of no differences between the right and left big toes was viewed as support for the role of differential practice. However, the findings of Gardner (1941) are contradictory as he found an asymmetry in foot tapping.

Provins also supports his position by comparing the dart throwing ability of women and men. While there was no asymmetry of skill between women's hands, the men had a right hand superiority. He reasoned that, since the men said they had played more darts and therefore had more practice than women, differential practice resulted in their asymmetry.

In a second study, Provins (1958) looked more directly at practice effects on skill development. Previous studies had indicated that practice did not affect performance level in finger tapping (Ream, 1922; Wells, 1908). Provins found that practice did increase the rate and regularity of oscillation for both the arm and finger leading him to conclude that the average improvement of skill "is more than enough to account for the average difference recorded between sides under comparable conditions (p. 39)." He is inferring that if practice can improve skill level on one side, it can also adequately account for the difference in skill levels between the two sides. The actual learning curves of the two sides or relative performance of the two sides was not explicitly addressed or reported.

A third study (Provins & Glencross, 1968) examined the performance level of experienced and nonexperienced typists in several typing tasks and a writing task. Experienced typists exhibited either no hand differences or else a left hand advantage in the speed of typing. This was true for typing words and scrambled letters or simply tapping keys as rapidly as possible. In contrast, the inexperienced typists showed a right hand advantage on all tasks except typing of words, which showed a left hand advantage. The left hand advantage for experienced typists was attributed to a greater number of common English words being composed by keys found on the left hand side. Consequently, the left hand received more practice. In nontypists, however, general differential experience would favour the right hand and so a right hand advantage was expected. Why the nontypists had a left hand advantage for words is not explained. These results were placed in contrast to those from writing where, obviously, a clear asymmetry was found for all subjects. Provins and Glencross viewed these findings as supporting the position that differential practice created a lack of asymmetries in experienced typists and was responsible for the other asymmetries seen in other tasks.

Additional support for the role of differential practice was found in an experiment using a fine motor manipulative task, the Crawford Small Parts Dexterity Test (Perelle, Ehrman & Manowitz, 1981). A small pin was picked up with tweezers and placed in one of a number of holes. A ring was then picked up and placed over the pin. The dependent measure was time-to-placement of a complete set of pins and rings. The design was a pre- and post-test evaluation with 30 learning trials per hand over a six day period. While both hands decreased their time, the non-preferred hand improved more, thereby resulting in no post-training differences between the hands. In the control group, pre- and post-test differences were significant. While these studies indicate that differential practice can result in performance asymmetries, they fail to provide any rationale explaining why most subjects would select the right hand to begin with and thus lead to its differential use on so many tasks.

Other studies have shown that while practice improves performance of both hands, hand differences are maintained. Annett, Hudson and Turner (1974) had three subjects perform five trials per day for 26 consecutive days on a peg shifting task. Both hands decreased time to complete the task. However, in contrast to Perelle et al., even with a greater number of practice trials, the left hand did not equal the right hand's performance. Similarly, Peters (1981b) evaluated training on a finger tapping task to asymptote. In 13 of 14 subjects, the left hand never equalled the right hand's performance. As discussed in the first section of this paper, it is on tasks such as these that hand differences have been found to be repeatedly observed if the dependent measures are carefully selected.

Recently, Peters (1983) proposed a developmental explanation for manual asymmetries that accounts for greater use by the right hand. In essence, he hypothesized that an innate asymmetry like that observed in the asymmetrical tonic neck reflex, shifts attention disproportionally to the right side leading to greater use. When the infant neurological system is rapidly developing and is highly plastic, increased use on one side may result in structural differences. These structural differences and the learned skill served to perpetuate and reinforce the asymmetry.

Summary and Implications

The first section of this paper demonstrated that, on selected tasks at least, it is possible to identify the task demands that maximize the observation of hand differences. On the types of tasks analyzed it appears that the hands differ in their ability to carry out the sequential processes necessary in adjusting movement trajectories. The general strategy of evaluating and manipulating task demands is viewed as a positive step in identifying the underlying nature of handedness. Extension of this strategy to different classes of movements would be most productive.

Identifying the aspect of the movement most responsible for hand differences provides a frame of reference from which to contrast experiments that use similar but not identical tasks. If, for example, experiments with "similar" tasks produce conflicting evidence of hand differences, they may differ in the extent to which the respective tasks taxed a common critical process. For this reason it seems prudent, where possible, to manipulate the component of the motor task believed to differentiate the hands (e.g., by varying accuracy demands of an aiming task). If experiments had different versions of a type of task or were varied procedurally, the relative hand difference across manipulations would still permit confirmation that the manipulated variable did indeed underlie hand differences.

It is apparent that the observation of hand differences, or for that matter, failure to observe hand differences in performance, across tasks, may be attributed to a number of interacting factors. The relative contribution of these factors is expected to vary across tasks and performance conditions.

The functional specialization of the cerebral hemispheres is a prominent contributor to hand differences in performance. However, at this time no model of hemispheric specialization is able to adequately account for the influence a number of interacting variables exert on performance. For this reason it is difficult to clearly delineate the relationship between hand differences in manual proficiency and asymmetries in cerebral function. This chapter attempts to illustrate how a number of such intervening variables impact on the observed performance of the hands.

If hemispheric specialization of function contributes to the relative dexterity of the hands, one would expect tasks differentially demanding right hemispheric functions to be performed better by the left hand. While right handed individuals infrequently, if ever, notice left hand superiority, it can be demonstrated on carefully selected tasks. Typically, these tasks require considerable spatial or manipulospatial processing, but do not, to any great extent, involve rapid sequencing of movement elements. This suggests that the hands may be stressed by different aspects of complex tasks and that their performance might reflect dissimilar strategies.

The extent to which the hands have had varying levels of experience with tasks certainly can affect the observed performance. However, differential practice or experience cannot account for all hand differences. On simple motor tasks or more complex movements where one hand has had considerably more practice, an inherent hand difference may be obscured or appear to be reversed. Additionally, through practice both hands may become proficient and appear equal on global measures of performance, yet a more fine grained analysis may reveal that the hands accomplish the task via different means (Peters, 1976).

As a consequence of disproportional use, the right hand may have an apparent learning-to-learn advantage. This is not to say that learning-to-learn is necessarily lateralized. Rather, as Fleishman and Hempel (1954) and Hein (1968) point out, it is through experience that sensory-motor processes become differentiated and integrated. Therefore, by virtue of more refined sensory-motor integration, the right hand should more readily acquire new skill. As a result of this superior sensory-motor integration, comparison of the hands in normal subjects may be confounded because the right hand's control processes may be more automated. As a number of investigators have demonstrated, automated tasks are less susceptible to dual-task interference (Rizzolatti et al., 1979) and control may shift to subcortical structures. Similarly, as is evident in the assessment of certain types of apraxia, highly overlearned tasks are often less disrupted. Yet, this shifting of control due to learning is not explicitly acknowledged when contrasting the performance of subjects with unilateral lesions.

Wyke (1967) and Finlayson and Reitan (1980) have demonstrated that when comparing lateralized lesion groups, failure to control for normal proficiency differences between the hands can lead to misleading conclusions. Similarly, Hellige and Longstreth (1981) have argued that in studies with normal subjects it is important to control for baseline differences when evaluating the impact of an experimental manipulation on the performance of the hands. While such techniques appear highly desirable under certain conditions, some caution is warranted. Through pretest training, Brodie (Note 4) was able to equalize the performance of the hands on single finger tapping, but there is the strong possibility that her training regime eliminated a critical element of hand differences. If this is true, it creates a significant problem for interpreting the effect of experimental manipulations designed to illuminate lateralized functions.

The nature of normal hand differences should provide some foundation from which to view disruptions to limb praxis. Further, the merits of using experimental procedures that manipulate motor task parameters or identify sensitive dependent measures, should be evident. Applying similar process oriented procedures to clinical populations should contribute significantly to our understanding of movement dysfunction. The movement sequencing task used by Kimura (1977) and Roy (1981) provides a good example of experiments that begin to identify the nature of the underlying performance deficit. Kimura (1977) found that more frequent persevera-tive movements were made by patients with left hmeisphere damage. On this basis, she concluded that the left hemisphere is not important for control of movement sequencing per se, but rather plays a critical role in execution of postural tran-sitions. Roy (1981) used a more refined qualitative analysis and confirmed the pro-pensity of left-side lesion patients to perseverate, but he also found evidence of sequencing errors.

A potentially informative extension of these studies would be to determine if perseverations involved ineffectual efforts to change the movement or a failure to appropriately generate a change in the motor plan. The potential for making such a distinction was pointed out by Todor et al. (Note 3). In rapid single finger tapping, subjects occassionally had abnormally long durations between sucessive key closure. Similarly, they observed key closures with two force peaks, indicating an ineffectual attempt to release the key. In both cases, the breakdown in performance occurred because of an inability to comply with the external task demands rather than a fail-ure to initiate an action.

REFERENCE NOTES

1. Maxwell, J.K. A neuropsychological assessment of cerebral interhemispheric communication during early childhood. Unpublished doctoral dissertation, Carleton University, Ottawa, Canada, 1981.

2. Todor, J.I. & Cisneros, J. Accommodation to increased accuracy demands by the right and left hands. Paper presented at the meeting of the North American Society for the Psychology of Sport and Physical Activity, East Lansing, Michigan, May 1983.

3. Todor, J.I., Smiley, A.L. & Price, H.L. Force modulation as a source of hand differences in rapid finger tapping. Unpublished manuscript, University of Michigan, 1983.

4. Brodie, D.A. The neuropsychology of dual task performance: a motor behaviour analysis. Unpublished doctoral dissertation, University of Michigan, Ann Arbor, Michigan, 1984.

5. McGlone, J. Hand preference and the performance of sequential movements of the fingers by the left and right hands. Research Bulletin No. 153, University of Western Ontario, London, Ontario, Canada, 1970.

REFERENCES

Allen, M. Models of hemispheric specialization. Psychological Bulletin, 1983, 93, 73-104.

Annett, J., Annett, M., Hudson, P.T.W. & Turner, A. The control of movement in the preferred and non-preferred hands. Quarterly Journal of Experimental Psychology, 1979, 31, 641-652.

Annett, J., Golby, C.W. & Kay, H. The measurement of elements in an assembly task: the information output of the human motor system. Quarterly Journal of Experimental Psychology, 1958, 20, 1-11.

Annett, M., Hudson, P.T.W. & Turner, A. The reliability of differences between the hands in motor skill. Neuropsychologia, 1974, 12, 527-531.

Annett, J. & Sheridan, M.R. Effects of S-R and R-R compatibility on bimanual movement time. Journal of Experimental Psychology, 1973, 25, 47-52.

Anzola, G.P., Pulimeno, R. & Rizzolatti, G. Interserenza Selettiva di un Conpito Motorio Sui Tempi di Reazone a Stimoli Presentali Nell'emicampo Visivo di Sinistra. Societa Italiano di Biologia Sperimentale, 1980, 56(14), 1440-1444.

Bahrick, H.P. & Shelley, C. Time sharing as an index of automation. Journal of Experimental Psychology, 1958, 56, 288-293.

Beaton, A.A. Hemispheric function and dual task performance. Neuropsychologia, 1979, 17, 629-635.

Benton, A.L., Levin, H.S. & Varney, N.R. Tactile perception of direction in normal subjects. Neurology, 1973, 23, 1248-1250.

Benton, A.L., Varney, N.R. & Hamsher, K. Lateral differences in tactile directional perception. Neuropsychologia, 1978, 16, 109-114.

Bogen, J.E. & Gazzaniga, M.S. Cerebral commissurotomy in man: minor hemispheric dominance for certain visuo-spatial functions. Journal of Neurosurgery, 1965, 23, 394-399.

Bowers, D., Heilman, K., Satz, P. & Altman, A. Simultaneous performance on verbal, nonverbal, and motor tasks by right handed adults. Cortex, 1978, 14, 540-556.

Brinkman, J. & Kuypers, H. Cerebral control of contralateral and ipsilateral arm, hand, and fingers movements in the split-brain Rhesus monkey. Brain, 1973, 96, 653-674.

Brown, S.H. & Cooke, J.D. EMG response to force perturbations preceding accurate arm movements in humans. Neuroscience Abstracts, 1981, 7, 477.

Carlton, L.G. Control processes in the production of discrete aiming responses. Journal of Human Movement Studies, 1979, 5, 115-124.

Carlton, L.G. Processing visual feedback information for movement control. Journal of Experimental Psychology: Human Perception and Performance, 1981, 7, 1019-1030.

Cress, R.H., Taylor, L.S., Allen, B.T. & Holden, R.W. Normal motor nerve conduction velocities in the upper extremities and their relation to handedness. Archives of Physical Medicine, 1963, 44, 216-219.

Crossman, E.R.F.W. & Goodeve, P.J. Feedback control of hand movement and Fitts' law. Proceedings of the Experimental Society, Oxford, 1963.

Di Stefano, M. Morelli, M. Marzi, C.A. & Berlucchi, G. Hemispheric control of unilateral and bilateral movements of proximal and distal parts of the arms as inferred from simple reaction time to lateralized light stimuli in man. Experimental Brain Research, 1980, 38, 197-204.

Doane, T. & Todor, J.I. Motor ability as a function of handedness. In D.M. Lander and R.W. Christina (Eds.), Psychology of motor behaviour and sport, 1978.

Finlayson, M.A. & Reitan, R.M. Effect of lateralized lesions on ipsilateral and contralateral motor functioning. Journal of Clinical Neuropsychology, 1980, 2(2), 237-243.

Fitts, P.M. The information capacity of the human motor system controlling the amplitude of movements. Journal of Experimental Psychology, 1954, 47, 381-391.

Fleishman, E.A. & Hempel, W.E. Changes in factor structure of a complex psychomotor test as a function of practice. Psychometrica, 1954, 18, 239-252.

Flowers, K. Handedness and controlled movement. British Journal of Psychology, 1975, 66, 39-52.

Friedman, A. & Polson, M.C. Hemispheres and independent resource systems: limited capacity processing and cerebral specialization. Journal of Experimental Psychology: Human Perception and Performance, 1981, 7(5), 1031-1058.

Galin, D. & Ornstein, R. Lateral specialization of cognitive mode: an EEG study. Psychophysiology, 1972, 9, 412-418.

Gardner, L.P. Experimental data on the problem of motor lateral dominance in feet and hands. Psychological Record, 1941, 5, 1-63.

Gazzaniga, M. The split brain in man. Scientific American, 1967, 217, 24-29.

Gazzaniga, M.S., Bogen, J.E. & Sperry, R.W. Dyspraxia following diminish of the cerebral commissures. Archives of Neurology, 1967, 16, 606-612.

Ghent, L. Developmental changes in tactual thresholds on dominant and nondominant sides. Journal of Comparitive and Physiological Psychology, 1961, 54(6), 670-673.

Haaland, K.Y., Cleeland, C.S. & Carr, D. Motor performance after unilateral hemispheric damage in patients with tumor. Archives of Neurology, 1977, 34, 556-559.

Hallett, M., Shahani, B.T. & Young, R.A. EMG analysis of stereotyped voluntary movements in man. Journal of Neurology, Neurosurgery, and Psychiatry, 1975, 38, 1154-1161.

Harriman, J. & Castell, L. Manual asymmetry for tactile discrimination. Perceptual and Motor Skills, 1979, 48, 290.

Hatta, T. The functional asymmetry of tactile pattern learning in normal subjects. Psychologica, 1978, 21, 83-89.

Heilman, K.M., Schwartz, H.D. & Geschwind, N. Defective motor learning in ideomotor apraxia. Neurology, 1975, 25, 1018-1020.

Hein, A. Exposure history in spatial-motor development. In: Perceptual-motor foundations: a multiple disciplinary concern. Washington, D.C.: American Alliance for Health, Physical Education and Recreation, 1968.

Hellige, J.B. & Longstreth, L.E. Effects of concurrent hemisphere -- specific activity on unimanual tapping rate. Neuropsychologia, 1981, 19(3), 395-405.

Herron, J. Neuropsychology of left-handedness. New York: Academic Press, 1980.

Hicks, R.E., Provenzani, F.J. & Rubstein, E.D. Generalized and lateralized effects of concurrent verbal rehearsal upon performance of sequential movements of the fingers by the left and right hands. Acta Psychologia, 1975, 39, 119-130.

Hiscock, M. & Kinsbourne, M. Asymmetries of selective listening and attention switching in children. Developmental Psychology, 1980, 16(1), 70-82.

Hiscock, M. & Kinsbourne, M. Ontogeny of cerebral dominance: evidence from time-sharing asymmetry in children. Developmental Psychology, 1978, 14(4), 321-329.

Howarth, C.I., Beggs, W.D.A. & Bowden, J.M. The relationship between speed and accuracy of movements aimed at a target. Acta Psychologica, 1971, 35, 207-218.

Kahneman, D. Attention and effort. Englewood Cliffs, N.J.: Prentice Hall, Inc., 1973.

Keele, S.W. Movement control in skilled motor performance. Psychological Bulletin, 1968, 70, 387-403.

Keele, S.W. Behavioural analysis of movement. In V.E. Brooks (Ed.), Handbook of physiology; Sec. 1, The nervous system, Vol. 2: Motor control (part 2). American Psychological Society, 1981.

Kertesz, A. & Geschwind, N. Patterns of pyramidal decussation and their relationship to handedness. Archives of Neurology, 1971, 24, 326-332.

Kimura, D. The symmetry of the human brain. Scientific American, 1973, 228, 70-78.

Kimura, D. Acquisition of a motor skill after left hemisphere damage. Brain, 1977, 100(300), 527-542.

Kimura, D. Neuromotor mechanisms in the evolution of human communication. In H.D. Steklis & M.J. Raleigh (Eds.), Neurobiology of social communication in primates: An evolutionary perspective. New York: Academic Press, 1979.

Kimura, D. & Davison, W. Right arm superiority for tapping with distal and proximal joints. Journal of Human Movement Studies. 1975, 1, 199-202.

Kimura, D. & Archibald, Y. Motor functions of the left hemisphere. Brain, 1974, 97, 337-350.

Kimura, D. & Vanderwolf, C.H. The relation between hand preference and the performance of individual finger movements by left and right hands. Brain, 1970, 93, 769-774.

Kinsbourne, M. The cerebral basis of lateral asymmetries in attention. Acta Psychologica, 1970, 33, 193-201.

Kinsbourne, M. The control of attention by interaction between the cerebral hemispheres. In S. Kornblum (Ed.), Attention and performance IV.. New York: Academic Press, 1973.

Kinsbourne, M. & Cook, J. Generalized and lateralized effects of concurrent cognitive activity on a unimanual skill. Cortex, 1970, 11, 283-290.

Kinsbourne, M. & Hicks, R.E. Functional cerebral space: A model for overflow, transfer, and interference effects in human performance. In J. Requin (Ed.), Attention and performance VII. New York: Academic Press, 1978.

Kreuter, C., Kinsbourne, M. & Trevarthen, C. Are deconnected cerebral hemispheres independent channels? A preliminary study of the effect of unilateral loading on bilateral finger tapping. Neuropsychologia, 1972, 10, 453-461.

Kuypers, H.G.J.M. Anatomy of the descending pathways. In V.E. Brooks (Ed.), Handbook of physiology; Sec 1, The nervous system, Vol. 2: motor control (part 2). American Physiological Society, 1981.

Kuypers, H.G.J.M. Brain systems providing motor control. Paper presented at the International Neuropsychological Society, Houston, February 1984.

Langolf, G.D., Chaffin, D.B. & Foulke, J.A. An investigation of Fitts' Law using a wide range of movement amplitudes. Journal of Motor Behaviour, 1976, 8, 113-128.

Lawrence, D.G. & Hopkins, D.A. The development of motor control in the rhesus monkey: evidence concerning the role of corticomotoneuronal connections. Brain, 1976, 99, 235-254.

LeDoux, J.E., Wilson, D.H. & Gazzaniga, M.S. Manipulo-spatial aspects of cerebral lateralization: Clues to the origin of lateralization. Neuropsychologia, 1977, 15, 743-750.

Lee, R.G., Lucier, G.E. & White. Modification of motor output to compensate for unexpected load conditions during ballistic movements. Neuroscience Abstracts, 1981, 7, 477.

Levy, J. & Reid, M. Variations in cerebral organization as a function of handedness, hand posture in writing and sex. Journal of Experimental Psychology: General, 1978, 107, 103-104.

Lezak, M. Neuropsychological assessment. New York: Oxford University Press, 1976.

Liepmann, H. Motor aphasia, anarthia, and apraxia. Trans. 17th. Int. Congr. Med., London, Section XI, pt2, 1913, 97-106.

Lomas, J. Competition within the left hemisphere between speaking and unimanual tasks performed without visual guidance. Neuropsychologia, 1980, 18, 141-149.

Lomas, J. & Kimura, D. Intrahemispheric interaction between speaking and sequential manual activity. Neuropsychologia, 1976, 14, 23-33.

McFarland, K.A. & Ashton, R. The lateralized effects of concurrent cognitive activity on a unimanual skill. Cortex, 1975, 11, 283-290.

McFarland, K.A. & Ashton, R. The influence of brain lateralization of function on a manual skill. Cortex, 1978, 14, 102-111.

Moscovitch, M. Information processing and the cerebral hemispheres. In M. Gazzaniga (Ed.), Handbook of behavioural neurobiology (Vol. 2), neuropsychology. New York: Plenum Press, 1979.

Myers, D.H. Right and left handed counting of Braille dots in subjects unaccustomed to Braille. British Journal of Psychology, 1976, 67(3), 407-412.

Nebes, R.D. Direct examination of cognitive function in the right and left hemispheres. In M. Kinsbourne (Ed.), Asymmetrical function of the brain. London: Cambridge Press, 1978.

Oldfield, R.C. Handedness and musicians. British Journal of Psychology, 1969, 60, 91-99.

Parlow, S. & Kinsbourne, M. Handwriting posture and manual motor asymmetry in sinistrals. Neuropsychologia, 1981, 19, 687-696.

Peters, M. Prolonged practice of a simple motor task by preferred and non-preferred hands. Perceptual and Motor Skills, 1976, 43, 447-450.

Peters, M. Simultaneous performance of two motor activities. Neuropsychologia, 1977, 15, 461-465.

Peters, M. Why the preferred hand taps more quickly than the non-preferred hand: Three experiments on handedness. Canadian Journal of Psychology, 1980, 34(1), 62-71.

Peters, M. Attentional asymmetries during concurrent bimanual performance. Quarterly Journal of Experimental Psychology, 1981a, 33A, 95-103.

Peters, M. Handedness: effects of prolonged practice on between hand performance differences. Neuropsychologia, 1981b, 19, 587-590.

Peters, M. Differentiation and lateral specialization in motor development. In G. Young, S.J. Segalovitz, C.M. Carter & S.E. Trehub (Eds.) Manual specialization and the developing brain. New York: Academic Press, 1983.

Peters, M. & Durding, B.M. Handedness measured by finger tapping: A continuous variable. Canadian Journal of Psychology, 1978, 32(4), 257-261.

Peters, M. & Durding, B.M. Left-handers and right-handers compared on a motor task. Journal of Motor Behaviour, 1979, 11, 2.

Perelle, I.B., Ehrman, L. & Manowitz, J.W. Human handedness: The influence of learning. Perceptual and Motor Skills, 1981, 53, 967-977.

Provins, K.A. Handedness and skill. Quarterly Journal of Experimental Psychology, 1956, 8, 79-95.

Provins, K.A. The effect of training and handedness on the performance of two simple motor tasks. Quarterly Journal of Experimental Psychology, 1958, 10, 29-39.

Provins, K.A. & Glencross, D.J. Handwriting, typewriting and handedness. Quarterly Journal of Experimental Psychology, 1968, 20, 282-289.

Ream, M.J. The tapping test: A measure of motility. Psychological Monogram, 1922, 31, 293-319.

Reitan, R. & Davison, L. Clinical Neuropsychology: Current Status and Applications. Washington, D.C.: V.H. Winston & Sons, 1974.

Rizzolatti, G., Bertoloni, G. & Buchtel, H.A. Interference of concomitant motor and verbal tasks on simple reaction time: A hemispheric difference. Neuropsychologia, 1979, 17, 323-330.

Roy, E.A. & MacKenzie, C. Handedness effects in kinesthetic spatial location judgements. Cortex, 1978, 14, 250-258.

342   *J.I. Todor and A.L. Smiley*

Roy, E.A. Action sequencing and lateralized damage: Evidence for asymmetries in control. In J. Long & A. Baddeley (Eds.), Attention and performance IX. Hillsdale, N.J.: Lawrence Erlbaum Associates, 1981.

Roy, E.A. Manual performance asymmetries and motor control processes: Subject-generated changes and response parameters. Human Movement Science, 1983, 2, 271-277.

Satz, P., Achenbach, K. & Fennel, E. Correlations between assessed manual laterality and predicted speech laterality in a normal population. Neuropsychologia, 1967, 5, 292-310.

Schmidt, R.A., Zelaznik, H.N., Hawkins, B., Franks, J.S. & Quinn, J.T. Jr. Motor-output variability: A theory for the accuracy of rapid motor acts. Psychological Review, 1979, 86, 415-451.

Semmes, J., Weinstein, S., Ghent, L. & Teuber, H.L. Somatosensory changes after penetrative brain wounds in man. Cambridge: Harvard University Press, 1960.

Sheridan, M.R. Effects of S-R compatibility and task difficulty on unimanual movement time. Journal of Motor Behaviour, 1973, 5, 199-205.

Simon, J.R. Steadiness, handedness and hand preference. Perceptual and Motor Skills, 1964, 18, 203-206.

Smith, M.O., Chu, J. & Edmonston, W.E. Cerebral lateralization of haptic perception: interaction of responses to Braille and music reveals a functional basis. Science, 1977, 197, 689-690.

Sperry, R.W. Lateralization in the surgically separated hemispheres. In F.O. Schmidt & F.G. Worden (Eds.), The neurosciences: Third study program. Cambridge, Mass.: The MIT Press, 1974.

Steingruber, H.S. Handedness as a function of test complexity. Perceptual and Motor Skills, 1975, 40, 263-266.

Summers, J.J. & Sharp, C.A. Bilateral effects of concurrent verbal and spatial rehearsal on complex motor sequencing. Neuropsychologia, 1979, 17, 331-343.

Thornton, C.D. & Peters, M. Interference between concurrent speaking and sequential finger tapping: Both hands show a performance decrement under both visual and non-visual guidance. Neuropsychologia, 1982, 20(2), 163-169.

Todor, J.I. Sequential motor ability of left-handed inverted and non-inverted writers. Acta Psychologica, 1980, 44, 119-124.

Todor, J.I. & Doane, T. Handedness classification: preference versus proficiency. Perceptual and Motor Skills, 1977, 45, 1041-1042.

Todor, J.I. & Doane, T. Handedness and hemispheric asymmetry in the control of movements. Journal of Motor Behaviour, 1978, 10, 295-300.

Todor, J.I. & Kyprie, P.M. Hand difference in the rate and variability of rapid tapping. Journal of Motor Behaviour, 1980, 12, 57-60.

Todor, J.I., Kyprie, P.M. & Price, H.L. Lateral asymmetries in arm, wrist, and finger movements. Cortex, 1982, 18, 515-523.

Todor, J.I. & Lazarus, J.C. Inhibitory influences on the emergence of motor competence in childhood. In Fuchs, C. Zui and Zaichowsky, L. (Eds.), The psychology of motor behaviour. Wingate Institute Press: Wingate, Israel, in press.

Vaughan, H.G. & Costa, L.D. Performance of patients with lateralized cerebral lesions: II. Sensory and motor tests. Journal of Nervous and Mental Disorders. 1962, 34, 237-243.

Wadman, W.J., Denier van der Gon, J.J., Geuze, R.H. & Mol, C.R. Control of fast goal-directed arm movements. Journal of Human Movement Studies, 1979, 5, 3-17.

Wang, P.L. Interaction between handedness and cerebral functional dominance. International Journal of Neuroscience, 1980, 11, 35-40.

Weinstein, S. & Sersen, E.A. Tactual sensitivity as a function of handedness and laterality. Journal of Comparative and Physiological Psychology, 1961, 51(6), 665-669.

Welch, J.C. On the measurement of mental activity through muscular activity and the determination of a constant attention. American Journal of Physiology, 1898, 1, 288-306.

Welford, A.T. Fundamentals of skill. London: Methuen. 1971.

Wells, F.L. Normal performance in the tapping test before and during practice with special reference to fatigue phenomena. American Journal of Psychology, 1977, 15, 539-546.

Wing, A.M. Perturbations of auditory feedback delay and the timing of movement. Journal of Experimental Psychology: Human Perception and Performance. 1977, 3(2), 175-186.

Wing, A.M. The long and short of timing in response sequence. In G.E. Stelmach and J. Requin (Eds.), Tutorials in motor behaviour. North Holland Publishing Company, 1980.

Wolff, P.H., Hurwitz, I. & Moss, H. Serial organization of motor skills in left- and right-handed adults. Neuropsychologia, 1977, 15, 539-546.

Woodworth, R.S. The accuracy of voluntary movements. Psychological Review, 1899, 3 (2, whole number 13).

Wyke, M. Postural arm drift associated with brain lesions in man. Archives of Neurology, 1966, 15, 329-334.

Wyke, M. Effect of brain lesions on the rapidity of arm movement. Neurology, 1967, 17, 1113-1120.

Wyke, M. The effect of brain lesions in the performance of an arm-hand precision task. Neuropsychologia, 1968, 6, 125-134.

Wyke, M. The effects of brain lesions on the performance of bilateral arm move-
    ments. Neuropsychologia, 1971, 9, 33-42.

Yakovlev, P.I. & Rakic, P. Patterns of decussation of bulbar pyramids and distribu-
    tion of pyramidal tracts on two sides of the spinal cord. American Neurologi-
    cal Association Transaction, 1966, 91, 366-367.

Young, A.W. & Ellis, A.W. Perception of numerical stimuli felt by fingers of the
    left and right hands. Quarterly Journal of Experimental Psychology, 1979, 31,
    263-272.

Neuropsychological Studies of Apraxia
and Related Disorders, E.A. Roy (ed.)
© Elsevier Science Publishers B.V. (North-Holland), 1985

BIMANUAL COORDINATION

Christie L. MacKenzie and Ronald G. Marteniuk

University of Waterloo

Bimanual coordination and coordination of a single
limb are viewed as special cases of multimovement
coordination. Thus, a more detailed examination of single and dual limb movements may provide insight into
the processes underlying normal and disordered limb
praxis. We identify a number of dimensions on which
bimanual tasks might be classified, noting that much of
the research indicates an intrinsic relationship between
the two limbs. Regardless of whether or not the task
places spatiotemporal contraints on the two limbs, there
appear to be internal constraints on bimanual movements
that give rise to preferred, stable modes of motor control. To understand these constraints we suggest that
bimanual coordination can be understood through sensorimotor integration processes where acquisition of
bimanual skill involves a specific sensorimotor integration, leading to the ability to verify relations among
limbs to achieve environmental goals. Finally, implications of this view for understanding motor deficits due to
apraxia are presented.

Apractic patients may be hemiparetic, and assessment may thus concern only
the hand ipsilateral to the lesion (usually the nonpreferred hand). Where possible,
both preferred and nonpreferred hands should be examined in unimanual tasks. In
addition, a complementary series of bimanual coordination tasks may help to elucidate the planning and motor deficits seen. An understanding of the neurobehavioral
factors involved in bimanual coordination may provide additional insight into the
processes underlying normal and disordered limb praxis.

One definition of coordination is harmonious adjustment or functioning. Our
intent in this chapter is to provide some ideas about: the dimensions on which
bimanual tasks may vary; the underlying information processing and interaction
between the limbs; how this may change as a function of the symmetry of the task
requirements and control system; and a framework for viewing bimanual coordination as a special case of multimovement coordination (Abbs & Gracco, 1983). Making no claims to be exhaustive, we selectively review pertinent research using normal or pathological populations.

Let us start with the observation that some bimanual activities are simpler or
easier than others; for example, it is easier to strike a match than to juggle, play
the piano, or rub your head while patting your stomach. Task difficulty may be
defined in terms of the requirements of the task (what the criteria are for success)

as well as the skill level (amount of practice coupled with "innate ability"), motivation and strategy of the performer/patient. In the following section, we focus on the task requirements and the plans and sensorimotor processes of the human nervous system. In a latter section we will focus on the processes underlying increasing expertise in the acquisition of bimanual coordination to achieve specific environmental goals.

How Shall We Classify Bimanual Coordination Tasks?

To our knowledge, no one has provided a complete taxonomy of bimanual coordination tasks, and we will not provide an exhaustive or mutually exclusive taxonomy here. We exclude from consideration bimanual coordination in locomotor activities such as swimming and walking. In Table 1, we present many dimensions (continua) on which bimanual tasks might vary. Several of the dimensions apply to bimanual as well as other skills. In examining these continua, we will consider constraints on and of information processing for bimanual coordination.

Table 1

Dimensions for Classification of Bimanual Coordination Tasks

     A.   Open vs. Closed Tasks
     B.   Discrete vs. Serial vs. Continuous
     C.   Movements Alternating in Time vs. Same Time
     D.   Two Hands Same vs. Two Hands Different
     E.   Spatiotemporal Symmetry vs. Asymmetry
     F.   Symbolic vs. "Meaningless"

Open vs. Closed Tasks

After Poulton (1957), an open skill differs from a closed one in that the environment is unpredictable. Thus placing a cup on a counter or imitating a gesture (after viewing is complete) are closed tasks while shooting a moving bird is an open task. Preparing an omelet might be viewed as intermediate on the continuum of closed vs. open tasks since although the stove and frying pan are not moving the inexperienced cook is unable to judge when/how the eggs will change consistency (a structural transformation) with the addition of heat or other ingredients.

Another critical difference between the hunting task and the cooking one is that the hunter's environmental information is exafferent, i.e., changes in the environment are not controlled by the individual whereas the cook's information is both exafferent and reafferent, since the individual is bringing about the environmental change (Bruner, 1971). The extent and rate at which information about environmental change must be monitored, the nature of the information, and through which modalities the information is symbolically represented are all important considerations in bimanual coordination tasks.

Discrete vs. Serial vs. Continuous Movements

The second main task dimension concerns whether movements have a recognizable beginning and end. According to Schmidt (1982), discrete movements include striking a match or pushing an elevator button, while continuous movements include tracking. Serial movements are viewed as intermediary on the continuum, consisting of a series of discrete movements strung together as in playing a piano, making instant coffee, or filling and lighting a pipe.

Whether a series of discrete movements is different from a series of discrete actions may be an important theoretical and empirical question. We define an action as a movement or series of movements with a well defined environmental goal. Thus making instant coffee may be viewed as a series of discrete actions, such as fill kettle, place on stove, place a teaspoon of coffee in cup, fill cup with boiling water and stir. Each of these actions could be broken into a series of smaller subactions involving objects, e.g., to place a teaspoon of coffee in the cup, we must get the cup, get the coffee jar, open the jar, get a spoon, place the spoon in the jar, etc. For any of these subactions, we could describe the movements required of the hands, e.g., to open the jar, we could describe the finger flexions and hand rotations as the left hand grasps to stabilize, then the right hand grasps and twists the lid. With transitive, symbolic movements (involving objects), a description of the movements (flex the fingers and rotate the hand) is more detailed and cumbersome than a description of low level actions (remove the lid) which these movements compose. Nonetheless, apractics appear to have problems with both serial movements and serial actions.

Movements Alternating in Time vs. Same Time

A third dimension concerns the extent to which movements of the two hands alternate in time or whether left and right hands move simultaneously. This may be both a function of the task requirements and the individual's strategy/control. The two hands may alternate in time when one hand is stabilizing and the preferred hand manipulating (as in opening the jar, explained above). In serial keyboard skills (e.g., typing), although the two hands may alternate in striking the keys, there is considerable overlap in left and right hand and finger movements (Gentner, 1981). The two hands may be moving simultaneously to pick up a large sack, in a continuous series of alternating flexion-extension movements, or in simultaneous keyboard skills (e.g., piano chords).

Of interest here is the finding of Podbros (Note 1) that Parkinson patients, in a pattern opposite to normals, showed greater decrements in the execution of "same" tasks with the two hands than with bimanual execution of "different" tasks (versions of the Purdue pegboard task). For the symmetrical, "same" tasks, the two hands moved synchronously, but very slowly; in the "different", cooperative tasks, the patients (unlike normal controls) clearly alternated between hands, with the head turned and eyes focused on each hand. The recent report that Parkinson patients show planning deficits similar to apractics (Sharpe, Cermak & Sax, 1983) suggests that this dimension is certainly worthy of further investigation, both as a specified task requirement and as a control strategy.

Two Hands Same vs. Two Hands Different

We next consider whether the two hands have the same or different task requirements. It is important to consider the goals of the movements, and the movements themselves. With respect to the goals, the two hands are normally coordinated to attain one environmental goal, (e.g., make instant coffee) even if the goals of the subactions are different (e.g., stabilize jar with one hand and remove lid with the other hand). An obvious exception is a mother with babe in arms when the phone is ringing and dinner burning on the stove! In this triple task, the arms may have three separate goals to reconcile! We are unaware of any research on patients with unilateral brain damage which has required subjects to use both arms for separate goals. Only in early reports of split brain research was there any indication that the hands do not "cooperate" to achieve one desired result (Gazzaniga, 1970; Sperry, 1974, but see also Zaidel & Sperry, 1977); initial reports indicated that the hands may work against one another.

In considering the movements themselves, it becomes appropriate to question whether the spatiotemporal morphology of the left and right hand movements is similar. The left and right limb movements required to attain the goal(s) may demonstrate varying degrees of spatiotemporal symmetry, giving rise to "R-R compatibility" effects (Fitts, 1964), and it is to a more detailed consideration of this issue that we now turn.

Spatiotemporal Symmetry – External and Internal Constraints

Here, we consider spatiotemporal symmetry or compatibility in bimanual tasks in which we view the movements of the two hands anchored in time and space in a variety of contexts: with respect to one another, with respect to the body midline, with respect to the plane of movement and with respect to whole body orientation. In all of these contexts, there appear to be critical interactions between the control processes underlying right and left hand movements.

A number of investigators have examined the temporal compatibility of finger tapping by right and left hands, with and without a rhythmic driving stimulus. For instance, Peters (1981) found that right-handed university students performed better on a dual task which required them to follow the beat of a metronome with their left hand while tapping as quickly as possible with the right hand than with the converse arrangement. Klapp (1979) examined university students and showed that when left and right hands pressed telegraph keys, "the two responses interfered with each other if their periods were not harmonically related" (p. 380). The relative rhythmic relations between the two hands has been more extensively investigated for simple rhythms and polyrhythms by Deutsch (1983) who suggests that accuracy in generating left and right hand rhythmic sequences in parallel depends on the development of an integrated pattern representation.

Several comments on the externally imposed temporal contraints are in order here. First, it appears that with increasing expertise, a highly skilled musician can overcome the mutual interference expected for complex polyrhythms (e.g., playing 3 against 4 rhythms, see Shaffer, 1981). This implies that with learning, there is "insulation" against mutual interference between what were initially two incompatible rhythmic processes. Alternatively, the sensorimotor integration achieved must permit a singular representation of a complex, coherent rhythmic structure. Second, the temporal compatibility of two rhythms has been examined in other response systems besides the two hands (e.g., nodding head, articulation, silent verbalization, tapping foot), suggesting greater generality to the temporal/rhythmic compatibility effects (Bowers, Heilman, Satz & Altman, 1976; Hicks, Provenzano & Rybstein,

1975). Finally, none of the above studies have examined systematically the kinematics of the movements. A more complete picture of two hand movements (with respect to one another) would reveal the phasing relationships (i.e., the relative position-time characteristics).

Such a picture was provided by Yamanishi, Kawato and Suzuki (1979,1980) who proposed that bimanual coordination in finger tapping is achieved through coupled neural oscillators, one for each finger. In their first paper (1979), they showed that single finger tapping in the vertical plane may lose its original rhythm (Type 0 phase transition) when a perturbation is due to a single keypress with the other hand; in contrast, perturbations due to vocal responses or pattern recognition tasks do not affect the original rhythm of single finger tapping (Type 1 phase transitions). In their second paper, Yamanishi et al. (1980) used paired visual driving stimuli (repeated every 1000 msec.) for right and left hands, where the required time between pairs of responses was 0 - 900 msec., in 100 msec. intervals. Results indicated that over the above range of rhythmic driving stimuli, subjects tended to tap either synchronously (together) or alternately with the two hand, and the authors argue that the two stable rhythm patterns are alternating (L-flex, R-extend; L-extend, R-flex) and synchronous (L-flex, R-flex; L-extend, R-extend).

Kelso, Holt, Rubin and Kugler (1981) also examined the kinematics of bimanual flexion-extension movements about the metacarpophalangeal joint in the horizontal plane. The repetitive index finger movements were symmetrical about the midline; left and right index fingers flexed together, then extended together. Over a series of manipulations including constraints on movement amplitude and load perturbations to one or the other finger, they found that the frequency of movements remained constant, and that the two fingers maintained tight phasing relationships, before and after perturbations. They also footnote that when the two limbs are operating out-of-phase (L-flex, R-extend), they will change phase abruptly to an in-phase pattern when driven to a certain critical frequency (See also Kelso, Note 2).

To determine the effects of spatial orientation of the two hands, MacKenzie & Patla (Note 3) recently investigated this abrupt change in the phasing relationship between the two hands. Subjects made bimanual flexion and extension movements with the index fingers in time with binaurally presented clicks. The frequency of movements (clicks) increased over the 32 second trial. We found that the orientation of the hands (relative to the body midline, and to one another) and the initial phasing relationships (in-phase or 180 degrees out-of-phase) interacted statistically in the analysis of the number of trials on which phasing relationships changed, and in the analysis of the frequency of movement (in Hz) when phase transitions occurred. That orientation of the hands should affect the phasing relationships of the two hands is important because it argues strongly that the neural interaction giving rise to the effect is not simply due to flexor-extensor switches or "confusions". Several qualitative aspects of our results may be of interest. On trials where changes in the phasing relationship occurred, usually the nonpreferred hand became entrained with the preferred hand; phase switching was not always abrupt, but occasionally gradual; there was often more than one switching of the phasing relationship--lending support to Yamanishi's claim that both alternating (180 degrees out-of-phase) and synchronous (in-phase) rhythm patterns are stable modes.

Before leaving the task of temporally constrained bimanual tapping, it is noteworthy that split brain patients have difficulty with both synchronous and especially alternate tapping. Kreuter, Kinsbourne and Trevarthen (1972) report that synchronous tapping only occurred at very slow rates, and the two hands might tap at completely independent rates! When they attempted to move their fingers alternately, the patients commonly lost voluntary coordination and the rates achieved were much slower than normal control subjects (see also Zaidel and Sperry, 1977 and Preilowski, 1975 for a complete description of motor deficits in these patients).

All of the above researchers used tasks with externally defined temporal constraints in the form of relative timing or rhythmic relations between the two hands. In addition, some researchers have examined bimanual coordination in tasks which place external spatial constraints on the two limbs.

This research has examined how the two hands move simultaneously when aiming at two separate visual targets in space. We have found that the reaction time to initiate two hand movements is longer than the reaction time to initiate one hand movement (Marteniuk & MacKenzie, 1980). Of greater interest here is how the hands perform when the spatial requirements are symmetric or asymmetric. Kelso and his colleagues (Kelso, Southard & Goodman, 1979; Kelso, Putnam & Goodman, 1983) have argued that under symmetric and asymmetric conditions, the underlying temporal structure remains invariant and the limbs are constrained to act as a single unit. Our own research (Marteniuk & MacKenzie, 1980; Marteniuk, MacKenzie & Baba, in press) suggests that when there is spatial symmetry in the task requirements, there is indeed an invariance in the temporal parameters (movement time and time to peak velocity); however, with asymmetric spatial requirements, there are significant (10-30 msec.) departures from temporal synchrony between the two hands.

An important aspect of the results concerns the systematic interference effects when the spatial requirements are different for the two hands. Relative to symmetric control data, for asymmetric bimanual movements, movement time for a short movement increases when the other hand makes a long one, and movement time for a long movement decreases when the other hand makes a short one. This effect is not sufficient to produce simultaneity in movement termination; furthermore the interference effects are not always the same for left and right hands when "mirror image comparisons" are made (Kelso, et al., 1983; Marteniuk et al., in press).

A neurobehavioural interpretation of the interference effects suggests that for this task there might be separate streams of commands which engage in "neural crosstalk" at many levels within the central nervous system. Neurophysiologically, the proximal musculature involved in the movements required by our task is subserved by both contralateral and ipsilateral descending pathways (Brinkman & Kuypers, 1972; Lawrence and Kuypers, 1968a,b). In terms of efferent commands to both upper limbs, this means that any activity from the left motor cortex, or other neural structures destined for proximal musculature of the right arm will also affect the left arm through ipsilateral descending pathways and segmental neural interaction. Preilowski (1975) used a similar structural model to interpret the interference effects in his bimanual task. Indeed, we adapted his model (Marteniuk & MacKenzie, 1980), to explain the interference effects. Alternatively, the neural interaction could affect perceptual aspects of the spatial specification process (i.e., a perceptual-motor bias; see Arbib, 1980) when there are disparate distances for the two limbs to move.

As a complement to studies with external temporal constraints, or external spatial constraints, Wing (1982) examined bimanual coordination in a task with external temporal and spatial constraints. The task required subjects to make repetitive movements to targets, under instructions to arrive at targets synchronously. From his analysis of the variance and covariance of interresponse intervals and response asynchronies of "simultaneous", aiming movements of left and right hands, Wing concluded that the two hands are coordinated prior to a timer which initiates a pair of time constrained responses.

In all the above research, the tasks have had explicit external constraints on the spatial locations or temporal structure of bimanual movements. In a task without external temporal or spatial constraints, Morasso (1983) examined coordination in the simultaneous horizontal trajectories of the two hands, while making "aim-less" movements on verbal commands. The following movements were examined: "synkinetic" or mirror image movements, defined as "simultaneous trajectories with a specular spatial similarity, which involve similar activities of homologous muscles of the arms"; "homokinetic" or same direction movements, defined as "simultaneous trajectories with direct spatial similarity, which involve different activities of homologous muscles of the two arms"; "heterokinetic" movements, defined as "trajectories alternated in time"; and "allokinetic" movements, defined as "trajectories with unrelated timing and shape" (p. 199).

From the velocity time profiles (in the horizontal plane) for left and right hands, Morasso defined a synchronization coefficient, which takes on a value of 0 if a time to peak velocity in one hand coincides with a time to peak velocity in the other hand, and a value of ± 1 if a positive velocity peak in one hand coincides with minimum velocity in the other. Put simply, the results indicate that the velocity peaks coincide for homokinetic and synkinetic movements (a coefficient of 0), and that for heterokinetic movements, the time instants of peak velocity in one hand coincide with the time at which the other hand goes to or leaves the rest position (a coefficient of ± 1). Interestingly, for allokinetic movements, the coefficients cluster about 0 and ± 1, indicating that the movements are not unrelated as initially defined and instructed to the subjects. Rather, the synchronization of allokinetic movements appears to shift between the mode seen for homokinetic and synkinetic movements and the mode characteristic of heterokinetic movements.

There is a striking parallel between these modes defined by Morasso for spatiotemporal characteristics of the trajectories in "aim-less" movements and the synchronous and alternating modes of tapping defined by Yamanishi et.al. (1979, 1980). Thus, it appears that regardless of whether or not the upper limb movements are task-constrained through externally specified spatial or temporal structure, there is an intrinsic relationship between the two limbs, giving rise to preferred, stable modes of operation. The integrative processes of this intrinsic relationship are central for bimanual coordination.

Symbolic vs. "Meaningless" Movements

The final dimension, alluded to earlier, concerns the meaning associated with upper limb movements. Symbolic movements have a goal with respect to object manipulation or gestural communication, whereas in "meaningless" movements, the goals are the movements themselves (see DeRenzi, this volume for a more extensive discussion). Thus, symbolic movements are actions (with environmental goals) which usually provide a context or facilitating set of conditions (hence activation, see McKay, this volume) for movements. Thus, one might predict that (both symmetrical and asymmetrical) bimanual movements would show fewer deficits with damage to the cerebral hemispheres or corpus callosum when they are symbolic (in a rich context) than when they are "meaningless". We are unaware of extensive empirical evidence on this issue except that split brain patients have few problems with highly learned, symbolic skills like playing the piano and buttoning clothing, yet they are unable to perform "meaningless" alternating movements (Preilowski, 1975; Zaidel & Sperry, 1977).

Acquisition of Bimanual Coordination

The previous section established the relative ease of execution of bimanual movements that were symmetrical with respect to the body midline and/or movement parameters like movement extent, intensity and rhythm. However, it was noted that when a task required the upper limbs to assume movements that were asymmetrical, achievement of coordination between the limbs became more difficult and there were systematic interactions between left and right limbs. While there may be several reasons for bimanual control being easier for symmetrical movements, one simple explanation is that they are easier because they have received the most practice during ones lifetime. The purpose of this section is to review literature relevant to how bimanual coordination is acquired. Not included in this review are issues relevant to motor development--that is, how motor coordination is changed as a result of maturational changes.

Any explanation of the underlying processes involved in the acquisition of coordinated movement must address how the central nervous system deals with the large number of degrees of freedom (Bernstein, 1967) represented by the joints and the permissable motions of the complex biokinematic chains that are represented in the skeletomuscular systems of human beings. There are two concerns here: First, is the observation that despite the apparent complexity involved in controlling the large number of degrees of freedom, the mature, normal human being has no problem in mastering complex skills. Second, highly skilled individuals exhibit flexibility in that they can realize the same result in a large number of ways (e.g., one can throw an object in a large number of different ways but still hit the target).

Traditionally, mastering of the degrees of freedom in motor control while at the same time allowing for flexibility in skill attainment, has been explained by the acquisition of motor programs (e.g., Schmidt, 1975). From this view, classes of movement have generalized motor programs and before execution these programs are parameterized with movement parameters specific to the needs of the task. Central to this idea is the notion that the "executive" is directly involved in all aspects of the movement planning and execution processes. Recently, motor programming theory has been criticized on the grounds that one executive cannot possibly compute the necessary detail to plan and execute movements with large degrees of freedom. To overcome this limitation, distributed processing views are advocated (Allport, 1980) where the control of movement is distributed over autonomous subsystems. These subsystems have the ability to control certain aspects of the total movement and the responsibility of the executive is to coordinate appropriate subsystems so that the complete task can be carried out. The executive in a distributed processing system does not directly enter into the control process (executive ignorance) and hence its computational load is relatively light.

While distributed processing views have come from disciplines like Artificial Intelligence, psychologists have approached the degrees of freedom problem in a similar way. Bruner (1971), for example, described skilled activity as a program specifying an objective to be obtained and requiring the serial ordering of a set of modular subroutines. The subroutines initially come from an innate repertoire of reflex-based patterns. These patterns are evoked by the appropriate interaction with the environment, and are derived from the differentiation of initially gross acts into component elements that achieve independence from their original context. A similar approach has been advocated by Fitts (1964) where he maintains that past the age of six, all human beings have the necessary subroutines (automatic sequences of activity) to learn any novel movement.

One way of viewing bimanual performance, then, would be to postulate that the upper limbs are two relatively independent subsystems that, perhaps, each have subsystems within them. Evidence for this comes from the work of Jeannerod (1981) who has shown two components to a single arm reaching task; one component concerned with moving the hand to the object and another concerned with orienting the hand to the object. Also, as Greene (1982) points out, arm movements can be likened to a spring model of control that allows the relatively easy specification of such movement parameters as end location and speed. Thus, by invoking the concept of relatively autonomous subsystems underlying movement control, one aspect of the degrees of freedom problem (i.e., the large number) for bimanual performance can be solved. That is, relatively large numbers of degrees of freedom are controlled collectively through an autonomous subsystem. However, to explain the flexibility a skilled person demonstrates in achieving a given goal still requires further elaboration.

This latter problem deals with the question of how the various subsystems are brought together to produce flexible but coordinated movement. The contention here is that this problem, central to understanding bimanual coordination, can be understood by considering that at the base of all coordinated movement is an integrated store of sensory and motor information that defines relations among body parts for the achievement of goals. The actual expression of coordinated movement, however, is modified by an interplay of motor and sensory information that fine tunes movement to the specific content of the situation. Thus, bimanual coordination can be described as a type of multimovement coordination where the process of sensorimotor integration underlies coordination of movement components.

An example of multimovement coordination can be found in insect flight. Altman (1982) has discussed the relationship between the concepts of the central pattern generator and sensory inputs in terms of their contributions to insect flight. Evidence shows that phasic sensory inputs play a crucial role in regulating the output of the central pattern generator. These sensory inputs come not only from wing receptors but also from the head, tail, and, perhaps, the entire body surface. More importantly, the inputs from the central pattern generator and sensory receptors during flight summate to produce a stable yet flexible motor output. In fact Altman raises the possibility that there may be no such thing as a central pattern generator but rather a flying insect might be more properly thought of as a combination of components, mechanical, sensory, and central neurons, all oscillating in resonance at flight frequency.

Analogous examples to the above can be fou;d in human motor behavior. The work of Abbs and his colleagues, summarized in Abbs and Gracco (1983), shows that coordination of multiple speech movements is not entirely preprogrammed but is subject to refinement through sensorimotor feedforward adjustments. Evidence for this comes from data showing that during speech, when the lower lip is perturbed, not only does adjustment to the perturbation occur in the lower lip, but consistent compensations occur in synergistic movements of the upper lip. This is significant since the lower and upper lips are controlled independently, thus ruling out a closed-loop feedback process. As Abbs and Gracco (1983) state, "This open-loop adjustment is based upon a pre-established sensorimotor translation between lower-lip afferent signals and upper-lip motor actions. This intermovement sensorimotor translation has been referred to as a predictive or feedforward process..." (p. 393).

Feedforward processes have also been implicated in the interaction of postural muscles with muscles involved in rapid arm movements. Work (e.g., Nashner & Cordo, 1981) has shown that leg stabilizers produce EMG responses about 50 msec prior to EMG appearance in an arm that must be rapidly moved. Data like these implicate a feedforward anticipation of the kinematic consequences of the muscular contractions in the prime mover.

If this type of multimovement coordination model were to be applied to bimanual coordination, the question of how open-loop,feedforward processes are acquired becomes central. As Ito (1975) has noted, this type of process is one where a movement is generated to cancel a previously generated error before that error can cause a functional disturbance in the motor output. This process involves prediction and does not necessitate the presence of a closed-loop error detection and correction mechanism. Houk and Rymer (1981) postulate that in multimovement coordination, an open-loop, feedforward process involves a feedforward controller (a neural model of the motor system) that translates a predicted error in one component of the multicomponent movement to an adjustment in a synergistic movement, which cancels the effect of the error on the functional output of a multicomponent movement.

Abbs, Gracco, and Cole (In press) have recently commented on how such a system might be acquired. They reason that in order to operate in a predictive manner such a system must have an experience based representation of the relationship between afferent signals from the movement where a potential error is detected and the motor output of a parallel synergistic movement where an adjustment is made. Invoking the concept of a feedforward controller (i.e., a neural model of the motor system - Houk & Rymer, 1981), Abbs et al. (in press) postulate that the role of experience is in the establishment of the representation (i.e., the neural model) which translates between motor and sensory events. Learning, then, involves establishing, in multimovement motor behaviors, a neural model which involves a highly integrated system of motor and sensory information among the components of the movement. Once such a rich store of information is established, Abbs, Graco and Cole (in press) point out that to implement the interdependent actions that make up a compound motor gesture, a motor program is constructed which results in the establishment of pertinent sensorimotor contingencies which ensure coordination of the multiple movements to a common goal. When executed the movement is dependent on the exact demands of the environment in that the program only sets up the correct patterns of interaction among the components of the movement. To achieve the goal, then, requires the individual movement spatial goals to be subordinate to the overall goal. Hence, one might expect movement outcomes (i.e., the achievement of the goal) to be consistently attained but the exact manner by which these outcomes are achieved would be quite variable (cf. Lacquaniti & Soechting, 1982).

Summary and Implications

In this chapter we have presented ideas relevant to the notion that a more detailed examination of bimanual coordination and control may provide some insight into the nature of apractic disorders. While evaluation of practic functioning has typically included unimanual tasks, many daily activities (e.g., use of tools and utensils) require bimanual coordination for their efficient or successful execution.

We have suggested that it is important to consider some of the dimensions on which bimanual tasks may be described. It may well be that performance in apractic patients is selectively affected on certain of these dimensions, e.g., perhaps in closed tasks where reafferent information is not integrated with exafferent (possibly visual) information, patients have particular sequencing difficulties.

Greatest consideration was given to the symmetry of spatiotemporal aspects of the movements, as defined by external task requirements. With symmetry or asymmetry, we saw an intrinsic relationship between the two hands, manifested as mutual interference when the task requirements were asymmetric. Further, this intrinsic coordinative relationship between the two hands holds for tasks without external spatiotemporal constraints, where we see preferred relative modes of movement for the two limbs.

We suggest that coordination of the two limbs occurs through sensorimotor integration processes, and that bimanual coordination may be viewed as a special case of multimovement coordination. Recent evidence on reciprocal interactions of position sense in the two arms by Lackner and Taublieb (1983) suggests that dynamic awareness of limb position is not dependent on afferent and efferent information of that limb in isolation, but involves a cross referencing of information from other body parts. Learning may well involve task (or component process) - specific sensorimotor integration, leading to the ability to specify relations among component movements to achieve environmental goals.

In traditional views of apraxia (see Faglioni et al., this volume for historical perspectives), the motor deficits are seen as being due to disorders in the planning or execution of motor programs. More recent versions of motor programming theory include the specification of feedforward and feedback contingencies: some problems in apraxia may well be due to deficits in planning for, or the on-line use of feedback and feedforward information. This might account for omissions, or improper sequencing, timing and phasing of movements/actions, improper plane of movement, improper spatial orientation of the hands; and, poorly calibrated manipulative components, particularly in the absence of the appropriate eliciting situational context.

A closer examination of coordination within and between limbs in normal individuals and patients with lateralized brain damage in the range of tasks outlined in Table 1 may help to elucidate the role of feedforward and feedback processes in coordination. In addition to evaluating earlier ideas of cross-education, this endeavour might also assess the potential for facilitation in praxis when one hand provides the intentional, or spatial or temporal context for the other.

REFERENCE NOTES

1. Podbros, L.Z. Bimanual performance of Parkinson patients: simultaneous vs. concurrent tasks. Presented at the 13th Annual Meeting of the Society for Neuroscience, Boston, MA, November 6-11, 1983.

2. Kelso, J.A.S. Phase transitions and critical behaviour in human bimanual coordination. Haskins Laboratories Status Report, SR-75, 1983. Also personal communication, June, 1983.

3. MacKenzie, C.L. & Patla, A.E. Breakdown in rapid bimanual finger tapping as a function of orientation and phasing. Presented at the 13th Annual Meeting of the Society for Neuroscience, Boston, MA, November 6-11, 1983.

REFERENCES

Abbs, J.H. & Gracco, V.L. Sensorimotor actions in the control of multi-movement speech gestures. Trends in Neurosciences, 1983, 6, 391-395.

Abbs, J.H., Gracco, V.L. & Cole, K.J. Control of multimovement coordination: sensorimotor mechanisms in speech motor programming. Journal of Motor Behavior, In press.

Allport, A.A. Patterns and actions: cognitive mechanisms are content-specific. In G. Claxton (Ed.), Cognitive Psychology. London: Routledge & Kegan Paul, 1980.

Altman, J. The role of sensory inputs in insect flight motor pattern generation. Trends in Neurosciences, 1982, 5, 257-260.

Arbib, M.A. Perceptual structures and distributed motor control. In Brooks, V.B. (Ed.), Handbook of Physiology, Vol. III, Motor Control. Bethesda, Md.: American Physiological Society, 1980.

Bernstein, N. The coordination and regulation of movements. Oxford: Pergamon Press, 1967.

Bowers, D., Heilman, K., Satz, P. & Altman, A. Simultaneous performance on verbal, nonverbal and motor tasks. Neuropsychologia, 1977.

Brinkman, J. & Kuypers, H. Splitbrain monkeys: cerebral control of ipsilateral and contralateral arm, hand and finger movements. Science, 1972, 197, 536-539.

Bruner, J.S. The growth and structure of skill. In K.J. Connolly (Ed.), Motor Skills in Infancy. New York: Academic Press, 1971.

Deutsch, D. The generation of two isochronous sequences in parallel. Perception & Psychophysics, 1983, 34, 331-337.

Fitts, P.M. Perceptual-motor skill learning. In A.W. Melton (Ed.), Categories of Human Learning. New York: Academic Press, 1964.

Gazzaniga, M.S. The bisected brain. New York: Appleton-Century-Crofts, 1970.

Gentner, D.R. Skilled finger movements in typing (Technical Report CHIP 104), La Jolla, CA: University of California, San Diego, Centre for Human Information Processing, 1981.

Greene, P.H. Why is it easy to control your arms? Journal of Motor Behavior, 1982, 14, 260-286.

Hicks, R.E., Provenzano, F.J. & Rybstein, E.D. Generalized and lateralized effects of concurrent verbal rehearsal upon performance of sequential movements of the fingers by the left and right hands. Acta Psychologica, 1975, 39, 119-130.

Houk, J.C. & Rymer, W.Z. Neural control of muscle length and tension. In V.B. Brooks (Ed.), Handbook of Physiology, Section 1 (Vol. II: Motor control, Part 1). Bethesda, Md.: American Physiological Society, 1981, 257-323.

Ito, M. The control mechanisms of cerebellar motor systems. In E.V. Evarts (Ed.), Central Processing of Sensory Input Leading to Motor Output. Cambridge, Mass.: MIT Press, 1975, 293-304.

Jeannerod, M. Intersegmental coordination during reaching at natural visual objects. In J. Long and A. Baddeley (Eds.), Attention and Performance IX. Hillsdale, N.J.: Erlbaum, 1981, 153-169.

Kelso, J.A.S., Holt, K.A., Rubin, P. & Kugler, P.N. Patterns of human interlimb coordination emerge from the properties of non-linear, limit cycle oscillatory processes: theory and data. Journal of Motor Behavior, 1981, 13, 226-261.

Kelso, J.A.S., Putnam, C.A. & Goodman, D. On the space-time structure of human interlimb coordination. Quarterly Journal of Experimental Psychology: Human Experimental Psychology, 1983, 35, 347-375.

Kelso, J.A.S., Southard, D.L. & Goodman, D. On the coordination of two-handed movements. Journal of Experimental Psychology: Human Perception and Performance, 1979, 5, 229-238.

Klapp, S.T. Doing two things at once: the role of temporal compatibility. Memory and Cognition, 1979, 7, 375-381.

Kreuter, C., Kinsbourne, M. & Trevarthen, C. Are disconnected cerebral hemispheres independent channels? A preliminary study of the effect of unilateral loading on bilateral finger tapping. Neuropsychologia, 1972, 10, 453-461.

Lackner, J.R. and Taublieb, A.B. Reciprocal interactions between the position sense representations of the two forearms. The Journal of Neuroscience, 1983, 3(11), 2280-2285.

Lacquaniti, F. & Soechting, J.F. Coordination of arm and wrist motion during a reaching task. Journal of Neuroscience, 1982, 2, 399-408.

Lawrence, D.G. & Kuypers, H.G.J.M. The functional organization of the motor system of the monkey. I. The effects of bilateral pyramidal lesions. Brain, 1968a, 91, 1-14.

Lawrence, D.G. & Kuypers, H.G.J.M. The functional organization of the motor system of the monkey. II. The effects of lesions of the descending brain stem pathways. Brain, 1968b, 91, 15-33.

Marteniuk, R.G. & MacKenzie, C.L. A preliminary theory of two-handed coordinated control. In G.E. Stelmach and J. Requin (Eds.), Tutorials in Motor Behavior. Amsterdam: North-Holland Publishing Co., 1980.

Marteniuk, R.G., MacKenzie, C.L. & Baba, S.M. Bimanual movement control: Information processing and interaction effects. Quarterly Journal of Experimental Psychology: Human Experimental Psychology, in press.

Morasso, P. Coordination aspects of arm trajectory formation. Human Movement Science, 1983, 2, 197-200.

Nashner, L.M. & Cordo, P.J. Relation of automatic postural responses and reaction-time voluntary movements of human leg muscles. Experimental Brain Research, 1981, 43, 395-405.

Peters, M. Attentional asymmetries during concurrent bimanual performance. Quarterly Journal of Experimental Psychology, 1981, 33A, 95-103.

Poulton, E.C. On prediction in skilled movements. Psychological Bulletin. 1957, 54, 467-478.

Preilowski, B. Bilateral motor interaction: Perceptual-motor performance of partial and complete split-brain patients. In K.S. Zulch, O. Creutzfeldt, & G.C. Galbraith, (Eds.), Cerebral Localization. Berlin: Springer, 1975.

Schmidt, R.A. A schema theory of discrete motor skill learning. Psychological Review, 1975, 82, 225-260.

Schmidt, R.A. Motor control and learning. Champaign, Ill.: Human Kinetics Publishers, 1982.

Shaffer, L.H. Performance of Chopin, Bach and Bartoli: studies in motor programming. Cognitive Psychology, 1981, 326-376.

Sharpe, M.H., Cermak, S.A.,& Sax, D.S. Motor planning in Parkinson patients. Neuropsychologia, 1983, 21, 455-462.

Sperry, R.W. Lateral specialization in the surgically separated hemispheres. In F.O. Schmitt and F.G. Worden (Eds.), The Neurosciences: Third Study Program. Cambridge, Mass.: MIT Press, 1974.

Wing, A.M. Timing and co-ordination of repetitive bimanual movements. Quartery Journal of Experimental Psychology, 1982, 34A, 339-348.

Yamanishi, J., Kawato, M. & Suzuki, R. Studies on human finger tapping neural networks by phase transition curves. Biological Cybernetics, 1979, 33, 199-208.

Yamanishi, J., Kawato, M. & Suzuki, R. Two coupled oscillators as a model for the coordinated finger tapping by both hands. Biological Cybernetics, 1980, 37, 219-225.

Zaidel, D. & Sperry, R.W. Some long-term motor effects of cerebral commissurotomy in man. Neuropsychologia, 1977, 15, 193-204.

AUTHOR INDEX

A

Abbie, A.	251, 252
Abbie, M.H.	232
Abbs, J.H.	126, 127, 128, 131, 134, 140, 141, 142, 345, 353, 354
Abelson, R.P.	293
Abramson, A.S.	133
Achenbach, K.	310
Ackerman, R.H.	184
Adams, M.	126, 236
Adams, R.D.	236
Akelaitis, A.J.	24, 81, 82
Ajuriaguerra, J. de	77, 85, 86, 89
Alajouanine, T.H.	8, 79, 133, 164, 165
Alavi, A.	184
Albert, M.L.	117, 205, 214, 241
Alcala, H.	182
Alexander, M.P.	19, 138, 183, 184
Allen, B.T.	319
Allen, M.	317, 320, 329
Allport, A.A.	352
Alpert, N.M.	184
Altman, A.	321, 348
Altman, J.	353
Ambrose, J.	181
Angevine, J.B. Jr.	19
Angelergues, R.	13, 18, 77, 85, 86, 89
Annett, J.	310, 311, 312, 313, 314, 316

Annett, M.	313, 314, 316, 333
Anzola, G.P.	324, 325, 326
Apsimon, T.T.	227, 232
Arbib, M.A.	255, 261, 350
Archibald, Y.	10, 46, 51, 84, 90, 119, 168, 212, 237, 329
Arnheim, D.D.	239
Aronson, A.E.	135
Arseni, C.	5, 13, 19
Ashton, R.	327
Assal, G.	14, 57, 78
Ayres, A.J.	226, 227, 228, 231, 232, 233, 234, 235, 236, 237, 238, 240, 241, 242

B

Baba, S.M.	350
Bahrick, H.P.	325
Bailey, P.	12, 256, 257
Baker, E.	112, 118
Baldy, R.	23
Balegdier, C.	259
Balint, R.	83
Bancaud, J.	19
Barrett, G.	30
Baron, J.C.	184
Barron, D.W.	100
Basso, A.	19, 21, 171, 184, 185, 193, 195
Bauman, J.	134, 136
Bay, E.	165
Bear, D.M.	255

Beaton, A.A.	321, 327
Bech Skriver, E.	182
Bechterew, W. von	12
Beck, C.H.M.	236, 238
Becker, H.	182
Becker, J.M.T.	184
Beggs, W.D.A.	310
Bellugi, U.	175
Bennett, E.L.	240
Benson, D.F.	133, 180, 236
Benson, W.E.	183
Benton, A.L.	13, 309, 331
Berges, J.	227, 236, 237
Bergstrom, K.	227, 232
Berlucchi, G.	319
Bernstein, N.A.	259, 261, 352
Bertoloni, G.	318, 324, 325, 334
Bertrand, C.	77
Bigeur, B.	255, 259
Biggerstaff, A.	228
Bilaniuk, L.T.	182
Bille, B.	227, 232
Birdwhistle, R.L.	100
Bisiach, E.	184
Blakemore, C.B.	24
Blanco, E.	182
Bland, B.H.	305
Blauenstein, U.W.	27
Blumstein, S.	132, 135, 136, 138, 139

Blunk, R.   183

Bogen, J.E.   24, 25, 26, 54, 81, 82, 170, 317, 327

Boller, F.   135, 180, 183

Bogliun, G.   183

Bonhoeffer, K.   23, 76, 81

Bonin, G. von   256, 257

Boomer, D.S.   125

Botez, M.I.   19

Bousser, M.G.   184

Bowden, J.M.   310

Bower, G.   294

Bowers, D.   321, 348

Boyes-Braem, P.   112

Braak, H.   256

Brain, R.   77

Bransford, J.D.   112

Breland, K.   220

Breland, M.   220

Bremer, F.   12

Brinkman, C.   80, 261

Brinkman, J.   103, 208, 217, 235, 318, 350

Brion, S.   23, 82

Brodal, A.   304

Brodie, D.A.   316, 323, 324, 325, 326, 334

Brodmann, K.   255

Brooks, R.   229, 231

Brooks, V.B.   205, 261

Brookshire, R.H.   146

Brown, J.   70, 237, 241

Brown, J.D.   261

Brown, J.K.   135, 233

Brown, J.W.   14, 48, 49, 50, 133, 138

Brown, S.H.   311

Brun, R.   8, 9, 10, 12, 18, 20, 21, 31, 77

Bruner, J.S.   346, 352

Bryan, W.L.   268

Buchtel, H.A.   318, 324, 325, 334

Buckingham, H.W.   140

Bucy, P.C.   255

Burns, M.S.   103

Buschke, H.   68, 69, 70

Buyssens, E.   134

Brownell, G.L.   184

Brunner, R.J.   183

Bychowski, Z.   12

C

Cail, W.S.   184

Campbell, A.W.   255

Canter, G.J.   103, 131, 132, 140

Cancilla, P.A.   182

Capitani, E.   184

Caplan, P.J.   238, 240

Cappa, S.   184

Caramazza, A.   118, 133, 138

Cardu, B.   24

Carr, D.   329

Carrieri, G.   19

Carlton, L.G.   310, 311, 312,

Carmon, A.   54

Castell, L.   331

Castaigne, P.   184

Caveness, W.F.   181

Cermak, S.A.   231, 235, 236, 237, 241, 347

Chaffin, D.B.   310

Chapin, C.   135

Chase, R.A.   126

Chiarello, C.   87

Chiu, L.C.   182

Christie, J.H.   182

Christman, D.   184

Chu, J.   326

Ciarla, E.   18, 23

Cisneros, J.   311, 313, 314

Claude, M.   23

Cleeland, C.S.   329

Clements, S.J.   230

Cole, K.J.   354

Cole, M.   183

Collins, M.   138

Coetes, R.   183

Comar, D.   184

Consoli, S.   139

Conrad, K.   231, 237, 241

Cook, J.   320, 321

Cooke, J.D.   261, 311

Cooper, F.S.   125

Cooper, R.   79, 180

Cooper, W.   133, 138

Cordo, P.J.   353

Correia, J.A.   184

Costa, L.D.   329

Coster, W.   235, 236, 237, 241

Court, S.D.M.   226

Coyle, J.M.   8, 102

Cratty, B.J.   239

Cress, R.H.   319

Critchley, M.   9

Crossman, E.R.F.W.   310

Crouzel, C.   184

Crow, H.J.   79, 180

D

Damasio, A.R.   13, 19, 23, 183, 259

Damasio, H.   183

Dann, R.   184

Daniloff, R.G.   128, 137

Dare, M.T.   238

Darley, F.L.   131, 132, 134, 135, 137, 138, 141, 142, 230

Dart, D.A.   251, 252

David, N.J.   183

Davis, K.R.   138, 140, 182

Davis, R.   14

Davidson, W.   54, 309

Davison, L.   315, 331

Dawdy, S.C.   226, 241

De Ajuriaguerra, J.   13, 18, 241

Deal, J.   132, 133, 135

De Bleser, R.   183

DeClerk, J.   126, 137

Defran, R.H.   141

Degos, C.   131

Delaney, H.D.   84, 121, 122

Delis, D.C.   8

Deloche, G.   131

DeLong, M.R.   205, 209

Denckla, M.B.   237

Denier, van der Gon, J.J.   311

Denny-Brown, D.   77, 79, 80, 89, 105, 118

Deonna, R.W.   24

De Renzi, E.   10, 13, 14, 18, 30, 31, 46, 48, 51, 52, 54, 58, 78,
                                    85, 86, 88, 90, 100, 103, 111, 118, 138, 142, 144,
                                    145, 165, 168, 186, 194, 214

De Recondo, J.   83

Desch, H.   182

Deuel, R.K.   80, 218

Deutsch, D.   348

Deutsch, S.E.   138, 140

De Vito, J.L.   80

Diamond, M.C.   240

Dibrell, J.W.   133, 139

DiSimoni, F.G.   134, 142

Di Stefano, M.   319

Doane, T.   310, 314, 322

Dobbing, J.   233

Dolinskas, C.A.   182

Dorsen, M.M.   24

Douglas, M.H.   232

Drake, C.   231, 235, 236, 237, 241

Dreyer, D.R.   135

Driscoll, L.A.   234

Druker, R.   227, 236, 237

Du Boulay, G.   183, 184

Duffy, J.R.   133, 134, 137, 139

Duncan, G.W.   14, 138, 140

Dunlop, J.M.   136

Durand, M.   133

Durding, B.M.   316

E

Easton, T.   115

Ebbinghaus, H.E.   70

Eccles, J.C.   208, 304

Edes, A.D.   19

Edmonston, W.E.   326

Efron, D.   101

Efron, R.   146, 302

Ehrman, L.   332

Eichling, J.C.   180

Elfeki, G.   121

Ellis, A.W.   331

Ellis, E.   226

Ettlinger, G.   9, 24, 26, 100

Eustis, R.   227

F

Fager, K.	138
Faglioni, P.	8, 10, 12, 13, 14, 18, 30, 31, 46, 48, 52, 58, 88, 90, 100, 186, 194
Fahn, S.	209
Fairbairn, D.	183
Farinholt, J.W.	103
Farmer, A.	136, 137
Faro, M.D.	233
Fennel, E.	310
Ferrier, D.	255
Ferris, G.S.	241
Ferro, J.M.	168, 171
Finger, S.	232, 240
Finkelburg, R.	75, 85
Finkelstein, S.	138, 140
Finlayson, M.A.	334
Fischer, E.D.	25
Fitts, P.M.	310, 348, 352
Fleishman, E.A.	234, 334
Fleming, W.R.	103
Flourens, P.	203, 204, 217
Flowers, C.	71
Flowers, K.	259, 309, 310, 312, 313
Foix, C.	12, 23, 77, 81
Folkins, J.W.	20, 22, 126, 127
Ford, F.R.	23, 225
Forster, E.	23
Foulke, J.A.	310

Fowler, J.   184

Frackowiak, R.S.J.   184

Franks, J.S.   313, 314

Freeman, F.   133, 139

Freud, S.   299

Friedman, A.   318, 320

Fritsch, G.   75

Fromkin, V.A.   125, 126

Fromm, D.   134, 139, 140, 142

Fry, D.B.   27, 32, 131, 136

Fugii, H.   181

Fuld, P.A.   68, 69, 70

Fullerton, G.D.   182

Fulton, J.F.   79, 255, 256

Funkenstein, H.   14, 19, 138, 140

Fusillo, M.   191

Fust, R.   175

Fuster, J.M.   252

G

Gaddes, W.H.   240

Gado, M.H.   180, 182

Gainotti, G.   90

Galaburda, A.M.   138, 255

Galin, D   327

Galkin, T.W   232

Galluscio, E.H   237

Garcin, R   8, 83

Gardner. L.P.   332

Gattoni,A.   183, 184, 186

Garvey,M.   227

Garrett,M.F.   125, 137

Gawle,C.   134, 138

Gay,T.   126, 127

Gazzaniga,M.S.   25, 26, 54, 81, 82, 170, 317, 321, 327, 331, 348

Geffen,G.   23

Gentile,A.M.   218

Gentillucci,M.   261

Gentner,D.R.   282, 347

Geoffroy,G.   24

Gersch, F.   23, 183

Geschwind,N.   8, 9, 11, 13, 14, 23, 26, 27, 31, 32, 47, 55, 57, 58,
                          78, 79, 81, 82, 84, 100, 102, 133, 145, 168, 174,
                          183, 191, 205, 211, 212, 226, 234, 235, 236, 237,
                          242, 302, 319, 329

Geuze,R.H.   311

Ghent,L.   122, 330, 331

Ghent,C.   180

Ghez,C.   209

Gibson,J.J.   112

Gimeno Alava,A.   5. 23

Glaser,J.S.   183

Gleniross,D.J.   310, 332

Golby,C.W.   311, 312

Godshalk,M.   257

Goldberg,G.   19, 183

Goldenberg,M.   5, 13

Goldman,P.S.   232, 240, 257

Goldman-Rakic, P.S.   26

Goldstein,K.	12, 23, 31, 77, 79, 82, 117
Gonyea,E.F.	8, 102
Goodeve,P.J.	310
Goodglass,H.	47, 55, 85, 112, 117, 118, 133, 135, 140, 164, 167, 236
Goodman, D.	350
Goodwin,W.L	234
Gordon,H.W.	24
Goree,J.A.	180
Gott,P.S.	24
Gottleib,J.	133
Gottsdanker,R.	116
Gouliamos,A.	184
Gracco,V.L.	345, 353, 354
Gray,W.	112
Graziani,L.	230
Green,J.R.	19
Green,S.	218
Greenberg,J.H.	184
Greene,P.H.	353
Gregory,R.L.	259
Greywalter,W.	180
Grotta,J.C.	184
Grubb,R.L.	180
Grudin,J.T.	276, 279, 282
Grunbaum,A.A.	77
Gubbay,S.S.	226, 227, 230, 231, 232, 324, 236, 238, 239, 241
Guidetti,B.	19
Guillain,G.	8

H

Haaland,K.Y.	9, 84, 121, 122, 142, 329
Haaxma,R.	14, 83, 217
Hacker,H.	182
Hall,D.	231, 241
Halle,M.	125
Hallett,M.	311
Halliday,E	30
Halliday,A.M.	30
Halsey,J.H.	27
Ham,R	126
Hamada,I.	257
Hamanaka,T.	79
Hamsher,S.K.De.	309, 331,
Hamuy,T.P.	257
Hand,	184
Hanson,R.	126
Hanson,W.R.	185
Hardison,D.	136
Harlock,W.	183
Harriman,J.	331
Harris,K.S.	125, 126, 131, 133
Harter,N.	268
Hartmann,F.	8, 12, 22, 23, 31, 79
Hatta,T.	331
Hawkins,B.	313, 314
Hayashi,M.	181
Hayward,R.W.	183, 184

Heather,J.D.	184
Hecaen,H.	5, 9, 13, 18, 23, 50, 77, 78, 79, 85, 86, 89, 104, 117, 139, 167, 205, 214, 241
Heene,R,	24
Heilman,K.M.	12, 23, 31, 54, 58, 60, 65, 66, 67, 68, 70, 78, 84, 100, 102, 115, 117, 118, 120, 122, 138, 142, 183, 184, 205, 214, 300, 302, 303, 321, 329, 348
Hein,A.	334
Hellige,J.B.	318, 320, 321, 322, 324, 326, 327, 334
Helms-Estabrooks,N.	183
Hempel,W.E.	334
Henderson,S.E.	231, 241
Henke,W.L.	128
Henneaux,J,	28, 30, 134
Henry,F.M.	290
Herren,R.Y.	24, 81, 82
Herron,J.	310
Hicks,R.E.	320, 321, 326, 329, 348
Hildebrandt, T.	8
Hillemand,P.	23, 81
Hirose,H.	134, 139, 140
Hisada,K.	181
Hiscock,M.	322
Hitzig,E.	75
Ho,M.	208
Hoff,H.	23
Holden,R.W.	319
Holt,K.A.	349
Holtzman,J.O.	25, 54
Hondek,P.Y.	181

Hooper,P.   166

Hopewell,J.W.   233

Hopkins,D.A.   318

Horenstein,S.   180

Hosokawa,S.   181

Hotopf,W.H.N.   125

Houk,J.C.   354

House,A.S.   126

Howarth,C.I.   310

Howes,D.   180

Hughes,O.   131

Hulme,C.   228

Hung,D.L.   301

Hurwitz,I.   237, 316, 323

Huton,J.I.A.   37, 140

Hyland,H.H.   19

I

Iliff,L.D.   182

Ingram,D.   237

Ingvar,D.H.   28

Iraqui,V.   175

Ireland,J.V.   136

Ito,M.   354

Itoh,M.   134, 139, 140

J

Jackson.C.V.   9

Jackson.J.H.   59, 104, 142, 235, 236, 255

Jacobs,L.	182
Jacobs,M.S.	255
Jaffee,J.W	133, 139
Jakobson,R.	87
James,M,	78
James,W.	296
Jason,G.	9
Jeannerod, M.	255, 259, 353
Jedynak, C.P.	23, 82
Jeeves,M.A.	23
Jernigan,T.L.	184
Jesduowich,B.	136
Johns,D.F.	131, 132, 137
Johnson,D.N.	112
Johnson-Laird,P.N.	114
Jones,T.	184

K

Kahneman, D.	322
Kalil, K.	259
Kaplan, E.	11, 23, 47, 55, 81, 82, 85, 117, 133, 140, 164, 167, 235, 236
Karis, R.	180
Kaufman, L.	299
Kawato, M.	349, 351
Kay, H.	311, 312
Keele, S.W.	115, 310
Keller, E.	132
Kellershohn C.	184

Kelly, A.B.   24

Kelso, J.A.S.   122, 125, 128, 131, 141, 349, 350

Kennard, M.A.   26

Kent, R.D.   126, 134, 137, 139, 140

Kephar , N.C.   228, 239

Kerschensteiner, M.   8, 101, 102, 143, 144, 145, 146, 147

Kertesz, A.   10, 71, 111, 118, 166, 168, 170, 171, 180, 183, 319

Kido, D.K.   183

Kim, Y.   183

Kimura, D.   10, 18, 19, 29, 46, 50, 51, 52, 53, 54, 65, 66, 84,
                                     90, 91, 100, 101, 111, 117, 118, 119, 120, 121, 122,
                                     123, 138, 140, 142, 144, 145, 147, 168,204, 210,
                                     212, 218, 226, 236, 237, 309, 315, 320, 322, 324,
                                     325, 326, 328, 329, 330, 335

Kinkel, W.R.   182

Kinsbourne, M.   78, 238, 240, 310, 318, 320, 321, 322, 329, 349

Klapp, S.T.   268, 348

Klein, R.   13, 57

Kleist, K.   3, 4, 8, 10, 12, 18, 19, 23, 24, 31, 32, 33, 47, 76,
                                     77, 79, 100, 195

Klich, R.J.   136

Knight, R.T.   8, 87

Knuckey, N.W.   227, 232

Kolb, B.   10, 13, 18, 19, 52, 53, 60, 111, 204, 210, 211, 212,
                                     213, 216, 217, 218, 219, 237, 268, 301, 304, 305

Koff, E.   172

Kohlmeyer, K.   181

Konich, A.W.   71

Kornhuber, H.H.   183, 208

Kornse, D.D.   230

Kots, Y.M.   141

Kowell, A.P.   185

Kreuter, C.	321, 349
Kroll, M.	12
Krones, R.	126
Kubota, K.	257, 258, 259
Kudlek, F.	20, 21
Kugler, P.N.	349
Kuhl, D.E.	182, 184, 185
Kunzle, H.	259
Kuypers, H.G.J.M.	14, 81, 83, 103, 205, 208, 217, 235, 257, 318, 319, 350
Kwan, H.C.	257, 259
Kyprie, P.M.	54, 309, 315, 316, 319, 323, 324

L

Labov, W.	293
Lackner, J.R.	355
Lacquaniti, F.	354
Ladefoged, P.	126
Ladurner, G.	182
Lange, J.	9, 10, 20, 49
Langolf, G.D.	310
Laplane, D.	19
LaPointe, L.L.	131, 132, 137, 142
Larsen, B.	27, 28, 29, 79, 181, 185, 257
Lashley, K.S.	146, 276
Lassen, N.A.	27, 28, 29, 79, 181, 185, 257
Lassonde, M.C.	24
Laughlin, S.A.	183, 184
Laver, J.D.M.	125

Lawrence, D.G.   103, 205, 208, 217, 235, 318, 350

Lazarus, J.C.   319, 330

Lebrun, Y.   133, 134, 138

LeCours, A.R.   37, 131, 133, 136, 195

Lechner, H.   182

LeDoux, J.E.   25, 26, 331

Lee, R.G.   311

Legg, G.   184

Lehmkuhl, G.   8, 48, 49, 61, 90, 100, 101, 102, 104, 105, 114, 119,
                                  183, 184, 236

Lehtinen, C.E.   226

Le May, M.   172, 183

Lenzi, G.L.   184

Lemmo, M.A.   90

Lemon, R.N.   257

Lesk, D.   180

Lesney, I.A.   234

Levine, H.L.   172, 183

Levin, H.S.   331

Levine, M.   229, 231

Levinson, A.W.   183

Levy, J.   84, 310

Levy, R.S.   8, 170, 184

Lezak, M.   324

Lezine, I.   227, 236, 237

Lhermitte, F.   77, 79, 133, 136, 138, 164, 165, 262

Liberman, A.M.   125

Liepmann, H.   3, 4, 5, 8, 9, 10, 11, 12, 14, 18, 20, 21, 22, 23, 24,
                                  29, 31, 32, 46, 47, 49, 53, 58, 59, 65, 66, 76, 77,
                                  81, 85, 100, 101, 105, 120, 163, 164, 171, 174, 194,
                                  211, 329

Lindblom, B.   126, 127

Linde, C.   293

Lisker, L.   133

Loc'h, C.   184

Lodesani, M.   13, 18, 31, 52, 195

Logue, R.D.   126

Logue, V.   137

Lomas, J.   100, 322, 325, 326, 328

Longstreth, L.E.   318, 320, 321, 322, 324, 326, 327, 334

LoVerme, S.R. Jr.   184

Loyez, M.   23

Lozano, R.A.   135

Lu, C.H.   182

Lubker, J.   22, 126

Lucier, G.E.   311

Lupert, N.   236

Luria, A.R.   12, 52, 84, 114, 117, 121, 140, 237, 241, 242, 262

Luzzatti, C.   19, 21, 171, 183, 184, 185, 186, 193

Lynch, A.   233

Lysaught, G.F.   126

M

Maas, O.   3, 5, 8, 15, 22, 81, 171

Mace, W.   115, 116, 122

MacGregor, B.   184

MacKay, D.G.   125, 267, 270, 277, 279, 290, 293, 295, 297

MacKay, W.A.   257, 259

MacKenzie, C.L.   309, 331, 349, 350

MacKenzie, R.   183

MacNeilage, L.A.   125

MacNeilage, P.F.   116, 123, 124, 126, 127, 137, 141, 146

Mack, J.L.   183

Maddison, S.   261

Maeda, T.   181

Mahowald, M.W.   9, 23

Mailloux, Z.   227

Malmo, R.   77

Mandel, M.   87

Manni, J.   230

Manowitz, J.W.   332

Maraschini, S.   195

Marcuse, H.   49

Margolin, D.I.   8

Marquardt, J.P.   133, 136, 139

Marshall, T.   184

Martin, A.D.   28, 31, 32, 33, 132, 135, 136

Marteniuk, R.G.   350

Marzi, C.A.   319

Masdeu, J.C.   19

Massonnet, J.   77

Mastri, A.   9, 23

Masure, L.   83

Mateer, C.   8, 29, 30, 101, 138, 141, 142, 144, 145, 146, 147,
                           180

Matsuda, H.   181

Matsumura, M.   257, 259, 258

Mattelli, M.   257, 259, 261, 262

Mauguiere, F.   259

Maurach, R.	183
Maxwell, A.E.	189
Maxwell, J.K.	309, 331
Mayer, N.H.	19, 183, 296, 297
Mazziotta, J.C.	184
Mazzocchi, F.	138, 139, 184
McAllister, R.	126
McAuley, D.L.	183
McCabe, P.	180
McCarrell, N.S.	112
McClean, M.	141
McConkie, A.	116
McFarland, K.A.	327
McFarling, D.	184
McFie, J.	77
McGlone, J.	185, 192, 329
McKinlay, I.	228, 230, 232, 233, 238
McNeil, M.R.	134
Meininger, V.	19
Meissner, B.	135
Melzack, R.	233
Mendelson, M.J.	240
Meringer, G.	296, 297
Mesulam, M.M.	175
Metter, E.J.	185
Meynert, H.	76, 85
Meyer, D.R.	257
Meyer, E.	27, 28, 29, 184
Meyer, J.S.	100

Miller, G.A.   114

Milner, A.D.   24

Milner, B.   10, 13, 18, 19, 52, 53, 60, 111, 210, 211, 212, 213, 216, 218, 237

Mingazzini, G.   8, 21, 23

Miranda, F.   9

Mishkin, M.   255, 259

Mlcoch, A.G.   133, 137, 138

Mohr, J.P.   14, 138, 139

Mol, C.R.   311

Moll, K.L.   123, 126, 128, 137

Moll, L.   81, 217

Monakow, O. von   8, 10, 12, 19, 20, 21, 22, 26, 31, 77, 171

Monroe, M.A.   180

Moore, W.   126

Moran, C.   228

Morasso, P.   351

Morelli, M.   319

Mori, H.   181, 182

Morgane, P.J.   255

Morlaas, J.   5, 8, 12, 13, 18, 23, 49, 50, 77, 90

Morris, C.B.   112

Morris, J.L.   184

Moscovitch, M.   329

Moss, H.   316, 323

Moss, M.   237

Motti, F.   10, 45, 46, 51, 52, 54, 186

Muakassa, K.F.   80, 257, 258, 259

Muller, R.   102

Murphy, J.T.   257, 259

Myers, D.H.   331

Myers, R.E.   219

N

Naeser,M.A.   9, 138, 172, 183, 184

Nathan,P.W.   79, 165

Nashner,L.M.   353

Nauta,W.J.H.   252

Nebes,R.D.   327

Neelley,J.M.   126

Nelson,K.   112

Netsell,R.   126, 141

New,P.F.J.   182

Newell,A.   112

Nichelli,P.   10, 45, 46, 51, 52, 54, 186

Nichols,A.C.   141

Nieburgs,A.   218

Nielson,J.M.   8, 79, 81

Nijs,H.G.T.   257

Noll,D.   137

Nonneman,A.J.   219

Nooteboom,S,G.   125

Norman,D.A.   112, 116, 269, 280, 296, 297, 299

North,P.   8, 9, 12

O

O'Connell,P.   136

Ohashi,H.   79

Ohigashi,Y.   79

Ohmam,S.   126, 137

Ojemann,G.A.   8, 29, 30, 143, 180

Oldfield,R.C.   185, 329

Oleson,J.   27, 79

Olmstead,C.E.   218

Olson,T.S.   182

Ombredane,A.   133

Orgogozo,J.M.   19, 27, 29, 257

Ornstein,R.   327

Orton,S.T.   225, 232, 238, 239

Osterag,C.B.   183

Ottenbacher,K.   240

Otani,K.   183

Overton,W.   235, 236

P

Paden,R.S.   183

Paillard,J.   255, 259

Pandya,D.M.   14, 24, 80, 259, 260

Papez,J.   259

Papp,K.R.   125

Parlow,S.   310

Patawaran,C.   183

Patla,A.E.   349

Patten,D.H.   180

Patton,H.D.   131

Pavesi,G.   257, 259, 261, 262,

Paxton.R.   181

Pencz,A.	182
Penfield,W.	28, 77, 79, 180, 257,
Perani,D.	184
Perelle,I.B.	332
Perkell,J.S.	128, 140, 141
Perret,D.	261
Pessin,M.S.	138, 140
Peters,M.	315, 316, 318, 319, 321, 322, 323, 324, 325, 328, 329, 330, 333, 334, 348
Peterson,A.	136
Peterson,J.M.	70
Peterson,L.R.	70
Petrides,M.	259,260
Phelps,M.E.	184, 185
Philipson,L.	28
Piaget,J.	89
Pick,A.	3, 49, 76, 100, 105
Pieczuro,A.	10, 14, 48, 50, 51, 54, 78, 85, 86,100, 103, 111, 118, 122, 142, 144, 165, 168, 214
Pieniadz,J.M.	9, 172
Pierce,C.S.	87
Piercy,M.F.	77
Pineas,H.	23
Pizzini,G.	183
Plummer,D.	184
Podbros,L.Z.	347
Poeck,K.	8, 48, 49, 61, 90, 100, 101, 102, 104, 105, 114, 119, 143, 144, 145, 146, 147, 236
Pocock,P.V.	30
Poizner,H.	175

Polson,M.C.   318, 320

Poncet,M.   131

Poole,F.   180

Poppelreuter,W.   77

Porch,B.E.   84, 121, 122

Porter,R.   261

Posner,M.I.   71

Poulton,E.C.   346

Pozzilli, K.   184

Pratt,R.T.C.   137

Preilowski,B.   24, 350, 351

Prescott,T.   134

Price,H.L.   54, 309, 315, 316, 319, 323, 324, 325, 329, 335

Provenzano, F.J.   321, 326, 329, 348

Provins, K.A.   309, 310, 332

Puerto, A.   261

Pulimeno, R.   324, 325, 326

Putnam, C.A.   350

Q

Quinn,J.T.Jr.   313, 314

De Quiros,J.   235

R

Rakic,P.   319, 320

Raichle,M.E.   180

Ream,M.J.   332

Reason,J.T.   112, 114, 116, 299

Regli,F.   14, 57

Reid,M.   310

Reitan,R.M.   315, 331, 334

Reivich,M.   181, 184

Ribadeau Dumas,J.L.   53

Rigrodsky,S.   132, 136

Ringel,R.L.   127

Rintelmann,W.   184

Risteen,W.A,   24, 81, 82

Risse,G.L.   8, 170, 184

Rizzo,M   183

Rizzolatti,G.   257, 259, 261, 262, 318, 324, 325, 326, 334

Roberson,G.H.   182

Roberts,L.   180

Robinson,G.M.   302

Robinson,R.G.   183

Roland,P.E.   27, 28, 29, 79, 181, 184, 185, 257

Rolls,E.T.   261

Romanul,F.C.   24

Rondot,P.   83

Roper-Hall,A.   261

Rosvold,H.E.   257

Rosch,E.H.   112

Rose,F.   8, 79

Rosenbek,J.   134, 137, 139, 141, 142

Rosenfield,D.B.   180

Rosenquist,A.   184

Rosenweig,M.R.   240

Ross,K.E.   232

Ross,E.D.   184

Ross Russell,R.W.   183

Rothi,L.J.   58, 60, 65, 66, 67, 68, 70, 78, 118, 183, 184

Rothmann,M.   8

Roy,C.S.   180

Roy,E.A.   52, 61, 100, 111, 112, 113, 114, 116, 117, 118, 119,
                                 120, 121, 122, 139, 141, 142, 214, 218, 226, 227,
                                 237, 241, 242,268, 295, 300, 309, 329, 331, 335

Rubens,A.B.   8, 9,19, 23, 170, 184

Rubin,P.   349

Rubstein,E.D.   321, 326, 329

Rubenstein,H.   230

Ruch,T.C.   26, 131

Rumelhart,D.E.   269, 280

Russell,W.R.   242

Rybstein,E.D.   348

Rymer,W.Z.   354

S

Sager,W.D.   182

Sakai,M.   257

Salvolini,U.   184

Sands,E.   133, 139

Sanides,F.   251, 252, 253

Sasanuma,S.   132, 134

Satz,P.   310, 348

Sauerwein,H.C.   24

Saul,R.E.   24

Sauguet,J.   9

Sax,D.S.   347

Scandolla,C.   261

Schaffer,K.	20, 21
Schank,R.C.	293
Scharlock,D.P.	26
Schell,G.R.	257, 259
Schilder,P.	77, 235
Schinshy,L.	175
Schiff,H.P.	35, 37, 138
Schmelzer,W.	218
Schmidt,R.A.	117, 285, 304, 313, 314, 347, 352
Schmitt,M.A.	19, 183
Schnur,J.A.	182
Schoene,W.C.	19
Schrager,O.	235
Schvey,M.M.	126
Schwartz,H.D.	84, 100, 329
Scott,C.M.	127
Scotti,G.	183, 184, 186
Seemuller,E.	183
Selin,D.	185
Selnes,C.A.	8, 170, 184
Seltz,O.	287
Seltzer,B.	14
Semmes,J.	122, 330
Sencer,W.	257
Sersen,E.A.	331
Settlage,P.H.	257
Skinhoj,E.	257
Shaffer,L.H.	348
Shahani,B.T.	311

Shallice, T.   137

Shane, H.C.   135

Shankweiler, D.   131, 134

Sharp, C.A.   321, 322, 328

Sharpe, M.H.   347

Shaw, R.E.   115, 116, 122

Shelley, C.   325

Sheppard, A.   183

Sheremata, W.A.   24

Sheridan, M.R.   310, 312, 313

Sherrington, C.S.   180

Shewan, C.M.   168

Shibasaki, H.   30

Shibasaki, T.   27, 28, 29, 184

Shipley, J.E.   218

Shonkoff, J.P.   229, 231

Shulman, H.G.   7, 116

Sidtis, J.J.   25, 54

Signoret, J.L.   8, 9, 12

Simon, H.A.   112

Simon, J.R.   309

Simpson, D.A.   23

Simpson,G.   8

Sinclair, W.A.   239

Sittig,O.   23, 47,49, 77

Skelly,M.   175

Skinhoj,E.   27, 28, 29, 79, 181, 185

Slager,U.T.   24

Smart.J.   233

Smiley,A.L.	315, 316, 323, 324, 325, 329, 335
Smith,A.	123
Smith,G.E.	255, 256
Smith,L.E.	290
Smith,O.	80
Smith,M.O.	326
Smith,R.	175
Smith,R.D.	19
Smith,V.O.	77
Sobel,L.	180
Soechting,J.F.	354
Soh,K	4
Sokoloff,L.	79
Solomon,D.J.	302
Sommers,R.K.	138
Sorgato,P.	10, 14, 30, 46, 48, 58, 88, 90, 100, 186
Southard,D.L.	350
Southmayd,J.E.	233
Soussaline,F.	184
Spector,R.H.	183
Sperry,R.W.	24, 25, 26, 54, 81, 82, 84, 170, 212, 317, 348, 350, 351
Spinnler,H.	19, 21, 171, 184, 185, 193
Square,P.A.	132, 133, 136, 137, 138, 140, 141, 142, 145
Statlender,S.	133
Stauffenberg, W.F. von	12
Steer,M.O.	126
Stein,A.	184
Stein,D.G.	218, 232, 240

Steingruber,H.S   310

Steinthal,P.   75

Stelmach,G.E.   214

Stevens,K.N.   125, 126, 128

Stolz,W.   116

Strauss,A.A.   226

Strauss,H.   77

Strian,F.   183

Strick,P.L.   80, 257, 258, 259

Strohmayer,W.   12, 13, 76

Strominger,N.L.   26

Studdert-Kennedy,M.   125

Suger,G.   183

Sugushita,M.   23

Summers,J.J.   115, 321, 322, 328

Sussman,H.M.   116, 142

Sutton,S.   126

Suzuki,R.   349, 351

Sweet,W.H.   23

Szetela,B.   183

Szentagothai,J.   208

T

Tagliabue,M.   183

Talairach,J.   19

Takase,M.   183

Taterka,H.   8, 23

Taubleib,A.B.   355

Taylor.L.S.   319

Taylor,M.L.	37, 134
Ter-Pogossian,M.M.	180
Teuber,H.L.	122, 330
Texeira,L.A.	141
Thompson,C.J.	27, 28, 29, 184
Thorpe, S.J.	261
Thornton, C.D.	321, 328
Tissot, R.	241
Todor, J.I.	54, 309, 310, 313, 314, 315, 316, 319, 322, 323, 324, 329, 330, 335
Toglia, J.U.	19, 183
Tognola, G.	145, 168, 171, 184
Tokunaga, A.	183
Tonami, N.	181
Torach, R.M.	182
Towbin, A.	232
Towe, A.L.	131
Toyokura, Y.	23
Travis, A.M.	79, 257
Tredici, G.	183
Trefler, M.	181
Trescher, J.H.	23
Trevarthen, C.	84, 116, 139, 321, 349
Trost, J.E.	131, 132
Tsaveras,J.M.	182, 184
Tucker, T.J.	26
Tuller, B.	122, 125, 128, 131, 141
Tulving, E.	11, 119
Turner, A.	313, 314, 316, 333

Turnier, H.   181

Turvey, M.T.   115, 116, 122, 127

Tusa, R.   184

Tzavaras, A.   12, 80, 83

Tzeng, O.J.L.   301

U

Ueno, H.   181

Ungerleider, L.G.   255, 259

Unsold, R.   183

Ushijima, T.   134

V

Valenstein, E.   8, 58, 60, 65, 66, 67, 70, 78, 118, 183

Vanderwolf, C.H.   220, 305, 324, 326

Varnier, M.   194

Van Hosen, G.W.   19, 259

Van Vleuten, C.F.   22

Van Wagenen, W.P.   24, 81, 82

Varney, N.R.   183, 309, 331

Vaughan, H.G.   329

Vecchi, A.   13, 18, 31, 52, 194

Victor, M.   236

Vierck, C.J.   233, 235

Vignolo, L.A.   14, 24, 48, 50, 51, 54, 78, 80, 85, 86, 100, 103, 111, 118, 122, 138, 139, 142, 145, 165, 168, 171, 182, 184, 214

Vilensky, J.   259

Villablanca, J.R.   218

Vining, D.Q.   183

Vleuten, C.F. van	82
Vogel, P.J.	25
Vogt, C.	255, 256, 257
Vogt, O.	55, 256, 257
Voinesco, I.	5, 13
Volpe, B.T.	25, 54

W

Wadman, W.J.	311
Wagner, J.A.	24
Wall, P.D.	233, 235
Wallesch, C.W.	183
Walton, J.N.	226
Wang, P.L.	330
Wang, W.S-Y	301
Wangler, H.H.	134
Warren, J.M.	217
Warrington, E.K.	78, 137
Wasterlain, O.G.	185
Webster, W.	218
Weidner, W.E.	136
Weinrich, J.	257
Weinstein, S.	122, 330, 331
Welch, J.C.	330
Welch, K.	28, 79, 257
Welford, A.T.	298, 311
Wells, F.L.	332
Wendenburg, K.	20, 21
Weniger, D.	102

Wernicke, C.   76

Wertz, R.T.   138, 141, 142, 144

Westphal, A.   23

Wickelgren, W.   280, 281, 282

Wiesendanger, M.   257

Willmes, K.   100, 101, 102, 104, 183, 236

Wills, E.H.   27

Wilson, D.H.   25, 54, 331

Wilson, E.M.   27

Wilson, J.   24

Wilson, S.A.K.   12, 142

Windle, W.F.   233

Wing, A.M.   323, 350

Wingate, M.E.   126

Winter, J.   185

Wise, S.P.   257

Whishaw, I.Q.   204, 217, 218, 219, 268, 301, 304, 305

White, J.C.   19, 311

Whitely, J.D.   290

Whitehouse, P.   118

Wolf, A.   184

Wolff, P.H.   237, 316, 323

Wong, Y.C.   257, 259

Woodbury, J.W.   131

Woodworth, R.S.   310

Woolsey, C.N.   257

Wyatt, E.P.   268

Wyke, M.   54, 84, 100, 329, 334

Y

Yakovlev, P.I.	319, 320
Yamada, R.	23
Yamadori, A.	47
Yamamoto, S.	181
Yamamoto, Y.L.	27, 28, 29, 184
Yamanishi, J.	349, 351
Yamashita, Y.	181
Yarnell, P.	180
Yoshioka, H.	134
Yoshioka, M.	23
Yoss, K.A.	230
Young, A.W.	331
Young, R.A.	311

Z

Zaidel, D.	25, 54, 82, 212, 348, 350, 351
Zangwill, O.L.	9, 47, 77, 89, 242
Zatz, L.M.	183, 184
Zelaznik, H.N.	313, 314
Zeumer, H.	183
Zimmerman, G.N.	123
Zimmerman, R.A.	182
Zurif, E.	118, 133, 138

SUBJECT INDEX

A

Action
  cognitive control, 267, 268

  context, 112, 123, 279–280, 300

  fields, 112

  memory structures, 112

  nodes (see Action Nodes)

  programs, 114, 116 (see also Motor Programs)

  projectional, 259, 261

  representation of action (see Action Nodes)

  responsive, 261

  speech and, 293, 301, 321

  systems controlling action (see Action Systems)

Action Nodes, 269
  activation, 269, 277–278

  content nodes, 272–275

  linkage strength, 270

  mental nodes, 272

  muscle movement nodes, 272

  priming, 270, 300

  sensory analysis nodes, 272

  sequence nodes, 274–276, 301

  timing nodes, 276–277

Action Systems
  action plan system, 291–293

  conceptual system, 112–114

  movement concept system, 290–291

  muscle movement system, 290

  production system, 114–117

pragmatic system, 293-295

Animal Models in Neuroscience
    behaviours to study, 217-220

    body-part-as-object errors, 220 (see also Errors)

    motor systems, 216

    species typical behaviour, 218

    structural similarities, 216

Aphasia
    anomic aphasia, 166

    apraxia and, 8, 45, 56, 85, 101, 104, 118, 163-176, 190, 232, 301

    Broca's, 14, 101, 131, 136, 138, 165, 166, 167, 168

    Conduction, 138, 166

    transcortical aphasia, 166, 167, 168

    Wernicke's, 101, 138, 165, 166, 167, 170

Apractagnosia, 77

Attention, 114, 125, 233, 295-300, 329

Apraxia
    activities of daily living, 228

    agraphia and, 191, 230

    alexia and, 191

    animal models of, 100, 203-221

    angular gyrus, 18, 171

    antilocalization theory, 20

    aphasia and (see aphasia)

    asymbolia, 75

    basal ganglia, 19, 210

    bimanual coordination and, 347, 354

    body schema, 228

    CAT correlates, 171, 173, 174, 179-195

    centre theory, 11

comprehension, 101, 168

conceptual disorder, 118, 135

corpus callosum, 22, 24, 25, 55, 81, 302

crossed dominance, 8

deep lesions, 190, 193

developmental disorders, 225-242

disconnection theory, 11, 22, 24, 53, 174

dressing, 99

environmental susceptibility, 300

error types (see errors)

facial/oral (see facial/oral apraxia)

fine motor control, 230

frontal, 12, 174, 191, 192, 210

gait, 100, 103

gross motor skills, 229

ideational, 3, 46, 48, 51, 76, 83, 85, 90, 164, 302

ideomotor, 4, 47, 48, 51, 65, 76, 83, 90, 101, 171, 173, 303

in left handers, 8, 172

input modalities, 14, 56

internal capsule, 190

intransitive gestures, 46, 165

kinetic, 77, 80

learning, 84, 144, 218

learning disabilities, 230

left hand only, 23

left hemisphere, 4, 52, 55, 77

Liepmann's theory, 3, 65, 76

limb vs. axial movements (see movements)

manual asymmetries, 212

melokinetic, 4, 76, 79, 164

methods of examination, 45, 101, 214

motor, 54

occipital lobe, 18, 190, 191, 193

parietal lobe, 12, 165, 191, 192, 210, 303

pathological process, 25

performance conditions, 4, 13, 14, 22, 46, 57, 88, 103, 145, 164, 212, 227, 236, 302

premotor area, 14

production disorder, 120

recovery, 170

right hemisphere, 5, 9, 55, 77

severity, 215-216

sex differences, 192

space, 27, 99, 228, 235

supplementary motor area, 19, 79

supramarginal gyrus, 168, 171

sympathetic, 80

temporal lobe, 18, 190, 191, 193

thalamus, 19, 210

therapy, 104, 238-240

transitive gestures, 46, 49, 165

verbal, 131

volume of lesion, 171, 187, 193

B

Basal ganglia, 19, 210, 234, 259, 321

Bimanual coordination, 25, 330, 345-356
     acquisition, 352-354

     coupled oscillators, 349

discrete vs. serial vs. continuous movements, 347

kinematics, 349

movements alternating in time vs. same time, 347

open vs. closed tasks, 346, 353

spatiotemporal symmetry vs. asymmetry, 348-351

symbolic vs. meaningless movements

two hands same vs. two hands different movement, 348

visual aiming, 350, 351, 353

C

CAT scan
    apraxia, 171, 173, 174

    artifacts and partial volume phenomenon, 181

    localization of lesions, 182-184

    skull asymmetries in, 172

    time post onset, 182

    type and size of lesion, 182

Clumsiness, 4

Command (performance to), 4, 57, 212, 302

Conceptual system
    disorders to, 118, 135

    knowledge of action, 113, 119

    knowledge of object function, 113, 118

    knowledge of serial order, 114, 119

Constructional apraxia, 99

Contralateral control, 25

Corpus callosum, 4, 22, 25, 81, 212, 317, 321

D

Developmental apraxia, 226-242
    activities of daily living, 229

    aphasia and, 232

    articulation, 230

    attention, 233

    body schema, 228

    cerebellum, 233

    clumsiness, 228

    etiology, 232-234

    evaluation, 234

    fine motor skills, 230, 234

    gross motor skills, 229, 234

    IQ and, 227, 231, 233

    language and, 227

    learning disabilities, 230

    performance conditions, 227, 236

    planning, 228, 230, 233, 234

    tactile perception, 228, 233

    thalamus, 233

    treatment, 238

    vs. adult onset, 226-227

    writing, 230

Dressing apraxia, 99

Dual task paradigm, 320-327, 348

E

Effector space, 117

Engrams, 4, 65, 68

Errors
  additions, 132

  anticipatory, 137

  body-part-as-object, 55, 220

  capture errors, 296

  clumsiness, 4, 117, 225, 226, 233, 303

  data driven errors, 296

  decay of priming errors, 296, 300

  distortions, 132

  inappropriate responses, 117

  omissions, 117, 132

  perseverations, 103, 120, 141, 303

  relation to attention and intention, 295-300

  sequencing, 120, 137, 141, 218-221, 303

  spatial errors, 141

  spoonerisms, 125, 137

  substitutions, 132, 303

F

Facial/oral apraxia, 79, 101, 142, 165
  anterior and central lesions in, 168, 170

  aphasia and, 103, 144, 165, 167

  conceptual disorder, 145

  errors observed, 142, 167

  learning sequences, 144

  limb apraxia and, 103, 112, 143, 165, 211

  memory and, 146

  production disorder, 147

  verbal apraxia and, 143

Frontal area, 321
    apraxia, 4, 12, 52, 174, 191, 192, 210, 216, 218

    evolutionary trends, 251–255

    protogradations, 251–255

    rCBF, 29

Fitts' Law, 310
    index of difficulty, 310, 314

    multiple error correction model, 311

    output variability model, 313

G

Gesture
    comprehension of, 66

    development, 89

    discrimination, 68

    encoding, 70

    execution of, 3

    facial (see facial/oral apraxia)

    graphic, 87

    intransitive, 46, 86, 165, 168

    learning, 68

    meaningless, 50, 70, 227, 236, 237

    memory for, 65, 71

    object use, 13, 46, 47, 51, 87

    representation of, 3

    symbolic, 50, 70, 87, 227, 236, 237

    transitive, 46, 165

I

Ideational apraxia, 3, 46, 47, 76, 83, 85, 90, 104, 302
    aphasia and, 104

    planning, 49

sequencing, 49, 104

 vs. ideomotor apraxia, 47, 104

Ideomotor apraxia, 4, 47, 48, 76, 83, 85, 90, 101, 171, 173, 186
 angular gyrus, 171

 CT correlates, 186-195

 meaningless gestures in, 50

 sequential movements, 51, 53

 single movements, 51, 53

 supramarginal gyrus, 171

 symbolic gestures in, 50

 two forms of, 65, 78

 vs. ideational apraxia, 47

Imagery, 28

Imitation (performance to), 4, 57

Ipsilateral control, 25

K

Kinematics, 349

Kinetic apraxia, 77

L

Left hemisphere
 apraxia, 44, 52, 77, 268

M

Manual asymmetries, 309-336, 350
 cerebral specialization and, 320-327

 dual task paradigms, 320-327

 finger tapping, 315-317

 handedness, 309, 320

 hemispheric asymmetries and, 317-318

 implications for apraxia, 334

in visually aimed movements, 310-315

index of difficulty, 310

motor pathways and, 318-320

practice, 332

task demands and, 309

Melokinetic apraxia, 4

Memory, 4, 52, 65, 146
        action and, 112

consolidation, 69

primary, 71

secondary, 68

Motor control processes
        bimanual coordination, 165

bottom-up control, 116, 300

closed loop, 117, 123, 353, 354

coalitional comtrol, 116, 127

context, 123, 279-280, 300

coupled oscillators, 349

data-driven control, 116

distributed control, 352

feedback, 117, 127, 139, 141, 260, 311, 314, 354

feedforward, 260, 353, 354

hemispheric asymmetries, 301, 317-330

open loop, 117, 123, 353, 354

programming, 147, 259

sequencing, 111, 120, 138, 144, 212, 237, 257, 261, 267-306

systems controlling action (see Action Systems)

timing, 276-277

top-down control, 115, 123, 146, 300

Motor pathways, 205-209
    basal ganglia input, 208

    cerebellar input, 208

    corticospinal, 205, 318, 319, 350

    dorsolateral, 206

    implications for apraxia, 209-213

    ventromedial, 207

Motor programs, 3, 69, 352
    activation of programs, 116, 278

    left hemisphere in, 3

    network representation, 116

    node structures, (see Action Nodes)

Movements (types of), 25, 51, 53, 54, 103, 166, 210, 212, 214, 227
    allokinetic, 351

    axial, 55, 103

    ballistic, 311, 314

    bimanual, 25, 103, 166, 330, 345-356

    habitual vs. nonhabitual, 237

    heterokinetic, 351

    homokinetic, 351

    meaningful vs. non-meaningful, (see gestures)

    proximal vs. distal, 25, 53, 210, 235, 319, 330, 350

    repetitive, 54, 348

    sequential, 51, 53, 166, 212, 218, 233, 238, 257, 267-306

    simultaneous, 284, 347

    single, 51, 53, 217, 238

    static vs. dynamic, 237

    synkinetic, 351

    visually aimed, 310, 322, 350, 351, 353

N

Neuroradiological techniques
    CAT scan, 171, 172, 181-184

    radioisotope brain scan, 180

    rCBF, 27, 179-180, 185, 257

    PET scan, 184-185

O

Object space, 117

Object use, 13, 46, 47, 57, 87

Occipital area
    apraxia, 11, 12, 18, 190, 191, 193

Optic ataxia, 81, 83

Oral apraxia (see facial/oral apraxia)

P

Parkinson's disease, 347
    210, 260, 303

Parietal area, 11, 12, 18, 29, 52, 139, 165, 191, 192,
    limb apraxia, 11, 12, 18, 52, 165, 191, 192, 210

    rCBF, 29

    verbal apraxia, 139, 165

Pathology
    angular gyrus, 18

    basal ganglia, 19, 210, 234

    cerebellum, 233, 234

    corpus callosum, 4, 22

    frontal, 4, 12, 14, 145, 174, 191, 216, 218

    left hemisphere, 4, 44, 52, 77, 268

    occipital lobe, 11, 12, 18, 190, 191

    parietal, 11, 12, 18, 52, 139, 145, 165, 191, 303

    postcentral gyrus, 4

precentral gyrus, 4, 218

premotor, 14

right hemisphere, 5, 9

supplementary motor area, 19

temporal lobe, 18, 139, 190, 191

thalamus, 19, 210, 233

Perceptual attributes, 113, 115

Performance conditions
command, 4, 22, 88, 103, 145

imitation, 4, 14, 22, 88, 103, 145, 164

object use, 13, 22, 88

Personal-extrapersonal space, 27, 235

Perseverations (see errors)

Planning, 320, 345, 347
apraxia, 49, 225, 227, 230, 234, 237, 345

right hemisphere in, 10

Postcentral gyrus, 4

Precentral gyrus, 4, 218, 251-255, 350

Premotor area, 251-262

Production system, 114, 117, 120
action programs, 114

activation of programs, 117

attention, 114

bottom-up control, 117, 126

coordinative structures, 117

effector space, 117

levels of control, 117

object space, 117

top-down control, 117

R

rCBF technique
     frontal area, 29

     imagery, 27

     language areas, 28

     parietal area, 29

     premotor area, 29

     sequences, 27

     thalamic area, 29

Right hemisphere
     apraxia, 5, 9, 77

     comprehension, 10

     planning, 10

RT-MT studies, 350

S

Sequencing, 3, 27, 49, 84, 90, 120, 139, 144, 212, 233, 237, 257, 261, 274, 267-306, 322

Speech production
     attention, 125

     central rules, 123, 125

     context, 126

     feedback, 127

     lexical selection processes, 125

     motor control, 123

     phonological system, 123

     target hypothesis, 125

Split brain studies, 321, 349

Supplementary motor area, 19, 28, 79, 251-262, 321

Supramarginal gyrus, 168

Sympathetic apraxia, 80

T

Temporal area, 139, 190, 191, 193, 259
    limb apraxia, 190, 191, 193

    verbal apraxia, 139

Thalamic area
    apraxia, 19, 210, 233

    rCBF, 29

V

Verbal apraxia, 131
    Broca's aphasia, 131, 136

    conceptual disorder, 135, 138

    conduction aphasia, 138

    disruptions to fine control, 142

    environmental factors, 134, 140

    errors in, 132

    instrumental analyses, 133

    limb apraxia and, 147

    oral apraxia and, 143

    parietal damage, 139

    perceptual analyses, 131

    physiological analyses, 133

    production disorder, 139

    spatial disorder, 141

    temporal damage, 139

    Wernicke's aphasia, 138